Explorations in CORE MATH

for Common Core GPS Georgia Accelerated Analytic Geometry B/ Advanced Algebra

Image Credits: (saw palmetto plants and pine trees) ©Cyrille Gibot/Alamy; (peach) ©Danny Smythe/Alamy Images.

Printed in the U.S.A.

4 5 6 7 8 9 10 0982 23 22 21 20 19 18 17 16 15 14

4500483797 C D E F G H I

Contents

UNIT 8 Exponential and Logarithms 407

UNIT 9 Trigonometric Functions 463

UNIT 10 Mathematical Modeling 521

Learning the Standards for Mathematical Practice

The Common Core Georgia Performance Standards include eight Standards for Mathematical Practice. Here's how *Explorations in Core Math* helps you learn those standards as you master the Standards for Mathematical Content.

1 Make sense of problems and persevere in solving them.

In *Explorations in Core Math*, you will work through Explores and Examples that present a solution pathway for you to follow. You will be asked questions along the way so that you gain an understanding of the solution process, and then you will apply what you've learned in the Practice for the lesson.

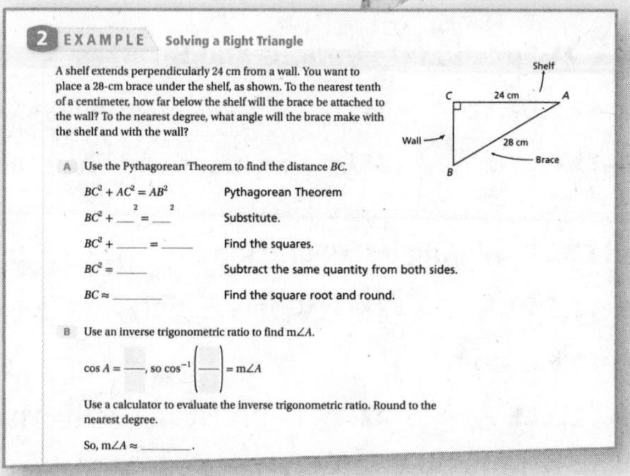

2 EXAMPLE Solving a Right Triangle

A shelf extends perpendicularly 24 cm from a wall. You want to place a 28-cm brace under the shelf, as shown. To the nearest tenth of a centimeter, how far below the shelf will the brace be attached to the wall? To the nearest degree, what angle will the brace make with the shelf and with the wall?

A Use the Pythagorean Theorem to find the distance BC.

$BC^2 + AC^2 = AB^2$ Pythagorean Theorem

$BC^2 + \_\_^2 = \_\_^2$ Substitute.

$BC^2 + \_\_\_ = \_\_\_$ Find the squares.

$BC^2 = \_\_\_$ Subtract the same quantity from both sides.

$BC \approx \_\_\_$ Find the square root and round.

B Use an inverse trigonometric ratio to find $m\angle A$.

$\cos A = \_\_$, so $\cos^{-1}\left(\_\_\right) = m\angle A$

Use a calculator to evaluate the inverse trigonometric ratio. Round to the nearest degree.

So, $m\angle A \approx \_\_\_$.

2 Reason abstractly and quantitatively.

When you solve a real-world problem in *Explorations in Core Math*, you will learn to represent the situation symbolically by translating the problem into a mathematical expression or equation. You will use these mathematical models to solve the problem and then state your answer in terms of the problem context. You will reflect on the solution process in order to check your answer for reasonableness and to draw conclusions.

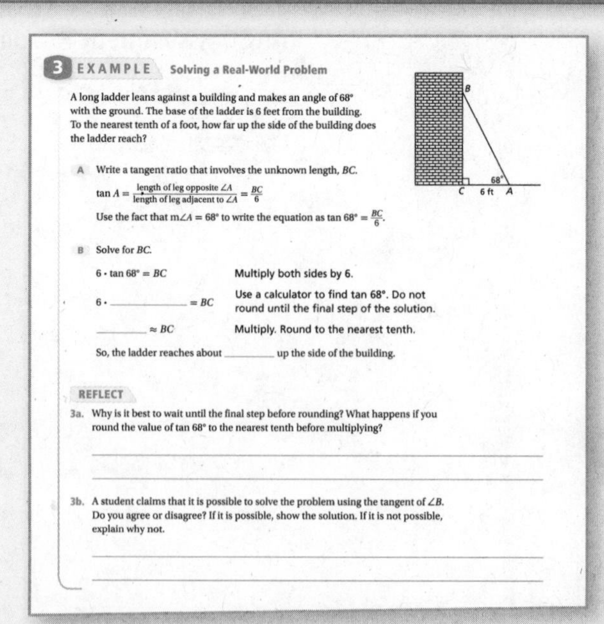

3 EXAMPLE Solving a Real-World Problem

A long ladder leans against a building and makes an angle of 68° with the ground. The base of the ladder is 6 feet from the building. To the nearest tenth of a foot, how far up the side of the building does the ladder reach?

A Write a tangent ratio that involves the unknown length, BC.

$\tan A = \frac{\text{length of leg opposite } \angle A}{\text{length of leg adjacent to } \angle A} = \frac{BC}{6}$

Use the fact that $m\angle A = 68°$ to write the equation as $\tan 68° = \frac{BC}{6}$.

B Solve for BC.

$6 \cdot \tan 68° = BC$ Multiply both sides by 6.

$6 \cdot \_\_\_ = BC$ Use a calculator to find tan 68°. Do not round until the final step of the solution.

$\_\_\_ \approx BC$ Multiply. Round to the nearest tenth.

So, the ladder reaches about ___ up the side of the building.

REFLECT

3a. Why is it best to wait until the final step before rounding? What happens if you round the value of tan 68° to the nearest tenth before multiplying?

3b. A student claims that it is possible to solve the problem using the tangent of $\angle B$. Do you agree or disagree? If it is possible, show the solution. If it is not possible, explain why not.

3 Construct viable arguments and critique the reasoning of others.

Throughout *Explorations in Core Math*, you will be asked to make conjectures, construct a mathematical argument, explain your reasoning, and justify your conclusions. Reflect questions offer opportunities for cooperative learning and class discussion. You will have additional opportunities to critique reasoning in Error Analysis problems.

REFLECT

2a. Given that $\triangle PQR \cong \triangle STU$, $PQ = 2.7$ ft, and $PR = 3.4$ ft, is it possible to determine the length of $\overline{TU}$? If so, find the length. If not, explain why not.

2b. A student claims that any two congruent triangles must have the same perimeter. Do you agree or disagree? Why?

3. **Error Analysis** A student who is 72 inches tall wants to find the height of a flagpole. He measures the length of the flagpole's shadow and the length of his own shadow at the same time of day, as shown in his sketch below. Explain the error in the student's work.

The triangles are similar by the AA Similarity Criterion, so corresponding sides are proportional.

$\frac{x}{72} = \frac{48}{128}$

$x = 72 \cdot \frac{48}{128}$, so $x = 27$ in.

72 in. 48 in. x 128 in.

4 Model with mathematics.

Explorations in Core Math presents problems in a variety of contexts such as science, business, and everyday life. You will use models such as equations, tables, diagrams, and graphs to represent the information in the problem and to solve the problem. Then you will interpret your results in context.

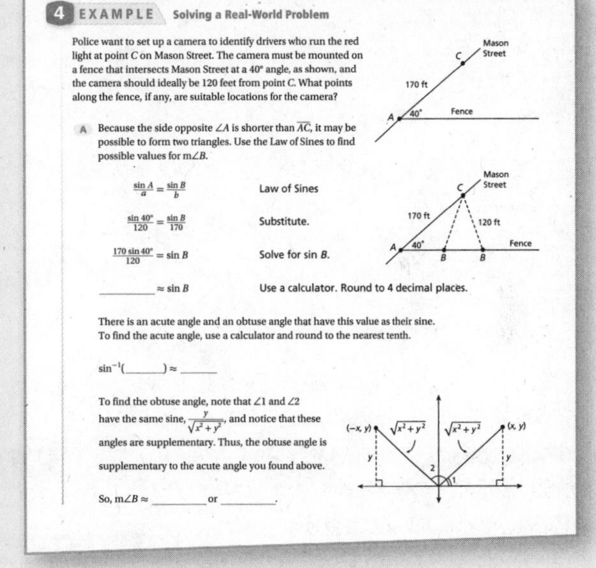

4 EXAMPLE **Solving a Real-World Problem**

Police want to set up a camera to identify drivers who run the red light at point *C* on Mason Street. The camera must be mounted on a fence that intersects Mason Street at a 40° angle, as shown, and the camera should ideally be 120 feet from point *C*. What points along the fence, if any, are suitable locations for the camera?

A Because the side opposite $\angle A$ is shorter than $\overline{AC}$, it may be possible to form two triangles. Use the Law of Sines to find possible values for m$\angle B$.

$\frac{\sin A}{a} = \frac{\sin B}{b}$ Law of Sines

$\frac{\sin 40^\circ}{120} = \frac{\sin B}{170}$ Substitute.

$\frac{170 \sin 40^\circ}{120} = \sin B$ Solve for sin *B*.

________ ≈ sin *B* Use a calculator. Round to 4 decimal places.

There is an acute angle and an obtuse angle that have this value as their sine. To find the acute angle, use a calculator and round to the nearest tenth.

$\sin^{-1}($______$) \approx$ ______

To find the obtuse angle, note that $\angle 1$ and $\angle 2$ have the same sine, $\frac{y}{\sqrt{x^2+y^2}}$, and notice that these angles are supplementary. Thus, the obtuse angle is supplementary to the acute angle you found above.

So, m$\angle B \approx$ ________ or ________.

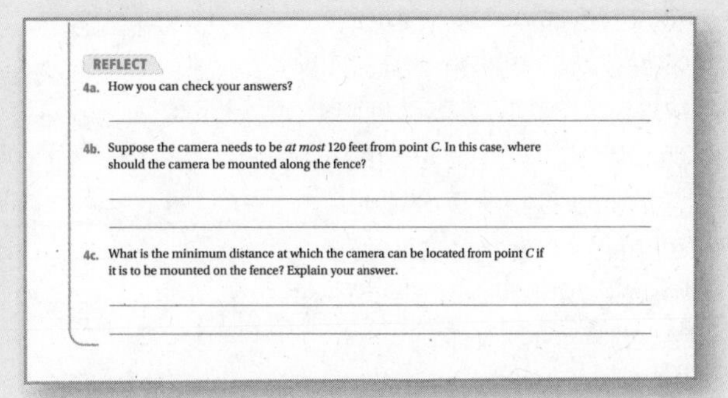

REFLECT

4a. How you can check your answers?

4b. Suppose the camera needs to be *at most* 120 feet from point *C*. In this case, where should the camera be mounted along the fence?

4c. What is the minimum distance at which the camera can be located from point *C* if it is to be mounted on the fence? Explain your answer.

5 Use appropriate tools strategically.

You will use a variety of tools in *Explorations in Core Math*, including manipulatives, paper and pencil, and technology. You might use manipulatives to develop concepts, paper and pencil to practice skills, and technology (such as graphing calculators, spreadsheets, or geometry software) to investigate more complicated mathematical ideas.

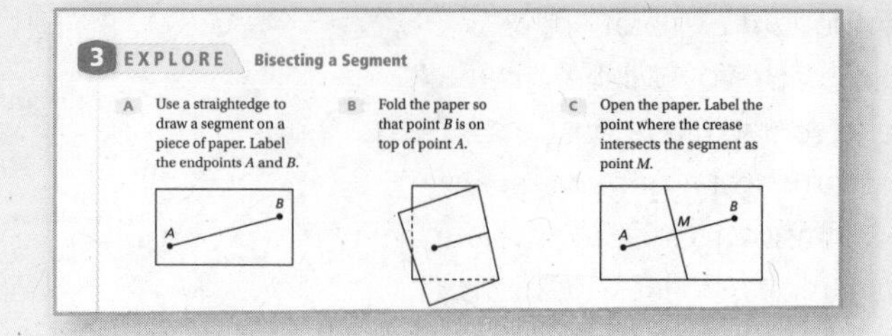

3 EXPLORE Bisecting a Segment

A Use a straightedge to draw a segment on a piece of paper. Label the endpoints *A* and *B*.

B Fold the paper so that point *B* is on top of point *A*.

C Open the paper. Label the point where the crease intersects the segment as point *M*.

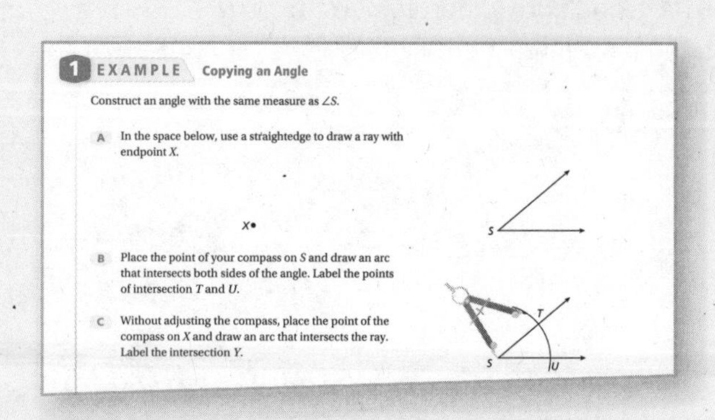

1 EXAMPLE Copying an Angle

Construct an angle with the same measure as $\angle S$.

A In the space below, use a straightedge to draw a ray with endpoint *X*.

B Place the point of your compass on *S* and draw an arc that intersects both sides of the angle. Label the points of intersection *T* and *U*.

C Without adjusting the compass, place the point of the compass on *X* and draw an arc that intersects the ray. Label the intersection *Y*.

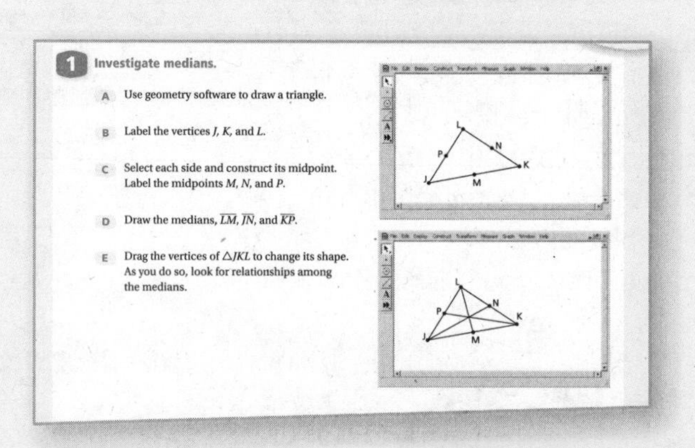

1 Investigate medians.

A Use geometry software to draw a triangle.

B Label the vertices *J*, *K*, and *L*.

C Select each side and construct its midpoint. Label the midpoints *M*, *N*, and *P*.

D Draw the medians, $\overline{LM}$, $\overline{JN}$, and $\overline{KP}$.

E Drag the vertices of $\triangle JKL$ to change its shape. As you do so, look for relationships among the medians.

6 Attend to precision.

Precision refers not only to the correctness of arithmetic calculations, algebraic manipulations, and geometric reasoning but also to the proper use of mathematical language, symbols, and units to communicate mathematical ideas. Throughout *Explorations in Core Math* you will demonstrate your skills in these areas when you are asked to calculate, describe, show, explain, prove, and predict.

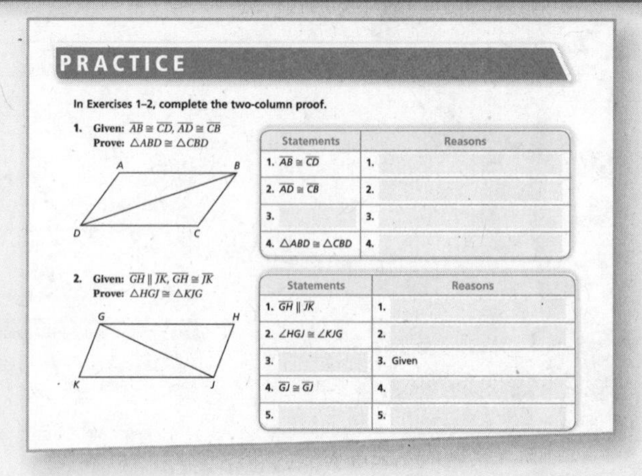

PRACTICE

In Exercises 1–2, complete the two-column proof.

1. Given: $\overline{AB} \cong \overline{CD}$, $\overline{AD} \cong \overline{CB}$
Prove: $\triangle ABD \cong \triangle CBD$

Statements	Reasons
1. $\overline{AB} \cong \overline{CD}$	1.
2. $\overline{AD} \cong \overline{CB}$	2.
3.	3.
4. $\triangle ABD \cong \triangle CBD$	4.

2. Given: $\overline{GH} \parallel \overline{JK}$, $\overline{GH} \cong \overline{JK}$
Prove: $\triangle HGJ \cong \triangle KJG$

Statements	Reasons
1. $\overline{GH} \parallel \overline{JK}$	1.
2. $\angle HGJ \cong \angle KJG$	2.
3.	3. Given
4. $\overline{GJ} \cong \overline{GJ}$	4.
5.	5.

7 Look for and make use of structure.

In *Explorations in Core Math*, you will look for patterns or regularity in mathematical structures such as expressions, equations, geometric figures, and graphs. Becoming familiar with underlying structures will help you build your understanding of more complicated mathematical ideas.

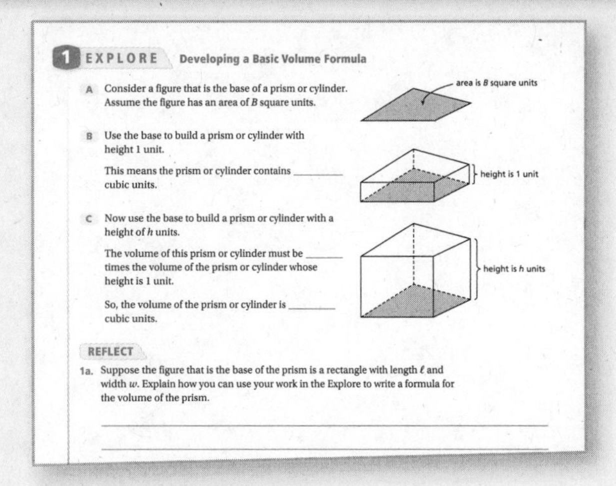

1 EXPLORE Developing a Basic Volume Formula

A Consider a figure that is the base of a prism or cylinder. Assume the figure has an area of B square units.

B Use the base to build a prism or cylinder with height 1 unit.

This means the prism or cylinder contains ________ cubic units.

C Now use the base to build a prism or cylinder with a height of h units.

The volume of this prism or cylinder must be ________ times the volume of the prism or cylinder whose height is 1 unit.

So, the volume of the prism or cylinder is ________ cubic units.

REFLECT

1a. Suppose the figure that is the base of the prism is a rectangle with length ℓ and width w. Explain how you can use your work in the Explore to write a formula for the volume of the prism.

8 Look for and express regularity in repeated reasoning.

In *Explorations in Core Math*, you will have the opportunity to explore and reflect on mathematical processes in order to come up with general methods for performing calculations and solving problems.

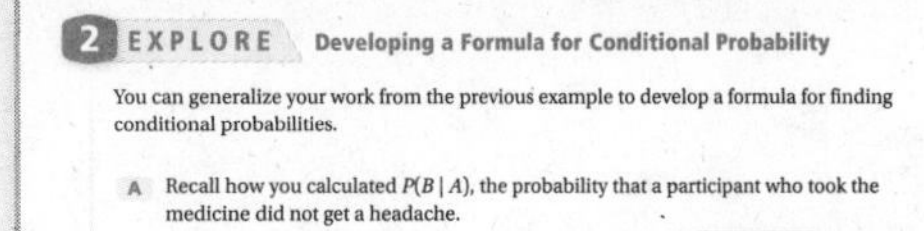

2 EXPLORE Developing a Formula for Conditional Probability

You can generalize your work from the previous example to develop a formula for finding conditional probabilities.

A Recall how you calculated $P(B \mid A)$, the probability that a participant who took the medicine did not get a headache.

You found that $P(B \mid A) = \frac{48}{60}$.

Use the table shown here to help you write this quotient in terms of events A and B.

$P(B \mid A) =$ ________

		Event A		
		Took Medicine	No Medicine	TOTAL
Event B	Headache	12	15	27
	No Headache	48 = $n(A \cap B)$	25	73 = $n(B)$
	TOTAL	60 = $n(A)$	40	100

B Now divide the numerator and denominator of the quotient by $n(S)$, the number of outcomes in the sample space. This converts the counts to probabilities.

$P(B \mid A) = \frac{\ \ /n(S)}{\ \ /n(S)} =$ ________

REFLECT

2a. Write a formula for $P(A \mid B)$ in terms of $n(A \cap B)$ and $n(B)$.

2b. Write a formula for $P(A \mid B)$ in terms of $P(A \cap B)$ and $P(B)$.

PhotoDisc/Getty Images

Extending the Number System

Module 1 Complex Numbers, Rational Exponents, and Closure

1-1	Complex Numbers and Roots	**MCC9-12.N.CN.1**
1-2	Operations with Complex Numbers	**MCC9-12.N.CN.2, MCC9-12.N.CN.3(+)**
	Performance Tasks	
	PARCC Assessment Readiness	

Unpacking the Standards

Understanding the standards and the vocabulary terms in the standards will help you know exactly what you are expected to learn in this unit.

GPS COMMON CORE **MCC9-12.N.CN.2**

Use the relation $i^2 = -1$ and the commutative, associative, and distributive properties to add, subtract, and multiply complex numbers.

Key Vocabulary

complex number *(número complejo)* Any number that can be written as $a + bi$, where a and b are real numbers and $i = \sqrt{-1}$.

What It Means For You

Whole numbers, integers, real numbers, and so on, are all members of a larger set called the complex numbers. You can use the same properties of operations with all of them.

EXAMPLE

$(4 + i)(3 - 2i)$

$= 4(3 - 2i) + i(3 + 2i)$	*Distributive Property*
$= 12 - 8i + 3i - 2i^2$	*Distributive Property*
$= 12 - 8i + 3i + 2$	$i^2 = -1$
$= (12 + 2) + (-8i + 3i)$	*Associative/ Commutative Properties*
$= 14 - 5i$	*Add real parts and imaginary parts.*

UNIT 1

MCC9-12.A.APR.2

Know and apply the Remainder Theorem: For a polynomial $p(x)$ and a number a, the remainder on division by $x - a$ is $p(a)$, so $p(a) = 0$ if and only if $(x - a)$ is a factor of $p(x)$.

What It Means For You

You can use the Remainder Theorem to find factors of polynomials.

EXAMPLE

To check whether $(x - 2)$ is a factor of $P(x) = x^3 - 19x + 30$, find the value of $P(2)$. If $P(2) = 0$, then $(x - 2)$ is a factor of P by the Remainder Theorem. You can substitute as shown below, or use a shortcut called synthetic substitution.

$$P(x) = x^3 - 19x + 30$$

$$P(2) = 2^3 - 19(2) + 30$$

$$P(2) = 8 - 38 + 30$$

$$P(2) = 0$$

Because $P(2) = 0$, $(x - 2)$ is a factor of P.

You can instead divide $x^3 - 19x + 30$ by $(x - 2)$ to check that $(x - 2)$ is a factor, using either long division or synthetic division. You will find that $\frac{x^3 - 19x + 30}{x - 2} = x^2 + 2x - 15$ or $(x + 5)(x - 3)$.

UNIT 1

Key Vocabulary

absolute value of a complex number *(valor absoluto de un número complejo)* The absolute value of $a + bi$ is the distance from the origin to the point (a, b) in the complex plane and is denoted $|a + bi| = \sqrt{a^2 + b^2}$.

complex conjugate *(conjugado complejo)* The complex conjugate of any complex number $a + bi$, denoted $\overline{a + bi}$, is $a - bi$.

complex number *(número complejo)* Any number that can be written as $a + bi$, where a and b are real numbers and $i = \sqrt{-1}$.

complex plane *(plano complejo)* A set of coordinate axes in which the horizontal axis is the real axis and the vertical axis is the imaginary axis; used to graph complex numbers.

imaginary unit *(unidad imaginaria)* The unit in the imaginary number system, $\sqrt{-1}$.

imaginary number *(número imaginario)* The square root of a negative number, written in the form bi, where b is a real number and i is the imaginary unit, $\sqrt{-1}$. Also called a *pure imaginary number*.

MATHEMATICAL PRACTICE

The Common Core Standards for Mathematical Practice describe varieties of expertise that mathematics educators at all levels should seek to develop in their students. Opportunities to develop these practices are integrated throughout this program.

1. **Make sense of problems and persevere in solving them.**
2. **Reason abstractly and quantitatively.**
3. **Construct viable arguments and critique the reasoning of others.**
4. **Model with mathematics.**
5. **Use appropriate tools strategically.**
6. **Attend to precision.**
7. **Look for and make use of structure.**
8. **Look for and express regularity in repeated reasoning.**

UNIT 1

Name______________________ Class______________ Date__________

1-1

Complex Numbers and Roots

Going Deeper

Essential question: *What is a complex number?*

MCC9-12.N.CN.1

Video Tutor

1 EXPLORE Understanding Complex Numbers

Consider the quadratic equations $x^2 - 1 = 0$ and $x^2 + 1 = 0$. You can solve the equations using square roots.

$$x^2 - 1 = 0 \qquad x^2 + 1 = 0$$
$$x^2 = 1 \qquad x^2 = -1$$
$$x = \pm\sqrt{1} = \pm 1 \qquad x = \pm\sqrt{-1}$$

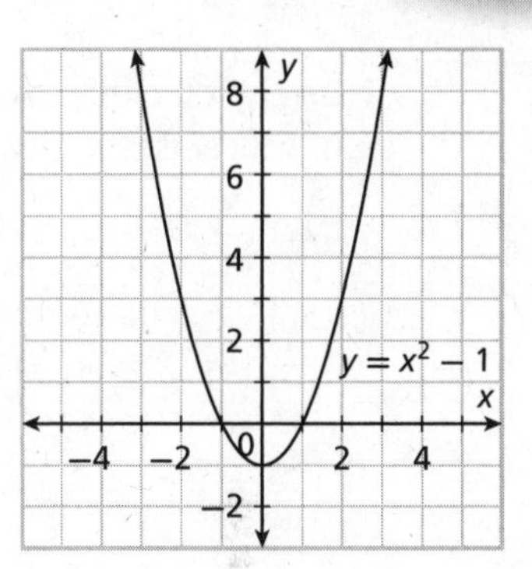

A The first equation has two solutions, 1 and -1. The second equation also has two solutions, $\sqrt{-1}$ and $-\sqrt{-1}$. Which of these four solutions are real numbers?______________________

B The graphs of $y = x^2 - 1$ and $y = x^2 + 1$ are shown. How do the graphs confirm your answer to part **A**?

____

____

____

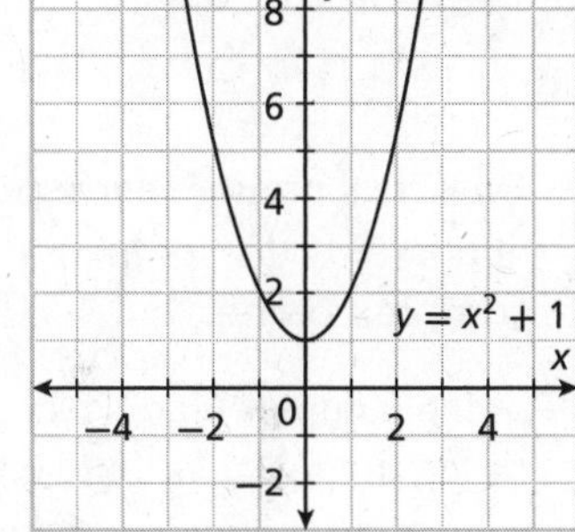

When the graph of a quadratic function $f(x)$ does not cross the x-axis, the solutions of $f(x) = 0$ involve the *imaginary unit i.*

C Previously you have used the Product Property $\sqrt{ab} = \sqrt{a} \cdot \sqrt{b}$ to simplify square roots of nonnegative numbers. Now extend the property to situations where $a = -1$ or $b = -1$. Simplify the following square roots by writing them in terms of the so-called **imaginary unit** i, which equals $\sqrt{-1}$.

$$\sqrt{-2} = \sqrt{-1 \cdot 2} = \sqrt{-1} \cdot \sqrt{\quad} = i\sqrt{2} \qquad \sqrt{-4} = \sqrt{\qquad} = \sqrt{4} \cdot \sqrt{-1} = 2i$$

A **complex number** is a number that can be written in the form $a + bi$, where a and b are real numbers and $i = \sqrt{-1}$. The set of real numbers is a subset of the complex numbers $\mathbb{C}$. Every complex number has a real part a and an imaginary part b.

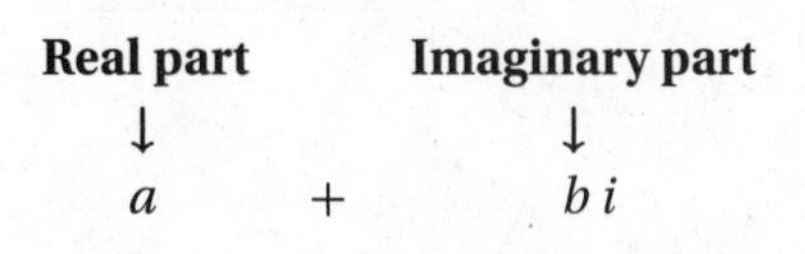

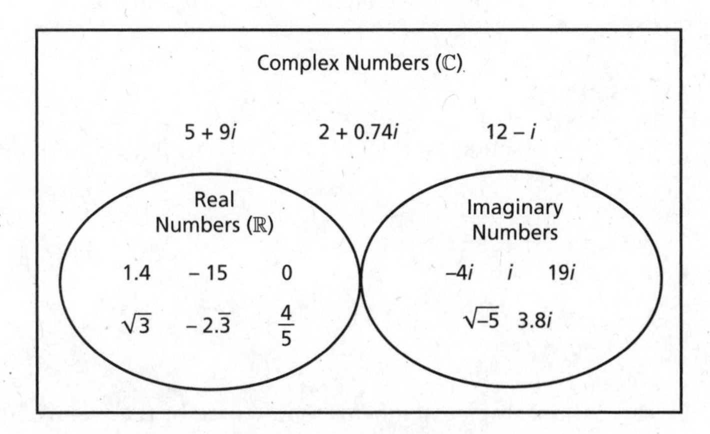

Real numbers are complex numbers where $b = 0$. Imaginary numbers are complex numbers where $a = 0$ and $b \neq 0$. These are sometimes called **pure imaginary numbers**.

The complex numbers that are neither real nor imaginary, such as $5 + 9i$, are called *nonreal numbers*. In general, the nonreal numbers $a + bi$ are those in which both $a \neq 0$ and $b \neq 0$.

REFLECT

1a. How many real solutions does $x^2 + 4 = 0$ have? How many nonreal solutions? Explain.

____

1b. What is the value of i^2? Explain.

____

1c. Using just the three set names shown in the Venn diagram on the previous page, name all sets to which each of the following numbers belong.

$1 - 2i$ ______________________________

$-2i$ ______________________________

-2 ______________________________

MCC9–12.N.CN.1

2 ENGAGE The Complex Plane

Every real number corresponds to a point on the real number line. Similarly, every complex number corresponds to a point in the **complex plane**.

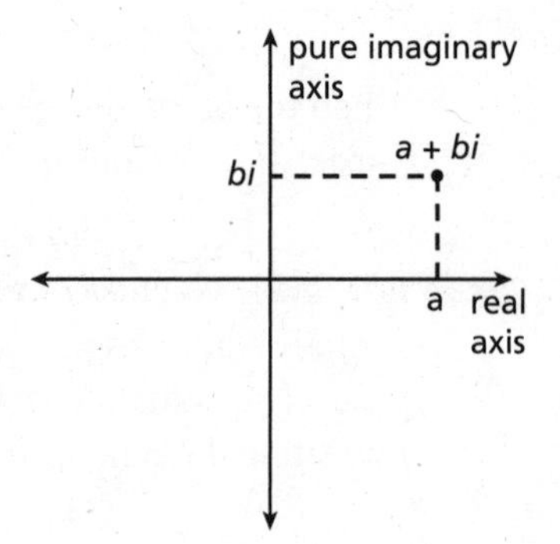

In the complex plane, real numbers are represented on a horizontal axis called the *real axis*. Pure imaginary numbers are represented on a vertical axis called the *pure imaginary* axis. Complex numbers that are neither real numbers nor pure imaginary numbers are represented in the plane formed by these axes.

It is important to recognize that the complex plane is not the same as the x-y coordinate plane that you are familiar with. In the x-y plane, real numbers are represented on both the x-axis and the y-axis.

REFLECT

2a. Describe how you would plot the following points in the complex plane.

7 ______________________________

$-4i$ ______________________________

$-6 + 2i$ ______________________________

2b. What complex number is represented by the origin of the complex plane?

____

The **complex conjugate** of any real number $a + bi$ is the complex number $a - bi$.

MCC9–12.N.CN.1

3 EXAMPLE Finding Complex Conjugates

Find each complex conjugate.

A $3 + 5i$ B $-6 - i$ C 12 D $-2i$

REFLECT

3a. What is the conjugate of the conjugate of a complex number $a + bi$? Explain.

MCC9–12.N.CN.1

4 EXPLORE Graphing Complex Conjugates

A Use the quadratic formula to solve $x^2 - 4x + 5 = 0$.

$x_1 = \dfrac{-\square + \sqrt{\square^2 - 4 \bullet \square \bullet \square}}{2 \bullet \square}$ $x_2 = \dfrac{-\square - \sqrt{\square^2 - 4 \bullet \square \bullet \square}}{2 \bullet \square}$

$= \dfrac{\square + \sqrt{\square}}{\square}$ $= \dfrac{\square - \sqrt{\square}}{\square}$

$= \square + i$ $= \square - i$

B Graph the solutions on the complex plane.

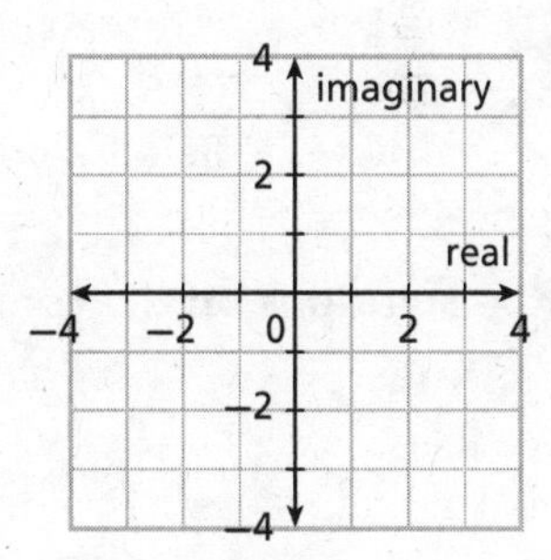

REFLECT

4a. Why are nonreal roots of a quadratic equation complex conjugates?

4b. Describe the locations of the graphs of a complex number and its conjugate relative to the real axis. Explain why the relationship exists.

PRACTICE

Write each number in its proper location in the Venn diagram.

1. $3 + i$

2. -17

3. $\sqrt{7}$

4. $9i$

5. $-6 - 5\text{i}$

6. $-\frac{7}{8}$

7. 6.492

8. $-\sqrt{-25}$

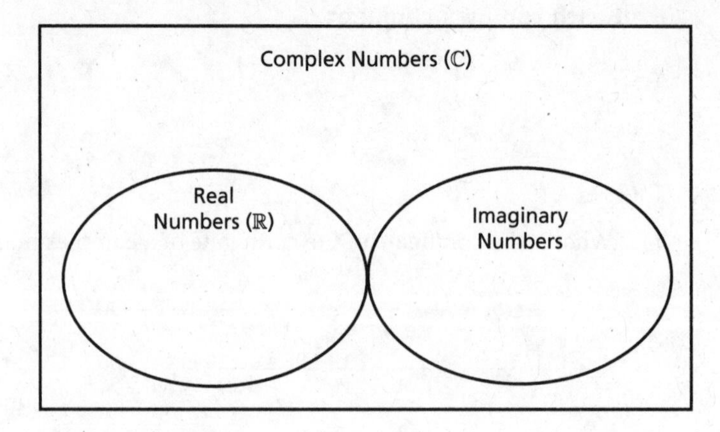

Write the square roots of each number in terms of *i*.

9. -9 ______ and ______

10. -7 ______ and ______

11. -1 ______ and ______

12. -100 ______ and ______

Solve.

13. $x^2 - 16 = 0$ ______ and ______

14. $x^2 + 16 = 0$ ______ and ______

15. $x^2 - 5 = 0$ ______ and ______

16. $x^2 + 5 = 0$ ______ and ______

Find each complex conjugate.

17. $7 - 2i$ ______

18. 9 ______

19. $6i$ ______

20. $-8i$ ______

21. $-1 - 9i$ ______

22. $12 + 5i$ ______

Solve. Then graph the solutions on the complex plane.

23. $x^2 + 2x + 5 = 0$

$x =$ ______

$x =$ ______

24. $x^2 - 6x + 13 = 0$

$x =$ ______

$x =$ ______

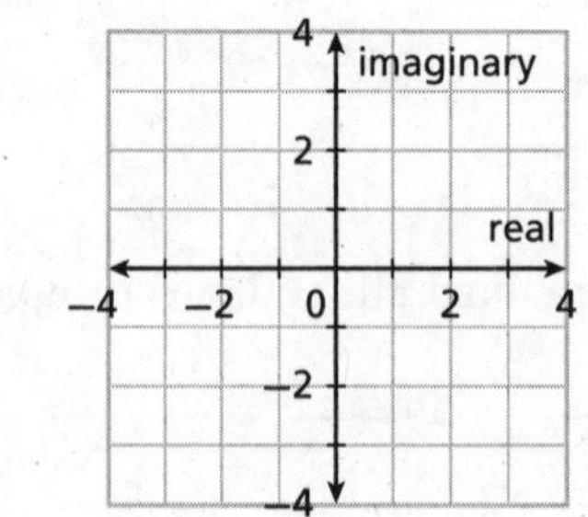

Name ____________ Class ____________ Date ____________

1-1

Additional Practice

Express each number in terms of *i*.

1. $\sqrt{-32}$
2. $2\sqrt{-18}$
3. $\sqrt{-\frac{1}{9}}$

Solve each equation.

4. $3x^2 + 81 = 0$
5. $4x^2 = -28$
6. $\frac{1}{4}x^2 + 12 = 0$
7. $6x^2 = -126$

Find the values of *x* and *y* that make each equation true.

8. $2x - 20i = 8 - (4y)i$
9. $5i - 6x = (10y)i + 2$

Find the zeros of each function.

10. $f(x) = x^2 - 2x + 4$
11. $g(x) = x^2 + 6x + 14$

Find each complex conjugate.

12. $i - 3$
13. $3i - 4$
14. $11i$

Solve.

15. The impedance of an electrical circuit is a way of measuring how much the circuit impedes the flow of electricity. The impedance can be a complex number. A circuit is being designed that must have an impedance that satisfies the function $f(x) = 2x^2 - 12x + 40$, where x is a measure of the impedance. Find the zeros of the function.

Problem Solving

At a carnival, a new attraction allows contestants to jump off a springboard onto a platform to be launched vertically into the air. The object is to ring a bell located 20 feet overhead. The distance from the bell in feet is modeled by the function $dt = 16t^2 - bt + 20$, where t is the time in seconds after leaving the platform, and b is the takeoff velocity from the platform.

1. Kate watches some of the contestants. She theorizes that if the platform launches a contestant with a takeoff velocity of at least 32 feet per second, the contestant can ring the bell.
   a. Find the zeros for the function using 32 feet per second as the takeoff velocity. ____________
   b. Is Kate's theory valid? Explain.

____

2. Mirko suggests they vary the value of b and determine for which values of b the roots are real.
   a. Complete the table to show the roots for different values of b.
   b. For which values of b in the table are the roots real?

____

   c. What difference does it make if the roots are real?

b	Function	Roots
24	$d(t) = 16t^2 - 24t + 20$	
32	$d(t) = 16t^2 - \_\_t + 20$	
40	$d(t) = 16t^2 - \_\_t + 20$	
48	$d(t) = 16t^2 - \_\_t + 20$	

____

3. Using the results from the table, and the function, estimate the minimum takeoff velocity needed for a contestant to be able to ring the bell. ____________

Choose the letter for the best answer.

4. Mirko suggests using four bells at heights of 15, 20, 25, and 30 feet from the platform. How many of the bells can a contestant reach if the takeoff velocity is 32 feet per second?
   A 3
   B 2
   C 1
   D 0

5. At what height must a bell be placed for a contestant to reach it with a takeoff velocity of 48 feet per second?
   A 20 feet or less
   B 25 feet or less
   C 30 feet or less
   D 36 feet or less

Name________________________ Class______________ Date__________

1-2

Operations with Complex Numbers

Going Deeper

Video Tutor

Essential question: *How do you add, subtract, and multiply complex numbers?*

To add or subtract complex numbers, add or subtract their real parts and add or subtract their nonreal parts. You can use the distributive property to add or subtract the nonreal parts. For instance, $3i + 2i = (3 + 2)i = 5i$.

MCC9–12.N.CN.2

1 EXAMPLE Adding and Subtracting Complex Numbers

A $(8 + 3i) + (7 + 5i) = (\ \_\_ + \_\_\ ) + (\ \_\_ + \_\_\ )$ Collect real parts, and collect nonreal parts.

$= \_\_ + \_\_$ Add real parts, and add nonreal parts.

B $(8 + 3i) - (7 + 3i) = (\ \_\_ - \_\_\ ) + (\ \_\_ - \_\_\ )$ Collect real parts, and collect nonreal parts.

$= \_\_ + (\ \_\_\ )$ Subtract real parts, and subtract nonreal parts.

$= \_\_ - \_\_$ Write the number without parentheses.

REFLECT

1a. Give an example of two complex numbers whose sum is a real number. Find the sum of the numbers.

____

1b. Give an example of two complex numbers whose sum is an imaginary number. Find the sum of the numbers.

____

1c. What properties (extended to nonreal numbers) allow you to collect the real parts and nonreal parts of two complex numbers being added?

____

To multiply two complex numbers, use the distributive property to multiply each part of one of the numbers with each part of the other. Then simplify by using the fact that $i^2 = -1$ and combining like terms. The general multiplication pattern is shown below.

$$(a + bi)(c + di) = ac + adi + bci + bdi^2$$

MCC9–12.N.CN.2

2 EXAMPLE Multiplying Complex Numbers

A $(5 + 3i)(9 + 8i) = 45 + \square + \square + 24i^2$ Multiply.

$= 45 + \square + \square + 24(-1)$ $i^2 = -1$

$= 21 + \square$ Combine like terms.

B $(8 + 12i)(4 - 2i) = \square - 16i + 48i + (\square)$ Multiply.

$= \square + 32i + \square$ $i^2 = -1$

$= \square + 32i$ Combine like terms.

REFLECT

2a. How is multiplying $(5 + 3i)(9 + 8i)$ like multiplying $(5 + 3x)(9 + 8x)$? How is it different?

2b. What is the product of $a + bi$ and $a - bi$ where a and b are real numbers, $a \neq 0$, and $b \neq 0$? Classify the product as a real number or a nonreal number. Explain.

2c. What is the square of $a + bi$ where a and b are real numbers, $a \neq 0$, and $b \neq 0$? Classify the square as a real number, an imaginary number, or neither.

2d. If you multiply a nonzero real number and a nonreal number, is the product real or nonreal? Explain.

Let $z = a + bi$ be a complex number. The **conjugate** of z is $\overline{z} = a - bi$. For example, the conjugate of $4 + 7i$ is $4 - 7i$.

MCC9-12.N.CN.3(+)

3 EXPLORE Finding Products of Complex Numbers and Their Conjugates

A Complete the table.

z	$\overline{z}$	$z \cdot \overline{z}$
$4 + 7i$		
$5 - 2i$		
$3i$		
-6		

B Generalize the results: If $z = a + bi$, then in terms of a and b,
$z \cdot \overline{z} = (a + bi)(a - bi) = a^2 - (bi)^2 = a^2 - b^2i^2 = a^2 - b^2(-1) =$ ________.

REFLECT

3a. Is the product $z \cdot \overline{z}$ a real number or an nonreal number? Explain.

MCC9-12.N.CN.3(+)

4 ENGAGE Understanding the Absolute Value of a Complex Number

A complex number can be represented by a point in the *complex plane* having real numbers on its horizontal axis and pure imaginary numbers on its vertical axis. If $z = a + bi$, then the coordinates of the point representing z are (a, bi).

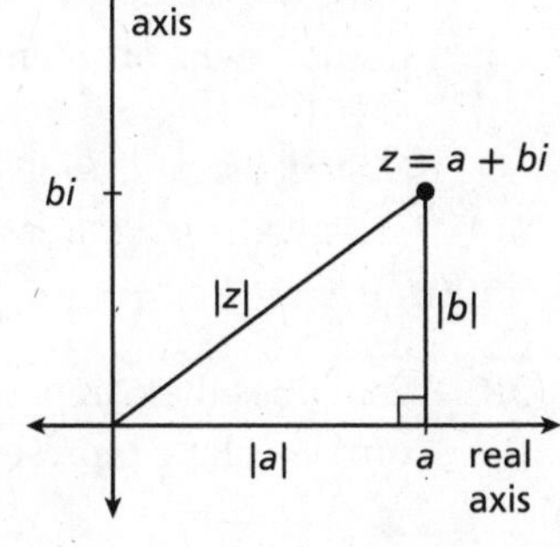

For any complex number not on one of the axes, you can draw a right triangle as shown. The lengths of the legs are the real numbers $|a|$ and $|b|$. The **absolute value** of the complex number z, written as $|z|$, is the length of the hypotenuse. The absolute value of z is also called the *modulus* of z.

For the special case of $z = a + 0i$, the graph of z is a point on the real axis, and $|z| = |a|$. Similarly, for the special case of $z = 0 + bi$, the graph of z is a point on the pure imaginary axis, and $|z| = |b|$.

REFLECT

4a. If $z = a + bi$, use the Pythagorean Theorem to express $|z|$ in terms of a and b. (Note that $|a|^2$ can simply be written as a^2 and $|b|^2$ as b^2.)

4b. Show that the formula you wrote for Question 2a also applies to the special cases $z = a + 0i$ and $z = 0 + bi$. Use the fact that if x is a real number, then $\sqrt{x^2} = |x|$.

4c. How is $|z|$ related to $z \cdot \bar{z}$?

Comparing Absolute Values The set of real numbers is an *ordered set* because for any two real numbers a and b, you can determine whether $a < b$, $a = b$, or $a > b$. The set of complex numbers, however, is not an ordered set. For instance, you cannot compare the numbers $3 + 4i$ and $1 - 5i$ other than to say that they are not equal.

Because the absolute value of a complex number is a real number, you *can* compare the absolute values of two complex numbers. Just as you can interpret the absolute value of a real number geometrically as the number's distance from 0 on the real number line, you can interpret the absolute value of a complex number geometrically as the number's distance from the origin of the complex plane.

MCC9–12.N.CN.3(+)

5 EXAMPLE Comparing Absolute Values of Complex Numbers

Compare the absolute values of $3 + 4i$ and $1 - 5i$.

A Find each absolute value.

$$|3 + 4i| = \sqrt{\square^2 + \square^2} = \sqrt{\square} = \square$$

$$|1 - 5i| = \sqrt{\square^2 + (\square)^2} = \sqrt{\square}$$

B Compare the absolute values.

$|3 + 4i|$ $\square$ $|1 - 5i|$ because ____________.

REFLECT

5a. What does the comparison of $|3 + 4i|$ and $|1 - 5i|$ tell you about the points in the complex plane representing $3 + 4i$ and $1 - 5i$?

5b. In part A you found that $|3 + 4i| = 5$. Give three other complex numbers that have an absolute value of 5.

Dividing Complex Numbers To divide two complex numbers $a + bi$ and $c + di$, express the quotient as $\frac{a + bi}{c + di}$. You can write this fraction as a single complex number by multiplying the numerator and denominator by the conjugate of the denominator and then simplifying.

MCC9–12.N.CN.3(+)

6 EXAMPLE Dividing Complex Numbers

Divide.

A $\frac{6 - 4i}{2i} = \frac{6 - 4i}{2i} \cdot \frac{\quad}{\quad}$ Multiply the numerator and denominator by the conjugate of the denominator.

$= \frac{\quad}{\quad}$ Multiply the numerators, and multiply the denominators. Simplify each product.

$=$ Write in the form $a + bi$.

B $\frac{10 - 15i}{2 + i} = \frac{10 - 15i}{2 + i} \cdot \frac{\quad}{\quad}$ Multiply the numerator and denominator by the conjugate of the denominator.

$= \frac{\quad}{\quad}$ Multiply the numerators, and multiply the denominators. Simplify each product.

$=$ Write in the form $a + bi$.

C $\frac{1}{2 + 2i} = \frac{1}{2 + 2i} \cdot \frac{\quad}{\quad}$ Multiply the numerator and denominator by the conjugate of the denominator.

$= \frac{\quad}{\quad}$ Multiply the numerators, and multiply the denominators. Simplify each product.

$=$ Write in the form $a + bi$.

REFLECT

6a. How can you use multiplication to check the quotient that you obtain when you divide one complex number by another? Illustrate this procedure using the quotient from part A.

6b. Find the absolute values of the dividend, the divisor, and the quotient in part A. How are these absolute values related?

PRACTICE

Add or subtract.

1. $10i - 2i$ ________

2. $9i - (13 + 7i)$ ________

3. $(9 - 8i) - (6 - 4i)$ ________

4. $(3 + 15i) - (-5 + i)$ ________

Multiply.

5. $-2(1 - 3i)$ ________

6. $5i(-5 + 2i)$ ________

7. $(4 - 8i)(5 - 6i)$ ________

8. $(5 + 4i)(3 + 9i)$ ________

9. $(1 + 2i)^2$ ________

10. $(2 - i)^2$ ________

11. Find the values i^1, i^2, i^3, and i^4. Use these to find the product $i^{18} \cdot i^{23}$ two ways: (1) by simplifying each power before multiplying, and (2) by using the product of powers property and then simplifying.

____

____

Find the absolute value of each complex number.

12. $4 + 3i$ ________

13. $5i$ ________

14. $-3 - 2i$ ________

Compare the absolute values of each pair of complex numbers.

15. $1 + 2i, 2 - i$ ________

16. $7 - 2i, 6 + 4i$ ________

Divide.

17. $\frac{-3 - 2i}{i}$ ________

18. $\frac{8 - 12i}{5 + 3i}$ ________

19. $\frac{5 + 2i}{3 + 6i}$ ________

20. For a complex number z, compare $|z|$ and $|\overline{z}|$. Explain the relationship two ways: using algebra and using a geometric interpretation.

____

____

____

____

21. For a real number a, $|a| = |-a|$. Show that this property also applies to a complex number and its opposite.

____

____

Name________________________ Class______________ Date__________ **1-2**

Additional Practice

Graph each complex number.

1. -6
2. $4i$
3. $6 + 7i$
4. $-8 - 5i$
5. $-3i$

Imaginary axis

Real axis

Find each absolute value.

6. $|4 + 2i|$ ________

7. $|5 - i|$ ________

8. $|-3i|$ ________

Add or subtract. Write the result in the form $a + bi$.

9. $(-1 + 2i) + (6 - 9i)$ ________

10. $(3 - 3i) - (4 + 7i)$ ________

11. $(-5 + 2i) + (-2 + 8i)$ ________

Multiply. Write the result in the form $a + bi$.

12. $3i(2 - 3i)$ ________

13. $(4 + 5i)(2 + i)$ ________

14. $(-1 + 6i)(3 - 2i)$ ________

Simplify.

15. $\dfrac{2 + 4i}{3i}$ ________

16. $\dfrac{3 + 2i}{4 + i}$ ________

17. $2i^{11}$ ________

Solve.

18. In electronics, the total resistance to the flow of electricity in a circuit is called the impedance, Z. Impedance is represented by a complex number. The total impedance in a series circuit is the sum of individual impedances. The impedance in one part of a circuit is $Z_1 = 3 + 4i$. In another part of a circuit, the impedance is $Z_1 = 5 - 2i$. What is the total impedance of the circuit?

____

Problem Solving

Hannah and Aoki are designing fractals. Aoki recalls that many fractals are based on the Julia Set, whose formula is $Z_{n+1} = (Z_n)^2 + c$, where c is a constant. Hannah suggests they make their own fractal pattern using this formula, where $c = 1$ and $Z_1 = 1 + 2i$.

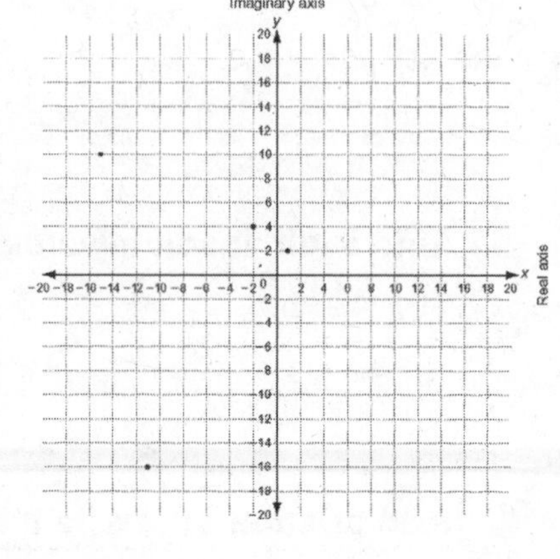

1. Complete the table to show values of n and Z_n.

n	$Z_{n+1} = (Z_n)^2 + c$	Z_n
0	$Z_1 = 1 + 2i$	$Z_1 = 1 + 2i$
1	$Z_2 = (1 + 2i)^2 + 1$	$Z_2 =$
2	$Z_3 = (\_\_\_\_\_\_\_\_)^2 + 1$	$Z_3 =$
3	$Z_4 = (\_\_\_\_\_\_\_\_)^2 + 1$	$Z_4 =$

2. Four points are shown on the complex plane. Which point is not part of the fractal pattern they have created? Explain.

____

Choose the letter for the best answer.

3. Aoki creates a second pattern by changing the value of c to 3. What happens to Z_n as n increases?
   - A The imaginary part is always twice the real part.
   - B The real and imaginary parts become equal.
   - C The real part becomes zero.
   - D The imaginary part becomes zero.

4. Hannah changes the formula to $Z_{n+1} = \frac{1}{(Z_n)^2} + c$. Leaving $c = 1$ and $Z_1 = 1 + 2i$, what is the value of Z_2?
   - A $0.48 - 0.16i$
   - B $0.88 - 0.16i$
   - C $1.2 - 0.4i$
   - D $2.2 - 0.4i$

5. Aoki takes Hannah's new formula, leaves $c = 1$, and sets $Z_1 = \frac{1}{1+2i}$. What is the value of Z_3?
   - A $Z_3 = -11 - 16i$
   - B $Z_3 = 2 + 2i$
   - C $Z_3 = 0.48 - 0.16i$
   - D $Z_3 = 147.4 + i$

6. Hannah reverts to $Z_{n+1} = (Z_n)^2 + c$. She sets $Z_1 = i$ and $c = i$. Which statement is NOT true?
   - A Z_n flip-flops between $(-1 + i)$ and $(-i)$.
   - B The coefficient of i never reaches 2.
   - C The imaginary part becomes zero.
   - D On a graph $Z_1 - Z_3$ create a triangle.

Name____________________ Class_______________ Date________

Performance Tasks

GPS COMMON CORE

MCC9-12.N.CN.1
MCC9-12.N.CN.2
MCC9-12.N.CN.3(+)

★ **1.** Give an argument that a complex number, $a + bi$, multiplied by its conjugate, always results in a real number.

★★ **2.** Simplify $\frac{-2 + 2i}{5 + 3i}$.

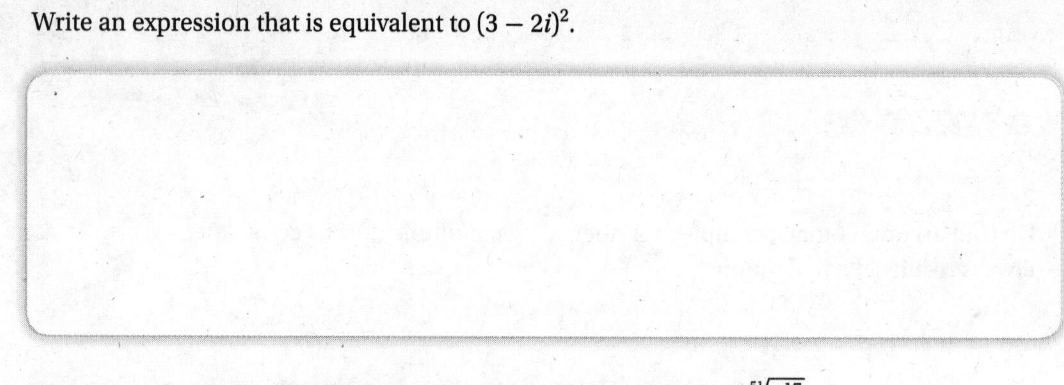

3. Write an expression that is equivalent to $(3 - 2i)^2$.

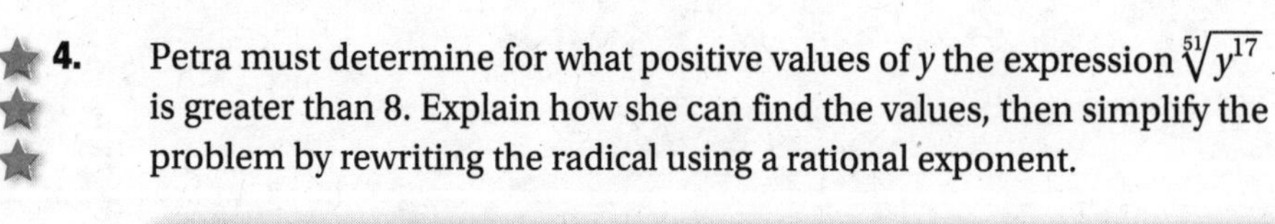

4. Petra must determine for what positive values of y the expression $\sqrt[51]{y^{17}}$ is greater than 8. Explain how she can find the values, then simplify the problem by rewriting the radical using a rational exponent.

Name ______________________ Class ______________ Date ________

SELECTED RESPONSE

1. What is the definition of a complex number?

A. A number of the form $a + bi$ where a and b are real

B. A number of the form $a + bi$ where $a = 0$ and b is real

C. A number of the form $a + bi$ where a is real and $b = 0$

D. A number of the form $a + bi$ where $a = 0$, b is real, and $b \neq 0$

2. What is the simplified form of the product $(-4 + 2i)(3 - 9i)$?

F. $6 - 42i$ **H.** $6 + 42i$

G. $-30 - 42i$ **J.** $-6 + 42i$

3. What is the conjugate of $2 - 3i$?

A. $-2 - 3i$ **C.** $3 + 2i$

B. $2 + 3i$ **D.** $3 - 2i$

4. What is the simplified form of the quotient $\frac{1 - 4i}{-2 + i}$?

F. $-2 + \frac{7}{3}i$ **H.** $\frac{2}{3} + 3i$

G. $-\frac{6}{5} + \frac{7}{5}i$ **J.** $\frac{2}{5} + \frac{9}{5}i$

5. What is $|-1 - i|$?

A. $1 + i$ **C.** $\sqrt{2}$

B. 1 **D.** 0

6. Solve the equation $2x^2 + 18 = 0$.

F. $x = 3 \pm i$ **H.** $x = \pm 3i$

G. $x = \pm 3$ **J.** $x = \pm 3 + i$

7. Find the zeros of the function $f(x) = x^2 + 6x + 18$.

A. $x = 3i$ or $-3i$ **C.** $x = -3 + 3i$

B. $x = -3 + 3i$ or $-3 - 3i$ **D.** $x = -6 + 3i$ or $-6 - 3i$

8. Find the complex conjugate of $3i + 4$.

F. $-4 - 3i$ **H.** $4 + 3i$

G. $-4 + 3i$ **J.** $4 - 3i$

CONSTRUCTED RESPONSE

9. Graph the complex number $4 + 2i$.

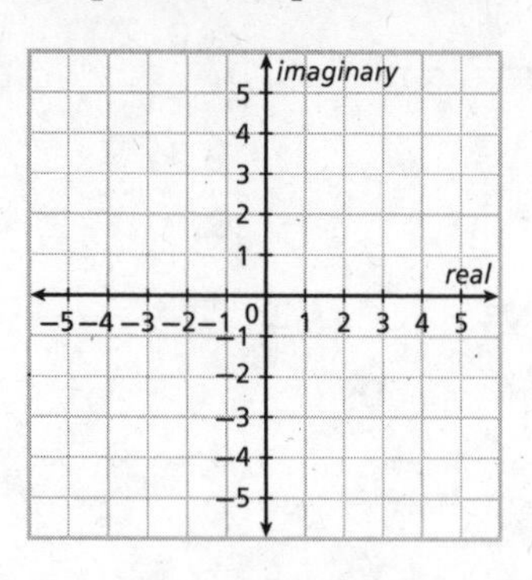

10. Graph the complex number $-5 + i$.

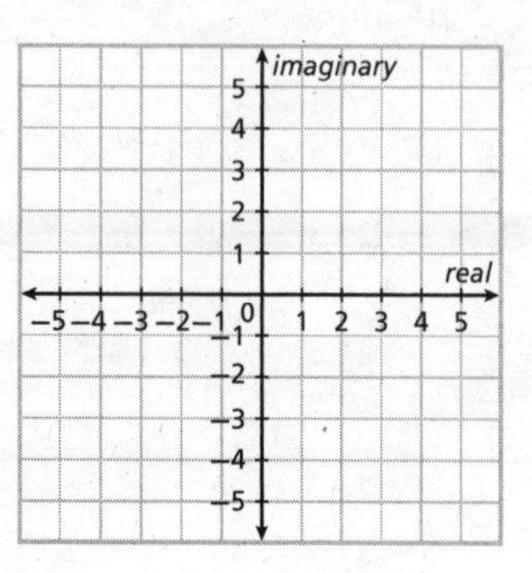

11. Find $(-3 + 6i) + (-4 - 2i)$ by graphing on the complex plane.

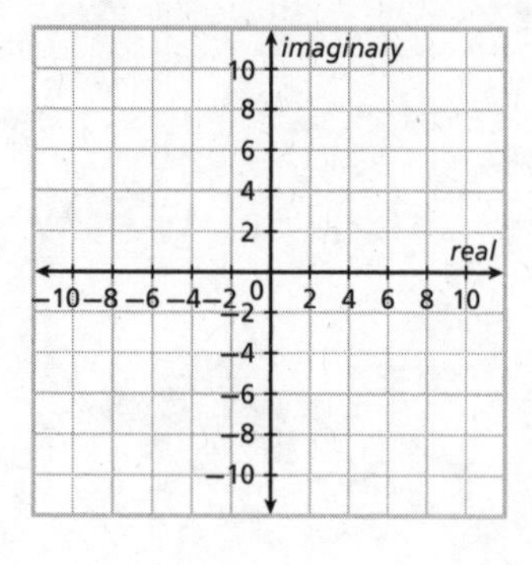

12. Consider the equation $x^2 - 4x + 5 = 0$.

a. Without solving the equation, tell whether it has real or imaginary solutions. Explain how you know.

____

____

____

b. What are the solutions of the equation?

____

c. Evaluate $x^2 - 4x + 5$ for each solution. Show your results each time you perform an operation (squaring, multiplying, subtracting, and adding). What can you conclude?

____

____

____

____

____

____

____

UNIT 2

Quadratic Functions

GPS COMMON CORE

Module 2 Factoring Quadratic Expressions

2-1	Factoring $x^2 + bx + c$	MCC9-12.A.SSE.2
2-2	Factoring $ax^2 + bx + c$	MCC9-12.A.SSE.2
2-3	Factoring Special Products	MCC9-12.A.SSE.2

Module 3 Graphing Quadratic Functions

3-1	Using Transformations to Graph Quadratic Functions	MCC9-12.A.CED.4, MCC9-12.F.IF.7a, MCC9-12.F.BF.3
3-2	Properties of Quadratic Functions in Standard Form	MCC9-12.A.SSE.1, MCC9-12.A.SSE.2, MCC9-12.F.IF.4, MCC9-12.F.IF.7a, MCC9-12.F.IF.8a
3-3	Curve Fitting with Quadratic Models	MCC9-12.A.CED.1, MCC9-12.A.CED.2, MCC9-12.S.ID.6a

Module 4 Solving Quadratic Equations

4-1	Solving Quadratic Equations by Graphing and Factoring	MCC9-12.A.SSE.1, MCC9-12.A.SSE.2, MCC9-12.A.SSE.3a, MCC9-12.A.CED.2, MCC9-12.A.REI.4
4-2	Completing the Square	MCC9-12.A.SSE.1, MCC9-12.A.SSE.2, MCC9-12.A.SSE.3b, MCC9-12.A.CED.2, MCC9-12.A.REI.4a, MCC9-12.A.REI.4b
4-3	The Quadratic Formula	MCC9-12.A.REI.4a, MCC9-12.A.REI.4b, MCC9-12.N.CN.7, MCC9-12.A.CED.1
4-4	Nonlinear Systems	MCC9-12.A.REI.7
	Performance Tasks	
	PARCC Assessment Readiness	

Unpacking the Standards

Understanding the standards and the vocabulary terms in the standards will help you know exactly what you are expected to learn in this unit.

GPS COMMON CORE **MCC9-12.A.SSE.2**

Use the structure of an expression to identify ways to rewrite it.

Key Vocabulary

expression *(expresión)* A mathematical phrase that contains operations, numbers, and/or variables.

UNIT 2

What It Means For You

You will learn to *factor* expressions, which means you will rewrite them as a product of two or more expressions. Being able to recognize patterns will help you decide which method to use.

EXAMPLE **Factor $x^2 + 7x + 6$**

The algebra tiles below show that $x^2 + 7x + 6 = (x + 1)(x + 6)$.

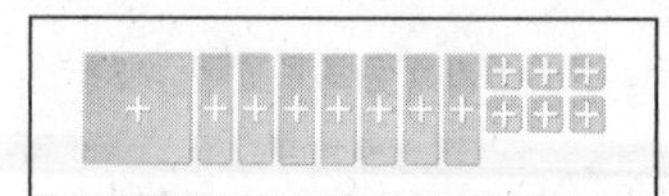

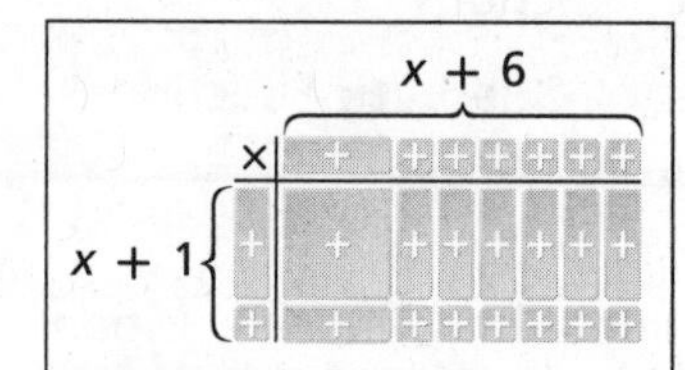

EXAMPLE **Factor $6x^2 - 11x + 3$**

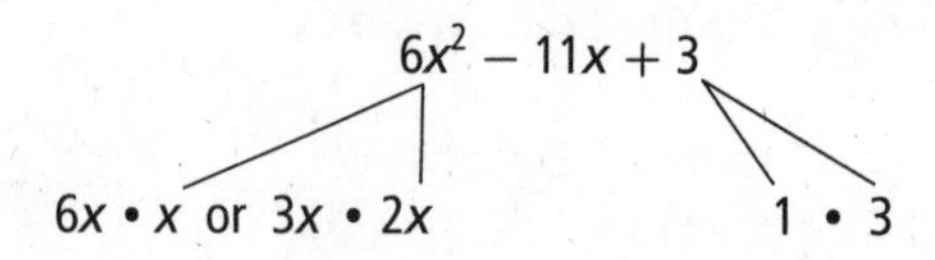

Guess and check: $(6x - 1)(x - 3) = 6x^2 - 18x - x + 3$

$= 6x^2 - 19x + 3$ ✗

Guess and check: $(3x - 1)(2x - 3) = 6x^2 - 9x - 2x + 3$

$= 6x^2 - 11x + 3$ ✓

EXAMPLE **Factor $x^2 - 49$**

Use the difference of two squares pattern:

$$a^2 - b^2 = (a + b)(a - b)$$

$$x^2 - 49 = (x + 7)(x - 7)$$

GPS COMMON CORE **MCC9-12.F.IF.7a**

Graph … quadratic functions and show intercepts, maxima, and minima.

Key Vocabulary

quadratic function *(función cuadrática)* A function that can be written in the form $f(x) = ax^2 + bx + c$, where a, b, and c are real numbers and $a \neq 0$, or in the form $f(x) = a(x - h)^2 + k$, where a, h, and k are real numbers and $a \neq 0$.

x-intercept *(intersección con el eje x)* The x-coordinate(s) of the point(s) where a graph intersects the x-axis.

y-intercept *(intersección con el eje y)* The y-coordinate(s) of the point(s) where a graph intersects the y-axis.

maximum/minimum value of a function *(máximo/mínimo de una función)* The y-value of the highest/lowest point on the graph of the function.

What It Means For You

The graph of a quadratic function has key features that are helpful when interpreting a real-world quadratic model: the intercepts and the maximum or minimum value.

EXAMPLE **Graph of $y = x^2 + 2x - 3$**

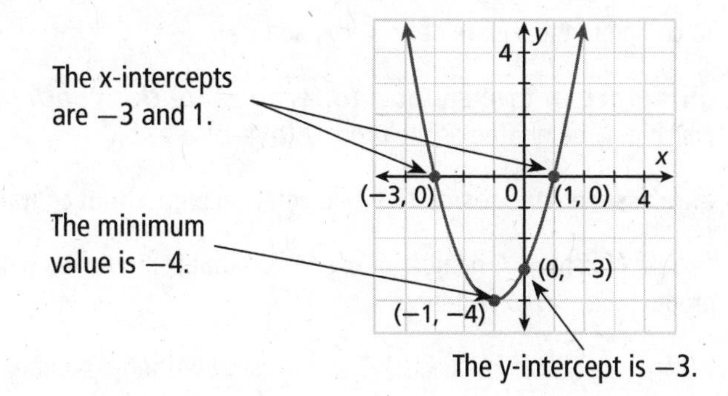

GPS COMMON CORE **MCC9-12.F.BF.3**

Identify the effect on the graph of replacing $f(x)$ by $f(x) + k$, $k\,f(x)$, $f(kx)$, and $f(x + k)$ for specific values of k (both positive and negative); …

Key Vocabulary

function notation *(notación de función)* If x is the independent variable and y is the dependent variable, then the function notation for y is $f(x)$, read "f of x," where f names the function.

What It Means For You

You can change a function by adding or multiplying by a constant. The result will be a new function that is a transformation of the original function.

EXAMPLE **Compression and Stretch/Reflection of $f(x)$**

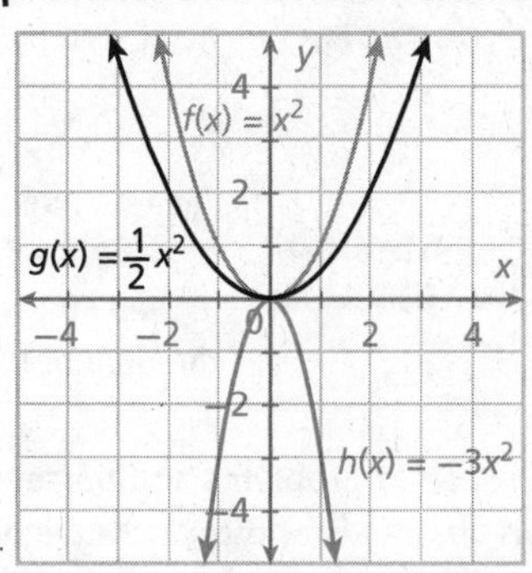

UNIT 2

Key Vocabulary

binomial *(binomio)* A polynomial with two terms.

completing the square *(completar el cuadrado)* A process used to form a perfect-square trinomial. To complete the square of $x^2 + bx$, add $\left(\frac{b}{2}\right)^2$.

difference of two squares *(diferencia de dos cuadrados)* A polynomial of the form $a^2 - b^2$, which may be written as the product $(a + b)(a - b)$.

expression *(expresión)* A mathematical phrase that contains operations, numbers, and/or variables.

factor *(factor)* A number or expression that is multiplied by another number or expression to get a product. *See also* factoring.

factoring *(factorización)* The process of writing a number or algebraic expression as a product.

monomial *(monomio)* A number or a product of numbers and variables with whole-number exponents, or a polynomial with one term.

perfect-square trinomial *(trinomio cuadrado perfecto)* A trinomial whose factored form is the square of a binomial. A perfect-square trinomial has the form $a^2 - 2ab + b^2 = (a - b)^2$ or $a^2 + 2ab + b^2 = (a + b)^2$.

UNIT 2

polynomial *(polinomio)* A monomial or a sum or difference of monomials.

quadratic equation *(ecuación cuadrática)* An equation that can be written in the form $ax^2 + bx + c = 0$, where a, b, and c are real numbers and $a \neq 0$.

Quadratic Formula *(fórmula cuadrática)* The formula $x = \frac{-b \pm \sqrt{b^2 - 4ac}}{2a}$ which gives solutions, or roots, of equations in the form $ax^2 + bx + c = 0$, where $a \neq 0$.

quadratic function *(función cuadrática)* A function that can be written in the form $f(x) = ax^2 + bx + c = 0$, where a, b, and c are real numbers and $a \neq 0$, or in the form $f(x) = a(x - h)^2 + k$, where a, h, and k are real numbers and $a \neq 0$.

trinomial *(trinomio)* A polynomial with three terms.

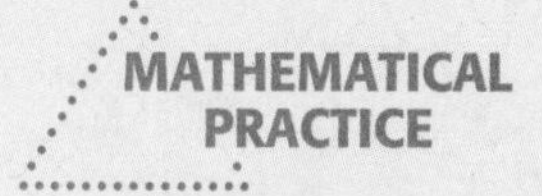

The Common Core Standards for Mathematical Practice describe varieties of expertise that mathematics educators at all levels should seek to develop in their students. Opportunities to develop these practices are integrated throughout this program.

1. **Make sense of problems and persevere in solving them.**
2. **Reason abstractly and quantitatively.**
3. **Construct viable arguments and critique the reasoning of others.**
4. **Model with mathematics.**
5. **Use appropriate tools strategically.**
6. **Attend to precision.**
7. **Look for and make use of structure.**
8. **Look for and express regularity in repeated reasoning**

Name________________ Class__________ Date__________

2-1

Factoring $x^2 + bx + c$

Going Deeper

Essential question: *How can you factor $x^2 + bx + c$?*

Video Tutor

MCC9-12.A.SSE.2

1 ENGAGE Factoring Trinomials

You know how to multiply binomials: for example, $(x + 3)(x - 5) = x^2 - 2x - 15$. In this lesson, you will learn how to reverse this process and factor trinomials.

There are several important things you should remember from multiplying binomials.

- Using FOIL, the constant term in the trinomial is a result of multiplying the *last* terms in the two binomials.
- Using FOIL, the x-term results from adding the products of the *outside* terms and *inside* terms.

You can factor $x^2 + 10x + 21$ by working FOIL backward. Both signs in the trinomial are plus signs, so you know both binomials are of the form *x plus something*. Therefore, you can set up the factoring as shown below.

$$x^2 + 10x + 21 = (x + \boxed{?})(x + \boxed{?})$$

To find the constant terms in the binomials, use the information above and follow the steps below.

1) The constant term in the trinomial, 21, is the product of the last terms in the two binomials. Factor 21 into pairs. The factor pairs are shown in the table at the right.

Factors of 21	Sum of Factors
1 and 21	22
3 and 7	10 ✓

2) The correct factor pair is the one whose sum is the coefficient of x in the trinomial.

3) Complete the binomial expression with the appropriate numbers.

$$x^2 + 10x + 21 = \left(x + \quad\right)\left(x + \quad\right)$$

REFLECT

1a. You want to factor $x^2 - 6x + 8$. What factoring pattern would you set up to begin the process? Explain.

____

____

1b. You want to factor $x^2 - 2x - 15$. What factoring pattern would you set up to begin the process? Explain. Would this pattern also work for $x^2 + 2x - 15$? Explain.

1c. Use factoring patterns to factor $x^2 + 8x + 16$ and $x^2 - 6x + 9$. What do you notice about the factored forms? What special type of trinomials are $x^2 + 8x + 16$ and $x^2 - 6x + 9$?

MCC9-12.A.SSE.2

2 EXAMPLE Factoring Trinomials

A **Factor $x^2 + 3x - 10$.**

The constant is negative, so you know one binomial will have a subtraction sign.

$$x^2 + 3x - 10 = (x + \boxed{?})(x - \boxed{?})$$

Complete the table at the right. Note that you are finding the factors of -10, not 10. Since the coefficient of x is positive, the factor with the greater absolute value will be positive (and the other factor will be negative).

Factors of −10	Sum of Factors
−1 and 10	

$$x^2 + 3x - 10 = (x + \quad)(x - \quad)$$

B **Factor $x^2 - 8x - 48$.**

The constant is negative, so you know one binomial will have a subtraction sign.

$$x^2 - 8x - 48 = (x + \boxed{?})(x - \boxed{?})$$

Complete the table at the right. Since the coefficient of x is negative, the factor with the greater absolute value will be negative (and the other factor will be positive).

Factors of −48	Sum of Factors
1 and −48	
2 and	

$$x^2 - 8x - 48 = (x + \quad)(x - \quad)$$

REFLECT

2a. Complete the table below. Assume that b, c, p, and q are positive numbers.

Trinomial	Form of Binomial Factors
$x^2 + bx + c$	$(x \quad p)(x \quad q)$
$x^2 - bx + c$	$(x \quad p)(x \quad q)$
$x^2 - bx - c$ or $x^2 + bx - c$	$(x \quad p)(x \quad q)$

For the last row in the table, explain how to determine which factor contains a + sign and which factor contains a – sign.

PRACTICE

Complete the factorization of the polynomial.

1. $t^2 + 6t + 5 = (t + 5)(t + \quad)$

2. $z^2 - 121 = (z + 11)(z \quad \quad)$

3. $d^2 + 5d - 24 = (d + \quad)(d - \quad)$

4. $x^4 - 4 = (x^2 + \quad)(\quad - 2)$

Factor the polynomial.

5. $y^2 + 3y - 4$

6. $x^2 - 2x + 1$

7. $p^2 - 2p - 24$

8. $g^2 - 100$

9. $z^2 - 7z + 12$

10. $q^2 + 25q + 100$

11. $m^2 + 8m + 16$

12. $n^2 - 10n - 24$

13. $x^2 + 25x$

14. $y^2 - 13y - 30$

Factor the polynomial.

15. $z^2 - 9$

16. $p^2 + 3p - 54$

17. $x^2 + 11x - 42$

18. $g^2 - 14g - 51$

19. $n^2 - 81$

20. $y^2 - 25y$

21. $x^2 + 11x + 30$

22. $x^2 - x - 20$

23. $x^2 + 6x - 7$

24. $x^2 + 2x + 1$

Name________________ Class________________ Date________________

Additional Practice

Factor each trinomial.

1. $x^2 + 7x + 10$
2. $x^2 + 9x + 8$
3. $x^2 + 13x + 36$
4. $x^2 + 9x + 14$
5. $x^2 + 7x + 12$
6. $x^2 + 9x + 18$
7. $x^2 - 9x + 18$
8. $x^2 - 5x + 4$
9. $x^2 - 9x + 20$
10. $x^2 - 12x + 20$
11. $x^2 - 11x + 18$
12. $x^2 - 12x + 32$
13. $x^2 + 7x - 18$
14. $x^2 + 10x - 24$
15. $x^2 + 2x - 3$
16. $x^2 + 2x - 15$
17. $x^2 + 5x - 6$
18. $x^2 + 5x - 24$
19. $x^2 - 5x - 6$
20. $x^2 - 2x - 35$
21. $x^2 - 7x - 30$
22. $x^2 - x - 56$
23. $x^2 - 2x - 8$
24. $x^2 - x - 20$
25. Factor $n^2 + 5n - 24$. Show that the original polynomial and the factored form describe the same sequence of numbers for $n = 0, 1, 2, 3,$ and 4.

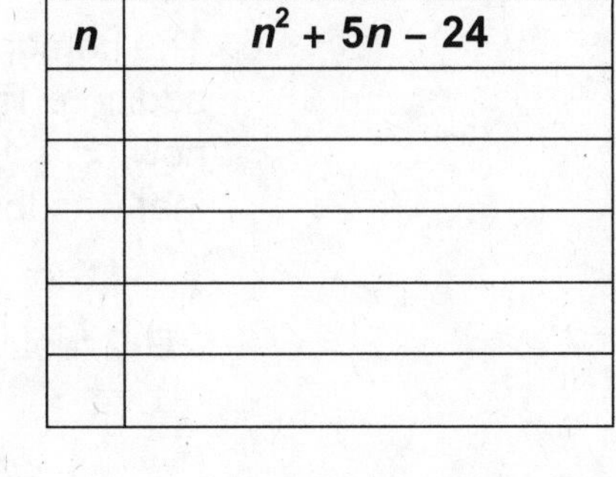

n	$n^2 + 5n - 24$

n	

Problem Solving

Write the correct answer.

1. A plot of land is rectangular and has an area of $x^2 - 5x - 24$ m^2. The length is $x + 3$ m. Find the width of the plot.

____

____

2. An antique Persian carpet has an area of $(x^2 + x - 20)$ ft^2 and a length of $(x + 5)$ feet. The rug is displayed on a wall in a museum. The wall has a width of $(x + 2)$ feet and an area of $(x^2 + 17x + 30)$ ft^2. Write expressions for the length and width of both the rug and wall. Then find the dimensions of the rug and the wall if $x = 20$ feet.

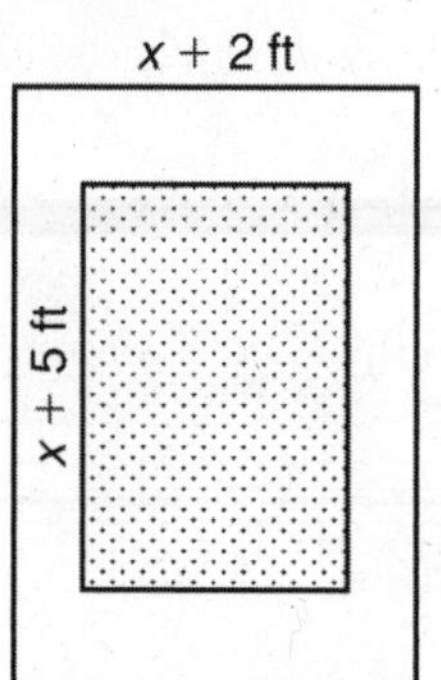

____

____

3. The area of a poster board is $x^2 + 3x - 10$ inches. The width is $x - 2$ inches.
   a. Write an expression for the length of the poster board.

   ____

   b. Find the dimensions of the poster board when $x = 14$.

   ____

   c. Write a polynomial for the area of the poster board if one inch is removed from each side.

   ____

The figure shows the plans for an addition on the back of a house. Use the figure to answer questions 4–6. Select the best answer.

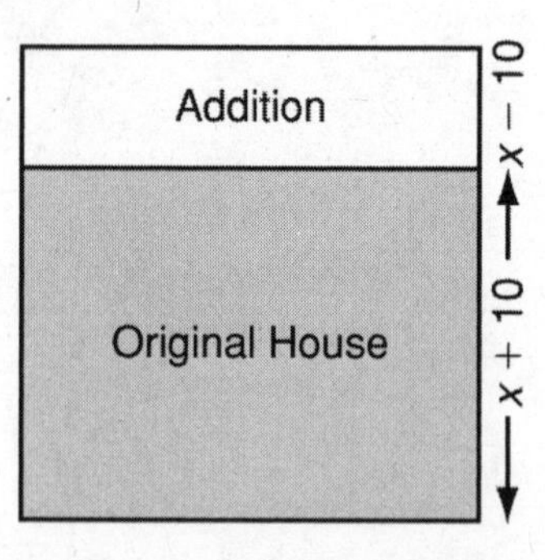

4. The area of the addition is $(x^2 + 10x - 200)$ ft^2. What is its length?
   A $(x - 20)$ feet
   B $(x - 2)$ feet
   C $(x + 2)$ feet
   D $(x + 20)$ feet

5. What is the area of the original house?
   F $(x^2 - 10x - 200)$ ft^2
   G $(x^2 + 8x - 20)$ ft^2
   H $(x^2 + 12x + 200)$ ft^2
   J $(x^2 + 30x + 200)$ ft^2

6. The homeowners decide to extend the addition. The area with the addition is now $(x^2 + 12x - 160)$ ft^2. By how many feet was the addition extended?
   A 1 foot
   B 2 feet
   C 3 feet
   D 4 feet

Name__________________ Class__________ Date__________

2-2

Factoring $ax^2 + bx + c$

Going Deeper

Video Tutor

Essential question: *How can you factor $ax^2 + bx + c$?*

You have learned how to factor $ax^2 + bx + c$ when $a = 1$ by identifying the correct pair of factors of c whose sum is b. But what if the coefficient of x^2 is not 1?

First, review binomial multiplication. The product $(2x + 5)(3x + 2)$ is found by using FOIL.

$$(2x + 5)(3x + 2) = \underset{\textbf{F}}{6x^2} + \underset{\textbf{O}}{4x} + \underset{\textbf{I}}{15x} + \underset{\textbf{L}}{10} = 6x^2 + 19x + 10$$

F The product of the coefficients of the **first** terms is a.

O, **I** } The sum of the coefficients of the **outer** and **inner** products is b.

L The product of the **last** terms is c.

To factor $ax^2 + bx + c$, you need to reverse this process. Start by listing the possible factor pairs of a and c. Then use trial and error to find a sum of b for the outer and inner products.

MCC9–12.A.SSE.2

1 EXAMPLE Factoring $ax^2 + bx + c$

Factor $5n^2 + 11n + 2$.

A First list the possible factor pairs for both a and c. All of the signs of the terms are positive, so the factors of a and c must all be positive.

The only factor pair for a is _____, _____. The only factor pair for c is _____, _____.

B Choose the arrangement of the factor pairs that makes $b = 11$. Check your result by multiplying.

$$5n^2 + 11n + 2 = (\quad n + \quad)(\quad n + \quad)$$

REFLECT

1a. What other arrangement of factor pairs is possible for a and c? What is the resulting product, and how is it different from $5n^2 + 11n + 2$?

____

1b. If a is positive, b is negative, and c is positive, what are the signs of the factors of a and c that you are looking for?

____

1c. If a is positive, b is negative, and c is negative, what are the signs of the factors of a and c that you are looking for?

____

If a and c have a lot of factors, there are many possible arrangements. One way to quickly check each arrangement is shown below, using the trinomial $5n^2 + 11n + 2$. List the factor pairs of a and c vertically, then multiply diagonally, and add.

Factors of a		Factors of c		Inner and Outer products
1	⤫	2	=	10
5		1	=	1
				11 ← Sum

If the sum is correct, the factors are read across: $(1n + 2)$ and $(5n + 1)$.

MCC9–12.A.SSE.2

2 EXAMPLE Factoring $ax^2 + bx + c$

Factor $6x^2 - 13x - 8$.

A First list the possible factor pairs for both a and c. Because c is negative, one of the factors of c must be positive, and the other must be negative.

The factor pairs for a are: _____, _____ and _____, _____.

The factor pairs for c are: _____, _____; _____, _____; _____, _____; _____, _____.

B Choose the arrangement of factor pairs that makes $b = -13$. Each factor pair of a can be arranged in two ways with each factor pair of c, so there are 16 possible arrangements. Three are shown below.

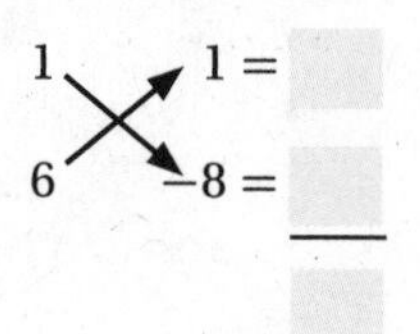

2 ⤫ 2 = ____
3 ⤫ −4 = ____
____

2 ⤫ 1 = ____
3 ⤫ −8 = ____
____

$6x^2 - 13x - 8 = (\_\_x + \_\_)(\_\_x - \_\_)$

REFLECT

2a. If you know the factors of $6x^2 - 13x - 8$, how could you easily factor $6x^2 + 13x - 8$?

____

2b. What fact about the sign of the sum can you use so that you need to test at most half of the possible arrangements?

____

____

PRACTICE

Factor.

1. $2x^2 + 15x + 7$

2. $7z^2 - 30z + 27$

3. $8x^2 - 10x - 3$

4. $30d^2 + 7d - 15$

5. $10g^2 + 23g + 12$

6. $5y^2 - 2y - 7$

7. $2n^2 - 11n + 15$

8. $6a^2 + 7a - 10$

9. $12x^2 - x$

10. $9z^2 - 25$

11. $36h^2 - 12h + 1$

12. $3n^2 - 20n + 12$

13. $9x^2 + 12x + 4$

14. $4y^2 + y - 18$

To factor a polynomial of the form $ax^2 + bx + c$ where a is negative, you first factor out -1 from all the terms. Factor each polynomial.

15. $-6x^2 + 11x + 10$

16. $-3x^2 + 5x + 22$

17. $-4x^2 - 12x + 7$

18. $-8x^2 + 6x + 9$

19. $-6x^2 + 7x + 5$

20. $-6x^2 - 25x + 9$

21. $-5x^2 + 17x - 6$

22. $-15x^2 + 2x + 8$

23. A dolphin bounces a ball off its nose at an initial upward velocity of 6 m/s to a trainer lying on a 1-meter high platform. The polynomial $-5t^2 + 6t - 1$ models the ball's height (in meters) above the platform.

a. Factor the polynomial.

____

b. When $t = 0$, what is the value of the polynomial? What does this value mean in the context of the situation?

____

____

c. For what values on t does the polynomial equal 0?

$t =$ __________ or $t =$ __________

d. Explain the two values for t in the context of the situation.

____

____

____

Name________________________ Class________________ Date______________

2-2

Additional Practice

Factor each trinomial.

1. $2x^2 + 13x + 15$ ________

2. $3x^2 + 10x + 8$ ________

3. $4x^2 + 24x + 27$ ________

4. $5x^2 + 21x + 4$ ________

5. $4x^2 + 11x + 7$ ________

6. $6x^2 - 23x + 20$ ________

7. $7x^2 - 59x + 24$ ________

8. $3x^2 - 14x + 15$ ________

9. $8x^2 - 73x + 9$ ________

10. $2x^2 + 11x - 13$ ________

11. $3x^2 + 2x - 16$ ________

12. $2x^2 + 17x - 30$ ________

13. $8x^2 + 29x - 12$ ________

14. $11x^2 + 25x - 24$ ________

15. $9x^2 - 3x - 2$ ________

16. $12x^2 - 7x - 12$ ________

17. $9x^2 - 49x - 30$ ________

18. $6x^2 + x - 40$ ________

19. $-12x^2 - 35x - 18$ ________

20. $-20x^2 + 29x - 6$ ________

21. $-2x^2 + 5x + 42$ ________

22. The area of a rectangle is $20x^2 - 27x - 8$. The length is $4x + 1$. What is the width? ________

Problem Solving

Write the correct answer.

1. A rectangular painting has an area of $(2x^2 + 8x + 6)$ cm^2. Its length is $(2x + 2)$ cm. Find the width of the painting.

____

2. A ball is kicked straight up into the air. The height of the ball in feet is given by the expression $-16t^2 + 12t + 4$, where t is time in seconds. Factor the expression. Then find the height of the ball after 1 second.

____

____

3. Instructors led an exercise class from a raised rectangular platform at the front of the room. The width of the platform was $(3x - 1)$ feet and the area was $(9x^2 + 6x - 3)$ ft^2. Find the length of this platform. After the exercise studio is remodeled, the area of the platform will be $(9x^2 + 12x + 3)$ ft^2. By how many feet will the width of the platform change?

____

____

4. A clothing store has a rectangular clearance section with a length that is twice the width w. During a sale, the section is expanded to an area of $(2w^2 + 19w + 35)$ ft^2. Find the amount of the increase in the length and width of the clearance section.

____

____

Select the best answer.

5. The area of a soccer field is $(24x^2 + 100x + 100)$ m^2. The width of the field is $(4x + 10)$ m. What is the length?

   A $(3x + 10)$ m
   B $(6x + 1)$ m
   C $(6x + 10)$ m
   D $(8x + 2)$ m

6. A square parking lot has an area of $(4x^2 + 20x + 25)$ ft^2. What is the length of one side of the parking lot?

   F $(2x + 5)$ ft
   G $(2x + 10)$ ft
   H $(5x + 4)$ ft
   J $(5x + 2)$ ft

7. For a certain college, the number of applications received after x recruiting seminars is modeled by the polynomial $3x^2 + 490x + 6000$. What is this expression in factored form?

   A $(3x - 40)(x - 150)$
   B $(3x + 40)(x + 150)$
   C $(3x - 30)(x - 200)$
   D $(3x - 30)(x + 200)$

8. Jin needs to fence in his rectangular backyard. The fence will have one long section away from, but parallel to, the length of his house and two shorter sides connecting that section to the house. The length of Jin's house is $(3x + 4)$ yd and the area of his backyard is $(9x^2 + 15x + 4)$ yd^2. How many yards of fencing will Jin need?

   F $(6x + 2)$ yd
   G $(9x + 6)$ yd
   H $(9x + 9)$ yd
   J $(12x + 10)$ yd

Factoring Special Products

Connection: Area

Essential question: *How can you represent factoring special products geometrically?*

Recall that perfect square trinomials and the difference of two squares are special polynomials.

Video Tutor

Representing the Factoring of a Perfect Square Trinomial

Use area models to factor $a^2 + 2ab + b^2$.

A Finish labeling this model of $a^2 + 2ab + b^2$. Use a and b.

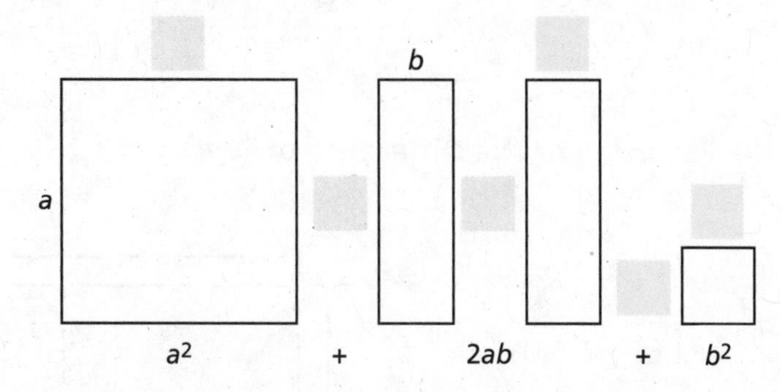

B Draw dashed lines inside the square below to show how the squares and rectangles from Step A could be placed together to form a larger square. Label the dimension of each part of the length and width of the larger square.

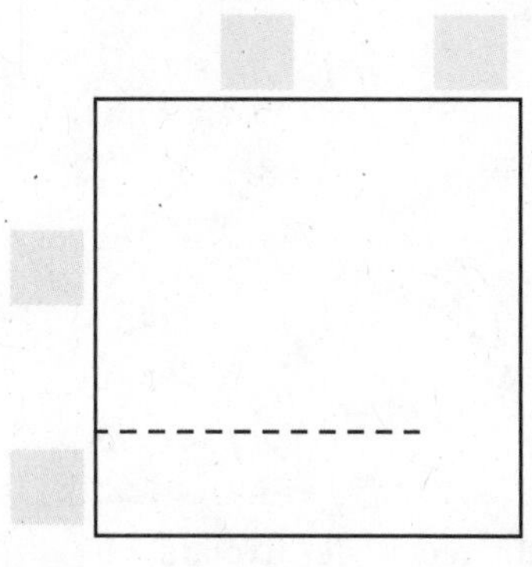

C Use the dimensions of the square in Step B to write the area of the square in Step B.

$A =$ (__________)(__________)

D Because the square has the same area as the model of the polynomial, the factorization of $a^2 + 2ab + b^2$ is ________________.

REFLECT

1a. How does the model at the right show that the factorization of $a^2 - 2ab + b^2$ is $(a - b)(a - b)$?

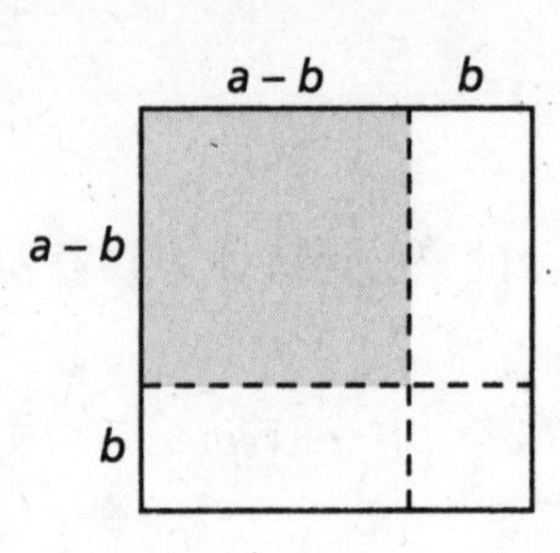

____

____

____

____

____

MCC9–12.A.SSE.2

2 EXPLORE Representing the Factoring of the Difference of Two Squares

Use area models to factor $a^2 - b^2$.

A Finish labeling this model of $a^2 - b^2$. Use a and b.

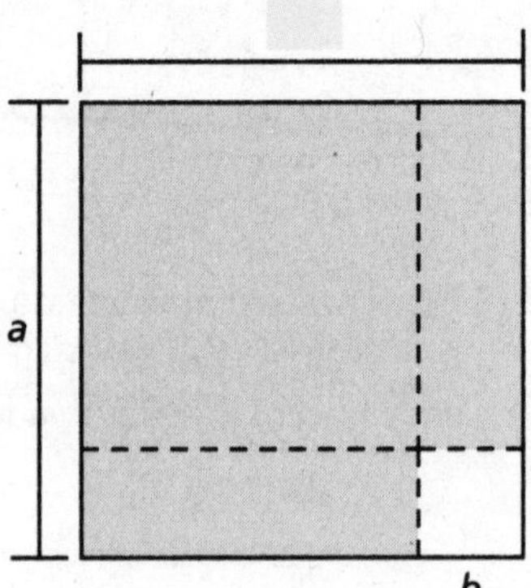

B Make a drawing that shows the shaded parts of the model arranged to show a rectangle. Label each segment of the length and width of the rectangle.

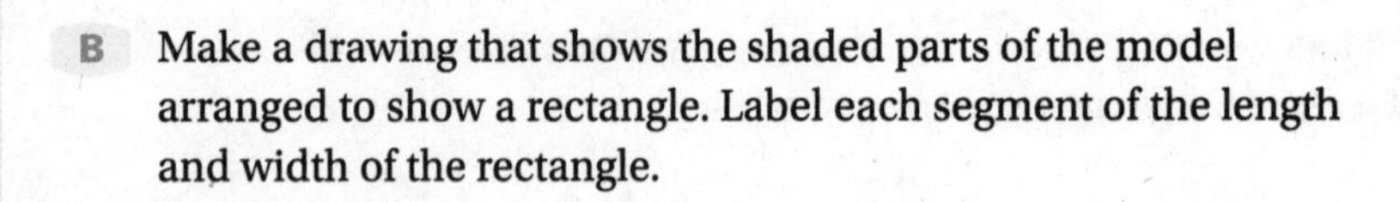

C What is the length of the longer side of the rectangle? Explain.

____

What is the length of the shorter side of the rectangle? __________

What is the area of the rectangle? (__________)(__________)

D Because the rectangle has the same area as the model of the polynomial, the factorization of $a^2 - b^2$ is ______________.

Name________________________ Class______________ Date__________

2-3

Additional Practice

Determine whether each trinomial is a perfect square. If so, factor it. If not, explain why.

1. $x^2 + 6x + 9$

____

2. $4x^2 + 20x + 25$

____

3. $36x^2 - 24x + 16$

____

4. $9x^2 - 12x + 4$

____

5. A rectangular fountain in the center of a shopping mall has an area of $(4x^2 + 12x + 9)$ ft^2. The dimensions of the fountain are of the form $cx + d$, where c and d are whole numbers. Find an expression for the perimeter of the fountain. Find the perimeter when $x = 2$ ft.

____

Determine whether each binomial is the difference of perfect squares. If so, factor it. If not, explain why.

6. $x^2 - 16$

____

7. $9b^4 - 200$

____

8. $1 - m^6$

____

9. $36s^2 - 4t^2$

____

10. $x^2y^2 + 196$

____

Problem Solving

Write the correct answer.

1. A rectangular fountain has an area of $(16x^2 + 8x + 1)$ ft^2. The dimensions of the rectangle have the form $ax + b$, where a and b are whole numbers. Write an expression for the perimeter of the fountain. Then find the perimeter when $x = 2$ feet.

____

____

2. A square tabletop has an area of $(9x^2 - 90x + 225)$ cm^2. The dimensions of the tabletop have the form $cx - d$, where c and d are whole numbers. Write an expression for the perimeter of the tabletop. Then find the perimeter when $x = 25$ centimeters.

____

____

3. The floor plan of a daycare center is shown.

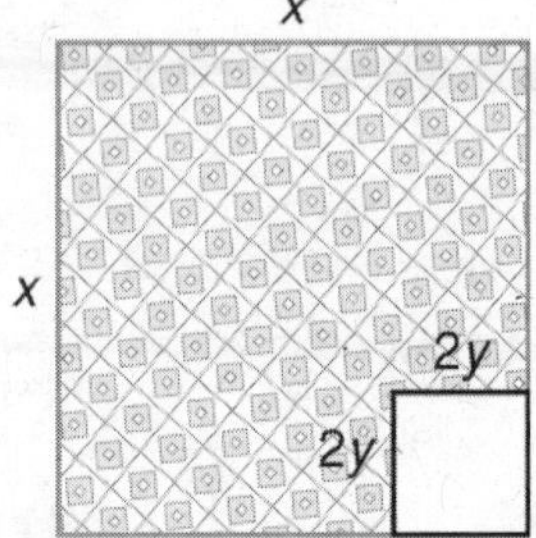

The arts and crafts area in the lower right corner is not carpeted. The rest of the center is carpeted. Write an expression, in factored form, for the area of the floor that is carpeted.

____

4. A plate with a decorative border is shown.

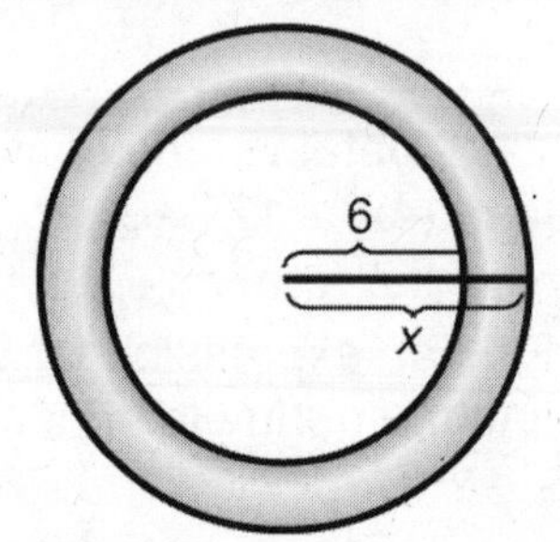

Write an expression, in factored form, for the area of the border. (*Hint:* First factor out the GCF.)

____

Nelson is making open top boxes by cutting out corners from a sheet of cardboard, folding the edges up, and then taping them together. Select the best answer.

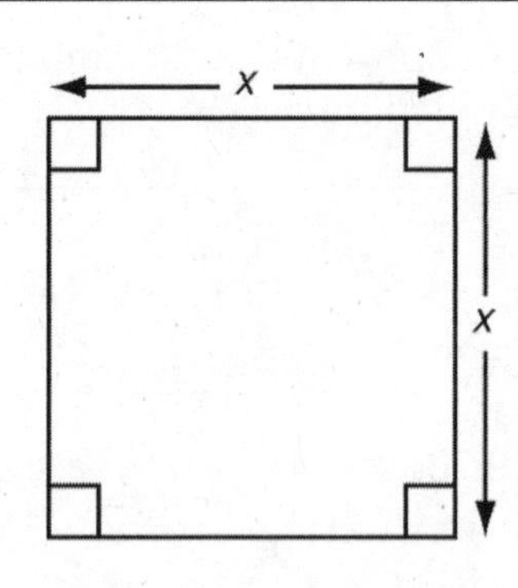

5. Nelson cut corners so that each corner was a square with side lengths of 4. What is the total area of the remaining piece of cardboard?

A $x^2 - 8x + 16$ C $x^2 - 16x + 64$

B $x^2 + 8x + 16$ D $x^2 + 16x + 64$

6. What are the dimensions of the square corners if the total remaining area is $x^2 - 4x + 4$?

F 1 by 1 H 4 by 4

G 2 by 2 J 8 by 8

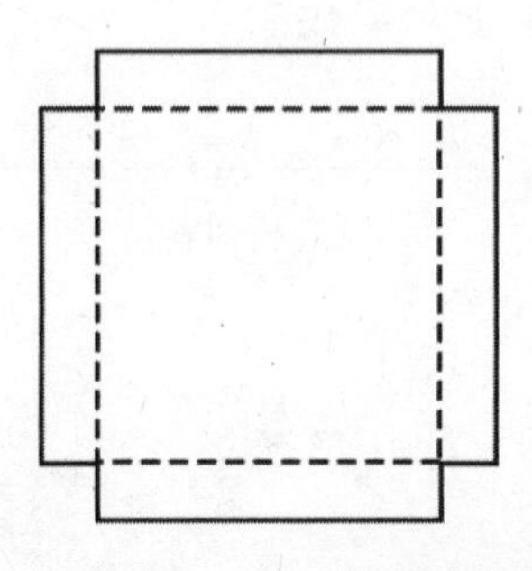

Name______________________ Class__________ Date________

3-1

Using Transformations to Graph Quadratic Functions

Extension: Graphing Quadratic Functions in Vertex Form

Video Tutor

Essential question: *How can you graph the function* $f(x) = a(x - h)^2 + k$?

MCC9–12.F.BF.3

1 ENGAGE Understanding Vertex Form

The **vertex form** of a quadratic function is $f(x) = a(x - h)^2 + k$. The vertex of the graph of a quadratic function in vertex form is (h, k).

$$f(x) = a(x - h)^2 + k$$

a indicates a vertical stretch or shrink and/or a reflection across the *x*-axis.	*h* indicates a horizontal translation.	*k* indicates a vertical translation.

A **zero of a function** is an input value x that makes the output value $f(x)$ equal 0. You can estimate the zeros of a quadratic function by observing where the graph crosses the x-axis.

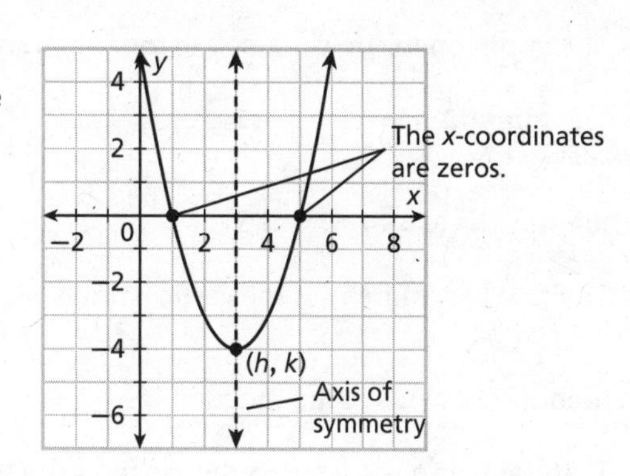

REFLECT

1a. For the function $f(x) = 2(x - 3)^2 + 1$, what are the values of a, h, and k? What do each of these values indicate about the graph of the function?

____

____

____

1b. Explain why the vertex of the graph of a quadratic function in vertex form is (h, k).

____

____

1c. If you estimate a zero of a quadratic function from a graph, how could you use algebra to check your answer?

____

____

MCC9–12.F.IF.7a

2 EXAMPLE Graphing $f(x) = a(x - h)^2 + k$

Graph the function $f(x) = 2(x + 1)^2 - 2$. Identify the vertex, minimum or maximum, axis of symmetry, and zeros of the function.

A Identify and graph the vertex.

$h =$

$k =$

The vertex of the graph is ______________ .

B Identify the coordinates of points to the left and right of the vertex.

x	−3	−2	0	1
$f(x)$				

C Graph the points and connect them with a smooth curve.

D Identify the minimum or maximum.

The graph opens upward, so the function has a ______________ .

The minimum is ______________ .

E Identify the axis of symmetry.

The axis of symmetry is the vertical line $x =$ ______________ .

F Identify the zeros of the function.

The graph appears to cross the x-axis at the points ______________ and ______________, so the zeros of the function appear to be __________ and __________ .

REFLECT

2a. How could you use the value of a to determine whether the function $f(x) = 2(x + 1)^2 - 2$ has a minimum or a maximum?

2b. How could you use the table in part B to confirm that you correctly identified the zeros of the function from its graph?

MCC9–12.F.BF.3

3 EXAMPLE Writing Equations in Vertex Form

Write the vertex form of the quadratic function whose graph is shown.

A Use the vertex of the graph to identify the values of h and k.

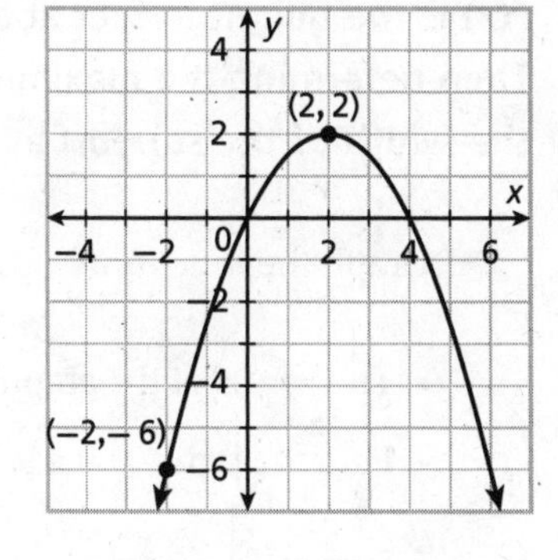

The vertex of the graph is ________.

$h =$ ____

$k =$ ____

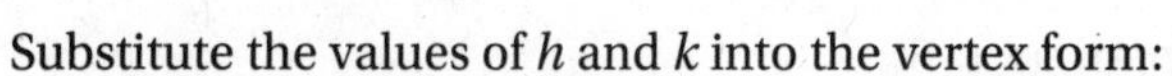
Substitute the values of h and k into the vertex form:

$f(x) = a\left(x - \text{\_\_\_\_}\right)^2 + \text{\_\_\_\_}$

B Use the point $(-2, -6)$ to identify the value of a.

$f(x) = a(x - 2)^2 + 2$	Vertex form
$\text{\_\_\_\_} = a\left(\text{\_\_\_\_} - 2\right)^2 + 2$	Substitute -6 for $f(x)$ and -2 for x.
$-6 = a\left(\text{\_\_\_\_}\right) + 2$	Simplify.
$\text{\_\_\_\_} = a(16)$	Subtract 2 from both sides.
$\text{\_\_\_\_} = a$	Divide both sides by 16.

Substitute the value of a into the vertex form:

$f(x) = \text{\_\_\_\_}(x - 2)^2 + 2$

So, the vertex form of the function shown in the graph is

________________________.

REFLECT

3a. How can you tell by looking at the graph that the value of a is negative?

____

____

____

3b. Describe the graph of the given function as a transformation of the parent quadratic function.

____

____

MCC9–12.F.IF.7a

4 EXAMPLE Modeling Quadratic Functions in Vertex Form

The shape of a bridge support can be modeled by $f(x) = -\frac{1}{600}(x - 300)^2 + 150$, where x is the horizontal distance in feet from the left end of the bridge and $f(x)$ is the height in feet above the bridge deck. Sketch a graph of the support. Then determine the maximum height of the support above the bridge deck and the width of the support at the level of the bridge deck.

A Graph the function.

- The vertex of the graph is ______________.
- Find the point at the left end of the support ($x = 0$).

  Since $f(0) =$ __________, the point __________ represents the left end.

- Use symmetry to find the point at the right end of the support.

  Since the left end is 300 feet to the left of the vertex, the right end will be 300 feet to the right of the vertex.

  The point __________ represents the right end.

- Find two other points on the support.

  (120, ____) and (480, ____)

- Sketch the graph.

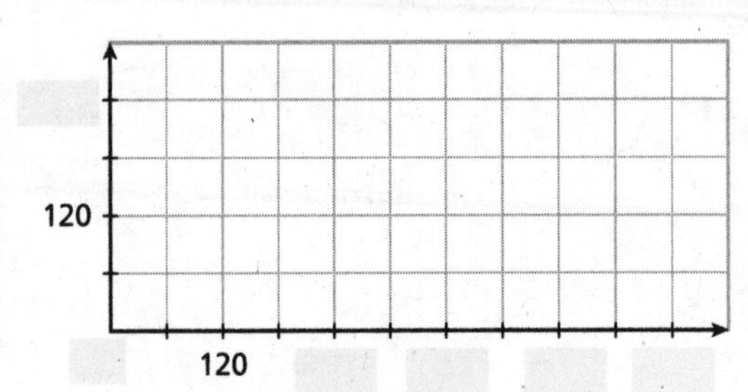

B Determine the maximum height of the support.

The maximum of the function is __________.

So, the maximum height of the bridge support is __________ feet.

C Determine the width of the bridge support at the level of the bridge deck.

The distance from the left end to the right end is __________ feet.

So, the width is __________ feet at the level of the bridge deck.

REFLECT

4a. Explain how you know that the y-coordinate of the right end of the support is 0.

____

____

4b. What does the vertex represent in this situation?

____

____

PRACTICE

Graph each quadratic function. Identify the vertex, minimum or maximum, axis of symmetry, and zeros of the function.

1. $f(x) = -2x^2 + 8$

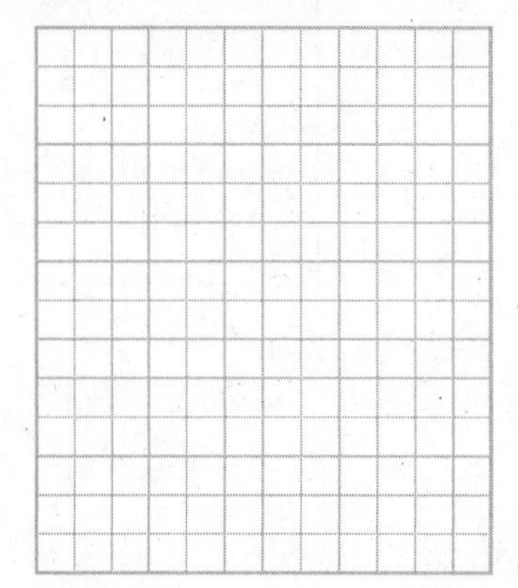

2. $f(x) = (x - 2)^2 - 4$

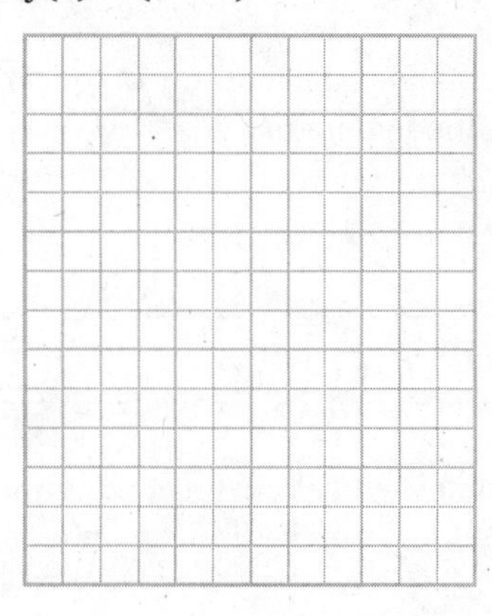

3. $f(x) = -(x + 4)^2 + 1$

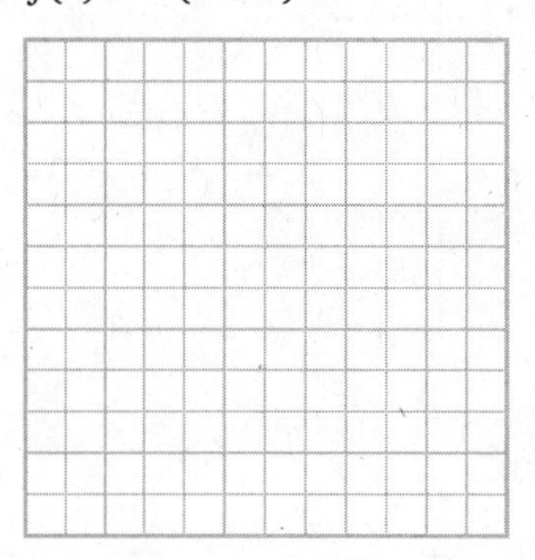

4. $f(x) = \frac{1}{3}(x - 2)^2 - 3$

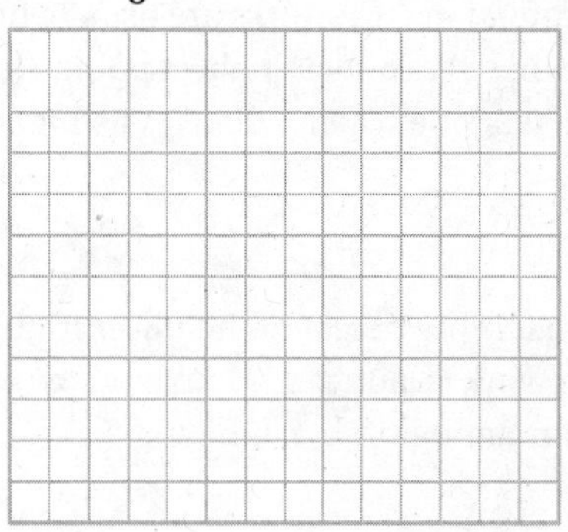

Write the vertex form of each quadratic function.

5.

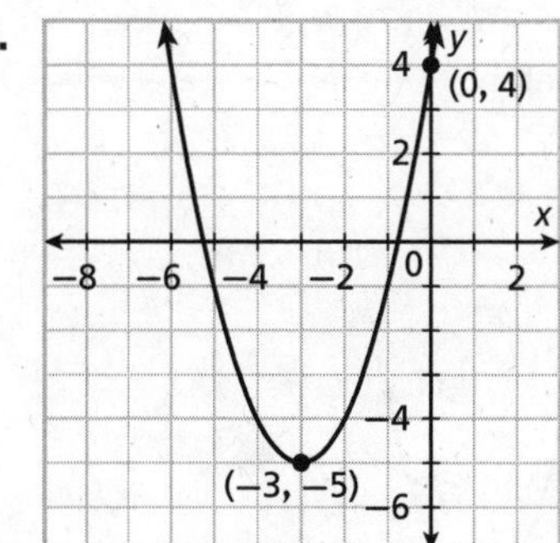

6.

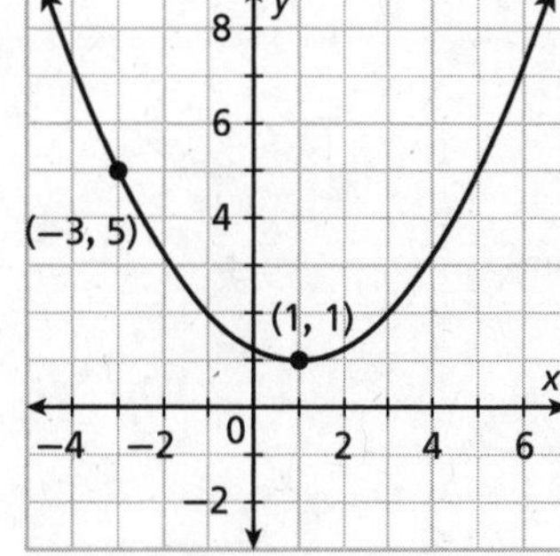

7. The function $f(x) = -16(x - 1)^2 + 16$ gives the height in feet of a football x seconds after it is kicked from ground level.

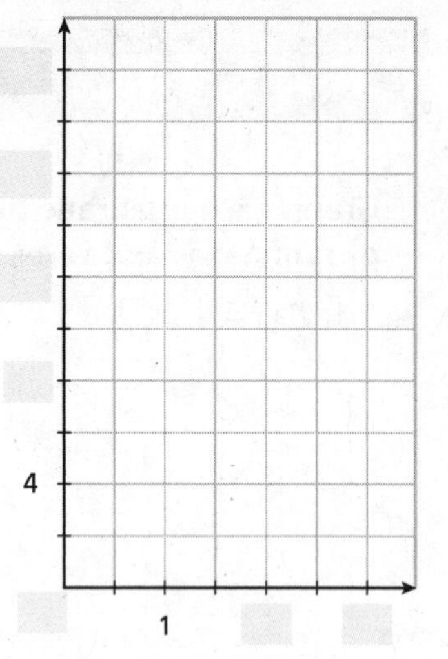

a. Sketch a graph of the function.

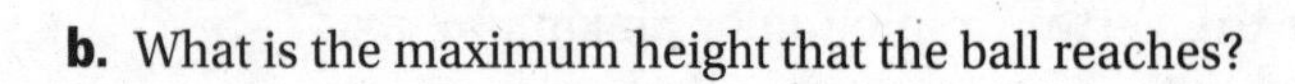

b. What is the maximum height that the ball reaches?

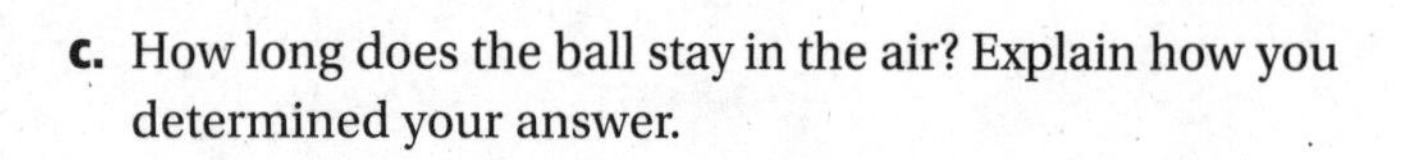

c. How long does the ball stay in the air? Explain how you determined your answer.

8. A technician is launching an aerial firework from a tower. The height of the firework in feet is modeled by the function $f(x) = -16(x - 3)^2 + 256$ where x is the time in seconds after the firework is launched.

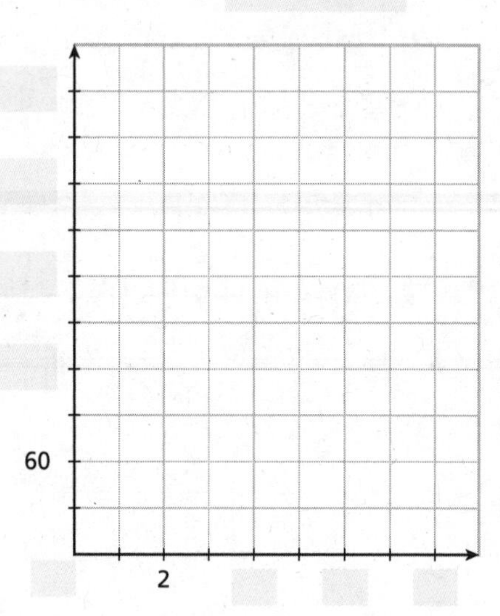

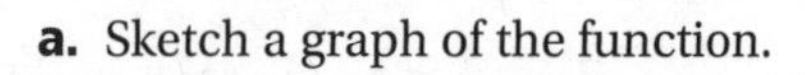

a. Sketch a graph of the function.

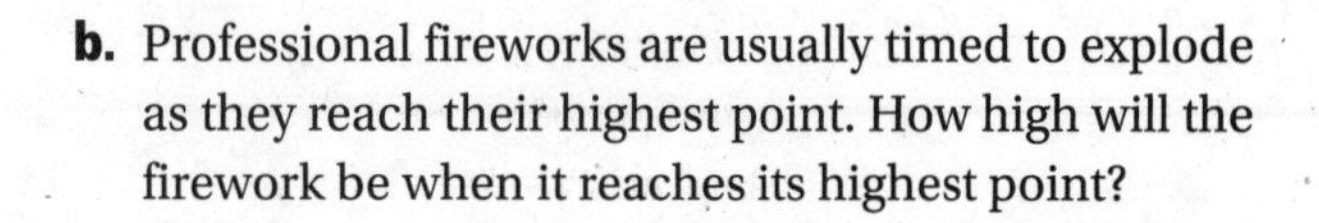

b. Professional fireworks are usually timed to explode as they reach their highest point. How high will the firework be when it reaches its highest point?

c. What is the height of the tower from which the firework is launched? Explain how you determined your answer.

9. Which quadratic function has a greater maximum: the function $f(x) = -(x - 5)^2 + 4$ or the function graphed below?

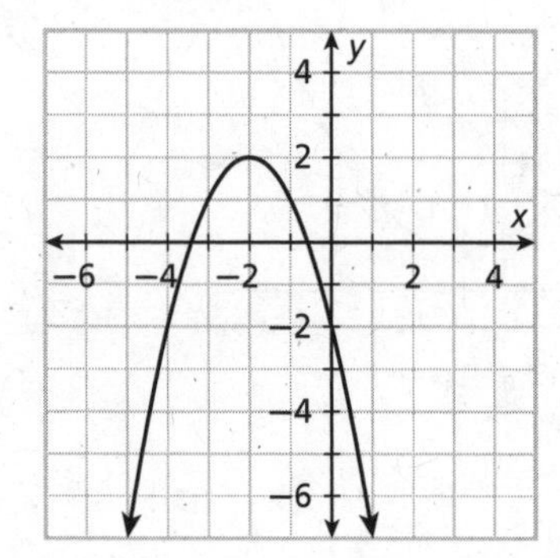

10. Which quadratic function has a lesser minimum: a function whose graph has a vertex at $(-5, -1)$ or the function graphed below?

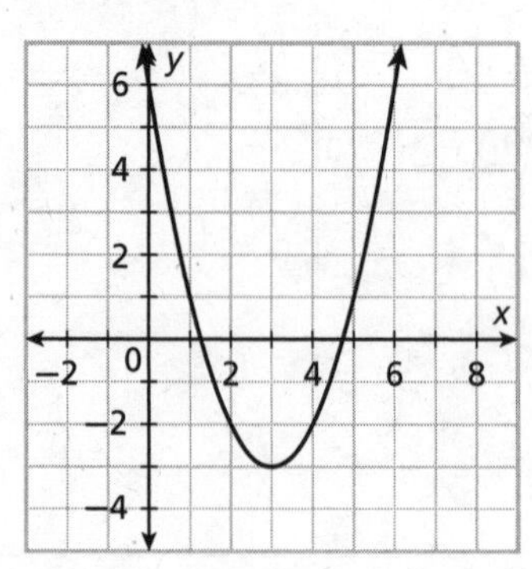

Name________________________ Class______________ Date__________

3-1

Additional Practice

Graph the function by using a table.

1. $f(x) = x^2 + 2x - 1$

x	$f(x) = x^2 + 2x - 1$	$(x, f(x))$
−2		
−1		
0		
1		
2		

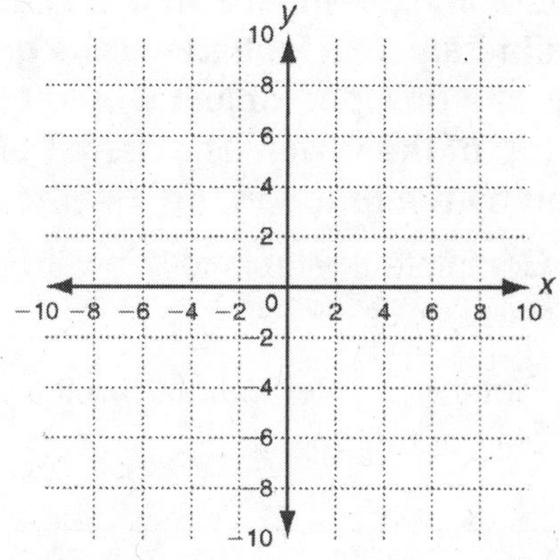

Using the graph of $f(x) = x^2$ as a guide, describe the transformations, and then graph each function. Label each function on the graph.

2. $h(x) = (x - 2)^2 + 2$

____

3. $h(x) = -(3x)^2$

____

4. $h(x) = \left(\frac{1}{2}x\right)^2$

____

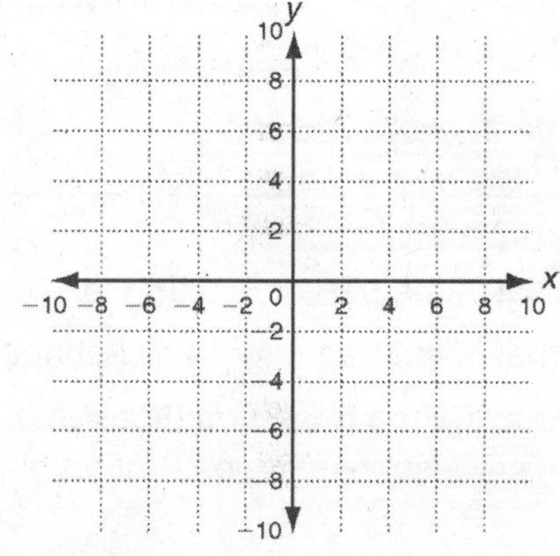

Use the description to write a quadratic function in vertex form.

5. The parent function $f(x) = x^2$ is reflected across the x-axis, horizontally stretched by a factor of 3 and translated 2 units down to create function g.

____

6. A ball dropped from the top of tower A can be modeled by the function $h(t) = -9.8t^2 + 400$, where t is the time after it is dropped and $h(t)$ is its height at that time. A ball dropped from the top of tower B can be modeled by the function $h(t) = -9.8t^2 + 200$. What transformation describes this change? What does this transformation mean?

____

Problem Solving

Christa and Jelani are standing at the top of the Leaning Tower of Pisa in Italy, 185 feet above the ground. Jelani wonders what the path of a dropped object would be as it falls to the ground from the top of the tower. The height of an object after *t* seconds is given by the function, $f(t) = -16t^2 + 185$.

1. Complete the table to show the height, $f(t)$, of the object for different values of t.

2. Plot the ordered pairs from the table and draw the graph to show the path of the object.

Time (t)	$f(t) = -16t^2 + 185$	$(t, f(t))$
0	$f(0) = -16(0)^2 + 185$	
1	$f(1) = -16(1)^2 + 185$	
2		
3		
4		

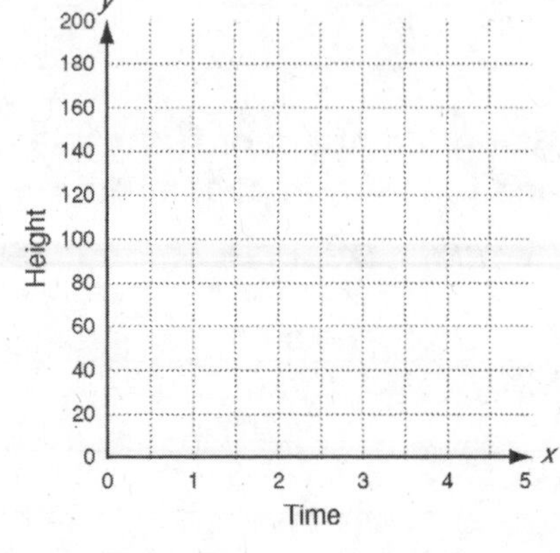

3. What is the parent function for the graph? __________________

4. What is the name for this U-shaped curve? __________________

5. Describe the transformations of the parent function into $f(t) = -16t^2 + 185$, which describes the path of an object falling from 185 feet.

____

Choose the letter for the best answer.

6. Mario dropped a wrench from the top of a sailboat mast 58 feet high. Which function describes the path of the falling wrench?

   A $f(t) = 16(t - 58)^2 - 185$

   B $f(t) = -16(t - 58)^2 + 185$

   C $f(t) = 16t^2 - 58$

   D $f(t) = -16t^2 + 58$

7. Delle wants to transform the parent function $f(t) = t^2$ into $f(t) = -4(t - 0.6)^2 + 6$. Which is NOT a step in that transformation?

   A Translation 6 units up

   B Translation 0.6 unit left

   C Reflection across the x-axis

   D Vertical stretch by a factor of 4

Name ______________________ Class ______________ Date ________

3-2

Properties of Quadratic Functions in Standard Form

Going Deeper

Video Tutor

Essential question: *How is the structure of a quadratic equation related to the structure of the parabola it describes?*

The standard form of a quadratic function is $f(x) = ax^2 + bx + c$, where a, b and c are constants and $a \neq 0$. The graph of a quadratic function is a parabola.

MCC9–12.F.IF.7a

1 EXPLORE Find the Axis of Symmetry and Vertex from a Graph

Find the axis of symmetry and vertex by graphing.

A Complete the table of values below. Sketch the graph of $y = x^2 - 4x + 5$.

x	$y = x^2 - 4x + 5$
0	
1	
2	
3	
4	

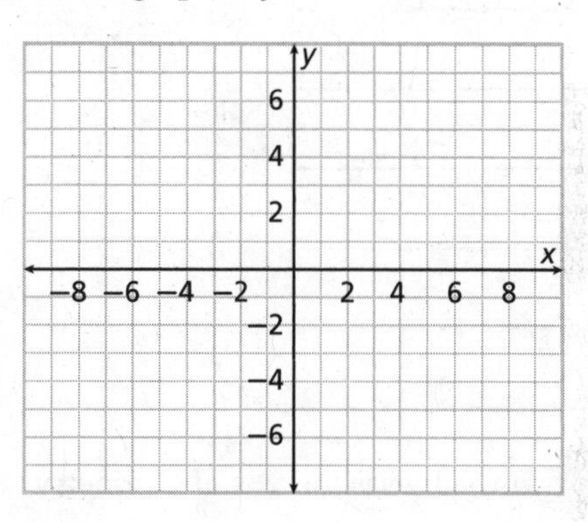

What is the axis of symmetry of the parabola? ____________

What is the vertex of the parabola? ____________

What is the y-intercept of the parabola? ____________

In which direction does the parabola open? ____________

B Complete the table of values below. Sketch the graph of $y = 2x^2 + 4x + 1$.

x	$y = 2x^2 + 4x + 1$
−3	
−2	
−1	
0	
1	

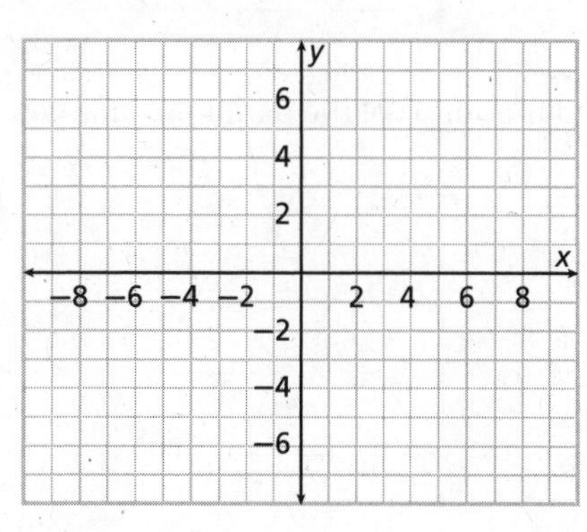

What is the axis of symmetry of the parabola? ____________

What is the vertex of the parabola? ____________

What is the y-intercept of the parabola? ____________

In which direction does the parabola open? ____________

REFLECT

1. How is the equation of the axis of symmetry related to coefficients a and b in Part A? How is the equation of the axis of symmetry related to coefficients a and b in Part C? Write a rule for the equation of the axis of symmetry based on the values of a and b.

MCC9–12.F.IF.7

2 EXAMPLE Find the Axis of Symmetry and Vertex from a Table

A Complete the table of values below.

x	$y = x^2 + x + 2$
−2	
−1	
0	
1	
2	

B Between which two x-values is the axis of symmetry located? ___________

What is the axis of symmetry of the parabola? ___________

How did you find the axis of symmetry?

How can you find the vertex of the parabola once you know the axis of symmetry?

What is the vertex of the parabola? ___________

REFLECT

2a. How might you find the axis of symmetry of a parabola if you are given a table of values?

____

____

2b. Why is the axis of symmetry halfway between two points on the parabola that have the same y-value?

____

____

PRACTICE

Complete the table of values and sketch the graph. Identify the axis of symmetry, vertex, and *y*-intercept of each parabola.

1. $y = x^2 + 6x - 1$

x	$y = x^2 + 6x - 1$
−5	
−4	
−3	
−2	
−1	

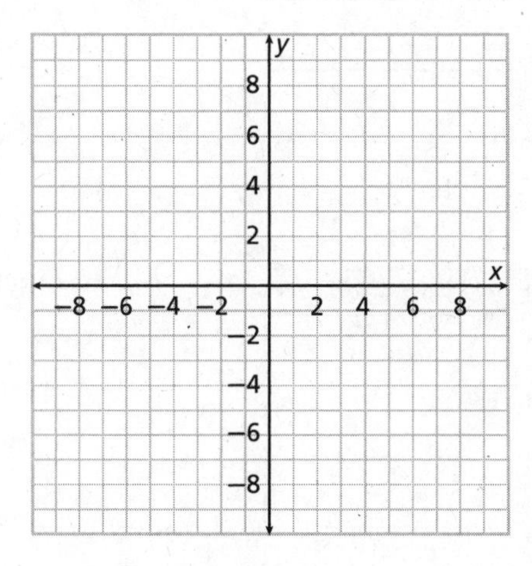

Axis of symmetry: ____________

Vertex: ____________

y-intercept: ____________

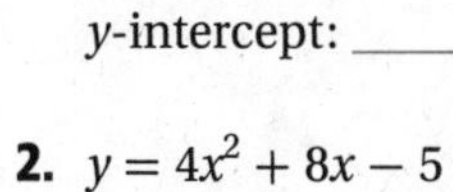

2. $y = 4x^2 + 8x - 5$

x	$y = 4x^2 + 8x - 5$
−3	
−2	
−1	
0	
1	

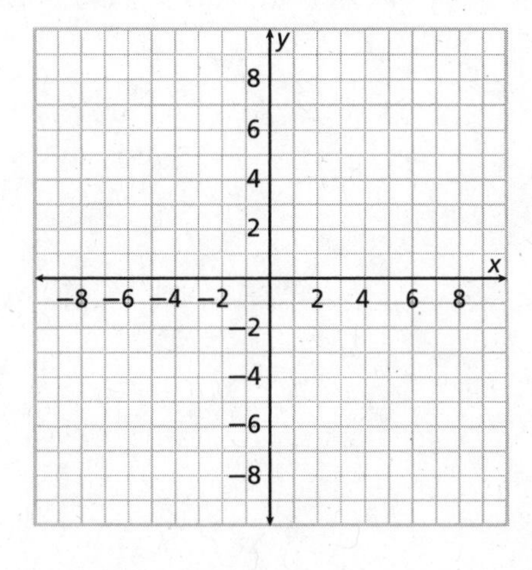

Axis of symmetry: ____________

Vertex: ____________

y-intercept: ____________

Complete the table of values. Identify the axis of symmetry, vertex, and *y*-intercept of each parabola.

3. $y = -2x^2 + 2x + 1$

x	$y = -2x^2 + 2x + 1$
−2	
−1	
0	
1	
2	

Axis of symmetry: ____________

Vertex: ____________

y-intercept: ____________

4. $y = x^2 + 3x - 2$

x	$y = x^2 + 3x - 2$
−4	
−3	
−2	
−1	
0	

Axis of symmetry: ____________

Vertex: ____________

y-intercept: ____________

5. $y = -x^2 - x - 4$

x	$y = -x^2 - x - 4$
−3	
−2	
−1	
0	
1	

Axis of symmetry: ____________

Vertex: ____________

y-intercept: ____________

Name________________________ Class______________ Date__________

3-2

Additional Practice

Identify the axis of symmetry for the graph of each function.

1. $g(x) = x^2 - 4x + 2$ ______
2. $h(x) = -8x^2 + 12x - 11$ ______
3. $k(x) = -4(x + 3)^2 + 9$ ______

For each function, (a) determine whether the graph opens upward or downward, (b) find the axis of symmetry, (c) find the vertex, and (d) find the *y*-intercept. Then graph the function.

4. $f(x) = -x^2 + 3x + 1$
   a. Upward or downward ______
   b. Axis of symmetry ______
   c. Vertex ______
   d. *y*-intercept ______
5. $g(x) = 2x^2 + 4x - 2$
   a. Upward or downward ______
   b. Axis of symmetry ______
   c. Vertex ______
   d. *y*-intercept ______

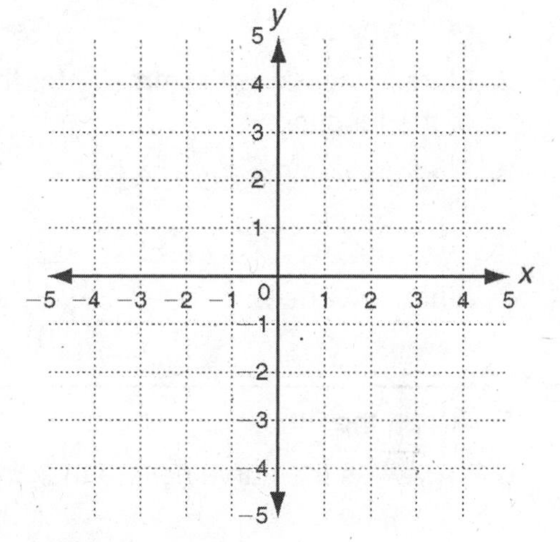

Find the minimum or maximum value of each function. Then state the domain and range of the function.

6. $g(x) = x^2 - 2x + 1$ ______
7. $h(x) = -5x^2 + 15x - 3$ ______

Solve.

8. A record label uses the following function to model the sales of a new release.

$$a(t) = -90t^2 + 8100t$$

The number of albums sold is a function of time, *t*, in days. On which day were the most albums sold? What is the maximum number of albums sold on that day?

______

Problem Solving

Kim wants to buy a used car with good gas mileage. He knows that the miles per gallon, or mileage, varies according to various factors, including the speed. He finds that highway mileage for the make and model he wants can be approximated by the function $f(s) = -0.03s^2 + 2.4s - 30$, where s is the speed in miles per hour. He wants to graph this function to estimate possible gas mileages at various speeds.

1. Determine whether the graph opens upward or downward. ________________

2. Identify the axis of symmetry for the graph of the function. ________________

3. Find the y-intercept.

____

4. Find the vertex.

____

5. Graph the function.

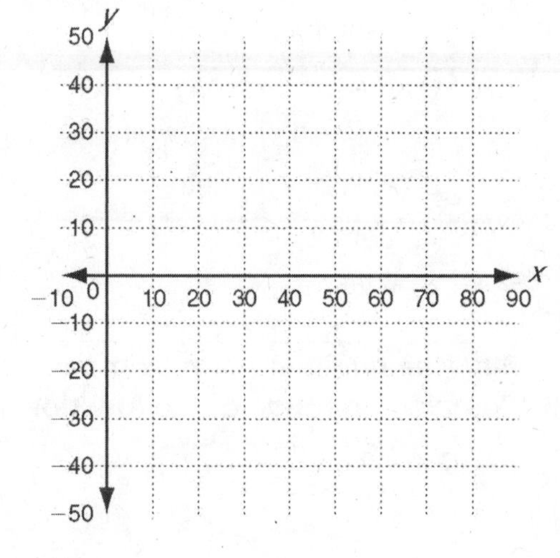

6. a. Does the curve have a maximum or a minimum value?

____

b. What is the value of the y-coordinate at the maximum or minimum?

____

c. Explain what this point means in terms of gas mileage.

____

A ball is hit into the air from a height of 4 feet. The function $g(t) = -16t^2 + 120t + 4$ can be used to model the height of the ball where t is the time in seconds after the ball is hit. Choose the letter for the best answer.

7. About how long is the ball in the air?

A 3.5 seconds

B 3.75 seconds

C 7 seconds

D 7.5 seconds

8. What is the maximum height the ball reaches?

A 108 feet

B 124 feet

C 229 feet

D 394 feet

Name________________________ Class______________ Date________

3-3

Curve Fitting with Quadratic Models

Focus on Modeling

Essential question: *How can you model changes in revenue from season-ticket sales using a quadratic function?*

Video Tutor

A community theater currently sells 200 season tickets at $50 each. In order to increase its season-ticket revenue without increasing the number of season tickets that it sells, the theater surveys its season-ticket holders to see if they would be willing to pay more. The survey finds that for every $5 increase in the price of a season ticket, the theater would lose 10 season-ticket holders. What action, if any, should the theater take to increase revenue?

1 Create a revenue function from the survey information.

A Let n be the number of $5 price increases in the cost of a season ticket. Write an expression for the cost of a season ticket after n price increases.

____

B Write an expression for the number of season-ticket holders after n price increases.

____

C The revenue generated from season-ticket sales is given below in words. Use this verbal model and your expressions from steps 1A and 1B to write an algebraic rule for the revenue function $R(n)$.

Revenue from season tickets	=	Number of season-ticket holders	·	Price of a season ticket

$R(n)$ = ______________________________

D As a check on your function rule, find the value of $R(0)$. Tell what this number represents and whether it agrees with the problem statement.

____

REFLECT

1a. What units are associated with the expressions that you wrote in steps 1A and 1B?

____

1b. When you multiply the units for the expressions, what units do you get for the revenue? Are they the units you expect?

____

2 Determine the domain of the revenue function.

A Because n is the number of \$5 price increases in the cost of a season ticket, you might think that the domain of the revenue function $R(n)$ is the set of whole numbers. However, given that increases in price result in losses of customers, what eventually happens to the number of season-ticket holders as n increases?

B Determine a constraint on the values of n. That is, write and solve an inequality that represents an upper bound on the values of n.

C State a reasonable domain for the revenue function.

REFLECT

2. When the value of n reaches its upper bound, what will happen to the value of $R(n)$? Why?

3 Graph the revenue function.

A Complete the tables of values for the revenue function.

n	$R(n)$
0	10,000
1	
2	
3	
4	
5	
6	
7	
8	
9	
10	

n	$R(n)$
11	
12	
13	
14	
15	
16	
17	
18	
19	
20	

B Graph the revenue function. Be sure to label the axes with the quantities they represent and indicate the axis scales by showing numbers for some grid lines.

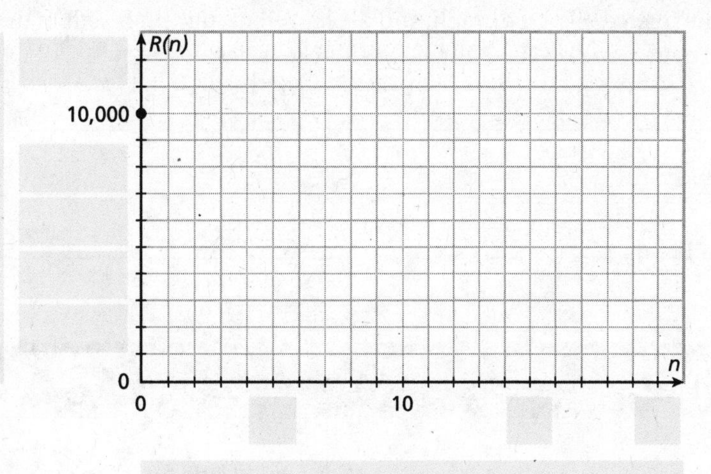

REFLECT

3. Enter the revenue function on a graphing calculator. Set the viewing window to match that of the grid above, then graph the function. Is your graph identical to the one on the graphing calculator? If not, describe and explain any differences. Which graph is correct, and why?

____

____

____

4 Analyze the revenue function.

A For what values of n does $R(n)$ increase? For what values of n does $R(n)$ decrease?

____

B At what value of n does $R(n)$ take on its maximum value? What is the maximum value?

____

C Write a brief paragraph describing what action the theater should take to maximize revenue. Include what happens to the number of season-ticket holders as well as the season-ticket price.

____

____

____

REFLECT

4. Identify the intercepts of the graph, and explain what they represent in the context of generating revenue from season-ticket sales.

EXTEND

1. Show that the revenue function from step 1C is a quadratic function by multiplying the two factors and collecting like terms to obtain a function of the form $R(n) = an^2 + bn + c$ where a, b, and c are constants.

2. A quadratic function $f(x) = ax^2 + bx + c$ has a maximum value at $x = -\frac{b}{2a}$ if $a < 0$ or a minimum value at $x = -\frac{b}{2a}$ if $a > 0$. Confirm that this property is true for the rewritten revenue function from Exercise 1.

3. Complete the square on the rewritten revenue function from Exercise 1 to obtain a function of the form $R(n) = a(n - h)^2 + k$ where a, h, and k are constants. Using this vertex form, identify the vertex of the graph of $R(n)$ and check to see whether it agrees with your answers for step 4B.

4. When graphing the revenue function in step 3B, you may have noticed that $R(0) = R(10)$, $R(1) = R(9)$, $R(2) = R(8)$, $R(3) = R(7)$, and $R(4) = R(6)$. Use the rewritten revenue function from Exercise 3 to explain those observations.

5. Using your tables of values from step 3A, calculate the rate of change in $R(n)$ for consecutive values of n. (The rate of change in $R(n)$ is given by the fraction $\frac{\text{change in } R(n)}{\text{change in } n}$, but because the values of n are consecutive whole numbers, the change in n is always 1 and the rate of change in $R(n)$ is just the change in $R(n)$.) Describe what happens to the rates of change in $R(n)$, and relate them to your answers to the questions in step 4A.

n	R(n)	Change in R(n)
0	10,000	—
1		
2		
3		
4		
5		
6		
7		
8		
9		
10		

n	R(n)	Change in R(n)
11		
12		
13		
14		
15		
16		
17		
18		
19		
20		

6. Rather than maximize season-ticket revenue, suppose the theater wants to increase the current revenue by just 8%. Using the revenue function from step 1C, write and solve a quadratic equation, and interpret the solution(s).

7. Predict what would happen to revenue if the theater lost fewer than 10 season-ticket holders for every $5 increase in the price of a ticket. Then check your prediction by creating and analyzing a model for the situation.

Additional Practice

Determine whether each data set could represent a quadratic function. Explain.

1.

x	–1	0	1	2	3
y	35	22	11	2	–5

____

2.

x	–2	0	2	4	6
y	18	10	6	2	1

____

Write a quadratic equation that fits each set of points.

3. (0, –8), (2, 0), and (–3, –5)

____

4. (–1, –16), (2, 5), and (5, 8)

____

5. (–2, 6), (0, –6), and (3, –9)

____

6. (1, 4), (–2, 13), and (0, 3)

____

Solve.

7. The data table shows the energy, *E*, of a certain object in joules at a given velocity, *v*, in meters per second.

Energy (joules)	4.5	12.5	24.5	40.5
Velocity (m/s)	1.5	2.5	3.5	4.5

a. Find the quadratic relationship between the energy and velocity of the object. _______________________

b. What is the energy of an object with a speed of 5 m/s? _______________________

c. What is the velocity of the object if the energy is 128 joules? _______________________

Problem Solving

Ellen and Kelly test Ellen's new car in an empty parking lot. They mark a braking line where Ellen applies the brakes. Kelly then measures the distance from that line to the place where Ellen stops, for speeds from 5 miles per hour to 25 miles per hour.

Brake Test					
Speed (mi/h)	5	10	15	20	25
Stopping Distance (ft)	7	17	30	46	65

1. Ellen wants to know the stopping distance at 60 miles per hour. She cannot drive the car at this speed in the parking lot, so they decide to try curve fitting, using the data they have collected.

   a. Can you use a quadratic function to represent the data in the table? Explain how you know.

   ____

   b. Use three points to write a system of equations to find a, b, and c in $f(x) = ax^2 + bx + c$. ______________

   c. Use any method to solve 3 equations with 3 variables. Find the values for a, b, and c. ______________

   d. Write the quadratic function that models the stopping distance of Ellen's car. ______________

   e. What is the stopping distance of Ellen's car at 60 miles per hour? ______________

The table shows the sizes and prices of decorative square patio tiles. Choose the letter for the best answer.

Patio Tiles Sale					
Side Length (in.)	6	9	12	15	18
Price Each ($)	1.44	3.24	5.76	9.00	12.96

2. What quadratic function models the price of the patio tiles?

   A $P(x) = 0.4x^2$

   B $P(x) = 0.04x^2$

   C $P(x) = 0.04x^2 + 0.4x$

   D $P(x) = 0.04x^2 + x + 0.4$

3. What is the second difference constant for the data in the table?

   A 1.44

   B 1.08

   C 0.72

   D 0.36

Name ______________________ Class ______________ Date __________

4-1

Solving Quadratic Equations by Graphing and Factoring

Extension: Intercept Form

Essential question: *How do you determine where the graph of a quadratic function crosses the x-axis?*

Video Tutor

PREP FOR MCC9–12.F.IF.8

1 EXPLORE Writing Different Forms of Quadratic Expressions

Write the expression in the form described.

A Rewrite $(x + 2)(x + 5)$ in standard form by multiplying.

$(x + 2)(x + 5)$	Write the original expression.
$(x + 2)x + (x + 2)$ ☐	Distribute $(x + 2)$.
$x(x) + x(2) + 5(x) + 5($ ☐ $)$	Distribute x and distribute 5.
$x^2 + 2x +$ ☐ $+$ ☐	Multiply.
$x^2 +$ ☐ $+ 10$	Combine like terms.

So, $(x + 2)(x + 5)$ is equivalent to ________________.

B Rewrite $x^2 - 3x - 4$ in factored form by factoring.

- You can factor a quadratic trinomial of the form $x^2 + bx + c$ by looking for factors of c whose sum is b.

  In the given expression, $b =$ ______ and $c =$ ______.

  So, look for factors of ______ whose sum is ________.

- Complete the table.

  The factors needed are ________ and ________.

Factors of −4	Sum
4 and −1	3
2 and −2	
1 and	

- Rewrite the given expression as a product of binomial factors with 1 and −4 as constants.

  $(x +$ ☐ $)(x -$ ☐ $)$

So, $x^2 - 3x - 4$ is equivalent to ________________.

REFLECT

1a. Describe the product you get when you multiply two linear binomials of the form $(x + p)$ and $(x + q)$ where p and q are constants.

____

____

REFLECT

1b. In part B, how could you check that you factored the given expression correctly?

____

____

The **intercept form** of a quadratic function is $f(x) = a(x - p)(x - q)$. The values of p and q are the x-intercepts of the function's graph, or the zeros of the function.

You can multiply to change a quadratic function in intercept form to standard form, and you can factor to change a quadratic function in standard form to intercept form.

MCC9–12.F.IF.8a

2 EXAMPLE Graphing $f(x) = a(x - p)(x - q)$

Write each function in intercept form. Identify the x-intercepts and vertex of the function's graph. Then graph the function.

A $f(x) = x^2 - 8x + 12$

- Write the function in intercept form by factoring the trinomial.

$f(x) = \left(x - \square\right)\left(x - \square\right)$ Factor the trinomial.

- Identify the x-intercepts.

The x-intercepts are __________ and __________.

So, the graph includes the points (2, 0) and $\left(\square, 0\right)$.

- Identify the vertex.

Based on the symmetry of the parabola, the x-coordinate of the vertex must be halfway between the x-coordinates of the points (2, 0) and (6, 0).

The x-coordinate of the vertex is $\frac{2 + 6}{2} = \square$.

Substitute this value of x into the function rule to find the y-coordinate of the vertex.

$f(4) = \left(\square - 2\right)\left(\square - 6\right)$ Substitute 4 for x.

$f(4) = \left(\square\right)\left(\square\right)$ Simplify the factors.

$f(4) = \square$ Multiply.

So, the vertex is $\left(\square, \square\right)$.

- Graph the function using the x-intercepts and the vertex.

B $f(x) = -\frac{1}{3}x^2 + \frac{4}{3}x + \frac{5}{3}$

- Write the function in intercept form by factoring the trinomial.

$f(x) = -\frac{1}{3}\left(x^2 - \square x - \square\right)$ Factor out $-\frac{1}{3}$ so that the coefficient of x^2 is 1.

$f(x) = -\frac{1}{3}\left(x - \square\right)\left(x + \square\right)$ Factor the trinomial.

- Identify the x-intercepts.

The x-intercepts are __________ and __________.

So, the graph includes the points $\left(\square, 0\right)$ and $\left(\square, 0\right)$.

- Identify the vertex.

The x-coordinate of the vertex must be halfway between the x-coordinates of the points (5, 0) and $\left(\square, 0\right)$.

The x-coordinate of the vertex is $\frac{\square + \square}{2} = \square$.

Substitute this value of x into the function rule to find the y-coordinate of the vertex.

$f(2) = -\frac{1}{3}\left(\square - 5\right)\left(\square + 1\right)$ Substitute 2 for x.

$f(2) = -\frac{1}{3}\left(\square\right)\left(\square\right)$ Simplify the factors.

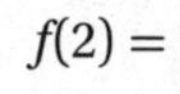

$f(2) = \square$ Multiply.

So, the vertex is $\left(\square, \square\right)$.

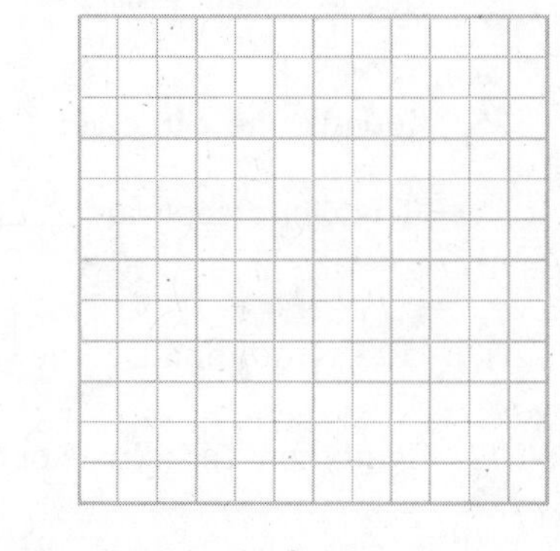

- Graph the function using the x-intercepts and the vertex.

REFLECT

2a. Describe another way that you could have found the vertex of the graph of the function in part A.

____

____

2b. In part B, how could you tell that the parabola opens downward by looking at the standard form of the quadratic function?

____

____

2c. A student claims that you can find the x-coordinate of the vertex of the graph of a quadratic function by averaging the values of p and q from the intercept form of the function. Is the student's claim correct? Explain.

____

____

____

Writing a Quadratic Model in Intercept Form

The cross-sectional shape of the archway of a bridge is modeled by the function $f(x) = -0.5x^2 + 2x$, where $f(x)$ is the height in meters of a point on the arch and x is the distance in meters from the left end of the arch's base. How wide is the arch at its base? Will a wagon that is 2 meters wide and 1.75 meters tall fit under the arch?

A Write the function in intercept form.

$f(x) = -0.5\left(x^2 - \square x\right)$ Factor out −0.5 so that the coefficient of x^2 is 1.

$f(x) = -0.5(x)\left(x - \square\right)$ Factor the binomial.

$f(x) = -0.5(x - 0)\left(x - \square\right)$ Write the intercept form.

B Identify the x-intercepts and the vertex.

The x-intercepts are ____________ and ____________.

The x-coordinate of the vertex is $\dfrac{\square + \square}{2} = \square$.

Find the y-coordinate of the vertex.

$f(2) = -0.5\left(\square - 0\right)\left(\square - 4\right)$ Substitute 2 for x.

$f(2) = -0.5\left(\square\right)\left(\square\right) = \square$ Simplify.

The vertex is $\left(\square, \square\right)$.

C Graph the function using the x-intercepts and the vertex.

D Use the graph to solve the problem.

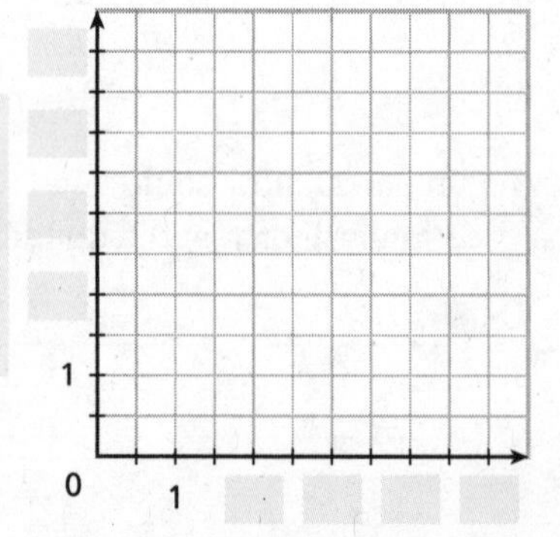

The width of the arch at its base is ____________ meters.
Sketch the wagon on your graph. Will the wagon fit under the arch? Explain.

____

____

REFLECT

3a. What do the x-intercepts represent in this situation?

3b. Explain how you used the graph to find the width of the arch at its base.

3c. Explain how you modeled the shape of the wagon on the graph.

3d. What are the x-coordinates of the left and right sides of the model of the wagon? Evaluate the function modeling the arch for these x-values. Do the results verify your conclusion about whether the wagon will fit under the arch? Explain.

PRACTICE

Write each function in intercept form. Identify the x-intercepts and vertex of the function's graph. Then graph the function.

1. $f(x) = x^2 + 6x + 5$

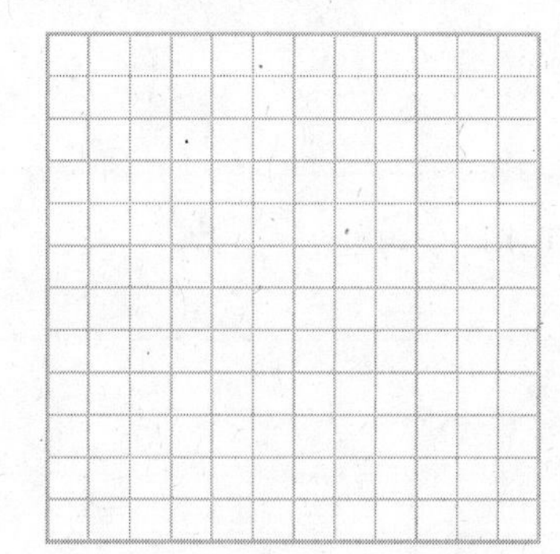

2. $f(x) = x^2 - 2x - 8$

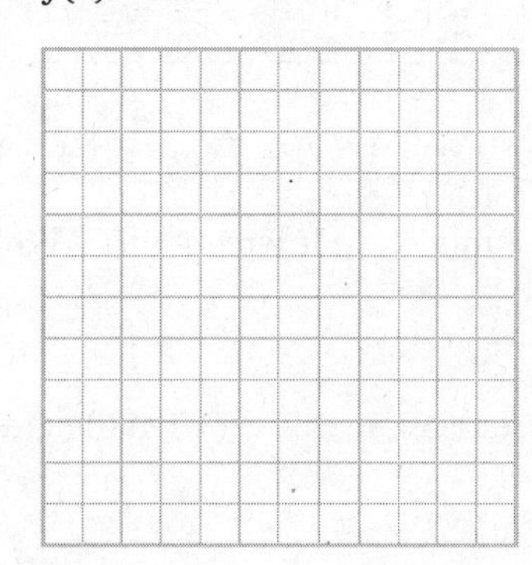

Write each function in intercept form. Identify the *x*-intercepts and vertex of the function's graph. Then graph the function.

3. $f(x) = 2x^2 - 8x + 6$

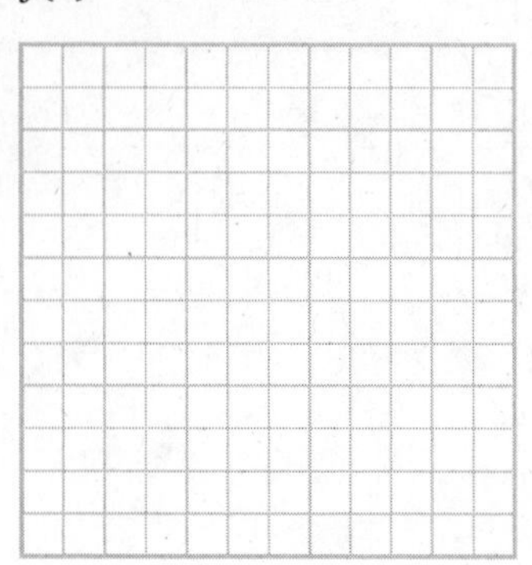

4. $f(x) = -3x^2 + 24x - 45$

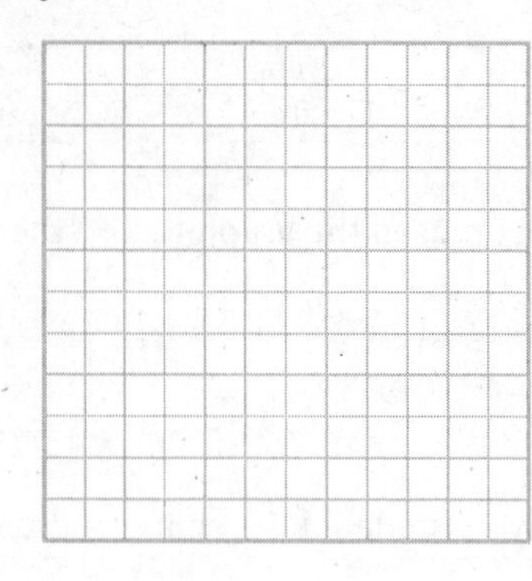

5. In a football game, Tony attempts to kick a field goal at a distance of 40 yards from the goal post. The path of the kicked football is given by the equation $y = -0.02x^2 + 0.9x$ where x is the horizontal distance in yards and y is the vertical distance in yards.

a. Write the equation in intercept form.

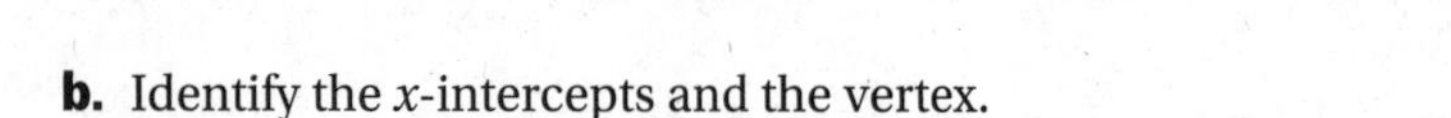

b. Identify the x-intercepts and the vertex.

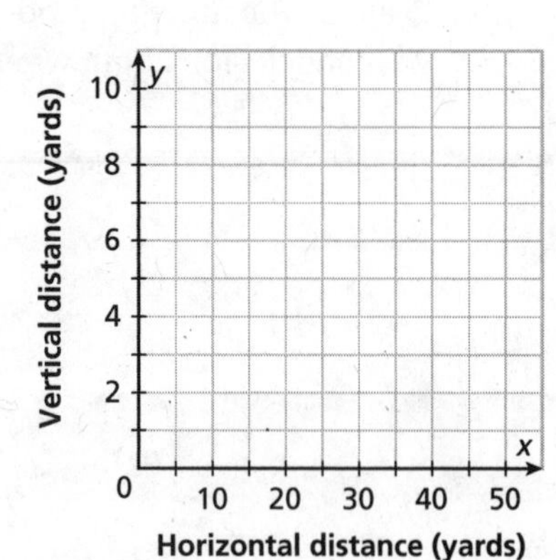

c. Graph the equation in the first quadrant.

d. The horizontal bar of the goal post is 10 feet above the ground. Does the ball go over the bar? Explain.

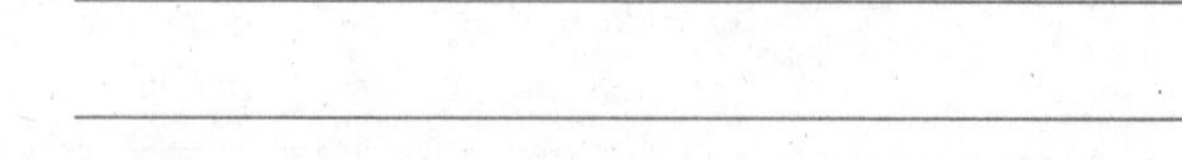

6. Consider the function $f(x) = 2x^2 + 12x + 18$.

a. Write the function in intercept form. What is the relationship between p and q?

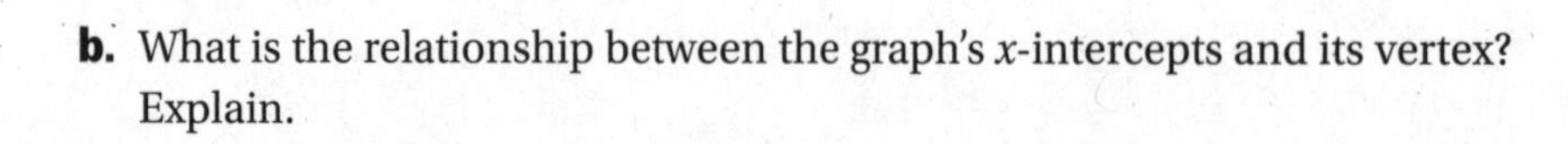

b. What is the relationship between the graph's x-intercepts and its vertex? Explain.

c. What is the vertex form of a quadratic function if $p = q$ in the intercept form of the function?

Name________________________ Class______________ Date__________ **4-1**

Additional Practice

Find the zeros of each function by using a graph and a table.

1. $f(x) = x^2 + 5x + 6$

x	–4	–3	–2	–1	0
$f(x)$					

____

2. $g(x) = -x^2 + 4x + 5$

x	–2	0	2	4	6
$f(x)$					

____

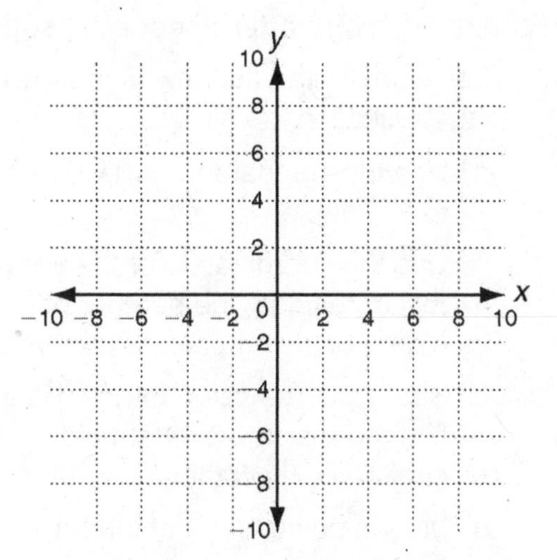

Find the zeros of each function by factoring.

3. $h(x) = -x^2 - 6x - 9$

4. $f(x) = 2x^2 + 9x + 4$

5. $g(x) = x^2 + x - 20$

______________________ ______________________ ______________________

Find the roots of each equation by factoring.

6. $12x = 9x^2 + 4$

7. $16x^2 = 9$

______________________ ______________________

Write a quadratic function in standard form for each given set of zeros.

8. –2 and 7

9. 1 and –8

______________________ ______________________

Solve.

10. The quadratic function that approximates the height of a javelin throw is $h(t) = -0.08t^2 + 4.48$, where t is the time in seconds after it is thrown and h is the javelin's height in feet. How long will it take for the javelin to hit the ground?

____

Problem Solving

Erin and her friends launch a rocket from ground level vertically into the air with an initial velocity of 80 feet per second. The height of the rocket, $h(t)$, after t seconds is given by $h(t) = -16t^2 + 80t$.

1. They want to find out how high they can expect the rocket to go and how long it will be in the air.
   a. Use the standard form $f(x) = ax^2 + bx + c$ to find values for a, b, and c. ________________
   b. Use the coordinates for the vertex of the path of the rocket to find t, the number of seconds the rocket will be in the air before it starts its downward path. ________________
   c. Substitute the value for t in the given function to find the maximum height of the rocket. How high can they expect their rocket to go? ________________
   d. Megan points out that the rocket will have a height of zero again when it returns to the ground. How long will the rocket stay in the air? ________________
2. Megan gets ready to launch the same rocket from a platform 21 feet above the ground with the same initial velocity. How long will the rocket stay in the air this time?
   a. Write a function that represents the rocket's path for this launch. ________________
   b. Factor the corresponding equation to find the values for t when h is zero. ________________
   c. Erin says that the roots of the equation are $t = 5.25$ and $t = -20.25$ and that the rocket will stay in the air 5.5 seconds. Megan says she is wrong. Who is correct? How do you know?

____

____

Choose the letter for the best answer.

3. Which function models the path of a rocket that lands 3 seconds after launch?
   A $h(t) = -16t^2 + 32t + 48$
   B $h(t) = -16t^2 + 32t + 10.5$
   C $h(t) = -16t^2 + 40t + 48$
   D $h(t) = -16t^2 + 40t + 10.5$
4. Megan reads about a rocket whose path can be modeled by the function $h(t) = -16t^2 + 100t + 15$. Which could be the initial velocity and launch height?
   A 15 ft/s; 100 ft off the ground
   B 16 ft/s; 100 ft off the ground
   C 100 ft/s; 15 ft off the ground
   D 171 ft/s; 15 ft off the ground

Name__________ Class__________ Date__________

4-2

Completing the Square

Connection: Vertex Form of Quadratic Equations

Essential question: *How do you convert quadratic functions to vertex form, $f(x) = a(x - h)^2 + k$?*

Video Tutor

MCC9–12.F.IF.8

1 EXPLORE Writing Quadratic Functions in Different Forms

Write the quadratic function in the form described.

A Write the function $f(x) = 2(x - 4)^2 + 3$ in the form $f(x) = ax^2 + bx + c$.

$f(x) = 2(x - 4)^2 + 3$

$f(x) = 2\left(x^2 - \square + \square\right) + 3$ Multiply to expand $(x - 4)^2$.

$f(x) = 2(x^2) - \square(8x) + \square(16) + 3$ Distribute 2.

$f(x) = 2x^2 - \square + \square + 3$ Multiply.

$f(x) = 2x^2 - 16x + \square$ Combine like terms.

So, $f(x) = 2(x - 4)^2 + 3$ is equivalent to ____________________.

B Write the function $f(x) = x^2 + 6x + 4$ in vertex form.

Recall that the vertex form of a quadratic function is $f(x) = a(x - h)^2 + k$. Write the given function in vertex form by completing the square.

$f(x) = x^2 + 6x + 4$

$f(x) = \left(x^2 + 6x + \square\right) + 4 - \square$ Set up for completing the square.

$f(x) = (x^2 + 6x + 9) + 4 - 9$ Add a constant so the expression inside the parentheses is a perfect square trinomial. Subtract the constant to keep the equation balanced.

$f(x) = \left(x + \square\right)^2 + 4 - 9$ Write $(x^2 + 6x + 9)$ as a binomial squared.

$f(x) = (x + 3)^2 - \square$ Combine like terms.

So, $f(x) = x^2 + 6x + 4$ is equivalent to ____________________.

REFLECT

1a. In part A, how does the value of a of the function in vertex form compare with the value of a when the function is in the form $f(x) = ax^2 + bx + c$?

____

1b. In part B, how could you check that you found the vertex form of the quadratic equation correctly?

____

____

1c. Describe how to complete the square for the quadratic expression $x^2 + 8x + \square$.

____

____

The **standard form** of a quadratic equation is $f(x) = ax^2 + bx + c$. Any quadratic function in standard form can be written in vertex form, and any quadratic function in vertex form can be written in standard form.

MCC9–12.F.IF.8a

2 EXAMPLE Graphing by Completing the Square

Graph the function by first writing it in vertex form. Then give the maximum or minimum of the function and identify its zeros.

A $f(x) = x^2 - 8x + 12$

- Write the function in vertex form.

$f(x) = \left(x^2 - 8x + \square\right) + 12 - \square$ Set up for completing the square.

$f(x) = \left(x^2 - 8x + \square\right) + 12 - \square$ Add a constant to complete the square. Subtract the constant to keep the equation balanced.

$f(x) = \left(x - \square\right)^2 + 12 - 16$ Write the expression in parentheses as a binomial squared.

$f(x) = (x - 4)^2 - \square$ Combine like terms.

- Sketch a graph of the function.

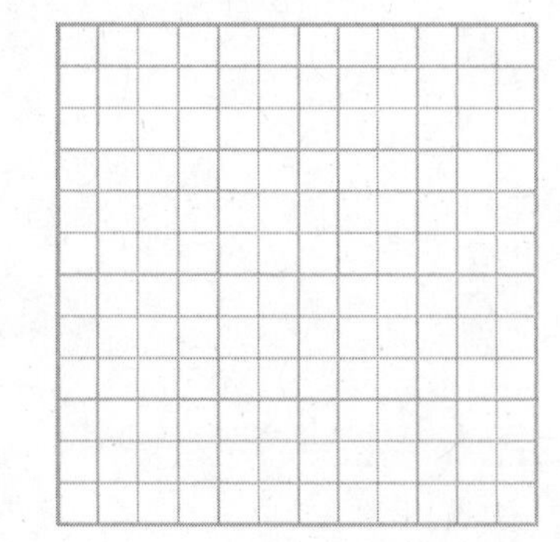

The vertex is __________.

Two points to the left of the vertex are $\left(2, \square\right)$ and $\left(3, \square\right)$.

Two points to the right of the vertex are $\left(5, \square\right)$ and $\left(6, \square\right)$.

- Describe the function's properties.

The minimum is __________.

The zeros are __________ and __________.

B $f(x) = -2x^2 - 12x - 16$

- Write the function in vertex form.

$f(x) = \square(x^2 + 6x) - 16$	Factor the variable terms so that the coefficient of x^2 is 1.
$f(x) = -2\left(x^2 + 6x + \square\right) - 16 - \square$	Set up for completing the square.
$f(x) = -2\left(x^2 + 6x + \square\right) - 16 - (-2)\square$	Complete the square. Since the constant is multiplied by −2, subtract the product of −2 and the constant to keep the equation balanced.
$f(x) = -2\left(x + \square\right)^2 - 16 - (-2)9$	Write the expression in parentheses as a binomial squared.
$f(x) = -2(x + 3)^2 - 16 - \left(\square\right)$	Simplify (−2)9.
$f(x) = -2(x + 3)^2 + \square$	Combine like terms.

- Sketch a graph of the function.

The vertex is __________.

Two points to the left of the vertex are

$\left(-5, \square\right)$ and $\left(-4, \square\right)$.

Two points to the right of the vertex are

$\left(-2, \square\right)$ and $\left(-1, \square\right)$.

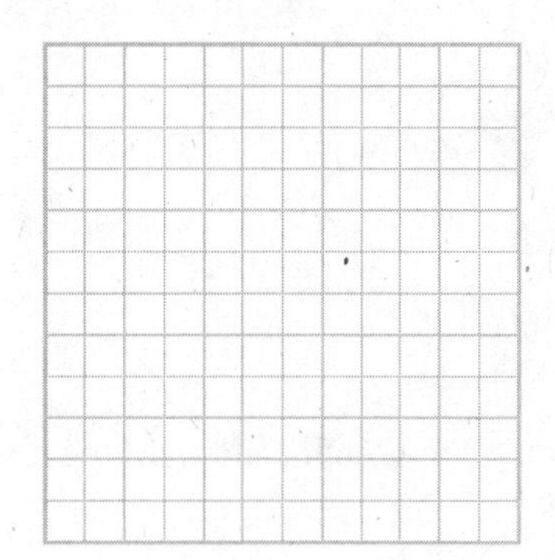

- Describe the function's properties.

The maximum is __________.

The zeros are __________ and __________.

REFLECT

2a. How do you keep the equation of a quadratic function balanced when completing the square?

____

____

2b. In part B, why do you factor out −2 from the variable terms before completing the square?

____

____

2c. Why might the vertex form of a quadratic equation be more useful in some situations than the standard form?

MCC9–12.F.IF.8a

3 EXAMPLE Modeling Quadratic Functions in Standard Form

The function $h(t) = -16t^2 + 64t$ gives the height h in feet of a golf ball t seconds after it is hit. The ball has a height of 48 feet after 1 second. Use the symmetry of the function's graph to determine the other time at which the ball will have a height of 48 feet.

A Write the function in vertex form.

$h(t) = \square(t^2 - 4t)$ — Factor so that the coefficient of t^2 is 1.

$h(t) = -16\left(t^2 - 4t + \square\right) - (-16)\square$ — Complete the square and keep the equation balanced.

$h(t) = -16\left(t - \square\right)^2 - (-16)4$ — Write the expression in parentheses as a binomial squared.

$h(t) = -16(t - 2)^2 + \square$ — Simplify.

B Use symmetry to sketch a graph of the function and solve the problem.

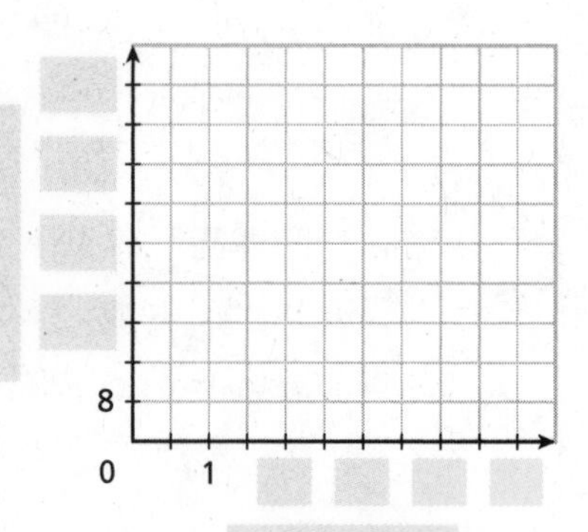

The vertex is ______.

The point $\left(0, \square\right)$ is on the graph.

This point is 2 units to the left of the vertex. Based on symmetry, there is a point 2 units to the right of the vertex with the same y-coordinate at $\left(\square, 0\right)$.

The point (1, 48) is on the graph. Based on symmetry, the point $\left(\square, 48\right)$ is also on the graph.

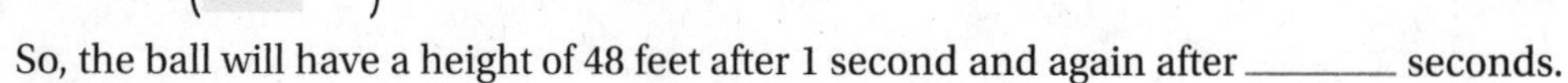

So, the ball will have a height of 48 feet after 1 second and again after ______ seconds.

REFLECT

3a. How can you check your answer to the problem?

3b. What is the maximum height that the ball reaches? How do you know?

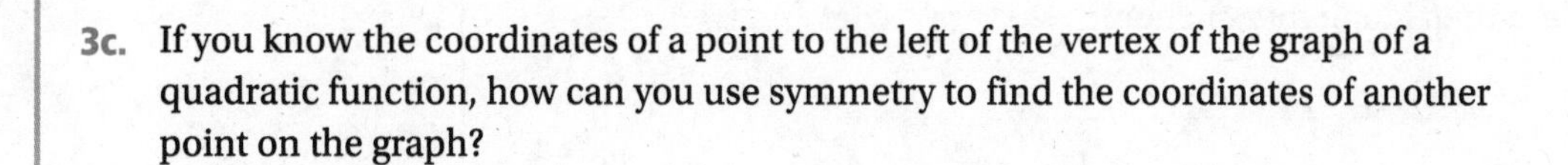

3c. If you know the coordinates of a point to the left of the vertex of the graph of a quadratic function, how can you use symmetry to find the coordinates of another point on the graph?

PRACTICE

Graph each function by first writing it in vertex form. Then give the maximum or minimum of the function and identify its zeros.

1. $f(x) = x^2 - 6x + 9$

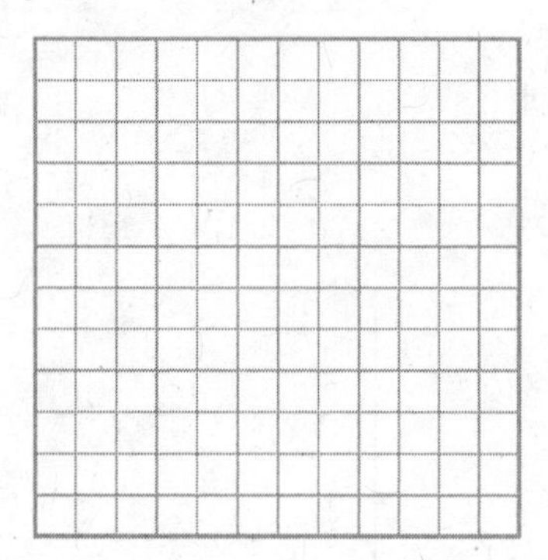

2. $f(x) = x^2 - 2x - 3$

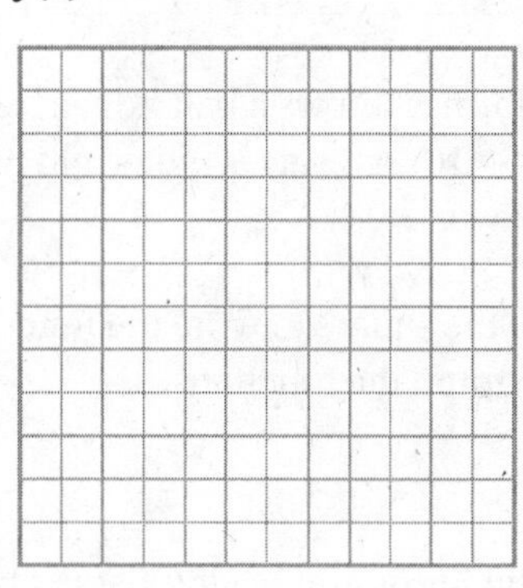

3. $f(x) = -7x^2 - 14x$

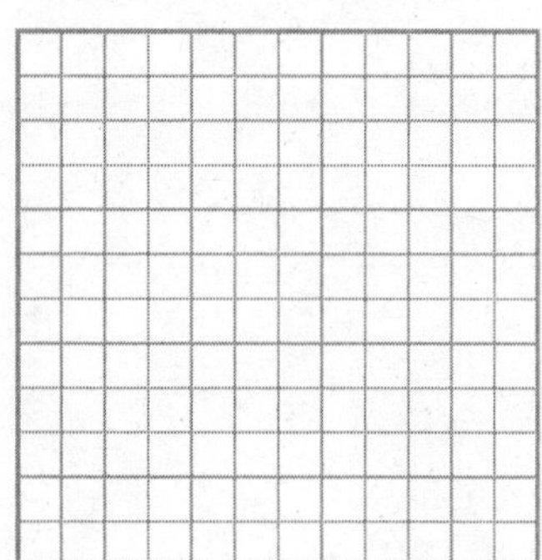

4. $f(x) = 3x^2 - 12x + 9$

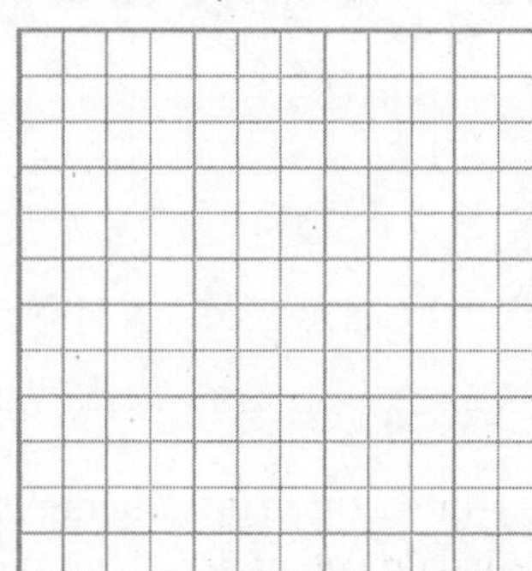

5. A company is marketing a new toy. The function $s(p) = -50p^2 + 3000p$ models how the total sales s of the toy, in dollars, depend on the price p of the toy, in dollars.

a. Complete the square to write the function in vertex form and then graph the function.

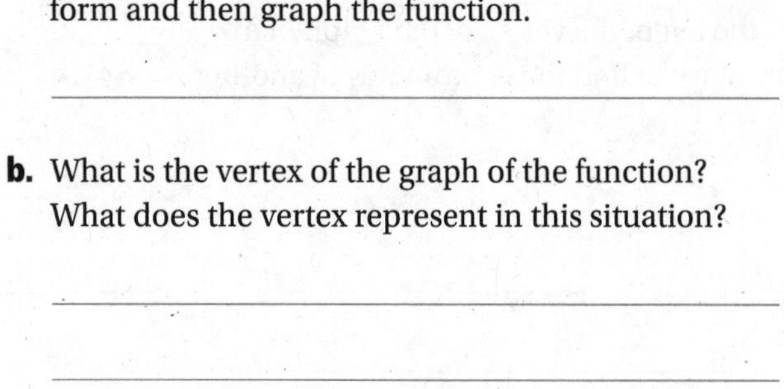

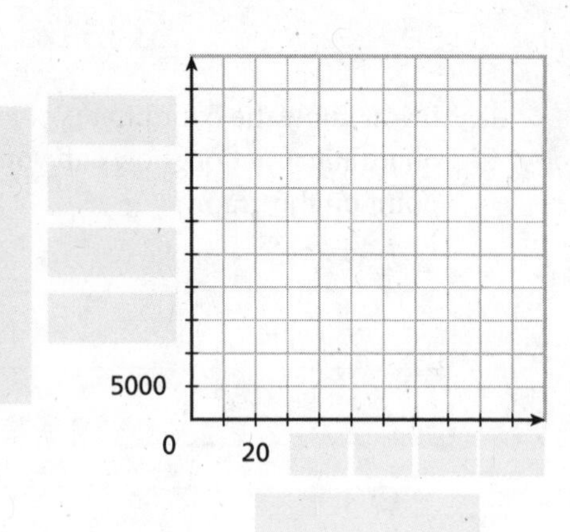

b. What is the vertex of the graph of the function? What does the vertex represent in this situation?

c. The model predicts that total sales will be \$40,000 when the toy price is \$20. At what other price does the model predict that total sales will be \$40,000? Use the symmetry of the graph to support your answer.

6. A circus performer throws a ball from a height of 32 feet. The model $h(t) = -16t^2 + 16t + 32$ gives the height of the ball in feet t seconds after it is thrown.

a. Complete the square to write the function in vertex form and then graph the function.

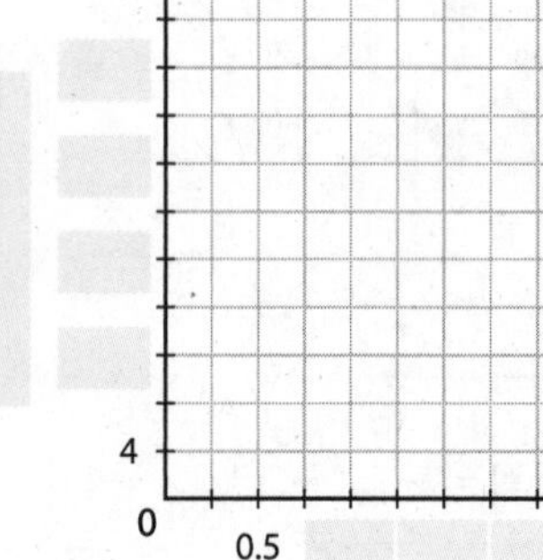

b. What is the maximum height that the ball reaches?

c. What is a reasonable domain of the function? Explain.

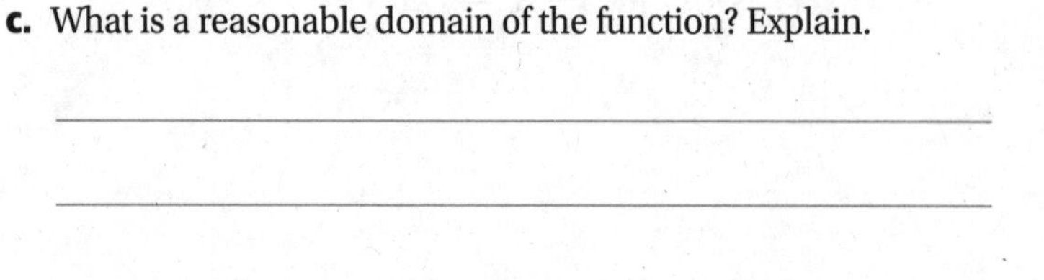

d. What is the y-intercept of the function's graph? What does it represent in this situation? What do you notice about the y-intercept and the value of c when the function is written in standard form?

Name________________ Class__________ Date__________

4-2

Additional Practice

Solve each equation.

1. $2x^2 - 6 = 42$

2. $x^2 - 14x + 49 = 18$

Complete the square for each expression. Write the resulting expression as a binomial squared.

3. $x^2 - 4x +$ _____

4. $x^2 + 12x +$ _____

Solve each equation by completing the square.

5. $2d^2 = 8 + 10d$

6. $x^2 + 2x = 3$

7. $-3x^2 + 18x = -30$

8. $4x^2 = -12x + 4$

Write each function in vertex form, and identify its vertex.

9. $f(x) = x^2 - 6x - 2$

10. $f(x) = x^2 - 4x + 1$

11. $h(x) = 3x^2 - 6x - 15$

12. $f(x) = -2x^2 - 16x + 4$

Solve.

13. Nathan made a triangular pennant for the band booster club. The area of the pennant is 80 square feet. The base of the pennant is 12 feet shorter than the height.

    a. What are the lengths of the base and height of the pennant?

    b. What are the dimensions of the pennant if the base is only 6 feet shorter than the height?

Problem Solving

Sean and Mason run out of gas while fishing from their boat in the bay. They set off an emergency flare with an initial vertical velocity of 30 meters per second. The height of the flare in meters can be modeled by $h(t) = -5t^2 + 30t$, where t represents the number of seconds after launch.

1. Sean thinks the flare should reach at least 15 meters to be seen from the shore. They want to know how long the flare will take to reach this height.
   a. Write an equation to determine how long it will take the flare to reach 15 meters. ________________
   b. Simplify the function so you can complete the square. ________________
   c. Solve the equation by completing the square. ________________
   d. Mason thinks that the flare will reach 15 meters in 5.4 seconds. Is he correct? Explain.

   ____

   e. Sean thinks the flare will reach 15 meters sooner, but then the flare will stay above 15 meters for about 5 seconds. Is he correct? Explain.

   ____

2. Sean wants to know how high the flare will reach above the surface of the water.
   a. Write the function in vertex form, factoring so the coefficient of t^2 is 1. ________________
   b. Complete the square using the vertex form of the function. ________________
   c. How high will the flare reach? ________________

Choose the letter for the best answer.

3. Use the vertex form of the function to determine how long after firing the flare it will reach its maximum height.

   A 3 s

   B 5 s

   C 9 s

   D 15 s

4. The boys fire a similar flare from the deck 5 meters above the water level. Which statement is correct?

   A The flare will reach 45 m in 3 s.

   B The flare will reach 50 m in 3 s.

   C The flare will reach 45 m in 3.5 s.

   D The flare will reach 50 m in 3.5 s.

Name ______________________ Class ______________ Date __________

4-3

The Quadratic Formula

Going Deeper

Essential question: *When does a quadratic equation have nonreal solutions, and how do you find them?*

Video Tutor

MCC9–12.A.REI.4b

1 ENGAGE Revisiting the Quadratic Formula

You have solved quadratic equations of the form $ax^2 + bx + c = 0$, where the coefficients a, b, and c are real numbers and $a \neq 0$, in several ways. One way was by using the *quadratic formula*:

$$x = \frac{-b \pm \sqrt{b^2 - 4ac}}{2a}$$

The radical $\sqrt{b^2 - 4ac}$ has meaning in the real number system only if the radicand $b^2 - 4ac$ is nonnegative. The radicand determines the number of real solutions and for this reason is called the *discriminant* for the quadratic equation. The table below summarizes the possible numbers of real solutions of a quadratic equation.

Value of Discriminant	Number of Real Solutions
$b^2 - 4ac > 0$	Two real solutions: $x = \frac{-b + \sqrt{b^2 - 4ac}}{2a}$ and $x = \frac{-b - \sqrt{b^2 - 4ac}}{2a}$
$b^2 - 4ac = 0$	One real solution: $x = -\frac{b}{2a}$
$b^2 - 4ac < 0$	No real solutions

When you solve a quadratic equation in the complex number system, where the radical $\sqrt{b^2 - 4ac}$ has meaning no matter what the value of the radicand is, the equation always has solutions. The table below summarizes the possible numbers of complex solutions of a quadratic equation.

Value of Discriminant	Number of Complex Solutions
$b^2 - 4ac > 0$	Two real solutions
$b^2 - 4ac = 0$	One real solution
$b^2 - 4ac < 0$	Two nonreal solutions

The table below gives three simple quadratic equations having different numbers and types of complex solutions.

Equation	Value of Discriminant	Solutions
$x^2 - 1 = 0$	$0^2 - 4(1)(-1) = 4$	$x = \pm 1$ (two real solutions)
$x^2 = 0$	$0^2 - 4(1)(0) = 0$	$x = 0$ (one real solution)
$x^2 + 1 = 0$	$0^2 - 4(1)(1) = -4$	$x = \pm i$ (two nonreal solutions)

REFLECT

1a. Use the discriminant to explain why the equation $x^2 + 2x - 3 = 0$ has two real solutions while the equation $x^2 + 2x + 3 = 0$ has no real solutions.

____

____

1b. For what value of c does the equation $x^2 + 2x + c = 0$ have exactly one real solution? Explain.

____

MCC9–12.N.CN.7

2 EXAMPLE Finding the Complex Solutions of a Quadratic Equation

Tell whether the solutions of $x^2 + 4 = 0$ are real or imaginary. Then find the solutions.

A Use the discriminant to determine the number and type of solutions.

$b^2 - 4ac = \square^2 - 4(\square)(\square) = \square$

Because $b^2 - 4ac$ $\square$ 0, there are two ______________ solutions.

B Use the quadratic formula to solve the equation.

$x = \dfrac{-b \pm \sqrt{b^2 - 4ac}}{2a}$ Write the quadratic formula.

$= \dfrac{-\square \pm \sqrt{\square}}{2(\square)}$ Substitute values. For the radicand $b^2 - 4ac$, use the value from part A.

Simplify the numerator, and simplify the denominator.

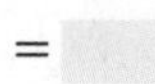

Simplify the fraction.

REFLECT

2a. Describe how you can check the solutions of a quadratic equation. Use the method to check the solutions of $x^2 + 4 = 0$.

____

____

2b. Why is it important to write a quadratic equation in the form $ax^2 + bx + c = 0$ before identifying the values of a, b, and c? For instance, why should you write $x^2 = -4$ as $x^2 + 4 = 0$ before using the quadratic formula to solve the equation?

____

____

____

3 EXAMPLE Finding the Complex Solutions of a Quadratic Equation

Tell whether the solutions of $x^2 - 4x + 13 = 0$ are real or imaginary. Then find the solutions.

A Use the discriminant to determine the number and type of solutions.

$b^2 - 4ac = (\quad)^2 - 4(\quad)(\quad) = \quad$

Because $b^2 - 4ac$ ____ 0, there are two ____________ solutions.

B Use the quadratic formula to solve the equation.

$x = \frac{-b \pm \sqrt{b^2 - 4ac}}{2a}$ Write the quadratic formula.

$= \frac{-(\quad) \pm \sqrt{\quad}}{2(\quad)}$ Substitute values. For the radicand $b^2 - 4ac$, use the value from part A.

$= \frac{\quad}{\quad}$ Simplify the numerator, and simplify the denominator.

$= \quad$ Simplify the fraction.

C One of the solutions is $x_1 = 2 + 3i$. Check this solution by substituting it into the equation to see if it produces a true statement.

$x^2 - 4x + 13 = (\quad)^2 - 4(\quad) + 13$ Substitute.

$= (\quad) - 4(\quad) + 13$ Square.

$= (\quad) + (\quad) + 13$ Multiply.

$= \quad$ Simplify.

REFLECT

3a. Describe what will change in each step of the check in part C when you substitute the other solution, x_2.

____

____

3b. Does the equation $x^2 + 4x + 13 = 0$ have the *same number and type of solutions* as $x^2 - 4x + 13 = 0$? Does it have the *same solutions*? Explain.

____

____

3c. Use the solutions x_1 and x_2 to write the expression $(x - x_1)(x - x_2)$. Multiply the binomials. What do you notice?

____

____

PRACTICE

Find the number and type of solutions of each equation.

1. $x^2 - 9 = 0$

2. $x^2 + 16 = 0$

3. $x^2 = 0$

4. $x^2 - 2x + 4 = 0$

5. $x^2 - 10x + 25 = 0$

6. $x^2 - 3x - 10 = 0$

7. $x^2 + 12x = -36$

8. $2x^2 + 5 = -3x$

9. $3x^2 = 7 - 4x$

Find the complex solutions of each equation.

10. $x^2 + 49 = 0$

11. $x^2 + 5 = 0$

12. $4x^2 + 9 = 0$

13. $x^2 - 2x + 2 = 0$

14. $x^2 - 6x + 13 = 0$

15. $x^2 + 10x + 29 = 0$

16. $5x^2 - 2x + 1 = 0$

17. $9x^2 + 12x + 5 = 0$

18. $2x^2 - 6x + 7 = 0$

19. Multiplying the binomials in $(x - x_1)(x - x_2)$ gives $x^2 - (x_1 + x_2)x + x_1x_2$.

a. Explain why x_1 and x_2 are solutions of the equation $(x - x_1)(x - x_2) = 0$ as well as the equation $x^2 - (x_1 + x_2)x + x_1x_2 = 0$.

b. For the equation $x^2 - (x_1 + x_2)x + x_1 x_2 = 0$, how is the coefficient of the x-term related to the equation's solutions? How is the constant term related to the solutions?

c. Describe a quick way to check the solutions x_1 and x_2 of an equation in the form $x^2 + bx + c = 0$. Then check to see if $x_1 = 2 + i$ and $x_2 = 2 - i$ are solutions of the equation $x^2 - 4x + 5 = 0$.

Name ______________________ Class ____________ Date ________

4-3

Additional Practice

Find the zeros of each function by using the Quadratic Formula.

1. $f(x) = x^2 + 10x + 9$

2. $g(x) = 2x^2 + 4x - 12$

3. $h(x) = 3x^2 - 3x + \frac{3}{4}$

4. $f(x) = x^2 + 2x - 3$

5. $g(x) = 2x^2 + 3x + 1$

6. $g(x) = x^2 + 5x - 3$

Find the type and number of solutions for each equation.

7. $x^2 - 3x = -8$

8. $x^2 + 4x = -3$

9. $2x^2 - 12x = -18$

Solve.

10. A newspaper delivery person in a car is tossing folded newspapers from the car window to driveways. The speed of the car is 30 feet per second, and the driver does not slow down. The newspapers are tossed horizontally from a height of 4 feet above the ground. The height of the papers as they are thrown can be modeled by $y = -16t^2 + 4$, and the distance they travel to the driveway is $d = 30t$.

    a. How long does it take for a newspaper to land?

    b. From how many feet before the driveway must the papers be thrown?

    c. The delivery person starts to throw the newspapers at an angle and the height of the papers as they travel can now be modeled by $y = -16t^2 + 12t + 4$. How long does it take the papers to reach the ground now?

Problem Solving

In a shot-put event, Jenna tosses her last shot from a position of about 6 feet above the ground with an initial vertical and horizontal velocity of 20 feet per second. The height of the shot is modeled by the function $h(t) = -16t^2 + 20t + 6$, where t is the time in seconds after the toss. The horizontal distance traveled after t seconds is modeled by $d(t) = 20t$.

1. Jenna wants to know the exact distance the shot travels at a velocity of 20 feet per second.

   a. Use the Quadratic Formula $t = \dfrac{-b \pm \sqrt{b^2 - 4ac}}{2a}$ to solve the height function for t. ________________

   b. Use the value for t and the distance function to find the distance her shot travels. ________________

2. Jenna is working to improve her performance. She makes a table to show how the horizontal distance varies with velocity. Complete the table.

	Velocity (ft/s)	Formula	Time (s)	Distance (ft)
a.	22	$t = \dfrac{-22 \pm \sqrt{(22)^2 - 4(-16)(6)}}{2(-16)}$		
b.	25			
c.	28			

Jenna has not reached her full potential yet. Her goal is to toss the shot from a height of 6 feet 6 inches with a vertical and horizontal velocity of 30 feet per second. Choose the letter for the best answer.

3. If she achieves her goal, how long will her shot stay in the air?

   A 1.65 s

   B 1.87 s

   C 2.07 s

   D 2.27 s

4. If she achieves her goal, what horizontal distance will the shot travel?

   A 41.4 ft

   B 56.1 ft

   C 62.1 ft

   D 68.1 ft

Name________________________ Class______________ Date________

4-4

Nonlinear Systems

Going Deeper

Video Tutor

Essential question: *How can you solve a system of equations when one equation is linear and the other is quadratic?*

To estimate the solution to a system of equations, you can graph both equations on the same coordinate plane and find the intersection points. Or you can solve the equations algebraically using substitution or elimination.

MCC9-12.A.REI.7

1 EXAMPLE Solving by Graphing and Algebraically

Solve the system of equations.

$$f(x) = -8x + 48$$
$$g(x) = -2(x - 2)^2 + 32$$

A Solve the system of equations by graphing.

Start by graphing the quadratic function. The vertex is (___ , ___). Describe the transformation of the parent quadratic function that produces the graph of $g(x)$.

____

____

To make the graph more accurate, plot the points where the x-intercepts occur. The x-intercepts are the solutions of the equation $g(x) = 0$:

$-2(x - 2)^2 + 32 = 0$

$-2(x - 2)^2 =$ ___

$(x - 2)^2 =$ ___

$x - 2 = \pm$ ___

$x =$ ___ $\pm$ ___ $=$ ___ or ___

So, the points (___ , 0) and (___ , 0) are on the graph.
Use these points and the vertex to draw the graph.

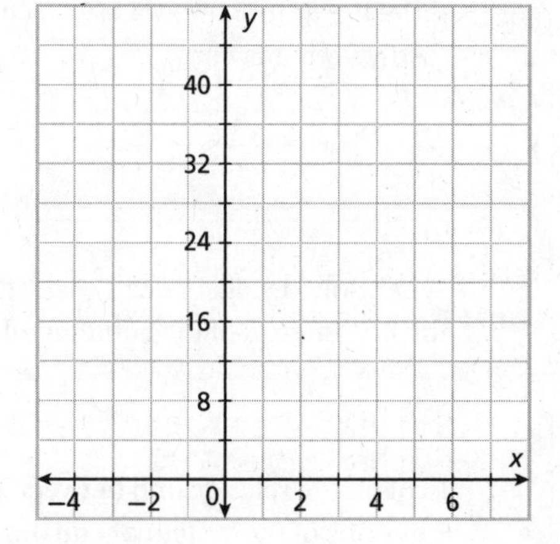

Now graph the linear function. The y-intercept is ______, and the slope is ______.

The line and the parabola intersect at two points. Identify the coordinates of those points.

(___ , ___) and (___ , ___)

B Solve the system of equations algebraically.

Write the functions in terms of y.

$$y = -8x + 48$$
$$y = -2(x - 2)^2 + 32$$

Both equations are solved for y, so set the right sides equal to each other and solve for x.

$-8x + 48 = -2(x - 2)^2 + 32$

$-8x + 48 =$ ______ Simplify the right side.

$\underline{8x - 48} = \underline{\qquad 8x - 48}$ Add $8x - 48$ to both sides.

$0 =$ ______ Simplify both sides.

$0 = -2(\quad)(\quad)$ Factor the right side.

$x =$ ___ or $x =$ ___ Use the zero-product property to solve for x.

Substitute these values of x into the equation of the line to find the corresponding y-values.

$y = -8(2) + 48 =$ ______

$y = -8(6) + 48 =$ ______

The solutions are $(\quad, \quad)$ and $(\quad, \quad)$.

REFLECT

1a. If the linear function was $f(x) = 8x + 48$, how many solutions would there be? Justify your answer.

______

______

1b. When solving algebraically, why do you substitute the x-values into the equation of the line instead of the equation of the parabola?

______

1c. Explain the relationship between the intersection points of the graphs and the solutions of the system of equations.

______

______

1d. Describe how to check that the solutions are correct.

______

______

Determining the Possible Number of Solutions

In the previous example, the system of equations had two solutions. You can use a graph to understand other possible numbers of solutions of a system of equations involving a linear equation and a quadratic equation.

The graph of the quadratic function $f(x) = -x^2 + 10x - 27$ is shown below.

Graph each linear function below on the same coordinate plane as the parabola.

Line 1: $g(x) = 2x - 11$

Line 2: $h(x) = -2x + 14$

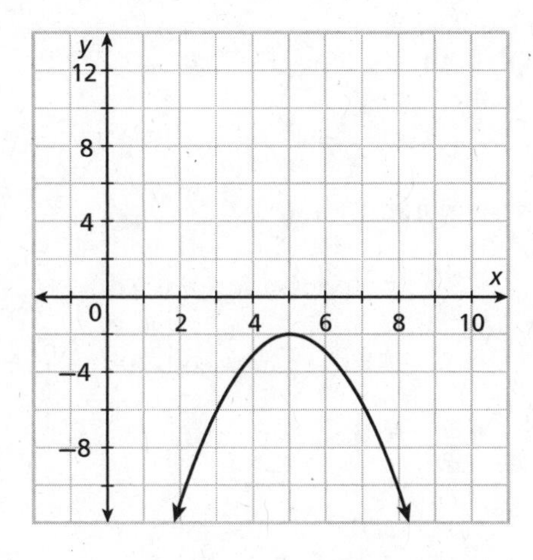

REFLECT

2a. At how many points do the parabola and Line 1 intersect? ___________

How many solutions are there for the system consisting of the quadratic function and the first linear function? ___________

2b. At how many points do the parabola and Line 2 intersect? ___________

How many solutions are there for the system consisting of the quadratic function and the second linear function? ___________

2c. A system of equations consisting of one quadratic equation and one linear equation can have ___________, ___________, or 2 real solutions.

2d. How many solutions does the following system of equations have? Explain your reasoning.

$$f(x) = -x^2 + 10x - 27$$
$$k(x) = -x + 1$$

____

____

2e. How many solutions does the following system of equations have? Explain your reasoning.

$$f(x) = -x^2 + 10x - 27$$
$$p(x) = -2$$

____

____

You can use the Intersect feature on a graphing calculator to solve systems of equations.

Solving Systems Using Technology

Use a graphing calculator to solve the system of equations.

$$f(x) = -4.9x^2 + 50x + 25$$
$$g(x) = 30x$$

A Enter the functions as Y_1 and Y_2 on a graphing calculator. Then graph both functions. Sketch the graphs on the coordinate plane at the right.

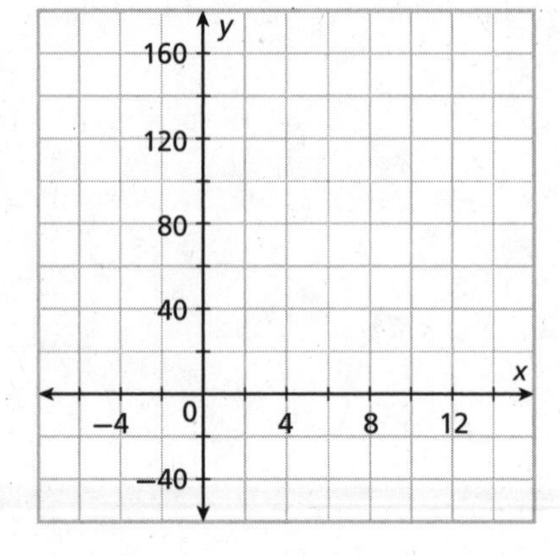

Estimate the solutions of the system from the graph.

____

B Solve the system directly by using the Intersect feature of the graphing calculator.

Press 2nd and CALC, then select Intersect. Press Enter for the first curve and again for the second curve. For Guess?, press the left or right arrows to move the cursor close to one of the intersections, then press Enter again. Repeat, moving the cursor close to the other intersection to find the second solution. Round your solutions to the nearest tenth.

____

REFLECT

3a. Are the solutions you get using the Intersect feature of a graphing calculator always exact? Explain.

____

3b. How can you check the accuracy of your estimated solutions?

____

3c. Use a graphing calculator to solve the system of equations $f(x)$ and $h(x)$ where $h(x) = 30x + 50$. What is the result? Explain.

____

____

PRACTICE

Solve the system of equations algebraically. Round to the nearest tenth, if necessary.

1. $f(x) = x^2 - 2$
$g(x) = -2$

____

2. $y = (x - 3)^2$
$y = x$

____

3. $y = -2x^2 - 4x + 1$
$y = -\frac{1}{2}x + 3$

____

4. $f(x) = x^2$
$g(x) = 1$

____

5. $y = x^2 + 4x - 5$
$y = 3x - 2$

____

6. $f(x) = -16x^2 + 15x + 10$
$g(x) = 14 - x$

____

The graph of a system of equations is shown. State how many solutions the system has. Then estimate the solution(s).

7. ______________________

____

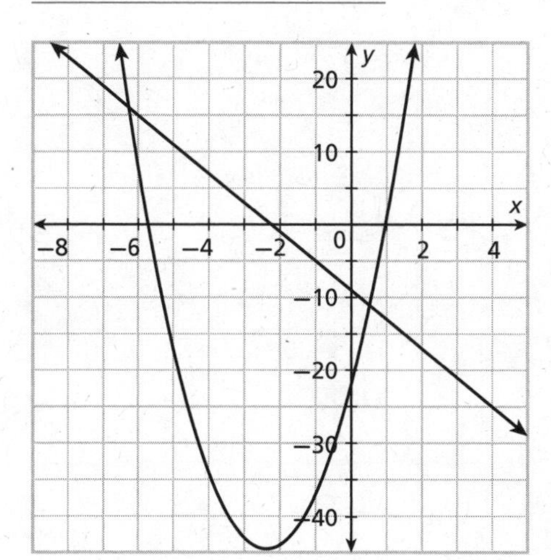

8. ______________________

____

Estimate the solutions to the system of equations graphically. Confirm the solutions by substituting the values into the equations.

9. $f(x) = x^2$

$g(x) = 1$

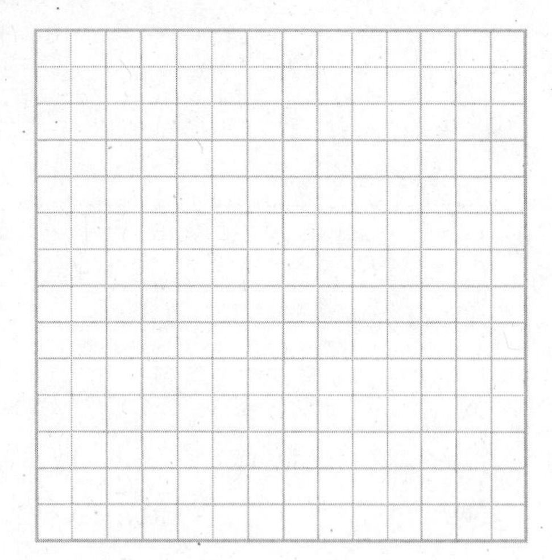

---

10. $y = x^2 - 1$

$y = 0.5x - 3$

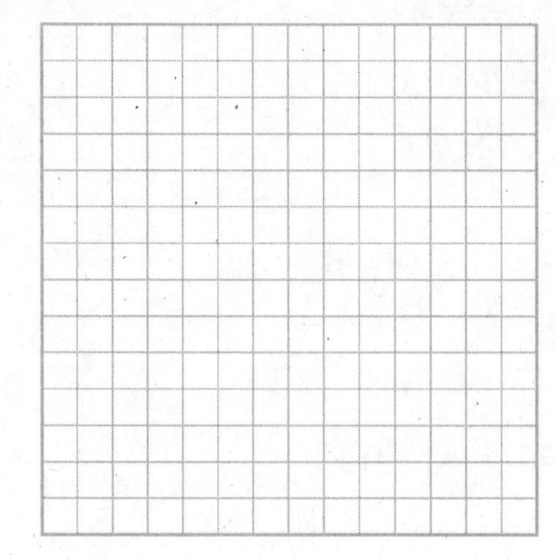

---

11. $f(x) = -16x^2 + 15x + 10$

$g(x) = 14 - x$

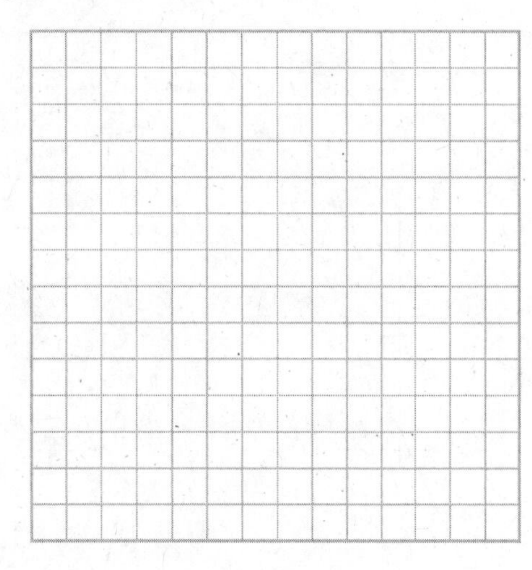

---

12. $f(x) = 3(x - 1)^2 + 4$

$g(x) = -4x + 9$

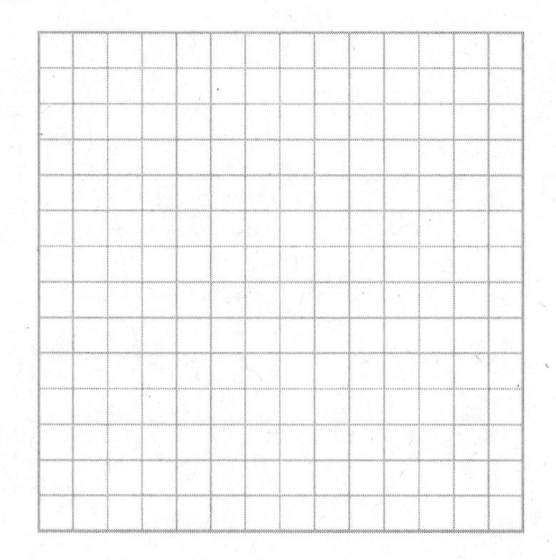

Solve the system of equations using the Intersect feature of a graphing calculator. Round your answers to the nearest tenth.

13. $y = -x^2 + 6x + 7$

$y = 2x + 6$

---

14. $f(x) = -x^2 + x - 2$

$g(x) = 2x - 3$

Name________________________ Class________________ Date____________ 4-4

Additional Practice

Solve each system by graphing. Check your answers.

1. $\begin{cases} y = x^2 - x - 2 \\ y = -x + 2 \end{cases}$

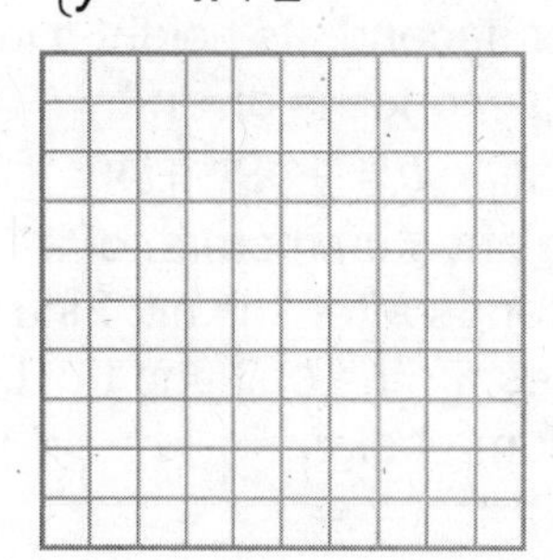

____

2. $\begin{cases} y = x^2 + x - 6 \\ y = -x - 3 \end{cases}$

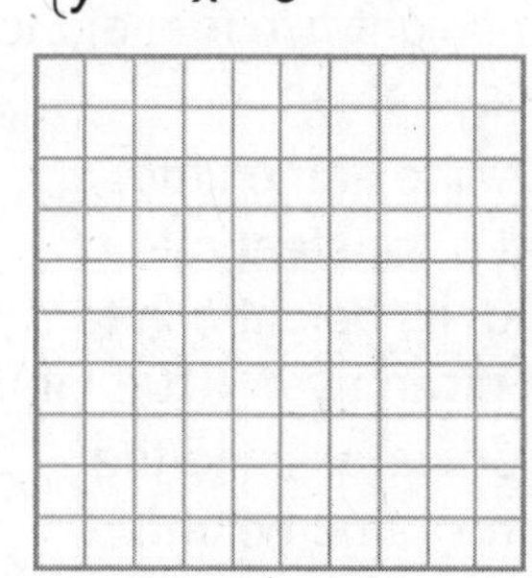

____

Solve each system by substitution. Check your answers.

3. $\begin{cases} y = -2x^2 + x + 4 \\ y = -5x + 8 \end{cases}$

____

4. $\begin{cases} y = -2x^2 - 3x + 2 \\ y = -x + 6 \end{cases}$

____

5. $\begin{cases} y = 3x^2 + 2x - 1 \\ x + y = 5 \end{cases}$

____

6. $\begin{cases} y = x^2 - 16 \\ y = x + 4 \end{cases}$

____

7. $\begin{cases} y = x^2 - 1 \\ x + 2y = 8 \end{cases}$

____

8. $\begin{cases} y = x^2 + 3x + 2 \\ 2x + y = -4 \end{cases}$

____

9. $\begin{cases} y = 2x^2 + 3x - 1 \\ 2x + y = -4 \end{cases}$

____

10. $\begin{cases} y = -x^2 + 2x - 4 \\ 3x + y = -4 \end{cases}$

____

Problem Solving

Write the correct answer.

1. A ball is thrown upward with an initial velocity of 40 feet per second from ground level. The height h in feet of the ball after t seconds is given by $h = -16t^2 + 40t$. At the same time, a balloon is rising at a constant rate of 10 feet per second. Its height h in feet after t seconds is given by $h = 10t$. Find the time it takes for the ball and the balloon to reach the same height.

 ____

2. A bird starts flying up from the grass in a park and climbs at a steady rate of 0.5 meters per second. Its height h in meters after t seconds is given by $h = 0.5t$. The equation $h = -4.9t^2 + 40t + 3$ models the height h, in meters, of a baseball t seconds after it is hit. Find the time it takes for the ball and the bird to reach the same height.

 ____

3. A skateboard company's monthly sales income can be modeled by the equation $C(s) = 0.5s^2 + 25s + 500$, where s represents the number of skateboards sold. The monthly cost of running the business is $C(s) = 25s + 812.5$. How many skateboards must the company sell in a month before the sales income equals or exceeds the cost of running the business?

 ____

4. The deer population in a park can be modeled by the equation $P(y) = 4y^2 - 10y + 60$, where y is the number of years after 2010. The deer population in another park can be modeled by $P(y) = 10y + 80$, where y is the number of years after 2010. In which year will the two parks have approximately the same number of deer?

 ____

Select the best answer.

5. A seagull is flying upwards such that its height h in feet above the sea after t seconds is given by $h = 3t$. At the same time, the height h in feet of a rock falling off a cliff above the sea after t seconds is given by $h = -16t^2 + 50$. Find the approximate time it takes for the rock and the bird to be at the same height.

 A 1.68 seconds C 3.36 seconds

 B 3.13 seconds D 16.67 seconds

6. A juggler at a fun park throws a ball upwards such that the ball's height h in feet above the ground after t seconds is given by $h = -16t^2 + 20t + 5$. At the same time, a scenic elevator begins climbing a tower at a constant rate of 20 feet per second. Its height h in feet after t seconds is given by $h = 20t$. Find the approximate time it takes for the ball and the elevator to reach the same height.

 F 0.56 seconds H 4 seconds

 G 1.12 seconds J 11.18 seconds

Name____________________ Class______________ Date__________

UNIT 2

Performance Tasks

GPS COMMON CORE

MCC9-12.A.SSE.1
MCC9-12.A.SSE.2
MCC9-12.A.SSE.3a
MCC9-12.A.CED.2
MCC9-12.A.REI.4

★ **1.** A football quarterback throws a long pass whose height h in meters can be modeled by $h = 15t - 4.9t^2 + 2$ where t is the time in seconds. A camera hangs from a wire 20 meters off the ground. Could the ball hit the camera? Explain your reasoning.

★ **2.** Baljit builds a square frame that is 1 inch wider than twice the width of a square frame from the store. He writes the area enclosed by his frame with the polynomial $4x^2 + 4x + 1$.

a. Factor the polynomial that Baljit wrote. Explain how the factorization yields an expression for the width of the frame Baljit builds.

b. What is a variable expression for the area enclosed by the frame from the store? Explain how you know.

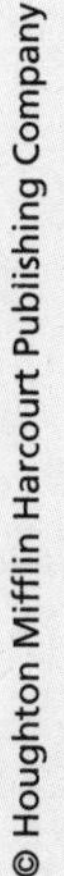

★★ **3.** Vehicle braking performance data uses 60 mph (or 28 m/s) to 0 mph. However, the published data is often unrealistic for the average driver and road conditions. To calculate how long it takes a vehicle to stop, assuming a constant deceleration, you can use the formula $d = \frac{1}{2}at^2$, where d is the distance traveled while stopping, a is the acceleration (deceleration), and t is the time. For a new hybrid car the published stopping distance is 75 meters and its constant deceleration is 6 m/s^2.

a. Substitute the given values into $d = \frac{1}{2}at^2$ and simplify the equation. Group all the terms on one side of the equation and use factoring to solve.

b. What do the solutions represent? Are all solutions meaningful? Explain.

continued

c. The stopping time provided does not include the driver recognition and reaction time, which can add about 2 seconds to the stopping time. Find the reaction distance by multiplying the speed (before stopping begins) times the reaction time. What is the total distance the vehicle travels, including the reaction distance? Convert this distance to feet using 1 m = 3.3 ft.

4. There are two square workout mats at a gym.

a. Let x represent the length of the larger mat, and let y represent the length of the smaller mat. Write a binomial that represents how much more area the larger mat has than the smaller mat.

b. Factor the binomial for the difference in the mat areas. Interpret what the factors could mean in this context.

c. One mat has 4 times the area of the other mat. Use this to rewrite the binomial from part **a** using only the variable y.

Name ______________________ Class ______________ Date ________

SELECTED RESPONSE

1. The graph of which function is a reflection and vertical stretch of the parent quadratic function?

   A. $f(x) = 3x^2$
   C. $f(x) = -3x^2$
   B. $f(x) = 0.3x^2$
   D. $f(x) = -0.3x^2$

2. Which of the following describes the graph of $f(x) = -2x^2$ as a transformation of the graph of the parent quadratic function?

   F. reflection across the x-axis and vertical stretch by a factor of 2
   G. reflection across the y-axis and vertical shrink by a factor of 2
   H. translation 2 units left
   J. translation 2 units down

3. What is the minimum value of $f(x) = 5x^2 + 10x + 10$?

   A. -5
   C. 1
   B. -1
   D. 5

4. Jon has rewritten the expression $15x^3 - 10x^2 + 27x - 18$ in order to factor it. Which is a reasonable next step for Jon to perform?

   F. Use the Commutative Property to rewrite the terms in a different order.
   G. Factor 2 from the second and fourth terms.
   H. Group the first two terms and factor out the greatest common factor, $5x^2$.
   J. Factor x from each of the four terms.

5. What is the factored form of $n^2-5n + 6$?

   A. $(n - 6)(n + 1)$
   B. $(n + 6)(n - 1)$
   C. $(n + 2)(n + 3)$
   D. $(n - 2)(n - 3)$

6. What is the factored form of $3c^2 + c - 4$?

   F. $(3c - 2)(c + 2)$
   G. $(3c + 2)(c + 2)$
   H. $(3c + 4)(c - 1)$
   J. $(3c - 1)(c + 4)$

7. Which of the following polynomials have a common binomial factor?

   A. $(x^2 + 4)$ and $(x^2 + 4x + 4)$
   B. $(x^2 + 4)$ and $(x^2 - 4x + 4)$
   C. $(x^2 - 4)$ and $(x^2 + 4x - 4)$
   D. $(x^2 - 4)$ and $(x^2 + 4x + 4)$

8. Which expression is not equivalent to the polynomial $6x^3 + 15x^2 - 9x$?

   F. $3(2x^3 + 5x^2 - 3x)$
   G. $3x(2x^2 + 5x - 3)$
   H. $3x(x + 3)(x - 1)$
   J. $3x(2x - 1)(x + 3)$

CONSTRUCTED RESPONSE

9. Amanda is adding a border to a rectangular quilt with a length of 4 feet and a width of 3 feet. The border has a width of x feet. Write a quadratic function $f(x)$ in standard form for the area of the border in square feet. What is $f(0.5)$ and what does it represent?

10. The function $f(x) = -16x^2 + 40x$ models the height in feet of a football x seconds after it is kicked from the ground.

a. Graph the function.

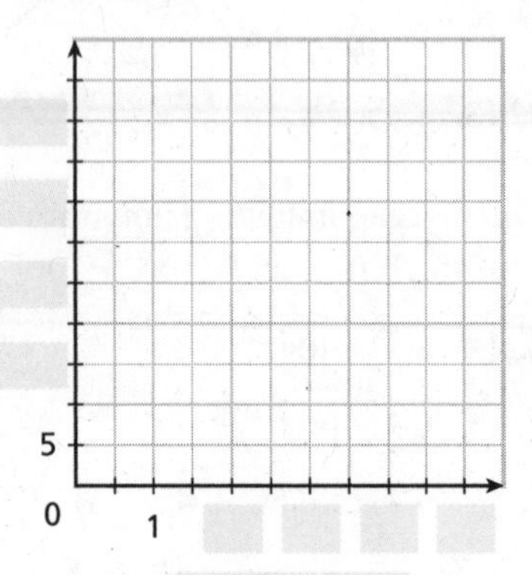

b. What does the origin of the graph represent?

c. What is a reasonable domain of the function? Explain.

d. What is the maximum of the function, and what does it represent in this situation?

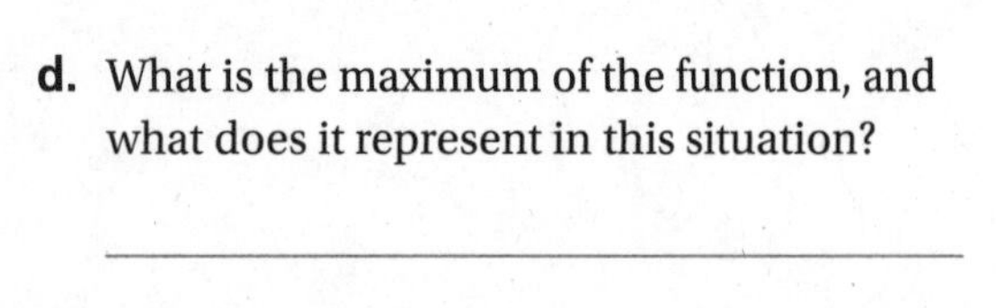

11. Complete the diagram and the equation that represent the binomial multiplication shown by the algebra tiles.

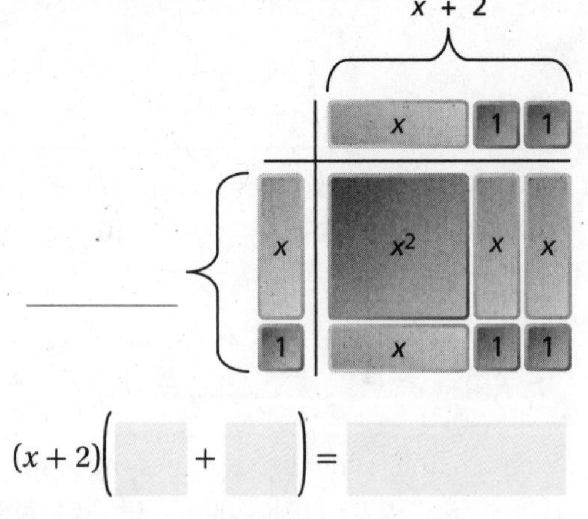

$(x + 2)(\quad + \quad) = \quad$

12. Show how to factor the polynomial $10a^2b - 20ab - 12b + 6ab$ completely.

13. The area of a square room (in square feet) is given by the polynomial $16x^2 + 40x + 25$. The length of each wall can be written in the form $cx + d$, where c and d are whole numbers.

a. Show how to write an expression in terms of x for the perimeter of the room.

b. Find the perimeter when $x = 2$ feet.

UNIT 3

Modeling Geometry

Module 5 Coordinate Geometry

UNIT 3

Unpacking the Standards

Understanding the standards and the vocabulary terms in the standards will help you know exactly what you are expected to learn in this unit.

GPS COMMON CORE **MCC9-12.G.GPE.1**

Derive the equation of a circle of given center and radius using the Pythagorean Theorem; ...

Key Vocabulary

circle *(círculo)* The set of points in a plane that are a fixed distance from a given point called the *center of the circle*.

radius of a circle *(radio de un círculo)* A segment whose endpoints are the center of a circle and a point on the circle; the distance from the center of a circle to any point on the circle.

Pythagorean Theorem *(Teorema de Pitágoras)* If a right triangle has legs of lengths a and b and a hypotenuse of length c, then $a^2 + b^2 = c^2$.

What It Means For You

You can use the Pythagorean Theorem to derive the Distance Formula. In turn, you can use the Distance Formula to derive the general form of the equation of a circle.

EXAMPLE

For the circle shown, the distance from the center (h, k) to any point (x, y) on the circle is the radius. The center is at $(-1, 2)$ and the radius is 3. Using the Distance Formula:

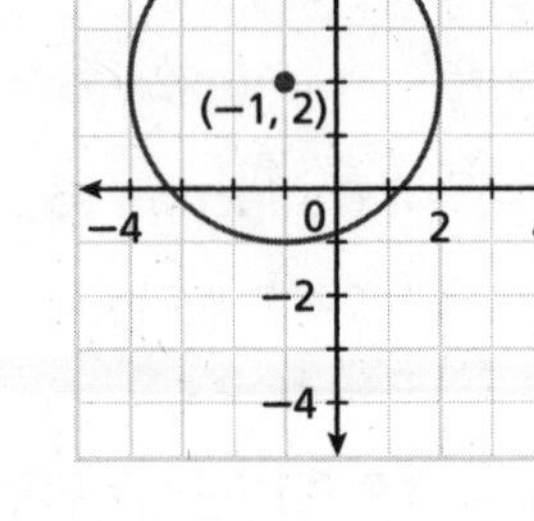

$$\sqrt{(x-h)^2 + (y-k)^2} = r$$

$$\sqrt{(x-(-1))^2 + (y-2)^2} = 3$$

$$\sqrt{(x+1)^2 + (y-2)^2} = 3$$

Squaring both sides of the equation gives the equation of the circle, $(x + 1)^2 + (y - 2)^2 = 9$.

UNIT 3

GPS COMMON CORE **MCC9-12.G.GPE.2**

Derive the equation of a parabola given a focus and directrix.

Key Vocabulary

directrix *(directriz)* A fixed line used to define a *parabola*. Every point on the parabola is equidistant from the directrix and a fixed point called the *focus*.

focus of a parabola *(foco de una parábola)* A fixed point F used with a directrix to define a parabola.

parabola *(parábola)* The shape of the graph of a quadratic function. Also, the set of points equidistant from a point F, called the *focus*, and a line d, called the directrix.

What It Means For You

You can use the Distance Formula to derive the general form of the equation of a parabola with focus $F(0, p)$ and directrix $y = p$.

EXAMPLE

y
F(0, p)
P(x, y)
A point: the *focus*
x
A line: the *directrix*
$y = -p$

The equation of a parabola with focus $F(0, p)$ and directrix $y = -p$ is $y = \frac{1}{4p}(x^2)$. It is sometimes written $x^2 = 4py$.

GPS COMMON CORE **MCC9-12.G.GPE.4**

Use coordinates to prove simple geometric theorems algebraically.

Key Vocabulary

coordinate *(coordenada)* A number used to identify the location of a point. On a number line, one coordinate is used. On a coordinate plane, two coordinates are used, called the *x*-coordinate and the *y*-coordinate. In space, three coordinates are used, called the *x*-coordinate, the *y*-coordinate, and the *z*-coordinate.

What It Means For You

Positioning geometric diagrams on a coordinate grid makes algebraic tools such as the Midpoint and Distance Formulas available to you to prove geometric relationships.

EXAMPLE

You can use coordinates and the Distance Formula to prove that $\overline{AB}$, which joins the midpoints of $\overline{PR}$ and $\overline{QR}$, is half as long as $\overline{PQ}$.

$$AB = \sqrt{(4-0)^2 + (0-3)^2}$$
$$= \sqrt{16+9}$$
$$= 5$$
$$PQ = \sqrt{(8-0)^2 + (0-6)^2}$$
$$= \sqrt{64+36}$$
$$= 10$$

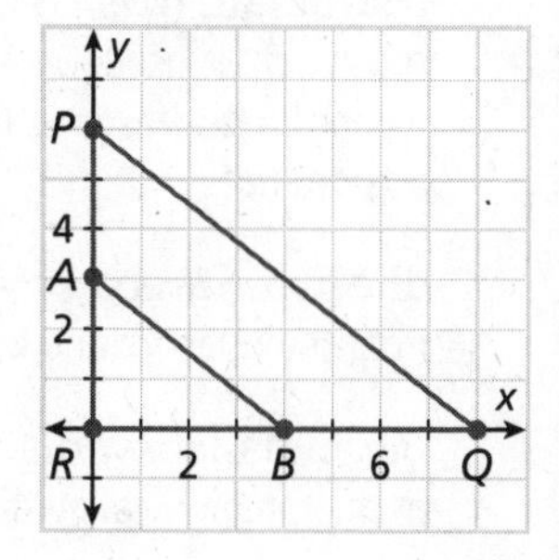

UNIT 3

Key Vocabulary

axis of symmetry *(eje de simetría)* A line that divides a plane figure or a graph into two congruent reflected halves.

circle *(círculo)* The set of points in a plane that are a fixed distance from a given point called the center of the circle.

coordinate *(coordenada)* A number used to identify the location of a point. On a number line, one coordinate is used. On a coordinate plane, two coordinates are used, called the x-coordinate and the y-coordinate. In space, three coordinates are used, called the x-coordinate, the y-coordinate, and the z-coordinate.

directrix *(directriz)* A fixed line used to define a *parabola*. Every point on the parabola is equidistant from the directrix and a fixed point called the *focus*.

parabola *(parábola)* The shape of the graph of a quadratic function. Also, the set of points equidistant from a point F, called the *focus*, and a line d, called the directrix.

radius of a circle *(radio de un círculo)* A segment whose endpoints are the center of a circle and a point on the circle; the distance from the center of a circle to any point on the circle.

vertex of a parabola *(vértice de una parábola)* The highest or lowest point on the parabola.

UNIT 3

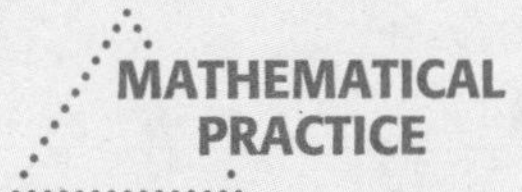

The Common Core Standards for Mathematical Practice describe varieties of expertise that mathematics educators at all levels should seek to develop in their students. Opportunities to develop these practices are integrated throughout this program.

1. **Make sense of problems and persevere in solving them.**
2. **Reason abstractly and quantitatively.**
3. **Construct viable arguments and critique the reasoning of others.**
4. **Model with mathematics.**
5. **Use appropriate tools strategically.**
6. **Attend to precision.**
7. **Look for and make use of structure.**
8. **Look for and express regularity in repeated reasoning**

Name________________________ Class______________ Date__________

5-1

Introduction to Coordinate Proof

Going Deeper

Video Tutor

Essential question: *How do you write a coordinate proof?*

You have already seen a wide range of purely geometric proofs. These proofs used postulates and theorems to build logical arguments. Now you will learn how to write coordinate proofs. These proofs also use logic, but they apply ideas from algebra to help demonstrate geometric relationships.

MCC9–12.G.GPE.4

1 EXAMPLE Proving or Disproving a Statement

Prove or disprove that the triangle with vertices $A(4, 2)$, $B(-1, 4)$, and $C(2, -3)$ is an isosceles triangle.

A Plot the vertices and draw the triangle.

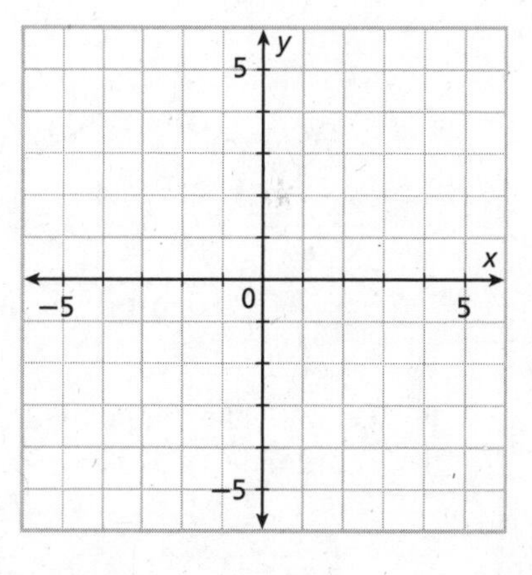

B Use the distance formula to find the length of each side of $\triangle ABC$.

$AB = \sqrt{(-1-4)^2 + (4-2)^2} = \sqrt{(-5)^2 + 2^2} = \sqrt{29}$

$BC =$ ______________________________

$AC =$ ______________________________

C Draw a conclusion based on your results. State whether or not the triangle is isosceles and why.

____

REFLECT

1a. What other conclusion(s) can you make about the sides or angles of $\triangle ABC$? Explain.

____

____

1b. Suppose you map $\triangle ABC$ to $\triangle A'B'C'$ by the translation $(x, y) \rightarrow (x - 3, y - 2)$. Is $\triangle A'B'C'$ an isosceles triangle? Why or why not?

____

____

You can write a coordinate proof to prove general facts about geometric figures. The first step in such a proof is using variables to assign general coordinates to a figure using only what is known about the figure.

MCC9–12.G.GPE.4

2 EXAMPLE Writing a Coordinate Proof

Prove that in a right triangle, the midpoint of the hypotenuse is equidistant from all three vertices.

A Assign coordinates to the figure.

Let the triangle be $\triangle ABC$. Since the triangle is a right triangle, assume $\angle B$ is a right angle. Place $\angle B$ at the origin and place the legs along the positive x- and y-axes.

Since the proof involves a midpoint, use multiples of 2 in assigning coordinates to A and C, as shown.

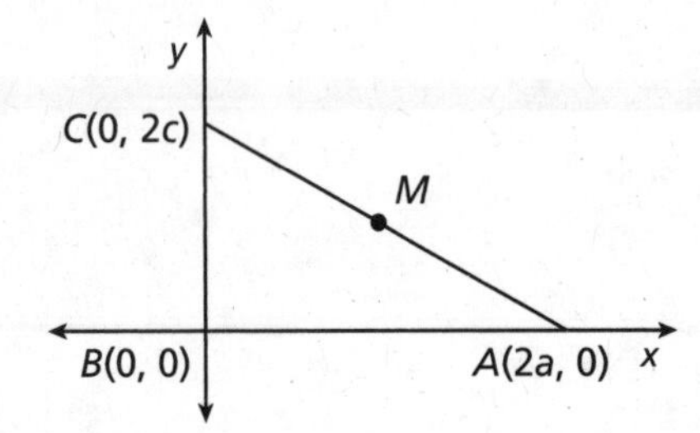

B Let M be the midpoint of the hypotenuse, $\overline{AC}$. Use the midpoint formula to find the coordinates of M.

$$M\left(\frac{\square + \square}{2}, \frac{\square + \square}{2}\right) = M\left(\square, \square\right)$$

C Use the distance formula to find MA, MB, and MC.

$$MA = \sqrt{\left(\square - \square\right)^2 + \left(\square - \square\right)^2} = \sqrt{\square^2 + \square^2}$$

$$MB = \sqrt{\left(\square - \square\right)^2 + \left(\square - \square\right)^2} = \sqrt{\square^2 + \square^2}$$

$$MB = \sqrt{\left(\square - \square\right)^2 + \left(\square - \square\right)^2} = \sqrt{\square^2 + \square^2}$$

So, the midpoint of the hypotenuse is equidistant from all three vertices because

____

____

REFLECT

2a. Explain why it is more convenient to assign the coordinates as $A(2a, 0)$ and $C(0, 2c)$ rather than $A(a, 0)$ and $C(0, c)$.

2b. Can you write the proof by assigning the coordinates as $A(2n, 0)$ and $C(0, 2n)$?

PRACTICE

1. Prove or disprove that the triangle with vertices $R(-2, -2)$, $S(1, 4)$, and $T(4, -5)$ is an equilateral triangle.

2. Refer to the triangle you drew in Exercise 1 to prove or disprove that the triangle with vertices $R(-2, -2)$, $S(1, 4)$, and $T(4, -5)$ is a right triangle.

3. $\triangle ABC$ has vertices $A(-4, 1)$, $B(-3, 4)$, and $C(-1, 1)$. $\triangle DEF$ has vertices $D(2, -3)$, $E(5, -2)$, and $F(2, 0)$. Prove or disprove that the triangles are congruent.

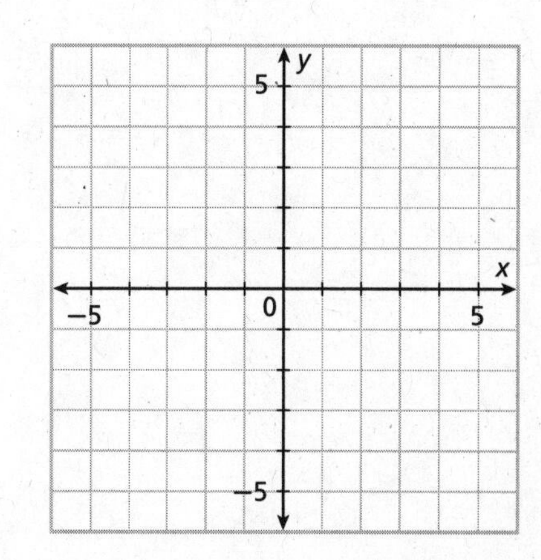

4. Write a coordinate proof to prove that the diagonals of a rectangle are congruent. Use the space at right to show how to assign coordinates. Then write the proof below.

5. **Error Analysis** A student proves that every right triangle is isosceles by assigning coordinates as shown at right and by using the distance formula to show that $PQ = a$ and $RQ = a$. Explain the error in the student's proof.

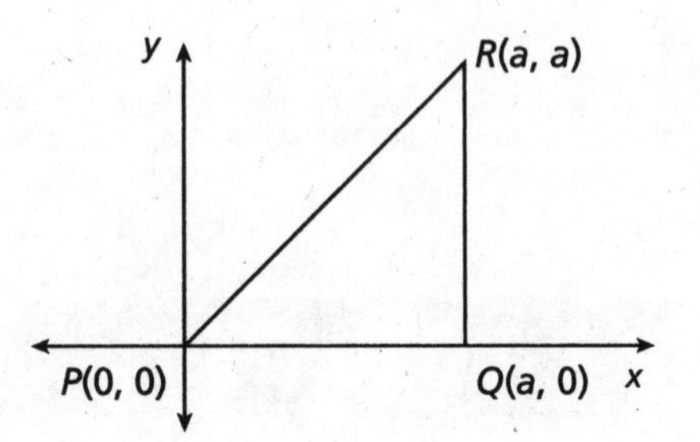

Name______________________________ Class________________ Date____________

Additional Practice

Position an isosceles triangle with sides of 8 units, 5 units, and 5 units in the coordinate plane. Label the coordinates of each vertex. (*Hint:* Use the Pythagorean Theorem.)

1. Center the long side on the *x*-axis at the origin.

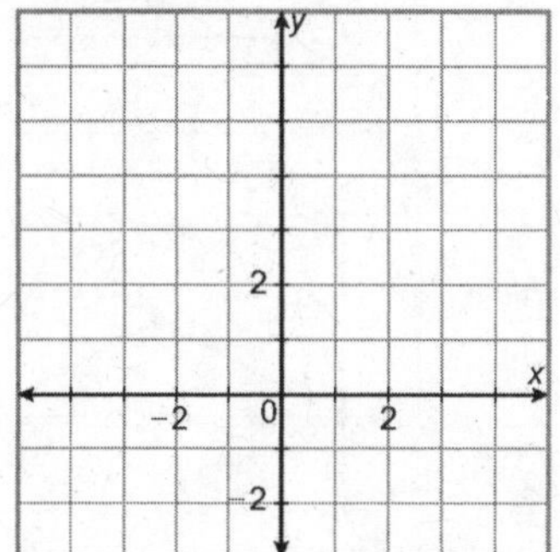

2. Place the long side on the *y*-axis centered at the origin.

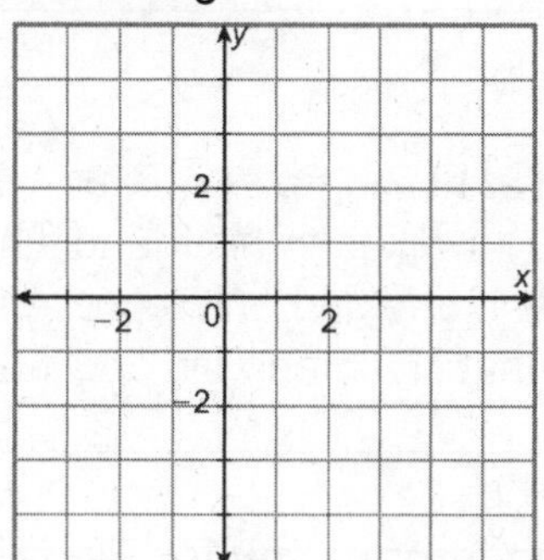

Write a coordinate proof.

3. **Given:** Rectangle *ABCD* has vertices *A*(0, 4), *B*(6, 4), *C*(6, 0), and *D*(0, 0). *E* is the midpoint of $\overline{DC}$. *F* is the midpoint of $\overline{DA}$.

   Prove: The area of rectangle *DEGF* is one-fourth the area of rectangle *ABCD*.

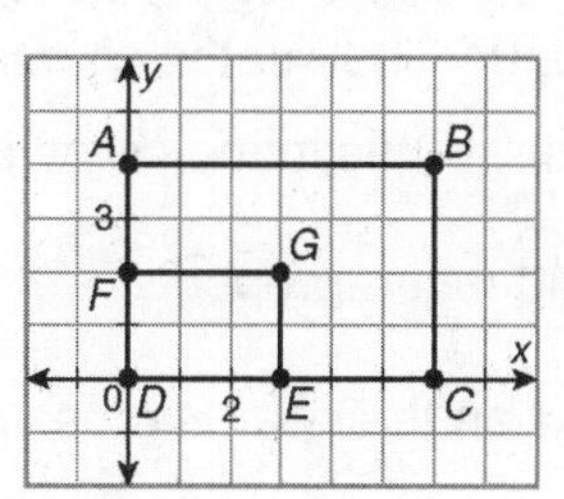

Problem Solving

Round to the nearest tenth for Exercises 1 and 2.

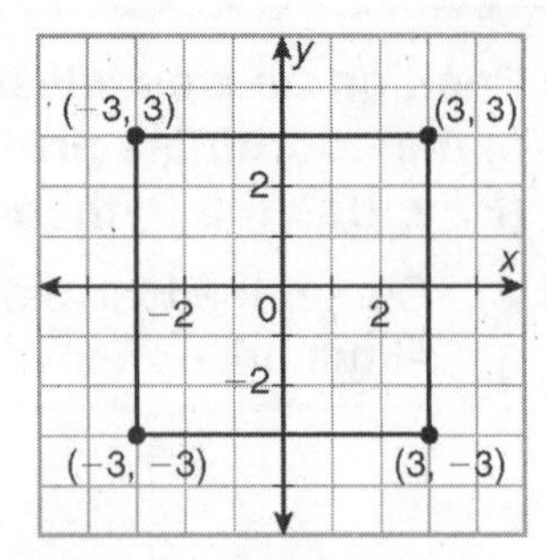

1. A fountain is at the center of a square courtyard. If one grid unit represents one yard, what is the distance from the fountain at (0, 0) to each corner of the courtyard?

____

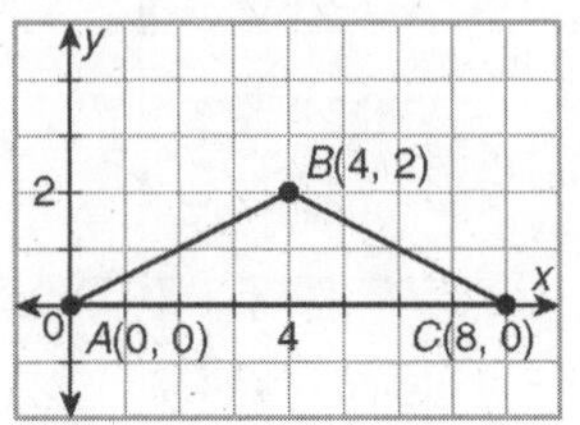

2. Noah started at his home at $A(0, 0)$, walked with his dog to the park at $B(4, 2)$, walked to his friend's house at $C(8, 0)$, then walked home. If one grid unit represents 20 meters, what is the distance that Noah and his dog walked?

____

Use the following information for Exercises 3 and 4.

Rachel started her cycling trip at $G(0, 7)$. Malik started his trip at $J(0, 0)$. Their paths crossed at $H(4, 2)$.

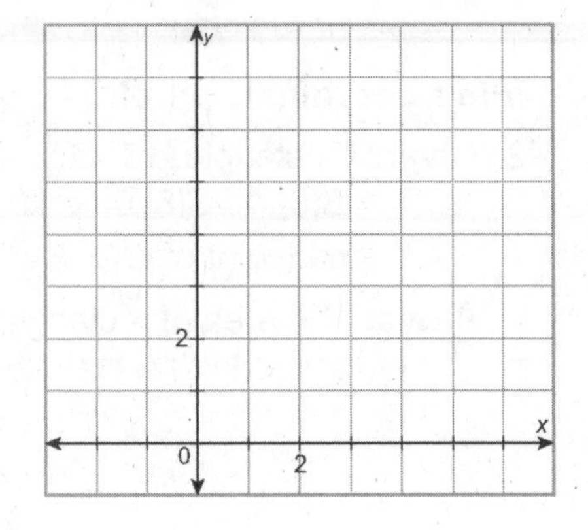

3. Draw their routes in the coordinate plane.

4. If one grid unit represents $\frac{1}{2}$ mile, who had ridden farther when their paths crossed? Explain.

____

____

Choose the best answer.

5. Two airplanes depart from an airport at $A(9, 11)$. The first airplane travels to a location at $N(-250, 80)$, and the second airplane travels to a location at $P(105, -400)$. Each unit represents 1 mile. What is the distance, to the nearest mile, between the two airplanes?

   A 335.3 mi　　　C 490.3 mi

   B 477.9 mi　　　D 597.0 mi

6. A corner garden has vertices at $Q(0, 0)$, $R(0, 2d)$, and $S(2c, 0)$. A brick walkway runs from point Q to the midpoint M of $\overline{RS}$. What is QM?

   F (c, d)　　　H $\sqrt{c+d}$

   G $c^2 + d^2$　　　J $\sqrt{c^2 + d^2}$

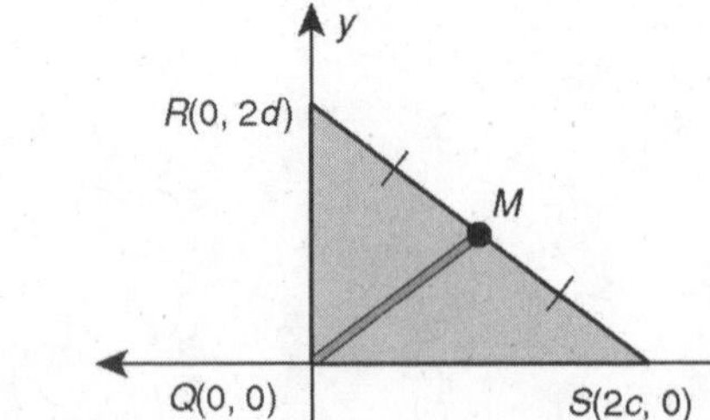

Name ________________ Class ________ Date ________

5-2

Circles in the Coordinate Plane

Connection: Completing the Square

Essential question: *How can you write and use equations of circles in the coordinate plane?*

Video Tutor

Recall that a circle is the set of all points in a plane that are a fixed distance from a given point. Now you will investigate circles in a coordinate plane.

MCC9–12.G.GPE.1

1 EXPLORE Deriving the Equation of a Circle

Consider the circle in a coordinate plane that has its center at $C(h, k)$ and that has radius r.

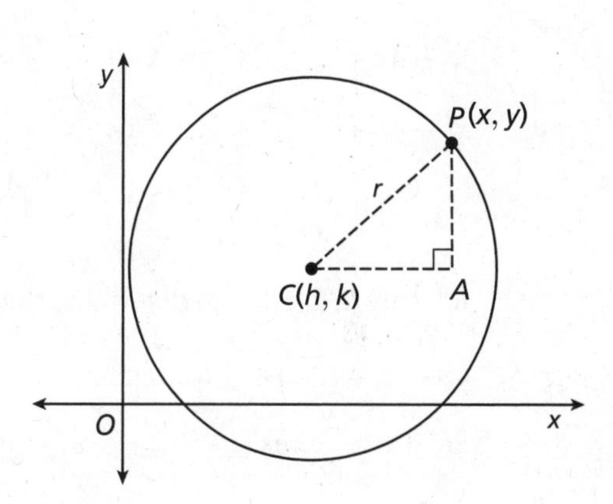

A Let P be any point on the circle and let the coordinates of P be (x, y).

Create a right triangle by drawing a horizontal line through C and a vertical line through P, as shown.

What are the coordinates of point A? ____________

Write expressions for the lengths of the legs of $\triangle CAP$.

$CA =$ ____________; $PA =$ ____________

B Use the Pythagorean Theorem to write a relationship among the side lengths of $\triangle CAP$.

____________ + ____________ = ____________

REFLECT

1a. Compare your work with that of other students. Then write the equation of a circle with center (h, k) and radius r.

____

1b. Why do you need absolute values when you write expressions for the lengths of the legs in Step A, but not when you write the relationship among the side lengths in Step B?

____

____

1c. Suppose a circle has its center at the origin. What is the equation of the circle in this case?

____

Equation of a Circle

The equation of a circle with center (h, k) and radius r is $(x - h)^2 + (y - k)^2 = r^2$.

MCC9–12.G.GPE.1

2 EXAMPLE Finding the Center and Radius of a Circle

Find the center and radius of the circle whose equation is $x^2 - 4x + y^2 + 2y = 4$. Then graph the circle.

A Complete the square to write the equation in the form $(x - h)^2 + (y - k)^2 = r^2$.

$x^2 - 4x + \square + y^2 + 2y + \square = 4 + \square$ Set up to complete the square.

$x^2 - 4x + \_\_\_\_ + y^2 + 2y + \_\_\_\_ = 4 + \_\_\_\_\_\_$ Add $\left(\frac{-4}{2}\right)^2$ and $\left(\frac{2}{2}\right)^2$ to both sides.

$x^2 - 4x + \_\_\_\_ + y^2 + 2y + \_\_\_\_ = 4 + \_\_\_\_$ Simplify.

$(x - \_\_\_\_)^2 + (y + \_\_\_\_)^2 = \_\_\_\_\_\_$ Factor.

B Identify h, k, and r to determine the center and radius.

$h =$ ______ $k =$ ______ $r =$ ______

So, the center is (______, ______) and the radius is ______.

C Graph the circle.

- Locate the center of the circle.
- Place the point of your compass at the center.
- Open the compass to the radius.
- Use the compass to draw the circle.

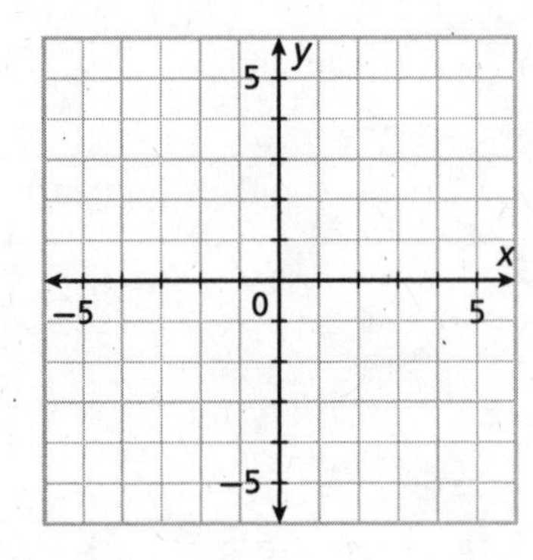

REFLECT

2a. How can you check your graph by testing specific points from the graph in the original equation? Give an example.

____

____

2b. Suppose you translate the circle by the translation $(x, y) \rightarrow (x + 4, y - 1)$. What is the equation of the image of the circle? Explain.

____

____

MCC9–12.G.GPE.4

3 EXAMPLE Writing a Coordinate Proof

Prove or disprove that the point $(1, \sqrt{15})$ lies on the circle that is centered at the origin and contains the point $(0, 4)$.

A Plot a point at the origin and at $(0, 4)$. Use these to help you draw the circle centered at the origin that contains $(0, 4)$.

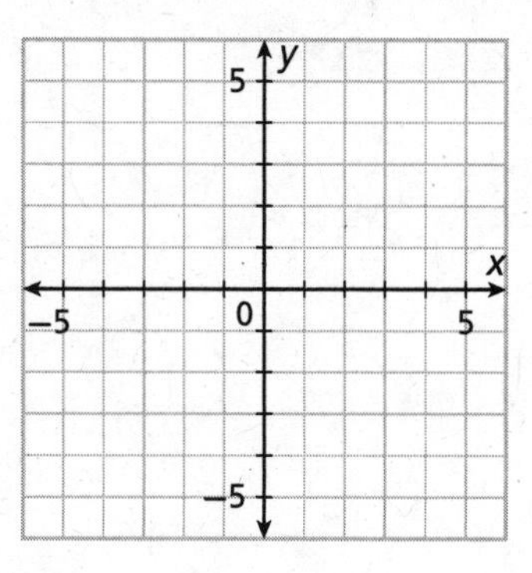

B Determine the radius: $r =$ ____________

C Use the radius and the coordinates of the center to write the equation of the circle.

____

D Substitute the x- and y-coordinates of the point $(1, \sqrt{15})$ in the equation of the circle to check whether they satisfy the equation.

$\_\_\_\_\_\_^2 + \_\_\_\_\_\_^2 \stackrel{?}{=} 16$ Substitute.

$\_\_\_\_\_\_ + \_\_\_\_\_\_ = 16$ Simplify.

E So, the point $(1, \sqrt{15})$ lies on the circle because

____

REFLECT

3a. Explain how to determine the radius of the circle.

____

____

3b. Name another point with noninteger coordinates that lies on the circle. Explain.

____

3c. Explain how you can prove that the point $(2, \sqrt{5})$ does *not* lie on the circle.

____

____

Recall that you can solve a system of two equations in two unknowns by graphing both equations and finding the point(s) of intersection of the graphs. You can also solve a system using the algebraic methods of substitution or elimination. In the next Examples, you will see how these techniques may be used with systems that include a quadratic equation.

MCC9–12.A.REI.7

4 EXAMPLE Solving a System by Graphing

Solve the system of equations. $\begin{cases} (x-1)^2 + (y-1)^2 = 16 \\ y = x + 4 \end{cases}$

A The equation $(x-1)^2 + (y-1)^2 = 16$ represents a circle with center ________ and radius ________.

The equation $y = x + 4$ represents a line with slope ________ and y-intercept ________.

B Graph the equations on the coordinate plane below.

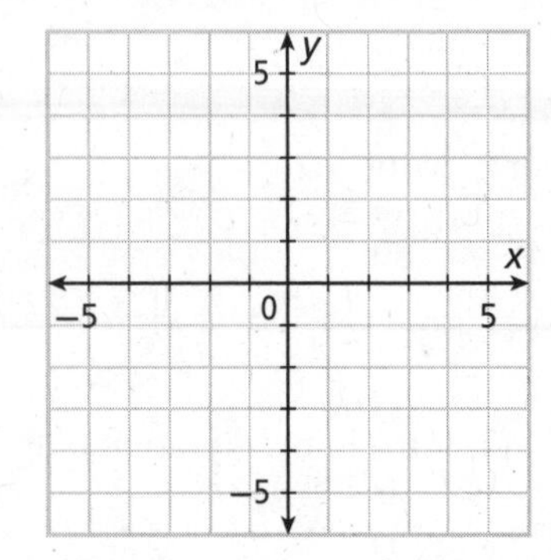

C The solutions of $(x-1)^2 + (y-1)^2 = 16$ are exactly the points on the circle. The solutions of $y = x + 4$ are exactly the points on the line. The solutions of the system are points that lie on both the circle and the line. These are the points of intersection of the circle and the line.

So, the solutions of the system are ________________________.

REFLECT

4a. How can you check your solutions? Check them.

____

____

____

4b. How many solutions are possible when a system of equations involves a circle and a line? Explain.

____

____

MCC9–12.A.REI.7

5 EXAMPLE Solving a System Algebraically

Solve the system of equations. $\begin{cases} x^2 + y^2 = 13 \\ y = -5x \end{cases}$

A Use substitution to write an equation in one variable. The second equation is already solved for y, so substitute this expression for y into the first equation.

$x^2 + y^2 = 13$ Write the first equation.

$x^2 + (\_\_\_\_\_\_)^2 = 13$ Substitute $-5x$ for y in the equation.

$x^2 + \_\_\_\_\_\_ = 13$ Square the expression in parentheses.

$\_\_\_\_\_\_ = 13$ Combine like terms.

$x^2 = \_\_\_\_\_\_$ Use the Division Property of Equality.

$x = \_\_\_\_\_\_$ Take the square root of both sides.

$x = \_\_\_\_\_\_$ Rationalize the denominator.

B Substitute each x-value into one of the original equations to find the corresponding y-values.

Substitute into the simpler equation, $y = -5x$.

When $x = \_\_\_\_\_\_$, $y = \_\_\_\_\_\_$.

When $x = \_\_\_\_\_\_$, $y = \_\_\_\_\_\_$.

So, the solutions of the system are ____________________.

REFLECT

5a. Is it possible to solve this system of equations by graphing? Explain.

____

____

5b. Based on what you know about the graphs of the equations in this system, why does it make sense that there are two solutions?

____

____

MCC9–12.A.REI.7

6 EXAMPLE Solving a System Involving a Parabola

Solve the system of equations. $\begin{cases} y = x^2 - 3 \\ y = 8x - 19 \end{cases}$

A Use substitution to write an equation in one variable. Substitute the expression for y from the second equation into the first equation.

$y = x^2 - 3$	Write the first equation.
________ $= x^2 - 3$	Substitute $8x - 19$ for y in the equation.
$0 =$ ________	Get 0 on one side of the equation.
$0 =$ ________	Combine like terms.
$0 =$ ________	Factor.
$0 =$ ________	Take the square root of both sides.
$x =$ ________	Solve for x.

B Substitute the x-value into one of the original equations to find the corresponding y-value.

Substitute into the equation $y = x^2 - 3$.

When $x =$ ______, $y =$ ______.

So, the solution of the system is ____________.

REFLECT

6a. In Step B, what would happen if you substituted the value of x in the other equation?

____

6b. Verify that the slope of the line that contains $(0, -19)$ and $(4, 13)$ is 8.

____

6c. Since there is only one solution of the system, what does this tell you about the line and the parabola that are represented by the equations?

____

6d. How many solutions are possible when a system of equations involves a parabola and a line? Explain.

____

____

PRACTICE

Write the equation of the circle with the given center and radius.

1. center: (0, 2); radius: 5

2. center: (−1, 3); radius 8

3. center: (−4, −5); radius: $\sqrt{2}$

4. center: (9, 0); radius $\sqrt{3}$

Find the center and radius of the circle with the given equation. Then graph the circle.

5. $x^2 - 2x + y^2 = 15$

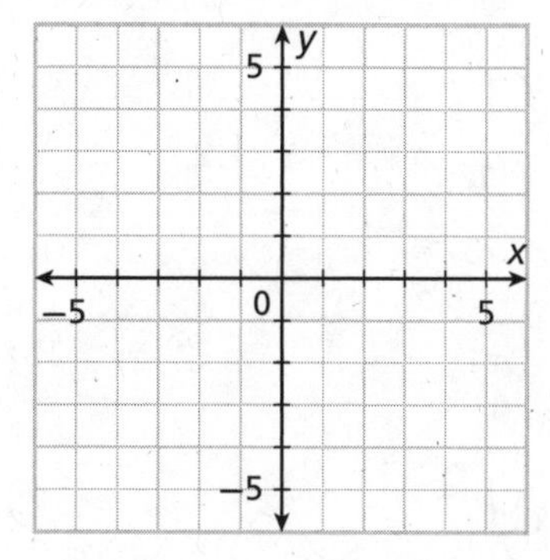

6. $x^2 + 4x + y^2 - 6y = -9$

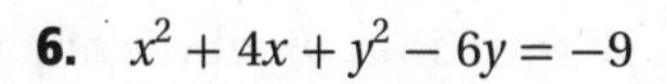

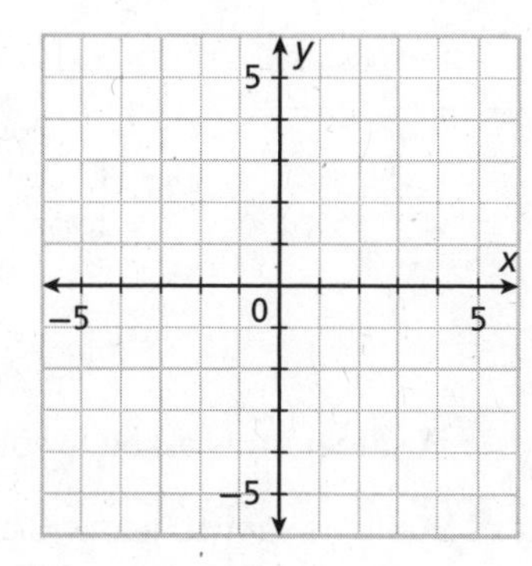

7. Prove or disprove that the point $(1, \sqrt{3})$ lies on the circle that is centered at the origin and contains the point (0, 2).

8. Prove or disprove that the point $(2, \sqrt{3})$ lies on the circle that is centered at the origin and contains the point (−3, 0).

9. Prove or disprove that the circle with equation $x^2 - 4x + y^2 = -3$ intersects the y-axis.

Solve each system of equations by graphing.

10. $\begin{cases} (x-2)^2 + y\text{^}2 = 4 \\ y = -x \end{cases}$

11. $\begin{cases} (x+1)^2 + (y-1)^2 = 9 \\ y = x - 1 \end{cases}$

12. $\begin{cases} y = x^2 - 1 \\ y = -x + 1 \end{cases}$

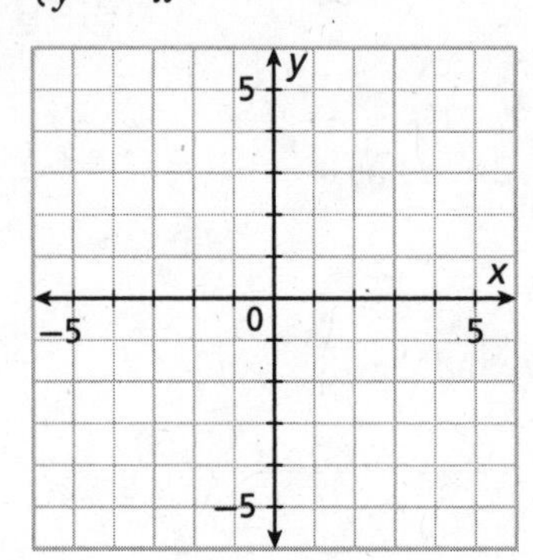

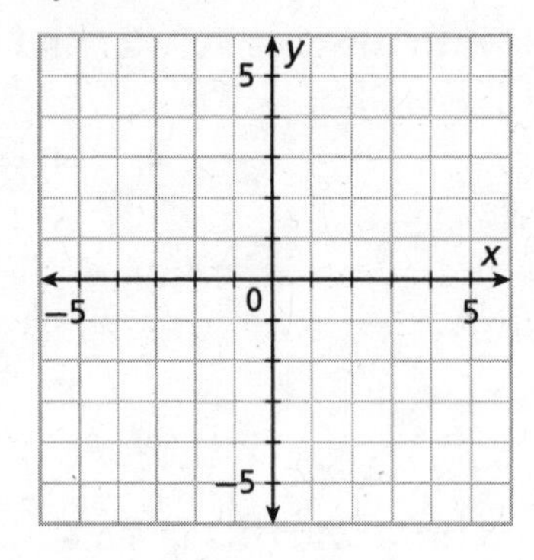

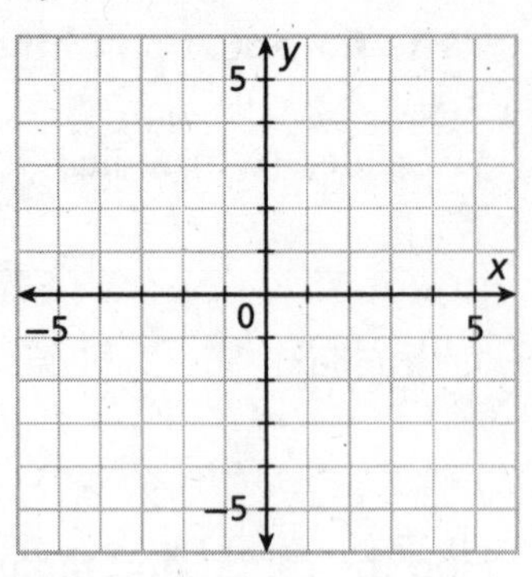

Solve each system of equations algebraically.

13. $\begin{cases} x^2 + y^2 = 10 \\ y = -3x \end{cases}$

14. $\begin{cases} x^2 + y^2 = 25 \\ y = 7x \end{cases}$

15. $\begin{cases} x^2 + y^2 = 13 \\ y = -8x \end{cases}$

16. $\begin{cases} y = x^2 \\ y = -x + 2 \end{cases}$

17. $\begin{cases} y = x^2 + 2 \\ y = 4 \end{cases}$

18. $\begin{cases} y = -x^2 + 2 \\ y = x - 4 \end{cases}$

19. **Error Analysis** A student was asked to solve the system $\begin{cases} x^2 + y^2 = 9 \\ y = x \end{cases}$.
The student's solution is shown below. Critique the student's work. If there is an error, give the correct solution.

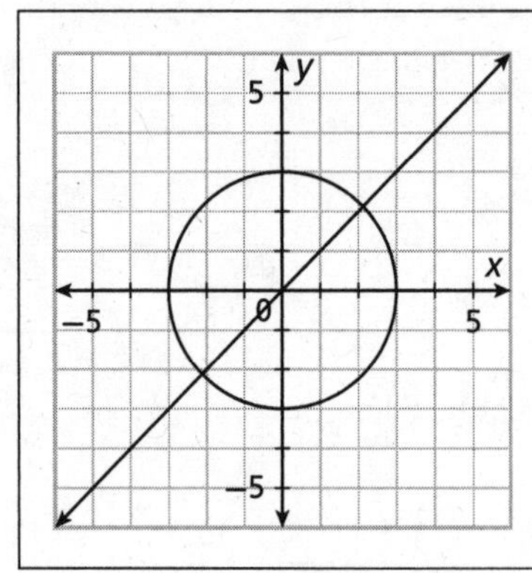

The graph of $x^2 + y^2 = 9$ is a circle centered at the origin with radius 3. The graph of $y = x$ is a straight line through the origin. The graphs intersect at (2, 2) and (−2, −2), so these are the solutions.

Name ______ Class ______ Date ______

5-2

Additional Practice

1. Write an equation of a circle with center $B(0, -2)$ that passes through $(-6, 0)$. ______

Complete the square to rewrite the given equation in the form $(x - h)^2 + (y - k)^2 = r^2$. Identify the center and radius of the circle. Then graph the circle.

2. $x^2 + 2x + y^2 - 6y = -6$

______

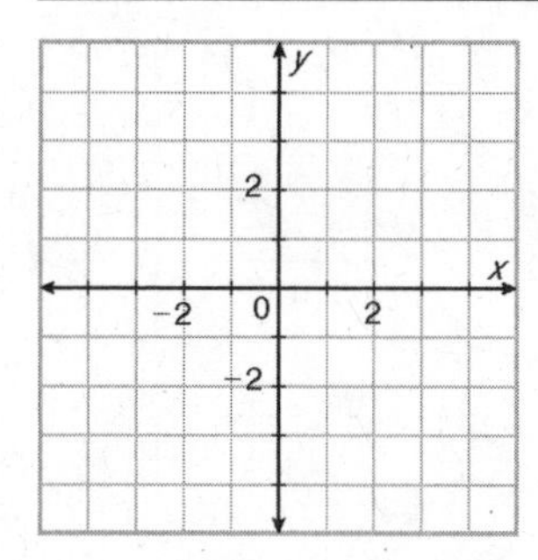

3. $x^2 + 4x + y^2 + 6y = -9$

______

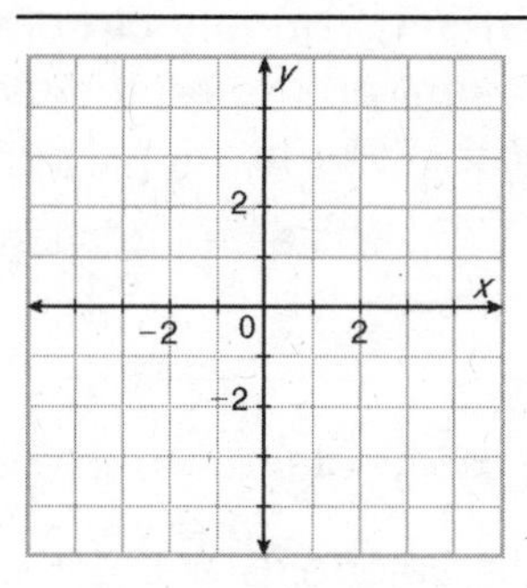

4. $x^2 - 2x + y^2 - 2y = 14$

______

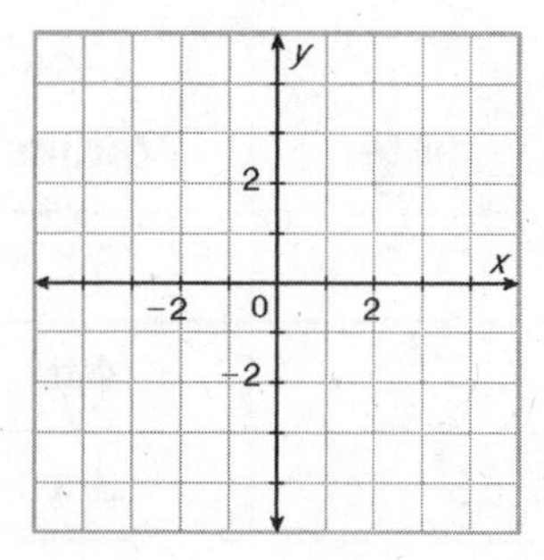

5. $x^2 + y^2 + 6y = -8$

______

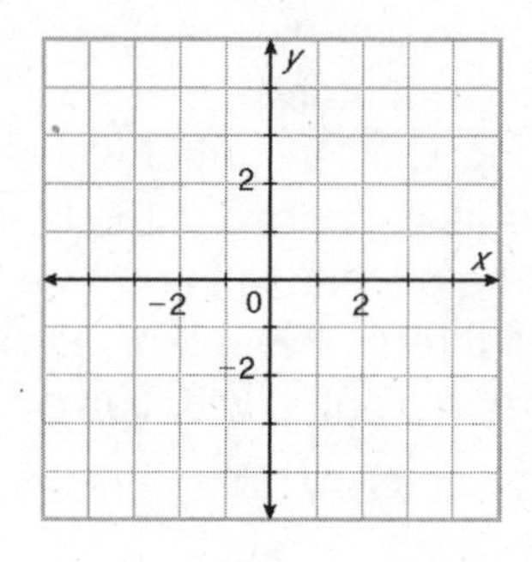

6. Solve the system of equations by graphing.

$$\begin{cases} x^2 + (y-2)^2 = 9 \\ y = x - 1 \end{cases}$$

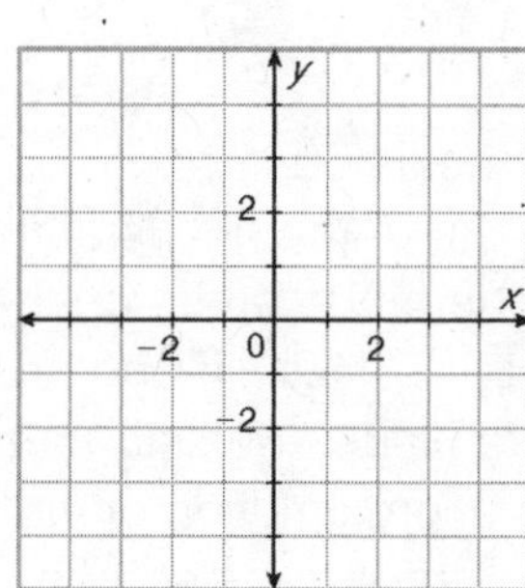

______

Solve each system of equations algebraically.

7. $\begin{cases} x^2 + y^2 = 25 \\ x - y = 5 \end{cases}$ ______

8. $\begin{cases} y = -x^2 \\ y = -x - 2 \end{cases}$ ______

9. $\begin{cases} (x-2)^2 + y^2 = 100 \\ y = -10 \end{cases}$ ______

Problem Solving

1. Prove or disprove that the circle that is centered at the origin and contains the point (–4, –3) intersects the line $x = 6$.

____

____

____

Crater Lake in Oregon is roughly circular. Suppose that *A*(–4, 1) and *B*(–2, –3) represent points on the circular shoreline of the lake. The center of the lake is at (1, 1).

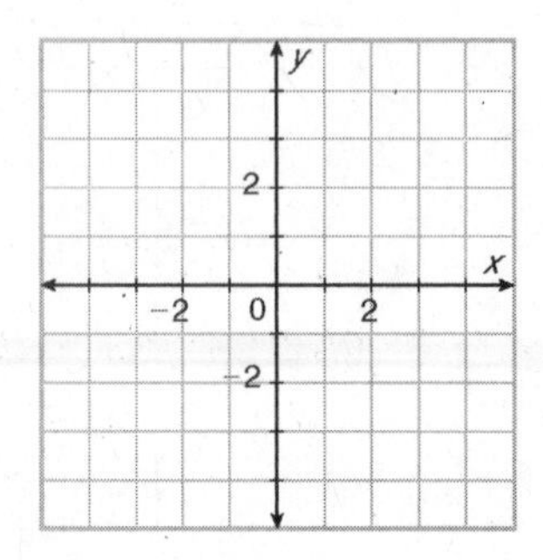

2. Does the point *C*(5, –2) lie on the shoreline of the lake?

____

3. Each unit of the coordinate plane represents $\frac{3}{5}$ mile. Find the diameter of Crater Lake.

____

Choose the best answer.

4. An English knot garden has hedges planted to form geometric shapes. A blueprint of a knot garden contains three circular hedges as described in the table. Flowers are to be planted in the space that is within all three circles. Which is a point that could be planted with flowers?

Circular Hedge	Center	Radius
A	(3, 2)	3 ft
B	(7, 2)	4 ft
C	(5, –1)	3 ft

A (7, 1) C (0, 5)
B (5, 1) D (0, 0)

5. An amusement park ride consists of a circular ring that holds 50 riders. Suppose the center of the ride is at the origin and that one of the riders on the circular ring is at (16, 15.1). If one unit on the coordinate plane equals 1 foot, which is a close approximation of the distance the rider travels during one complete revolution of the circle?

F 22 ft H 138 ft
G 44 ft J 1521 ft

6. Which of these circles intersects the circle that has center (0, 6) and radius 1?

A $(x-5)^2 + (y+3)^2 = 4$
B $(x-4)^2 + (y-3)^2 = 9$
C $(x+5)^2 + (y+1)^2 = 16$
D $(x+1)^2 + (y-4)^2 = 4$

7. The center of a circle is (9, 2), and the radius of the circle is 5 units. Which is a point on the circle?

F (4, 2) H (9, 4)
G (14, 0) J (9, –5)

Name________________ Class________________ Date________________

5-3

Parabolas

Going Deeper

Essential question: *What are the defining features of a parabola?*

Like the circle, the ellipse, and the hyperbola, the parabola can be defined in terms of distance. A parabola is the set of all points in a plane that are the same distance from a fixed point, called the **focus**, and a fixed line, called the **directrix**. The midpoint of the shortest segment connecting the focus and the directrix is the **vertex** of the parabola. The **axis of symmetry** is a line perpendicular to the directrix and passes through the focus and the vertex.

MCC9–12.G.GPE.2

1 EXPLORE Deriving the Equation of a Parabola

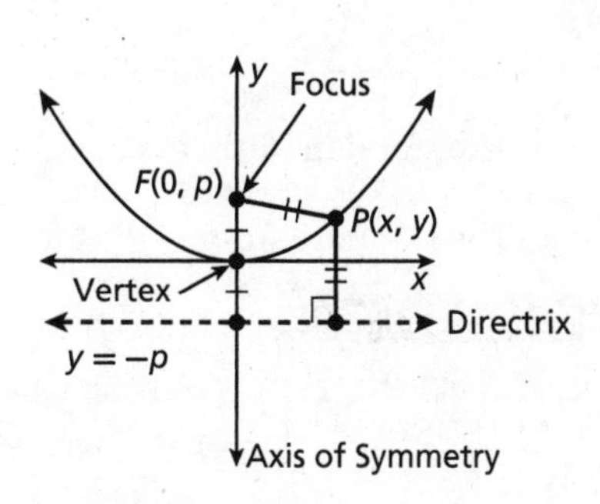

Use distance on the coordinate plane to find the equation of a parabola.

A In the figure, $P(x, y)$ on the parabola is equidistant from the focus $F(0, p)$ and the directrix $y = -p$.
A line perpendicular to the directrix from P intersects the directrix at $D(x, -p)$.

$\sqrt{(x - x_1)^2 + (y - y_1)^2} = \sqrt{(x - x_2)^2 + (y - y_2)^2}$ Distance Formula

$\sqrt{(\quad)^2 + (\quad)^2} = \sqrt{(\quad)^2 + (\quad)^2}$ Substitute $(0, p)$ for (x_1, y_1) and $(x, -p)$ for (x_2, y_2).

$\sqrt{\quad + (\quad)^2} = \sqrt{(\quad)^2}$ Simplify.

$\quad + (\quad)^2 = (\quad)^2$ Square both sides.

$\quad + \quad - \quad + \quad = \quad + \quad + \quad$ Expand the binomials.

$\quad - \quad = \quad$ Subtract y^2 and p^2 from both sides.

$x^2 = \quad$ Add $2yp$ to both sides.

$y = \frac{\quad}{\quad}(x^2)$ Solve for y.

This is the standard form of the equation of a parabola. Sometimes, the equation is given in the form $x^2 =$ ________.

B A parabola has its focus at $F(0, 6)$ and directrix $y = -6$.

The equation of the parabola is $y =$ ________.

C The focus of the parabola $x^2 = 18y$ is ________. The directrix is ________.

REFLECT

1. In the first step of the derivation of the equation of a parabola, the points $(0, p)$ and $(x, -p)$ were substituted for (x_1, y_1) and (x_2, y_2), yielding the equation $\sqrt{(x-0)^2+(y-p)^2}$ $=\sqrt{(x-x)^2+(y+p)^2}$. Compare that equation with the equation you would write if the parabola were rotated 90° so that its axis of symmetry were horizontal, as in the figure at the right. How would the remaining equations in the derivation be affected? What would the derivation yield as the standard form of the equation of a parabola with a horizontal axis of symmetry?

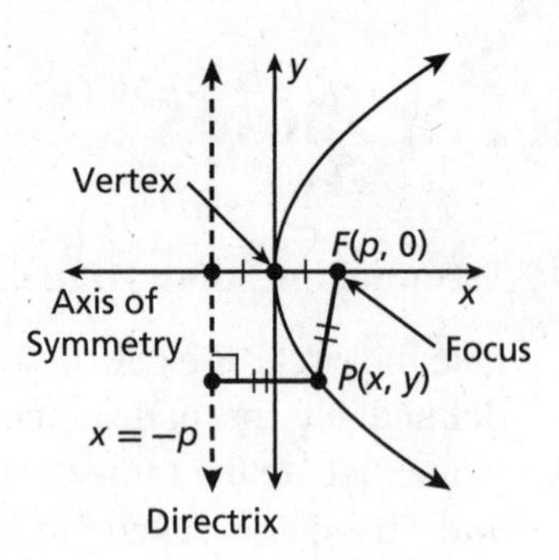

____

____

____

The standard form of the equation of a parabola with a vertical axis is $y = \frac{1}{4p}x^2$.

The standard form of the equation of a parabola with a horizontal axis is $x = \frac{1}{4p}y^2$.

MCC9–12.G.GPE.2

2 EXAMPLE Finding the Equation of a Parabola with its Vertex at the Origin

Write the equation of each parabola in standard form.

A

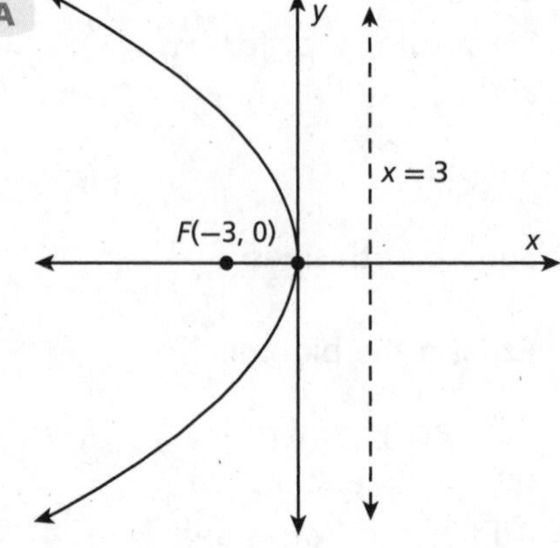

B

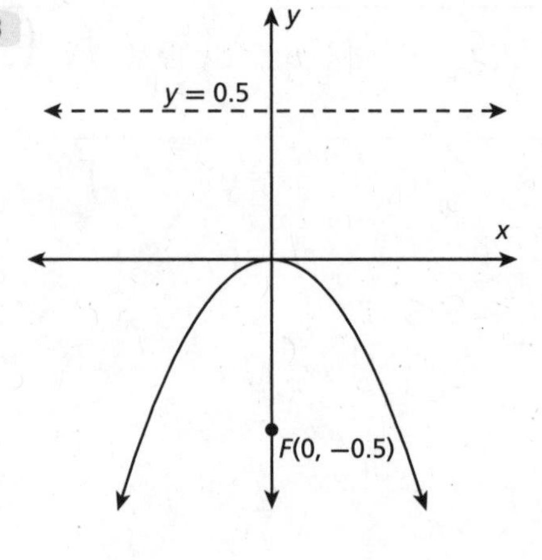

______________________ ______________________

REFLECT

2. Describe how the value of p relates to the shape of the parabola.

____

____

____

For the circle, the ellipse, and the hyperbola, translating the center of the conic section from (0, 0) to (h, k) changed x in the standard form of the equation of the figure to $x - h$ and changed y to $y - k$. A similar transformation takes place when the vertex of a parabola is translated from (0, 0) to (h, k).

Direction of Axis of Symmetry	Equation of Axis of Symmetry	Standard Form of the Equation of a Parabola with Vertex at (h, k)
Vertical	$x = h$	$y - k = \frac{1}{4p}(x - h)^2$
Horizontal	$y = k$	$x - h = \frac{1}{4p}(y - k)^2$

MCC9–12.G.GPE.2

3 EXAMPLE Finding the Equation of a Parabola with its Vertex Not at the Origin

Use the focus and directrix to sketch the parabola. Then find the equation of the parabola.

A A parabola has focus (3, 8) and directrix $y = 4$.

The vertex of the parabola is ________. So $h =$ ________ and $k =$ ________.

Use the fact that p equals the distance from the focus to the vertex to find p: $p =$ ________.

Standard form of the equation of the parabola: ____________________

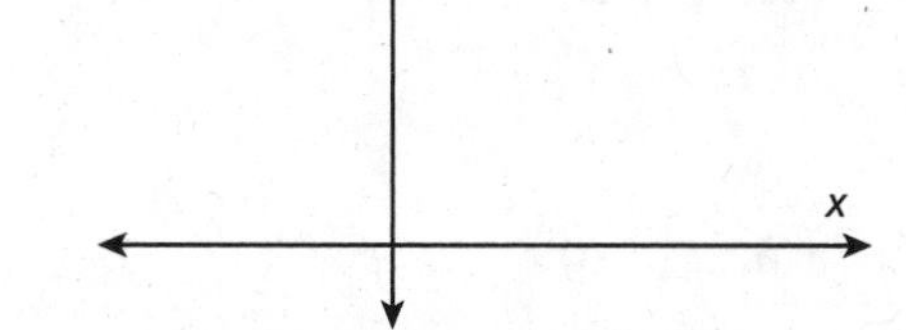

B A parabola has focus (3, −1) and directrix $x = -2$

The vertex of the parabola is ________. So $h =$ ________ and $k =$ ________.

Find p: $p =$ ________.

Standard form of the equation of the parabola: ____________________

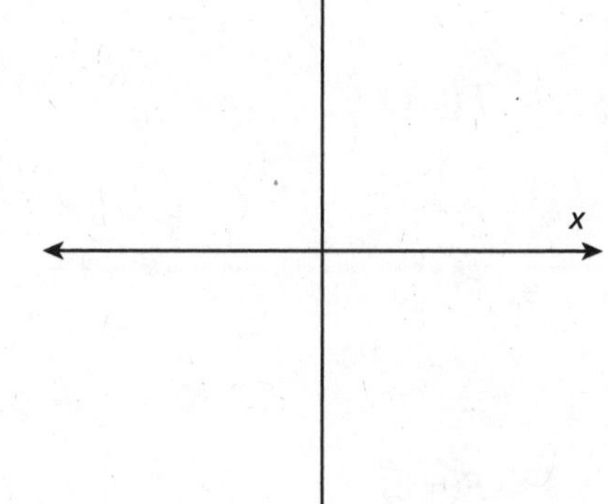

REFLECT

3. During the study of quadratic functions, the standard form of a quadratic function is given as $y = ax^2 + bx + c$. Find values of a, b, and c which show that this equation is equivalent to the standard form given in this lesson $y - k = \frac{1}{4p}(x - h)^2$. Explain how you found the values.

____

____

____

PRACTICE

Write the equation of each parabola in standard form.

	Focus	Directrix	Equation
1.	$F(2, 0)$	$x = -2$	______
2.	$F(0, 8)$	$y = -8$	______
3.	$F(-20, 0)$	$x = 20$	______
4.	$F\left(0, -\frac{1}{12}\right)$	$y = \frac{1}{12}$	______
5.	$F(5, 5)$	$y = -3$	______
6.	$F(3, 0)$	$x = -2$	______
7.	$F(4, -3)$	$y = 6$	______
8.	$F(8, 0)$	$y = 4$	______
9.	$F(10, -3)$	$x = 5$	______
10.	$F(6, 2)$	$x = 4$	______
11.	$F(7, -7)$	$x = -2$	______
12.	$F(-1, 2)$	$y = -1$	______

Name________________________ Class______________ Date__________

Additional Practice

Use the Distance Formula to find the equation of a parabola with the given focus and directrix.

1. $F(6, 0)$, $x = -3$

____

2. $F(1, 0)$, $x = -4$

____

Write the equation in standard form for each parabola.

3. Vertex (0, 0), directrix $y = -2$

____

4. Vertex (0, 0), focus (9, 0)

____

5. Focus (–6, 0), directrix $x = 6$

____

6. Vertex (0, 0), focus (0, –3)

____

Find the vertex, value of *p*, axis of symmetry, focus, and directrix of each parabola. Then graph.

7. $x - 1 = -\frac{1}{12}y^2$

____

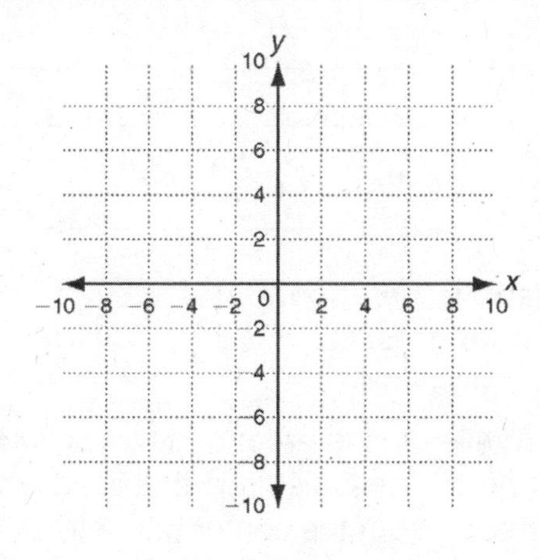

8. $y + 2 = \frac{1}{4}(x - 1)^2$

____

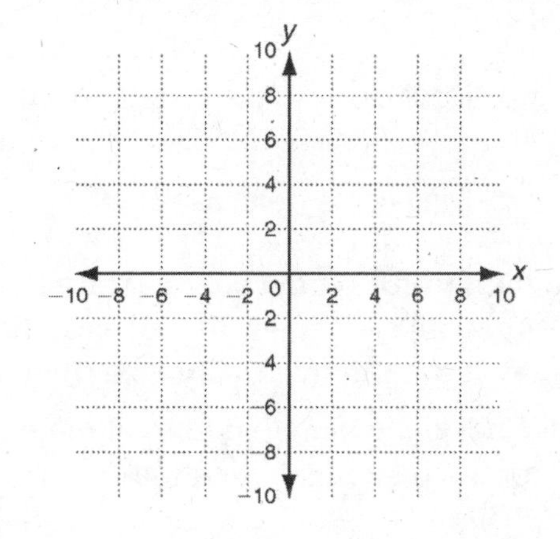

Solve.

9. A spotlight has parabolic cross sections.
   a. Write an equation for a cross section of the spotlight if the bulb is 6 inches from the vertex and the vertex is placed at the origin. _________________________
   b. If the spotlight has a diameter of 36 inches at its opening, find the depth of the spotlight if the bulb is 6 inches from the vertex. _________________________

Problem Solving

At a bungee-jumping contest, Gavin makes a jump that can be modeled by the equation $x^2 - 12x - 12y + 84 = 0$, with dimensions in feet.

1. Gavin wants to know how close he came to the ground during his jump.
   a. Classify the shape of his path. Identify the values for the coefficients of each term, and determine what conic section models his path.

   ____

   b. Write the equation of his path in standard form by completing the square.

   ____

   c. Which point on the path identifies the lowest point that Gavin reached? What are the coordinates of this point? How close to the ground was he?

   ____

2. Nicole makes a similar jump that can be modeled by the equation $x^2 - 4x - 8y + 84 = 0$. She wants to know whether she got closer to the ground than Gavin and by how much.
   a. Write the equation of Nicole's path in standard form.

   ____

   b. How close to the ground did she get? ______________

   c. Did Nicole get closer to the ground than Gavin? ______________

The design for a new auto racetrack can be modeled by the equation $x^2 + 4y^2 - 20x - 32y + 160 = 0$, with dimensions in kilometers. Tracey tests the track. Choose the letter for the best answer.

3. What is the standard form of the equation for the path of the racetrack?

   A $\frac{(x-10)^2}{1^2} + \frac{(y-4)^2}{2^2} = 1$

   B $\frac{(x-10)^2}{2^2} + \frac{(y-4)^2}{1^2} = 1$

   C $\frac{(x-4)^2}{2^2} + \frac{(y-10)^2}{1^2} = 1$

   D $\frac{(x-4)^2}{1^2} + \frac{(y-10)^2}{2^2} = 1$

4. While driving around the track, what is the greatest distance that Tracey will reach from the center of the track?

   F 1 km

   G 2 km

   H 10 km

   J 16 km

Performance Tasks

MCC9-12.G.GPE.1
MCC9-12.G.GPE.2
MCC9-12.G.GPE.4

★ **1.** Missy draws a map on the coordinate plane. She plots her house at the origin. She then draws a circle that represents all the places that are exactly 9 miles from the library.

a. The equation $x^2 - 8x + y^2 = 65$ represents the graph of the circle that Missy drew. Complete the square to find the center and radius of the circle.

b. How far does Missy live from the library? Explain.

2. A graphic artist is using a coordinate plane to design a company logo. The logo has an equilateral triangle inscribed in a circle. The circle lies in Quadrant I, is tangent to the x- and y-axes, and has a radius of 10 units. One side of the triangle is parallel to the y-axis, and one vertex is at (20, 10).

a. Write the equation for the circle.

b. What is the length of the sides of the inscribed triangle? Round your answer to the nearest hundredth of a unit and show your work.

c. Use the fact that the base opposite the vertex at (20, 10) is parallel to the y-axis, and your result from part **b** to find the coordinates of the other two vertices. Round the coordinates to the nearest hundredth of a unit and show your work. (*Hint*: The vertices will be the same distance above and below a horizontal line passing through (20, 10)).

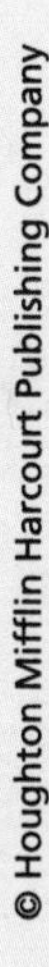

3. Chase wants to prove the following: Given a circle with radius r and center (0, 0), if (a, b) is on the circle, then the point $(-a, -b)$ is on the circle.

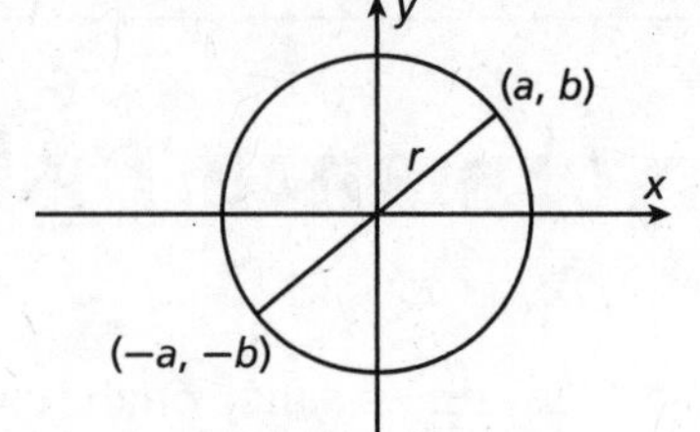

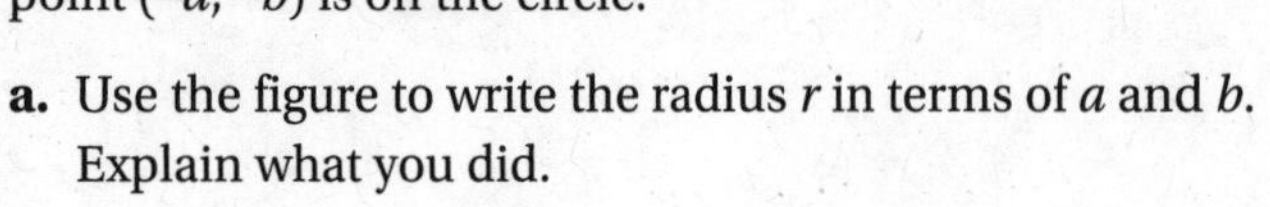

a. Use the figure to write the radius r in terms of a and b. Explain what you did.

b. Write the equation of the circle using your expression for the radius from part **a.**

c. Use the equation to prove Chase's statement. Justify your answer.

4. In the diagram, $\overline{AC}$ bisects $\overline{BD}$ at K and $\overline{BD}$ bisects $\overline{AC}$ at K.

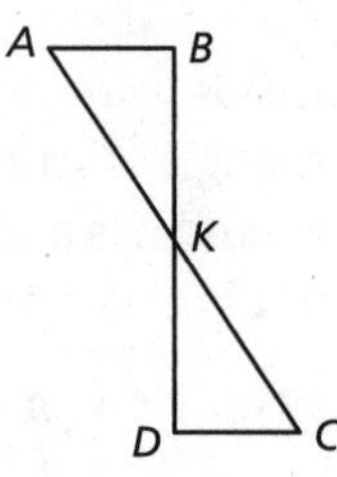

a. What must you know in order to prove that $\overline{AB} \parallel \overline{DC}$?

b. Write a plan to prove the criteria you gave in part **a.**

c. Prove $\overline{AB} \parallel \overline{DC}$.

Name ______________________ Class ____________ Date ________

SELECTED RESPONSE

1. Tyrell's teacher asks him to prove or disprove that the triangle with vertices $A(1, 1)$, $B(2, 5)$, and $C(6, 4)$ is an isosceles triangle. Which of the following should he do?

   A. Disprove the statement by using the distance formula to show that $\overline{AB}$, $\overline{BC}$, and $\overline{AC}$ all have different lengths.

   B. Prove the statement by using the distance formula to show that $AB = BC$.

   C. Prove the statement by using the distance formula to show that $AB = AC$.

   D. Prove the statement by using the distance formula to show that $BC = AC$.

2. What is the equation in standard form for the parabola with focus $F(0, -6,)$ and directrix $y = 6$?

   F. $y = \frac{1}{24}x^2$

   G. $x = \frac{1}{24}y^2$

   H. $x = -\frac{1}{24}y^2$

   J. $y = -\frac{1}{24}x^2$

3. What is an equation in standard form for the parabola shown?

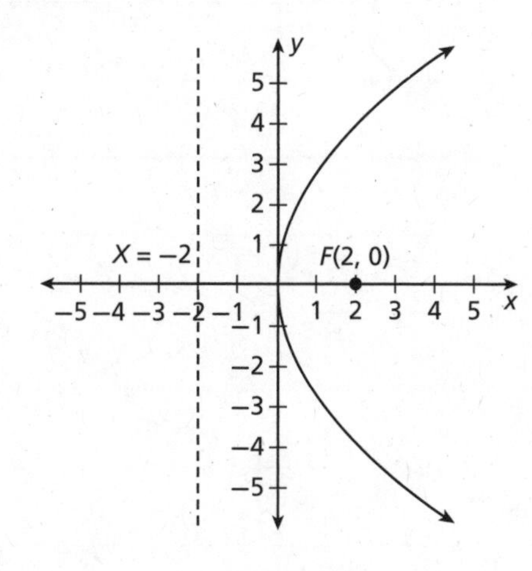

   A. $y = -\frac{1}{8}x^2$

   B. $y = \frac{1}{8}x^2$

   C. $x = \frac{1}{8}y^2$

   D. $x = -\frac{1}{8}y^2$

4. Three friends are planning to visit each other. To optimize travel time, they want the meeting place to be equidistant from the three different cities they live in. The cities are located at $A(-16, -1)$, $B(1, 6)$, and $C(1, -18)$. What are the coordinates where the meeting should take place?

   F. $(-7.5, 2.5)$

   G. $(-7, -9.5)$

   H. $(-4.3, -4.3)$

   J. $(-4, -6)$

5. Position a right triangle with leg lengths r and $2s + 4$ in the coordinate plane and give the coordinates of each vertex.

   A.

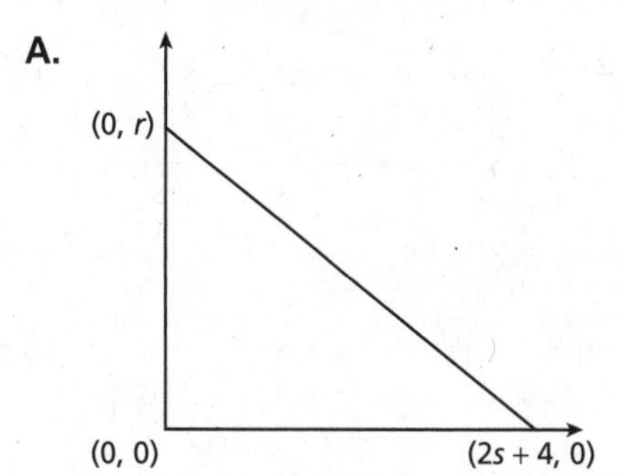

   B.

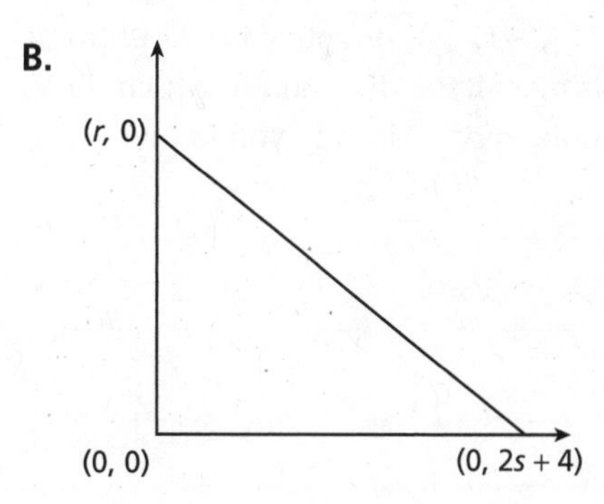

   C.

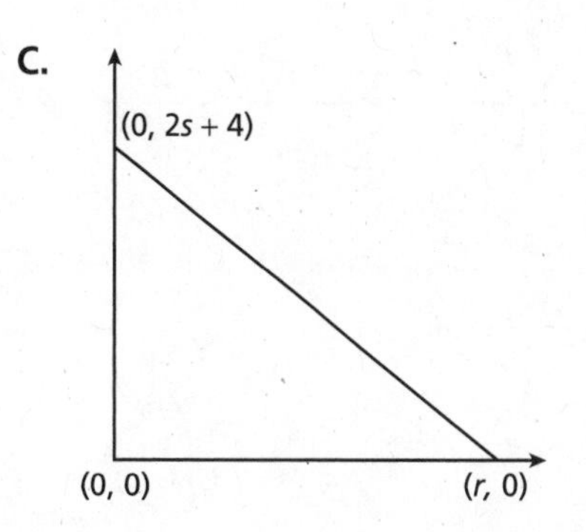

   D. Both a. and c.

CONSTRUCTED RESPONSE

6. Prove or disprove that the point $(2, \sqrt{5})$ lies on the circle that is centered at the origin and contains the point $(0, -3)$.

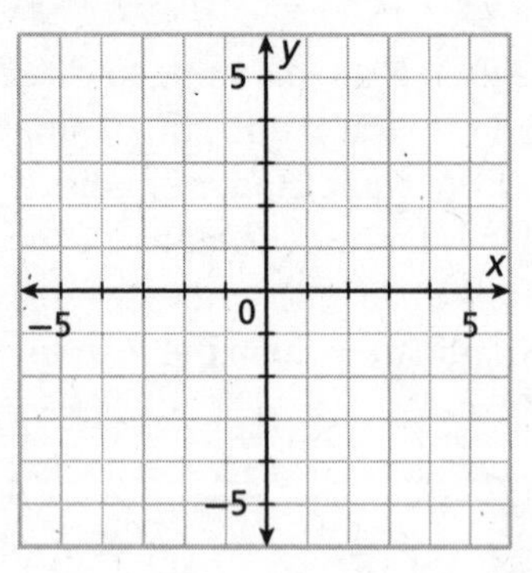

7. What is the equation of the parabola with focus $(4, -1)$ and directrix $x = 1$? Without graphing, tell the direction in which the parabola opens. How do you know?

8. Prove that the angle inscribed in a semicircle below is a right angle.

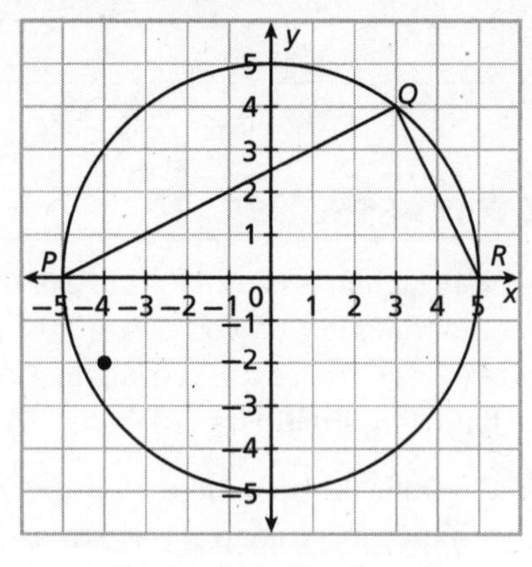

9. Find the point(s) of intersection of the line $x - y = -6$ and the circle $x^2 + y^2 = 18$ by solving the system of equations.

UNIT 4

Applications of Probability

Module 6 Probability

6-1	Geometric Probability	MCC9-12.S.CP.1
6-2	Permutations and Combinations	MCC9-12.S.CP.9(+)
6-3	Theoretical and Experimental Probability	MCC9-12.S.CP.1

Module 7 Conditional Probability

7-1	Independent and Dependent Events	MCC9-12.S.CP.2, MCC9-12.S.CP.3, MCC9-12.S.CP.5, MCC9-12.S.CP.6
7-2	Two-Way Tables	MCC9-12.S.CP.4
7-3	Compound Events	MCC9-12.S.CP.5, MCC9-12.S.CP.7
	Performance Tasks	
	PARCC Assessment Readiness	

UNIT 4

Unpacking the Standards

Understanding the standards and the vocabulary terms in the standards will help you know exactly what you are expected to learn in this unit.

MCC9-12.S.CP.9(+)

Use permutations and combinations to compute probabilities of compound events and solve problems.

Key Vocabulary

permutation *(permutación)* An arrangement of a group of objects in which order is important. The number of permutations of r objects from a group of n objects is denoted ${}_nP_r$.

combination *(combinación)* A selection of a group of objects in which order is *not* important. The number of combinations of r objects chosen from a group of n objects is denoted ${}_nC_r$.

probability *(probabilidad)* A number from 0 to 1 (or 0% to 100%) that is the measure of how likely an event is to occur.

event *(suceso)* An outcome or set of outcomes in a probability experiment.

compound event *(suceso compuesto)* An event made up of two or more simple events.

UNIT 4

What It Means For You

A permutation is an arrangement of objects in which order is important. A combination is an arrangement of objects in which order is not important. Both permutations and combinations can be used to find probabilities.

EXAMPLE **Permutations**

Lindsey will choose two of these pictures to hang next to each other on her bedroom wall.

This is an example of a permutation because the order is important. Hanging the mountain picture to the right of the sunset picture is different from hanging the mountain picture to the left of the sunset picture.

EXAMPLE **Combinations**

You can choose three toppings for your hamburger.

This is an example of a combination because the order is not important. Tomato, onions, and pickles is the same as pickles, tomato, and onions.

MCC9-12.S.CP.1

GPS COMMON CORE

Describe events as subsets of a sample space (the set of outcomes) using characteristics (or categories) of the outcomes, or as unions, intersections, or complements of other events ("or," "and," "not").

Key Vocabulary

sample space *(espacio muestral)*
The set of all possible outcomes of a probability experiment.

outcome *(resultado)* A possible result of a probability experiment.

union *(unión)* The union of two sets is the set of all elements that are in either set, denoted by $\cup$.

intersection *(intersección de conjuntos)* The intersection of two sets is the set of all elements that are common to both sets, denoted by $\cap$.

complement of an event *(complemento de un suceso)* All outcomes in the sample space that are not in an event E, denoted $\overline{E}$ or E^c.

What It Means For You

To calculate the probability of a particular event, you may need to find the sample space, which is the set of all possible outcomes. You may also need to determine which outcome(s) in the sample space make up the event.

EXAMPLE **Sample Spaces**

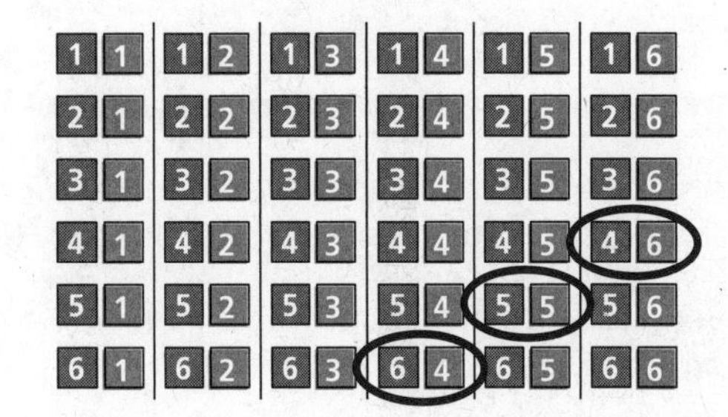

The sample space for rolling two standard number cubes is shown. The circled outcomes make up the event "rolling a sum of 10."

MCC9-12.S.CP.4

GPS COMMON CORE

Construct and interpret two-way frequency tables of data when two categories are associated with each object being classified. Use the two-way table as a sample space to decide if events are independent and to approximate conditional probabilities.

Key Vocabulary

frequency table *(tabla de frecuencia)*
A table that lists the number of times, or frequency, that each data value occurs.

independent events *(sucesos independientes)* Events for which the occurrence or non-occurrence of one event does not affect the probability of the other event.

conditional probability *(probabilidad condicional)* The probability of event B, given that event A has already occurred or is certain to occur, denoted $P(B|A)$.

What It Means For You

A two-way table organizes data about two variables. A two-way frequency table can be very helpful when finding probabilities.

EXAMPLE **Finding Conditional Probability**

		Owns a cat		
		Yes	No	Total
Owns a dog	Yes	0.15	0.24	0.39
	No	0.18	0.43	0.61
	Total	0.33	0.67	1

This two-way frequency table describes data collected by a sociologist who surveyed 100 randomly selected people about their pets. You can use this table to answer the question, "If a person in this survey has a dog, what is the probability that he or she also has a cat?"

Key Vocabulary

combination *(combinación)* A selection of a group of objects in which order is *not* important. The number of combinations of r objects chosen from a group of n objects is denoted ${}_nC_r$.

complement of an event *(complemento de un suceso)* All outcomes in the sample space that are not in an event E, denoted $\overline{E}$ or E^C.

compound event *(suceso compuesto)* An event made up of two or more simple events.

conditional probability *(probabilidad condicional)* The probability of event B, given that event A has already occurred or is certain to occur, denoted $P(B|A)$.

convenience sample *(muestra de conveniencia)* A sample based on members of the population that are readily available.

dependent events *(sucesos dependientes)* Events for which the occurrence or non-occurrence of one event affects the probability of the other event.

event *(suceso)* An outcome or set of outcomes in a probability experiment.

factorial *(factorial)* If n is a positive integer, then n factorial, written $n!$, is $n \bullet (n - 1) \bullet (n - 2) \bullet \ldots \bullet 2 \bullet 1$. The factorial of 0 is defined to be 1.

frequency table *(tabla de frecuencia)* A table that lists the number of times, or frequency, that each data value occurs.

independent events *(sucesos independientes)* Events for which the occurrence or non-occurrence of one event does not affect the probability of the other event.

intersection *(intersección de conjuntos)* The intersection of two sets is the set of all elements that are common to both sets, denoted by $\cap$.

mutually exclusive events *(sucesos mutuamente excluyentes)* Two events are mutually exclusive if they cannot both occur in the same trial of an experiment.

outcome *(resultado)* A possible result of a probability experiment.

permutation *(permutación)* An arrangement of a group of objects in which order is important. The number of permutations of r objects from a group of n objects is denoted ${}_nP_r$.

probability *(probabilidad)* A number from 0 to 1 (or 0% to 100%) that is the measure of how likely an event is to occur.

random sample *(muestra aleatoria)* A sample selected from a population so that each member of the population has an equal chance of being selected.

sample space *(espacio muestral)* The set of all possible outcomes of a probability experiment.

union *(unión)* The union of two sets is the set of all elements that are in either set, denoted by $\cup$.

UNIT 4

Name ______________________ Class ______________ Date ______________

6-1

Geometric Probability

Connection: Set Theory

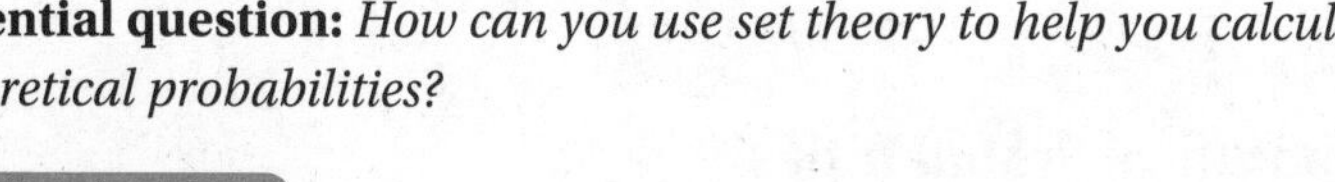

Essential question: *How can you use set theory to help you calculate theoretical probabilities?*

Video Tutor

MCC9–12.S.CP.1

1 ENGAGE Introducing the Vocabulary of Sets

You will see that set theory is useful in calculating probabilities. A **set** is a well-defined collection of distinct objects. Each object in a set is called an **element** of the set. A set may be specified by writing its elements in braces. For example, the set S of prime numbers less than 10 may be written as $S = \{2, 3, 5, 7\}$.

The number of elements in a set S may be written as $n(S)$. For the set S of prime numbers less than 10, $n(S) = 4$.

The set with no elements is the **empty set** and is denoted by $\varnothing$ or $\{\ \}$. The set of all elements under consideration is the **universal set** and is denoted by U. The following terms describe how sets are related to each other.

Term	Notation	Venn Diagram
Set A is a **subset** of set B if every element of A is also an element of B.	$A \subset B$	U, B, A
The **intersection** of sets A and B is the set of all elements that are in both A and B.	$A \cap B$	U, A, B
The **union** of sets A and B is the set of all elements that are in A or B.	$A \cup B$	U, A, B
The **complement** of set A is the set of all elements in the universal set U that are not in A.	A^c	U, A

REFLECT

1a. For any set A, what is $A \cap \varnothing$? Explain.

____

____

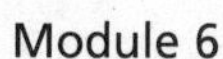

Recall that a *probability experiment* is an activity involving chance. Each repetition of the experiment is a *trial* and each possible result is an *outcome*. The *sample space* of an experiment is the set of all possible outcomes. An *event* is a set of outcomes.

When all outcomes of an experiment are equally likely, the **theoretical probability** that an event A will occur is given by $P(A) = \frac{n(A)}{n(S)}$, where S is the sample space.

MCC9–12.S.CP.1

2 EXAMPLE Calculating Theoretical Probabilities

You roll a number cube. Event *A* is rolling an even number. Event *B* is rolling a prime number. Calculate each of the following probabilities.

A $P(A)$ B $P(A \cup B)$ C $P(A \cap B)$ D $P(A^c)$

A $P(A)$ is the probability of rolling an even number. To calculate $P(A)$, first identify the sample space S.

$S =$ ________________, so $n(S) =$ ________.

$A =$ ________________, so $n(A) =$ ________.

So, $P(A) = \frac{n(A)}{n(S)} = \frac{\square}{\square} = \frac{\square}{\square}$.

B $P(A \cup B)$ is the probability of rolling an even number *or* a prime number.

$A \cup B =$ ________________, so $n(A \cup B) =$ ________.

So, $P(A \cup B) = \frac{n(A \cup B)}{n(S)} = \frac{\square}{\square}$.

C $P(A \cap B)$ is the probability of rolling an even number *and* a prime number.

$A \cap B =$ ________________, so $n(A \cap B) =$ ________.

So, $P(A \cap B) = \frac{n(A \cap B)}{n(S)} = \frac{\square}{\square}$.

D $P(A^c)$ is the probability of rolling a number that is *not* even.

$A^c =$ ________________, so $n(A^c) =$ ________.

So, $P(A^c) = \frac{n(A^c)}{n(S)} = \frac{\square}{\square} = \frac{\square}{\square}$.

REFLECT

2a. Explain what $P(S)$ represents and then calculate this probability. Do you think this result is true in general? Explain.

____

____

You may have noticed in the example that $P(A) + P(A^c) = 1$. To see why this is true in general, note that an event and its complement represent all outcomes in the sample space, so $n(A) + n(A^c) = n(S)$.

$$P(A) + P(A^c) = \frac{n(A)}{n(S)} + \frac{n(A^c)}{n(S)}$$ Definition of theoretical probability

$$= \frac{n(A) + n(A^c)}{n(S)}$$ Add.

$$= \frac{n(S)}{n(S)} = 1$$ $n(A) + n(A^c) = n(S)$

You can write this relationship as $P(A) = 1 - P(A^c)$ and use it to help you find probabilities when it is more convenient to calculate the probability of the complement of an event.

Probabilities of an Event and Its Complement

The probability of an event and the probability of its complement have a sum of 1. So, the probability of an event is one minus the probability of its complement. Also, the probability of the complement of an event is one minus the probability of the event.

$$P(A) + P(A^c) = 1$$

$$P(A) = 1 - P(A^c)$$

$$P(A^c) = 1 - P(A)$$

MCC9–12.S.CP.1

3 EXAMPLE Using the Complement of an Event

You roll a blue number cube and white number cube at the same time. What is the probability that you do not roll doubles?

A Let A be the event that you do not roll doubles. Then A^c is the event that you do roll doubles.

Complete the table at right to show all outcomes in the sample space.

Circle the outcomes in A^c (rolling doubles).

White Number Cube

Blue Number Cube	1	2	3	4	5	6
1	1-1	1-2	1-3	1-4	1-5	1-6
2	2-1					
3	3-1					
4	4-1					
5	5-1					
6	6-1					

B Find the probability of rolling doubles.

$$P(A^c) = \frac{n(A^c)}{n(S)} = \frac{\quad}{\quad} = \frac{\quad}{\quad}$$

C Find the probability that you do not roll doubles.

$$P(A) = 1 - P(A^c) = 1 - \frac{\quad}{\quad} = \frac{\quad}{\quad}$$

REFLECT

3a. Describe a different way you could have calculated the probability that you do not roll doubles.

PRACTICE

You have a set of 10 cards numbered 1 to 10. You choose a card at random. Event A is choosing a number less than 7. Event B is choosing an odd number. Calculate each of the following probabilities.

1. $P(A)$

2. $P(B)$

3. $P(A \cup B)$

4. $P(A \cap B)$

5. $P(A^c)$

6. $P(B^c)$

7. A bag contains 5 red marbles and 10 blue marbles. You choose a marble without looking. Event A is choosing a red marble. Event B is choosing a blue marble. What is $P(A \cap B)$? Explain.

8. A standard deck of cards has 13 cards (2, 3, 4, 5, 6, 7, 8, 9, 10, jack, queen, king, ace) in each of 4 suits (hearts, clubs, diamonds, spades). You choose a card from a deck at random. What is the probability that you do not choose an ace? Explain.

9. You choose a card from a standard deck of cards at random. What is the probability that you do not choose a club? Explain.

10. **Error Analysis** A bag contains white tiles, black tiles, and gray tiles. $P(W)$, the probability of choosing a tile at random and choosing a white tile, is $\frac{1}{4}$. A student claims that the probability of choosing a black tile, $P(B)$, is $\frac{3}{4}$ since $P(B) = 1 - P(W) = 1 - \frac{1}{4} = \frac{3}{4}$. Do you agree? Explain.

Name ______________________ Class ______________ Date ____________

Additional Practice

Set $A = \{2, 4, 6, 8, 10\}$ and Set B is the set of all prime numbers less than 20. List the elements in each of the following sets.

1. B ______________
2. $A \cup B$ ______________
3. $A \cap B$ ______________

A bag contains 26 tiles, one for each letter of the alphabet. Event A is drawing a tile with a vowel on it. Event B is drawing a tile with the letter A, B, C, D, E, or F on it. Calculate each of the following probabilities.

4. $P(A)$ ______________
5. $P(B)$ ______________
6. $P(A \cup B)$ ______________
7. $P(A \cap B)$ ______________
8. $P(A^C)$ ______________
9. $P(B^C)$ ______________

Find the probability of A^C for each of the following situations.

10. $P(A) = 0.3$ ______________
11. $P(A) = \frac{1}{4}$ ______________
12. A number cube with sides numbered 1–6 is rolled. A is rolling a 5.

____

13. A number cube with sides numbered 1–6 is rolled. A is rolling an even number.

____

14. Give an example of two sets A and B, for which A and $A \cup B$ both contain the exact same elements. Both sets should contain at least two elements, and the sets should not be the same.

____

Problem Solving

Write the correct answer.

1. The universal set U is the set of all integers from 1 through 20. You select one element of U at random. Event A is choosing 2, 6, or 18. What is $P(A^C)$?

____

2. A bag contains a total of 10 marbles. Four of the marbles are black, and 3 of the marbles are white. If Event A is drawing a black marble and Event B is drawing a white marble, what is $P(A \cup B)$?

____

3. Set $C = \{-2, -1, 0, 1, 2\}$ and Set D is the set of all positive integers. What elements are in the set $C \cap D$?

____

4. You roll two six-sided number cubes at the same time. Event A is rolling a 1 on both cubes. What is $P(A^C)$?

____

Select the best answer.

5. A spinner has four sections of equal size. The sections are painted blue, red, green, and yellow. Event A is spinning a yellow, and Event B is spinning a red. What is $P(A \cup B)$?

   A $\frac{1}{4}$ C $\frac{3}{4}$

   B $\frac{1}{2}$ D 1

6. What is $P(B^C)$ for the situation described in Exercise 5?

   F $\frac{1}{4}$ H $\frac{3}{4}$

   G $\frac{1}{2}$ J 1

7. Set $J = \{-\pi, \sqrt{2}, 0, 1\}$ and Set Q is the set of all rational numbers. Which set represents $J \cap Q$?

   A $\varnothing$

   B $\{0\}$

   C $\{0, 1\}$

   D Q

8. If you have two sets, A and B, and A and $A \cap B$ have the exact same elements, which statement must be true?

   F B is the null set.

   G Every element in A is also in B.

   H Every element in B is also in A.

   J $A \cup B$ is the null set.

Name ______________________ Class ______________ Date ________

6-2

Permutations and Combinations

Going Deeper

Essential question: *What are permutations and combinations and how can you use them to calculate probabilities?*

Video Tutor

A **permutation** is a selection of a group of objects in which order is important. For example, there are 6 permutations of the letters A, B, and C.

ABC	ACB
BAC	BCA
CAB	CBA

Finding Permutations

The members of a club want to choose a president, a vice-president, and a treasurer. Seven members of the club are eligible to fill these positions. In how many different ways can the positions be filled?

A Consider the number of ways each position can be filled.

There are __________ different ways the position of president can be filled.

Once the president has been chosen, there are __________ different ways the position of vice-president can be filled.

Once the president and vice-president have been chosen, there are __________ different ways the position of treasurer can be filled.

B Multiply to find the total number of different ways the positions can be filled.

President — Vice-President — Treasurer

__________ × __________ × __________ = __________ permutations

So, there are __________ different ways that the positions can be filled.

REFLECT

1a. Suppose the club members also want to choose a secretary from the group of 7 eligible members. In how many different ways can the four positions (president, vice-president, treasurer, secretary) be filled? Explain.

____

1b. Suppose 8 members of the club are eligible to fill the original three positions (president, vice-president, treasurer). In how many different ways can the positions be filled? Explain.

____

The process you used in the example can be generalized to give a formula for permutations. To do so, it is helpful to use factorials. For a positive integer n, n **factorial**, written $n!$, is defined as follows.

$$n! = n \cdot (n-1) \cdot (n-2) \cdot \ldots \cdot 3 \cdot 2 \cdot 1$$

That is, $n!$ is the product of n and all the positive integers less than n. Note that 0! is defined to be 1.

In the example, the number of permutations of 7 objects taken 3 at a time is

$$7 \cdot 6 \cdot 5 = \frac{7 \cdot 6 \cdot 5 \cdot \cancel{4} \cdot \cancel{3} \cdot \cancel{2} \cdot \cancel{1}}{\cancel{4} \cdot \cancel{3} \cdot \cancel{2} \cdot \cancel{1}} = \frac{7!}{4!} = \frac{7!}{(7-3)!}.$$

This can be generalized as follows.

Permutations

The number of permutations of n objects taken r at a time is given by

$${}_nP_r = \frac{n!}{(n-r)!}.$$

Recall that the probability of an event is equal to the number of outcomes that result in the event, divided by the number of all possible outcomes.

MCC9–12.S.CP.9(+)

2 EXAMPLE Using Permutations to Calculate a Probability

Every student at your school is assigned a four-digit code, such as 6953, to access the computer system. In each code, no digit is repeated. What is the probability that you are assigned a code with the digits 1, 2, 3, and 4 in any order?

A Let S be the sample space. Find $n(S)$.

The sample space consists of all permutations of 4 digits taken from the 10 digits 0 through 9.

$$n(S) = {}_{10}P_4 = \frac{10!}{(10-4)!} = \frac{10!}{6!} = \frac{10 \cdot 9 \cdot 8 \cdot 7 \cdot \cancel{6} \cdot \cancel{5} \cdot \cancel{4} \cdot \cancel{3} \cdot \cancel{2} \cdot \cancel{1}}{\cancel{6} \cdot \cancel{5} \cdot \cancel{4} \cdot \cancel{3} \cdot \cancel{2} \cdot \cancel{1}} = \_\_\_\_\_\_$$

B Let A be the event that your code has the digits 1, 2, 3, and 4. Find $n(A)$.

The event consists of all permutations of 4 digits chosen from the 4 digits 1 through 4.

$$n(A) = {}_4P_4 = \frac{4!}{(4-4)!} = \frac{4!}{0!} = \frac{\quad}{\quad} = \_\_\_\_\_\_$$

C Find $P(A)$.

$$P(A) = \frac{n(A)}{n(S)} = \frac{\quad}{\quad} = \_\_\_\_\_\_$$

So, the probability that your code has the digits 1, 2, 3, and 4 is ______.

REFLECT

2a. What is the probability that you are assigned the code 1234? Explain.

____

A **combination** is a grouping of objects in which order does not matter. For example, when you choose 3 letters from the letters A, B, C, and D, there are 4 different combinations.

ABC ABD ACD BCD

PREP FOR MCC9–12.S.CP.9(+)

3 EXAMPLE Finding Combinations

A restaurant offers 8 side dishes. When you order an entree, you can choose 3 of the side dishes. In how many ways can you choose 3 side dishes?

Side Dishes	
Beets	Rice
Potatoes	Broccoli
Carrots	Cole slaw
Salad	Apple sauce

A First find the number of ways to choose 3 sides dishes when order does matter. This is the number of permutations of 8 objects taken 3 at a time.

$$_8P_3 = \frac{8!}{(8-3)!} = \frac{8!}{5!} = \frac{\quad}{\quad} = \underline{\quad\quad}$$

B In this problem, order does not matter, since choosing beets, carrots, and rice is the same as choosing rice, beets, and carrots.

Divide the result from Step A by $_3P_3$, which is the number of ways the 3 side dishes can be ordered.

$$_3P_3 = \frac{\quad}{\quad} = \frac{\quad}{\quad} = \underline{\quad\quad}$$

So, the number of ways you can choose 3 side dishes is $\frac{\quad}{\quad} = \underline{\quad\quad}$.

REFLECT

3a. Suppose the restaurant offers a special on Mondays that allows you to choose 4 side dishes. In how many ways can you choose the side dishes?

____

3b. In general, are there more ways or fewer ways to select objects when order does not matter? Why?

____

____

The process you used in the example can be generalized to give a formula for combinations. In order to find ${}_8C_3$, the number of combinations of 8 objects taken 3 at a time, you first found the number of permutations of 8 objects taken 3 at a time, then you divided by 3! That is,

$${}_8C_3 = \frac{8!}{(8-3)!} \div 3! \text{ or } \frac{8!}{3!(8-3)!}.$$

This can be generalized as follows.

Combinations

The number of combinations of n objects taken r at a time is given by

$${}_nC_r = \frac{n!}{r!(n-r)!}.$$

MCC9–12.S.CP.9(+)

4 EXAMPLE Using Combinations to Calculate a Probability

There are 5 boys and 6 girls in a school play. The director randomly chooses 3 of the students to meet with a costume designer. What is the probability that the director chooses all boys?

A Let S be the sample space. Find $n(S)$.

The sample space consists of all combinations of 3 students taken from the group of 11 students.

$$n(S) = {}_{11}C_3 = \frac{11!}{3!(11-3)!} = \frac{11!}{3! \cdot 8!} = \frac{11 \cdot 10 \cdot 9 \cdot \cancel{8} \cdot \cancel{7} \cdot \cancel{6} \cdot \cancel{5} \cdot \cancel{4} \cdot \cancel{3} \cdot \cancel{2} \cdot \cancel{1}}{3 \cdot 2 \cdot 1 \cdot \cancel{8} \cdot \cancel{7} \cdot \cancel{6} \cdot \cancel{5} \cdot \cancel{4} \cdot \cancel{3} \cdot \cancel{2} \cdot \cancel{1}} = \_\_\_\_\_\_$$

B Let A be the event that the director chooses all boys. Find $n(A)$.

Suppose the 11 students are $B_1, B_2, B_3, B_4, B_5, G_1, G_2, G_3, G_4, G_5, G_6$, where the Bs represent boys and the Gs represent girls.

The combinations in event A are combinations like $B_2B_4B_5$ and $B_1B_3B_4$. That is, event A consists of all combinations of 3 boys taken from the set of 5 boys.

So, $n(A) = {}_5C_3 = \frac{\_\_\_\_}{\_\_\_\_} = \frac{\_\_\_\_}{\_\_\_\_} = \frac{\_\_\_\_}{\_\_\_\_} = \_\_\_\_\_\_$.

C Find $P(A)$.

$P(A) = \frac{n(A)}{n(S)} = \frac{\_\_\_\_}{\_\_\_\_} = \_\_\_\_\_\_$

So, the probability that the director chooses all boys is ______.

REFLECT

4a. Is the director more likely to choose all boys or all girls? Why?

PRACTICE

1. An MP3 player has a playlist with 12 songs. You select the shuffle option for the playlist. In how many different orders can the songs be played?

2. There are 10 runners in a race. Medals are awarded for 1st, 2nd, and 3rd place. In how many different ways can the medals be awarded?

3. There are 9 players on a baseball team. In how many different ways can the coach choose players for first base, second base, third base, and shortstop?

4. You have 15 photographs of your school. In how many different ways can you arrange 6 of them in a line for the cover of the school yearbook?

5. A bag contains 9 tiles, each with a different number from 1 to 9. You choose a tile, put it aside, choose a second tile, put it aside, and then choose a third tile. What is the probability that you choose tiles with the numbers 1, 2, and 3 in that order?

6. There are 11 students on a committee. To decide which 3 of these students will attend a conference, 3 names are chosen at random by pulling names one at a time from a hat. What is the probability that Sarah, Jamal, and Mai are chosen in any order?

7. **Error Analysis** A student solved the problem at right. The student's work is shown. Did the student make an error? If so, explain the error and provide the correct answer.

A bag contains 6 tiles with the letters A, B, C, D, E, and F. You choose 4 tiles one at a time without looking and line up the tiles as you choose them. What is the probability that your tiles spell BEAD?

Let S be the sample space and let A be the event that the tiles spell BEAD.

$$n(S) = {}_6P_4 = \frac{6!}{(6-4)!} = \frac{6!}{2!} = 360$$

$$n(A) = {}_4P_4 = \frac{4!}{(4-4)!} = \frac{4!}{0!} = 4! = 24$$

So, $P(A) = \frac{n(A)}{n(S)} = \frac{24}{360} = \frac{1}{15}$.

8. A cat has a litter of 6 kittens. You plan to adopt 2 of the kittens. In how many ways can you choose 2 of the kittens from the litter?

______

9. An amusement park has 11 roller coasters. In how many ways can you choose 4 of the roller coasters to ride during your visit to the park?

______

10. A school has 5 Spanish teachers and 4 French teachers. The school's principal randomly chooses 2 of the teachers to attend a conference. What is the probability that the principal chooses 2 Spanish teachers?

______

11. There are 6 fiction books and 8 nonfiction books on a reading list. Your teacher randomly assigns you 4 books to read over the summer. What is the probability that you are assigned all nonfiction books?

______

12. A bag contains 26 tiles, each with a different letter of the alphabet written on it. You choose 3 tiles from the bag without looking. What is the probability that you choose the tiles containing the letters A, B, and C?

______

13. You are randomly assigned a password consisting of 6 different characters chosen from the digits 0 to 9 and the letters A to Z. As a percent, what is the probability that you are assigned a password consisting of only letters?

______

14. Calculate ${}_{10}C_6$ and ${}_{10}C_4$.

a. What do you notice about these values? Explain why this makes sense.

______

______

______

b. Use your observations to help you state a generalization about combinations.

______

______

15. Use the formula for combinations to make a generalization about ${}_nC_n$. Explain why this makes sense.

______

______

______

Name________________ Class__________ Date__________ 6-2

Additional Practice

Use the Fundamental Counting Principle.

1. The soccer team is silk-screening T-shirts. They have 4 different colors of T-shirts and 2 different colors of ink. How many different T-shirts can be made using one ink color on a T-shirt? ________________

2. A travel agent is offering a vacation package. Participants choose the type of tour, a meal plan, and a hotel class from the table below.

Tour	Meal	Hotel
Walking	Restaurant	4-Star
Boat	Picnic	3-Star
Bicycle		2-Star
		1-Star

How many different vacation packages are offered? ________________

Evaluate.

3. $\frac{3!6!}{3!}$

4. $\frac{10!}{7!}$

5. $\frac{9!-6!}{(9-6)!}$

Solve.

6. In how many ways can the debate team choose a president and a secretary if there are 10 people on the team? ________________

7. A teacher is passing out first-, second-, and third-place prizes for the best student actor in a production of *Hamlet*. If there are 14 students in the class, in how many different ways can the awards be presented? ________________

Evaluate.

8. ${}_5P_4$

9. ${}_3C_2$

10. ${}_8P_3$

Solve.

11. Mrs. Marshall has 11 boys and 14 girls in her kindergarten class this year.
    a. In how many ways can she select 2 girls to pass out a snack? ________________
    b. In how many ways can she select 5 boys to pass out new books? ________________
    c. In how many ways can she select 3 students to carry papers to the office? ________________

Problem Solving

Rosalie is looking at locks. The label *combination lock* confuses her. She wonders about the number of possible permutations or combinations a lock can have.

1. She looks at one circular lock with 12 positions. To open it she turns the dial clockwise to a first position, then counterclockwise to a second position, then clockwise to a third position

   a. Write an expression for the number of 3-position codes that are possible, if no position is repeated.

   ____

   b. Explain how this represents a combination or a permutation.

   ____

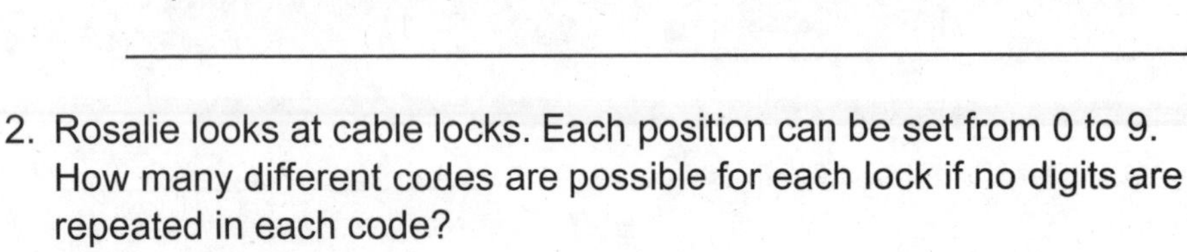

2. Rosalie looks at cable locks. Each position can be set from 0 to 9. How many different codes are possible for each lock if no digits are repeated in each code?

   a. a 3-digit cable lock

   ____

   b. a 4-digit cable lock

   ____

   c. a 6-digit cable lock

   ____

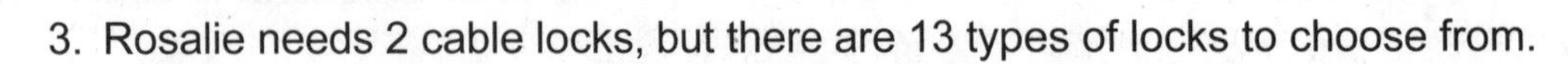

3. Rosalie needs 2 cable locks, but there are 13 types of locks to choose from.

   a. In how many ways can she choose 2 different locks? ____________

   b. Explain how this represents a permutation or a combination.

   ____

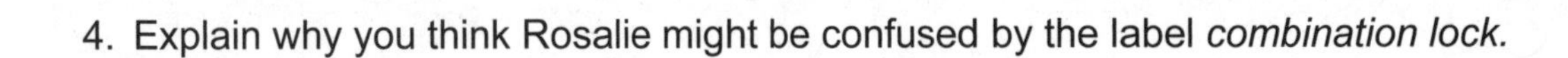

4. Explain why you think Rosalie might be confused by the label *combination lock.*

   ____

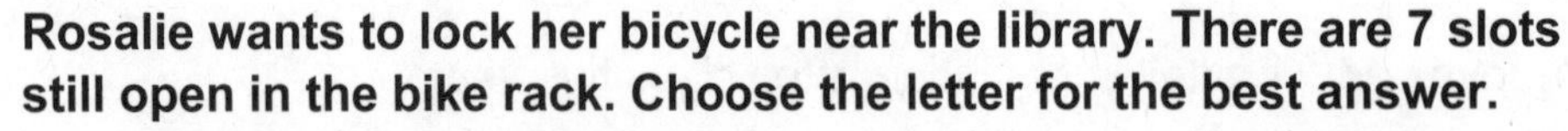

Rosalie wants to lock her bicycle near the library. There are 7 slots still open in the bike rack. Choose the letter for the best answer.

5. Rosalie arrives at the same time as 2 other cyclists. In how many ways can they arrange their bikes in the open slots?

   A 7　　C 210

   B 35　　D 343

6. Suppose Rosalie arrived just ahead of the 2 other cyclists and selected a slot. In how many ways can the others arrange their bikes in the open slots?

   F 2　　H 24

   G 15　　J 30

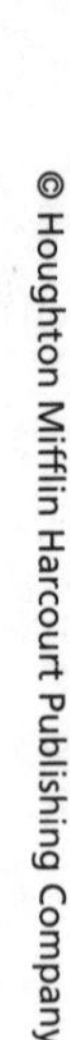

Name________________________ Class______________ Date__________

6-3

Theoretical and Experimental Probability

Connection: Sampling

Essential question: *How can you use probabilites to help you make fair decisions?*

Video Tutor

PREP FOR MCC9–12.S.MD.6(+)

1 ENGAGE Introducing a Decision-Making Problem

A small town has 25 residents. The state has given the town money that must be used for something that benefits the community. The town's mayor has decided that the money will be used to build a teen center or a senior center.

In order to make a decision about the type of community center to build, the mayor plans to survey a subset of town residents. There are two survey methods: a random sample and a convenience sample. The convenience sample will be conducted by surveying town residents at a local movie theater.

In the table below, each resident of the town is identified by a number from 1 to 25. The table shows each resident's preference: T for the teen center, S for the senior center. The table also gives the probability that each resident is at the movie theater when the convenience-sample survey is conducted.

1 S 0.2	**2** S 0.3	**3** T 0.8	**4** S 0.1	**5** T 0.8
6 T 0.7	**7** S 0.2	**8** T 0.8	**9** S 0.1	**10** S 0.3
11 S 0.1	**12** T 0.7	**13** S 0.2	**14** S 0.2	**15** S 0.4
16 T 0.6	**17** S 0.7	**18** S 0.1	**19** S 0.1	**20** T 0.6
21 S 0.3	**22** S 0.2	**23** S 0.3	**24** S 0.1	**25** T 0.9

REFLECT

1a. Based on the data in the table, what percent of all residents favor the teen center? the senior center?

____

1b. If it were possible for the mayor to survey every resident, what decision do you think the mayor would make? Why?

____

MCC9–12.S.MD.6(+)

2 EXPLORE Using a Random Sample

Suppose the mayor of the town is not able to survey every resident, so the mayor decides to survey a random sample of 10 residents.

A You can use your calculator to simulate the process of choosing and surveying a random sample of residents.

- Go to the MATH menu.
- Use the right arrow key to access the PRB menu.
- Use the down arrow key to select **5:randInt(** .
- Use "randInt(1,25)" as shown at the right.
- Each time you press Enter, the calculator will return a random integer from 1 to 25.

Generate 10 random integers in this way. For each integer, note the corresponding preference (T or S) of that resident of the town. (If a number is selected more than once, ignore the duplicates and choose a new number. This ensures that no resident is surveyed more than once.) Record your results in the table.

Resident Number										
Preference (T or S)										

B Based on the random sample, what percent of residents favor the teen center? the senior center?

____

REFLECT

2a. What is the probability that any resident is chosen to be part of the random sample? Explain.

____

____

2b. What decision do you think the mayor would make based on the random sample? Why?

____

2c. Compare your results with those of other students. In general, how well do the results of the random sample predict the preferences of the town as a whole?

____

MCC9–12.S.MD.6(+)

3 EXPLORE Using a Convenience Sample

The mayor of the town decides to use a convenience sample by surveying the first 10 residents of the town to leave a local movie theater.

A You can use slips of paper to simulate the process of choosing and surveying this convenience sample.

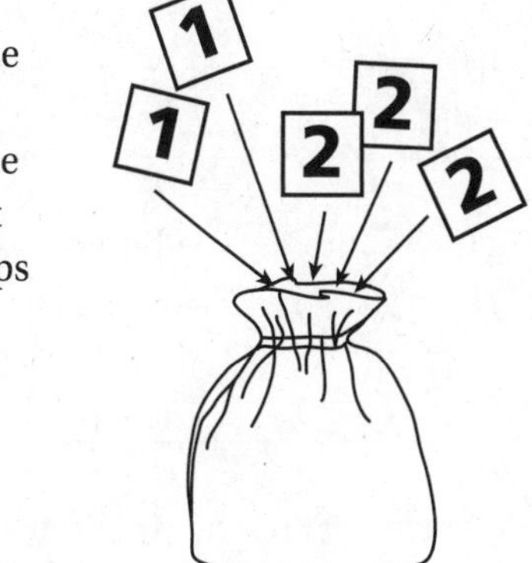

- For each resident, prepare 1 to 10 small slips of paper with the resident's number on them. The number of slips of paper is determined by the probability that the resident is at the movie theater when the survey is conducted. For example, Resident 1 has a 0.2 probability of being at the theater, so prepare 2 slips of paper with the number 1; Resident 2 has a 0.3 probability of being at the theater, so prepare 3 slips of paper with the number 2; and so on.
- Place all of the slips of paper in a bag and mix them well.
- Choose slips of paper one at a time without looking.

Choose 10 residents in this way. For each resident, note the corresponding preference (T or S) using the table on the first page of the lesson. (If a resident is selected more than once, ignore the duplicates and choose a new number from the bag. This ensures that no resident is surveyed more than once.) Record your results in the table.

Resident Number										
Preference (T or S)										

B Based on the convenience sample, what percent of residents favor the teen center? the senior center?

____

REFLECT

3a. Why do some residents of the town have more slips of paper representing them than other residents? How does this connect to the way the convenience sample is conducted?

____

____

____

____

3b. What decision do you think the mayor would make based on the convenience sample? Why?

3c. Compare your results with those of other students. In general, how well do the results of the convenience sample predict the preferences of the town as a whole?

3d. Which sampling method is more likely to lead to fair decision-making? Explain.

3e. What factors might explain why the results of the convenience sample are different from the results of the random sample?

3f. When you conduct the random-sample simulation is it possible that you might choose 10 residents who all favor the senior center? Is this result possible when you conduct the convenience-sample simulation? In which simulation do you think this result is more likely?

3g. What are some limitations or drawbacks of the simulations?

3h. In a town of 25 residents, it is likely that the mayor could actually survey all the residents, instead of using a random sample or convenience sample. What are some reasons that sampling might be used in situations involving populations that are much larger than 25?

Name________________________ Class________________ Date____________ 6-3

Additional Practice

The table represents a class of 30 students. Each student was asked if he or she would prefer having a written report (R) or an oral presentation (O) for the final. Use the table for Exercises 1–4.

1 R	2 R	3 O	4 R	5 O
6 R	7 R	8 R	9 O	10 R
11 O	12 O	13 R	14 R	15 R
16 R	17 O	18 R	19 R	20 R
21 R	22 R	23 O	24 R	25 R
26 O	27 R	28 O	29 R	30 R

1. Use a calculator or slips of paper to choose 10 random numbers from 1 to 30. Circle the 10 numbers you generate.
2. What is the probability of any given student being chosen for your sample?

____

3. According to your sample, what percent of the class would prefer to have a written report as the final?

____

4. What percent of the class would prefer to have a written report if you take into account *all* of the students? How does this compare to what you found in your sample?

____

____

5. Another teacher wants to survey his classes with the same question. He has three classes of 90 students each. Explain a way he could collect responses from a random sample of 10% of his students. The sample should have equal representation for each of the three classes.

____

____

Problem Solving

The council of a city of 200,000 people is deciding on one of two improvement projects. The two proposed projects are (1) creating bike lanes in the downtown area and (2) repairing a road that passes through the suburbs. An employee of the city takes a survey of 50 people near his house in the suburbs. Of those surveyed, 45 people said they would prefer the road repair. Use this information for Exercises 1–4.

1. According to the survey, what percent of the city residents prefer the road repair project?

____

2. The city employee calculates that every city resident had a $\frac{50}{200,000} = \frac{1}{4,000}$ probability of being chosen for his survey. Do you agree? Explain why or why not.

____

____

3. Is the sample a random sample or a convenience sample? Explain your reasoning.

____

____

4. Do you think it's likely that the sample represents the population as a whole? Explain why or why not.

____

____

____

Select the best answer.

5. A survey asks a question of 30 people out of a total of 3,000 visiting a mall in one day. If the sample is random, what is the probability of any given person being surveyed?

   A 1%   C 10%

   B 3%   D 30%

6. A survey finds that 65% of town residents support leash laws. If that number was found by taking a sample of 40 residents, how many people in the sample support leash laws?

   F 12   H 40

   G 26   J 6

Name________________ Class__________ Date________

7-1

Independent and Dependent Events

Going Deeper

Essential question: *How do you find the probability of independent and dependent events?*

Video Tutor

Two events are **independent events** if the occurrence of one event does not affect the occurrence of the other event. For example, rolling a 1 on a number cube and choosing an ace at random from a deck of cards are independent events.

If two events A and B are independent events, then the fact that event B has occurred does not affect the probability of event A. In other words, for independent events A and B, $P(A) = P(A \mid B)$. You can use this as a criterion to determine whether two events are independent.

MCC9–12.S.CP.4

1 EXAMPLE Determining If Events are Independent

An airport employee collects data on 180 random flights that arrive at the airport. The data is shown in the two-way table. Is a late arrival independent of the flight being an international flight? Why or why not?

	Late Arrival	On Time	TOTAL
Domestic Flight	12	108	120
International Flight	6	54	60
TOTAL	18	162	180

A Let event A be the event that a flight arrives late. Let event B be the event that a flight is an international flight.

To find $P(A)$, first note that there is a total of ________ flights.

Of these flights, there is a total of ________ late flights.

So, $P(A) = \frac{\square}{\square} =$ ________.

To find $P(A \mid B)$, first note that there is a total of ________ international flights.

Of these flights, there is a total of ________ late flights.

So, $P(A \mid B) = \frac{\square}{\square} =$ ________.

B Compare $P(A)$ and $P(A \mid B)$.

So, a late arrival is independent of the flight being an international flight because

____

____

REFLECT

1a. In the example, you compared $P(A)$ and $P(A \mid B)$. Suppose you compare $P(B)$ and $P(B \mid A)$. What do you find? What does this tell you?

____

You can use a tree diagram to help you understand the formula for the probability of independent events. For example, consider tossing a coin two times. The outcome of one toss does not affect the outcome of the other toss, so the events are independent.

The tree diagram shows that the probability of the coin landing heads up on both tosses is $\frac{1}{4}$ because this is 1 of 4 equally-likely outcomes at the end of Toss 2. This probability is simply the product of the probabilities of the coin landing heads up on each individual toss: $\frac{1}{2} \cdot \frac{1}{2} = \frac{1}{4}$.

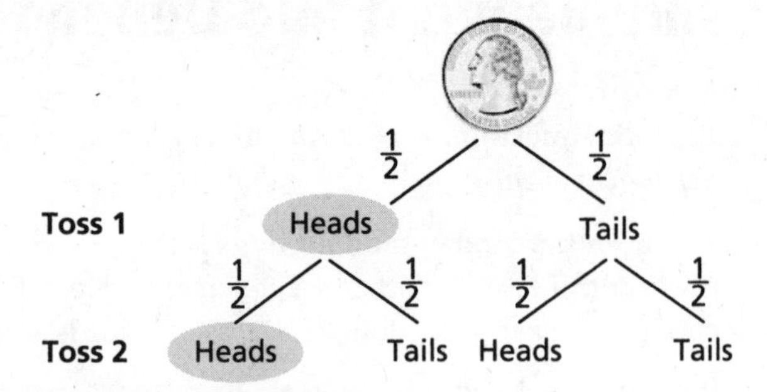

Probability of Independent Events

A and B are independent events if and only if $P(A \text{ and } B) = P(A) \cdot P(B)$.

MCC9–12.S.CP.3

2 EXAMPLE Using the Formula

You spin the spinner at right two times. What is the probability that you spin an even number on the first spin followed by an odd number on the second spin?

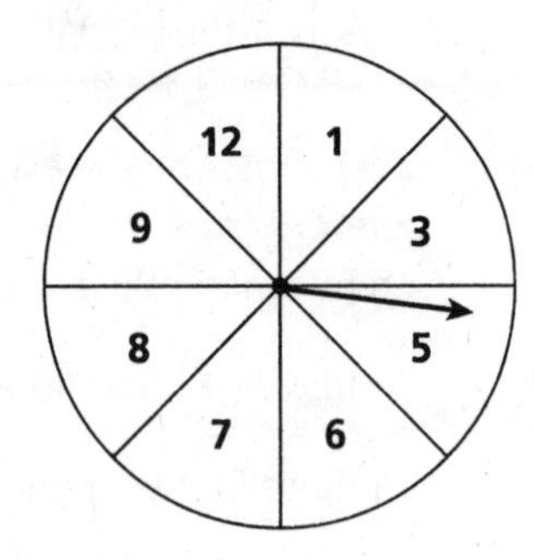

A Let event A be the event that you spin an even number on the first spin. Let event B be the event that you spin an odd number on the second spin.

$P(A) = \frac{\quad}{\quad}$ $P(B) = \frac{\quad}{\quad}$

B The outcome of the first spin does not affect the outcome of the second spin, so the events are independent events.

$P(A \text{ and } B) = P(A) \cdot P(B)$ Use the formula for independent events.

$= (\_\_\_\_\_) \cdot (\_\_\_\_\_)$ Substitute.

$= \_\_\_\_\_\_$ Simplify.

So, the probability that you spin an even number on the first spin followed by an odd number on the second spin is ________.

REFLECT

2a. What is the probability that you spin an odd number on the first spin followed by an even number on the second spin? What do you notice?

The formula for the probability of independent events gives you another way to determine whether two events are independent. That is, two events A and B are independent events if $P(A \text{ and } B) = P(A) \cdot P(B)$.

MCC9–12.S.CP.2

3 EXAMPLE Showing that Events are Independent

The two-way table shows the data from the first example. Show that a flight arriving on time and a flight being a domestic flight are independent events.

	Late Arrival	On Time	TOTAL
Domestic Flight	12	108	120
International Flight	6	54	60
TOTAL	18	162	180

A Let event A be the event that a flight arrives on time. Let event B be the event that a flight is a domestic flight.

To find $P(A)$, $P(B)$, and $P(A \text{ and } B)$ note that there is a total of ________ flights.

There is a total of ________ on-time flights.

So, $P(A) = \frac{\square}{\square} = \frac{\square}{\square}$.

There is a total of ________ domestic flights.

So, $P(B) = \frac{\square}{\square} = \frac{\square}{\square}$.

There is a total of ________ on-time domestic flights.

So, $P(A \text{ and } B) = \frac{\square}{\square} = \frac{\square}{\square}$.

B Compare $P(A \text{ and } B)$ and $P(A) \cdot P(B)$.

$P(A) \cdot P(B) = (\_\_\_\_) \cdot (\_\_\_\_) = \_\_\_\_$

So, the events are independent events because

____

REFLECT

3a. Describe a different way you can show that a flight arriving on time and a flight being a domestic flight are independent events.

____

____

PREP FOR MCC9–12.S.CP.8(+)

4 ENGAGE — Introducing Dependent Events

Two events are **dependent events** if the occurrence of one event affects the occurrence of the other event.

Suppose you have a bag containing 2 blue marbles and 2 black marbles. You choose a marble without looking, put it aside, and then choose a second marble. Consider the following events.

Event A: The first marble you choose is blue.

Event B: The second marble you choose is black.

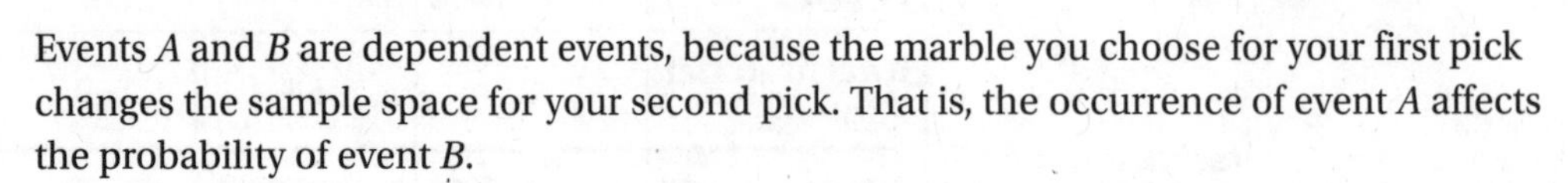

Events A and B are dependent events, because the marble you choose for your first pick changes the sample space for your second pick. That is, the occurrence of event A affects the probability of event B.

Recall that you developed the following formula for conditional probability.

$$P(B \mid A) = \frac{P(A \text{ and } B)}{P(A)}$$

Multiplying both sides by $P(A)$ results in $P(A) \cdot P(B \mid A) = P(A \text{ and } B)$. This is known as the Multiplication Rule.

Multiplication Rule

$P(A \text{ and } B) = P(A) \cdot P(B \mid A)$, where $P(B \mid A)$ is the conditional probability of event B, given that event A has occurred.

You can use the Multiplication Rule to find the probability of dependent or independent events. Note that when A and B are independent events, $P(B \mid A) = P(B)$ and the rule may be rewritten as $P(A \text{ and } B) = P(A) \cdot P(B)$, which is the rule for independent events.

REFLECT

4a. How can you write the Multiplication Rule in a different way by starting with the formula for the conditional probability $P(A \mid B)$ and multiplying both sides of that equation by $P(B)$?

____

____

MCC9–12.S.CP.8(+)

5 EXAMPLE — Finding the Probability of Dependent Events

There are 5 tiles with the letters A, B, C, D, and E in a bag. You choose a tile without looking, put it aside, and then choose another tile. Find the probability that you choose a consonant followed by a vowel.

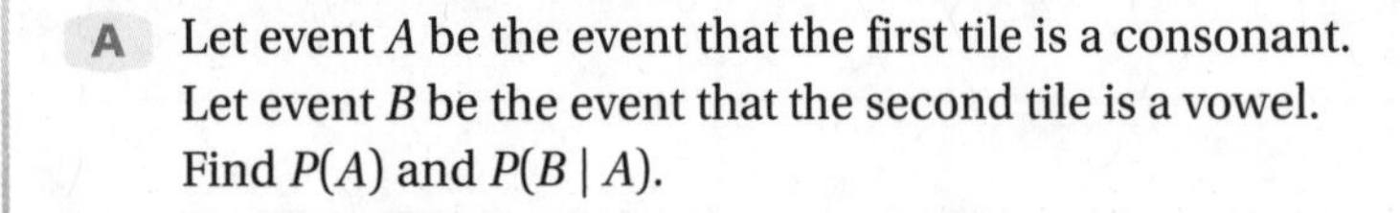

A Let event A be the event that the first tile is a consonant.
Let event B be the event that the second tile is a vowel.
Find $P(A)$ and $P(B \mid A)$.

$P(A) = \frac{\square}{\square}$ Of the 5 tiles, 3 are consonants.

$P(B \mid A) = \frac{\_\_\_}{\_\_\_} = \frac{\_\_\_}{\_\_\_}$ Of the 4 remaining tiles, 2 are vowels.

B Use the Multiplication Rule.

$P(A \text{ and } B) = P(A) \cdot P(B \mid A)$ Use the Multiplication Rule.

$= (\_\_\_\_\_) \cdot (\_\_\_\_\_)$ Substitute.

$= \_\_\_\_\_\_\_\_$ Multiply.

So, the probability that you choose a consonant followed by a vowel is ________.

REFLECT

5a. Complete the tree diagram below. Then explain how you can use it to check your answer.

1st tile A B C

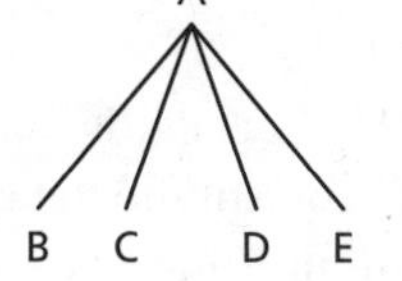

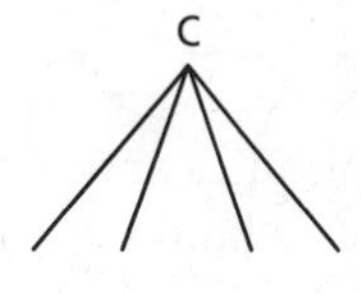

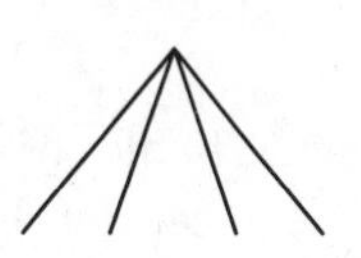

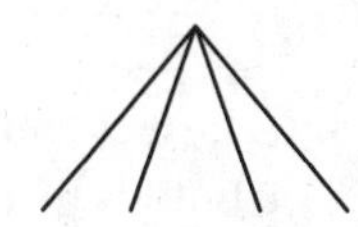

2nd tile B C D E A C D E

____

____

____

5b. What does your answer tell you about the likelihood of choosing a consonant followed by a vowel?

____

PRACTICE

1. A farmer wants to know if an insecticide is effective in preventing small insects called aphids from living on tomato plants. The farmer checks 80 plants. The data is shown in the two-way table. Is having aphids independent of being sprayed with the insecticide? Why or why not?

	Has Aphids	No Aphids	TOTAL
Was sprayed with insecticide	12	40	52
Was not sprayed with insecticide	14	14	28
TOTAL	26	54	80

____

____

2. A student wants to know if right-handed people are more or less likely to play a musical instrument than left-handed people. The student collects data from 250 people, as shown in the two-way table. Show that being right handed and playing a musical instrument are independent events.

	Right Handed	Left Handed	TOTAL
Plays a musical instrument	44	6	50
Does not play a musical instrument	176	24	200
TOTAL	220	30	250

____

____

____

3. A basket contains 6 bottles of apple juice and 8 bottles of grape juice. You choose a bottle without looking, put it aside, and then choose another bottle. What is the probability that you choose a bottle of apple juice followed by a bottle of grape juice?

____

4. You have a set of ten cards that are numbered 1 through 10. You shuffle the cards and choose a card at random. You put the card aside and choose another card. What is the probability that you choose an even number followed by an odd number?

____

5. There are 12 boys and 14 girls in Ms. Garcia's class. She chooses a student at random to solve a geometry problem at the board. Then she chooses another student at random to check the first student's work. Is she more likely to choose a boy followed by a girl, a girl followed by a boy, or are these both equally likely? Explain.

____

____

____

6. A bag contains 4 blue marbles and 4 red marbles. You choose a marble without looking, put it aside, and then choose another marble. Is there a greater than or less than 50% chance that you choose two marbles with different colors? Explain.

____

____

____

Name ______________________ Class ____________ Date __________

7-1

Additional Practice

Find each probability.

1. A bag contains 5 red, 3 green, 4 blue, and 8 yellow marbles. Find the probability of randomly selecting a green marble, and then a yellow marble if the first marble is replaced. ____________
2. A sock drawer contains 5 rolled-up pairs of each color of socks, white, green, and blue. What is the probability of randomly selecting a pair of blue socks, replacing it, and then randomly selecting a pair of white socks? ____________

Two 1–6 number cubes are rolled—one is black and one is white.

3. The sum of the rolls is greater than or equal to 6 and the black cube shows a 3.
   a. Explain why the events are dependent.
   ____
   b. Find the probability. ____________
4. The white cube shows an even number, and the sum is 8.
   a. Explain why the events are dependent.
   ____
   b. Find the probability. ____________

The table below shows numbers of registered voters by age in the United States in 2004 based on the census. Find each probability in decimal form.

Age	Registered Voters (in thousands)	Not Registered to Vote (in thousands)
18–24	14,334	13,474
25–44	49,371	32,763
45–64	51,659	19,355
65 and over	26,706	8,033

5. A randomly selected person is registered to vote, given that the person is between the ages of 18 and 24. ____________
6. A randomly selected person is between the ages of 45 and 64 and is not registered to vote. ____________
7. A randomly selected person is registered to vote and is at least 65 years old. ____________

A bag contains 12 blue cubes, 12 red cubes, and 20 green cubes. Determine whether the events are independent or dependent, and find each probability.

8. A green cube and then a blue cube are chosen at random with replacement. ____________
9. Two blue cubes are chosen at random without replacement. ____________

Problem Solving

The table shows student participation in different sports at a high school. Suppose a student is selected at random.

Sports Participation by Grade					
	Track	Volleyball	Basketball	Tennis	No Sport
Grade 9	12	18	15	9	66
Grade 10	6	20	12	2	95
Grade 11	15	11	8	5	61
Grade 12	7	6	10	12	50

1. What is the probability that a student is in grade 10 and runs track?
   a. Find the probability that a student is in grade 10, $P(10)$. ________________
   b. Find the probability that a student runs track, given that the student is in grade 10, $P(Tr \mid 10)$, ________________
   c. Find $P(10 \text{ and } Tr) = P(10) \cdot P(Tr \mid 10)$. ________________
2. What is the probability that a student is in grade 12 and runs track or plays tennis?
   a. Find the probability that a student is in grade 12, $P(12)$. ________________
   b. Find the probability that a student runs track or plays tennis, given that the student is in grade 12, $P(Tr \text{ or } Te \mid 12)$. ________________
   c. Find $P(12 \text{ or } (Tr \text{ or } Te))$. ________________
3. During a fire drill, the students are waiting in the parking lot. What is the probability that one student is in grade 12 and runs track or plays tennis, and the student standing next to her is in grade 10 and runs track?
   a. Find the probability for the first student. ________________
   b. Find the probability for the second student. ________________
   c. Find the probability for the event occurring. ________________
   d. Are these events independent or dependent? Explain.

____

Samantha is 1 of 17 students in a class of 85 who have decided to pursue a business degree. Each week, a student in the class is randomly selected to tutor younger students. Choose the letter for the best answer.

4. What is the probability of drawing a business student one week, replacing the name, and drawing the same name the next week?

   A 3.4
   B 0.2
   C 0.04
   D 0.002

5. What is the probability of drawing Samantha's name one week, not replacing her name, and drawing the name of another business student the next week?

   F $\frac{1}{85} \cdot \frac{16}{84}$
   G $\frac{1}{85} \cdot \frac{17}{84}$
   H $\frac{17}{85} \cdot \frac{16}{84}$
   J $\frac{17}{85} \cdot \frac{17}{84}$

Name ______________________ Class ______________ Date ________

7-2

Two-Way Tables

Going Deeper

Essential question: *How do you calculate a conditional probability?*

Video Tutor

The probability that event B occurs given that event A has already occurred is called the **conditional probability** of B given A and is written $P(B \mid A)$.

MCC9–12.S.CP.6

1 EXAMPLE Finding Conditional Probabilities

One hundred people who frequently get migraine headaches were chosen to participate in a study of a new anti-headache medicine. Some of the participants were given the medicine; others were not. After one week, the participants were asked if they got a headache during the week. The two-way table summarizes the results.

	Took Medicine	No Medicine	TOTAL
Headache	12	15	27
No Headache	48	25	73
TOTAL	60	40	100

A **To the nearest percent, what is the probability that a participant who took the medicine did not get a headache?**

Let event A be the event that a participant took the medicine. Let event B be the event that a participant did not get a headache.

To find the probability that a participant who took the medicine did not get a headache, you must find $P(B \mid A)$. You are only concerned with participants who took the medicine, so look at the data in the "Took Medicine" column.

There were ________ participants who took the medicine.

Of these participants, ________ participants did not get a headache.

So, $P(B \mid A) = \frac{\square}{\square} =$ ________.

B **To the nearest percent, what is the probability that a participant who did not get a headache took the medicine?**

To find the probability that a participant who did not get a headache took the medicine, you must find $P(A \mid B)$. You are only concerned with participants who did not get a headache, so look at the data in the "No headache" row.

There were ________ participants who did not get a headache.

Of these participants, ________ participants took the medicine.

So, $P(A \mid B) = \frac{\square}{\square} \approx$ ________.

REFLECT

1a. In general, do you think $P(B \mid A) = P(A \mid B)$? Why or why not?

1b. How can you use set notation to represent the event that a participant took the medicine and did not get a headache? Is the probability that a participant took the medicine and did not get a headache equal to either of the conditional probabilities you calculated in the example?

MCC9–12.S.CP.3

2 EXPLORE Developing a Formula for Conditional Probability

You can generalize your work from the previous example to develop a formula for finding conditional probabilities.

A Recall how you calculated $P(B \mid A)$, the probability that a participant who took the medicine did not get a headache.

You found that $P(B \mid A) = \frac{48}{60}$.

Use the table shown here to help you write this quotient in terms of events A and B.

		Event A		
		Took Medicine	No Medicine	TOTAL
	Headache	12	15	27
Event B	No Headache	48 = $n(A \cap B)$	25	73 = $n(B)$
	TOTAL	60 = $n(A)$	40	100

$P(B \mid A) = \frac{\square}{\square}$

B Now divide the numerator and denominator of the quotient by $n(S)$, the number of outcomes in the sample space. This converts the counts to probabilities.

$P(B \mid A) = \frac{\square / n(S)}{\square / n(S)} = \frac{\square}{\square}$

REFLECT

2a. Write a formula for $P(A \mid B)$ in terms of $n(A \cap B)$ and $n(B)$.

2b. Write a formula for $P(A \mid B)$ in terms of $P(A \cap B)$ and $P(B)$.

You may have discovered the following formula for conditional probability.

Conditional Probability

The conditional probability of B given A (the probability that event B occurs given that event A occurs) is given by the following formula:

$$P(B \mid A) = \frac{P(A \cap B)}{P(A)}$$

MCC9–12.S.CP.3

3 EXAMPLE Using the Conditional Probability Formula

In a standard deck of playing cards, find the probability that a red card is a queen.

A Let event Q be the event that a card is a queen. Let event R be the event that a card is red. You are asked to find $P(Q \mid R)$. First find $P(R \cap Q)$ and $P(R)$.

$R \cap Q$ represents cards that are both red and a queen; that is, red queens.

There are ________ red queens in the deck of 52 cards, so $P(R \cap Q) =$ ________.

There are ________ red cards in the deck, so $P(R) =$ ________.

B Use the formula for conditional probability.

$P(Q \mid R) = \frac{P(Q \cap R)}{P(R)} =$ ______ Substitute probabilities from above.

$=$ ______ Multiply numerator and denominator by 52.

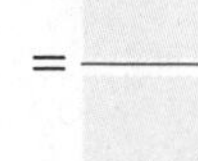

$=$ ______ Simplify.

So, the probability that a red card is a queen is ________.

REFLECT

3a. How can you interpret the probability you calculated above?

____

____

3b. Is the probability that a red card is a queen equal to the probability that a queen is red? Explain.

____

PRACTICE

1. In order to study the connection between the amount of sleep a student gets and his or her school performance, data was collected about 120 students. The two-way table shows the number of students who passed and failed an exam and the number of students who got more or less than 6 hours of sleep the night before.

	Passed Exam	Failed Exam	TOTAL
Less than 6 hours of sleep	12	10	22
More than 6 hours of sleep	90	8	98
TOTAL	102	18	120

a. To the nearest percent, what is the probability that a student who failed the exam got less than 6 hours of sleep? ________

b. To the nearest percent, what is the probability that a student who got less than 6 hours of sleep failed the exam? ________

c. To the nearest percent, what is the probability that a student got less than 6 hours of sleep and failed the exam? ________

2. A botanist studied the effect of a new fertilizer by choosing 100 orchids and giving 70% of these plants the fertilizer. Of the plants that got the fertilizer, 40% produced flowers within a month. Of the plants that did not get the fertilizer, 10% produced flowers within a month. Find each probability to the nearest percent. (*Hint:* Construct a two-way table.)

a. Find the probability that a plant that produced flowers got the fertilizer. ________

b. Find the probability that a plant that got the fertilizer produced flowers. ________

3. At a school fair, a box contains 24 yellow balls and 76 red balls. One-fourth of the balls of each color are labeled "Win a prize." Find each probability as a percent.

a. Find the probability that a ball labeled "Win a prize" is yellow. ________

b. Find the probability that a ball labeled "Win a prize" is red. ________

c. Find the probability that a ball is labeled "Win a prize" and is red. ________

d. Find the probability that a yellow ball is labeled "Win a prize." ________

In Exercises 4–9, consider a standard deck of playing cards and the following events: A: the card is an ace; B: the card is black; C: the card is a club. Find each probability as a fraction.

4. $P(A \mid B)$ ________

5. $P(B \mid A)$ ________

6. $P(A \mid C)$ ________

7. $P(C \mid A)$ ________

8. $P(B \mid C)$ ________

9. $P(C \mid B)$ ________

Additional Practice

1. The table shows the results of a customer satisfaction survey of 100 randomly selected shoppers at the mall who were asked if they would shop at an earlier time if the mall opened earlier. Complete the table below and use it to answer parts **a** and **b**.

	Ages 10–20	Ages 21–45	Ages 46–65	Ages Over 65
Yes	13	2	8	24
No	25	10	15	3

	Ages 10–20	Ages 21–45	Ages 46–65	Ages Over 65	Total
Yes					
No					
Total					

a. To the nearest whole percent, what is the probability that a shopper who is in the age range 21 to 45 said that he or she would shop earlier?

____

b. To the nearest whole percent, what is the probability that a shopper who would shop earlier is in the age range 65 and older?

____

2. Jerrod collected data on 100 randomly selected students, and summarized the results in a table.

		Owns an MP3 player	
		Yes	**No**
Owns a	**Yes**	28	12
Smart phone	**No**	34	26

a. If you are given that a student owns an MP3 player, what is the probability that the student also owns a smart phone? Round your answer to the nearest hundredth.

____

b. If you are given that a student owns a smart phone, what is the probability that the student also owns an MP3 player? Round your answer to the nearest hundredth.

____

Problem Solving

1. The table shows the number of students who would drive to school if the school provided parking spaces. Complete the table below and use it to answer parts **a** and **b**.

	Lowerclassmates	Upperclassmates
Always	32	122
Sometimes	58	44
Never	24	120

a. To the nearest whole percent, what is the probability that a student who said "always" is an upperclassmate?

____

b. To the nearest whole percent, what is the probability that a lowerclassmate said "always" or "sometimes"?

____

2. Gerry collected data and did a table of marginal relative frequencies on the number of students who participate in chorus and the number who participate in band.

		Chorus	
		Yes	**No**
Band	**Yes**	38	29
	No	9	24

a. If you are given that a student is in chorus, what is the probability that the student also is in band? Round your answer to the nearest hundredth.

____

b. If you are given that a student is not in band, what is the probability that the student is in chorus? Round your answer to the nearest hundredth.

____

Use the table in Exercise 2 to answer Exercises 3 and 4. Select the best answer.

3. What is the probability if a student is not in chorus, then that student is in band?

A 0.29　　B 0.38

C 0.43　　D 0.55

4. What is the probability that if a student is not in band then the student is not in chorus?

F 0.09　　G 0.33

H 0.44　　J 0.73

Name ____________________ Class ____________ Date ________

7-3

Compound Events

Going Deeper

Video Tutor

Essential question: *How do you find the probability of mutually exclusive events and overlapping events?*

Two events are **mutually exclusive events** if the events cannot both occur in the same trial of an experiment. For example, when you toss a coin, the coin landing heads up and the coin landing tails up are mutually exclusive events.

PREP FOR MCC9–12.S.CP.7

1 EXAMPLE Finding the Probability of Mutually Exclusive Events

A dodecahedral number cube has 12 sides numbered 1 through 12. What is the probability that you roll the cube and the result is an even number or a 7?

A Let event A be the event that you roll an even number. Let event B be the event that you roll a 7. Let S be the sample space.

Complete the Venn diagram by writing all outcomes in the sample space in the appropriate region.

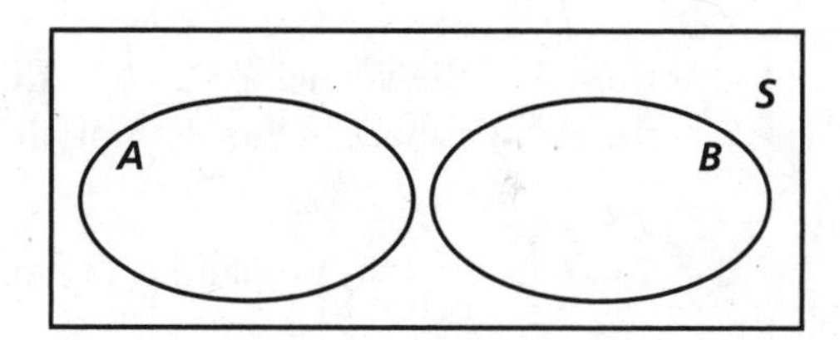

B You must find the probability of A or B.

$n(S) =$ ________

$n(A \text{ or } B) = n(A) + n(B)$ — A and B are mutually exclusive events.

$=$ ________ $+$ ________ — Use the Venn diagram to find $n(A)$ and $n(B)$.

$=$ ________ — Add.

So, $P(A \text{ or } B) = \frac{n(A \text{ or } B)}{n(S)} =$ ________.

REFLECT

1a. Does the probability you calculated seem reasonable? Why?

____

____

1b. Is it always true that $n(A \text{ or } B) = n(A) + n(B)$? Explain.

____

1c. How is $P(A \text{ or } B)$ related to $P(A)$ and $P(B)$? Do you think this is always true?

____

____

The process you used in the example can be generalized to give a formula for the probability of mutually exclusive events.

Mutually Exclusive Events

If A and B are mutually exclusive events, then $P(A \text{ or } B) = P(A) + P(B)$.

Two events are **overlapping events** (or *inclusive events*) if they have one or more outcomes in common.

PREP FOR MCC9–12.S.CP.7

2 EXAMPLE Finding the Probability of Overlapping Events

What is the probability that you roll a dodecahedral number cube and the result is an even number or a number greater than 7?

A Let event A be the event that you roll an even number. Let event B be the event that you roll a number greater than 7. Let S be the sample space.

Complete the Venn diagram by writing all outcomes in the sample space in the appropriate region.

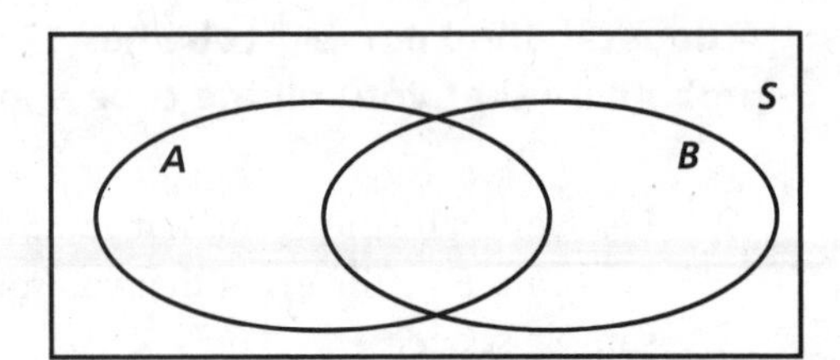

B You must find the probability of A or B.

$n(S) =$ ______

$n(A \text{ or } B) = n(A) + n(B) - n(A \text{ and } B)$ — A and B are overlapping events.

$=$ ______ $+$ ______ $-$ ______ — Use the Venn diagram.

$=$ ______ — Simplify.

So, $P(A \text{ or } B) = \frac{n(A \text{ or } B)}{n(S)} = \frac{\_\_\_}{\_\_\_} = \frac{\_\_\_}{\_\_\_}$.

REFLECT

2a. Why is $n(A \text{ or } B)$ equal to $n(A) + n(B) - n(A \text{ and } B)$?

____

____

____

____

2b. Is $P(A \text{ or } B)$ equal to $P(A) + P(B)$ in this case? Explain.

____

In the previous example you saw that for overlapping events A and B, $n(A \cup B) = n(A) + n(B) - n(A \cap B)$. You can convert these counts to probabilities by dividing each term by $n(S)$ as shown below.

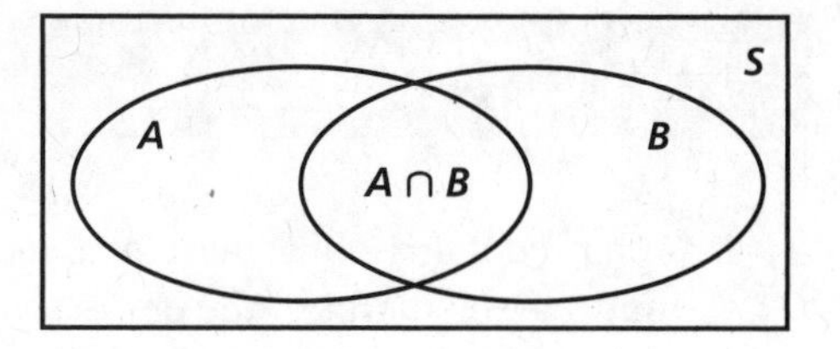

$$\frac{n(A \cup B)}{n(S)} = \frac{n(A)}{n(S)} + \frac{n(B)}{n(S)} - \frac{n(A \cap B)}{n(S)}$$

Rewriting each term as a probability results in the following rule.

Addition Rule

$P(A \text{ or } B) = P(A) + P(B) - P(A \text{ and } B)$

Notice that when A and B are mutually exclusive events, $P(A \text{ and } B) = 0$, and the rule becomes the simpler rule for mutually exclusive events on the previous page.

MCC9–12.S.CP.7

3 EXAMPLE Using the Addition Rule

You shuffle a standard deck of playing cards and choose a card at random. What is the probability that you choose a king or a heart?

A Let event A be the event that you choose a king. Let event B be the event that you choose a heart. Let S be the sample space.

There are 52 cards in the deck, so $n(S) =$ ________.

There are 4 kings in the deck, so $n(A) =$ ________ and $P(A) =$ ________.

There are 13 hearts in the deck, so $n(B) =$ ________ and $P(B) =$ ________.

There is one king of hearts in the deck, so $P(A \text{ and } B) =$ ________.

B Use the Addition Rule.

$P(A \text{ or } B) = P(A) + P(B) - P(A \text{ and } B)$

= ________ + ________ − ________ Substitute.

= ________ or ________ Simplify.

So, the probability of choosing a king or a heart is ________.

REFLECT

3a. What does the answer tell you about the likelihood of choosing a king or a heart from the deck?

____

____

PRACTICE

1. A bag contains 3 blue marbles, 5 red marbles, and 4 green marbles. You choose a marble without looking. What is the probability that you choose a red marble or a green marble?

2. An icosahedral number cube has 20 sides numbered 1 through 20. What is the probability that you roll the cube and the result is a number that is less than 4 or greater than 11?

3. A bag contains 26 tiles, each with a different letter of the alphabet written on it. You choose a tile without looking. What is the probability that you choose a vowel or a letter in the word GEOMETRY?

4. You roll two number cubes at the same time. Each cube has sides numbered 1 through 6. What is the probability that the sum of the numbers rolled is even or greater than 9?

5. You shuffle a standard deck of playing cards and choose a card at random. What is the probability that you choose a face card (jack, queen, or king) or a club?

6. You have a set of 25 cards numbered 1 through 25. You shuffle the cards and choose a card at random. What is the probability that you choose a multiple of 3 or a multiple of 4?

7. The two-way table provides data on the students at a high school. You randomly choose a student at the school. Find each probability.

	Freshman	Sophomore	Junior	Senior	TOTAL
Boy	98	104	100	94	396
Girl	102	106	96	108	412
TOTAL	200	210	196	202	808

a. The student is a senior. ________

b. The student is a girl. ________

c. The student is a senior and a girl. ________

d. The student is a senior or a girl. ________

8. A survey of the 1108 employees at a software company finds that 621 employees take a bus to work and 445 employees take a train to work. Some employees take both a bus and a train, and 312 employees take only a train. To the nearest percent, what is the probability that a randomly-chosen employee takes a bus or a train to work? (*Hint:* Make a Venn diagram.)

9. Suppose A and B are complementary events. Explain how you can rewrite the Addition Rule in a simpler form for this case.

Name__________ Class__________ Date__________

Additional Practice

A can of vegetables with no label has a $\frac{1}{8}$ chance of being green beans and a $\frac{1}{5}$ chance of being corn.

1. Explain why the events "green beans" and "corn" are mutually exclusive.

____

2. What is the probability that an unlabeled can of vegetables is either green beans or corn? __________

Ben rolls a 1–6 number cube. Find each probability.

3. Ben rolls a 3 or a 4. __________
4. Ben rolls a number greater than 2 or an even number. __________
5. Ben rolls a prime number or an odd number. __________

Of the 400 doctors who attended a conference, 240 practiced family medicine and 130 were from countries outside the United States. One-third of the family medicine practitioners were not from the United States.

6. What is the probability that a doctor practices family medicine or is from the United States? __________
7. What is the probability that a doctor practices family medicine or is not from the United States? __________
8. What is the probability that a doctor does not practice family medicine or is from the United States? __________

Use the data to fill in the Venn diagram. Then solve.

9. Of the 220 people who came into the Italian deli on Friday, 104 bought pizza and 82 used a credit card. Half of the people who bought pizza used a credit card. What is the probability that a customer bought pizza or used a credit card?

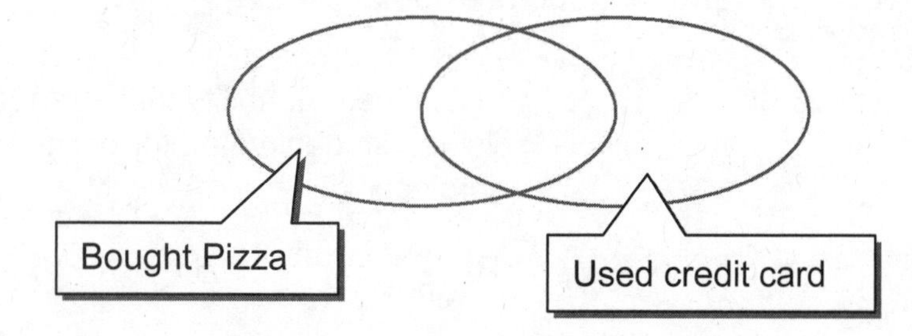

____

Solve.

10. There are 6 people in a gardening club. Each gardener orders seeds from a list of 11 different types of seeds available. What is the probability that 2 gardeners will order the same type of seeds? __________

Problem Solving

Of 100 students surveyed, 44 are male and 54 are in favor of a change to a 9-period, 4-day school week. Of those in favor, 20 are female. One student is picked at random from those surveyed.

1. What is the probability that the student is male or favors the change? Use the Venn diagram.

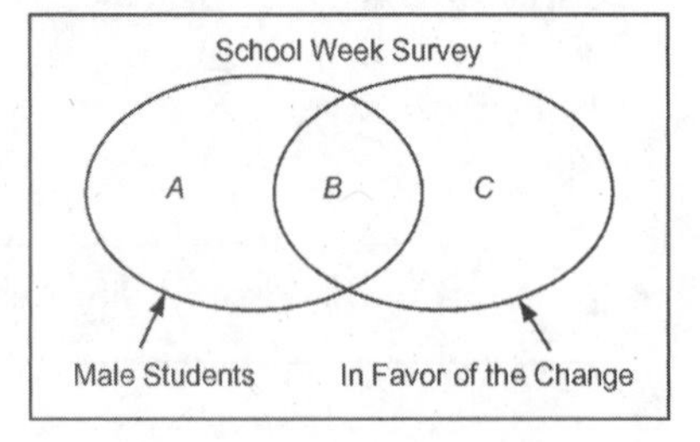

   a. What is represented by the total of $A + B$?

   ____

   b. What is represented by the total of $B + C$?

   ____

   c. How many of those in favor of the change are male? _______________

   d. Find the values for A, B, and C and label the diagram.

   e. Write and evaluate an expression for the probability that the student is male or favors the change. _______________

2. What is the probability that the student is female or opposes the change?

   a. How many students are female? _______________

   b. How many students oppose the change? _______________

   c. If you draw a Venn diagram to show females and those opposed to the change, what is the meaning and value of the overlapping area?

   ____

   d. Write and evaluate an expression for the probability that the student is female or opposes the change. _______________

3. Of the students surveyed, 27 plan to start their own businesses. Of those, 18 are in favor of the change to the school week. Write and evaluate an expression for the probability that a student selected at random plans to start his or her own business or favors the change.

   ____

Sean asks each student to cast a vote for the type of class he or she would prefer. Of the students, 55% voted for online classes, 30% voted for projects, and 15% voted for following the textbook. Choose the letter for the best answer.

4. Which description best describes Sean's experiment?

   A Simple events

   B Compound events

   C Mutually exclusive events

   D Inclusive events

5. What is the probability that a randomly selected student voted for online classes or projects?

   F $\frac{33}{200}$

   G $\frac{7}{10}$

   H $\frac{1}{4}$

   J $\frac{17}{20}$

Performance Tasks

GPS COMMON CORE
MCC9-12.S.CP.1
MCC9-12.S.CP.2
MCC9-12.S.CP.3
MCC9-12.S.CP.5
MCC9-12.S.CP.6
MCC9-12.S.CP.7
MCC9-12.S.CP.9(+)

★ **1.** Sam is playing a board game. He rolls a number cube to see how many spaces he can move. To win, he must land on the WIN! square. If he passes it, he must move back to the beginning of the board.

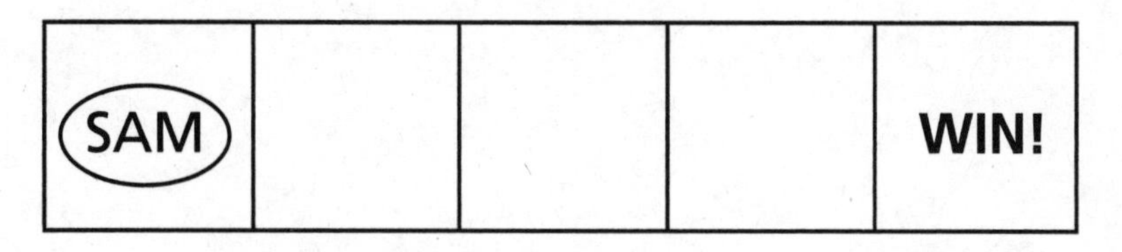

What is the probability that Sam wins on this roll? Is this event the complement of the event "Sam moves back to beginning"? Explain.

★ **2.** Kiki surveyed a random sample of 30 registered voters in a neighborhood and asked if they had voted in the last election. Twelve voters answered yes. The neighborhood has 525 registered voters. Based on this data, what is the probability that a person in the neighborhood voted in the last election given that he or she is a registered voter?

★★ **3.** The Teacup serves 20 different teas. Of the 20 teas, 14 of them contain caffeine, and 12 of them are organic. Alice selects a tea at random. Her friend Mel then randomly selects a different tea than Alice.

continued

a. Let A be the event that Alice selects a tea with caffeine, and B be the event that Mel selects a tea with caffeine. Are the events independent? Explain.

b. Two of the teas are neither caffeinated nor organic. Draw a Venn diagram to show how many of each type of tea there are.

c. A tea is selected at random. Determine $P(\text{tea is organic} \mid \text{tea is caffeinated})$.

4. Shannon is designing a target of 3 concentric circles. From inside to outside, the colors are yellow, blue, and white. She wants the probabilities of randomly hitting yellow to be 15%, of randomly hitting blue to be 35%, and of randomly hitting white to be 50%. The radius of the entire target will be 9 inches.

a. Find the radius of each concentric circle to the nearest tenth of an inch. Show your work.

b. How wide will the blue and white circular bands be? Round to the nearest tenth of an inch.

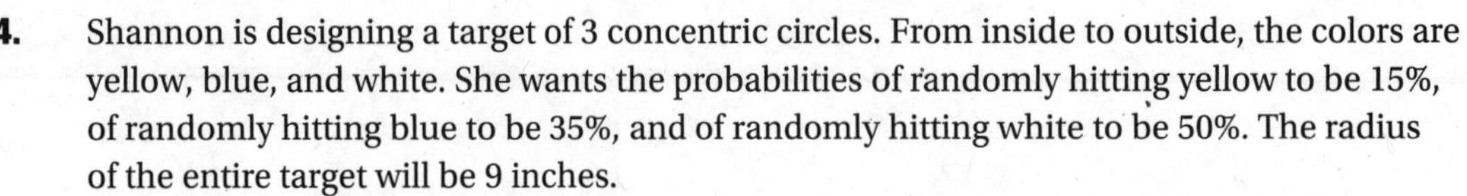

Name ________________________ Class ______________ Date ________

SELECTED RESPONSE

1. You spin a spinner with 10 equal sections that are numbered 1 through 10. Event A is rolling an odd number. Event B is rolling a number greater than 5. What is $P(A \cap B)$?

   A. $\frac{1}{8}$
   B. $\frac{1}{5}$
   C. $\frac{1}{2}$
   D. $\frac{4}{5}$

2. There are 9 players on a basketball team. For a team photo, 4 of the players are seated on a row of chairs and 5 players stand behind them. In how many different ways can 4 players be arranged on the row of chairs?

   F. 24
   G. 126
   H. 180
   J. 3024

3. There are 5 peaches and 4 nectarines in a bowl. You randomly choose 2 pieces of fruit to pack in your lunch. What is the probability that you choose 2 peaches?

   A. $\frac{5}{36}$
   B. $\frac{5}{18}$
   C. $\frac{2}{5}$
   D. $\frac{5}{9}$

4. You shuffle the cards shown below and choose one at random. What is the probability that you choose a gray card or an even number?

1	2 (gray)	4	5 (gray)	7 (gray)	9
10	11 (gray)	13 (gray)	16 (gray)	18	19 (gray)

   F. $\frac{1}{10}$
   G. $\frac{35}{144}$
   H. $\frac{5}{6}$
   J. 1

The two-way table provides data about 240 randomly chosen people who visit a movie theater. Use the table for Items 5 and 6.

	Discount Admission	Regular Admission	TOTAL
Purchases a snack	24	72	96
Purchases no snack	36	108	144
TOTAL	60	180	240

5. Consider the following events.

   Event A: Pays for a regular admission.
   Event B: Purchases a snack.

   Which is the best description of the two events?

   A. complementary events
   B. dependent events
   C. independent events
   D. mutually exclusive events

6. What is the probability that a visitor to the movie theater purchases a snack given that the visitor pays for a discount admission?

   F. 0.1
   G. 0.25
   H. 0.4
   J. 0.75

7. A bag contains 8 yellow marbles and 4 blue marbles. You choose a marble, put it aside, and then choose another marble. What is the probability that you choose two yellow marbles?

   A. $\frac{7}{18}$
   B. $\frac{14}{33}$
   C. $\frac{4}{9}$
   D. $\frac{2}{3}$

8. Events A and B are independent events. Which of the following must be true?

F. $P(A \text{ and } B) = P(A) \cdot P(B)$

G. $P(A \text{ and } B) = P(A) + P(B)$

H. $P(A) = P(B)$

J. $P(B|A) = P(A|B)$

9. Which expression can you use to calculate the conditional probability of event A given that event B has occurred?

A. $P(A) + P(B) - P(A \text{ and } B)$

B. $P(B) \cdot P(A|B)$

C. $\frac{P(A \text{ and } B)}{P(B)}$

D. $\frac{P(A)}{P(B)}$

CONSTRUCTED RESPONSE

10. It is known that 1% of all mice in a laboratory have a genetic mutation. A test for the mutation correctly identifies mice that have the mutation 98% of the time. The test correctly identifies mice that do not have the mutation 96% of the time. A lab assistant tests a mouse and finds that the mouse tests positive for the mutation. The lab assistant decides that the mouse must have the mutation. Is this a good decision? Explain.

11. Two students, Naomi and Kayla, play a game using the rules shown below. The winner of the game gets a box of 80 fruit chews.

Game Rules

- One student repeatedly tosses a coin.
- When the coin lands heads up, Naomi gets a point.
- When the coin lands tails up, Kayla gets a point.
- The first student to reach 8 points wins the game and gets the fruit chews.

The game gets interrupted when Naomi has 7 points and Kayla has 5 points. How should the 80 fruit chews be divided between the students given that the game was interrupted at this moment? Explain why your answer provides a fair way to divide the fruit chews.

Inferences and Conclusions from Data

GPS COMMON CORE

Unpacking the Standards

Understanding the standards and the vocabulary terms in the standards will help you know exactly what you are expected to learn in this unit.

MCC9-12.S.ID.2

Use statistics appropriate to the shape of the data distribution to compare center (median, ...) and spread (interquartile range, ...) of two or more different data sets.

Key Vocabulary

statistic *(estadística)* A number that describes a sample.

median of a data set *(mediana de un conjunto de datos)* For an ordered data set with an odd number of values, the median is the middle value. For an ordered data set with an even number of values, the median is the average of the two middle values.

interquartile range (IQR) *(rango entre cuartiles)* The difference of the third (upper) and first (lower) quartiles in a data set, representing the middle half of the data.

What It Means For You

You can compare two data sets by comparing their medians and comparing how the data are spread around the medians.

EXAMPLE

Box-and-whisker plots help you compare the center and spread of two data sets.

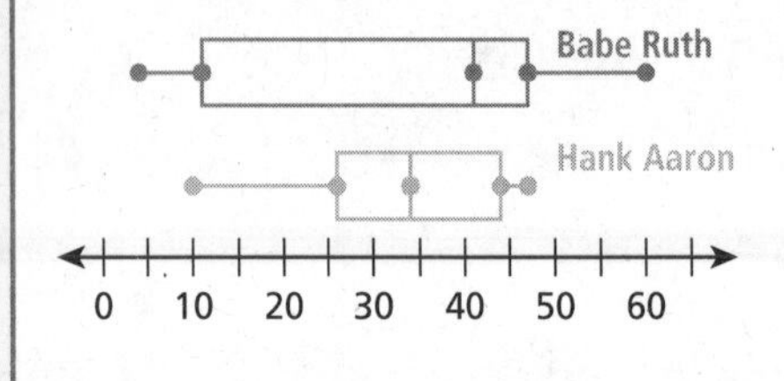

MCC9-12.S.IC.3

Recognize the purposes of and differences among sample surveys, experiments, and observational studies; explain how randomization relates to each.

Key Vocabulary

observational study *(estudio de observación)* A study that observes individuals and measures variables without controlling the individuals or their environment in any way.

What It Means For You

A survey allows you to measure a population variable. An observational study helps you look for associations between variables. An experiment may allow you to establish a cause-and-effect relationship between variables.

EXAMPLE

Survey: You choose 20 students at random from those taking a particular math course at your school, and you ask whether they take notes during class.

Observational Study: You observe whether 20 students taking a particular math course take notes during class, and you compare the test scores of those who take notes with those who don't.

Experiment: You randomly divide 20 students taking a particular math course into two groups of 10. One group is asked to take notes, and the other group is asked not to take notes. You then compare the test scores of the two groups to see if taking notes had an effect on the scores.

UNIT 5

GPS COMMON CORE **MCC9-12.S.IC.4**

Use data from a sample survey to estimate a population mean or proportion; develop a margin of error through the use of simulation models for random sampling.

Key Vocabulary

population *(población)* The entire group of objects or individuals considered for a survey.

margin of error *(margen de error)* In a random sample, it defines an interval, centered on the sample percent, in which the population percent is most likely to lie.

simulation *(simulación)* A model of an experiment, often one that would be too difficult or time-consuming to actually perform.

random sample *(muestra aleatoria)* A sample selected from a population so that each member of the population has an equal chance of being selected.

What It Means For You

You can use results from a sample of a population to predict the interval where the proportion for the population is likely to be.

EXAMPLE

In an opinion survey of a random sample of students, 54% agreed with a proposal, with a ±5% margin of error. So, the percent of the total population who agree is likely between 49% and 59%.

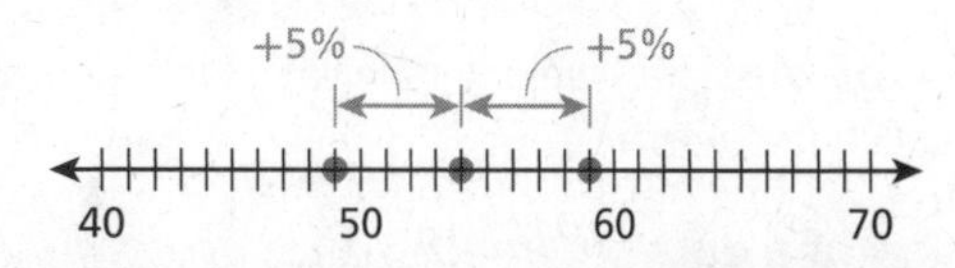

GPS COMMON CORE **MCC9-12.S.ID.4**

Use the mean and standard deviation of a data set to fit it to a normal distribution and to estimate population percentages. Recognize that there are data sets for which such a procedure is not appropriate. Use calculators, spreadsheets, and tables to estimate areas under the normal curve.

Key Vocabulary

mean *(media)* The sum of all the values in a data set divided by the number of data values. Also called the *average*.

standard deviation *(desviación estándar)* A measure of dispersion of a data set. The standard deviation σ is the square root of the variance.

What It Means For You

When the histogram for a data set is bell-shaped, the data can be represented by a normal distribution. You can use the mean and standard deviation to fit a *normal curve* to the data and then use the normal curve to make estimates.

EXAMPLE

A standardized test is designed so that the scores are normally distributed with a mean of 500 and a standard deviation of 100. So about 68% of the scores are between 400 and 600.

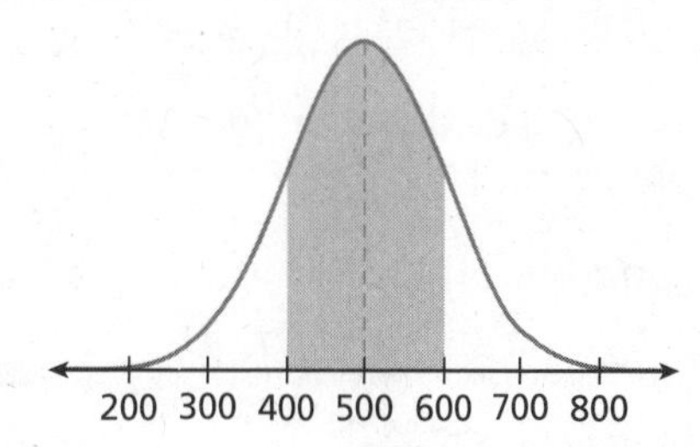

UNIT 5

Key Vocabulary

interquartile range (IQR) (*rango entre cuartiles*) The difference of the third (upper) and first (lower) quartiles in a data set, representing the middle half of the data.

margin of error *(margen de error)* In a random sample, it defines an interval, centered on the sample percent, in which the population percent is most likely to lie.

mean *(media)* The sum of all the values in a data set divided by the number of data values. Also called the *average*.

median of a data set *(mediana de un conjunto de datos)* For an ordered data set with an odd number of values, the median is the middle value. For an ordered data set with an even number of values, the median is the average of the two middle values.

normal curve *(curva normal)* A smooth, symmetrical, bell-shaped curve that can model normal distributions and approximate some binomial distributions.

observational study *(estudio de observación)* A study that observes individuals and measures variables without controlling the individuals or their environment in any way.

population *(población)* The entire group of objects or individuals considered for a survey.

probability distribution for an experiment *(distribución de probabilidad para un experimento)* The function that pairs each outcome with its probability.

random sample *(muestra aleatoria)* A sample selected from a population so that each member of the population has an equal chance of being selected.

random variable *(variable aleatoria)* A variable whose value is determined by the outcomes of a random event.

randomized comparative experiment *(experimento comparativo aleatorizado)* An experiment in which the individuals are assigned to the control group or the treatment group at random, in order to minimize bias.

sample *(muestra)* A part of the population.

simulation *(simulación)* A model of an experiment, often one that would be too difficult or time-consuming to actually perform.

standard deviation *(desviación estándar)* A measure of dispersion of a data set. The standard deviation σ is the square root of the variance.

standard normal distribution *(distribución normal típica)* The normal distribution with mean 0 and standard deviation 1.

statistic *(estadística)* A number that describes a sample.

z-score *(puntuación z)* The number z of standard deviations that a data value lies above or below the mean of the data set: $\frac{x - \bar{x}}{\sigma}$

UNIT 5

Name______________________ Class______________ Date__________

8-1

Measures of Central Tendency and Variation

Extension: Data Distributions

Video Tutor

Essential question: *How can you use shape, center, and spread to characterize a data distribution?*

A **data distribution** is a set of numerical data that you can graph using a data display that involves a number line, such as a line plot, histogram, or box plot. The graph will reveal the shape of the distribution.

MCC9–12.S.ID.1

1 EXPLORE Seeing the Shape of a Data Distribution

The table gives data about a random sample of 20 babies born at a hospital.

Baby	Birth month	Birth weight (kg)	Mother's age
1	5	3.3	28
2	7	3.6	31
3	11	3.5	33
4	2	3.4	35
5	10	3.7	39
6	3	3.4	30
7	1	3.5	29
8	4	3.2	30
9	7	3.6	31
10	6	3.4	32
11	9	3.6	33
12	10	3.5	29
13	11	3.4	31
14	1	3.7	29
15	6	3.5	34
16	5	3.8	30
17	8	3.5	32
18	9	3.6	30
19	12	3.3	29
20	2	3.5	28

A Make a line plot for the distribution of birth months.

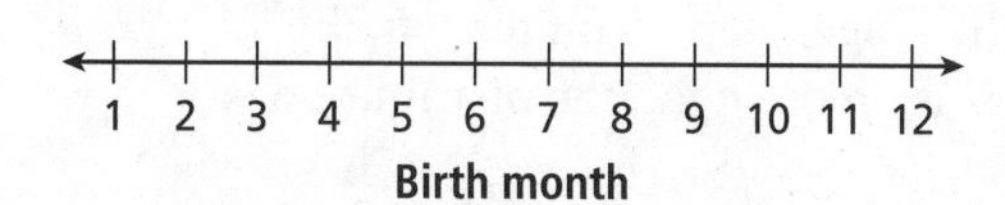

B Make a line plot for the distribution of birth weights.

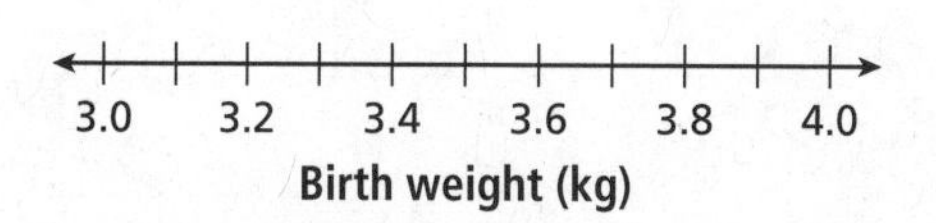

C Make a line plot for the distribution of mothers' ages.

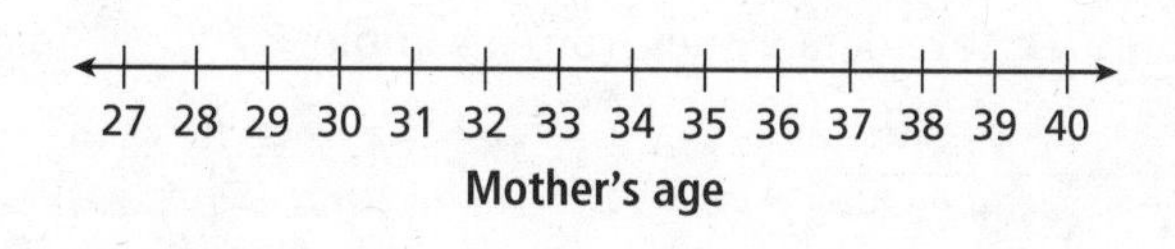

REFLECT

1a. Describe the shape of the distribution of birth months.

____

1b. Describe the shape of the distribution of birth weights.

____

1c. Describe the shape of the distribution of mothers' ages.

____

____

PREP FOR MCC9–12.S.ID.3

2 ENGAGE Understanding Shape, Center, and Spread

As you saw in the Explore, data distributions can have various shapes. Some of these shapes are given names in statistics.

- A distribution whose shape is basically level (that is, it looks like a rectangle) is called a **uniform distribution**.
- A distribution that is mounded in the middle with symmetric "tails" at each end (that is, it looks bell-shaped) is called a **normal distribution**. To be a normal distribution, a data distribution has to have some additional properties besides a bell shape. You will learn more about this in later lessons.
- A distribution that is mounded but not symmetric because one "tail" is much longer than the other is called a **skewed distribution**. When the longer "tail" is on the left, the distribution is called **skewed left**. When the longer "tail" is on the right, the distribution is called **skewed right**.

The figures below show the general shape of normal and skewed distributions.

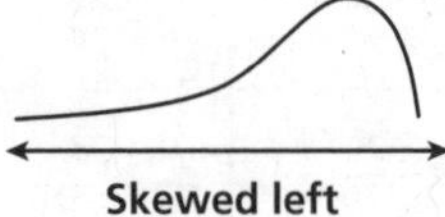

Skewed left

Symmetric

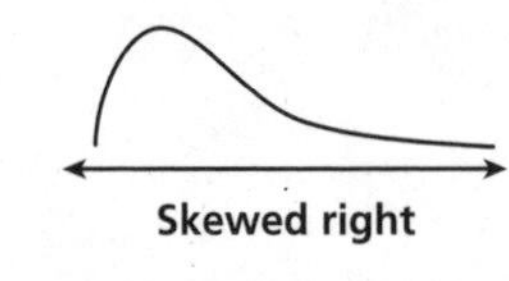

Skewed right

Shape is one way of characterizing a data distribution. Another way is by identifying the distribution's center and spread.

- The **mean** of n data values is the sum of the data values divided by n. If $x_1, x_2, \ldots, x_n$ are data values from a sample, then the mean $\bar{x}$ is given by:

$$\bar{x} = \frac{x_1 + x_2 + \cdots + x_n}{n}$$

- The **median** of n data values written in ascending order is the middle value if n is odd and is the mean of the two middle values if n is even.
- The **standard deviation** of n data values is the square root of the mean of the squared deviations from the distribution's mean. If $x_1, x_2, \ldots, x_n$ are data values from a sample, then the standard deviation s is given by:

$$s = \sqrt{\frac{(x_1 - \bar{x})^2 + (x_2 - \bar{x})^2 + \cdots + (x_n - \bar{x})^2}{n}}$$

- The **interquartile range**, or IQR, of data values written in ascending order is the difference between the median of the upper half of the data, called the *third quartile* or Q_3, and the median of the lower half of the data, called the *first quartile* or Q_1. So, IQR $= Q_3 - Q_1$.

The first quartile, the median, and the third quartile divide a set of data into four groups that each contain about 25% of the data, so the IQR tells you how spread out the middle 50% (or so) of the data are.

To distinguish a population mean from a sample mean, statisticians use the Greek letter mu, written μ, instead of $\bar{x}$. Similarly, they use the Greek letter sigma, written σ, instead of s to distinguish a population standard deviation from a sample standard deviation. Also, for a reason best left to a statistics course, the formula for the sample standard deviation sometimes has $n - 1$ rather than n in the denominator of the radicand. (In this book, n will always be used.)

REFLECT

2a. Describe the shape of each distribution in the Explore using the vocabulary defined on the previous page.

____

____

2b. When the center and spread of a distribution are reported, they are generally given either as the mean and standard deviation or as the median and IQR. Why do these pairings make sense?

____

MCC9–12.S.ID.3

3 EXPLORE Relating Center and Spread to Shape

Use a graphing calculator to compute the measures of center and the measures of spread for the distribution of baby weights and the distribution of mothers' ages.

A Enter the two sets of data into two lists on a graphing calculator as shown.

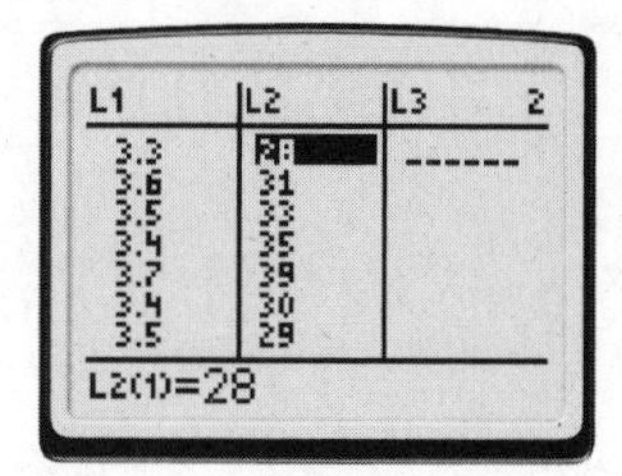

B Calculate the "1-Variable Statistics" for the distribution of baby weights. Record the statistics listed below. (Note: Your calculator may report the standard deviation with a denominator of $n - 1$ as "s_x" and the standard deviation with a denominator of n as "σ_x." Use the latter.)

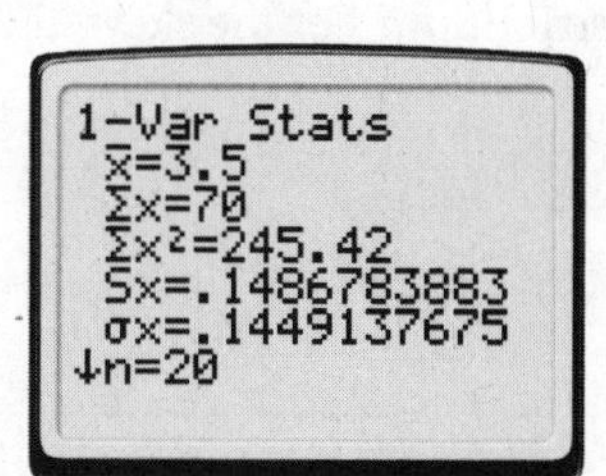

$\bar{x} =$ __________ Median = __________

$s \approx$ __________ IQR $= Q_3 - Q_1 =$ __________

C Calculate the "1-Variable Statistics" for the distribution of mothers' ages. Record the statistics listed below.

```
1-Var Stats
x̄=31.15
Σx=623
Σx²=19543
Sx=2.680828623
σx=2.612948526
↓n=20
```

$\bar{x}$ = __________ Median = __________

$s \approx$ __________ $\text{IQR} = Q_3 - Q_1 =$ __________

REFLECT

3a. What do you notice about the mean and median for the symmetric distribution (baby weights) as compared with the mean and median for the skewed distribution (mothers' ages)? Explain why this happens.

____

____

____

3b. One way to compare the spread of two distributions is to find the ratio (expressed as a percent) of the standard deviation to the mean for each distribution. Another way is to find the ratio (expressed as a percent) of the IQR to the median. Calculate these ratios, rounding each to the nearest percent if necessary, for the symmetric distribution (baby weights) and the skewed distribution (mothers' ages). What do you observe when you compare the corresponding ratios? Why does this make sense?

____

____

____

____

____

____

____

3c. Which measures of center and spread would you report for the symmetric distribution? For the skewed distribution? Explain your reasoning.

____

____

____

MCC9–12.S.ID.1

4 EXPLORE Making and Analyzing a Histogram

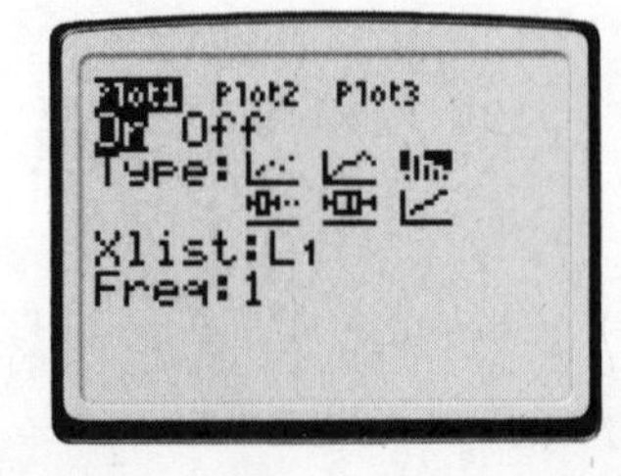

A Use a graphing calculator to make a histogram for the distribution of baby weights. Begin by turning on a statistics plot, selecting the histogram option, and entering the list where the data are stored.

B Set the viewing window. To obtain a histogram that looks very much like the line plot that you drew for this data set, use the values shown at the right. Xscl determines the width of each bar, so when Xscl = 0.1 and Xmin = 3.15, the first bar covers the interval $3.15 \le x < 3.25$, which captures the weight of 3.2 kg.

C Draw the histogram by pressing GRAPH. You can obtain the heights of the bars by pressing TRACE and using the arrow keys.

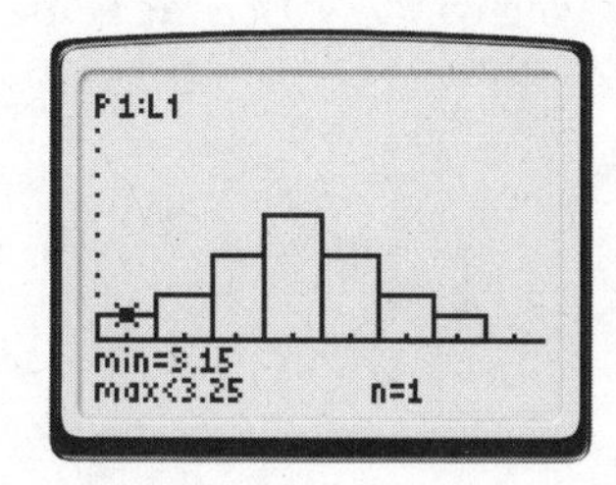

REFLECT

4a. By examining the histogram, determine the percent of the data that fall within 1 standard deviation ($s = 0.14$) of the mean ($\bar{x} = 3.5$). That is, determine the percent of the data in the interval $3.5 - 0.14 < x < 3.5 + 0.14$, or $3.36 < x < 3.64$. Explain your reasoning.

4b. Suppose one of the baby weights is chosen at random. By examining the histogram, determine the probability that the weight is more than 1 standard deviation ($s = 0.14$) above the mean ($\bar{x} = 3.5$). That is, determine the probability that the weight is in the interval $x > 3.5 + 0.14$, or $x > 3.64$. Explain your reasoning.

4c. Change Xscl from 0.1 to 0.2 and redraw the histogram. Notice that the histogram loses some of its symmetry. Explain why this happens.

4d. To create a histogram for the distribution of mothers' ages, what values of Xscl and Xmin would you use so that the histogram matches the line plot that you drew?

MCC9–12.S.ID.1

5 EXPLORE Making and Analyzing a Box Plot

A Use a graphing calculator to make a box plot for the distribution of mothers' ages. Begin by turning on a statistics plot, selecting the box plot option, and entering the list where the data are stored. (There are two box plot options: one that shows outliers and one that does not. Choose the second of these.)

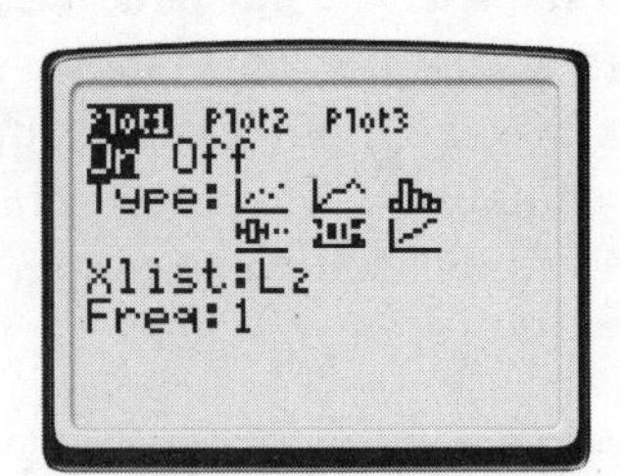

B Set the viewing window. Use the values shown at the right.

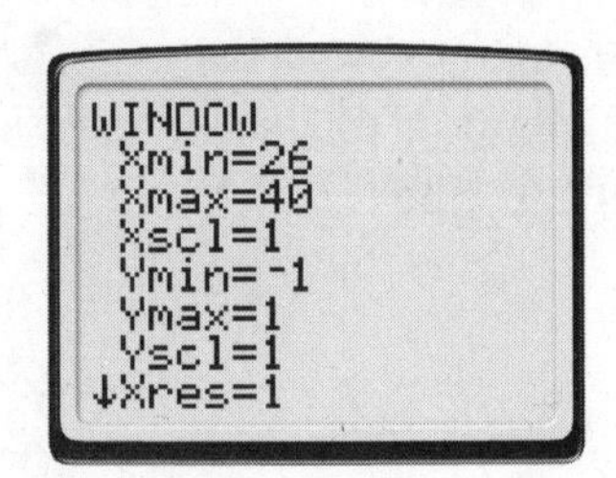

C Draw the box plot by pressing GRAPH. The box plot is based on five key values: the minimum data value, the first quartile, the median, the third quartile, and the maximum data value. You can obtain these values by pressing TRACE and using the arrow keys.

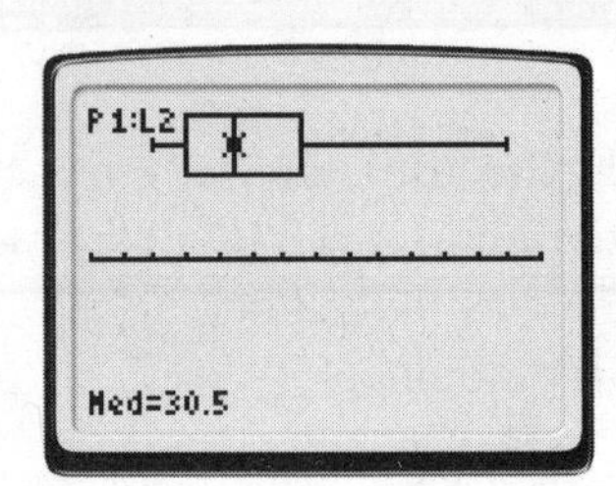

REFLECT

5a. How does the box plot show that the distribution is skewed right?

5b. Suppose one of the mothers' ages is chosen at random. Based on the box plot and not the original set of data, what can you say is the approximate probability that the age falls between the median, 30.5, and the third quartile, 32.5? Explain your reasoning.

5c. A data value x is considered to be an *outlier* if $x < Q_1 - 1.5(\text{IQR})$ or $x > Q_3 + 1.5(\text{IQR})$. Explain why a mother's age of 39 is an outlier for this data set. Redraw the box plot using the option for showing outliers. How does the box plot change?

Name__________ Class__________ Date__________

Additional Practice

Find the mean, median, and mode of each data set.

1. { 12, 11, 17, 3, 9, 14, 16, 2 }
   a. Mean __________
   b. Median __________
   c. Mode __________

2. { 6, 9, 9, 20, 4, 5, 9, 13, 10, 1 }
   a. Mean __________
   b. Median __________
   c. Mode __________

Make a box-and-whisker plot of the data. Find the interquartile range.

3. { 3, 7, 7, 3, 10, 1, 6, 6 }

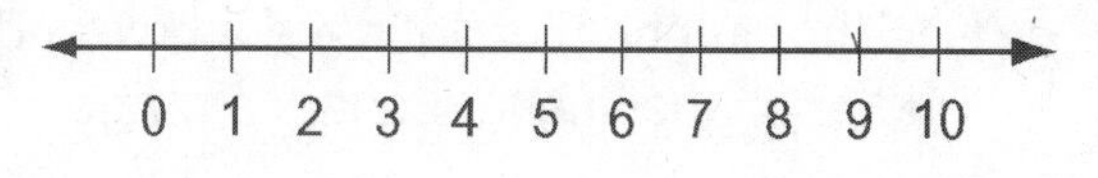

4. { 1, 2, 3, 5, 3, 5, 8, 2 }

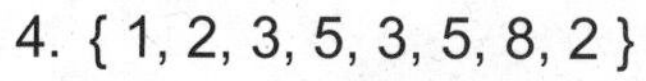

0 1 2 3 4 5 6 7 8 9 10

Find the variance and standard deviation.

5. { 7, 4, 3, 9, 2 }

6. { 35, 67, 21, 16, 24, 51, 18, 32 }

____

7. { 19, 23, 17, 20, 25, 19, 15, 22 }

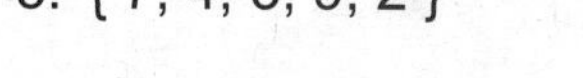

8. { 5, 12, 10, 13, 8, 11, 15, 12 }

____

Solve.

9. The probability distribution for the amount of rain that falls on Boston in May each year is given below. Find the expected amount of rain for Boston in May. __________

Inches of Rain, *n*	5	6	7	8
Probability	0.05	0.10	0.64	0.21

10. A biologist is growing bacteria in the lab. For a certain species of bacteria, she records these doubling times: 41 min, 45 min, 39 min, 42 min, 38 min, 88 min, 43 min, 40 min, 44 min, 39 min, 42 min, and 40 min.
    a. Find the mean of the data. __________
    b. Find the standard deviation. __________
    c. Identify any outliers. __________
    d. Describe how any outlier affects the mean and the standard deviation.

____

Problem Solving

Each week, Damien records the miles per gallon for his car, to the nearest whole number. Over a period of 10 weeks, the data are 18, 17, 19, 18, 18, 25, 29, 30, 26, 19. He wants to arrange and summarize his data so that he can analyze it.

1. Make a box-and-whisker plot of his data.
   a. Order the data from least to greatest. ______________________
   b. Identify the minimum, maximum, median, first quartile, and third quartile.

   ____

   c. Use the number line to make a box-and-whisker plot of the data. Find and label the interquartile range.

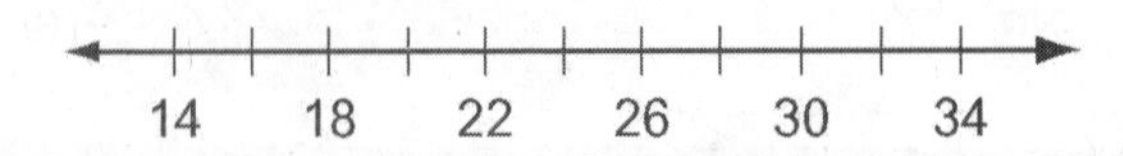

   d. Explain what the interquartile range represents in terms of the car's miles per gallon.

   ____

2. Find the standard deviation for the data.
   a. Write an equation and solve to find the mean. ______________________
   b. Complete the table to show the difference between the mean and each data value, and the square of that difference.

Data Value, x	18	17	19	18	18	25	29	30	26	19
$x - \overline{x}$										
$(x - \overline{x})^2$										

   c. Explain how to use the data from the table to find the standard deviation.

   ____

   d. What is the standard deviation for the data? ______________________
   e. Explain what the standard deviation represents in terms of the car's miles per gallon.

   ____

3. Damien thinks that the standard deviation is a more reliable measure of dispersion than the interquartile range. Is he correct? Explain.

____

____

____

Name________________________ Class________________ Date__________

8-2

Data Gathering

Going Deeper

Essential question: *What are the different methods for gathering data about a population?*

Video Tutor

PREP FOR MCC9–12.S.IC.1

1 ENGAGE Understanding Data-Gathering Techniques

In the branch of mathematics known as statistics, you work with data. Data can be **numerical**, such as heights or salaries, or **categorical**, such as eye color or political affiliation. You collect data about a **population** by surveying or studying some or all of the **individuals** in the population.

When *all* the individuals in a population are surveyed or studied, the data-gathering technique is called a **census**. A **parameter** is a number that summarizes a characteristic of the population.

When only some of the individuals in a population are surveyed or studied, the data-gathering technique is called **sampling**. A **statistic** is a number that summarizes a characteristic of a sample. Statistics can be used to estimate parameters. Samples that result in accurate estimates are said to be **representative** of the population.

There are a variety of sampling methods, characterized by how the individuals in the sample are chosen. The table below lists a few.

Sampling Method	Description
Random	Each individual in the population has an equal chance of being selected.
Self-selected	Individuals volunteer to be part of the sample.
Convenience	Individuals are selected based on how accessible they are.
Systematic	Members of the sample are chosen according to a rule, such as every *n*th individual in the population.
Stratified	The individuals are organized into groups, and individuals from each group are selected (typically through a random sample within each group).
Cluster	The individuals are organized into groups, and all of the individuals in just some of the groups are selected (typically through a random sample of the groups).

REFLECT

1a. Give an example of numerical data and an example of categorical data other than the examples listed in the first paragraph.

____

____

1b. Asking your friends is an example of what type of sampling method? Explain.

____

1c. Which sampling method do you think is most likely to result in a representative sample? Why?

1d. Which sampling method do you think would be least likely to result in a representative sample? Why?

1e. Explain why a researcher might use a sampling method rather than a census to gather information about a population.

MCC9-12.S.IC.1

2 EXPLORE Finding Statistics Using Various Sampling Methods

The salaries (in thousands of dollars) of all 30 employees at a small company are listed in the table.

Salaries at a Small Company									
21	24	26	28	30	32	33	35	37	41
44	46	47	49	50	51	52	54	55	57
58	62	62	64	64	65	70	71	73	80

Use the table to generate a sample of 6 individuals using each sampling method, and then use the sample to predict the mean of the population.

A Suppose individuals whose salaries are 51, 57, 58, 65, 70, and 73 volunteer to be in the sample. Compute the self-selected sample's mean, rounding to the nearest whole number.

B Take a convenience sample by choosing the 6 numbers in the first two columns of the table. Record the salaries, and then compute the sample's mean, rounding to the nearest whole number.

C Take a systematic sample by choosing every fifth number in the list, reading from left to right in each row. Record the salaries, and then compute the sample's mean, rounding to the nearest whole number.

D Take a random sample. Begin by labeling the data in the table with the identifiers 1–10 for the first row, 11–20 for the second row, and 21–30 for the third row. Then use a graphing calculator's random integer generator to generate 6 identifiers between 1 and 30, as shown. (If any identifiers are repeated, simply generate replacements for them until you have 6 unique identifiers.) Record the corresponding salaries, and then compute the sample's mean, rounding to the nearest whole number.

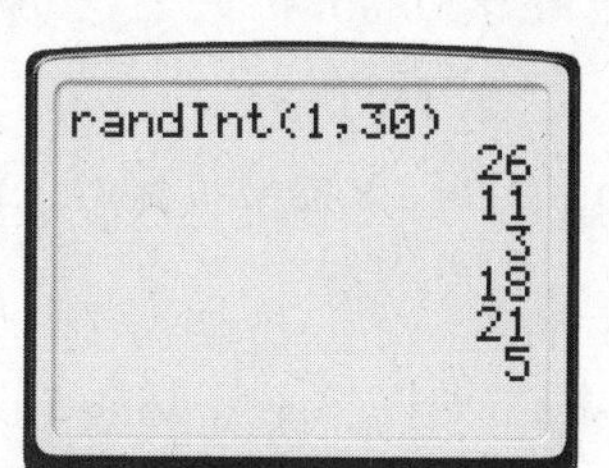

____

____

____

REFLECT

2a. Compute the mean of the population. Then list the four samples from best to worst in terms of how well each sample mean estimates the population mean.

____

2b. How do the best and worst sampling methods from your list compare with your answers to Reflect Questions 1c and 1d?

____

____

Some statistics, such as the mean, apply only to numerical data. For categorical data, an appropriate statistic is a **proportion**, which is the relative frequency of a category.

MCC9–12.S.IC.1

3 EXAMPLE Making Predictions from a Sample

A community health center surveyed a small random sample of adults in the community about their exercise habits. The survey asked whether the person engages in regular cardio exercise (running, walking, swimming, or other) and, if so, what the duration and frequency of exercise are.

Of the 25 people surveyed, 10 said that they do engage in regular cardio exercise. The table lists the data for those 10 people.

Calculate statistics from the sample, and use the statistics to make predictions about the exercise habits of the approximately 5000 adults living in the community.

Type of exercise	Duration (minutes spent exercising)	Frequency (times per week)
Running	30	4
Walking	20	5
Running	40	3
Running	60	6
Swimming	40	4
Other	90	2
Running	30	3
Walking	20	5
Running	30	4
Other	120	1

A Calculate the following two proportions from the sample data.

Proportion of adults who get regular cardio exercise $= \frac{\square}{25} = \square\,\%$

Proportion of runners among those who get regular cardio exercise $= \frac{\square}{10} = \square\,\%$

B Use the proportions from part A and the verbal model below to predict the number of runners among all adults living in the community.

Number of runners in the community	=	Number of adults in the community	×	Proportion of adults who get cardio exercise	×	Proportion of runners among those who get regular cardio exercise

____

C Calculate the following two means from the sample data.

Mean duration of exercise for those who get regular cardio exercise = ______________

Mean frequency of exercise for those who get regular cardio exercise = ______________

D Use the means from part C to predict, for those who get regular cardio exercise, the number of *hours* spent exercising each week. Show your calculations and include units.

____

REFLECT

3a. One of the *categorical variables* in the survey was regular cardio exercise. That variable had only two possible values: yes or no. What was the other categorical variable, and what were its possible values?

____

3b. What were the two *numerical variables* in the survey, and what were their possible values?

____

____

____

3c. How much confidence do you have in the predictions made from the results of the survey? Explain your reasoning.

____

____

____

PRACTICE

A student council wants to know whether students would like the council to sponsor a mid-winter dance or a mid-winter carnival this year. Classify each sampling method.

1. Survey every tenth student on the school's roster. ______________

2. Survey all freshmen and all juniors. ______________

3. Survey 20 freshmen, 20 sophomores, 20 juniors, and 20 seniors. ______________

4. Survey those who ask the council president for a questionnaire. ______________

5. Survey those who happen to be in the cafeteria at noon. ______________

Use the following information for Exercises 6–9.

The officers of a neighborhood association want to know whether residents are interested in beautifying the neighborhood and, if so, how much money they are willing to contribute toward the costs involved. The officers are considering the three sampling methods below.

A. Call and survey every tenth resident on the association's roster.

B. Randomly select and survey 10 residents from among those who come to the neighborhood block party.

C. Mail a survey to every resident with instructions to complete and mail the survey back.

6. Identify the population.

____

7. Which sampling method is most likely to result in a representative sample of the population? Explain.

____

____

____

8. Describe another sampling method that is likely to result in a representative sample of the population.

____

9. Describe the categorical and numerical data that the officers of the neighborhood association want to gather through a survey.

____

____

Use the following information for Exercises 10–14.

A community theater association plans to produce three plays for the upcoming season. The association surveys a random sample of the approximately 7000 households in the community to see if an adult member of the household is interested in attending plays and, if so, what type of plays the person prefers (comedy, drama, or musical), how many members of the household (including the person surveyed) might attend plays, and how many of the three plays those household members might attend.

Of the 50 adults surveyed, 12 indicated an interest in attending plays. The table lists the data for those 12 people.

Preferred type of play	Number of people attending	Number of plays attending
Comedy	2	1
Musical	3	2
Musical	1	2
Drama	2	3
Comedy	3	2
Comedy	2	3
Musical	4	1
Drama	2	3
Comedy	2	2
Musical	2	3
Comedy	5	1
Drama	1	2

10. Describe the categorical and numerical data gathered in the survey.

11. Calculate the proportion of adults who indicated an interest in attending plays. Then calculate the proportion of those interested in attending plays who prefer dramas.

12. Approximately 15,000 adults live in the community. Predict the number of adults who prefer plays that are dramas. Show your calculations.

13. For an adult with an interest in attending plays, calculate the mean number of household members who might attend plays. Then calculate the mean number of plays that those household members might attend. Round each mean to the nearest tenth.

14. The theater association plans to sells tickets to the plays for $40 each. Predict the amount of revenue from ticket sales. Show your calculations and include units.

Name________________________ Class________________ Date______________ 8-2

Additional Practice

Decide which sampling method, A or B, is less likely to result in a biased sample.

1. A representative of a mall wants to know whether the mall's customers would shop at a new audio equipment store in the mall.
   A. He asks every 5th person walking into an electronics store if they would shop at a new audio equipment store in the mall.
   B. He asks every 5th person walking into the main mall entrance if they would shop at a new audio equipment store in the mall.

   ____

2. A researcher wants to know the average amount of debt college students expect to have.
   A. She surveys 50 randomly-selected students on several college campuses with different tuitions and with different kinds of programs.
   B. She surveys 100 randomly-selected students at an expensive medical school.

   ____

Decide which survey is more likely to result in a sample that is representative of the population.

3. The manager of a movie theater wants to know what type of movies his customers prefer.
   A. He asks every 3rd customer coming out of a comedy movie.
   B. He asks every 10th customer who enters the theater during a day when the theater is showing an assortment of movie types.

   ____

4. The chef at a restaurant wants to get feedback on the quality of his food.
   A. He has each server at the restaurant survey 5 customers during each shift for a week.
   B. He has the servers at the restaurant survey every customer on a night when family members of employees get a discount.

   ____

100 students out of 1000 at a school were surveyed. The results are recorded in each problem below. Predict the number of students in the entire population that would answer similarly.

5. 50 ride the bus to school.

   ____

6. 10 transferred from another school.

   ____

____

Problem Solving

100 students out of 1100 at a school were surveyed. The results are recorded in each problem below. For Exercises 1–4, predict the number of students in the population that would answer similarly.

1. 82 students said they would take a study hall or resource period if it were offered. **Solution:** 82 x 11 = 902 ___902 students___
2. 12 students said they were members of the after-school music program. _____ x _____ = 132 ____________________
3. 94 students said they used the Internet for their homework. ____________________
4. 32 students said they drove to school. ____________________
5. The principal wanted to know if he should allow cell phones in the classroom. He surveyed the students in Algebra 2 class. Decide whether the sampling method could result in a biased sample. Explain your reasoning.

   ____

6. A discount store chain wants to know how often families in a certain area would shop regularly at a discount store. Their representative surveys 100 people at a mall in the same area. Are his results likely to be representative of the population? Explain.

   ____

Select the best answer.

7. The director of the Glee Club would like to know if her Booster Club parents would do a fundraiser. Which sampling method is most likely to yield an accurate prediction of the population?
   - A Survey every 3rd Booster Club parent who comes to a fundraiser meeting.
   - B Survey every 10th Booster Club parent who comes to a fundraiser meeting.
   - C Survey only the parents who respond to a letter from the director.

8. The principal of the school would like to determine if the cafeteria should sell snacks during non-lunch hour periods. Which sampling method is most likely to yield an accurate prediction of the population?
   - F Survey every 20th student who enters the cafeteria during lunch hour.
   - G Survey 50 random students each from the 9th, 10th, 11th, and 12th grades.
   - H Survey the first 25 students that walk into the school.

Name_______________ Class_______________ Date_______________

8-3

Video Tutor

Surveys, Experiments, and Observational Studies

Going Deeper

Essential question: *What kinds of statistical research are there, and which ones can establish cause-and-effect relationships between variables?*

A **survey** measures characteristics of interest about a population using a sample selected from the population. A sample needs to be representative of the population in order for the measurements obtained from the sample to be accurate. Random sampling is generally the best way to ensure representation.

Even when random sampling is used for a survey, the survey's results can have errors. Some of the sources of errors are:

- *Biased questions:* The wording of questions in a survey can influence the way people respond to the questions. Survey questions need to be worded in a neutral, unbiased way.
- *Interviewer effect:* If the questions in a survey are being asked by an interviewer, the person being interviewed may give inaccurate responses to avoid being embarrassed. For instance, if the questions involve sensitive issues, the person may not tell the truth, or if the questions involve complex or unfamiliar issues, the person may resort to guessing.
- *Nonresponse:* Some people may be difficult or impossible to contact, or they may simply refuse to participate once contacted. If nonresponse rates are higher for certain subgroups of a population, such as the elderly, then those subgroups will be underrepresented in the survey results.

MCC9–12.S.IC.3

1 EXAMPLE Detecting Errors in Surveys

Explain why the results of each survey are likely to be inaccurate and then suggest a way to improve the accuracy of the survey.

A Mrs. Ruben, the owner of a business, conducts one-on-one interviews with a random sample of employees to have them rate how satisfied they are with different aspects of their jobs.

____

____

____

B In a random sample of town residents, a survey asks, "Are you in favor of a special tax levy to renovate the dilapidated town hall?"

____

____

____

REFLECT

1a. Even if the survey question in part B is revised to give a factual list of repairs that need to be made to the town hall, do the people surveyed have enough information to give an informed and accurate response? Explain.

An **observational study** can be used to determine whether an existing condition, called a **factor**, in a population is related to a characteristic of interest. For instance, an observational study might be used to find the incidence of heart disease among those who smoke. In the study, being a smoker is the factor, and having heart disease is the characteristic of interest.

In an observational study, the condition already exists in the population. In an **experiment**, the condition is created by imposing a **treatment** on the sample. For instance, an experiment might be conducted by having a group of people with eczema take a vitamin E pill daily, and then observing whether their symptoms improve. In the experiment, taking the vitamin E pill is the treatment, and improvement of symptoms is the characteristic of interest.

MCC9–12.S.IC.3

2 EXAMPLE Identifying Observational Studies and Experiments

Determine whether each research study is an observational study or an experiment. Identify the factor if it is an observational study or the treatment if it is an experiment. Also identify the characteristic of interest.

A Researchers measure the cholesterol of 50 subjects who report that they eat fish regularly and 50 subjects who report that they do not eat fish regularly.

B Researchers have 100 subjects with high cholesterol take fish oil pills daily for two months. They monitor the cholesterol of the subjects during that time.

REFLECT

2a. Suppose the researchers in part A find that considerably more people who eat fish regularly have normal cholesterol levels than those who do not eat fish regularly. Is it reasonable to conclude that eating fish regularly has an effect on cholesterol? Explain.

2b. In medical research, subjects sometimes respond to a treatment even if the treatment, called a *placebo*, is designed not to have an effect. (For instance, a placebo may be a pill with no active ingredients.) If the researchers in part B find that taking fish oil pills lowers cholesterol, what should they do to rule out the possibility of a placebo effect?

____

____

Whether a study is observational or experimental, it should be *comparative* in order to establish a connection between the factor or treatment and the characteristic of interest. For instance, determining the rate of car accidents among people who talk on cell phones while driving is pointless unless you compare it with the rate of car accidents among people who don't talk on cell phones while driving and find that it is significantly different.

While a comparative observational study can suggest a relationship between two variables, such as cell phone use while driving and car accidents, it cannot establish a cause-and-effect relationship because there can be *confounding variables* (also called *lurking variables*) that influence the results. For instance, perhaps people who talk on cell phones while driving are more likely to drive aggressively, so it is the aggressive driving (not the cell phone use) that leads to a higher rate of car accidents.

In an experiment, randomization can remove the problem of a confounding variable by distributing the variable among the groups being compared so that its influence on the groups is more or less equal. Therefore, the best way to establish a cause-and-effect relationship between two variables is through a **randomized comparative experiment** where subjects are randomly divided into two groups: the **treatment group**, which is given the treatment, and the **control group**, which is not.

MCC9–12.S.IC.3

3 EXAMPLE Identifying Control Groups and Treatment Groups

Identify the control group and treatment group in each experiment. Assume all subjects of the research are selected randomly.

A To see whether zinc has an effect on the duration of a cold, half the subjects took tablets containing zinc at the onset of cold symptoms, and half took tablets without any zinc. The durations of the colds were then recorded.

Control group: _______________________________

Treatment group: _______________________________

B To see whether reviewing for a test with a classmate improves test scores, half the subjects studied with a classmate prior to taking a test, and half studied for the test alone. The test scores were then recorded.

Control group: _______________________________

Treatment group: _______________________________

REFLECT

3a. How does using a control group help a researcher interpret the results of an experiment? How does using randomization help?

When you encounter media reports of statistical research in your daily life, you should judge any reported conclusions on the basis of how the research was conducted. Among the questions you should consider are:

- Is the research a survey, an observational study, or an experiment? In broad terms, a survey simply measures variables, an observational study attempts to find a relationship between variables, and an experiment attempts to establish a cause-and-effect relationship between variables.
- Was randomization used in conducting the research? As you know, random sampling is considered the best way to obtain a representative sample from a population and therefore get accurate results. Randomization also helps to dilute the effect of confounding variables.
- Does the report include the details of the research, such as sample size, statistics, and margins of error?

MCC9–12.S.IC.6

4 EXAMPLE Evaluating a Media Report

Evaluate the article about the effect of doctor empathy on the duration and severity of a cold.

A Is this a survey, an observational study, or an experiment? How do you know?

B Was randomization used in the research? If so, how?

C Does the report include the details of the research? If not, what information is missing?

Caring Doctors Shorten and Ease the Common Cold

Researchers have found that among patients with colds, those who gave their doctors perfect scores on a questionnaire measuring empathy had colds that did not last as long and were less severe. Empathy on the part of doctors included making patients feel at ease, listening to their concerns, and showing compassion.

A total of 350 subjects who were experiencing the onset of a cold were randomly assigned to one of three groups: no doctor-patient interaction, standard interaction, and enhanced interaction. Only subjects in the third group saw doctors who had been coached on being empathetic.

REFLECT

4a. What information would you want to see before deciding on the validity of the study?

4b. Describe a confounding variable that might have affected the results of the research. How did the researchers deal with such confounding variables?

PRACTICE

Explain why the results of each survey are likely to be inaccurate and then suggest a way to improve the accuracy of the survey.

1. A store offers its customers a chance to win a cash prize if they call a toll-free number and participate in a survey of customer satisfaction.

2. In a random sample of parents in a school district, a survey asks, "Are you willing to pay a small fee for each school sport that your child participates in?"

For Exercises 3 and 4, determine whether each research study is an observational study or an experiment. Identify the factor if it is an observational study or the treatment if it is an experiment. Also identify the characteristic of interest.

3. Researchers found that of patients who had been taking a bone-loss drug for more than five years, a high percent also had an uncommon type of fracture in the thigh bone.

4. Researchers found that when patients with chronic illnesses were randomly divided into two groups, the group that got regular coaching by phone from health professionals to help them manage their illnesses had lower monthly medical costs than the group that did not get the coaching.

5. Is the research study in Exercise 4 a comparative randomized experiment? If so, identify the treatment group and the control group.

6. Evaluate the article about doctors working when sick.

Doctors Work When Sick

Doctors know that they can get sick from their patients, but when they are sick themselves, do they stay away from their patients? Researchers asked 537 doctors-in-training to anonymously report whether they had worked while sick during the past year. The researchers found that 58% said they had worked once while sick and 31% said they had worked more than once while sick.

a. Is this a survey, an observational study, or an experiment? How do you know?

b. Was randomization used in the research? If so, how?

c. Does the report include the details of the research? If not, what information is missing?

d. What is your overall evaluation of the report? Why?

7. Evaluate the article about antibiotic use in infants.

Antibiotic Use Tied to Asthma and Allergies

Antibiotic use in infants is linked to asthma and allergies, says a study involving 1401 children. Researchers asked mothers how many doses of antibiotics their children received before 6 months of age as well as whether their children had developed asthma or allergies by age 6. Children who received just one dose of antibiotics were 40% more likely to develop asthma or allergies. The risk jumped to 70% for children who received two doses.

a. Is this a survey, an observational study, or an experiment? How do you know?

b. Was randomization used in the research? If so, how?

c. Does the report include the details of the research? If not, what information is missing?

d. What is your overall evaluation of the report? Why?

Name________________________ Class________________ Date____________

8-3

Additional Practice

Explain whether each situation is an experiment or an observational study. The first problem has been completed for you.

1. A park ranger measures the change in height of all trees of a similar species and age over a month. Half the trees are within a quarter of a mile from a large lake and half are further away.

   Observational study; the park ranger gathers data without controlling the individuals or applying a treatment.

2. A park ranger plants 10 trees within a quarter of a mile from a large lake and 10 trees of a similar species and age further than half of a mile from the lake. He then measures the growth of all trees over a month.

   ____

3. A caretaker at a zoo records the sleeping habits of the wildcats at the zoo for a month.

   ____

The study described below is a randomized comparative experiment. Describe the treatment, the treatment group, and the control group. The first problem has been completed for you.

4. A researcher feeds one group of rats high-fat and high-calorie foods like cheesecake, bacon, and pastries. She feeds a second group of rats a normal, nutritious diet. For two weeks, the researcher records how many calories each rat eats daily, as well as how often it goes to its feeding bowl. She compares the data from the one group to the data from the other and finds that the rats that eat the nutritious food get hungry less often and eat a smaller number of calories overall.

   The treatment is *feeding high-fat and high-calorie foods*. The treatment group is the rats that were fed the diet that was not nutritious. The control group is the rats that were fed the nutritious diet.

5. A college professor wants to know if students learn as well in an online class as in person. He decides to offer the same course both online and in a classroom. Students who sign up for the course are told they will be assigned to either class randomly. The professor then gives the same test to both classes and compares the scores.

   ____

Explain whether the research topic is best addressed through an experiment or an observational study. Then explain how you would set up the experiment or observational study.

6. Does being a smoker cause people to get minor sicknesses more often?

   ____

   ____

Problem Solving

Explain whether each situation is an experiment or an observational study.

1. A teacher plays music during all tests given in a one-month period and compares the class grades with a similar class that does not have music played during tests.

   Solution: The teacher applies a treatment (playing music during tests) to some of the individuals (the class). This situation is an example of an experiment.

2. A real estate developer records the listing and selling prices of all homes in one area to determine the difference in the listing price and the selling price.

   Does the real estate developer control the individuals or apply a treatment? ____________

   Is the situation an experiment or an observational study? ____________________________

The study described below is a randomized controlled experiment. Describe the treatment, the treatment group, and the control group.

3. At a seed farm, 50 randomly chosen seeds were treated to temperatures above 100°F, and 50 other randomly chosen seeds were left at normal temperatures. At the end of the growing season, the heated group sprouted 20% faster than the non-heated group.

   ____

   ____

4. An engineer recruits 40 volunteers, and randomly assigns them to two groups. One group fills their cars with gasoline with an additive. The other group fills their cars with plain gasoline. The group that uses the additive sees a 5% decrease in fuel efficiency.

   ____

   ____

Choose the method that would be least biased.

5. An ice cream company wants to test whether the quality of ingredients it uses affects the taste of the product.

   A randomized comparative experiment

   B observational study

   C survey

6. An auto manufacturer wants to measure the fuel efficiency of a new hybrid car.

   F randomized comparative experiment

   G observational study

   H survey

Name_______________ Class_______________ Date_______________

9-1

Significance of Experimental Results

Going Deeper

Video Tutor

Essential question: *In an experiment, when is a difference between the control group and treatment group likely to be caused by the treatment?*

You can think of every randomized comparative experiment as a test of a *null hypothesis*. The **null hypothesis** states that any difference between the control group and the treatment group is due to chance. In other words, the null hypothesis is the assumption that the treatment has no effect.

In statistics, an experimental result is called **significant** if the likelihood that it occurred by chance alone is very low. A low probability of getting the result by chance is evidence in favor of rejecting the null hypothesis. A significant result, however, does not *prove* that the treatment has an effect; the null hypothesis may still be true, and a rare event may simply have occurred. Nevertheless, standard practice in statistics is to reject the null hypothesis in favor of the *alternative* hypothesis that the result is due to the treatment.

Formulating the Null Hypothesis

For each experiment, state the null hypothesis.

A A potential growth agent is sprayed on the leaves of 12 emerging ferns twice a week for a month. Another 12 emerging ferns are not sprayed with the growth agent. The mean stalk lengths of the two groups of ferns are compared after a month.

____

____

B Ten people with colds are treated with a new formula for an existing brand of cold medicine. Ten other people with colds are treated with the original formula. The mean recovery times for the two groups are compared.

____

____

REFLECT

1a. Suppose in part A that the treated ferns had a mean stalk length that is twice the mean stalk length of the untreated ferns. Should the researcher reject the null hypothesis? Does the experimental result prove that the growth agent works? Explain.

____

____

____

____

1b. Suppose in part B that the mean recovery time for both groups is 5 days. Should the researcher reject the null hypothesis? Does the experimental result prove that the new formula is no more effective than the original formula? Explain.

1c. In the U.S. legal system, a defendant is assumed innocent until guilt is proved beyond a reasonable doubt. How is this situation like rejecting a null hypothesis?

Suppose a company that offers an SAT prep course wants to demonstrate that its course raises test scores. The company recruits 20 students and randomly assigns half of them to a treatment group, where subjects take the course before taking the SAT, and half to a control group, where subjects do not take the course before taking the SAT. The table below shows the SAT scores of the 10 students in each group. How can you tell whether the course actually improved the scores of the students in the treatment group?

	SAT Scores				
Treatment Group	1440	1610	1430	1700	1690
	1570	1480	1620	1780	2010
Control Group	1150	1500	1050	1600	1460
	1860	1350	1750	1680	1330

One thing you could do is compute the mean SAT score for each group to see if the means are different. Obviously, the company expects the treatment group's mean to be greater than the control group's mean. But even if that is the case, how do you know that the difference in the means can be attributed to the treatment and not to chance? In other words, how do you know if the difference is *significant*?

The null hypothesis for this experiment is that the SAT prep course has no effect on a student's score. Under this assumption, it doesn't matter whether a student is in the treatment group or the control group. Since each group is a sample of the students, the means of the two samples should be about equal. In fact, any random division of the 20 students into two groups of 10 should result in two means whose difference is relatively small and a matter of chance. This technique, called **resampling**, allows you to create a distribution of the differences of means for every possible pairing of groups with 10 students in each. You can *test* the null hypothesis by using this distribution to find the likelihood, given that the null hypothesis is true, of getting a difference of means at least as great as the actual experimental difference. The test is called a **permutation test**.

MCC9–12.S.IC.5

2 EXAMPLE Using a Permutation Test

Use the table of SAT scores on the previous page to construct a resampling distribution for the difference of means, assuming that the null hypothesis is true. Then determine the significance of the actual experimental result.

A State the null hypothesis in terms of the difference of the two group means.

____

B Calculate the mean score for the treatment group, $\bar{x}_T$, and the mean score for the control group, $\bar{x}_C$. Then find the difference of the means.

$\bar{x}_T =$ ________ $\bar{x}_C =$ ________ $\bar{x}_T - \bar{x}_C =$ ________

C Label the data in the table on the previous page with the identifiers 1 through 20. Then follow these steps to complete each table below:

- Use a calculator's random integer generator to generate a list of 10 identifiers between 1 and 20 with no identifiers repeated.
- Record the scores that correspond to those identifiers as the scores for Group A. Record the remaining 10 scores as the scores for Group B.
- Find $\bar{x}_A$, $\bar{x}_B$, and $\bar{x}_A - \bar{x}_B$, and record them in the table.

	Simulation 1					Means	Difference of means
Group A						$\bar{x}_A =$	$\bar{x}_A - \bar{x}_B =$
Group B						$\bar{x}_B =$	

	Simulation 2					Means	Difference of means
Group A						$\bar{x}_A =$	$\bar{x}_A - \bar{x}_B =$
Group B						$\bar{x}_B =$	

	Simulation 3					Means	Difference of means
Group A						$\bar{x}_A =$	$\bar{x}_A - \bar{x}_B =$
Group B						$\bar{x}_B =$	

D Report the differences of means that you found for simulations 1–3 to your teacher so that he or she can create a frequency table and histogram of the class results. You should make your own copy of the frequency table and histogram using the table and the grid below.

Interval	Frequency
$-320 \le x < -240$	
$-240 \le x < -160$	
$-160 \le x < -80$	
$-80 \le x < 0$	
$0 \le x < 80$	
$80 \le x < 160$	
$160 \le x < 240$	
$240 \le x < 320$	

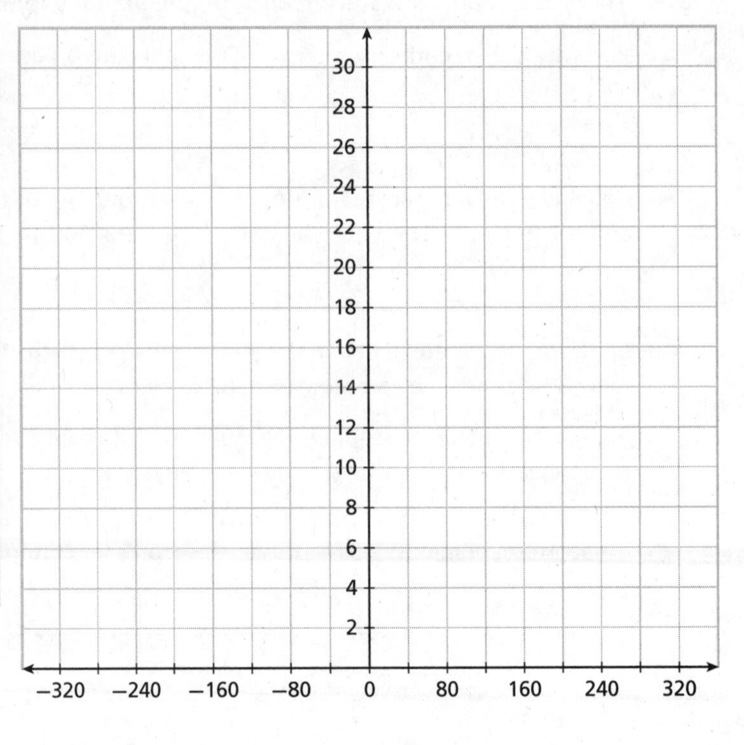

E Explain how you can use the frequency table or the histogram to find the probability that a difference of means is *at least as great* as the difference that you recorded in part B. Then find that probability.

______

______

______

F The probability that you found in part E is called a *P-value*. The *P*-value determines the significance of the experimental result. Statisticians commonly use the following levels of significance:

- When $P > 0.10$, the result is *not significant.*
- When $0.05 < P \le 0.10$, the result is *marginally significant.*
- When $0.01 < P \le 0.05$, the result is *significant.*
- When $P \le 0.01$, the result is *highly significant.*

Using the *P*-value that you obtained in part E, characterize the significance of the experimental result for the SAT scores.

______

G State the conclusion that you can draw from the permutation test.

______

______

REFLECT

2a. The reason that the test is called a *permutation* test is that the process of resampling assigns different permutations of the labels "treatment" and "control" to the 20 SAT scores. Although the number of permutations of n distinct objects is $n!$, the objects in this case are 10 "treatment" labels and 10 "control" labels, so the 20 labels are not distinct. When a set of n objects contains n_1 copies of the first object, n_2 copies of the second object, . . ., and n_L copies of the last object, then the formula for the number of permutations of the n objects becomes $\frac{n!}{n_1! \cdot n_2! \cdot \cdots \cdot n_L!}$. Use this formula to find the number of permutations of the labels for the SAT scores. Did your class generate all possible resamples?

2b. Suppose your class had generated all possible resamples. Explain why the distribution would be perfectly symmetric and centered on 0.

2c. Explain why it makes sense to call the test of significance in part F a *one-tailed* test?

PRACTICE

1. King County, Washington, recently required all restaurant chains to post Calorie counts for menu items. Researchers gathered data on the average Calories per transaction at a Mexican restaurant chain both before and after the regulation went into effect.

a. State the null hypothesis in terms of the difference in the average Calories per transaction before and after Calorie counts were posted.

b. The researchers found a slight increase in the average Calories per transaction once the regulation went into effect, but the result was not statistically different from 0. What does this result mean in terms of accepting or rejecting the null hypothesis?

For Exercises 2–4, use the following information.

A textbook company has created an electronic version of one of its books and wants to know what effect, if any, using the e-book has on student learning. With the permission of the school district, a teacher who has two classes that already use the textbook agrees to participate in a research study. One of the classes uses the e-book for the next unit of instruction while the other class continues to use the print version of the book. After teaching the unit, the teacher gives the same test to both classes. The mean score for the class using the e-book is 82.3, while the mean score for the class using the print book is 78.2.

2. State the null hypothesis in terms of the difference of the mean test scores.

3. Identify the treatment group and its mean test score, $\bar{x}_T$, as well as the control group and its mean test score, $\bar{x}_C$. Then find $\bar{x}_T - \bar{x}_C$.

4. The resampling distribution for the difference of mean test scores, given that the null hypothesis is true, is normal with a mean of 0 and a standard error of 2. The distribution is shown at the right.

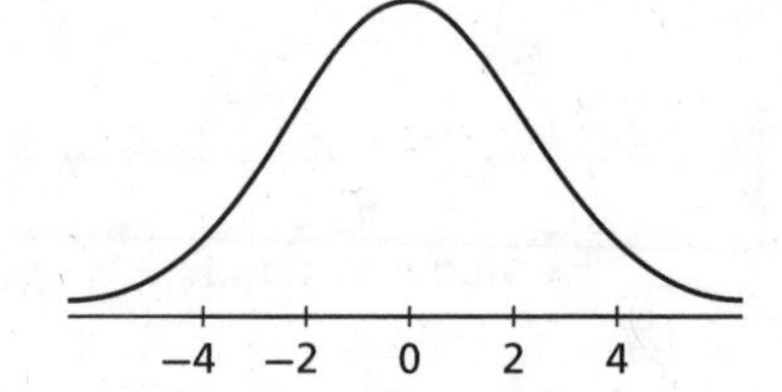

a. Describe how the resampling distribution is obtained from the students' test scores.

b. Write an interval that captures the middle 95% of the differences of means in the resampling distribution. If the experimental result falls within this interval, the result is not significant; if it falls outside the interval, the result is significant. Which is the case?

c. Explain why the test of significance in part b is called a *two-tailed* test.

d. Should the null hypothesis be accepted or rejected? What does acceptance or rejection mean in this situation?

Name________________________ Class______________ Date____________

9-1

Additional Practice

1. The makers of a light bulb claim that their light bulbs last longer than the leading brand. A researcher tests this claim by finding the mean length of time that 25 bulbs of each brand last. State the null hypothesis for the experiment.

____

2. A pharmaceutical company is testing a new drug to see whether it lowers cholesterol in women. They randomly divide 150 volunteers into two groups. The volunteers in each group have their cholesterol monitored for one month to establish a baseline. Then one group is given the drug for a one month period, and the other group is given a placebo for a one month period. The mean change in cholesterol before and after treatment is found for each group. State the null hypothesis for the experiment.

____

____

3. A study investigates how many numbers in a list a person can memorize in order in 30 seconds. Volunteers are randomly assigned either to a group simply shown the list or to a group taught a memorization strategy before being shown the list. A report on the study's results includes the statement, "After comparing the means of the groups, the null hypothesis is rejected with a *P*-value of 0.01." What does this statement say about the results of the study?

____

____

____

For Exercises 4 and 5, use the following information.

The results of an experiment are resampled 80 times by randomly assigning them to a "control" or a "treatment" group, and the differences in the means are found for each resampling. The table gives the results of the differences x.

Interval	Frequency
$-16 \le x < -12$	1
$-12 \le x < -8$	6
$-8 \le x < -4$	10
$-4 \le x < 0$	18
$0 \le x < 4$	23
$4 \le x < 8$	13
$8 \le x < 12$	7
$12 \le x < 16$	2

4. In the original experiment, the difference of the means was 8. What is the *P*-value for this result?

____

5. Using a one-tailed test, what is the significance of the experimental result?

____

Problem Solving

For Exercises 1–3, use the following information.

In a lab comparing handle strengths of two kinds of paper bags, students add weight to each bag and record the weight at which its handles fail. The results are shown below.

	Trial 1	Trial 2	Trial 3	Trial 4	Trial 5
Bag A	25 lb	22 lb	27 lb	26 lb	21 lb
Bag B	35 lb	37 lb	30 lb	31 lb	40 lb

1. What is the difference of the means for the two groups? ____________

2. State the null hypothesis of the experiment.

   ____

3. Dee uses a graphing calculator to randomly resample the data 100 times. The distribution of the resampling difference of means $\bar{x}_B - \bar{x}_A$ has a mean of –0.2 and a standard error of 3.8. Is the difference of means from Exercise 1 significant? Explain.

   ____

   ____

For Exercises 4 and 5, use the following information.

Students record how long it takes a given amount of water to boil using identical burners. Half of the students do not add salt to the water (control) and half add a teaspoon of salt (treatment). The boiling times in seconds are shown in the chart below.

Control	65	78	64	71	75
Treatment	61	70	73	69	64

4. The resampling distribution for the difference of mean boiling times is normal with a mean of 0 and a standard error of about 3.3. Are the experimental results significant? Explain.

   ____

   ____

5. Adding salt to water raises the boiling point a very small amount. Explain how this can be consistent with the information in Exercise 4.

   ____

   ____

Name________________________ Class______________ Date__________

9-2

Sampling Distributions

Extension: Confidence Intervals and Margins of Error

Essential question: *How do you calculate a confidence interval and a margin of error for a population proportion or mean?*

Video Tutor

MCC9-12.S.IC.4

1 EXPLORE Developing a Sampling Distribution

The table provides data about the first 50 people to join a new gym. For each person, the table lists his or her member ID number, age, and sex.

ID	Age	Sex	ID	Age	Sex	ID	Age	Sex	ID	Age	Sex	ID	Age	Sex
1	30	M	11	38	F	21	74	F	31	32	M	41	46	M
2	48	M	12	24	M	22	21	M	32	28	F	42	34	F
3	52	M	13	48	F	23	29	F	33	35	M	43	44	F
4	25	F	14	45	M	24	48	M	34	49	M	44	68	M
5	63	F	15	28	F	25	37	M	35	18	M	45	24	F
6	50	F	16	39	M	26	52	F	36	56	F	46	34	F
7	18	F	17	37	F	27	25	F	37	48	F	47	55	F
8	28	F	18	63	F	28	44	M	38	38	F	48	39	M
9	72	M	19	20	M	29	29	F	39	52	F	49	40	F
10	25	F	20	81	F	30	66	M	40	33	F	50	30	F

A Use your calculator to find the mean age μ and standard deviation σ for the population of the gym's first 50 members. Round to the nearest tenth.

$\mu =$ __________; $\sigma =$ __________

B Use your calculator's random number generator to choose a sample of 5 gym members. Find the mean age $\bar{x}$ for your sample. Round to the nearest tenth.

$\bar{x} =$ ______________________________

C Report your sample mean to your teacher. As other students report their sample means, create a class histogram below. To do so, shade a square above the appropriate interval as each sample mean is reported. For sample means that lie on an interval boundary (such as 39.5), shade a square on the interval to the right (39.5 to 40.5).

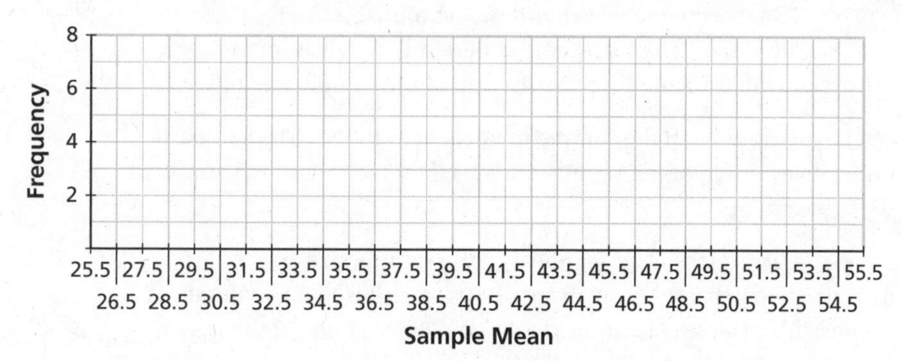

D Calculate the mean of the sample means $\mu_{\bar{x}}$ and the standard deviation of the sample means $\sigma_{\bar{x}}$.

$\mu_{\bar{x}} =$ __________; $\sigma_{\bar{x}} =$ __________

E Now use your calculator's random number generator to choose a sample of 15 gym members. Find the mean $\bar{x}$ for your sample. Round to the nearest tenth.

$\bar{x} =$ ____________

F Report your sample mean to your teacher and make a class histogram below.

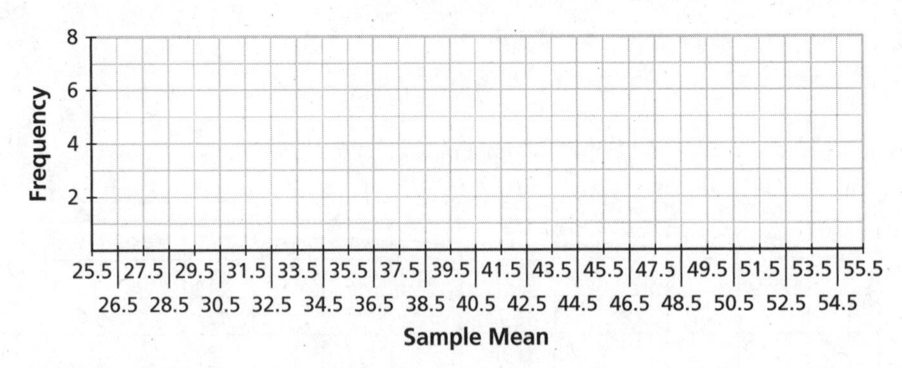

G Calculate the mean of the sample means $\mu_{\bar{x}}$ and the standard deviation of the sample means $\sigma_{\bar{x}}$.

$\mu_{\bar{x}} =$ ________; $\sigma_{\bar{x}} =$ ________

REFLECT

1a. In the class histograms, how does the mean of the sample means compare with the population mean?

____

1b. What happens to the standard deviation of the sample means as the sample size increases?

____

1c. What happens to the shape of the histogram as the sample size increases?

____

The histograms that you made are *sampling distributions*. A **sampling distribution** shows how a particular statistic varies across all samples of n individuals from the same population. You have worked with the sampling distribution of the sample mean, $\bar{x}$.

The mean of the sampling distribution of the sample mean is denoted $\mu_{\bar{x}}$. The standard deviation of the sampling distribution of the sample mean is denoted $\sigma_{\bar{x}}$ and is also called the **standard error of the mean**.

You may have discovered that $\mu_{\bar{x}}$ is close to $\bar{x}$ regardless of the sample size and that $\sigma_{\bar{x}}$ decreases as the sample size n increases. These observations were based on simulations. When you consider *all* possible samples of n individuals, you arrive at one of the major theorems of statistics.

Properties of the Sampling Distribution of the Sample Mean

If a random sample of size n is selected from a population with mean μ and standard deviation σ, then

(1) $\mu_{\bar{x}} = \mu$,

(2) $\sigma_{\bar{x}} = \frac{\sigma}{\sqrt{n}}$, and

(3) the sampling distribution of the sample mean is normal if the population is normal; for all other populations, the sampling distribution of the mean approaches a normal distribution as n increases.

The third property stated above is known as the Central Limit Theorem.

All normal distributions have the following properties, sometimes collectively called the *68-95-99.7 rule*:

- 68% of the data fall within 1 standard deviation of the mean.
- 95% of the data fall within 2 standard deviations of the mean.
- 99.7% of the data fall within 3 standard deviations of the mean.

You will learn more about the specific properties of normal distributions later in this chapter.

MCC9–12.S.IC.4

2 EXAMPLE Using the Sampling Distribution of the Sample Mean

Boxes of Cruncho cereal have a mean mass of 323 g with a standard deviation of 20 g. You choose a random sample of 36 boxes of the cereal. What interval captures 95% of the means for random samples of 36 boxes?

- Write the given information about the population and the sample.

$\mu =$ ________ $\sigma =$ ________ $n =$ ________

- Find the mean of the sampling distribution of the sample mean and the standard error of the mean.

$\mu_{\bar{x}} = \mu =$ ________ $\sigma_{\bar{x}} = \frac{\sigma}{\sqrt{n}} = \frac{\square}{\square} \approx$ ________

The sampling distribution of the sample mean is approximately normal. In a normal distribution, 95% of the data fall within 2 standard deviations of the mean.

$\mu_{\bar{x}} - 2\sigma_{\bar{x}} = \square - 2(\square) =$ ________

$\mu_{\bar{x}} + 2\sigma_{\bar{x}} = \square + 2(\square) =$ ________

So, 95% of the sample means fall between ________ g and ________ g.

REFLECT

2a. When you choose a sample of 36 boxes, is it possible for the sample to have a mean mass of 315 g? Is it likely? Explain.

____

____

MCC9–12.S.IC.4

3 EXPLORE Developing Another Sampling Distribution

Use the table of data from the first Explore. This time you will develop a sampling distribution based on a sample proportion rather than a sample mean.

A Find the proportion p of gym members in the population who are female.

$p =$ ________

B Use your calculator's random number generator to choose a sample of 5 gym members. Find the proportion of female members $\hat{p}$ for your sample.

$\hat{p} =$ ________

C Report your sample proportion to your teacher. As other students report their sample proportions, create a class histogram at right.

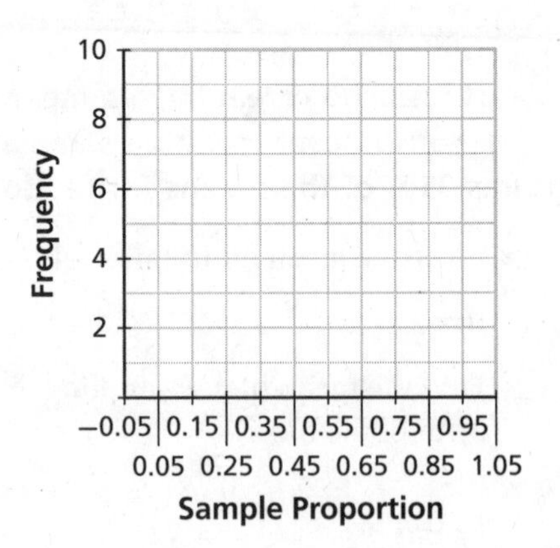

D Calculate the mean of the sample proportions $\mu_{\hat{p}}$ and the standard deviation of the sample proportions $\sigma_{\hat{p}}$. Round to the nearest hundredth.

$\mu_{\hat{p}} =$ ________; $\sigma_{\hat{p}} =$ ________

E Now use your calculator's random number generator to choose a sample of 10 gym members. Find the proportion of female members $\hat{p}$ for your sample.

$\hat{p} =$ ________

F Report your sample proportion to your teacher. As other students report their sample proportions, create a class histogram at right.

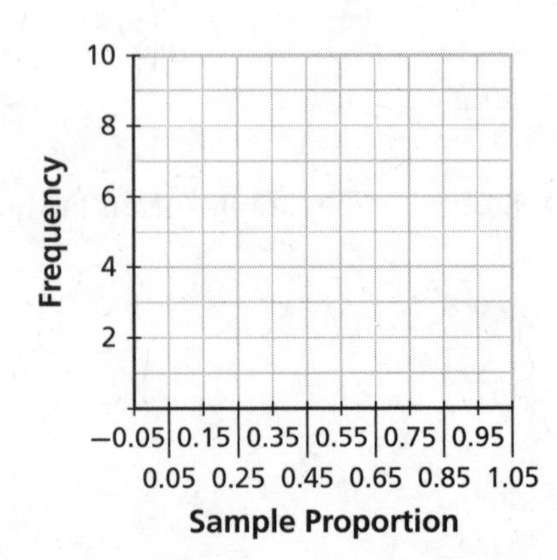

G Calculate the mean of the sample proportions $\mu_{\hat{p}}$ and the standard deviation of the sample proportions $\sigma_{\hat{p}}$. Round to the nearest hundredth.

$\mu_{\hat{p}} =$ ________; $\sigma_{\hat{p}} =$ ________

REFLECT

3a. In the class histograms, how does the mean of the sample proportions compare with the population proportion?

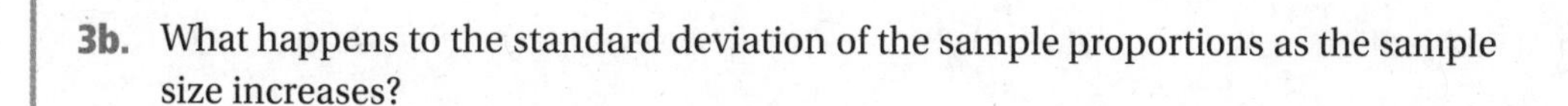

3b. What happens to the standard deviation of the sample proportions as the sample size increases?

____

When you work with the sampling distribution of a sample proportion, p represents the proportion of individuals in the population that have a particular characteristic (that is, the proportion of "successes") and $\hat{p}$ is the proportion of successes in a sample. The mean of the sampling distribution of the sample proportion is denoted $\mu_{\hat{p}}$. The standard deviation of the sampling distribution of the sample proportion is denoted $\sigma_{\hat{p}}$ and is also called the **standard error of the proportion**.

Properties of the Sampling Distribution of the Sample Proportion

If a random sample of size n is selected from a population with proportion of successes p, then

(1) $\mu_{\hat{p}} = p$,

(2) $\sigma_{\hat{p}} = \sqrt{\frac{p(1-p)}{n}}$, and

(3) if both np and $n(1-p)$ are at least 10, then the sampling distribution of the sample proportion is approximately normal.

MCC9–12.S.IC.4

4 EXAMPLE Using the Sampling Distribution of the Sample Proportion

About 40% of the students at a university live off campus. You choose a random sample of 50 students. What interval captures 95% of the proportions for random samples of 50 students?

A Write the given information about the population and the sample, where a success is a student who lives off campus.

$p =$ _______ $n =$ _______

B Find the mean of the sampling distribution of the sample proportion and the standard error of the proportion.

$\mu_{\hat{p}} = p =$ _______ $\sigma_{\hat{p}} = \sqrt{\frac{p(1-p)}{n}} = \sqrt{\frac{\square\left(1-\square\right)}{\square}} \approx$ _______

C Check that np and $n(1-p)$ are both at least 10.

$np =$ ☐ • ☐ = ______ $n(1-p) =$ ☐ • ☐ = ______

Since np and $n(1-p)$ are both greater than 10, the sampling distribution is approximately normal.

D In a normal distribution, 95% of the data fall within 2 standard deviations of the mean.

$\mu_{\hat{p}} - 2\sigma_{\hat{p}} =$ ☐ $- 2($☐$) =$ ______

$\mu_{\hat{p}} + 2\sigma_{\hat{p}} =$ ☐ $+ 2($☐$) =$ ______

So, 95% of the sample proportions fall between ______ and ______.

REFLECT

4a. How likely is it that a random sample of 50 students includes 31 students who live off campus? Explain.

______

______

Previously, you investigated sampling from a population whose parameter of interest (mean or proportion) is known. In many real-world situations, you collect sample data from a population whose parameter of interest is not known. Now you will learn how to use sample statistics to make inferences about population parameters.

MCC9–12.S.IC.4

5 EXPLORE Analyzing Likely Population Proportions

You survey a random sample of 50 students at a large high school and find that 40% of the students have attended a school football game. You cannot survey the entire population of students, but you would like to know what population proportions are reasonably likely in this situation.

A Suppose the proportion p of the population that has attended a school football game is 30%. Find the reasonably likely values of the sample proportion $\hat{p}$.

In this case, $p =$ ______ and $n =$ ______.

$\mu_{\hat{p}} = p =$ ______ and $\sigma_{\hat{p}} = \sqrt{\frac{p(1-p)}{n}} = \sqrt{\frac{☐(1-☐)}{☐}} \approx$ ______

The reasonably likely values of $\hat{p}$ fall within 2 standard deviations of $\mu_{\hat{p}}$.

$\mu_{\hat{p}} - 2\sigma_{\hat{p}} =$ ☐ $- 2($☐$) =$ ______

$\mu_{\hat{p}} + 2\sigma_{\hat{p}} =$ ☐ $+ 2($☐$) =$ ______

B On the graph, draw a horizontal line segment at the level of 0.3 on the vertical axis to represent the interval of likely values of $\hat{p}$ that you found above.

C Now repeat the process for $p = 0.35$, 0.4, 0.45, and so on to complete the graph. You may wish to divide up the work with other students and pool your findings.

D Draw a vertical line at 0.4 on the horizontal axis. This represents $\hat{p} = 0.4$. The line segments that this vertical line intersects are the population proportions for which a sample proportion of 0.4 is reasonably likely.

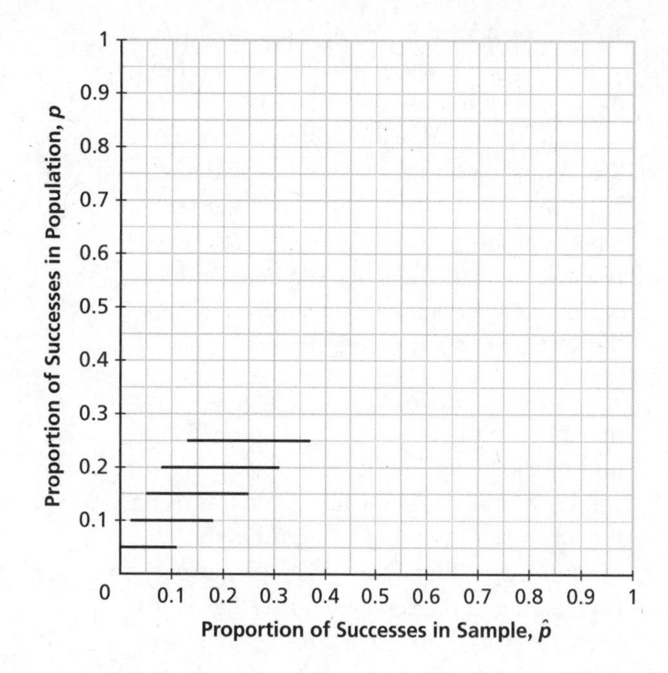

REFLECT

5a. Given that the sample proportion is $\hat{p} = 0.4$, is it possible that 30% of all students at the school have attended a football game? Is it likely? Explain.

5b. Is it possible that 60% of all students at the school have attended a football game? Is it likely? Explain.

5c. Based on your graph, which population proportions do you think are reasonably likely? Why?

A **confidence interval** is an approximate range of values that is likely to include an unknown population parameter. The *level* or *degree* of a confidence interval, such as 95%, gives the probability that the interval includes the true value of the parameter.

Recall that when data are normally distributed, 95% of the values fall within 2 standard deviations of the mean. Using this idea in the Explore, you found a 95% confidence interval for the proportion of all students who have attended a school football game.

To develop a formula for a confidence interval, notice that the vertical bold line segment in the figure, which represents the 95% confidence interval you found in the Explore, is about the same length as the horizontal bold line segment. The horizontal bold line segment has endpoints $\mu_{\hat{p}} - 2\sigma_{\hat{p}}$ and $\mu_{\hat{p}} + 2\sigma_{\hat{p}}$ where $\hat{p} = 0.4$. Since the bold line segments intersect at (0.4, 0.4), the vertical bold line segment has these same endpoints.

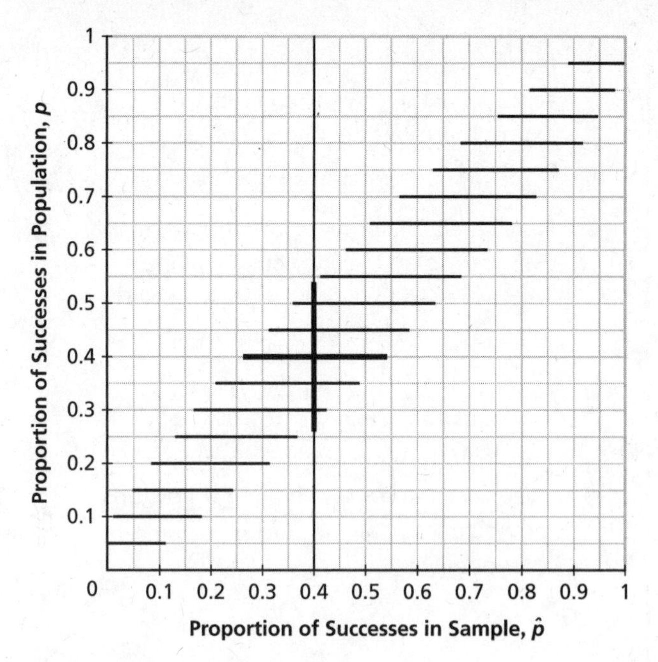

The above argument shows that you can find the endpoints of the confidence interval by finding the endpoints of the horizontal segment centered at $\hat{p}$. You know how to do this using the formula for the standard error of the sampling distribution of the sample proportion from earlier in this lesson. Putting these ideas together gives the following result.

A Confidence Interval for a Population Proportion

A c% confidence interval for the proportion p of successes in a population is given by

$$\hat{p} - z_c\sqrt{\frac{\hat{p}(1-\hat{p})}{n}} \leq p \leq \hat{p} + z_c\sqrt{\frac{\hat{p}(1-\hat{p})}{n}}$$

where $\hat{p}$ is the sample proportion, n is the sample size, and z_c depends upon the desired degree of confidence.

In order for this interval to describe the value of p reasonably accurately, three conditions must be met.

1. There are only two possible outcomes associated with the parameter of interest. The population proportion for one outcome is p, and the proportion for the other outcome is $1 - p$.
2. $n\hat{p}$ and $n(1 - \hat{p})$ must both be at least 10.
3. The size of the population must be at least 10 times the size of the sample, and the sample must be random.

Use the values in the table below for z_c. (Note that for greater accuracy you should use 1.96 rather than 2 for $z_{95\%}$.)

Desired degree of confidence	90%	95%	99%
Value of z_c	1.645	1.96	2.576

MCC9–12.S.IC.4

6 EXAMPLE Finding a Confidence Interval for a Proportion

In a random sample of 100 four-year-old children in the United States, 76 were able to write their name. Find a 95% confidence interval for the proportion *p* of four-year-olds in the United States who can write their name.

A Determine the sample size n, the proportion $\hat{p}$ of four-year-olds in the sample who can write their name, and the value of z_c for a 95% confidence interval.

$n =$ ________ $\hat{p} =$ ________ $z_c =$ ________

B Substitute the values of n, $\hat{p}$, and z_c into the formulas for the endpoints of the confidence interval. Then simplify and round to two decimal places.

$$\hat{p} - z_c\sqrt{\frac{\hat{p}(1-\hat{p})}{n}} = \square - \square\sqrt{\frac{\square(1-\square)}{\square}} \approx \_\_\_\_\_\_$$

$$\hat{p} + z_c\sqrt{\frac{\hat{p}(1-\hat{p})}{n}} = \square + \square\sqrt{\frac{\square(1-\square)}{\square}} \approx \_\_\_\_\_\_$$

So, you can state with 95% confidence that the proportion of all four-year-olds in the United States who can write their name lies between ________ and ________.

REFLECT

6a. Find the 99% confidence interval for p and describe how increasing the degree of confidence affects the range of values. Why does this make sense?

____

____

____

____

You can use reasoning similar to the argument in the Explore to develop a formula for a confidence interval for a population mean.

A Confidence Interval for a Population Mean

A $c\%$ confidence interval for the mean μ in a normally distributed population is given by

$$\bar{x} - z_c\frac{\sigma}{\sqrt{n}} \le \mu \le \bar{x} + z_c\frac{\sigma}{\sqrt{n}}$$

where $\bar{x}$ is the sample mean, n is the sample size, σ is the population standard deviation, and z_c depends upon the desired degree of confidence.

Note that it is assumed that the population is normally distributed and that you know the population standard deviation σ. In a more advanced statistics course, you can develop a confidence interval formula that does not depend upon a normally distributed population or knowing the population standard deviation.

MCC9–12.S.IC.4

7 EXAMPLE Finding a Confidence Interval for a Mean

In a random sample of 20 students at a large high school, the mean score on a standardized test is 610. Given that the standard deviation of all scores at the school is 120, find a 99% confidence interval for the mean score among all students at the school.

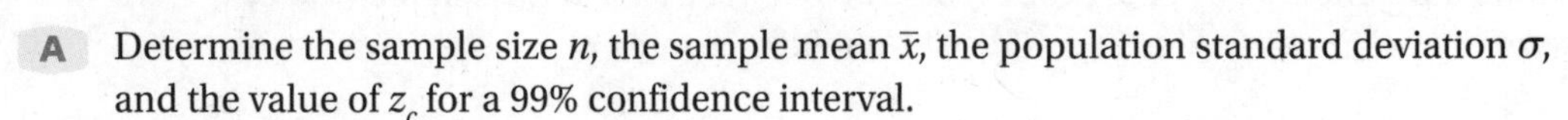

A Determine the sample size n, the sample mean $\bar{x}$, the population standard deviation σ, and the value of z_c for a 99% confidence interval.

$n =$ ________ $\bar{x} =$ ________

$\sigma =$ ________ $z_c =$ ________

B Substitute the values of n, $\bar{x}$, σ, and z_c into the formulas for the endpoints of the confidence interval. Then simplify and round to the nearest whole number.

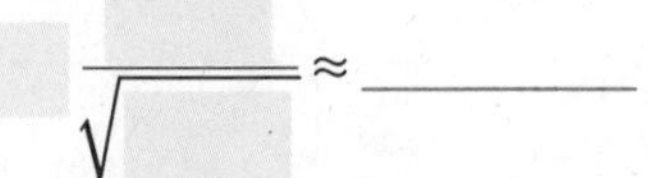

$\bar{x} - z_c \frac{\sigma}{\sqrt{n}} = \square - \square \frac{\square}{\sqrt{\square}} \approx$ ________

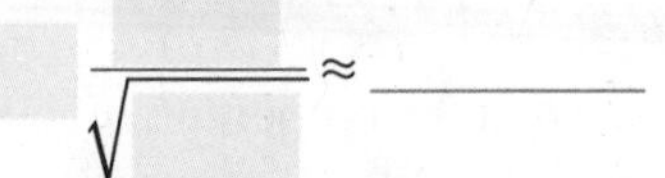

$\bar{x} + z_c \frac{\sigma}{\sqrt{n}} = \square + \square \frac{\square}{\sqrt{\square}} \approx$ ________

So, you can state with 99% confidence that the mean score among all students at the school lies between ________ and ________.

REFLECT

7a. What is the 99% confidence interval when the sample size increases to 50? Describe how increasing the sample size affects the confidence interval.

____

____

7b. What do you assume about the test scores of all students at the school in order to use the formula for the confidence interval?

____

In the previous example, you found the 99% confidence interval $541 \leq \mu \leq 679$, which is a range of values centered at $\mu = 610$. You can write the confidence interval as 610 ± 69, where 69 is the *margin of error*. The **margin of error** is half the length of a confidence interval.

Margin of Error for a Population Proportion

The margin of error E for the proportion of successes in a population with sample proportion $\hat{p}$ and sample size n is given by

$$E = z_c\sqrt{\frac{\hat{p}(1-\hat{p})}{n}}$$

where z_c depends on the degree of the confidence interval.

Margin of Error for a Population Mean

The margin of error E for the mean in a normally distributed population with standard deviation σ and sample size n is given by

$$E = z_c\frac{\sigma}{\sqrt{n}}$$

where z_c depends on the degree of the confidence interval.

From the above formulas, it is clear that the margin of error decreases as the sample size n increases.

PRACTICE

Bags of SnackTime Popcorn have a mean mass of 15 ounces with a standard deviation of 1.5 ounces. A quality control inspector selects a random sample of 40 bags of popcorn at the factory. Find each of the following.

1. What is the population mean? ____________

2. What is the mean of the sampling distribution of the sample mean? ____________

3. What is the standard error of the sample mean? ____________

4. What interval captures 95% of the sample means for random samples of 40 bags of popcorn?

____

5. In a random sample of 100 U.S. households, 37 had a pet dog.

a. Do the data satisfy the three conditions for the confidence interval formula for a population proportion? Why or why not?

____

____

____

____

b. Find a 90% confidence interval for the proportion p of U.S. households that have a pet dog.

____

c. Find a 95% confidence interval for the proportion p of U.S. households that have a pet dog.

6. In a quality control study, 200 cars made by a particular company were randomly selected and 13 were found to have defects in the electrical system.

a. Give a range for the percent p of all cars made by the company that have defective electrical systems, assuming you want to have a 90% degree of confidence.

b. What is the margin of error?

c. How does the margin of error change if you want to report the range of percents p with a 95% degree of confidence?

7. The mean annual salary for a random sample of 300 kindergarten through 12th grade teachers in a particular state is $50,500. The standard deviation among the state's entire population of teachers is $3,700. Find a 95% confidence interval for the mean annual salary μ for all kindergarten through 12th grade teachers in the state.

8. You survey a random sample of 90 students at a university whose students' grade-point averages (GPAs) have a standard deviation of 0.4. The surveyed students have a mean GPA of 3.1.

a. How likely is it that the mean GPA among all students at the university is 3.25? Explain.

b. What are you assuming about the GPAs of all students at the university? Why?

9. The margin of error E for the proportion of successes in a population may be estimated by $\frac{1}{\sqrt{n}}$ where n is the sample size. Explain where this estimate comes from. (*Hint:* Assume a 95% confidence interval.)

Name________________________ Class______________ Date__________ 9-2

Additional Practice

For Exercises 1–3, use the following information: The mean height of the population of male high school students in a school district is 67.2 inches with a standard deviation of 2.8 inches.

1. Random samples are drawn from the population. What is the mean of the sampling distribution of the sample mean?

   ____

2. What is the standard error of the mean for a random sample of 25 students? for a random sample of 64 students?

   ____

3. What interval captures 95% of the sample means for a sample size of 64 students?

   ____

For Exercises 4 and 5, use the following information: From a random sample of 30 customers who bought a soft-serve frozen yogurt cone, 26% chose chocolate-vanilla swirl.

4. Find $n\hat{p}$ and $n(1 - \hat{p})$ where n is the sample size and $\hat{p}$ is the sample proportion.

   ____

5. Is it reasonable to use this sample to construct a confidence interval for the population proportion of customers who would choose chocolate-vanilla swirl? Explain.

   ____

6. In a random sample of 44 students from a school of 1290 students, 60% chose red and blue for the new school colors over red and white. Find a 90% confidence interval for the proportion p of students at the school who prefer red and blue. Can you conclude with 90% confidence that the majority of students prefer red and blue?

   ____

7. In a random sample of 550 students in a state, the mean math score on a standardized test was 22.6. Find a 95% confidence interval for the population mean score μ for the state given that the standard deviation is 4.8.

   ____

Find the margin of error *E* for the statistic at the given confidence level.

8. population proportion, if sample proportion $\hat{p} = 0.11$ and sample size $n = 124$; 99% ________

9. population mean, if standard deviation $\sigma = 6.8$ and sample size $n = 1000$; 95% ________

Problem Solving

Out of a random sample of $n = 40$ students from a high school with more than 2000 students, $\hat{p} = 58\%$ say that their morning travel time to school is less than 30 minutes.

1. Can you use the data to construct a reasonably accurate confidence interval for the proportion of students with a morning travel time of less than 30 minutes? Explain.

2. Can you conclude that the morning travel time for the majority of the students is less than 30 minutes at the 90%, 95%, or 99% confidence level? Explain.

3. If you increase the sample size to $n = 125$ students and obtain the same sample proportion of $\hat{p} = 0.58$, does this change your answer to Exercise 2? Explain.

For Exercises 4 and 5, a random sample is drawn from a population with a normally distributed statistic with mean μ and standard deviation $\sigma = 20$.

4. What is the margin of error E for estimating μ from the sample mean at the 95% confidence level for a sample size of $n = 100$?

5. How can you use the margin of error formula to find the minimum sample size so that $E \leq 2.0$ at the 95% confidence level? What is this sample size?

6. What is the relationship between the margin of error E for a population proportion when the sample proportion is $\hat{p} = 0.2$ and when the sample proportion is $\hat{p} = 0.5$ for a given confidence level and sample size?

Name______________________ Class______________ Date__________

9-3

Fitting to a Normal Distribution

Going Deeper

Essential question: *How do you find percents of data and probabilities of events associated with normal distributions?*

Video Tutor

MCC9–12.S.ID.4

1 EXPLORE Substituting a Normal Curve for a Symmetric Histogram

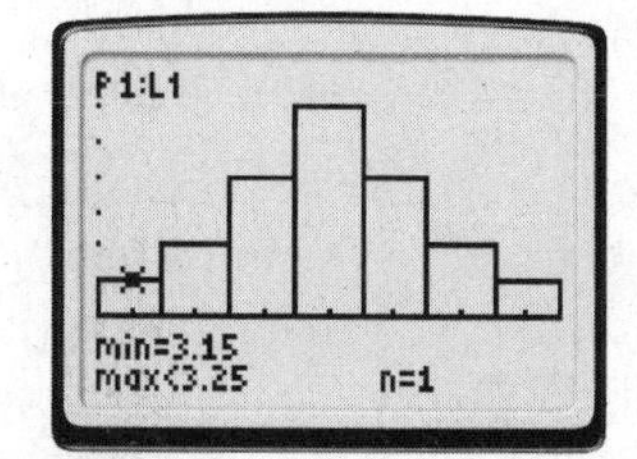

Previously, you used a graphing calculator to create a histogram for a set of 20 baby weights. The baby weights had a mean of 3.5 kg and a standard deviation of 0.14 kg. Because the histogram was perfectly symmetric, you learned that it represents a *normal distribution*. The table below gives the frequency of each weight from the data set.

Weight (kg)	3.2	3.3	3.4	3.5	3.6	3.7	3.8
Frequency	1	2	4	6	4	2	1

You can use a graphing calculator to draw a smooth bell-shaped curve, called a *normal curve*, that captures the shape of the histogram. A normal curve has the property that the area under the curve (and above the x-axis) is 1. This means that you must adjust the heights of the bars in the histogram so that the sum of the areas of the bars is 1.

A Convert the frequency table above to a relative frequency table by using the fact that there are 20 data values.

Weight (kg)	3.2	3.3	3.4	3.5	3.6	3.7	3.8
Relative frequency	$\frac{1}{20} = 0.05$						

What is the sum of the relative frequencies? __________

B For a given baby weight, the relative frequency is the area that you want the bar to have. Since you used a bar width of 0.1 when you created the histogram, the area of the bar is $0.1h$ where h is the height of the bar. You want $0.1h$ to equal the relative frequency f, so solve $0.1h = f$ for h to find the adjusted bar height.

Weight (kg)	3.2	3.3	3.4	3.5	3.6	3.7	3.8
Adjusted bar height	$\frac{0.05}{0.1} = 0.5$						

C Enter each weight from the table in part B into L_1 on your graphing calculator. Then enter each adjusted bar height into L_2.

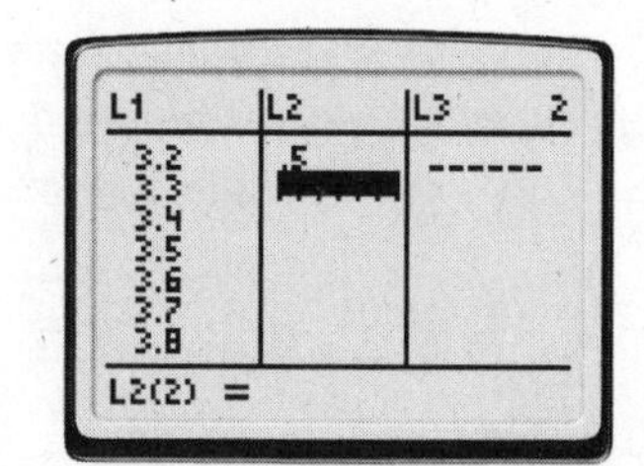

D Turn on a statistics plot and select the histogram option. For Xlist, enter L_1. For Freq, enter L_2. Set the graphing window as shown. Then press GRAPH.

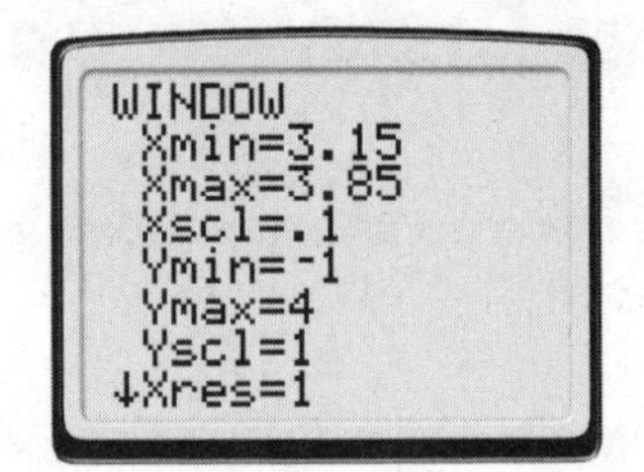

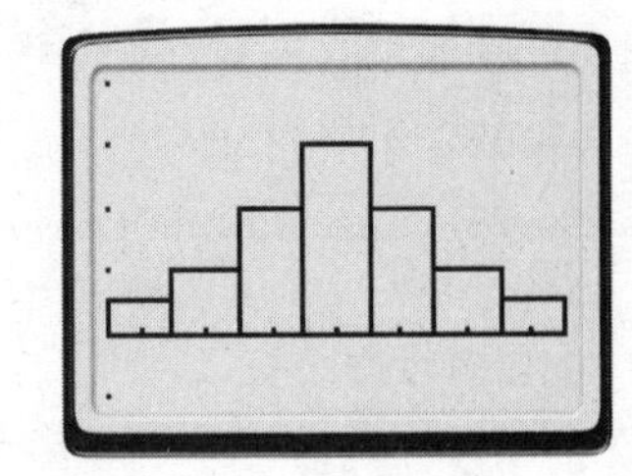

E Your calculator has a built-in function called a *normal probability density function,* which you can access by pressing 2nd VARS (DISTR) and selecting the first choice from the DISTR (distribution) menu. When entering this function to be graphed, you must include the mean and standard deviation of the distribution as shown below. When you press GRAPH, the calculator will draw a normal curve that fits the histogram.

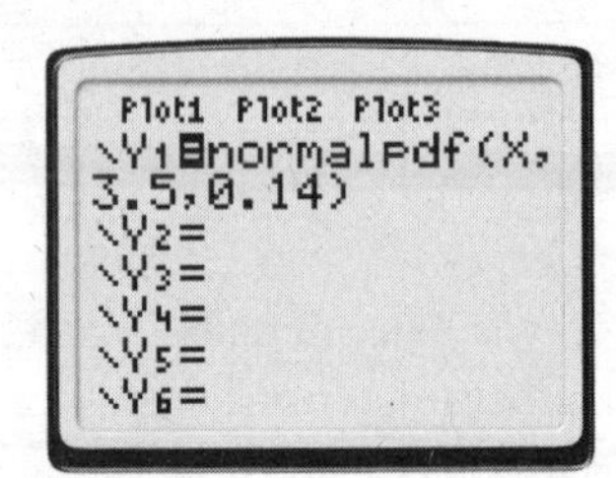

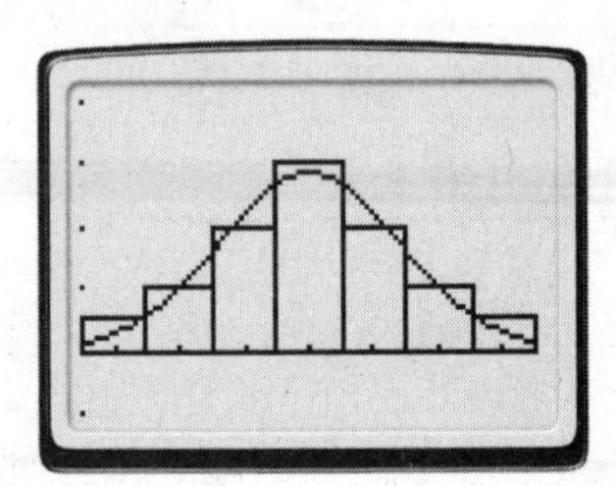

REFLECT

1a. Describe the end behavior of the normal probability density function.

____

1b. If the area under the normal curve is 1, then what is the area under the curve to the left of the mean, 3.5? Describe how to obtain this area using the bars in the histogram. Show that your method gives the correct result.

____

____

1c. Explain how you can use the bars in the histogram to estimate the area under the curve within 1 standard deviation of the mean, which is the interval from $3.5 - 0.14 = 3.36$ to $3.5 + 0.14 = 3.64$ on the x-axis. Then find the estimate.

____

____

1d. Explain how you can use the bars in the histogram to estimate the area under the curve within 2 standard deviations of the mean, which is the interval from $3.5 - 2(0.14) = 3.22$ to $3.5 + 2(0.14) = 3.78$ on the x-axis. Then find the estimate.

____

____

Normal Curves All normal curves have the following properties, sometimes collectively called the *68-95-99.7 rule*:

- 68% of the data fall within 1 standard deviation of the mean.
- 95% of the data fall within 2 standard deviations of the mean.
- 99.7% of the data fall within 3 standard deviations of the mean.

The figure at the left below illustrates the 68-95-99.7 rule.

A normal curve's symmetry allows you to separate the area under the curve into eight parts and know the percent of the data in each part, as shown at the right below.

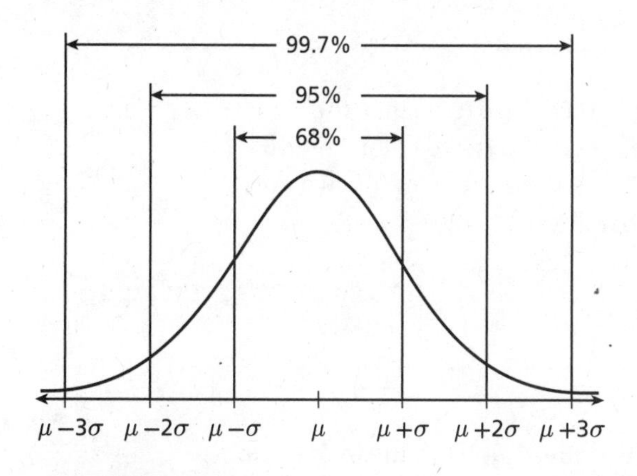

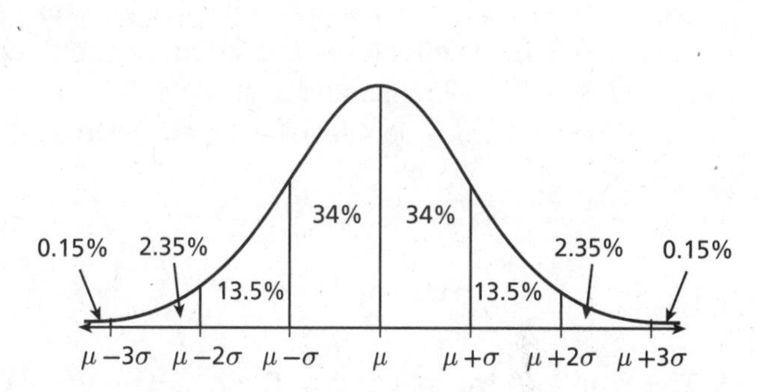

MCC9–12.S.ID.4

2 EXAMPLE Finding Areas Under a Normal Curve

Suppose the masses (in grams) of pennies minted in the United States after 1982 are normally distributed with a mean of 2.50 g and a standard deviation of 0.02 g. Find each of the following.

A **The percent of pennies that have a mass between 2.46 g and 2.54 g**

- How far below the mean is 2.46 g?
  How many standard deviations is this? ____________________
- How far above the mean is 2.54 g?
  How many standard deviations is this? ____________________
- What percent of the data in a normal distribution fall within n standard deviations of the mean where n is the number of standard deviations you found in the preceding questions? ____________________

B **The probability that a randomly chosen penny has a mass greater than 2.52 g**

- How far above the mean is 2.52 g?
  How many standard deviations is this? ____________________
- When the area under a normal curve is separated into eight parts as shown above, which of those parts satisfy the condition that the penny's mass be greater than 2.52 g? (Give the percent of data that fall within each part.) ____________________
- Find the sum of the percents. Express this probability as a decimal as well. ____________________

REFLECT

2a. In the second normal curve shown on the previous page, explain how you know that the area under the curve between $\mu + \sigma$ and $\mu + 2\sigma$ represents 13.5% of the data if you know that the percent of the data within 1 standard deviation of the mean is 68% and the percent of the data within 2 standard deviations of the mean is 95%.

2b. Another way to approach part B of the Example is to recognize that since the mound in the middle of the distribution (between $\mu - \sigma$ and $\mu + \sigma$) represents 68% of the data, the remainder of the data, 100% − 68% = 32%, must be in the two tails. Complete the reasoning to obtain the desired probability.

The Standard Normal Curve The **standard normal distribution** has a mean of 0 and a standard deviation of 1. A data value x from a normal distribution with mean μ and standard deviation σ can be standardized by finding its **z-score** using the formula

$$z = \frac{x - \mu}{\sigma}.$$

Areas under the *standard normal curve* to the left of a given z-score have been computed and appear in the *standard normal table* below. This table allows you to find a greater range of percents and probabilities than you can using μ and multiples of σ as on the previous page. For instance, the intersection of the shaded row and column of the table tells you that the value of $P(z \leq 1.3)$ is 0.9032. (In the table, ".0000+" means slightly more than 0, and "1.0000−" means slightly less than 1.)

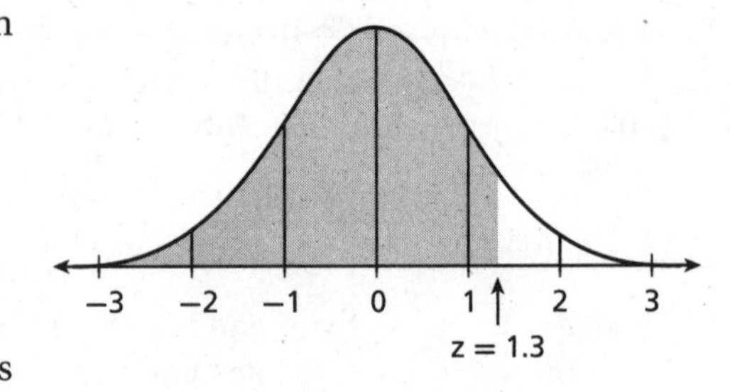

Standard Normal Table

z	.0	.1	.2	.3	.4	.5	.6	.7	.8	.9
−3	.0013	.0010	.0007	.0005	.0003	.0002	.0002	.0001	.0001	.0000+
−2	.0228	.0179	.0139	.0107	.0082	.0062	.0047	.0035	.0026	.0019
−1	.1587	.1357	.1151	.0968	.0808	.0668	.0548	.0446	.0359	.0287
−0	.5000	.4602	.4207	.3821	.3446	.3085	.2743	.2420	.2119	.1841
0	.5000	.5398	.5793	.6179	.6554	.6915	.7257	.7580	.7881	.8159
1	.8413	.8643	.8849	.9032	.9192	.9332	.9452	.9554	.9641	.9713
2	.9772	.9821	.9861	.9893	.9918	.9938	.9953	.9965	.9974	.9981
3	.9987	.9990	.9993	.9995	.9997	.9998	.9998	.9999	.9999	1.000−

MCC9–12.S.ID.4

3 EXAMPLE Using the Standard Normal Table

Suppose the heights (in inches) of adult females in the United States are normally distributed with a mean of 63.8 inches and a standard deviation of 2.8 inches. Find each of the following.

A **The percent of women who are no more than 65 inches tall**

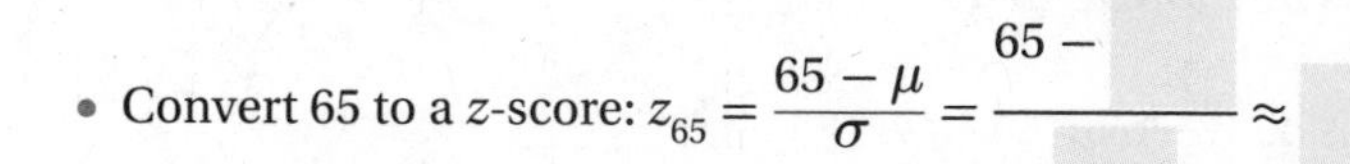

- Convert 65 to a *z*-score: $z_{65} = \frac{65 - \mu}{\sigma} = \frac{65 - \square}{\square} \approx \square$

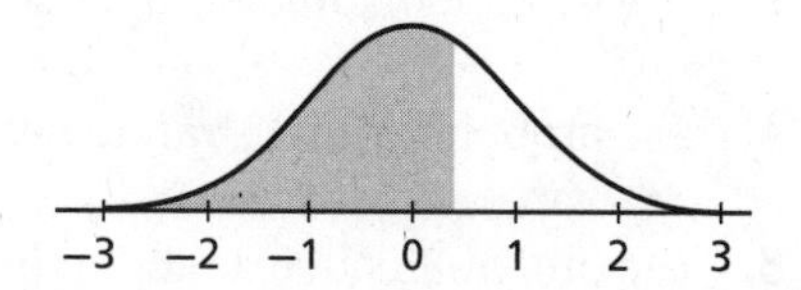

- Recognize that the phrase “no more than 65 inches” means that $z \le z_{65}$. Read the decimal from the appropriate row and column of the standard normal table: ________
- Write the decimal as a percent, rounding to the nearest whole percent: ________

B **The probability that a randomly chosen woman is between 60 inches and 63 inches tall**

- Convert 60 to a *z*-score: $z_{60} = \frac{60 - \mu}{\sigma} = \frac{60 - \square}{\square} \approx \square$
- Convert 63 to a *z*-score: $z_{63} = \frac{63 - \mu}{\sigma} = \frac{63 - \square}{\square} \approx \square$

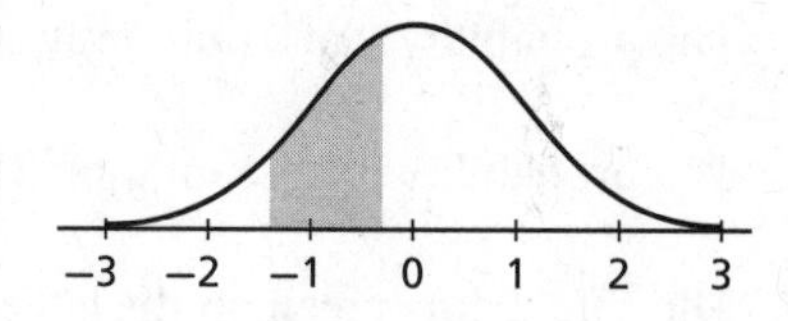

- Because the standard normal table gives areas under the standard normal curve to the left of a given *z*-score, you find $P(z_{60} \le z \le z_{63})$ by subtracting $P(z \le z_{60})$ from $P(z \le z_{63})$. Complete the following calculation using the appropriate values from the table:

$P(z_{60} \le z \le z_{63}) = P(z \le z_{63}) - P(z \le z_{60}) =$ ________ − ________ = ________

- Round the decimal to the nearest hundredth: ________

REFLECT

3a. Using the result of part A, you can find the percent of females who are at least 65 inches tall without needing the table. Find the percent and explain your reasoning.

____

____

____

3b. How does the probability that a randomly chosen female has a height between 64.6 inches and 67.6 inches compare with your answer in part B? Why?

____

PRACTICE

Suppose the scores on a test given to all juniors in a school district are normally distributed with a mean of 74 and a standard deviation of 8. Find each of the following.

1. The percent of juniors whose score is no more than 90 ____________

2. The percent of juniors whose score is between 58 and 74 ____________

3. The percent of juniors whose score is at least 74 ____________

4. The probability that a randomly chosen junior has a score above 82 ____________

5. The probability that a randomly chosen junior has a score between 66 and 90 ____________

6. The probability that a randomly chosen junior has a score below 74 ____________

Suppose the heights (in inches) of adult males in the United States are normally distributed with a mean of 69.4 inches and a standard deviation of 3.2 inches. Find each of the following.

7. The percent of men who are no more than 68 inches tall ____________

8. The percent of men who are between 70 and 72 inches tall ____________

9. The percent of men who are at least 66 inches tall ____________

10. The probability that a randomly chosen man is greater than 71 inches tall ____________

11. The probability that a randomly chosen man is between 63 and 73 inches tall ____________

12. The probability that a randomly chosen man is less than 76 inches tall ____________

13. The calculator screen on the left shows the probability distribution when six coins are flipped and the number of heads is counted. The screen on the right shows the probability distribution when six dice are rolled and the number of 1s is counted. For which distribution is it reasonable to use a normal curve as an approximation? Why?

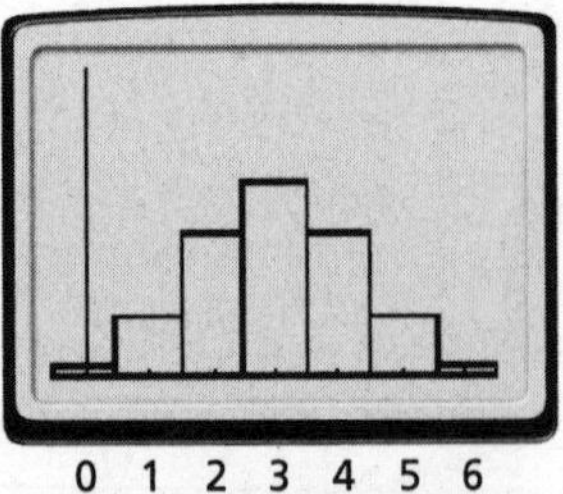

0 1 2 3 4 5 6
Probability of getting a given number of heads when 6 coins are flipped

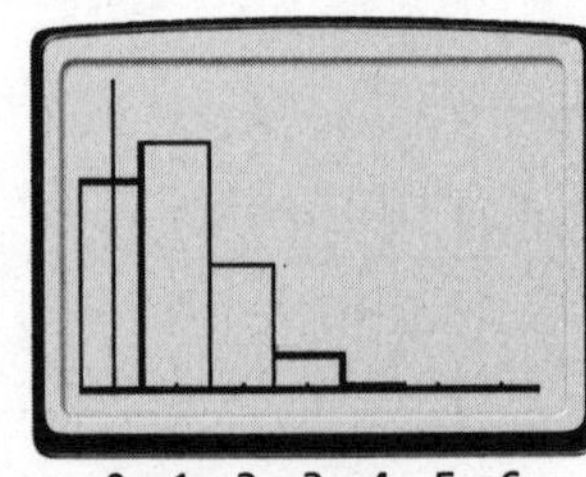

0 1 2 3 4 5 6
Probability of getting a given number of 1s when 6 dice are rolled

____

____

Name________________________________ Class________________ Date______________

9-3

Additional Practice

1. In a plant shop, the heights of young plants are normally distributed with a mean of 50 mm and a standard deviation of 4 mm. Count grid squares in the graph to estimate the probability that a plant chosen at random by a customer will be less than 54 mm tall.

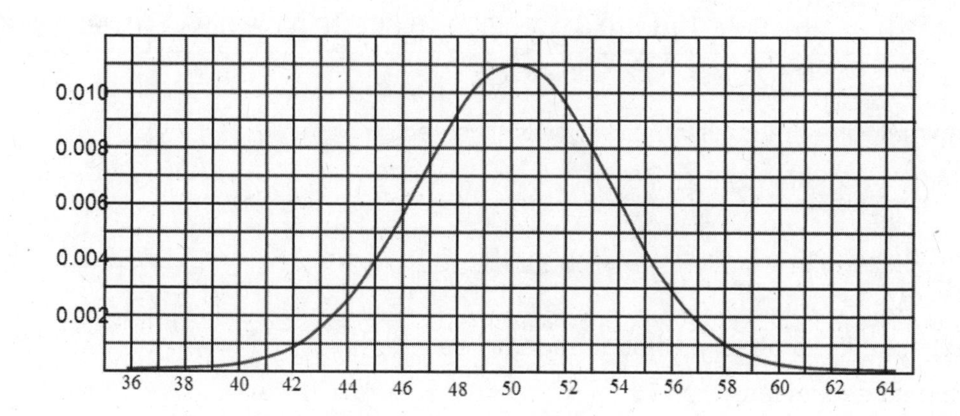

____

Scores on a test are normally distributed with a mean of 80 and a standard deviation of 5. Use the table below to find each probability. The first probability has been found for you.

$z = \frac{x - \mu}{\sigma}$	–2	–1	0	1	2
Area Under Standard Normal Curve	0.02	0.16	0.5	0.84	0.98

2. A randomly selected student scored below 80. $z = \frac{80 - 80}{5} = 0$, so P(below 80) = 0.5

3. A randomly selected student scored above 90. ________________________

4. A randomly selected student scored below 75. ________________________

5. A randomly selected student scored between 75 and 85. ________________________

6. The wait times, in minutes, of 10 customers in line at a grocery store are given below. The mean wait time is 7 minutes. How many data points fall below the mean? Use your answer to explain whether the data appear to be normally distributed.

16	15	10	7	5
5	4	3	3	2

Problem Solving

The scores on a test are normally distributed with a mean of 70 and a standard deviation of 6. Use the table below to answer the questions.

z	−2.5	−2	−1.5	−1	−0.5	0	0.5	1	1.5	2	2.5
Area	0.01	0.02	0.07	0.16	0.31	0.5	0.69	0.84	0.93	0.98	0.99

1. a. Estimate the probability that a randomly selected student scored less than 76.

   Solution: $z = \frac{76 - 70}{6} = \frac{6}{6} = 1$ ______0.84______

   b. Estimate the probability that a randomly selected student scored less than 79.

   $z = \frac{\_\_\_ - 70}{6} = \frac{\_\_\_}{6}$ ____________

   c. Estimate the probability that a randomly selected student scored greater than 82. ____________

   d. Estimate the probability that a randomly selected student scored greater than 55. ____________

   e. Estimate the probability that a randomly selected student scored between 64 and 76. ____________

   f. Estimate the probability that a randomly selected student scored between 67 and 79. ____________

A student is analyzing a set of normally distributed data, but the data provided is incomplete. The student knows that the mean of the data is 120. The student also knows that 84% of the data are less than 130.

2. What is the standard deviation for this data?

   A −10

   B 10

   C 120

3. Use the table of *z*-scores above to determine which statement about this data is true.

   F About 90% of the values are greater than 140.

   G About 50% of the values are greater than 130.

   H About 68% of the values are between 110 and 130.

Name________________________ Class______________ Date__________

9-4

Analyzing Decisions

Going Deeper

Essential question: *How can you use probability to help you analyze decisions?*

You can use a two-way table and what you know about probability to help you evaluate decisions.

Video Tutor

MCC9–12.S.MD.7(+)

1 EXAMPLE Analyzing a Decision

A test for a virus correctly identifies someone who has the virus (by returning a positive result) 99% of the time. The test correctly identifies someone who does not have the virus (by returning a negative result) 99% of the time. It is known that 0.5% of the population has the virus. A doctor decides to treat anyone who tests positive for the virus. Is this a good decision?

A In order to analyze the decision, you need to know the probability that someone who tests positive actually has the virus.

Make a two-way table. Begin by assuming a large overall population of 1,000,000. This value appears in the cell at the lower right, as shown.

- Use the fact that 0.5% of the population has the virus to complete the rightmost column.
- Use the fact that the test correctly identifies someone who has the virus 99% of the time to complete the "Has the virus" row.
- Use the fact that the test correctly identifies someone who does not have the virus 99% of the time to complete the "Does not have the virus" row.
- Finally, complete the bottom row of the table by finding totals.
- Check your work by verifying that the numbers in the bottom row have a sum of 1,000,000.

	Tests Positive	Tests Negative	TOTAL
Has the virus			
Does not have the virus			
TOTAL			1,000,000

B Use the table to find the the probability that someone who tests positive actually has the virus.

There is a total of ____________ people who test positive.

Of these people, ____________ people actually have the virus.

So, the probability that some who tests positive has the virus is ____________.

REFLECT

1a. Do you think the doctor made a good decision in treating everyone who tests positive for the virus? Why or why not?

____

____

The method that you used in the example can be generalized. The generalization is known as Bayes's Theorem.

Bayes's Theorem

Given two events A and B with $P(B) \neq 0$, $P(A|B) = \dfrac{P(B|A) \cdot P(A)}{P(B)}$.

The following example shows how you can use Bayes's Theorem to help you analyze a decision.

MCC9–12.S.MD.7(+)

2 EXAMPLE Using Bayes's Theorem

The principal of a school plans a school picnic for June 2. A few days before the event, the weather forecast predicts rain for June 2, so the principal decides to cancel the picnic. Consider the following information.

- **In the school's town, the probability that it rains on any day in June is 3%.**
- **When it rains, the forecast correctly predicts rain 90% of the time.**
- **When it does not rain, the forecast incorrectly predicts rain 5% of the time.**

Do you think the principal made a good decision? Why or why not?

A Let event A be the event that it rains on a day in June. Let event B be the event that the forecast predicts rain. To evaluate the decision to cancel the picnic, you want to know $P(A|B)$, the probability that it rains given that the forecast predicts rain.

In order use Bayes's Theorem to calculate $P(A|B)$, you must find $P(B|A)$, $P(A)$, and $P(B)$. For convenience, find these probabilities as decimals.

$P(B|A)$ is the probability of a prediction of rain given that it actually rains. This value is provided in the given information.

$P(B|A) =$ ____________

$P(A)$ is the probability of rain on any day in June. This value is also provided in the given information.

$P(A) =$ ____________

$P(B)$ is the probability of a prediction of rain. This value is not provided in the given information. In order to calculate $P(B)$, make a tree diagram, as shown on the following page.

B Make a tree diagram to find $P(B)$. The values on the "branches" show the probability of the associated event. Complete the right side of the tree diagram by writing the correct probabilities. Remember that the probabilities of events that are complements must add up to 1.

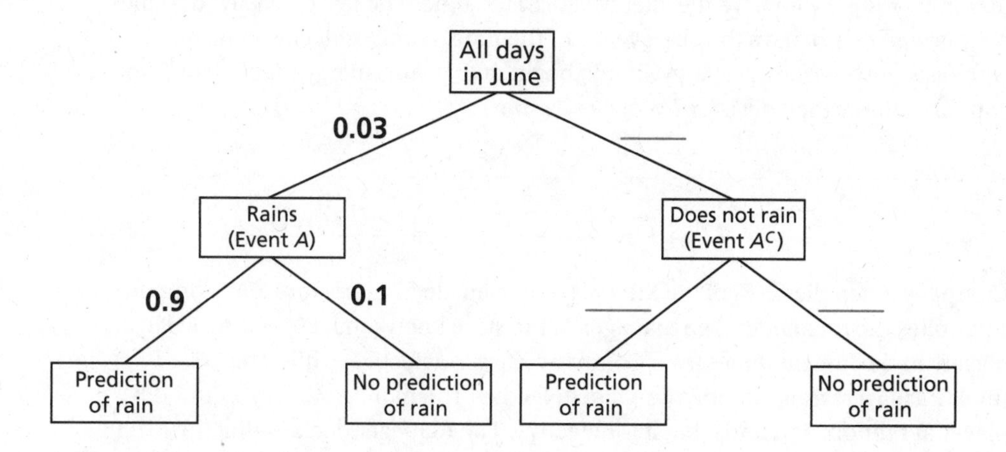

$P(B)$ is the probability that there is a prediction of rain when it actually rains plus the probability that there is a prediction of rain when it does not rain.

$P(B) = P(A) \cdot P(B \mid A) + P(A^c) \cdot P(B \mid A^c)$

$= 0.03 \cdot 0.9 +$ ________ $\cdot$ ________ Substitute values from the tree diagram.

$=$ ________ Simplify.

C Use Bayes's Theorem to find $P(A \mid B)$.

$P(A \mid B) = \dfrac{P(B \mid A) \cdot P(A)}{P(B)}$ Use Bayes's Theorem.

$= \dfrac{\square \cdot \square}{\square}$ Substitute.

$\approx$ ________ Simplify. Round to the nearest thousandth.

So, as a percent, the probability that it rains given that the forecast predicts rain is approximately ________.

REFLECT

2a. Do you think the principal made a good decision when canceling the picnic? Why or why not?

____

____

2b. What would $P(A)$, the probability that it rains on any day in June, have to be for the value of $P(A \mid B)$ to be greater than 50%? Explain.

____

____

PRACTICE

1. It is known that 2% of the population has a certain allergy. A test correctly identifies people who have the allergy 98% of the time. The test correctly identifies people who do not have the allergy 94% of the time. A doctor decides that anyone who tests positive for the allergy should begin taking anti-allergy medication. Do you think this a good decision? Why or why not?

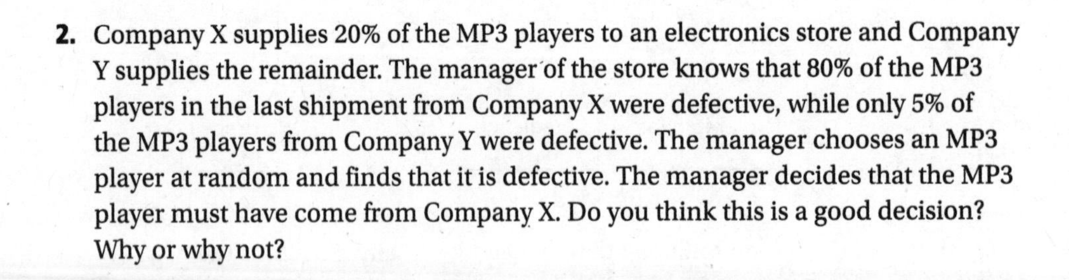

2. Company X supplies 20% of the MP3 players to an electronics store and Company Y supplies the remainder. The manager of the store knows that 80% of the MP3 players in the last shipment from Company X were defective, while only 5% of the MP3 players from Company Y were defective. The manager chooses an MP3 player at random and finds that it is defective. The manager decides that the MP3 player must have come from Company X. Do you think this is a good decision? Why or why not?

3. You can solve Example 2 using a two-way table. Consider a population of 10,000 randomly chosen June days. Complete the table. Then explain how to find the probability that it rains given that the forecast predicts rain.

	Rains	Does not rain	TOTAL
Prediction of rain			
No prediction of rain			
TOTAL			10,000

4. Explain how to derive Bayes's Theorem using the Multiplication Rule. (*Hint:* The Multiplication Rule can be written as $P(A \text{ and } B) = P(B) \cdot P(A \mid B)$ or as $P(A \text{ and } B) = P(A) \cdot P(B \mid A)$.)

Name__________ Class__________ Date__________

Additional Practice

1. Bayes's Theorem can be applied to filter for spam e-mail messages. These filters often look for the presence of specific phrases. Write an equation showing how to calculate the probability that a given message is spam, given that it contains a certain phrase.

   ____

2. Suppose a test for a drug returns true positive results for 99% of users and 99% true negative results for non-users. What percentage of the population would have to be users of the drug in order to say that a positive test result was more likely than not to indicate use of the drug? Set up an equation and solve it.

   ____

   __________ % of the population

3. A certain test for a genetic condition correctly identifies a person with the condition 96% of the time and correctly identifies a person without the condition 93% of the time. It is known that 0.3% of the population has the condition. In order to improve accuracy, a researcher runs the test twice on each subject. Fill out the tree diagram.

   ____

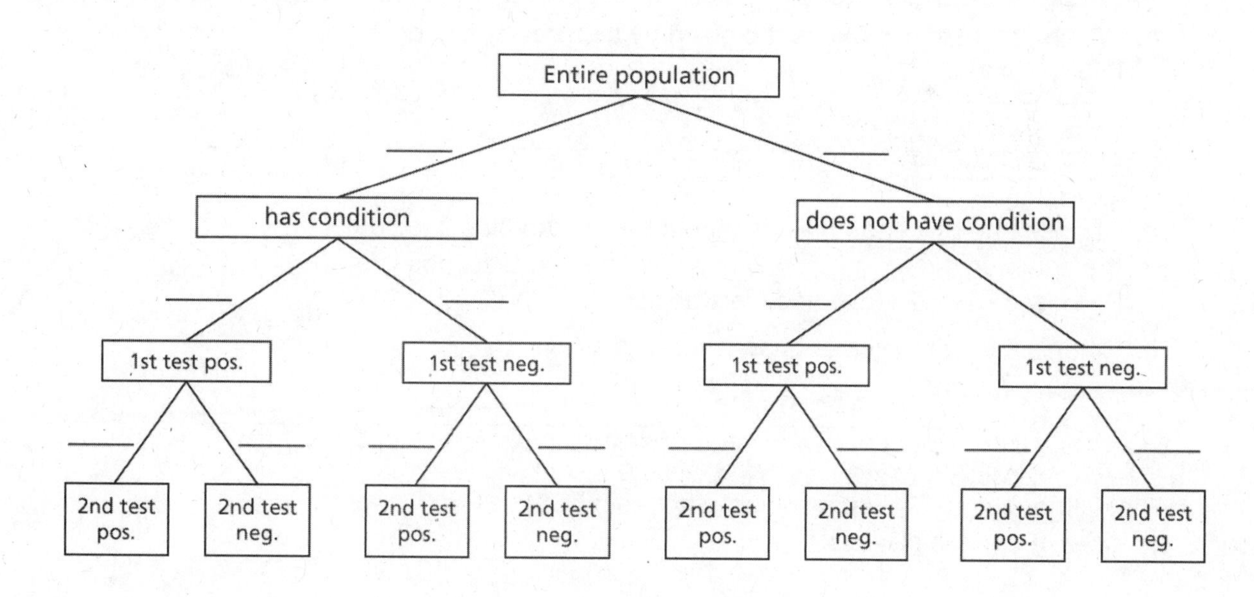

Problem Solving

1. Suppose a medical screening test for a disease always returns a positive result if the subject has the disease, but also returns false positives in 55% of subjects without the disease. Draw a Venn diagram to illustrate this situation.

2. Let A be the event "tests positive for the disease" and let B be the event "has the disease". The disease occurs naturally in 2% of the population.
   a. What is the meaning of P(A)?

   ____

   b. What is the meaning of P(B)?

   ____

   c. What is the meaning of P(A|B)?

   ____

   d. What is the meaning of P(B|A)?

   ____

   e. Which of these four values are given by the problem, and what is their value?

   ____

3. a. Choose one of the four values mentioned in exercise 2 to complete the equation. __________ = P(has disease and tests positive) + P(doesn't have disease and tests positive)
   b. What is the value of your answer for part a?

   ____

4. What is the probability that a subject who tests positive for the disease has the disease?

   ____

Name________________ Class________________ Date________

UNIT 5

Performance Tasks

GPS COMMON CORE

MCC9-12.S.ID.2
MCC9-12.S.ID.4
MCC9-12.S.IC.3
MCC9-12.S.IC.6

★ **1.** Samples of the ages of members of two different athletic clubs in Smithville are shown.

Membership Information	
Power-Pump Gym	24, 28, 44, 50, 31, 20, 25, 54, 27, 19, 23, 37, 42, 25, 29, 40
Smithville Racket Club	14, 49, 30, 17, 28, 71, 64, 29, 12, 28, 60, 51, 23, 59, 66, 23

a. Determine the mean and standard deviation for each data set. Round to the nearest whole year.

b. What do the samples say about the age of a typical member at each club? Explain.

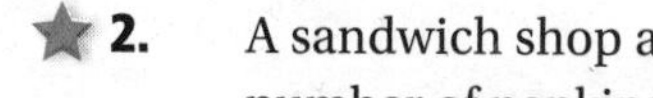

★ **2.** A sandwich shop at the airport wants to determine if there is a correlation between the number of napkins taken and the type of sandwich that is ordered.

a. Which of the following should the manager conduct—a survey, an experiment, or an observational study? Justify your answer.

b. Name a factor other than sandwich type that might affect how many napkins a customer takes.

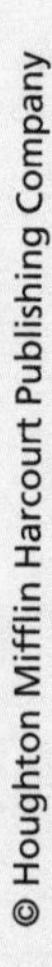

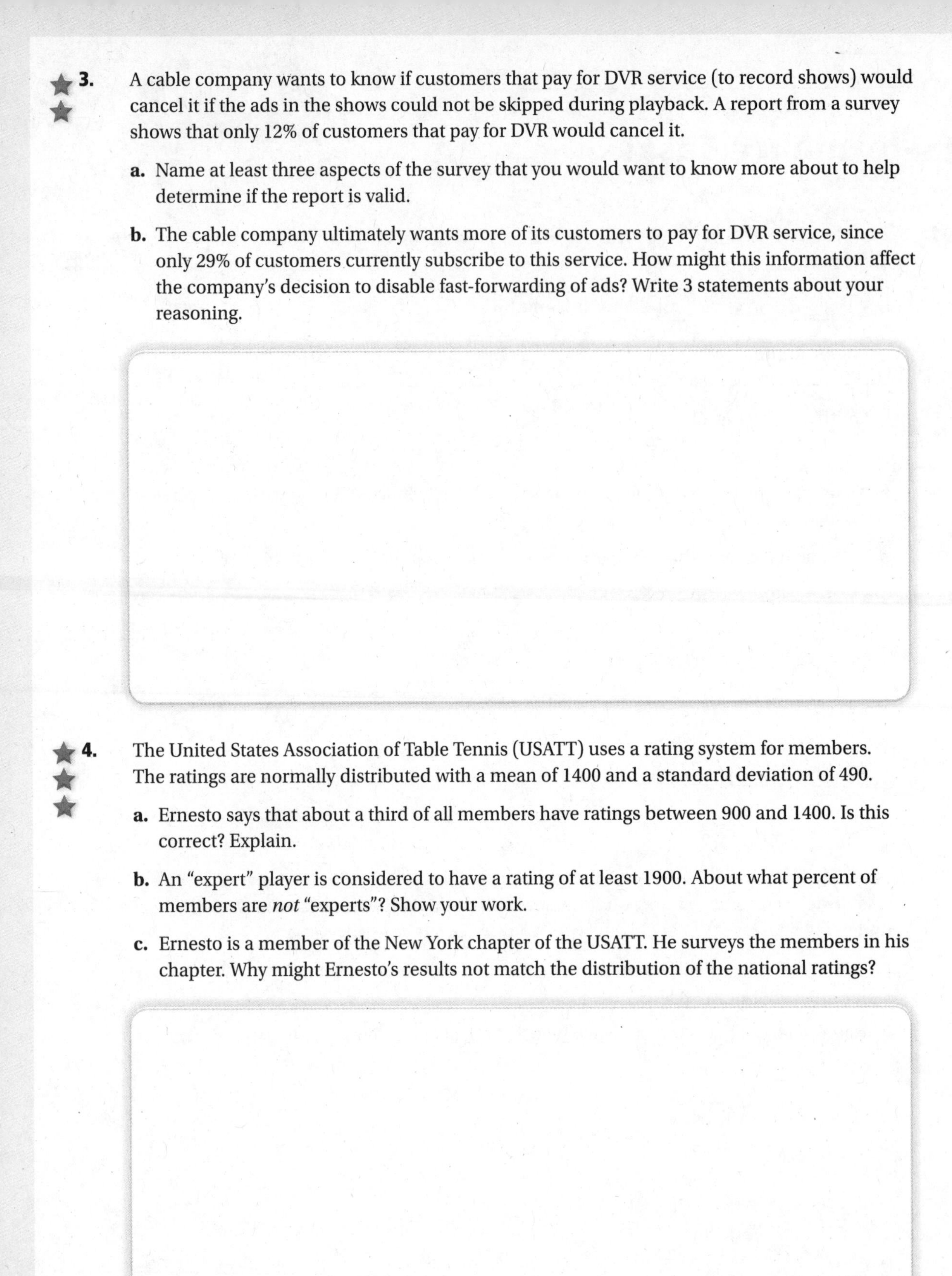

★★ **3.** A cable company wants to know if customers that pay for DVR service (to record shows) would cancel it if the ads in the shows could not be skipped during playback. A report from a survey shows that only 12% of customers that pay for DVR would cancel it.

a. Name at least three aspects of the survey that you would want to know more about to help determine if the report is valid.

b. The cable company ultimately wants more of its customers to pay for DVR service, since only 29% of customers currently subscribe to this service. How might this information affect the company's decision to disable fast-forwarding of ads? Write 3 statements about your reasoning.

★★★ **4.** The United States Association of Table Tennis (USATT) uses a rating system for members. The ratings are normally distributed with a mean of 1400 and a standard deviation of 490.

a. Ernesto says that about a third of all members have ratings between 900 and 1400. Is this correct? Explain.

b. An "expert" player is considered to have a rating of at least 1900. About what percent of members are *not* "experts"? Show your work.

c. Ernesto is a member of the New York chapter of the USATT. He surveys the members in his chapter. Why might Ernesto's results not match the distribution of the national ratings?

Name ______________________ Class ______________ Date ________

SELECTED RESPONSE

1. What type of research, described below, is being conducted?

A researcher recruits 50 people with colds and measures the level of stress they were under during the week prior to the start of the cold.

A. Experiment

B. Observational study

C. Survey

D. None of these

2. Identify the word or phrase that completes this statement: The mean of the data in the distribution shown is greater than the median because the distribution is __?__.

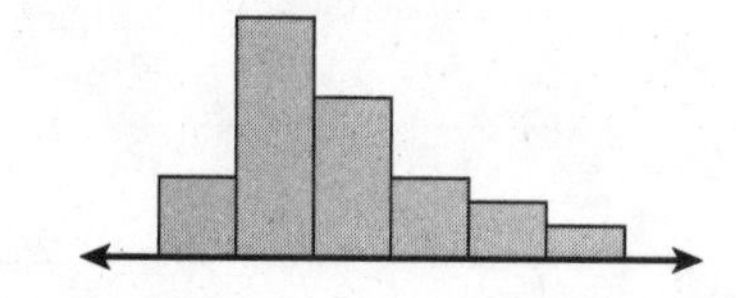

F. normal **H.** skewed right

G. skewed left **J.** uniform

3. You want to estimate a population mean by taking a sample from the population and finding the sample's mean. Which sampling technique gives the best estimate?

A. Convenience sampling

B. Random sampling

C. Self-selected sampling

D. Systematic sampling

4. Suppose you roll a die repeatedly and make a histogram of the results (number of 1s, number of 2s, and so on). If the die is fair, which shape will the histogram have?

F. Normal **H.** Skewed right

G. Skewed left **J.** Uniform

5. A normal distribution has a mean of 10 and a standard deviation of 1.5. In which interval does the middle 95% of the data fall?

A. $-3 \le x \le 3$ **C.** $7 \le x \le 13$

B. $8.5 \le x \le 11.5$ **D.** $5.5 \le x \le 14.5$

6. A researcher recorded the heights of 5 plants grown in soil treated with a fertilizer and 5 plants grown in soil not treated with the fertilizer. The mean height of the treatment group was 24 cm, while the mean height of the control group was 22 cm. A histogram of the differences of means for 50 resamples of the data under the assumption that the fertilizer had no effect on the plants' growth is shown.

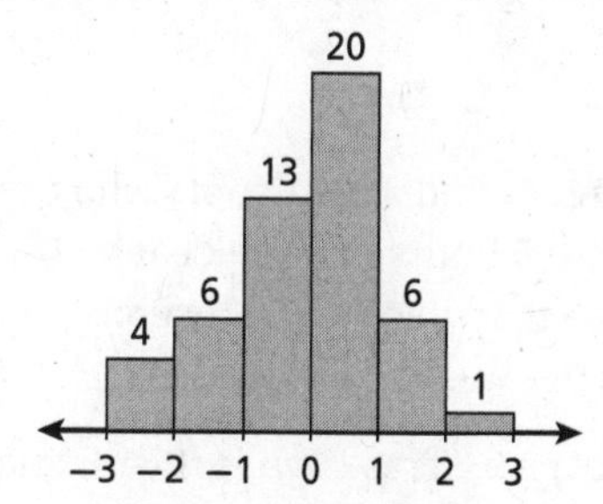

Based on the histogram, what is the probability that a difference of means is *at least as great* as the experimental result?

F. 0.01 **H.** 0.1

G. 0.02 **J.** 0.2

7. A newspaper reports on a survey of likely voters in an upcoming local election. The survey showed that 57% support candidate Robertson with a margin of error of 4%. Which statement about all voters in the election is most likely to be accurate?

A. Between 55% and 59% favor Robertson.

B. Between 53% and 61% favor Robertson.

C. Between 53% and 57% favor Robertson.

D. Between 57% and 61% favor Robertson.

CONSTRUCTED RESPONSE

8. Researchers plan to use a survey to find the percent of workers who are employed full-time in a state. The researchers are aiming for a 3% margin of error at a 95% confidence level. Can they attain this result by polling 1000 randomly selected workers? Justify your answer. (*Hint:* Use the margin of error formula with 0.5 as an estimate for $\hat{p}$.)

9. A researcher finds that people who exercise for at least 5 hours per week eat high-fat foods less often than people who exercise less than 5 hours per week.

   a. What type of research is this? Explain how you know.

   b. Can the researcher conclude that exercise causes people to eat high-fat foods less frequently? Explain.

10. In a randomized comparative experiment, 100 people used a hair growth agent for two months and 100 people did not. The mean hair growth among people who used the agent was 1.3 inches, and the mean hair growth among people who did not use it was 1.0 inch.

    a. State the null hypothesis for this experiment in terms of the effect of the treatment and in terms of the difference of the means.

    b. Given that the null hypothesis is true, the resampling distribution for the difference of means is normal with a mean of 0 inches and a standard deviation of 0.14 inch. State the interval that captures the middle 95% of the differences of the means.

    c. Should the null hypothesis be rejected? Explain why or why not.

11. Suppose the upper arm length (in centimeters) of adult males in the United States is normally distributed with a mean of 39.4 cm and a standard deviation of 2.3 cm.

    a. What percent of adult males have an upper arm length no greater than 41.7 cm? Explain how you know.

    b. What is the probability that a randomly chosen adult male has an upper arm length greater than 44 cm? Explain how you know.

Polynomial Functions

Module 10 Polynomials		
10-1	Polynomials	MCC9-12.A.APR.1
10-2	Multiplying Polynomials	MCC9-12.A.APR.5(+)
10-3	Binomial Distributions	MCC9-12.A.APR.5(+)
10-4	Dividing Polynomials	MCC9-12.A.APR.6
10-5	Factoring Polynomials	MCC9-12.A.APR.2, MCC9-12.A.SSE.1, MCC9-12.A.SSE.2, MCC9-12.F.IF.8
Module 11 Polynomial Functions		
11-1	Finding Real Roots of Polynomial Equations	MCC9-12.A.APR.2, MCC9-12.F.IF.8
11-2	Fundamental Theorem of Algebra	MCC9-12.N.CN.8, MCC9-12.N.CN.9(+)
11-3	Investigating Graphs of Polynomial Functions	MCC9-12.F.IF.4, MCC9-12.F.IF.7c, MCC9-12.F.IF.8
Module 12 Geometric Sequences and Series		
12-1	Introduction to Sequences	MCC9-12.F.BF.2
12-2	Series and Summation Notation	MCC9-12.F.BF.1a
12-3	Geometric Sequences and Series	MCC9-12.A.SSE.4
	Performance Tasks	
	PARCC Assessment Readiness	

Unpacking the Standards

Understanding the standards and the vocabulary terms in the standards will help you know exactly what you are expected to learn in this unit.

GPS COMMON CORE **MCC9-12.A.APR.5(+)**

Know and apply the Binomial Theorem for the expansion of $(x + y)^n$ in powers of x and y for a positive integer n, where x and y are any numbers, with coefficients determined for example by Pascal's Triangle.

Key Vocabulary

Binomial Theorem *(Teorema de los binomios)* For any positive integer n, $(x + y)^n = {}_nC_0 x^n y^0 + {}_nC_1 x^{n-1} y^1 + {}_nC_2 x^{n-2} y^2 + \ldots + {}_nC_{n-1} x^1 y^{n-1} + {}_nC_n x^0 y^n$

Pascal's triangle *(triángulo de Pascal)* A triangular arrangement of numbers in which every row starts and ends with 1 and each other number is the sum of the two numbers above it.

What It Means For You

You can use the number patterns in Pascal's Triangle to find the coefficients when you raise a binomial like $(x + y)$ to a power.

EXAMPLE **Pascal's triangle and binomial expansion**

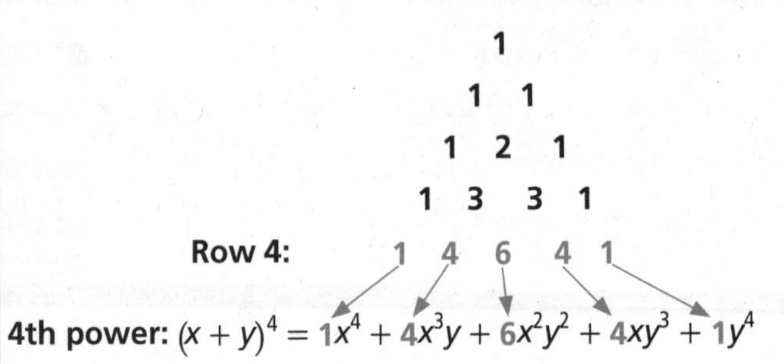

GPS COMMON CORE **MCC9-12.A.APR.2**

Know and apply the Remainder Theorem: For a polynomial $p(x)$ and a number a, the remainder on division by $x - a$ is $p(a)$, so $p(a) = 0$ if and only if $(x - a)$ is a factor of $p(x)$.

What It Means For You

You can use the Remainder Theorem to find factors of polynomials.

EXAMPLE

To check whether $(x - 2)$ is a factor of $P(x) = x^3 - 19x + 30$, find the value of $P(2)$. If $P(2) = 0$, then $(x - 2)$ is a factor of P by the Remainder Theorem. You can substitute as shown below, or use a shortcut called synthetic substitution.

$P(x) = x^3 - 19x + 30$

$P(2) = 2^3 - 19(2) + 30$

$P(2) = 8 - 38 + 30$

$P(2) = 0$

Because $P(2) = 0$, $(x - 2)$ is a factor of P.

You can instead divide $x^3 - 19x + 30$ by $(x - 2)$ to check that $(x - 2)$ is a factor, using either long division or synthetic division. You will find that $\frac{x^3 - 19x + 30}{x - 2} = x^2 + 2x - 15$ or $(x + 5)(x - 3)$.

UNIT 6

GPS COMMON CORE **MCC9-12.N.CN.9(+)**

Know the Fundamental Theorem of Algebra; show that it is true for quadratic polynomials.

Key Vocabulary

Fundamental Theorem of Algebra *(Teorema fundamental del álgebra)* Every polynomial function of degree $n \geq 1$ has at least one zero, where a zero may be a complex number.

quadratic polynomial *(polinomio cuadrático)* A polynomial of degree 2.

What It Means For You

The Fundamental Theorem of Algebra leads to the result that the degree of a polynomial function indicates the number of zeros. More generally, as with quadratic functions, zeros may be repeated or complex. Real zeros indicate x-intercepts of the graph.

EXAMPLE

The graph shows $f(x) = x^4 + x^3 + 2x^2 + 4x - 8$. There are two x-intercepts, so you know that $f(x)$ has two real zeros. Because the degree of $f(x)$ is 4, there must be 4 zeros in all. So, $f(x)$ also must have two complex zeros.

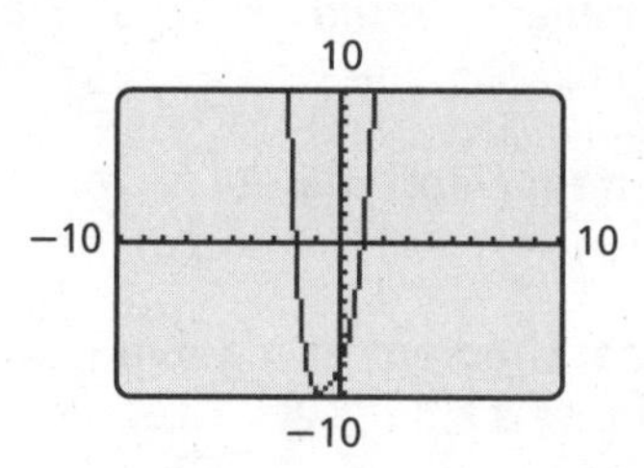

GPS COMMON CORE **MCC9-12.F.IF.7c**

Graph polynomial functions, identifying zeros when suitable factorizations are available, and showing end behavior.

Key Vocabulary

polynomial function *(función polynomial)* A function whose rule is a polynomial.

zero of a function *(cero de una función)* For the function f, any number x such that $f(x) = 0$.

What It Means For You

You can find zeros of a polynomial function by locating where the graph of the function crosses the x-axis.

EXAMPLE

The volume of a box is modeled by the function

$V(x) = 4x^3 - 20x^2 + 24x$, or
$V(x) = 4x(x - 2)(x - 3)$.

The zeros of $V(x)$ are also the x-intercepts of the graph: $x = 0$, $x = 2$, and $x = 3$.

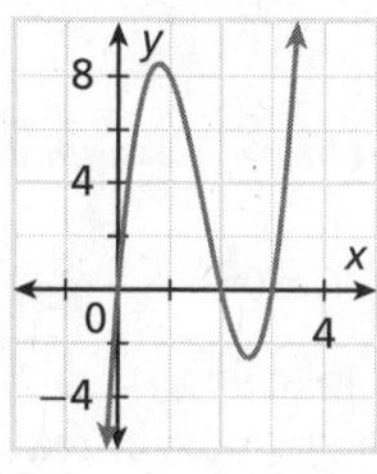

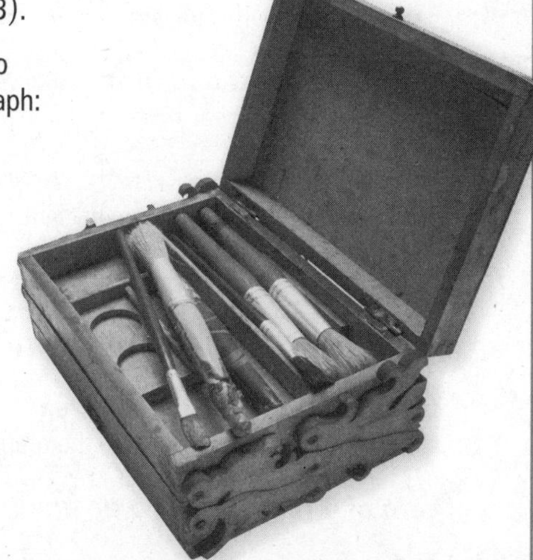

UNIT 6

Key Vocabulary

Binomial Theorem *(Teorema de los binomios)* For any positive integer n,
$(x + y)^n = {}_nC_0 x^n y^0 + {}_nC_1 x^{n-1} y^1 + {}_nC_2 x^{n-2} y^2 + \dots + {}_nC_{n-1} x^1 y^{n-1} + {}_nC_n x^0 y^n$.

common ratio *(rázon común)* In a geometric sequence, the constant ratio of any term and the previous term).

degree of a monomial *(grado de un monomio)* The sum of the exponents of the variables in the monomial.

degree of a polynomial *(grado de un polonomia)* The degree of the term of the polynomial with the greatest degree.

explicit formula *(fórmula explícita)* A formula that defines the nth term a_n, or general term, of a sequence as a function of n.

Factor Theorem *(Teorema del factor)* For any polynomial $P(x)$, $(x - a)$ is a factor of $P(x)$ if and only if $P(a) = 0$.

Fundamental Theorem of Algebra *(Teorema fundamental del álgebra)* Every polynomial function of degree $n \geq 1$ has at least one zero, where a zero may be a complex number.

geometric sequence *(sucesión geométrica)* A sequence in which the ratio of successive terms is a constant r, called the common ratio, where $r \neq 0$.

geometric series *(serie geométrica)* The indicated sum of the terms of a geometric sequence.

partial sum *(suma parcial)* Indicated by $S_n = \sum_{i=1}^{n} a_i$, the sum of a specified number of terms n of a sequence whose total number of terms is greater than n.

Pascal's triangle *(triángulo de Pascal)* A triangular arrangement of numbers in which every row starts and ends with 1 and each other number is the sum of the two numbers above it.

polynomial *(polinomio)* A monomial or a sum or difference of monomials.

quadratic polynomial *(polinomio cuadrático)* A polynomial of degree 2.

sequence *(sucesión)* A list of numbers that often form a pattern.

series *(serie)* The indicated sum of the terms of a sequence.

summation notation *(notación de sumatoria)* A method of notating the sum of a series using the Greek letter Σ (capital *sigma*).

synthetic division *(división sintética)* A shorthand method of dividing by a linear binomial of the form $(x - a)$ by writing only the coefficients of the polynomials.

synthetic substitution *(sustitución sintética)* A method used to evaluate a polynomial function.

transformation *(transformación)* A change in the position, size, or shape of a figure or graph.

turning point *(punto de inflexión)* A point on the graph of a function that corresponds to a local maximum (or minimum) where the graph changes from increasing to decreasing (or vice versa).

zero of a function *(cero de una función)* For the function f, any number x such that $f(x) = 0$.

Name________________________ Class____________ Date________

10-1

Polynomials

Going Deeper

Video Tutor

Essential question: *How do you add and subtract polynomials?*

A **monomial** is a number or a product of numbers and variables with whole-number exponents. For example, 6, $3x^5$, and $-2xy^2$ are all monomials. A **polynomial** is a monomial or a sum of monomials. For example, $-4x^9 + 5x^2 + 1$ is a polynomial.

The **degree of a monomial** is the sum of the exponents of the variables. The **degree of a polynomial** is the degree of the term with the greatest degree. For example, the polynomial $-4x^9 + 5x^2 + 1$ has degree 9.

To add or subtract polynomials, you combine like terms. You can add or subtract horizontally or vertically.

MCC9–12.A.APR.1

1 EXAMPLE Adding Polynomials

Add.

A $(3x^3 + 12x^2 + 9x + 6) + (5x^2 - 6x + 7)$

Use a vertical arrangement.

$3x^3 + \quad 12x^2 + \quad 9x + \quad 6$ Write the polynomials, aligning like terms.

$\qquad\qquad 5x^2 - \quad 6x + \quad 7$

$\_\_\_x^3 + \_\_\_x^2 + \_\_\_x + \_\_\_$ Add the coefficients of like terms.

B $(2x - 7x^2) + (x^2 - 2x + 1)$

Use a horizontal arrangement.

$(-7x^2 + 2x) + (x^2 - 2x + 1)$ Write the polynomials in standard form.

$= (-7x^2 + \_\_\_) + (2x - \_\_\_) + \_\_\_$ Group like terms.

$= \_\_\_ + 0x + \_\_\_$ Add the coefficients of like terms.

$= \_\_\_ + \_\_\_$ Simplify.

REFLECT

1a. Do you get the same results whether you add polynomials vertically or horizontally? Why or why not?

____

____

1b. Is the sum of two polynomials always another polynomial? Explain.

____

____

1c. Is the sum of two polynomials of degree 5 always a polynomial of degree 5? Give an example to explain your answer.

____

To subtract polynomials, you add the opposite of the subtracted polynomial. The following example shows how to use this method with the vertical and horizontal formats.

MCC9–12.A.APR.1

2 EXAMPLE Subtracting Polynomials

Subtract.

A $(2 + 9x^2) - (-6x^2 - 2x + 1)$

Use a vertical arrangement.

$9x^2 \quad\quad\quad + 2$	Write the first polynomial in standard form.
$6x^2 + \quad 2x - 1$	Add the opposite of the second polynomial.
$\_\_\_ x^2 + \_\_\_ x + \_\_\_$	Add the coefficients of like terms.

B $(6x^3 + 3x^2 + 2x + 9) - (4x^3 + 8x^2 - 2x + 5)$

Use a horizontal arrangement.

$(6x^3 + 3x^2 + 2x + 9) - (4x^3 + 8x^2 - 2x + 5)$	Write the polynomials.
$= (6x^3 + 3x^2 + 2x + 9) + (-4x^3 - 8x^2 + 2x - 5)$	Add the opposite.
$= (6x^3 - \_\_\_) + (3x^2 - \_\_\_) + (\_\_\_ + 2x) + (\_\_\_ - 5)$	Group like terms.
$= \_\_\_ x^3 - \_\_\_ x^2 + \_\_\_ x + \_\_\_$	Add the coefficients of like terms.

REFLECT

2a. How is subtracting polynomials similar to subtracting integers?

____

____

2b. In part A, you leave a gap in the polynomial $9x^2 + 2$ when you write the subtraction problem vertically. Why?

____

____

2c. Is the difference of two polynomials always another polynomial? Explain.

____

____

____

MCC9–12.F.BF.1b

3 EXAMPLE Modeling High School Populations

According to data from the U.S. Census Bureau for the period 2000–2007, the number of male students enrolled in high school in the United States can be approximated by the function $M(x) = -0.004x^3 + 0.037x^2 + 0.049x + 8.11$ where x is the number of years since 2000 and $M(x)$ is the number of male students in millions. The number of female students enrolled in high school in the United States can be approximated by the function $F(x) = -0.006x^3 + 0.029x^2 + 0.165x + 7.67$ where x is the number of years since 2000 and $F(x)$ is the number of female students in millions. Estimate the total number of students enrolled in high school in the United States in 2007.

A Make a plan. The problem asks for the total number of students in 2007. First find $T(x) = M(x) + F(x)$ to find a model for the total enrollment. Then evaluate $T(x)$ at an appropriate value of x to find the total enrollment in 2007.

B Add the polynomials.

$-0.004x^3 + \quad 0.037x^2 + \quad 0.049x + 8.11$ Write the polynomials, aligning like terms.

$\underline{-0.006x^3 + \quad 0.029x^2 + \quad 0.165x + 7.67}$

$\_\_\_\_\_ x^3 + \_\_\_\_\_ x^2 + \_\_\_\_\_ x + \_\_\_\_\_$ Add the coefficients of like terms.

$T(x) = \_\_\_\_\_\_\_\_\_\_\_\_\_\_\_\_$

C Evaluate $T(x)$.

For 2007, $x = 7$. Use a calculator to evaluate $T(7)$. Round to one decimal place.

$T(7) \approx \_\_\_\_\_\_\_\_\_\_$

So, there were approximately ____________ high school students in 2007.

REFLECT

3a. Is it possible to solve this problem without adding the polynomials? Explain.

____

____

3b. Explain how you can use the given information to estimate how many more male high school students than female high school students there were in the United States in 2007.

____

____

____

____

PRACTICE

Add or subtract.

1. $(2x^4 - 6x^2 + 8) + (-x^4 + 2x^2 - 12)$

2. $(7x^2 - 2x + 1) + (8x^3 + 2x^2 + 5x - 4)$

3. $(5x^2 - 6x^3 + 16) + (9x^3 + 3x + 7x^4)$

4. $(-3x^3 - 7x^5 - 3) + (5x^2 + 3x^3 + 7x^5)$

5. $(2x^4 - 6x^2 + 8) - (-x^4 + 2x^2 - 12)$

6. $(x^3 + 25) - (-x^2 - 18x - 8)$

7. $(2x^2 + 3x + 1) - (7x^2 - 2x + 7x^3)$

8. $(12x^2 + 3) - (15x^2 - 4x + 9x^4 + 7)$

9. $(14x^4 - x^3 + 2x^2 + 5x + 15) - (10x^4 + 3x^3 - 5x^2 - 6x + 4)$

10. $(-6x^3 + 10x + 26) + (5x^2 - 6x^5 + 7x) + (3 - 22x^4)$

11. According to data from the U.S. Census Bureau, the total number of people in the United States labor force can be approximated by the function $T(x) = -0.011x^2 + 2x + 107$, where x is the number of years since 1980 and $T(x)$ is the number of workers in millions. The number of women in the United States labor force can be approximated by the function $W(x) = -0.012x^2 + 1.26x + 45.5$.

a. Write a polynomial function $M(x)$ that models the number of men in the labor force.

b. Estimate the number of men in the labor force in 2008. Explain how you made your estimate.

12. **Error Analysis** A student was asked to find the difference $(4x^5 - 3x^4 + 6x^2) - (7x^5 - 6x^4 + x^3)$. The student's work is shown at right. Identify the student's error and give the correct difference.

$$\begin{array}{r} 4x^5 - 3x^4 \qquad\quad + 6x^2 \\ -7x^5 - 6x^4 + x^3 \qquad\quad \\ \hline -3x^5 - 9x^4 + x^3 + 6x^2 \end{array}$$

Name________________ Class________ Date________

Additional Practice

Identify the degree of each monomial.

1. $6x^2$ ________
2. $3p^3m^4$ ________
3. $2x^8y^3$ ________

Rewrite each polynomial in standard form. Then identify the leading coefficient, degree, and number of terms. Name the polynomial.

4. $6 + 7x - 4x^3 + x^2$

____

5. $x^2 - 3 + 2x^5 + 7x^4 - 12x$

____

Add or subtract. Write your answer in standard form.

6. $(2x^2 - 2x + 6) + (11x^3 - x^2 - 2 + 5x)$ ________
7. $(x^2 - 8) - (3x^3 - 6x - 4 + 9x^2)$ ________
8. $(5x^4 + x^2) + (7 + 9x^2 - 2x^4 + x^3)$ ________
9. $(12x^2 + x) - (6 - 9x^2 + x^7 - 8x)$ ________

10. Find and correct the error in Tom's calculation below.

$$(2x^4 - 3x^2 + 5x + 1) - (3x^4 + 5x^2 - 3x + 2) = ?$$

$$\begin{array}{r} (2x^4 - 3x^2 + 5x + 1) \\ -\underline{(3x^4 + 5x^2 - 3x + 2)} \\ -x^4 - 2x^2 + 2x - 1 \end{array}$$

Solve.

11. The height, h, in feet, of a baseball after being struck by a bat can be approximated by $h(t) = -16t^2 + 100t + 5$, where t is measured in seconds.

a. Evaluate $h(t)$ for $t = 3$ and $t = 5$. ________

b. Describe what the values of the function from part a represent.

____

Problem Solving

As part of a project to build a model castle, Julian wants to find the surface area of solid towers of various sizes, shaped like the one shown in the figure below. The diameter of the circular base is *d* inches, the height of the cylinder is $d + 4$ inches, and the slant height of the right circular cone is $d - 0.6$ inch.

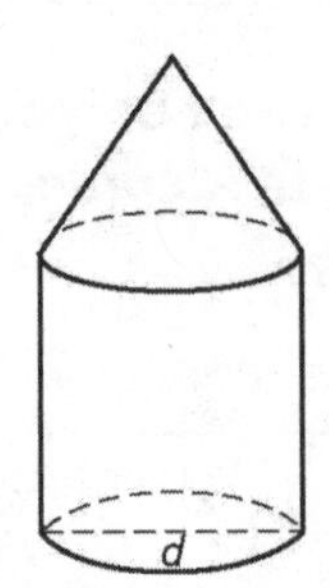

1. The general formula for the lateral surface area of a cone is $SA = \pi r^2 - \pi rs$, where r is the radius of the base, and s is the slant height of the cone.

   a. Write the formula in terms of d.

   ____

   b. What part of the formula will you use to find the surface area of the cone part of the model? Why?

   ____

   ____

   ____

2. The general formula for the surface area of a cylinder (with radius r and height h) is $SA = 2\pi r^2 + 2\pi rh$.

   a. Write the formula in terms of d. _______________

   b. What part of the formula will you use to find the surface area of the cylinder part of the model? Why?

   ____

3. Write a general polynomial expression for the surface area of the model tower.

   ____

Choose the letter for the best answer.

4. What is the approximate surface area in square inches of a tower with a diameter of 5 inches?

   A 278 C 44

   B 196 D 38

5. What is the approximate surface area in square inches of a tower with a diameter of 10 inches?

   A 176 C 666

   B 278 D 1174

6. What is the approximate surface area in square inches of a tower where the height of the cylinder is 12 inches?

   A 931 C 445

   B 716 D 395

7. What is the approximate surface area in square inches of a tower where the slant height of the cone is 3.4 inches?

   A 103 C 158

   B 134 D 268

Name ________________ Class ________ Date ________

10-2

Multiplying Polynomials

Going Deeper

Video Tutor

Essential question: *How do you multiply polynomials?*

To multiply two polynomials, you use the distributive property so that every term in the first factor is multiplied by every term in the second factor. You also use the product of powers property ($a^m \cdot a^n = a^{m+n}$) each time you multiply two terms.

MCC9–12.A.APR.1

1 EXAMPLE Multiplying Polynomials

Find the product.

A $(4x^2)(2x^3 - x^2 + 5)$

$= (4x^2)(2x^3) + (4x^2)(-x^2) + (4x^2)(5)$ — Distributive property

$= 8x^5 -$ ______ $+$ ______ — Multiply monomials.

B $(x - 3)(-x^2 + 2x + 1)$

Method 1: Use a horizontal arrangement.

$(x - 3)(-x^2 + 2x + 1)$

$= x(-x^2) + x(2x) + x(1) - 3(-x^2) - 3(2x) - 3(1)$ — Distribute x and then -3.

$= -x^3 +$ ______ $+ x +$ ______ $-$ ______ $- 3$ — Multiply monomials.

$= -x^3 +$ ______ $-$ ______ $-$ ______ — Combine like terms.

Method 2: Use a vertical arrangement.

$-x^2 + 2x + 1$	Write the polynomials vertically.
$x - 3$	
$3x^2 - 6x - 3$	Multiply $(-x^2 + 2x + 1)$ by -3.
$-x^3 +$ ______ $+$ ______	Multiply $(-x^2 + 2x + 1)$ by x.
$-x^3 +$ ______ $-$ ______ $-$ ______	Add.

REFLECT

1a. Is the product of two polynomials always another polynomial? Explain.

____

____

1b. If one polynomial has m terms and the other has n terms, how many terms does the product of the polynomials have before it is simplified?

____

There are several special products that occur so frequently that it is helpful to recognize their patterns and develop rules for the products. These rules are summarized in the table.

Special Product Rules	
Sum and Difference	$(a + b)(a - b) = a^2 - b^2$
Square of a Binomial	$(a + b)^2 = a^2 + 2ab + b^2$ $(a - b)^2 = a^2 - 2ab + b^2$
Cube of a Binomial	$(a + b)^3 = a^3 + 3a^2b + 3ab^2 + b^3$ $(a - b)^3 = a^3 - 3a^2b + 3ab^2 - b^3$

MCC9–12.A.APR.4

2 EXAMPLE Justifying and Applying a Special Product Rule

Justify the sum and difference rule. Then use it to find the product $(4x^2 + 15)(4x^2 - 15)$.

A Justify the rule.

$(a + b)(a - b) = a \cdot a + a(-b) +$ ______ $+$ ______ Distribute a and then b.

$= a^2 \quad - ab \quad +$ ______ $+$ ______ Multiply monomials.

$=$ ______ $-$ ______ Combine like terms.

B Find the product $(4x^2 + 15)(4x^2 - 15)$.

$(4x^2 + 15)(4x^2 - 15) = ($______$)^2 - ($______$)^2$ Sum and difference rule

$=$ ____________ Simplify.

REFLECT

2a. Error Analysis A student was asked to find the square of $7x + 3$. The student quickly wrote $(7x + 3)^2 = 49x^2 + 9$. Identify the student's error and provide the correct answer.

____

____

2b. Show how to justify the rule for the cube of a binomial, $(a + b)^3$.

____

____

____

____

MCC9–12.A.APR.4

3 EXAMPLE Applying Special Products

Recall that a *Pythagorean triple* is a set of positive integers, *a*, *b*, and *c*, such that $a^2 + b^2 = c^2$. Euclid's formula states that if *x* and *y* are positive integers with $x > y$, then $x^2 - y^2$, $2xy$, and $x^2 + y^2$ form a Pythagorean triple.

$$(x^2 - y^2)^2 + (2xy)^2 = (x^2 + y^2)^2$$

Verify Euclid's formula. Then use the formula to generate a Pythagorean triple with $x = 5$ and $y = 3$.

A Show that $(x^2 - y^2)^2 + (2xy)^2 = (x^2 + y^2)^2$.

Step 1: Simplify the left side of the equation.

$(x^2 - y^2)^2 = (\_\_\_\_)^2 - 2 \cdot \_\_\_\_ \cdot \_\_\_\_ + (\_\_\_\_)^2$ Square of a binomial

$= \_\_\_\_\_\_\_\_\_\_\_\_\_\_\_\_\_\_\_\_.$ Simplify.

$(2xy)^2 = \_\_\_\_\_\_\_\_\_\_\_\_\_\_\_\_\_\_\_\_$ Simplify.

So, $(x^2 - y^2)^2 + (2xy)^2 = \_\_\_\_\_\_\_\_\_\_\_\_\_\_\_\_.$ Add.

Step 2: Simplify the right side of the equation.

$(x^2 + y^2)^2 = (\_\_\_\_)^2 + 2 \cdot \_\_\_\_ \cdot \_\_\_\_ + (\_\_\_\_)^2$ Square of a binomial

$= \_\_\_\_\_\_\_\_\_\_\_\_\_\_\_\_\_\_\_\_$ Simplify.

Step 3: Compare the expressions on both sides of the equation.

The expressions on both sides of the equation equal ________________.

So, Euclid's formula is valid.

B Use the formula to generate a Pythagorean triple with $x = 5$ and $y = 3$.

$a = x^2 - y^2 = (\_\_\_\_)^2 - (\_\_\_\_)^2 = \_\_\_\_ - \_\_\_\_ = \_\_\_\_$

$b = 2xy = 2 \cdot \_\_\_\_ \cdot \_\_\_\_ = \_\_\_\_$

$c = x^2 + y^2 = (\_\_\_\_)^2 + (\_\_\_\_)^2 = \_\_\_\_ + \_\_\_\_ = \_\_\_\_$

So, the Pythagorean triple is $a =$ ____, $b =$ ____, and $c =$ ____.

REFLECT

3a. Describe how you can check the Pythagorean triple. Then perform the check.

____

____

Pascal's Triangle is a famous number pattern named after the French mathematician Blaise Pascal (1623–1662). You can use Pascal's Triangle to help you expand a power of a binomial of the form $(a + b)^n$.

PREP FOR MCC9–12.A.APR.5(+)

4 EXPLORE Generating Pascal's Triangle

You can generate Pascal's Triangle by making a tree diagram as shown below. Starting at the top of the diagram, there are two paths from each node to the nodes beneath it, the left path (L) and the right path (R). You can describe a path from the top down to any node using lefts and rights.

There is only one possible path to each node in row 1. In row 2, there is only one possible path (LL) to the first node and only one possible path (RR) to the last node, but there are two possible paths (LR and RL) to the center node.

A Complete rows 3 and 4 of Pascal's Triangle. In each node, write the number of possible paths from the top down to that node.

B Look for patterns in the tree diagram.

What is the value in the first and last node in each row? ___________

For the other nodes, what is the relationship of the value in the node to the two values above it?

____

____

C Use the patterns to complete rows 5 and 6 of Pascal's Triangle.

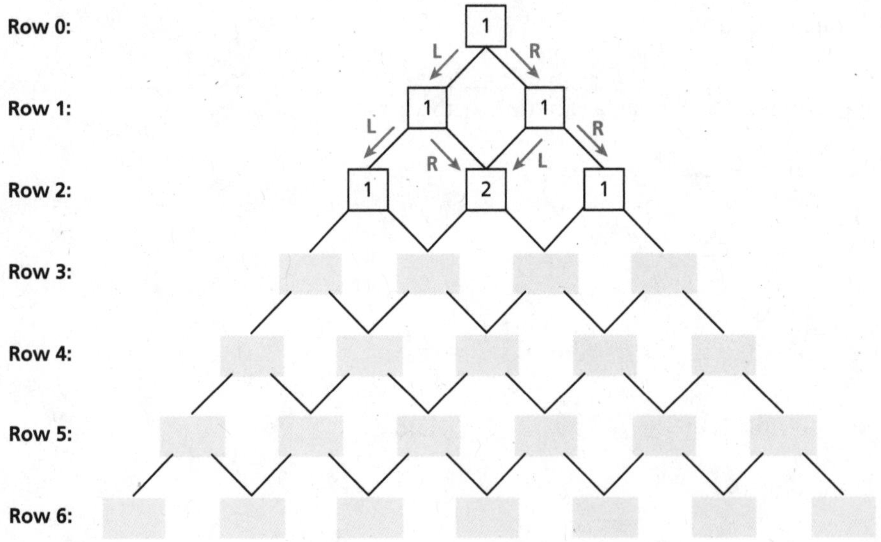

Row 0: 1

L R

Row 1: 1 1

L R L R

Row 2: 1 2 1

Row 3:

Row 4:

Row 5:

Row 6:

REFLECT

4a. What are all the paths to get to the second node in row 3? Write the paths in terms of L and R. How are the paths alike? How are they different?

____

____

4b. Which node in which row of Pascal's Triangle is located by the path LLRLR? What is the value at that node?

____

The value in position r of row n of Pascal's Triangle is written as ${}_nC_r$, where the position numbers in each row start with 0. In the next Explore, you will see how the values in Pascal's Triangle are related to powers of a binomial.

Row 0 ⟶ ${}_0C_0$

Row 1 ⟶ ${}_1C_0$ ${}_1C_1$

Row 2 ⟶ ${}_2C_0$ ${}_2C_1$ ${}_2C_2$

Row 3 ⟶ ${}_3C_0$ ${}_3C_1$ ${}_3C_2$ ${}_3C_3$

MCC9–12.A.APR.5(+)

5 EXPLORE Expanding a Power of a Binomial

A Expand each power.

$(a + b)^0 =$ ______

$(a + b)^1 =$ ______

$(a + b)^2 =$ ______ Square of a binomial

$(a + b)^3 =$ ______ Multiply $(a + b)^2$ by $(a + b)$.

$(a + b)^4 =$ ______ Multiply $(a + b)^3$ by $(a + b)$.

B Identify patterns in the expanded power $(a + b)^n$.

What do you notice about the exponents of a?

____

What do you notice about the exponents of b?

____

What is the sum of the exponents in each term? ______

What is the pattern in the coefficients of the terms?

____

____

____

REFLECT

5a. In the expanded power $(a + b)^n$, if you replace a with L and b with R, then the terms describe the lefts and rights in the paths to each node.

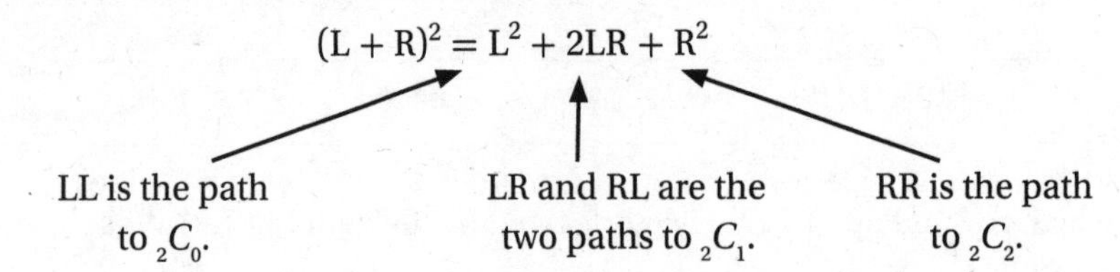

Describe the paths to each node in row 4 using the expanded form of $(L + R)^4$.

$(L + R)^4 =$ ______ + ______ + ______ + ______ + ______

Path(s) to ${}_4C_0$: ______________________

Path(s) to ${}_4C_1$: ______________________

Path(s) to ${}_4C_2$: ______________________

Path(s) to ${}_4C_3$: ______________________

Path(s) to ${}_4C_4$: ______________________

5b. How many terms are in the expanded form of $(a + b)^n$? ______________________

5c. Without expanding the power, what is the middle term of $(a + b)^6$? Explain how you found your answer.

____

____

____

5d. Without expanding the power, what is the first term of $(a + b)^{15}$? Explain how you found your answer.

____

____

The Binomial Theorem states the connection between the terms of the expanded binomial $(a + b)^n$ and Pascal's Triangle.

Binomial Theorem

For any whole number n, the binomial expansion of $(a + b)^n$ is given by

$$(a + b)^n = {}_nC_0a^nb^0 + {}_nC_1a^{n-1}b^1 + {}_nC_2a^{n-2}b^2 + \cdots + {}_nC_{n-1}a^1b^{n-1} + {}_nC_na^0b^n$$

where ${}_nC_r$ is the value in position r of the nth row of Pascal's Triangle.

MCC9–12.A.APR.5(+)

6 EXAMPLE Using the Binomial Theorem to Expand a Power

Use the Binomial Theorem to expand each power of a binomial.

A $(s - 2)^3$

Step 1: Identify the values in row 3 of Pascal's Triangle. ____________________

Step 2: Expand the power as described in the Binomial Theorem, using the values from Pascal's Triangle as coefficients.

$$\square s^{\square}(-2)^{\square} + \square s^{\square}(-2)^{\square} + \square s^{\square}(-2)^{\square} + \square s^{\square}(-2)^{\square}$$

Step 3: Simplify.

So, $(s - 2)^3 =$ ____________________.

B $(x + y)^5$

Step 1: Identify the values in row 5 of Pascal's Triangle. ____________________

Step 2: Expand the power as described by the Binomial Theorem, using the values from Pascal's Triangle as coefficients.

$$\square x^{\square}y^{\square} + \square x^{\square}y^{\square} + \square x^{\square}y^{\square} + \square x^{\square}y^{\square} + \square x^{\square}y^{\square} + \square x^{\square}y^{\square}$$

Step 3: Simplify.

So, $(x + y)^5 =$ ____________________.

REFLECT

6a. What do you notice about the signs of the terms in the expanded form of $(s - 2)^3$? Why does this happen?

____

____

____

6b. If the number 11 is written as the binomial $(10 + 1)$, how can you use the Binomial Theorem to find 11^2, 11^3, and 11^4? What is the pattern in the digits?

____

____

____

____

PRACTICE

Find each product.

1. $(2x^3)(2x^2 - 9x + 3)$

2. $(x + 5)(3x^2 - x + 1)$

3. $(x - 4)(x - 6)$

4. $(3 + x^3)(-x + x^2 + 7)$

5. $(4x^2 + 2x + 2)(2x^2 - x + 3)$

6. $(2x^4 - 5x^2)(6x + 4x^2)$

7. $(x + y)(2x - y)$

8. $(x + 2y)(x^2 + xy + y^2)$

9. $(3x^2 - x + 2x^3 - 2)(2x + 3)$

10. $(x^3)(x^2 - 3)(3x + 1)$

Use the Binomial Theorem to expand each power of a binomial.

11. $(x - 1)^4$

12. $(2m + 5)^3$

13. $(c + 2d)^3$

14. $(2x - 2)^4$

15. $(8 - m)^3$

16. $(3s + 2t)^4$

17. $(3 + t)^5$

18. $(x - y)^5$

19. $(2n + 1)^6$

20. $(p - 2q)^6$

21. Justify the rule for the square of a binomial, $(a + b)^2 = a^2 + 2ab + b^2$. Then use it to expand $(2x^3 + 6y)^2$.

22. The sum and difference rule is useful for mental-math calculations. Explain how you can use the rule and mental math to calculate $32 \cdot 28$. (*Hint:* $32 \cdot 28 = (30 + 2)(30 - 2)$.)

23. You can generate a Pythagorean triple by choosing a positive integer m and letting $a = 2m$, $b = m^2 - 1$, and $c = m^2 + 1$. Show that this formula generates a Pythagorean triple. Then use the formula to generate a Pythagorean triple with $m = 5$.

24. Previously, you graphed functions of the form $f(x) = a(x - h)^n + k$.

a. What is the expanded form of $a(x - h)^3 + k$?

b. Is this function a polynomial? Why or why not?

c. What is the constant term in the expanded form of $a(x - h)^3 + k$? What does this represent in the graph of the function?

25. What is the leading term of the expanded form of $f(x) = a(x - h)^n + k$? What is the constant term? Explain how you know.

26. If n is even, the expanded form of $(a + b)^n$ has an odd number of terms. For example, the expansion of $(a + b)^2$ is $a^2 + 2ab + b^2$ and the expansion of $(a + b)^4$ is $a^4 + 4a^3b + 6a^2b^2 + 4ab^3 + b^4$. Write an expression for the middle term of the expanded form of $(a + b)^n$ when n is an even number. Explain your reasoning.

27. You can use a graphing calculator to evaluate $_nC_r$. First enter the value of n, then press MATH, select **PRB**, then select **3:nCr**. Now enter the value of r, and then press ENTER. Use a calculator to help you expand $(x + 1)^9$.

Name ______________________ Class ______________ Date ___________

Additional Practice

Find each product.

1. $4x^2(3x^2 + 1)$

2. $-9x(x^2 + 2x + 4)$

3. $-6x^2(x^3 + 7x^2 - 4x + 3)$

4. $x^3(-4x^3 + 10x^2 - 7x + 2)$

5. $-5m^3(7n^4 - 2mn^3 + 6)$

6. $(x + 2)(y^2 + 2y - 12)$

7. $(p + q)(4p^2 - p - 8q^2 - q)$

8. $(2x^2 + xy - y)(y^2 + 3x)$

Expand each expression.

9. $(3x - 1)^3$

10. $(x - 4)^4$

11. $3(a - 4b)^2$

12. $5\left(x^2 - 2y^3\right)^3$

Solve.

13. A biologist has found that the number of branches on a certain rare tree in its first few years of life can be modeled by the polynomial $b(y) = 4y^2 + y$. The number of leaves on each branch can be modeled by the polynomial $l(y) = 2y^3 + 3y^2 + y$, where y is the number of years after the tree reaches a height of 6 feet. Write a polynomial describing the total number of leaves on the tree.

Problem Solving

Latesha is making an open wooden toy box to hold the building blocks at her day care center. She has a square panel of cedar with side length of 24 inches. The first step is to cut out congruent squares from each corner. She needs to know what the side length of the cutout square should be in order for the finished toy box to have the greatest volume possible.

1. Draw a sketch to help solve the problem.

2. The toy box will be square and x inches deep. Write an expression for the side length of the finished box. ______________________

3. Write an equation to represent the volume. ______________________

4. Express the volume as the sum of monomials. ______________________

5. Latesha decides to try some possible values for x. She knows that x must be less than 12. Explain why.

____

6. Complete the table for each value of x. Round each volume to the nearest square inch.

x (in.)	2	3	4	5	6
Volume (sq in.)					

7. Latesha decides that she will use an integer value for x, so that she does not have to cut fractions of an inch.

   a. What value for x should she choose? ______________________

   b. Explain why this is the best choice.

   ____

   c. What are the dimensions of her finished toy box?

   ____

Name________________________ Class______________ Date__________

10-3

Binomial Distributions

Extension: Probability Distributions

Essential question: *What is a probability distribution and how is it displayed?*

MCC9–12.S.MD.5(+)

1 ENGAGE Introducing Probability Distributions

A **random variable** is a variable whose value is determined by the outcome of a probability experiment. For example, when you roll a number cube, you can use a random variable X to represent the number you roll. The possible values of X are 1, 2, 3, 4, 5, and 6.

A **probability distribution** is a data distribution that gives the probabilities of the values of a random variable. A probability distribution can be represented by a histogram in which the values of the random variable—that is, the possible outcomes—are on the horizontal axis, and probabilities are on the vertical axis. The figure shows the probability distribution for rolling a number cube.

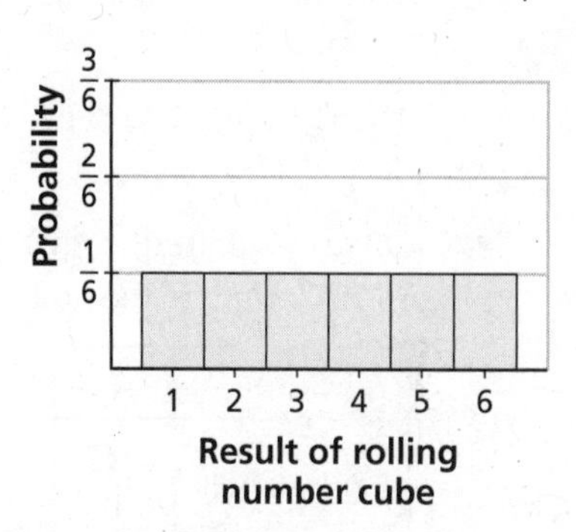

When the values of a random variable are consecutive whole numbers, as is the case for rolling a number cube, a histogram for the probability distribution typically shows bars that each have a width of 1 and is centered on a value of the variable. The area of each bar therefore equals the probability of the corresponding outcome, and the combined areas of the bars is the sum of the probabilities, which is 1.

A **cumulative probability** is the probability that a random variable is less than or equal to a given value. You can find cumulative probabilities from a histogram by adding the areas of the bars for all outcomes less than or equal to the given value.

REFLECT

1a. In an experiment in which a coin is tossed twice, the random variable X is the number of times that the coin lands heads up. What are the possible values of the random variable?

____

1b. A spinner has 8 equal sections, each labeled 1, 2, 3, or 4. The histogram shows the probability distribution for spinning the spinner. How many sections of the spinner are labeled with each number? How do you know?

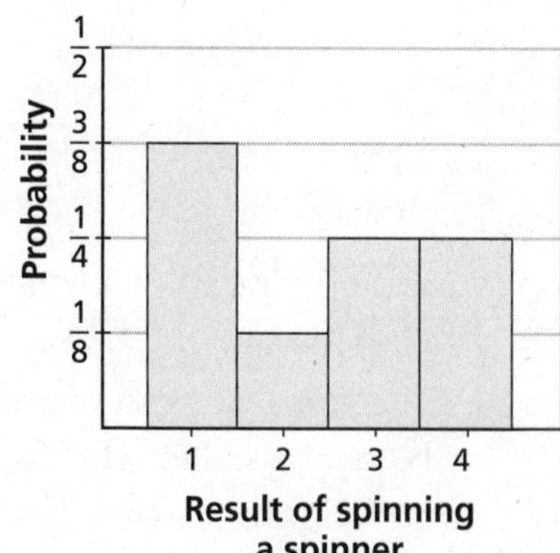

____

____

____

____

____

Displaying a Probability Distribution

You roll two number cubes at the same time. Let *X* be a random variable that represents the sum of the numbers rolled. Make a histogram to show the probability distribution for *X*.

A Complete the frequency table to show the number of ways that you can get each sum in one roll of the number cubes.

Sum	2	3	4	5	6	7	8	9	10	11	12
Frequency	1										

B Add the frequencies you found in part A to find the total number of possible outcomes.

The total number of possible outcomes is ___________.

C Divide each frequency by the total number of outcomes to find the probability of each sum. Complete the table.

Sum	2	3	4	5	6	7	8	9	10	11	12
Probability	$\frac{1}{36}$										

D Create a histogram with the sums on the horizontal axis and the probabilities on the vertical axis. Complete the histogram below by labeling the axes and drawing a bar to represent the probability of each sum.

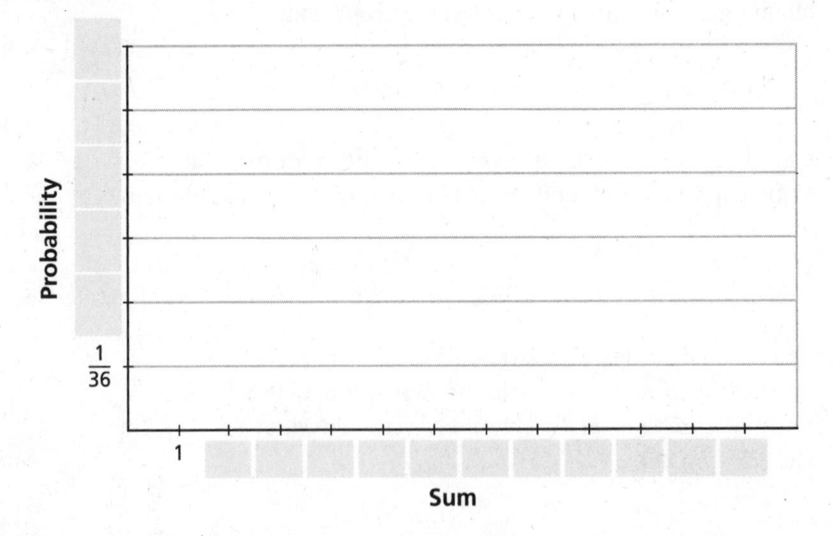

REFLECT

2a. The probability that you roll a sum less than or equal to 5 is written $P(X \leq 5)$. What is this probability? How is it represented in the histogram?

____

____

In the example, you used theoretical probabilities to define a probability distribution. You can also use experimental probabilities to define a probability distribution.

MCC9–12.S.IC.2

3 EXPLORE Using a Simulation

You flip a coin 7 times in a row. Use a simulation to determine the probability distribution for the number of times the coin lands heads up.

A When you flip a coin, the possible outcomes are heads and tails. You will use your calculator to generate random numbers between 0 and 1, assigning heads to numbers less than or equal to 0.5 and tails to numbers greater than 0.5.

To do the simulation, press MATH and then select **PRB**. Choose **1:rand** and press ENTER.

Now press ENTER 7 times to generate 7 random numbers. This simulates one trial (that is, one set of 7 coin flips). Record the number of heads in the table. For example, on the calculator screen shown here, there are 3 numbers less than or equal to 0.5, so there are 3 heads.

Carry out three more trials and record your results in the table.

Trial	1	2	3	4
Number of Heads				

B Report your results to your teacher in order to combine everyone's results. Use the combined class data to complete the table below. To find the relative frequency for an outcome, divide the frequency of the outcome by the total number of trials in the class.

Number of Heads	0	1	2	3	4	5	6	7
Frequency								
Relative Frequency								

C Enter the outcomes (0 through 7) into your calculator as list L_1. Enter the relative frequencies as list L_2.

D Make a histogram by turning on a statistics plot, selecting the histogram option, and using L_1 for Xlist and L_2 for Freq. Set the viewing window as shown. Then press GRAPH. A sample histogram is shown below.

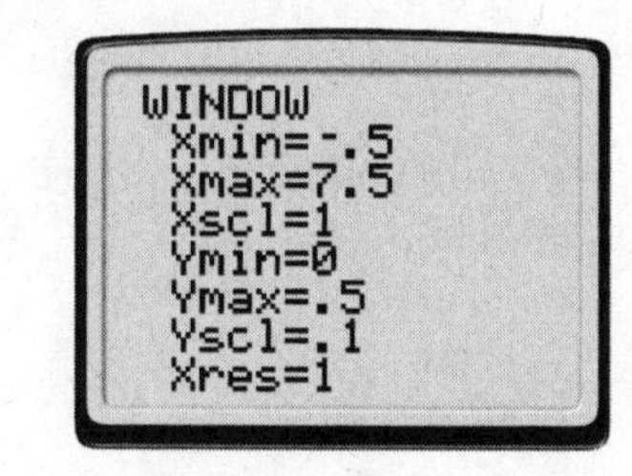

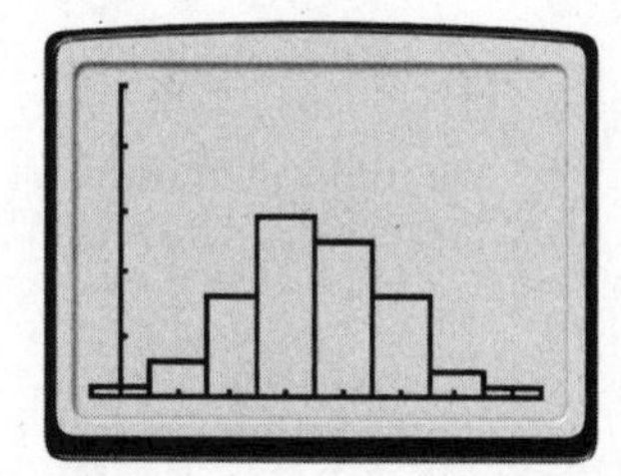

REFLECT

3a. Describe the shape of the probability distribution.

____

3b. Based on the histogram, what is $P(X \leq 3)$? That is, what is the probability of getting 3 or fewer heads when you flip a coin 7 times? Explain.

____

____

3c. If you flipped a coin 7 times and got 7 heads, would this cause you to question whether the coin is fair? Why or why not?

____

____

MCC9–12.S.MD.3(+)

4 EXAMPLE Analyzing a Probability Distribution

The histogram shows the theoretical probability distribution for the situation in the Explore. Use the distribution to answer each question.

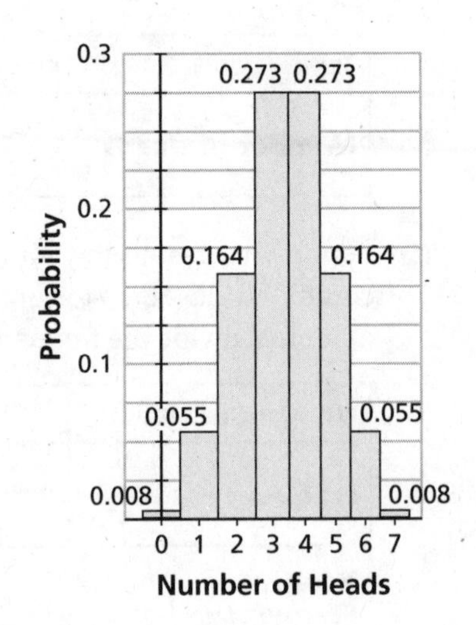

A **What is the probability of getting 4 or more heads?**

$P(X \geq 4) = P(X = 4) + P(X = 5) + P(X = 6) + P(X = 7)$

So, the probability of getting 4 or more heads is

_______ + _______ + _______ + _______ = _______.

B **What is the probability of getting at least 1 head?**

An easy way to calculate this probability is to use the complement of the event. The complement of getting at least 1 head is getting 0 heads. Use the histogram to find $P(X = 0)$ and subtract it from 1.

$P(X = 0) =$ _______

So, the probability of getting at least 1 head is

$1 -$ _______ $=$ _______.

REFLECT

4a. Why are the probabilities in the histogram you made in the Explore different from the probabilities given in the histogram above?

____

____

4b. What do you think would happen to the histogram you made in the Explore if you included data from 1000 additional trials?

4c. Why does it make sense that the histogram that shows the theoretical probabilities is symmetric?

PRACTICE

1. The spinner at right has three equal sections. You spin the spinner twice and find the sum of the two numbers the spinner lands on.

a. Let X be a random variable that represents the sum of the two numbers. What are the possible values of X?

b. Complete the table.

Sum					
Probability					

c. Make a histogram of the probability distribution.

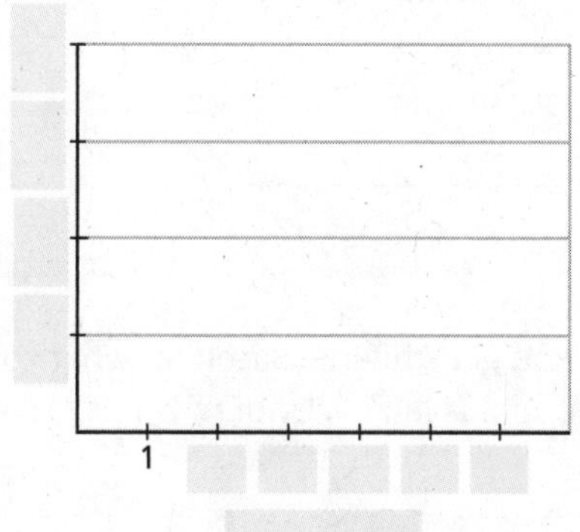

d. What is the probability that the sum is not 2? How is this probability represented in the histogram?

2. You roll two number cubes at the same time. Let X be a random variable that represents the absolute value of the difference of the numbers rolled.

a. What are the possible values of X?

____

b. Complete the table.

Difference						
Probability						

c. Is this probability distribution symmetric? Why or why not?

____

____

____

A trick coin is designed to land heads up with a probability of 80%. You flip the coin 7 times. The histogram shows the probability distribution for the number of times the coin lands heads up. ("0+" means slightly greater than 0.) Use the histogram for Exercises 3–6.

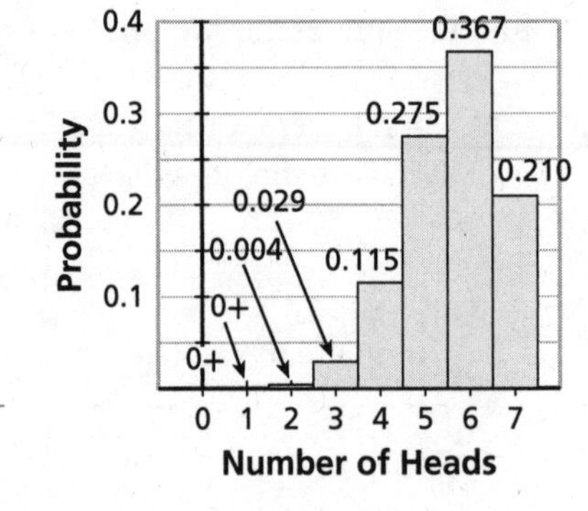

3. What is the probability of getting 6 or 7 heads?

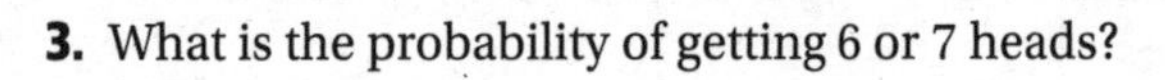

____

4. What is the probability of getting 4 or more heads? Explain.

____

____

5. Is the probability of getting an even number of heads the same as the probability of getting an odd number of heads? Explain.

____

____

____

6. Suppose you flip a coin 7 times and get 7 heads. Based on what you know now, would you question whether the coin is fair? Why or why not?

____

____

____

Name_______________ Class_______________ Date_______________

Additional Practice

1. You roll two four-sided number cubes at the same time. Let X be a random variable that represents the product of the numbers rolled.

   a. What are the possible values of X?

   ____

   b. Complete the table.

Control									
Probability									

   c. Draw a histogram of the probability distribution.

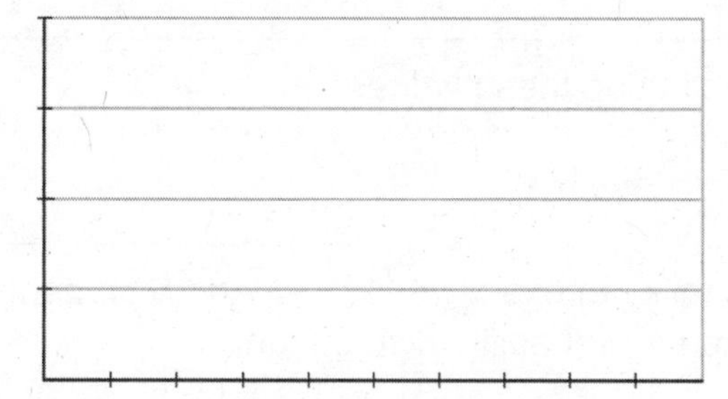

2. Describe the probability distribution for flipping a fair coin. Does this depend on the number of flips?

Problem Solving

Sales records for the snack machines show that 1 of every 6 students buys a bag of trail mix. There are 5 students waiting to use the machines. Melanie uses the formula for binomial probability, $P(r) = {}_nC_r p^r q^{n-r}$, to determine the number of students expected to buy trail mix. (The expression ${}_nC_r$ means $\frac{n!}{(r!)(n-r!)}$).

1. What is the probability of exactly 3 students buying a bag of trail mix?
   a. What is the probability of each student buying a bag of trail mix? ________________
   b. Define each variable used in the formula and give its value.
   ____
   c. Write the binomial formula, substituting these values. ________________
   d. Solve the equation to give the probability of exactly 3 students buying a bag of trail mix. ________________
2. Repeat the process to find the probability of exactly 0, 1, 2, 4, and 5 students buying a bag of trail mix. Use these results to graph a probability distribution.

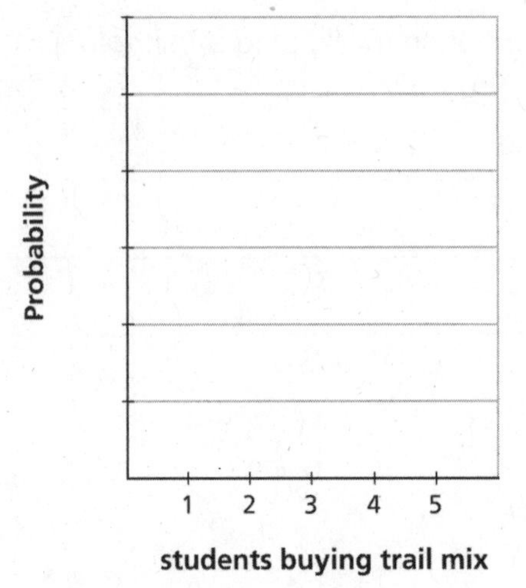

3. What is the probability of at least 1 student buying a bag of trail mix?
   a. Describe a method to solve involving the sum of probabilities.
   ____
   b. Describe a method to solve that uses the formula $P(E) + P(\text{not } E) = 1$.
   ____
   c. Use either method to determine the probability of at least 1 student buying a bag of trail mix. ________________

Name ______________________ Class ____________ Date ________

10-4

Dividing Polynomials

Going Deeper

Essential question: *What is the relationship between polynomial division and the Remainder Theorem?*

Video Tutor

You can use long division to divide a polynomial by another polynomial of a lower degree. The process is similar to dividing numbers.

PREP FOR MCC9–12.A.APR.2

1 EXAMPLE Using Long Division to Divide Polynomials

Divide $2x^3 + 4x^2 + 5$ by $x - 3$ using long division.

A Write the quotient in long division format with the polynomials written in standard form. Remember to include terms with a coefficient of 0.

$$\begin{array}{r} \square + \square + \square \\ x-3\overline{)2x^3 + 4x^2 + 0x + 5} \\ -(2x^3 - 6x^2) \\ \hline 10x^2 + 0x \\ -(10x^2 - 30x) \\ \hline 30x + 5 \\ -(30x - 90) \\ \hline \square \end{array}$$

Divide $2x^3$ by x. Write $2x^2$ above $2x^3$.

Multiply $2x^2$ by $x - 3$ and subtract.

Bring down the next term. Divide $10x^2$ by x.

Multiply $10x$ by $x - 3$ and subtract.

Bring down the next term. Divide $30x$ by x.

Multiply 30 by $x - 3$ and subtract.

Write the remainder.

B Write the quotient. The last term of the quotient is the remainder in fraction form.

$$\frac{2x^3 + 4x^2 + 5}{x - 3} = \square + \square + \square + \frac{\square}{\square}$$

REFLECT

1a. When you perform long division of polynomials, why must the degree of the remainder be less than the degree of the divisor?

____

____

____

1b. Is the set of polynomials closed under division? Why or why not?

____

____

MCC9–12.A.APR.2

2 ENGAGE Understanding the Remainder Theorem

When you divide $2x^3 + 4x^2 + 5$ by $x - 3$, you get a remainder of 95. If you evaluate the polynomial $2x^3 + 4x^2 + 5$ for $x = 3$, you get $2(3)^3 + 4(3)^2 + 5 = 2(27) + 4(9) + 5 = 95$. This is an illustration of the Remainder Theorem.

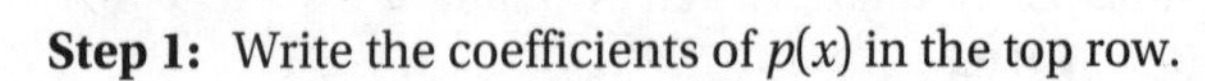

Remainder Theorem

If a polynomial $p(x)$ is divided by $x - a$, then the remainder r is $p(a)$.

You can use the Remainder Theorem to evaluate polynomials. To find $p(a)$, you divide the polynomial $p(x)$ by $x - a$ and find the remainder.

A shorthand method for dividing a polynomial by $x - a$ is called **synthetic division**. The process is similar to long division, but you work only with the coefficients. Here are the steps for using synthetic division to find the quotient $(2x^3 + 4x^2 + 5) \div (x - 3)$. In this case, $p(x) = 2x^3 + 4x^2 + 5$ and $a = 3$.

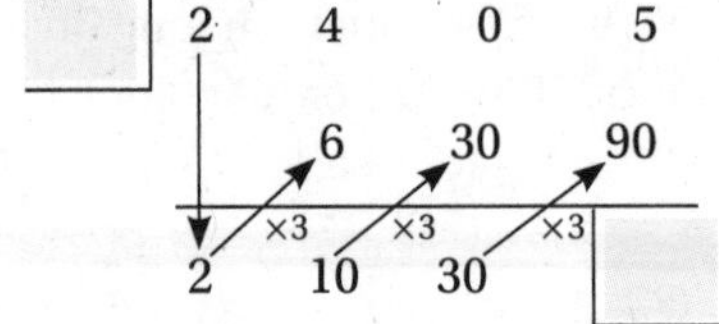

Step 1: Write the coefficients of $p(x)$ in the top row.

Step 2: Write the value of a to the left.

Step 3: Bring down the first coefficient.

Step 4: Multiply by a and place the result below the next coefficient, then add. Continue to the last column.

The coefficients of the quotient, $2x^2 + 10x + 30$, are shown in the bottom row, and the last value, 95, is the remainder. By the Remainder Theorem, this is also the value of $p(3)$. Because synthetic division may be used to evaluate polynomials, the process is also known as **synthetic substitution**.

REFLECT

2a. If a polynomial $p(x)$ is divided by $x - a$, then $\frac{p(x)}{x-a} = q(x) + \frac{r}{x-a}$, where $q(x)$ is the quotient and r is the remainder. This is the first step in the proof of the Remainder Theorem. Complete the proof.

$\frac{p(x)}{x-a} = q(x) + \frac{r}{x-a}$	Given
$(x-a)\frac{p(x)}{x-a} = (x-a)\left(q(x) + \frac{r}{x-a}\right)$	Multiply both sides by $x - a$.
$p(x) = (x-a)q(x) +$ ______	Distributive property and simplification
$p(a) = (a-a)q(a) +$ ______	Substitute a for x.
$p(a) =$ ______ $\cdot\, q(a) +$ ______	Simplify $a - a$.
$p(a) =$ ______	Simplify.

MCC9–12.A.APR.2

3 EXAMPLE Using Synthetic Division

Divide $3x^3 + 14x^2 - x + 20$ by $x + 5$ using synthetic division.

A Write the coefficients of $p(x)$ in the top row.

B Write the divisor in the form $x - a$.

$x + 5 = x - (-5)$, so $a =$ ________.

C Write the value of a in the upper left corner.

D Bring down the first coefficient. Multiply by a and place the result below the next coefficient, then add. Continue to the last column.

E Write the quotient: ____________________

	3	14	−1	20

REFLECT

3a. What is the remainder in this example? How do you know?

____

____

____

3b. Can you use synthetic division to divide $3x^3 + 14x^2 - x + 20$ by $x^2 + 5$? Why or why not?

____

____

____

PRACTICE

Divide using long division.

1. $(5x^3 - 8x^2 - x - 4) \div (x - 2)$

2. $(6x^3 + 16x^2 + 3x - 2) \div (x + 1)$

3. $(x^3 + 7x^2 + 5x + 35) \div (x + 7)$

4. $(7x^3 + 9x^2 + 13) \div (x - 3)$

5. $(4x^2 - 6x + 6) \div (2x + 1)$

6. $(15x^3 + 16x^2 + x - 2) \div (3x + 2)$

Divide using synthetic division.

7. $(4x^3 + 5x^2 + 2x + 16) \div (x + 2)$

8. $(2x^3 - 22x^2 + 3x - 33) \div (x - 11)$

9. $(4x^4 + 2x^2 - 3x - 9) \div (x + 1)$

10. $(6x^3 - 5x^2 - 3x + 2) \div \left(x - \frac{1}{2}\right)$

11. $(3x^3 - x + 7) \div (x + 3)$

12. $(6x^3 - 4x^2 + 2x + 17) \div (x - 4)$

13. Error Analysis A student was asked to find the quotient $(4x^3 + x^2 + 2x + 1) \div (x + 2)$. The student's work is shown at right. Identify the student's error and provide the correct quotient.

2	4	1	2	1
		8	18	40
	4	9	20	41

So, $(4x^3 + x^2 + 2x + 1) \div (x + 2) =$

$4x^2 + 9x + 20 + \frac{41}{x + 2}.$

14. The set of polynomials is analogous to a set of numbers you have studied. To determine which, consider the following questions about closure.

a. Under which operations is the set of polynomials closed?

b. Which set of the numbers discussed in Lesson 1-1 is closed under the same set of operations?

15. When the polynomial $p(x)$ is divided by $x - 1$, the quotient is $-2x^2 + 3x + 5 + \frac{12}{x - 1}$. What is $p(x)$? How did you find $p(x)$?

16. Determine the values of a, b, and c in the synthetic division shown at right. Then tell what polynomial division problem and quotient are represented by the synthetic division.

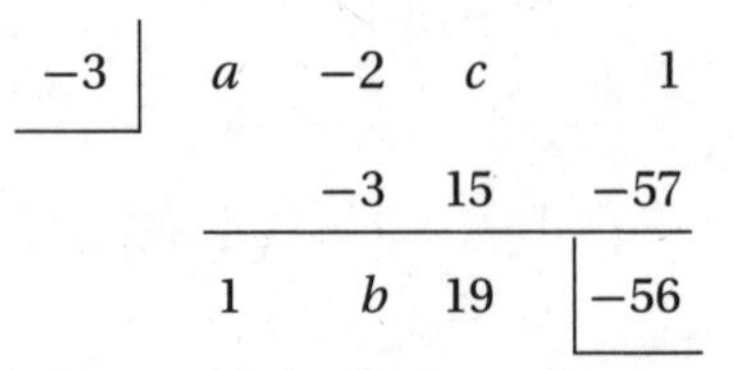

Name________________________ Class______________ Date__________

10-4

Dividing Polynomials

Going Deeper

Essential question: *What is the relationship between polynomial division and the Remainder Theorem?*

Video Tutor

You can use long division to divide a polynomial by another polynomial of a lower degree. The process is similar to dividing numbers.

PREP FOR MCC9–12.A.APR.2

1 EXAMPLE Using Long Division to Divide Polynomials

Divide $2x^3 + 4x^2 + 5$ by $x - 3$ using long division.

A Write the quotient in long division format with the polynomials written in standard form. Remember to include terms with a coefficient of 0.

$\square + \square + \square$	
$x - 3 \overline{)2x^3 + 4x^2 + 0x + 5}$	Divide $2x^3$ by x. Write $2x^2$ above $2x^3$.
$-(2x^3 - 6x^2)$	Multiply $2x^2$ by $x - 3$ and subtract.
$10x^2 + 0x$	Bring down the next term. Divide $10x^2$ by x.
$-(10x^2 - 30x)$	Multiply $10x$ by $x - 3$ and subtract.
$30x + 5$	Bring down the next term. Divide $30x$ by x.
$-(30x - 90)$	Multiply 30 by $x - 3$ and subtract.
$\square$	Write the remainder.

B Write the quotient. The last term of the quotient is the remainder in fraction form.

$$\frac{2x^3 + 4x^2 + 5}{x - 3} = \square + \square + \square + \frac{\square}{\square}$$

REFLECT

1a. When you perform long division of polynomials, why must the degree of the remainder be less than the degree of the divisor?

____

____

____

1b. Is the set of polynomials closed under division? Why or why not?

____

____

2 ENGAGE Understanding the Remainder Theorem

When you divide $2x^3 + 4x^2 + 5$ by $x - 3$, you get a remainder of 95. If you evaluate the polynomial $2x^3 + 4x^2 + 5$ for $x = 3$, you get $2(3)^3 + 4(3)^2 + 5 = 2(27) + 4(9) + 5 = 95$. This is an illustration of the Remainder Theorem.

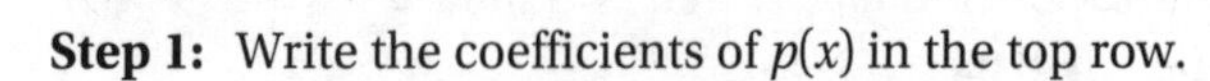

Remainder Theorem

If a polynomial $p(x)$ is divided by $x - a$, then the remainder r is $p(a)$.

You can use the Remainder Theorem to evaluate polynomials. To find $p(a)$, you divide the polynomial $p(x)$ by $x - a$ and find the remainder.

A shorthand method for dividing a polynomial by $x - a$ is called **synthetic division**. The process is similar to long division, but you work only with the coefficients. Here are the steps for using synthetic division to find the quotient $(2x^3 + 4x^2 + 5) \div (x - 3)$. In this case, $p(x) = 2x^3 + 4x^2 + 5$ and $a = 3$.

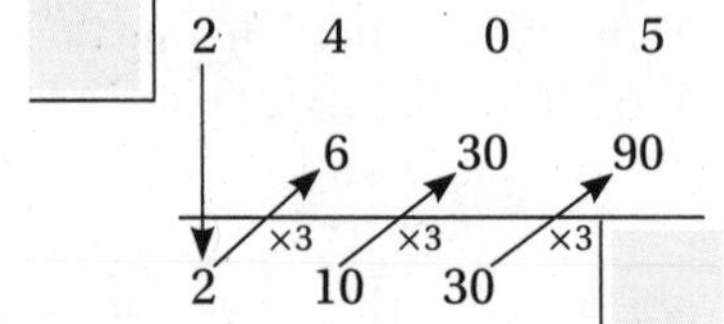

Step 1: Write the coefficients of $p(x)$ in the top row.

Step 2: Write the value of a to the left.

Step 3: Bring down the first coefficient.

Step 4: Multiply by a and place the result below the next coefficient, then add. Continue to the last column.

The coefficients of the quotient, $2x^2 + 10x + 30$, are shown in the bottom row, and the last value, 95, is the remainder. By the Remainder Theorem, this is also the value of $p(3)$. Because synthetic division may be used to evaluate polynomials, the process is also known as **synthetic substitution**.

REFLECT

2a. If a polynomial $p(x)$ is divided by $x - a$, then $\frac{p(x)}{x-a} = q(x) + \frac{r}{x-a}$, where $q(x)$ is the quotient and r is the remainder. This is the first step in the proof of the Remainder Theorem. Complete the proof.

$\frac{p(x)}{x-a} = q(x) + \frac{r}{x-a}$	Given
$(x-a)\frac{p(x)}{x-a} = (x-a)\left(q(x) + \frac{r}{x-a}\right)$	Multiply both sides by $x - a$.
$p(x) = (x-a)q(x) + \underline{\qquad}$	Distributive property and simplification
$p(a) = (a-a)q(a) + \underline{\qquad}$	Substitute a for x.
$p(a) = \underline{\qquad} \cdot q(a) + \underline{\qquad}$	Simplify $a - a$.
$p(a) = \underline{\qquad}$	Simplify.

Name________________________ Class______________ Date______________

Additional Practice

Divide using long division.

1. $(x^2 - x - 6) \div (x - 3)$

2. $(2x^3 - 10x^2 + x - 5) \div (x - 5)$

3. $(-3x^2 + 20x - 12) \div (x - 6)$

4. $(3x^3 + 9x^2 - 14) \div (x + 3)$

Divide using synthetic division.

5. $(3x^2 - 8x + 4) \div (x - 2)$

6. $(5x^2 - 4x + 12) \div (x + 3)$

7. $(9x^2 - 7x + 3) \div (x - 1)$

8. $(-6x^2 + 5x - 10) \div (x + 7)$

Use synthetic substitution to evaluate the polynomial for the given value.

9. $P(x) = 4x^2 - 9x + 2$ for $x = 3$

10. $P(x) = -3x^2 + 10x - 4$ for $x = -2$

Solve.

11. The total number of dollars donated each year to a small charitable organization has followed the trend $d(t) = 2t^3 + 10t^2 + 2000t + 10{,}000$, where d is dollars and t is the number of years since 1990. The total number of donors each year has followed the trend $p(t) = t^2 + 1000$. Write an expression describing the average number of dollars per donor.

Problem Solving

An art class is making pedestals in the shape of regular prisms to display sculptures in an art show. Blake is in charge of the mirrors for the tops of the pedestals. He needs to estimate the total area of the mirrored surfaces. He will use that total to help determine the amount of mirrored product to purchase.

The figures below show the shape of the bases for each of the three kinds of prisms that will be used for pedestals. Each regular polygon has a side length of *x*. Recall that, for a prism, $V = Bh$.

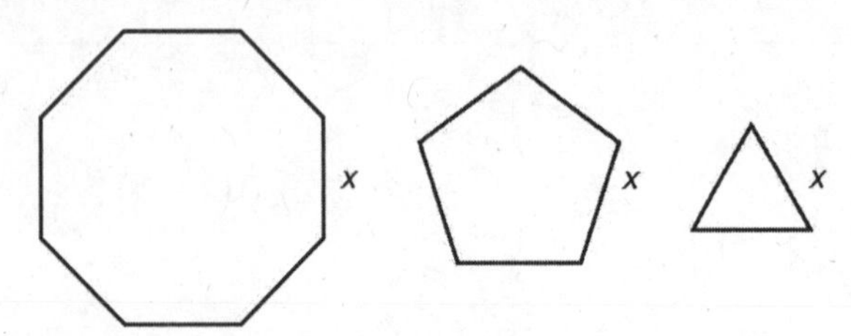

1. The triangular prism has a height of $2x + 1$ and its volume can be modeled by $V(x) = \frac{\sqrt{3}}{2}x^3 + \frac{\sqrt{3}}{4}x^2$. What is the area of the top of the pedestal?

____

Choose the letter for the best answer.

2. The volume of the pentagonal prism can be modeled by $V = 6.88x^3 - 1.72x^2$. Which expression represents the area of the top of the prism if the height is $4x - 1$?

   A $0.57x^2$

   B $1.72x^2$

   C $2.28x^2$

   D $6.88x^2$

3. The volume of the octagonal prism can be modeled by $V = 4.83x^3 - 24.15x^2$. Which expression represents the area of the top of the prism if the height is $x - 5$?

   A $48.3x^2$

   B $38.64x^2$

   C $4.83x^2$

   D $3.86x^2$

4. Which expression represents the total area that will be mirrored?

   A $A = x^2\left(\frac{\sqrt{3}}{4} + 6.55\right)$

   B $A = 6.98x$

   C $A = 12.58x^3 + 22.86x^2$

   D $A = \sqrt{6.98x}$

5. If $x = 5$, what is the total mirrored area in square units?

   A 6.98

   B 34.9

   C 69.8

   D 174.5

Name________________________________ Class________________ Date__________

10-5

Factoring Polynomials

Connection: The Remainder Theorem

Essential question: *What is the relationship between polynomial division and the Factor Theorem?*

Video Tutor

MCC9–12.A.APR.2

1 ENGAGE Understanding the Factor Theorem

When you use synthetic division to divide $3x^3 + 14x^2 - x + 20$ by $x + 5$, the remainder is 0. Therefore the divisor is a factor of the polynomial, as shown below.

$(x + 5)(3x^2 - x + 4) = x(3x^2) + x(-x) + x(4) + 5(3x^2) + 5(-x) + 5(4)$ Distribute each term.

$= 3x^3 - x^2 + 4x + 15x^2 - 5x + 20$ Multiply.

$= 3x^3 + 14x^2 - x + 20$ Combine like terms.

This shows that the product of $x + 5$ and $3x^2 - x + 4$ is the original polynomial, $3x^3 + 14x^2 - x + 20$. So, the divisor is a factor of the original polynomial.

The above observation is generalized in the Factor Theorem.

Factor Theorem

For any polynomial $p(x)$, $x - a$ is a factor if and only if $p(a) = 0$.

REFLECT

1a. Complete the proof of the Factor Theorem for a polynomial $p(x)$ divided by a linear binomial $x - a$ with quotient $q(x)$ and remainder r.

The proof has two parts: if $p(a) = 0$, then $x - a$ is a factor of $p(x)$, and if $x - a$ is a factor of $p(x)$, then $p(a) = 0$.

Part 1: Assume that $p(a) = 0$.

$p(a) = 0$	Given
$r =$ __________	Remainder Theorem
$p(x) = (x - a)q(x) +$ __________	Dividend = Divisor • Quotient + Remainder
$p(x) = (x - a)q(x) +$ __________	Substitute 0 for $p(a)$.
$p(x) =$ __________	Simplify.
$x - a$ is a factor of $p(x)$.	Definition of factor

Part 2: Assume that $x - a$ is a factor of $p(x)$.

$x - a$ is a factor of $p(x)$.	Given
$p(x) = (x - a)q(x)$	Definition of factor
$p(a) =$ __________	Substitute a for x.
$p(a) =$ __________	Simplify.

MCC9–12.A.APR.2

2 EXAMPLE Using the Factor Theorem

Show that $x - 4$ is a factor of $p(x) = x^3 + 2x^2 - 21x - 12$. Then write $p(x)$ as the product of $x - 4$ and another factor.

A Evaluate $p(4)$ by using synthetic substitution. Complete the process at the right.

	1	2	−21	−12

B The synthetic substitution shows that $p(4) =$ ________.

So, by the Factor Theorem, $x - 4$ is a factor of $p(x)$.

C Write the polynomial as the product of $x - 4$ and the quotient.

From the synthetic substitution, $(x^3 + 2x^2 - 21x - 12) \div (x - 4) =$ ____________.

So, $p(x) = x^3 + 2x^2 - 21x - 12 = ($__________$)($__________$)$.

REFLECT

2a. Show how to check the factorization you wrote in the last step.

PRACTICE

1. a. Show that $x + 6$ is a factor of $p(x) = x^3 + 6x^2 - 16x - 96$. Then write $p(x)$ as the product of $x + 6$ and another factor.

b. Factor $p(x) = x^3 + 6x^2 - 16x - 96$ completely. That is, write $p(x)$ as a product of linear factors. Describe the strategy you used.

2. Use the Table feature of your graphing calculator to complete the table of values for $p(x) = x^4 - 2x^3 - 9x^2 + 2x + 8$. Use your results to factor $p(x)$ completely. Justify your answer.

x	p(x)	x	p(x)
−4		1	
−3		2	
−2		3	
−1		4	
0		5	

Name ______________________ Class ______________ Date ______________ 10-5

Additional Practice

Determine whether the given binomial is a factor of the polynomial *P*(*x*).

1. $(x-4)$; $P(x) = x^2 + 8x - 48$

2. $(x+5)$; $P(x) = 2x^2 - 6x - 1$

3. $(x-6)$; $P(x) = -2x^2 + 15x - 18$

4. $(x+3)$; $P(x) = 2x^2 - x + 7$

Factor each expression.

5. $2x^4 + 2x^3 - x^2 - x$

6. $4x^3 + x^2 - 8x - 2$

7. $5x^6 - 5x^4 + x^3 - x$

8. $2x^4 + 54x$

9. $64x^3 - 1$

10. $3x^4 + 24x$

Solve.

11. Since 2006, the water level in a certain pond has been modeled by the polynomial $d(x) = -x^3 + 16x^2 - 74x + 140$, where the depth *d*, is measured in feet over *x* years. Identify the year that the pond will dry up. Use the graph to factor $d(x)$.

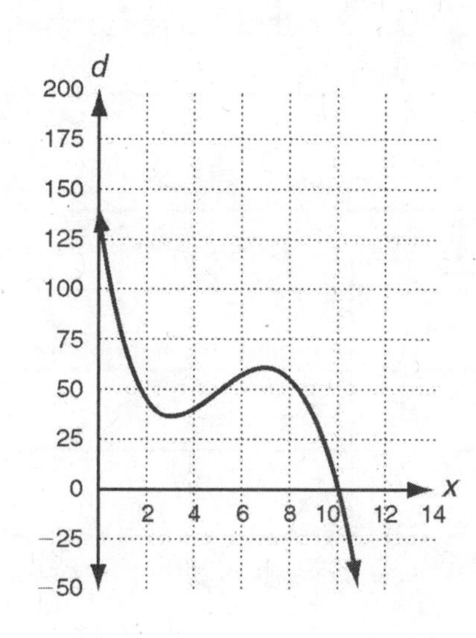

Problem Solving

Paulo is drawing plans for a set of three proportional nesting baskets, in the shape of open rectangular prisms.

1. The volume for the middle-sized basket (B) can be modeled by the function $V_B(x) = x^3 - 8x^2 + 4x + 48$. Use the graph to factor V_B.

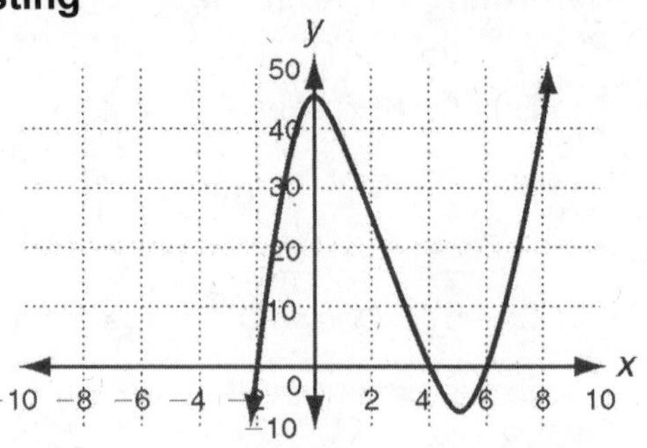

   a. What are the values of x where $V_B = 0$?

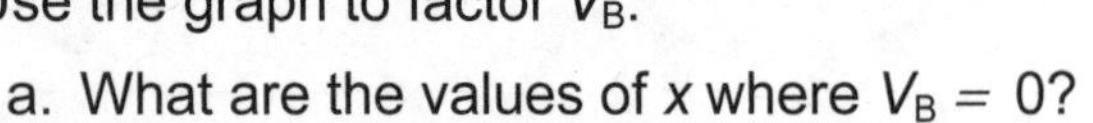

   ____

   b. Use these zeros to write the factors.

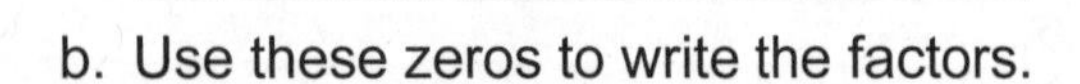

   ____

2. The volume for the largest basket (C) can be modeled by the function $V_C(x) = 2x^3 + 10x^2 + 8x$. Use the graph to factor V_C.

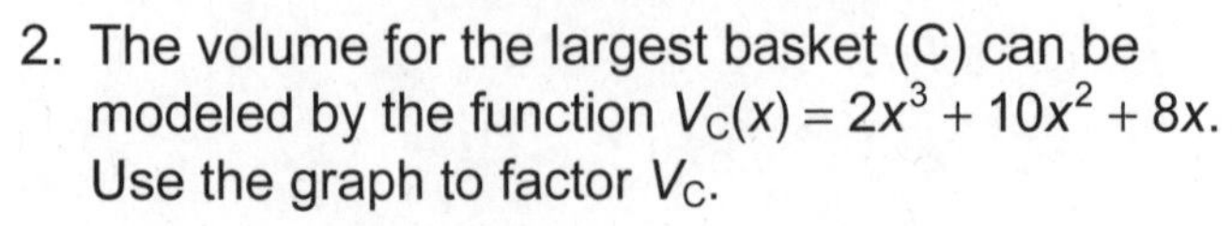

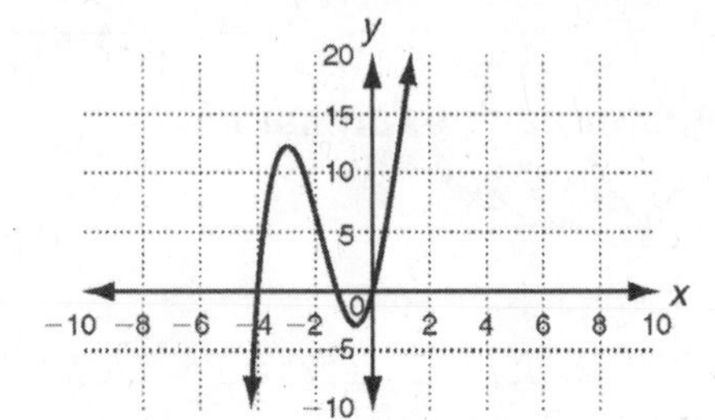

   a. What are the values of x where $V_C = 0$?

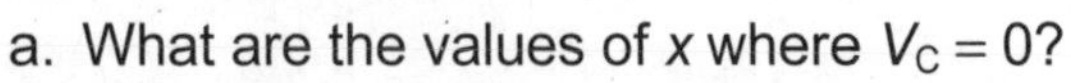

   ____

   b. Use these zeros to write the factors.

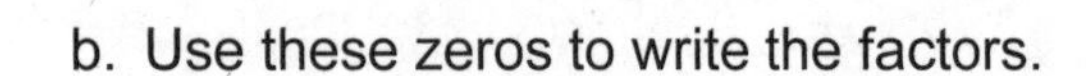

   ____

3. The volume for the smallest basket (A) can be modeled by the function $V_A(x) = x^3 - 22x^2 + 157x - 360$. Use the graph to factor V_A.

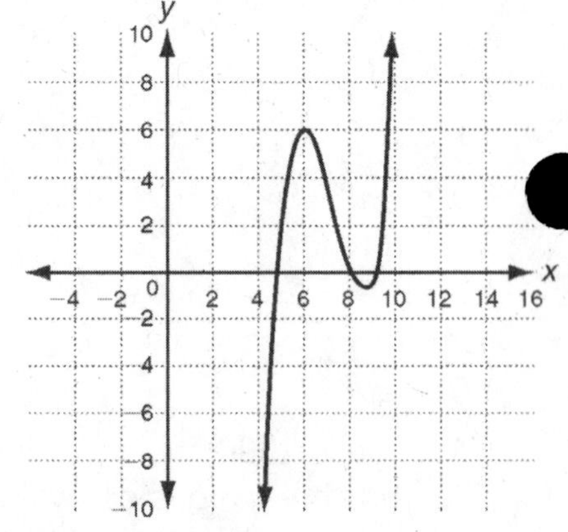

   a. What are the values of x where $V_A = 0$?

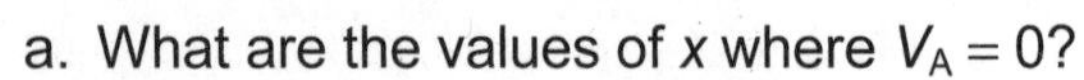

   ____

   b. Use these zeros to write the factors.

   ____

4. Complete the table. Use $x = 12$ units to find the actual dimensions and volume.

Basket	Dimensions (in terms of x)	Actual Dimensions	Volume
A			
B			
C			

5. Are the actual dimensions of the three baskets proportional? Explain.

____

6. Are the volumes of the three baskets proportional? Explain.

____

Name__________ Class__________ Date__________

11-1

Finding Real Roots of Polynomial Equations

Extension: Graphing Factorable Polynomial Functions

Essential question: *How do you use zeros to graph polynomial functions?*

Video Tutor

PREP FOR MCC9-12.F.IF.7c

1 ENGAGE Understanding Polynomial Functions

A **polynomial function** can be written as $f(x) = a_nx^n + a_{n-1}x^{n-1} + \cdots + a_1x + a_0$ where the coefficients $a_n, \ldots, a_1, a_0$ are real numbers. This is known as *standard form*. Note that linear functions are polynomial functions of degree 1 and quadratic functions are polynomial functions of degree 2. The functions you have graphed in the form $f(x) = a(x - h)^n + k$ are also polynomial functions, as you will see in later lessons.

The end behavior of a polynomial function $f(x) = a_nx^n + a_{n-1}x^{n-1} + \cdots + a_1x + a_0$ is determined by the term with the greatest degree, a_nx^n.

Polynomial End Behavior

n	a_n	As $x \to +\infty$	As $x \to -\infty$	Graph
Even	Positive	$f(x) \to +\infty$	$f(x) \to +\infty$	↖ ↗
Even	Negative	$f(x) \to -\infty$	$f(x) \to -\infty$	↙ ↘
Odd	Positive	$f(x) \to +\infty$	$f(x) \to -\infty$	↙ ↗
Odd	Negative	$f(x) \to -\infty$	$f(x) \to +\infty$	↖ ↘

You know how to use transformations to help you graph functions of the form $f(x) = a(x - h)^n + k$. If a polynomial function is not written in this form, then other graphing methods must be used. You will learn several methods throughout this unit, but the most basic is to plot points and connect them with a smooth curve, taking into account the end behavior of the function.

In general, the higher the degree of a polynomial, the more complex the graph. Here are some typical graphs for polynomials of degree n.

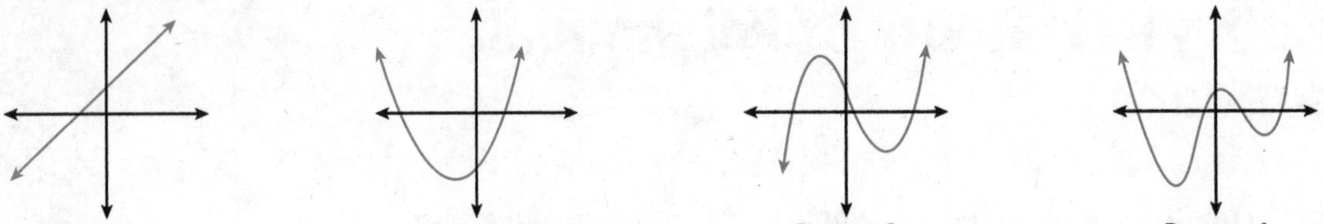

Degree 1
Linear

Degree 2
Quadratic

Degree 3
Cubic

Degree 4
Quartic

REFLECT

1a. Evaluate each term of the polynomial $f(x) = x^4 + 2x^3 - 5x^2 + 2x - 3$ for $x = 10$ and $x = -10$. Explain why the end behavior is determined by the term with the greatest degree.

____

____

____

____

1b. Describe the end behavior of $f(x) = -2x^3 + 3x^2 - x - 3$. Explain your reasoning.

____

____

____

The *nested form* of a polynomial has the form $f(x) = (((ax + b)x + c)x + d)x \dots)$. It is often simpler to evaluate polynomials in nested form.

MCC9–12.F.IF.2

2 EXAMPLE Writing Polynomials in Nested Form

Write $f(x) = x^3 + 2x^2 - 5x - 6$ in nested form.

$f(x) = x^3 + 2x^2 - 5x - 6$	Write the function.
$f(x) = (\_\_\_\_\_\_\_\_\_\_)x - 6$	Factor an x out of the first three terms.
$f(x) = ((\_\_\_\_\_\_\_\_)x - 5)x - 6$	Factor an x out of the first two terms in parentheses.

REFLECT

2a. Use the standard form and the nested form to evaluate the polynomial for $x = 3$. Then compare both methods. Which is easier? Why?

____

____

____

MCC9–12.F.IF.7c

3 EXAMPLE Graphing Polynomials

Graph $f(x) = x^3 + 2x^2 - 5x - 6$.

A Determine the end behavior of the graph. The end behavior is determined by the leading term, x^3.

So, as $x \to +\infty$, $f(x) \to$ ________, and as $x \to -\infty$, $f(x) \to$ ________.

B Complete the table of values. Use the nested form from the previous example to evaluate the polynomial.

x	−3	−2	−1	0	1	2	3
f(x)							

C Plot the points from the table on the graph, omitting any points whose y-values are much greater than or much less than the other y-values on the graph.

D Draw a smooth curve through the plotted points, keeping in mind the end behavior of the graph.

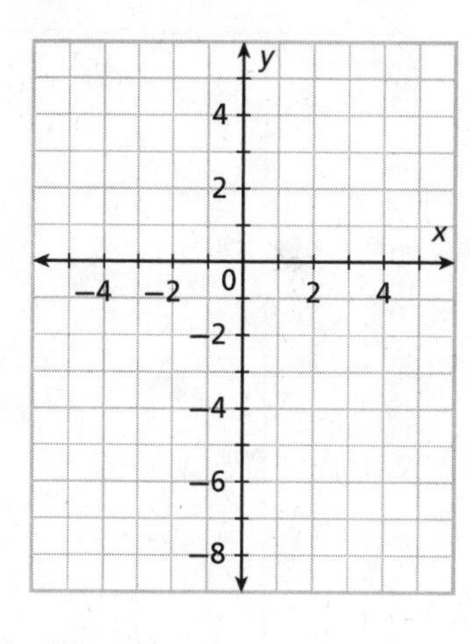

REFLECT

3a. What are the zeros of the function? How can you identify them from the graph?

____

3b. What are the approximate values of x for which the function is increasing? decreasing?

____

____

3c. A student wrote that $f(x)$ has a minimum value of approximately −8. Do you agree or disagree? Why?

____

____

3d. Without graphing, what do you think the graph of $g(x) = -x^3 - 2x^2 + 5x + 6$ looks like? Why?

____

____

Now you will sketch a variety of polynomial functions. You do not need to put values on the y-axis. The emphasis is on showing the overall shape of the graph and its x-intercepts.

MCC9–12.F.IF.7c

4 EXPLORE Investigating the Behavior of Graphs Near Zeros

Use a graphing calculator to graph each function. Sketch the graphs on the axes provided below. Then complete the table.

A $f(x) = (x - 1)(x - 2)(x - 3)(x - 4)$

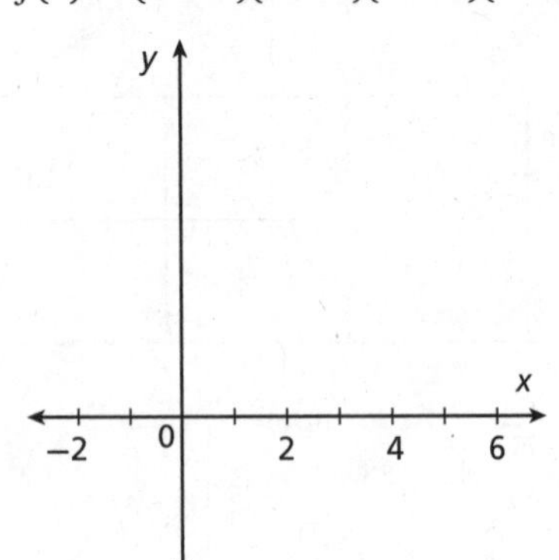

B $g(x) = (x - 1)^2(x - 2)(x - 3)$

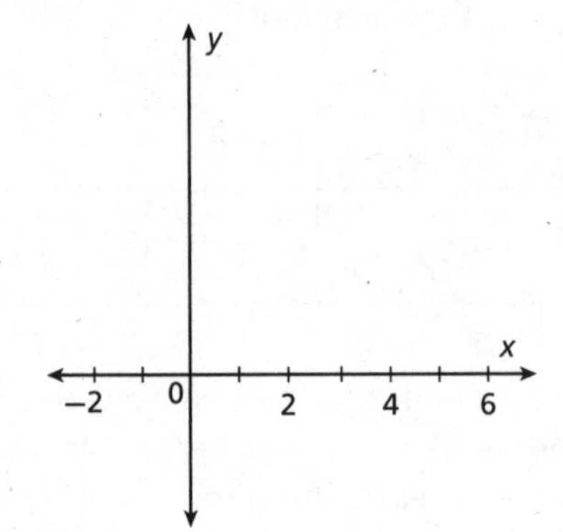

C $h(x) = (x - 1)^3(x - 2)$

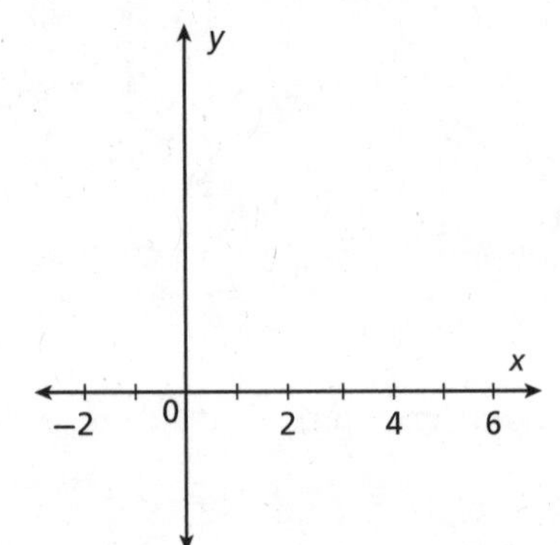

D $j(x) = (x - 1)^4$

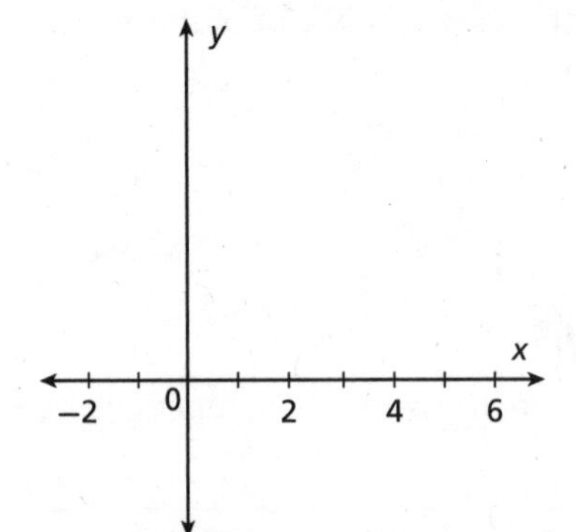

E

Examining Zeros	$f(x)$	$g(x)$	$h(x)$	$j(x)$
What are the zeros of the function?	1, 2, 3, 4			
How many times does each zero occur in the factorization?		1: 2 times 2, 3: 1 time		
At which zero(s) does the graph cross the x-axis?			1, 2	
At which zero(s) is the graph tangent to the x-axis?				1

REFLECT

4a. Based on your results, make a generalization about the number of times a zero occurs in the factorization of a function and whether the graph of the function crosses or is tangent to the x-axis at that zero.

The factored form of a polynomial is useful for graphing because the zeros can easily be determined. The degree of a polynomial in factored form is the sum of the degrees of the factors.

MCC9–12.F.IF.7c

5 EXAMPLE Sketching the Graph of a Factored Polynomial Function

Sketch the graph of $f(x) = (x + 2)^2(x + 1)(x - 2)(x - 3)$.

A Determine the end behavior.

The degree of the polynomial is the sum of the degrees of the factors.

So, the degree of $f(x)$ is ________.

If you multiply the factors to write $f(x)$ standard form, $a_nx^n + a_{n-1}x^{n-1} + \cdots + a_1x + a_0$, the leading coefficient a_n is ________.

Because the degree is odd and the leading coefficient is positive,

$f(x) \to$ ________ as $x \to +\infty$ and $f(x) \to$ ________ as $x \to -\infty$.

B Describe the behavior at the zeros.

The zeros of the function are ________________.

Identify how many times each zero occurs in the factorization.

____

Determine the zero(s) at which the graph crosses the x-axis.

____

Determine the zero(s) at which the graph is tangent to the x-axis.

____

C Sketch the graph at right. Use the end behavior to determine where to start and end. You may find it helpful to plot a few points between the zeros to help get the general shape of the graph.

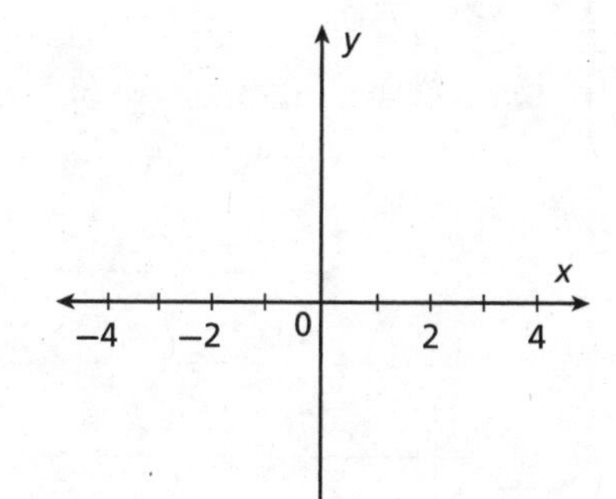

REFLECT

5a. Can you determine how many times a zero occurs in the factorization of a polynomial function just by looking at the graph of the function? Explain.

____

____

____

6 ENGAGE The Rational Zero Theorem

If you multiply the factors of the function $f(x) = (x - 1)(x - 2)(x - 3)(x - 4)$, you can write $f(x)$ in standard form as follows.

$$f(x) = x^4 - 10x^3 + 35x^2 - 50x + 24$$

So, $f(x)$ is a polynomial with integer coefficients that begins with the term x^4 and ends with the term 24. The zeros of $f(x)$ are 1, 2, 3, and 4. Notice that each zero is a factor of the constant term, 24.

Now consider the function $g(x) = (2x - 1)(3x - 2)(4x - 3)(5x - 4)$. If you multiply the factors, you can write $g(x)$ in standard form as follows.

$$g(x) = 120x^4 - 326x^3 + 329x^2 - 146x + 24$$

So, $g(x)$ is a polynomial with integer coefficients that begins with the term $120x^4$ and ends with the term 24. The zeros of $g(x)$ are $\frac{1}{2}, \frac{2}{3}, \frac{3}{4}$, and $\frac{4}{5}$. In this case, the numerator of each zero is a factor of the constant term, 24, and the denominator of each zero is a factor of the leading coefficient, 120.

These examples illustrate the Rational Zero Theorem.

Rational Zero Theorem

If $p(x) = a_nx^n + a_{n-1}x^{n-1} + \cdots + a_2x^2 + a_1x + a_0$ has integer coefficients, then every rational zero of $p(x)$ is a number of the following form:

$$\frac{c}{b} = \frac{\text{factor of constant term } a_0}{\text{factor of leading coefficient } a_n}$$

REFLECT

6a. If $\frac{c}{b}$ is a rational zero of a polynomial function $p(x)$, explain why $bx - c$ must be a factor of the polynomial.

____

____

____

MCC9-12.A.APR.3

7 EXAMPLE Using the Rational Zero Theorem

Sketch the graph of $f(x) = x^3 - x^2 - 8x + 12$.

A Use the Rational Zero Theorem to identify the possible rational zeros of $f(x)$.

The constant term is 12.

Integer factors of the constant term are $\pm1, \pm2, \pm3, \pm4, \pm6$, and ±12.

The leading coefficient is ________.

Integer factors of the leading coefficient are ______________.

By the Rational Zero Theorem, the possible rational zeros of $f(x)$ are all rational numbers of the form $\frac{c}{b}$ where c is a factor of the constant term and b is a factor of the leading coefficient.

List all the possible rational zeros.

Possible rational zeros: ______________________________

B Test the possible rational zeros until you find one that is an actual zero.

Use synthetic substitution to test 1 and 2.

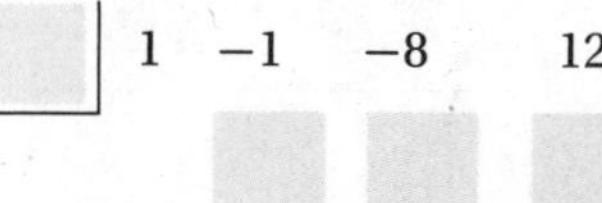

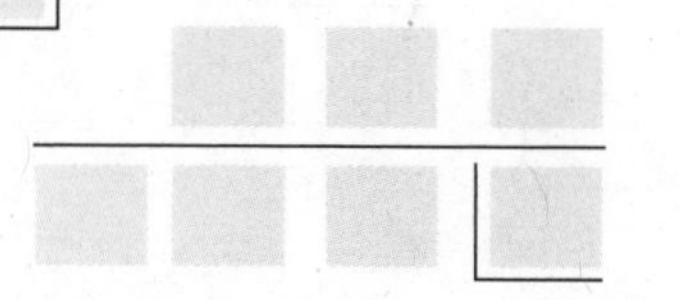

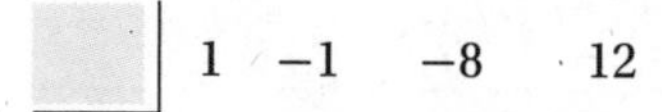

So, __________ is a zero, and therefore __________ is a factor of $f(x)$.

C Factor $f(x) = x^3 - x^2 - 8x + 12$ completely.

Use the results of the synthetic substitution to write $f(x)$ as the product of a linear factor and a quadratic factor.

$f(x) =$ (__________)(____________________)

Factor the quadratic factor to write $f(x)$ as a product of linear factors.

$f(x) =$ (__________)(__________)(__________)

Use the factorization to identify the other zeros of $f(x)$.

____

How many times does each zero occur in the factorization?

____

D Determine the end behavior.

$f(x) \rightarrow$ __________ as $x \rightarrow +\infty$ and $f(x) \rightarrow$ __________ as $x \rightarrow -\infty$.

E Sketch the graph of the function on the coordinate plane at right.

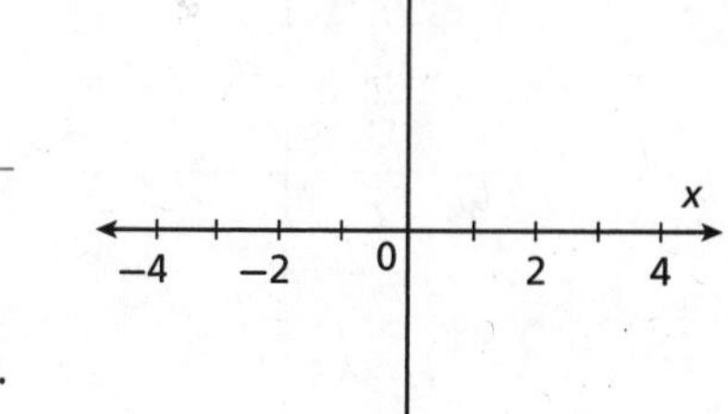

REFLECT

7a. How did you determine where the graph crosses the x-axis and where it is tangent to the x-axis?

____

____

____

____

7b. How did factoring the polynomial help you graph the function?

7c. How did using the Rational Zero Theorem to find one zero help you find the other zeros?

PRACTICE

Write each polynomial function in nested form. Then sketch the graph by plotting points and using end behavior.

1. $f(x) = x^4 - 4x^2$

$f(x) =$ ______

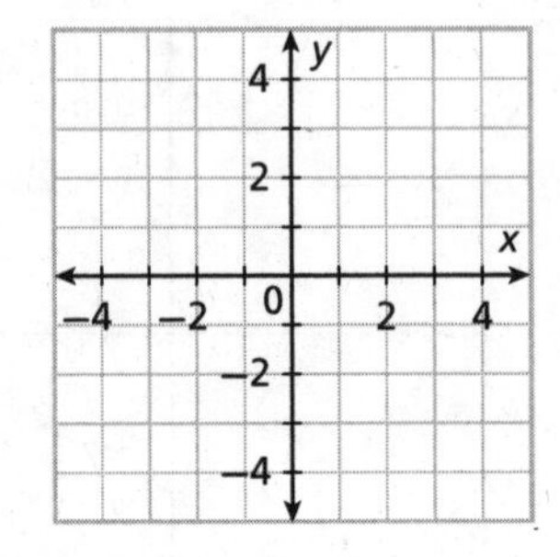

2. $f(x) = -x^3 + 4x^2 - x - 6$

$f(x) =$ ______

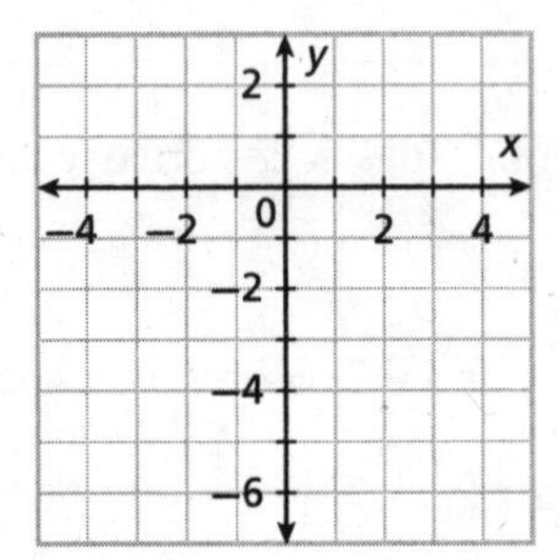

3. $f(x) = x^3 - x^2 - 4x + 4$

$f(x) =$ ______

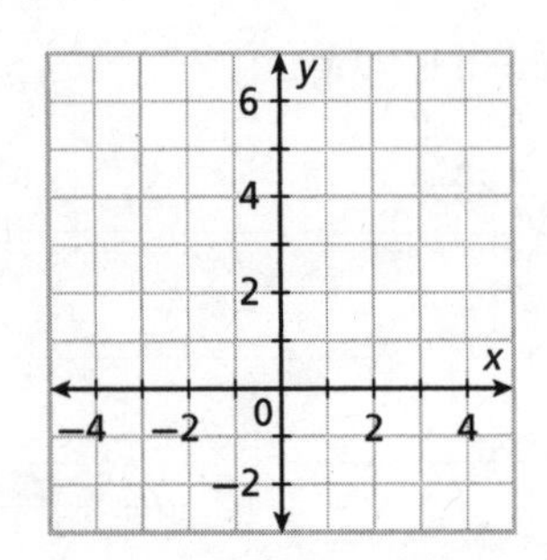

4. $f(x) = -x^4 + 4x^3 - 2x^2 - 4x + 3$

$f(x) =$ ______

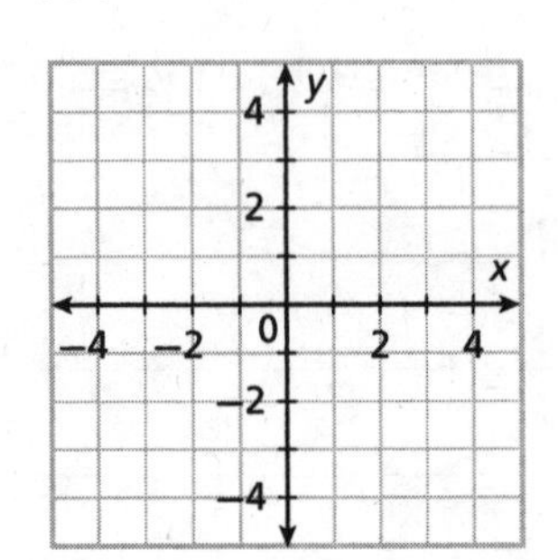

5. Given the graph of a polynomial function, how can you tell if a given zero occurs an even or an odd number of times?

Sketch the graph of each factored polynomial function.

6. $f(x) = (x - 3)(x + 2)^2$

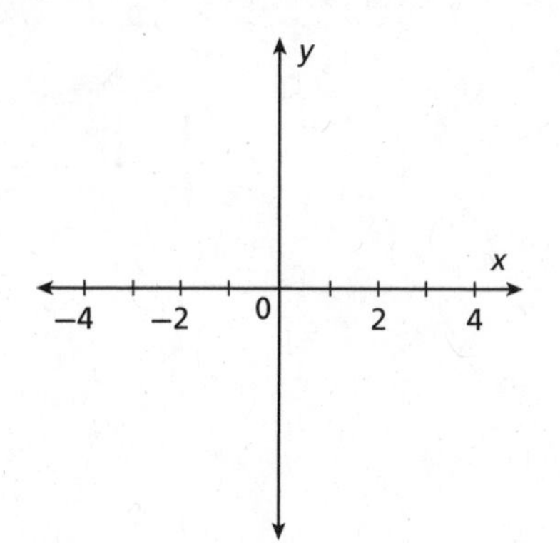

7. $g(x) = (x + 1)^6$

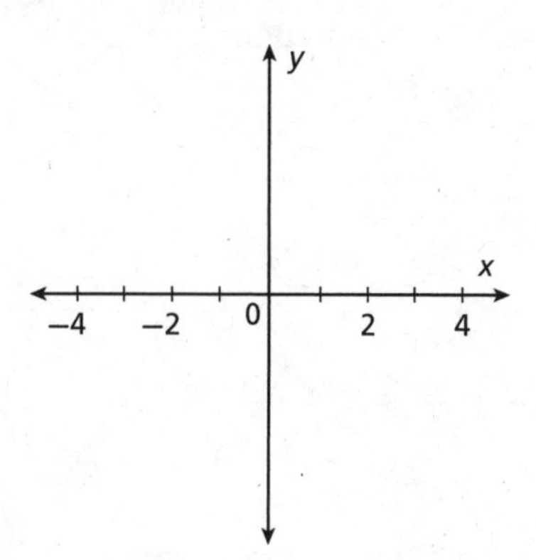

8. $h(x) = (x + 3)(x + 1)^2(x - 1)$

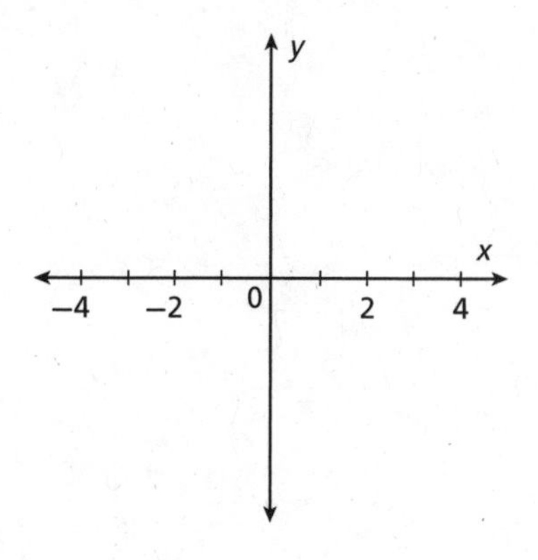

9. $j(x) = (x + 2)^3(x - 3)^2$

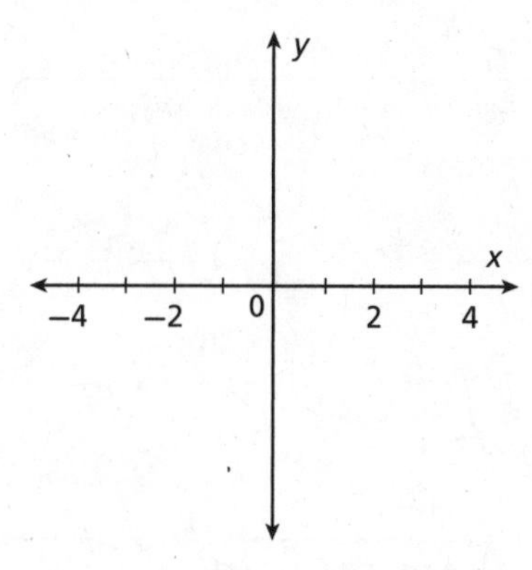

10. From 2000 to 2010, the profit (in thousands of dollars) for a small business is modeled by $P(x) = -x^3 + 9x^2 - 6x - 16$, where x is the number of years since 2000.

a. Sketch a graph of the function at right.

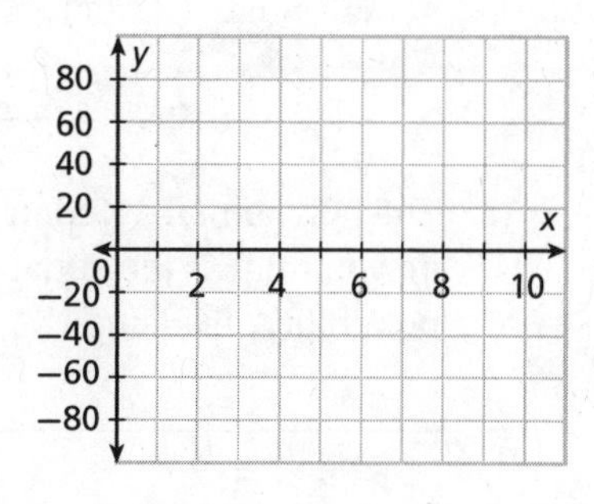

b. What are the zeros of the function in the domain $0 \leq x \leq 10$?

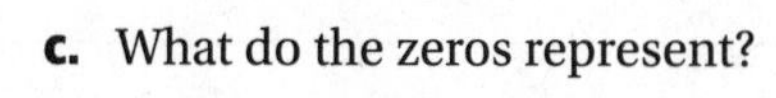

c. What do the zeros represent?

Use the Rational Zero Theorem to identify the possible zeros of each function. Then factor the polynomial completely. Finally, identify the actual zeros and sketch the graph of the function.

10. 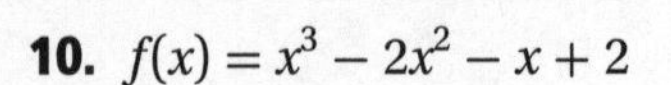
$f(x) = x^3 - 2x^2 - x + 2$

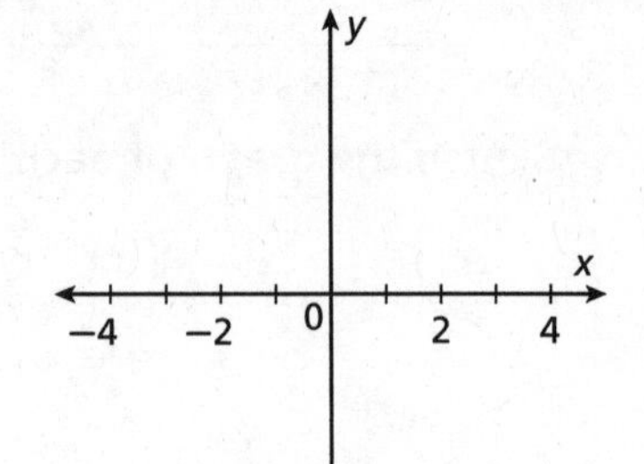

Possible zeros:

____

Factored form of function:

____

Actual zeros:

____

11. $g(x) = x^3 - 2x^2 - 11x + 12$

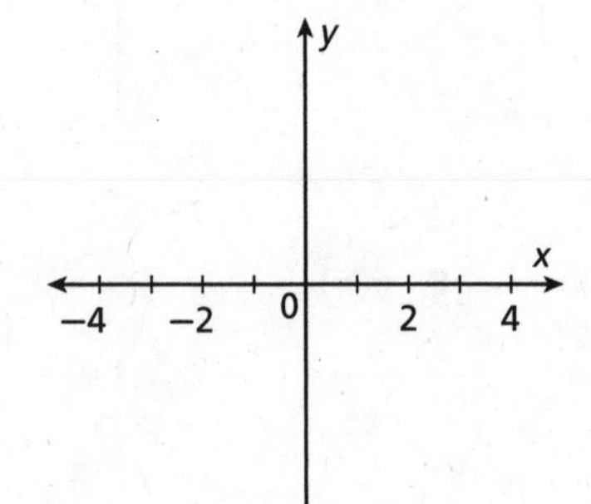

Possible zeros:

____

Factored form of function:

____

Actual zeros:

____

12. $h(x) = 2x^4 - 5x^3 - 11x^2 + 20x + 12$

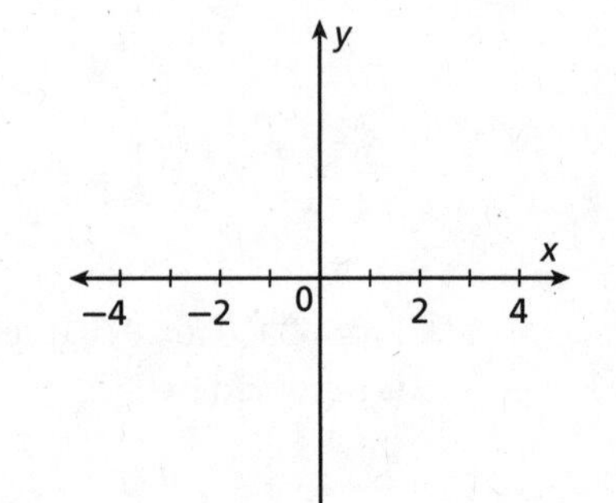

Possible zeros:

____

Factored form of function:

____

Actual zeros:

____

13. The polynomial function $p(x)$ has degree 3, and its zeros are −3, 4, and 6. What do you think is the equation of $p(x)$? Do you think there could be more than one possibility? Explain.

____

____

____

____

Additional Practice

Solve each polynomial equation by factoring.

1. $9x^3 - 3x^2 - 3x + 1 = 0$

____

2. $x^5 - 2x^4 - 24x^3 = 0$

____

3. $3x^5 + 18x^4 - 21x^3 = 0$

____

4. $-x^4 + 2x^3 + 8x^2 = 0$

____

Identify the roots of each equation. State the multiplicity of each root.

5. $x^3 + 3x^2 + 3x + 1 = 0$

____

6. $x^3 + 5x^2 - 8x - 48 = 0$

____

Identify all the real roots of each equation.

7. $x^3 + 10x^2 + 17x = 28$

____

8. $3x^3 + 10x^2 - 27x = 10$

____

Solve.

9. An engineer is designing a storage compartment in a spacecraft. The compartment must be 2 meters longer than it is wide and its depth must be 1 meter less than its width. The volume of the compartment must be 8 cubic meters.

   a. Write an equation to model the volume of the compartment.

   ____

   b. List all possible rational roots. _______________

   c. Use synthetic division to find the roots of the polynomial equation. Are the roots all rational numbers?

   ____

   d. What are the dimensions of the storage compartment? _______________

Problem Solving

Most airlines have rules concerning the size of checked baggage. The rules for Budget Airline are such that the dimensions of the largest bag cannot exceed 45 in. by 55 in. by 62 in. A designer is drawing plans for a piece of luggage that athletes can use to carry their equipment. It will have a volume of 76,725 cubic inches. The length is 10 in. greater than the width and the depth is 14 in. less than the width. What are the dimensions of this piece of luggage?

1. Write an equation in factored form to model the volume of the piece of luggage.

____

2. Multiply and set the equation equal to zero.

____

3. Think about possible roots of the equation. Could a root be a multiple of 4? ______________ a multiple of 5? ______________ a multiple of 10? ______________. How do you know?

____

4. Use synthetic substitution to test possible roots. Choose positive integers that are factors of the constant term and reasonable in the context of the problem.

Possible Root	**1 –4 –140 –76,725**

____

Choose the letter for the best answer.

5. Which equation represents the factored polynomial?
   A $(w + 55)(w^2 + 25w + 1550) = 0$
   B $(w - 35)(w^2 + 60w + 1405) = 0$
   C $(w - 45)(w^2 + 41w + 1705) = 0$
   D $(w - 4)(w^2 - 140w + 76{,}725) = 0$

6. Which could be the dimensions of this piece of luggage?
   A 31 in. by 45 in. by 55 in.
   B 45 in. by 55 in. by 55 in.
   C 45 in. by 45 in. by 55 in.
   D 45 in. by 55 in. by 62 in.

Name ____________ Class ____________ Date ____________

11-2

Fundamental Theorem of Algebra

Going Deeper

Video Tutor

Essential question: *How can you find zeros of polynomial functions?*

So far, you have found only rational zeros of polynomial functions. In this lesson you will review the various techniques for finding rational zeros and employ those techniques on polynomial functions whose zeros may not all be rational numbers.

MCC9–12.A.SSE.2

1 EXAMPLE Using the Binomial Theorem to Find Zeros

Find the zeros of $f(x) = x^3 + 3x^2 + 3x + 1$ and write the function in factored form.

A Write the coefficients of the terms of the polynomial.

____

How are these coefficients related to Pascal's Triangle?

____

Identify the corresponding binomial expansion.

$(a + b)^{\square} = a^3 + 3a^2b + 3ab^2 + b^3$

B Use the binomial expansion to rewrite the function in the form $(a + b)^n$.

$f(x) = (\square + \square)^{\square}$

C Identify the zero(s) of the function.

____

How many times does each zero occur? Explain.

____

So, the zero of $f(x)$ is ________.

The factored form of $f(x)$ is ______________________.

REFLECT

1a. Can you always use the Binomial Theorem in this way to find the zeros of a polynomial function? Explain.

____

____

1b. Without actually graphing, describe the graph of $f(x)$.

____

MCC9–12.A.APR.2

2 EXAMPLE Using the Rational Zero Theorem to Find Zeros

Find the zeros of $g(x) = x^3 - x^2 - 2x + 2$ and write the function in factored form.

A Use the Rational Zero Theorem to identify possible rational zeros.

Integer factors of the constant term are ________________.

Integer factors of the leading coefficient are ________________.

By the Rational Zero Theorem, the possible rational zeros of $g(x)$ are all rational numbers of the form $\frac{c}{b}$ where c is a factor of the constant term and b is a factor of the leading coefficient.

Possible rational zeros are ________________.

B Use synthetic substitution to test each possible rational zero to identify any actual rational zeros.

The function $g(x)$ has one rational zero, which is ________.

So, $x -$ ________ is a factor of $g(x)$.

C Use synthetic division to identify the other factors of the polynomial.

Divide $g(x)$ by $x -$ ________. Complete the synthetic division at right.

☐	1	−1	−2	2
		☐	☐	☐
	☐	☐	☐	☐

The quotient is ________ $x^2 +$ ________ $x -$ ________.

Write $g(x)$ as a product of two factors.

$g(x) = (x -$ ________ $)(x^2 -$ ________ $)$

The zeros of the quadratic factor are ________.

Write the quadratic factor as a product of two linear factors.

____

D Identify the zeros of the function.

The zeros of $g(x)$ are ________________.

E Write the function in factored form.

The factored form is $g(x) = (x -$ ________ $)(x -$ ________ $)(x +$ ________ $)$.

REFLECT

2a. When you used the Rational Zero Theorem, did your list of possible zeros include all of the actual zeros of $g(x)$? Why or why not?

____

____

2b. How can you check that you wrote the factored form of $g(x)$ correctly?

____

MCC9–12.A.SSE.2

3 EXAMPLE Using Special Products to Find Zeros

Find the zeros of $h(x) = x^4 - 16$ and write the function in factored form.

A Rewrite the function as a special product.

What type of special polynomial is $x^4 - 16$?

____

Factor the polynomial.

$f(x) = (x^2 + 4)(\_\_\_\_\_ - \_\_\_\_\_)$

B Find the zeros for each factor of the special product.

$x^2 + 4 = 0$ $\qquad$ $x^2 - \_\_\_\_\_ = 0$

$x^2 = -4$ $\qquad$ $x^2 = \_\_\_\_\_$

$x = \pm\sqrt{-4}$ $\qquad$ $x = \pm\sqrt{\quad}$

$x = \pm 2i$ $\qquad$ $x = \pm \_\_\_\_\_$

C Identify the zeros of the function.

The zeros of $h(x)$ are ______________.

D Write the function in factored form.

The factored form is $h(x) = (x + \_\_\_\_)(x - \_\_\_\_)(x + \_\_\_\_)(x - \_\_\_\_)$.

REFLECT

3a. How many x-intercepts does the graph of $h(x)$ have? What are they? Explain how you know.

____

____

3b. Show how you can check the imaginary zeros of $h(x)$.

____

____

3c. In general, how many zeros does the function $j(x) = x^4 - a$ have when a is a positive integer? What are the zeros?

____

3d. Could you use the method of the example to find the zeros of $k(x) = x^4 + 16$? Explain.

____

Understanding the Fundamental Theorem of Algebra

The table summarizes the functions from the three examples. Notice that the number of zeros equals the degree of the polynomial as long as repeated zeros are counted multiple times. Irrational and imaginary zeros must also be taken into account.

Function	Degree	Zeros	Number of Zeros
$f(x) = x^3 + 3x^2 + 3x + 1$	3	-1 (occurs 3 times)	3
$g(x) = x^3 - x^2 - 2x + 2$	3	$1, \sqrt{2}, -\sqrt{2}$	3
$h(x) = x^4 - 16$	4	$-2i, 2i, -2, 2$	4

The table can help you understand the Fundamental Theorem of Algebra.

Fundamental Theorem of Algebra

If $f(x)$ is a polynomial of degree n, then $f(x)$ has at least one zero in the set of complex numbers.

Corollary: If $f(x)$ is a polynomial of degree n, then $f(x)$ has exactly n zeros, provided that repeated zeros are counted multiple times.

REFLECT

4a. How does the quadratic formula prove the Fundamental Theorem of Algebra for the case $n = 2$?

4b. If you apply the Fundamental Theorem of Algebra to any polynomial function $f(x)$, you can conclude that $f(x)$ has one complex zero z_1. So, by the Factor Theorem, $x - z_1$ is a factor of $f(x)$. This means $f(x) = (x - z_1)q_1(x)$ where $q_1(x)$ is a polynomial whose degree is one less than the degree of $f(x)$. Explain how you can use this idea and repeatedly apply the Fundamental Theorem of Algebra to prove the corollary of the theorem.

4c. Can you conclude that $f(x) = x^5 - 4x^2 + \frac{1}{x}$ has 5 zeros? Why or why not?

PRACTICE

Find the zeros of the function and write the function in factored form.

1. $f(x) = x^4 + 4x^3 + 6x^2 + 4x + 1$

The zeros of $f(x)$ are

______________________.

The factored form is

$f(x) =$ ______________________.

2. $g(x) = x^3 - 3x^2 + 3x - 1$

The zeros of $g(x)$ are

______________________.

The factored form is

$g(x) =$ ______________________.

3. $f(x) = x^5 + 5x^4 + 10x^3 + 10x^2 + 5x + 1$

The zeros of $f(x)$ are

______________________.

The factored form is

$f(x) =$ ______________________.

4. $g(x) = x^3 - x^2 - 3x + 3$

The zeros of $g(x)$ are

______________________.

The factored form is

$g(x) =$ ______________________.

5. $f(x) = x^3 + 2x^2 - 5x - 10$

The zeros of $f(x)$ are

______________________.

The factored form is

$f(x) =$ ______________________.

6. $g(x) = x^4 - 81$

The zeros of $g(x)$ are

______________________.

The factored form is

$g(x) =$ ______________________.

7. $f(x) = x^4 - 8x^2 + 16$

The zeros of $f(x)$ are

______________________.

The factored form is

$f(x) =$ ______________________.

8. $g(x) = 16x^4 - 1$

The zeros of $g(x)$ are

______________________.

The factored form is

$g(x) =$ ______________________.

9. $f(x) = x^4 - 4x^3 - 6x^2 + 40x - 40$

The zeros of $f(x)$ are

______________________.

The factored form is

$f(x) =$ ______________________.

10. $g(x) = x^5 + 2x^3 + x$

The zeros of $g(x)$ are

______________________.

The factored form is

$g(x) =$ ______________________.

11. A polynomial function has exactly four zeros: 2, $-2, \sqrt{3}$, and $-\sqrt{3}$. Use standard form to write the simplest function with these zeros. Describe your method.

12. Suppose $p(x)$ is the product of a polynomial of degree 5 and a cubic polynomial. How many zeros does $p(x)$ have? Explain.

Suppose $q(x)$ is a polynomial function of degree 5 and you know that two of the zeros are $2i$ and $\sqrt{6}$.

13. How many other zeros does the function $q(x)$ have? Justify your answer.

14. Can you identify any of the other zeros of the function? If so, give them and explain how you know they are zeros.

Name________________________ Class:______________ Date____________ 11-2

Additional Practice

Write the simplest polynomial function with the given roots.

1. 1, 4, and –3

2. $\frac{1}{2}$, 5, and –2

3. $2i$, $\sqrt{3}$, and 4

4. $\sqrt{2}$, –5, and $-3i$

Solve each equation by finding all roots.

5. $x^4 - 2x^3 - 14x^2 - 2x - 15 = 0$

6. $x^4 - 16 = 0$

7. $x^4 + 4x^3 + 4x^2 + 64x - 192 = 0$

8. $x^3 + 3x^2 + 9x + 27 = 0$

Solve.

9. An electrical circuit is designed such that its output voltage, V, measured in volts, can be either positive or negative. The voltage of the circuit passes through zero at $t = 1$, 2, and 7 seconds. Write the simplest polynomial describing the voltage $V(t)$.

Problem Solving

A company that makes accessories for cars needs a container like that shown at the right to hold touch-up paint. The hemispherical top will be fitted with a brush applicator. The cylindrical part of the container should be 4 inches tall. The volume of the entire container is $\frac{13}{12}\pi$ cubic inches. Find the value of x, the radius of the hemisphere.

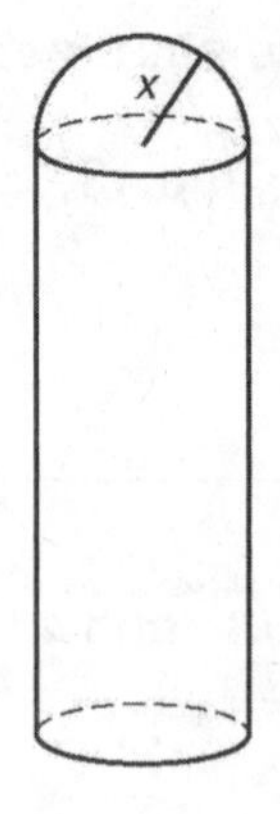

1. a. Write a formula for the volume of the cylindrical part of the container.

   ____

   b. Write a formula for the volume of the hemispherical part of the container.

   ____

2. Write an equation to represent the total volume of the container.

   ____

3. Write the equation in standard form.

   ____

4. Graph the equation with a graphing calculator. Hint: Use a window with x-values from –8 to 5 with a scale of 1, and y-values from –20 to 250 with a scale of 30 to see the general shape of the graph. Sketch the graph. Then focus on the area of the positive root by using a window of –8 to 3 on the x-axis and –20 to 20 on the y-axis. Use Trace to help you find a possible positive root.

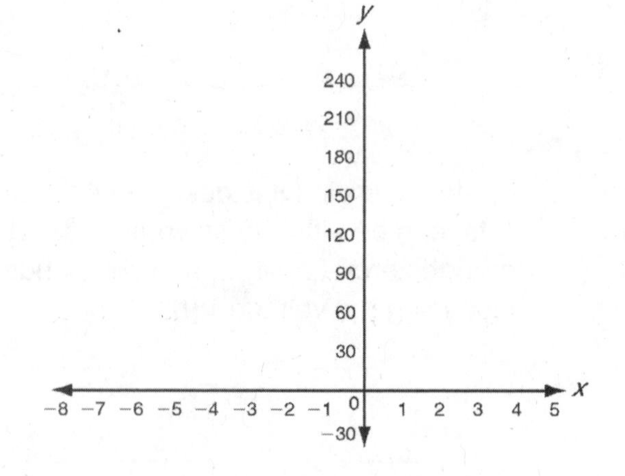

5. Verify the root using synthetic substitution. What is the positive root?

   ____

6. Use the Quadratic Formula to find approximate values for the other two roots. Explain why these two roots cannot also be solutions to the problem.

   ____

7. What is the value of x, the radius of the hemisphere, for this paint container?

   ____

Name________________________ Class________________ Date__________

11-3

Investigating Graphs of Polynomial Functions

Going Deeper

Video Tutor

Essential question: *How does the value of n affect the behavior of the function $f(x) = x^n$?*

MCC9–12.F.IF.7c

1 EXPLORE Graphing $f(x) = x^n$ When n is Even

Follow these steps to investigate the graphs of $f(x) = x^2$, $f(x) = x^4$, and $f(x) = x^6$.

A Set the viewing window of your graphing calculator as shown.

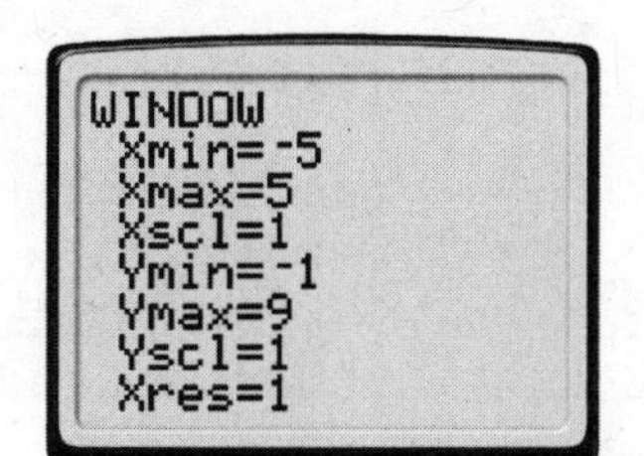

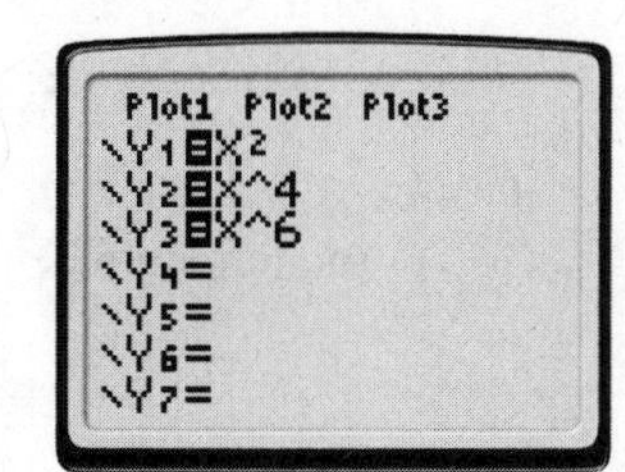

B Enter the functions $f(x) = x^2$, $f(x) = x^4$, and $f(x) = x^6$ in the equation editor as shown.

C Graph the functions on the coordinate plane at right by sketching what you see on your calculator.

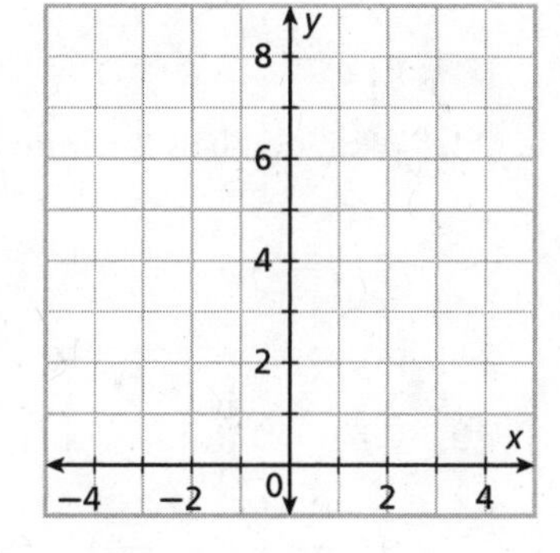

D Use your graphs to identify the zero(s) of the functions.

____

E Identify the minimum value of each function.

____

F Describe any symmetry of the graphs.

____

REFLECT

1a. What do all of the functions and their graphs have in common?

____

____

1b. For these functions, what happens to the values of $f(x)$ as x increases without bound? How is this displayed in the graph?

____

____

1c. For these functions, what happens to the values of $f(x)$ as x decreases without bound? How is this displayed in the graph?

____

____

MCC9–12.F.IF.7c

2 EXPLORE Graphing $f(x) = x^n$ When n is Odd

Follow these steps to investigate the graphs of $f(x) = x$, $f(x) = x^3$, and $f(x) = x^5$.

A Set the viewing window of your graphing calculator as shown.

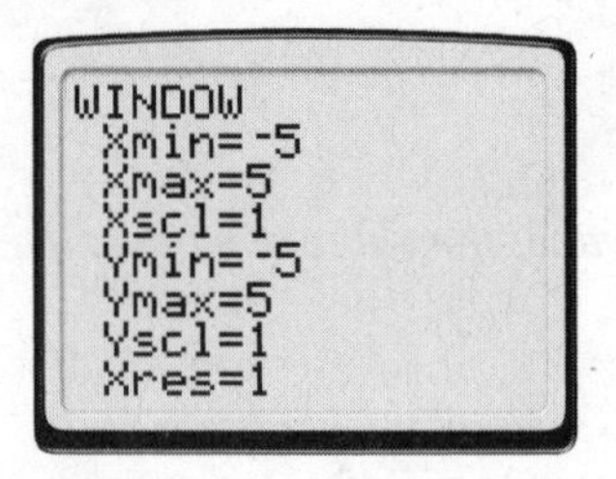

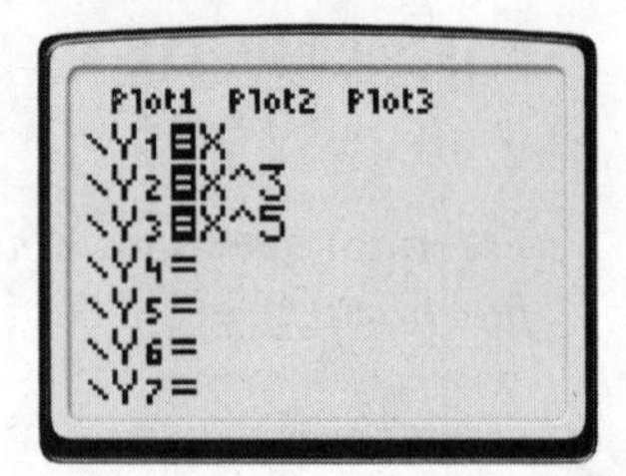

B Enter the functions $f(x) = x$, $f(x) = x^3$, and $f(x) = x^5$ in the equation editor as shown.

C Graph the functions on the coordinate plane at right by sketching what you see on your calculator.

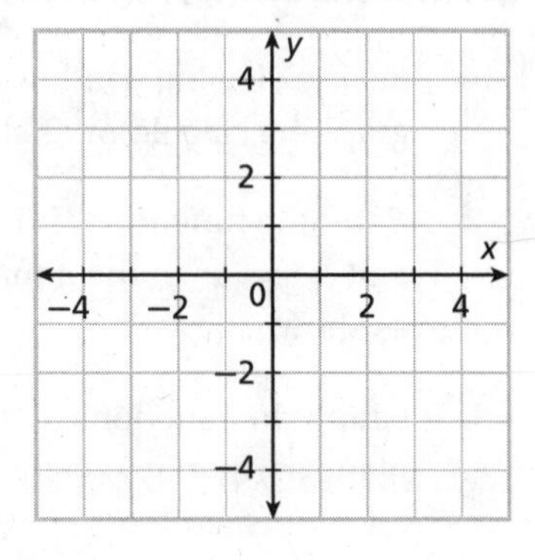

D Use your graphs to identify the zero(s) of the functions.

____

E Identify any maximum values or minimum values of each function.

____

F Describe any symmetry of the graphs.

____

REFLECT

2a. What do all of the functions and their graphs have in common?

____

____

2b. What points lie on all of the graphs?

____

2c. For these functions, what happens to the values of $f(x)$ as x increases without bound? How is this displayed in the graph?

____

____

2d. For these functions, what happens to the values of $f(x)$ as x decreases without bound? How is this displayed in the graph?

____

____

3 ENGAGE Describing Characteristics of Functions

The **end behavior** of a function is a description of the values of the function as x increases without bound or decreases without bound.

For example, for $f(x) = x^3$, the values of $f(x)$ increase without bound as x increases without bound. You can say that $f(x)$ approaches positive infinity as x approaches positive infinity. This may be abbreviated as "$f(x) \to +\infty$ as $x \to +\infty$."

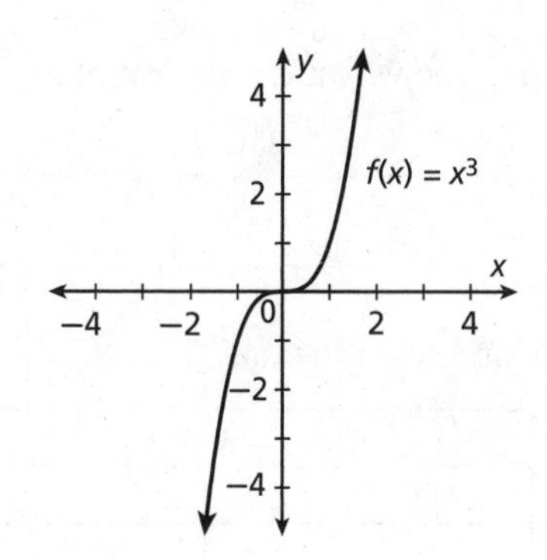

Also, the values of $f(x)$ decrease without bound as x decreases without bound. You can say that $f(x)$ approaches negative infinity as x approaches negative infinity. This may be abbreviated as "$f(x) \to -\infty$ as $x \to -\infty$."

A function is an **even function** if $f(-x) = f(x)$ for all values of x. This means that if the point (x, y) is on the graph, then the point $(-x, y)$ is also on the graph, so the graph is symmetric with respect to the y-axis.

A function is an **odd function** if $f(-x) = -f(x)$ for all values of x. This means that if the point (x, y) is on the graph, then the point $(-x, -y)$ is also on the graph, so the graph has 180° rotational symmetry about the origin.

The Graph of an Even Function	The Graph of an Odd Function
(−x, y) (x, y)	(x, y) (−x, −y)

REFLECT

3a. For the function $g(x)$, you are told that $g(1000) = 5{,}000{,}000$. Is it possible to make any conclusions about the end behavior of $g(x)$? Explain.

____

____

3b. What can you say about the end behavior of $f(x) = x^n$ when n is even?

____

3c. What can you say about the end behavior of $f(x) = x^n$ when n is odd?

____

3d. Explain why any function of the form $f(x) = x^n$ is an even function if n is even.

____

____

3e. Explain why any function of the form $f(x) = x^n$ is an odd function if n is odd.

____

____

3f. Complete the table.

Characteristics of $f(x) = x^n$		
	***n* is even**	***n* is odd**
Sketch of graph of $f(x) = x^n$	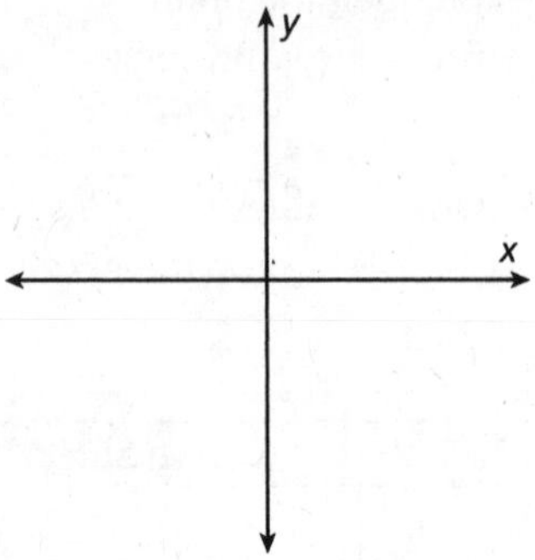	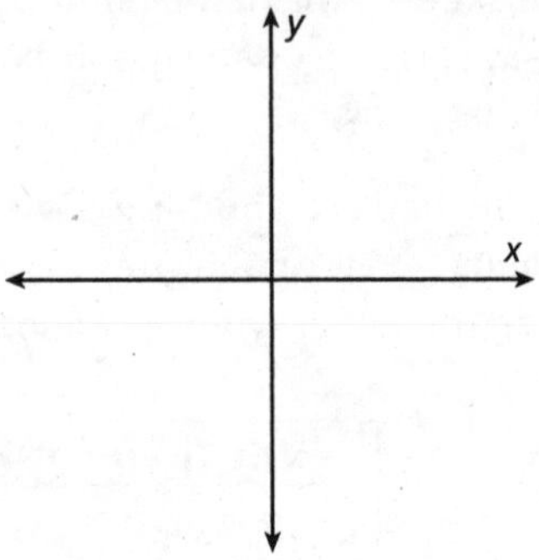
End behavior	As $x \to +\infty$, $f(x) \to$ ______. As $x \to -\infty$, $f(x) \to$ ______.	As $x \to +\infty$, $f(x) \to$ ______. As $x \to -\infty$, $f(x) \to$ ______.
Zeros	$x =$ ______	$x =$ ______
Maximum or minimum values	Maximum: ______ Minimum: ______	Maximum: ______ Minimum: ______
Symmetry		
Even or odd function		

Additional Practice

Identify the leading coefficient, degree, and end behavior.

1. $P(x) = 2x^5 - 6x^3 + x^2 - 2$

____

2. $Q(x) = -4x^2 + x - 1$

____

Identify whether the function graphed has an odd or even degree and a positive or negative leading coefficient.

3. 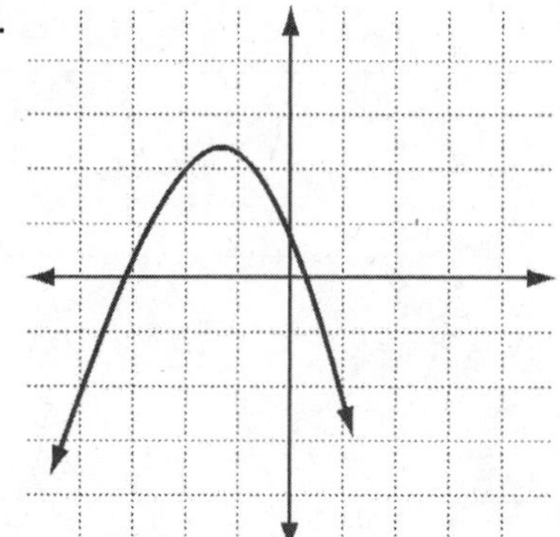

4. 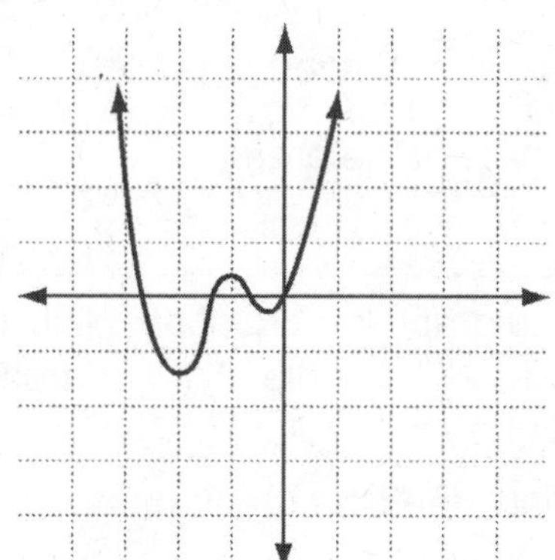

5. 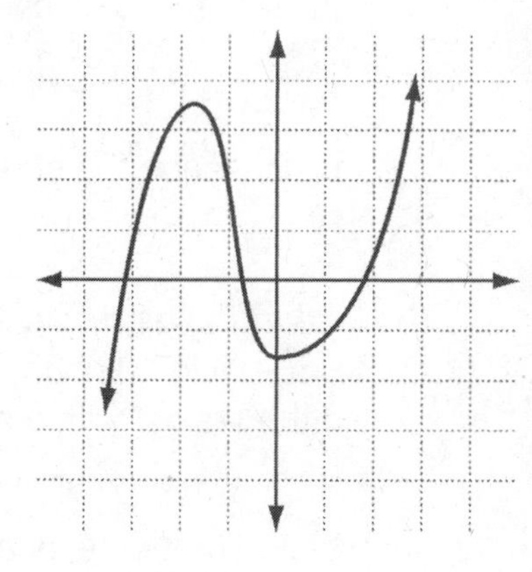

_______________ _______________ _______________

Graph the function $P(x) = x^3 + 6x^2 + 5x - 12$.

6. Identify the possible rational roots.

____

7. Identify the zeros.

____

8. Describe the end behavior of the function.

____

9. Sketch the graph of the function.

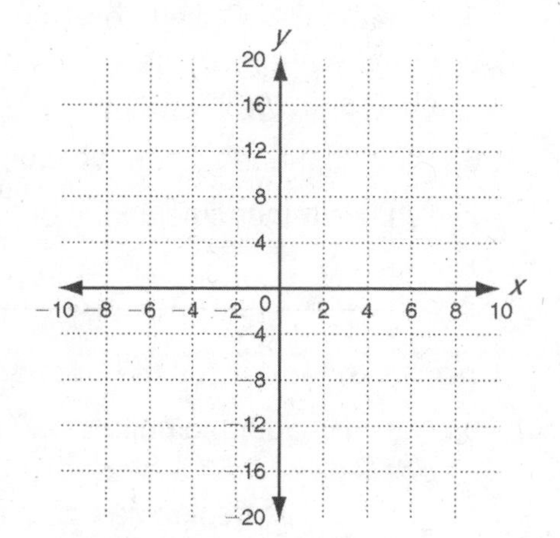

Solve.

10. The number, $N(y)$, of subscribers to a local magazine can be modeled by the function $N(y) = 0.1y^4 - 3y^3 + 10y^2 - 30y + 10{,}000$, where y is the number of years since the magazine was founded. Graph the polynomial on a graphing calculator and find the minimum number of subscribers and the year in which this occurs.

____

Problem Solving

The Spanish Club members are baking and selling fruit bars to raise money for a trip. They are going to make open boxes to display the bars from sheets of cardboard that are 11 inches by 17 inches. They will cut a square from each corner and fold up the sides and tape them. Find the maximum value for the volume of the box and find its dimensions.

1. Write a formula to represent the volume of the box. ________________

2. a. Write the equation in standard form. ________________

   b. Is the leading coefficient positive or negative? ________________

   c. Is the degree of the polynomial even or odd? ________________

   d. Describe the end behavior of the graph.

   ____

3. Use a graphing calculator to graph the equation. Hint: Try a window from –10 to 10 on the *x*-axis, with a scale of 1, and from –500 to 500 on the *y*-axis, with a scale of 100.

   a. How many turning points does the graph have? ________________

   b. Estimate the local maxima and minima from the graph. ________________

4. What values of *x* are excluded as solutions because they do not make sense for this problem? ________________

5. Use the CALC menu on your graphing calculator to find the approximate values of *x* and *y* at the local maximum for the graph. ________________

6. What is the maximum volume of the box? ________________

7. What are the dimensions of the box to the nearest tenth of an inch?

   ____

Choose the letter for the best answer.

8. Arturo is going to build a dog run using one side of his house and 100 feet of fencing. His design has an area that can be modeled by $A(x) = 100x - 7x^2$. What is the maximum area he can enclose?

   A 357 ft^2
   B 204 ft^2
   C 100 ft^2
   D 70 ft^2

9. In order to eliminate some choices on a standardized test, Ruth identifies which of these functions could NOT have a local maximum.

   A $F(x) = -7x^2 + 5x + 2$
   B $F(x) = -7x^3 + 5x - 11$
   C $F(x) = 7x^3 - 5x^2 - 2$
   D $F(x) = 7x^2 - 3x - 18$

Name________________________ Class______________ Date__________

12-1

Introduction to Sequences

Going Deeper

Essential question: *Why is a sequence a function?*

Video Tutor

MCC9–12.F.IF.3

1 ENGAGE Understanding Sequences

A **sequence** is an ordered list of numbers or other items. Each element in a sequence is called a **term**. For instance, in the sequence 1, 3, 5, 7, 9, …, the second term is 3.

Each term in a sequence can be paired with a position number, and these pairings establish a function whose domain is the set of position numbers and whose range is the set of terms, as illustrated below. The position numbers are consecutive integers that typically start at either 1 or 0.

Position number	n	1	2	3	4	5	Domain
Term of sequence	$f(n)$	1	3	5	7	9	Range

For the sequence shown in the table, you can write $f(4) = 7$, which can be interpreted as "the fourth term of the sequence is 7."

REFLECT

1a. The domain of the function f defining the sequence 2, 5, 8, 11, 14, … is the set of consecutive integers starting with 0. What is $f(4)$? Explain how you determined your answer.

1b. How does your answer to Question 1a change if the domain of the function is the set of consecutive integers starting with 1?

1c. Predict the next term in the sequence 48, 42, 36, 30, 24, …. Explain your reasoning.

1d. Why is the relationship between the position numbers and the terms of a sequence a function?

1e. Give an example of a sequence from your everyday life. Explain why your example represents a sequence.

Some numerical sequences can be described by using algebraic rules. An **explicit rule** for a sequence defines the nth term as a function of n.

MCC9–12.F.IF.2

2 EXAMPLE Using an Explicit Rule to Generate a Sequence

Write the first 4 terms of the sequence $f(n) = n^2 + 1$. Assume that the domain of the function is the set of consecutive integers starting with 1.

n	$n^2 + 1$	$f(n)$
1	$\square^2 + 1 = \square + 1$	$\square$
2	$\square^2 + 1 = \square + 1$	$\square$
3	$\square^2 + 1 = \square + 1$	$\square$
4	$\square^2 + 1 = \square + 1$	$\square$

The first 4 terms are ______________________.

REFLECT

2a. How could you use a graphing calculator to check your answer?

____

2b. Explain how to find the 20th term of the sequence.

____

A **recursive rule** for a sequence defines the nth term by relating it to one or more previous terms.

MCC9–12.F.IF.2

3 EXAMPLE Using a Recursive Rule to Generate a Sequence

Write the first 4 terms of the sequence with $f(1) = 3$ and $f(n) = f(n - 1) + 2$ for $n \geq 2$. Assume that the domain of the function is the set of consecutive integers starting with 1.

The first term is given: $f(1) = 3$. Use $f(1)$ to find $f(2)$, $f(2)$ to find $f(3)$, and so on. In general, $f(n - 1)$ refers to the term that precedes $f(n)$.

n	$f(n - 1) + 2$	$f(n)$
2	$f(2 - 1) + 2 = f(1) + 2 = 3 + 2$	$\square$
3	$f(\square - 1) + 2 = f(\square) + 2 = \square + 2$	$\square$
4	$f(\square - 1) + 2 = f(\square) + 2 = \square + 2$	$\square$

The first 4 terms are ______________________.

REFLECT

3a. Describe how to find the 12th term of the sequence.

____

3b. Suppose you want to find the 50th term of a sequence. Would you rather use a recursive rule or an explicit rule? Explain your reasoning.

____

____

____

____

MCC9–12.F.BF.1a

4 EXAMPLE Modeling a Sequence

A male honeybee has one female parent, and a female honeybee has one male and one female parent. In the diagram below, a male honeybee is represented by M in row 1. His parent is represented by F in row 2. Her parents are represented by M and F in row 3, and so on. Write a recursive rule for a sequence that describes the number of bees in each row.

A Extend the diagram to show rows 5, 6, and 7.

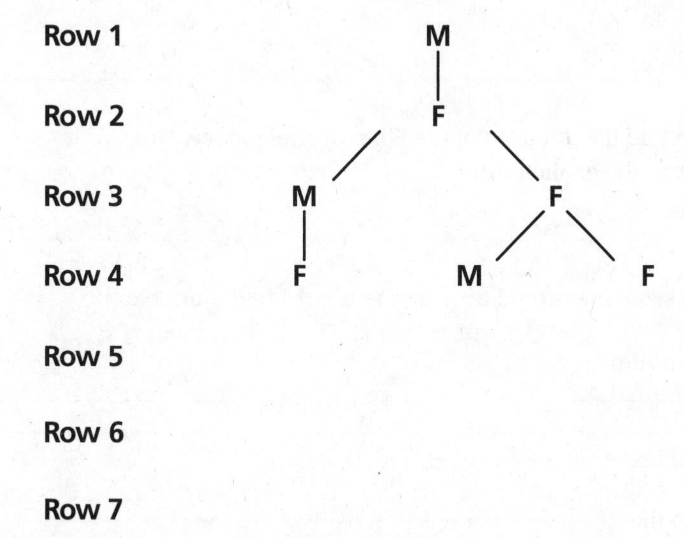

B Complete the table to show the number of bees in each row.

Row (position number)	1	2	3	4	5	6	7
Number of bees (term of sequence)	1	1	2				

C Write a recursive rule for the sequence in the table. Assume that the domain of the function is the set of consecutive integers starting with 1.

- First, write the rule in words.

  The first two terms are both ________. Every other term is the ________ of the previous two terms.

- Then, write the rule algebraically.

  $f(1) = f(2) =$ ☐ and — The first and second terms are both 1.

  $f(n) = f(n - \square) + f(n - 2)$ for $n \geq$ ☐ — Each successive term is the sum of the preceding two terms.

REFLECT

4a. If you continued the pattern in the diagram, how many bees would be in the 8th row? Explain how you determined your answer.

____

4b. The sequence given in the table, 1, 1, 2, 3, 5, 8, 13, . . ., is called the Fibonacci sequence. An explicit rule for the Fibonacci sequence is $f(n) = \frac{1}{\sqrt{5}}\left(\frac{1+\sqrt{5}}{2}\right)^n - \frac{1}{\sqrt{5}}\left(\frac{1-\sqrt{5}}{2}\right)^n$ where the values of n are consecutive integers starting with 1. Use the explicit rule to show that $f(1) = 1$. Then use a calculator and the explicit rule to find the 9th term of the Fibonacci sequence.

____

4c. Now use the recursive rule to find the 9th term of the Fibonacci sequence. Does your result agree with the result from the explicit rule?

____

4d. Which rule for the Fibonacci sequence would be easier to use if you did not have a calculator? Explain.

____

____

____

____

4e. The number of petals on many flowers is equal to a *Fibonacci number*, that is, one of the terms in the Fibonacci sequence. Based on this fact, is a flower more likely to have 20 petals or 21 petals? Explain.

____

PRACTICE

Write the first four terms of each sequence. Assume that the domain of the function is the set of consecutive integers starting with 1.

1. $f(n) = (n - 1)^2$

____

2. $f(n) = \frac{n + 1}{n + 3}$

____

3. $f(n) = 4(0.5)^n$

____

4. $f(n) = \sqrt{n - 1}$

____

5. $f(1) = 2$ and $f(n) = f(n - 1) + 10$ for $n \geq 2$ ________________

6. $f(1) = 16$ and $f(n) = \frac{1}{2} f(n - 1)$ for $n \geq 2$ ________________

7. $f(1) = 1$ and $f(n) = 2f(n - 1) + 1$ for $n \geq 2$ ________________

8. $f(1) = f(2) = 1$ and $f(n) = f(n - 2) - f(n - 1)$ for $n \geq 3$ ________________

9. Each year for the past 4 years, Donna has gotten a raise equal to 5% of the previous year's salary. Her starting salary was $40,000.

a. Complete the table to show Donna's salary over time.

b. Write a recursive rule for the sequence in the table. Assume that the domain of the function is the set of consecutive integers starting with 0, so the first term of the sequence is $f(0)$.

____

____

Year (position number)	Salary ($) (term of sequence)
0	40,000
1	
2	
3	
4	

c. What is $f(7)$, rounded to the nearest whole number? What does $f(7)$ represent in this situation?

____

____

Write the 12th term of each sequence. Assume that the domain of the function is the set of consecutive integers starting with 1.

10. $f(n) = 3n - 2$ ________________

11. $f(n) = 2n(n + 1)$ ________________

12. The diagram shows the first four figures in a pattern of dots.

a. Draw the next figure in the pattern.

b. Use the pattern to complete the table.

c. Write an explicit rule for the sequence in the table. Assume that the domain of the function is the set of consecutive integers starting with 1.

____

d. How many dots will be in the 10th figure of the pattern?

____

Figure (position number)	Number of dots (term of sequence)
1	1
2	
3	
4	
5	

Write an explicit rule for each sequence. Assume that the domain of the function is the set of consecutive integers starting with 1.

13.

n	$f(n)$
1	6
2	7
3	8
4	9
5	10

____

14.

n	$f(n)$
1	3
2	6
3	9
4	12
5	15

____

15.

n	$f(n)$
1	1
2	$\frac{1}{2}$
3	$\frac{1}{3}$
4	$\frac{1}{4}$
5	$\frac{1}{5}$

____

Write a recursive rule for each sequence. Assume that the domain of the function is the set of consecutive integers starting with 1.

16.

n	$f(n)$
1	8
2	9
3	10
4	11
5	12

____

____

17.

n	$f(n)$
1	2
2	4
3	8
4	16
5	32

____

____

18.

n	$f(n)$
1	27
2	24
3	21
4	18
5	15

____

____

Name______________ Class__________ Date__________

12-1

Additional Practice

Find the first 5 terms of each sequence.

1. $a_1 = 1$, $a_n = 3(a_{n-1})$
2. $a_1 = 2$, $a_n = 2(a_{n-1} + 1) - 5$
3. $a_1 = -2$, $a_n = (a_{n-1})^2 - 1$
4. $a_1 = 1$, $a_n = 6 - 2(a_{n-1})$
5. $a_1 = -1$, $a_n = (a_{n-1} - 1)^2 - 3$
6. $a_1 = -2$, $a_n = \dfrac{2 - a_{n-1}}{2}$
7. $a_n = (n - 2)(n + 1)$
8. $a_n = n(2n - 1)$
9. $a_n = n^3 - n^2$
10. $a_n = \left(\dfrac{1}{2}\right)^{n-3}$
11. $a_n = (-2)^{n-1}$
12. $a_n = n^2 - 2n$

Write a possible explicit rule for the *n*th term of each sequence.

13. 8, 16, 24, 32, 40, ...
14. 0.1, 0.4, 0.9, 1.6, 2.5, ...
15. 3, 6, 11, 18, 27, ...
16. $\dfrac{3}{2}, \dfrac{3}{4}, \dfrac{3}{8}, \dfrac{3}{16}, \dfrac{3}{32}, \ldots$
17. −2, 1, 4, 7, 10, ...
18. 5, 1, 0.2, 0.04, 0.008, ...

Solve.

19. Find the number of line segments in the next two iterations. ______________

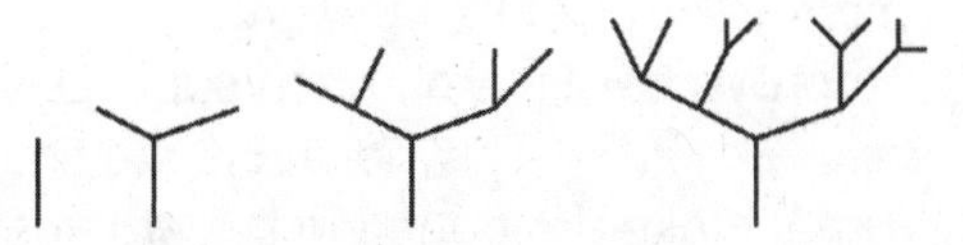

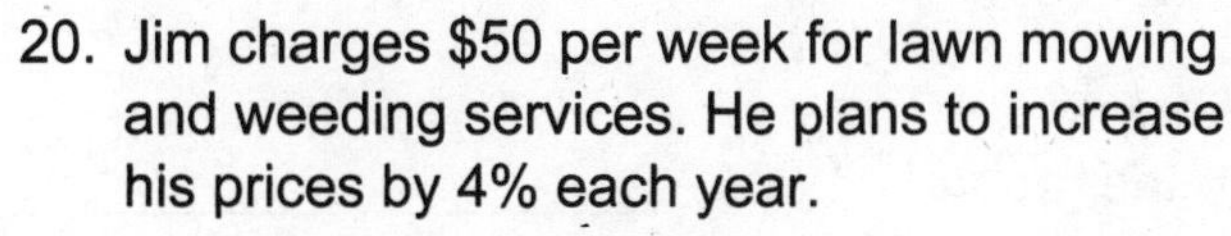

20. Jim charges $50 per week for lawn mowing and weeding services. He plans to increase his prices by 4% each year.

    a. Graph the sequence.

    b. Describe the pattern.

    ____

    c. To the nearest dollar, how much will he charge per week in 5 years?

    ____

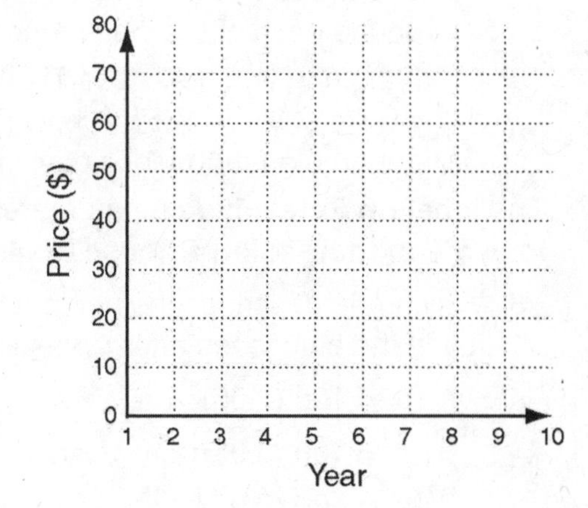

Problem Solving

Tina is working on some home improvement projects involving repeated tasks. She wants to analyze her work patterns.

1. Tina is hammering nails into wallboard. With the first hit, a nail goes in 13.5 millimeters; with the second, it goes in an additional 9 mm; with the third, it goes in an additional 6 mm; and with the fourth it goes in 4 mm further. Suppose this pattern continues. Predict how far the nail would go in with the seventh hit.

   a. Complete the table to find first differences, second differences, and ratios.

Distance	13.5mm	9mm	6mm	4mm
Ratios	$\frac{2}{3}$			
First Differences	–4.5			
Second Differences				

   b. How do you know whether the rule for the sequence of distances that the nail goes in is linear, quadratic, or exponential? ________________

   c. Write a possible rule for a_n , the nth term in the sequence. ________________

   d. If this pattern continues, how far would the nail go in with the seventh hit? ________________

2. Tina builds a fence for her neighbor. It takes her 10 minutes to pound the first fence post into the ground. The neighbor predicts that Tina should improve her time on each successive fence post according to the rule $a_n = F - 2(n - 1)$, where F is the time for the first fence post, and a_n is the time it takes to pound in the nth post.

   a. Use the rule to find the time it should take Tina to pound each of the first 4 fence posts into the ground. ________________

   b. If the rule that describes Tina's time on each successive post is $a_n = F - 1.\ 5^{n-1}$, how long will it take her to pound the fourth fence post into the ground? ________________

The label on Pete's blue jeans states that, when washed, the jeans will lose 5% of their color. Choose the letter for the best answer.

3. Which rule describes the percent of color left in the blue jeans after n washings?

   A $a_n = 100\ (0.05)^n$

   B $a_n = 100\ (0.95)^n$

   C $a_n = 100\ (0.95)^n$

   D $a_n = 100\ (0.05)^n$

4. How much of the original color will be left after 8 washings?

   F 66%

   G 60%

   H 40%

   J 34%

Name ________________ Class ________ Date ________

12-2

Series and Summation Notation

Extension: Summation of Linear and Quadratic Series

Essential question: *How can you derive and apply formulas for the sum of a linear or quadratic series?*

Video Tutor

MCC9–12.F.BF.1a

1 ENGAGE Investigating Series and Summation Notation

The sum of the terms of a sequence is called a **series**. Many sequences are infinite and therefore do not have defined sums. For these sequences, *partial sums* can be found. A **partial sum**, represented by S_n, is the sum of a specified number, n, of terms of a sequence. Examples of partial sums of a sequence of odd integers are shown below.

Sequence: 1, 3, 5, 7, 9, ...

$S_1 = 1$	Sum of first term
$S_2 = 1 + 3 = 4$	Sum of first 2 terms
$S_3 = 1 + 3 + 5 = 9$	Sum of first 3 terms
$S_4 = 1 + 3 + 5 + 7 = 16$	Sum of first 4 terms

A series can be represented using **summation notation**, in which the Greek letter $\sum$ (capital *sigma*) is used to represent the sum of a sequence defined by a rule. The series $1 + 3 + 5 + 7 + 9$ is written in summation notation below.

$$\sum_{k=1}^{5}(2k - 1)$$

5 ← Last value of k
$(2k - 1)$ ← Explicit formula for sequence
$k = 1$ ← First value of k

In summation notation, an explicit formula for the sequence is needed as shown above. When writing a formula for a sequence, it is helpful to examine the first and second differences of the terms and the ratios of the terms.

REFLECT

1a. Explain the difference between a sequence and a series.

____

____

1b. Without making any calculations, determine whether the two series below have the same sum. Explain your reasoning.

$$\sum_{k=1}^{7}4(k + 12) \qquad \sum_{k=3}^{9}4(k + 12)$$

____

____

____

____

MCC9–12.F.BF.1a

2 EXAMPLE Using Summation Notation and Evaluating Series

A Write the series $\frac{3}{5} + \frac{3}{10} + \frac{3}{15} + \frac{3}{20} + \frac{3}{25}$ in summation notation.

Find a rule for the kth term of the series. Notice that the denominators of the terms are multiples of ___. The numerator of each term is ___. So the terms of the series can be written as follows:

$$a_k = \frac{\quad}{\quad} \text{ where } k = \_\_, \_\_, \_\_, \_\_, \_\_$$

Notice that the first value of k is ___ and the last value of k is ___.

The summation notation for the series is $\sum_{k=1}^{5} \frac{3}{5k}$.

B Expand the series $\sum_{k=3}^{6} (-1)^k(k+4)$ and evaluate.

$$\sum_{k=3}^{6} (-1)^k(k+4) = \_\_\_$$

$$= \_\_\_$$

$$= \_\_\_$$

REFLECT

2a. In part B of Example 2, suppose the rule for the kth term of the series is $(-1)^{k+1}(k+4)$. How will this affect the answer? Explain.

______

______

______

2b. The first term of the series $\sum_{k=a}^{b} k$ is a and the last term of the series is b. Given that the series has c terms, write a rule for finding the value of b in terms of a and c.

______

Formulas can be used to find sums of some common series. In a *constant series*, such as $2 + 2 + 2 + 2$, each term has the same value.

$$\sum_{k=1}^{n} c = \underbrace{c + c + c + \ldots + c}_{n \text{ terms}} = nc$$

You can see that the sum of a constant series with n terms of value c can be expressed as nc. How can you find formulas for the sums of non-constant series?

MCC9–12.F.BF.1a

3 EXPLORE Deriving a Formula for the Sum of Positive Integers

Derive a formula for the sum of the first n positive integers.

A Consider the partial sum $\sum_{k=1}^{6} k$, which can be called S_6.

Write S_6 twice, the second time with the order reversed. Then add the two equations term by term.

$$S_6 = 1 + 2 + 3 + 4 + 5 + 6$$
$$S_6 = 6 + 5 + 4 + 3 + 2 + 1$$

$2S_6 =$ ______

Solve for S_6. Notice that the sum is the product of the number of terms, ____, and the sum of the first and last terms, ____, divided by ____.

$S_6 = \frac{6(7)}{2} =$ ____

B Now consider the general sum $\sum_{k=1}^{n} k$, which can be called S_n.

Write the series twice, as in part A, and then add the two equations.

$S_n = 1 \quad + \quad 2 \quad + \quad$ ____ $\quad + \ldots + \quad$ ____ $\quad + \quad$ ____ $\quad + \quad$ ____

$S_n = n \quad + (n - 1) \quad + \quad$ ____ $\quad + \ldots + \quad$ ____ $\quad + \quad$ ____ $\quad + \quad$ ____

$2S_n =$ ______ (n terms)

$2S_n =$ ____

$S_n =$ ____

REFLECT

3a. Expand and evaluate to find the sum of the series $\sum_{k=1}^{9} k$. Show that you get the same sum by using the formula in part B of Explore 3.

______

3b. The terms of the series at the right are rearranged to form 4 terms of 9. Explain how this suggests the formula for the sum of the first n integers in part B of Explore 3.

$$\sum_{k=1}^{8} k = 1 + 2 + 3 + 4 + 5 + 6 + 7 + 8$$
$$= (1 + 8) + (2 + 7) + (3 + 6) + (4 + 5)$$
$$= 9 + 9 + 9 + 9$$
$$= 4(9)$$
$$= 36$$

______

______

______

______

MCC9–12.F.BF.1a

4 EXPLORE Deriving a Formula for the Sum of Squares of Integers

Derive a formula for the sum of the squares of the first n positive integers.

A To derive the formula for $\sum_{k=1}^{n} k^2$, use the series $\sum_{k=1}^{n} k^3$ and $\sum_{k=1}^{n} (k-1)^3$.

Notice the result when you find the difference of these series.

$$\sum_{k=1}^{n} k^3 = 1^3 + 2^3 + \square + \dots + \square + \square + \square$$

$$\sum_{k=1}^{n} (k-1)^3 = 0^3 + 1^3 + \square + \square + \dots + \square + \square$$

$$\sum_{k=1}^{n} [k^3 - (k-1)^3] = 0 + 0 + \square + \square + \dots + \square + \square + \square$$

B Use the result from part A to find a formula for the sum of $= \sum_{k=1}^{n} k^2$.

$\square = \sum_{k=1}^{n} [k^3 - (k-1)^3]$ Write result from part A.

$\square = \sum_{k=1}^{n} \square$ Simplify the explicit rule.

$\square = \sum_{k=1}^{n} \square - \sum_{k=1}^{n} \square + \sum_{k=1}^{n} \square$ Separate into three sums.

$\square = \square \sum_{k=1}^{n} \square - \square \sum_{k=1}^{n} \square + \sum_{k=1}^{n} \square$ Move constant factors outside of sigma.

$\square = 3\sum_{k=1}^{n} k^2 - 3\left(\square\right) + \square$ Substitute formulas for $\sum_{k=1}^{n} k$ and $\sum_{k=1}^{n} 1$.

$\sum_{k=1}^{n} k^2 = \square + \square - \square$ Rewrite equation to isolate $\sum_{k=1}^{n} k^2$.

$\sum_{k=1}^{n} k^2 = \square$ Write expression with a common denominator.

$\sum_{k=1}^{n} k^2 = \dfrac{\square}{6}$ Factor numerator.

REFLECT

4a. Use the formula in part B to find the sum of the series $\sum_{k=1}^{5} k^2$. Show that you get the same sum by expanding and evaluating the series.

4b. One of the steps in part B uses the fact that $\sum_{k=1}^{n} ck = c\sum_{k=1}^{n} k$ for any constant c. Prove this fact by using the Distributive Property on the expanded series.

MCC9–12.F.BF.1a

5 EXAMPLE Using Summation Formulas

Evaluate each series.

A $\sum_{k=1}^{44} k$

$\sum_{k=1}^{44} k = \frac{n(n+1)}{2}$ Use the formula derived in Explore 3.

$=$ Substitute 44 for n.

$=$ Simplify.

B $\sum_{k=1}^{17} k^2$

$\sum_{k=1}^{17} k^2 = \frac{n(n+1)(2n+1)}{6}$ Use the formula derived in Explore 4.

$=$ Substitute 17 for n.

$=$ Simplify.

REFLECT

5a. Suppose the series in part A started with $k = 8$. Would you be able to use the formula derived in Explore 3 to find the sum of the series? Explain.

5b. Let n be any integer. Is the sum of the series $\sum_{k=1}^{n} k^2$ an integer? Explain.

PRACTICE

Write each series in summation notation.

1. $8 + 9 + 10 + 11 + 12 + 13 + 14 + 15$

2. $-3 + (-6) + (-9) + (-12) + (-15)$

3. $1 + \frac{1}{4} + \frac{1}{9} + \frac{1}{16}$

4. $\frac{1}{2} + \frac{2}{3} + \frac{3}{4} + \frac{4}{5} + \frac{5}{6} + \frac{6}{7}$

5. $11 + 101 + 1{,}001 + 10{,}001 + 100{,}001$

6. $-2 + 4 + (-6) + 8 + (-10) + 12$

Expand each series and evaluate.

7. $\sum_{k=1}^{5}(3k - 2)$

8. $\sum_{k=3}^{9}4k$

9. $\sum_{k=1}^{7}(-1)^k(11k)$

10. $\sum_{k=5}^{11}(k - 1)(k + 4)$

Evaluate each series using a summation formula.

11. $\sum_{k=5}^{14}6.2$

12. $\sum_{k=1}^{77}k$

13. $\sum_{k=1}^{20}k^2$

14. Follow the steps below to find the sum of the series $\sum_{k=16}^{31}k$.

a. Solve the equation $\sum_{k=1}^{31}k = \sum_{k=1}^{15}k + \sum_{k=16}^{31}k$ for $\sum_{k=16}^{31}k$.

b. Use your rewritten equation to find the sum of the series $\sum_{k=16}^{31}k$.

15. Do the series $\sum_{k=1}^{n}(k + 2)(k + 7)$ and $\sum_{k=1}^{n-1}(k + 3)(k + 8)$ have the same sum? Explain.

Name________________________ Class______________ Date__________ 12-2

Additional Practice

Write each series in summation notation.

1. $-2 + 4 - 8 + 16 - 32$

____

2. $\frac{1}{10} + \frac{1}{100} + \frac{1}{1{,}000} + \frac{1}{10{,}000}$

____

3. $-6 - 1 + 4 + 9 + 14 + 19$

____

4. $\frac{1}{3} + \frac{1}{6} + \frac{1}{9} + \frac{1}{12} + \frac{1}{15} + \frac{1}{18}$

____

5. $7 + 13 + 19 + 25 + 31$

____

6. $-1 + 1 - 1 + 1 - 1 + 1 - 1$

____

Expand each series and evaluate.

7. $\sum_{k=4}^{8} \frac{k}{4}$

a. Expand. _______________

b. Simplify. _______________

8. $\sum_{k=1}^{4} 5^{k-2}$

a. Expand. _______________

b. Simplify. _______________

9. $\sum_{k=2}^{6} \left(-2^{k}\right)$

a. Expand. _______________

b. Simplify. _______________

10. $\sum_{k=30}^{39} (70 - 2k)$

a. Expand. _______________

b. Simplify. _______________

Evaluate each series.

11. $\sum_{k=12}^{20} 3$

____

12. $\sum_{k=1}^{40} k$

____

13. $\sum_{k=1}^{10} k^2$

____

Solve.

14. One day, Hannah starts a new online Internet club by convincing two of her friends to join. The next day, each member convinces two more people to join. The third day of the club, each member convinces two more people to join, and so on for a full week.

a. Write a series that represents the number of club members at the end of *n* days. _______________

b. Write a series that represents the number of club members at the end of one week. _______________

c. How many members will the club have at the end of a week? _______________

Problem Solving

Todd joins a fitness club. During the first week of training, his biceps increase by 4 millimeters. The trainer says Todd can expect his biceps to continue to increase each week, but only by about 90% of the increase of the week before.

1. Todd wants to know how much his biceps will increase in 8 weeks.
   a. Write a rule for the *k*th term in the sequence that represents the amount of muscle increase each week. ____________________
   b. Write the summation notation using $\sum$ for the first 8 terms. ____________________
   c. Expand the series and evaluate to find the amount by which Todd's biceps will increase in 8 weeks. ____________________
2. Todd thinks that, if he works out extra hard each week, his biceps should increase by at least an additional half-millimeter each week. If this is true, how much will his biceps increase after 8 weeks? ____________________
   a. Write a rule for the *k*th term in the sequence that represents the minimum amount of muscle increase each week. ____________________
   b. Use summation notation to represent the minimum total amount of muscle increase after 8 weeks. ____________________
   c. What is the minimum increase in size in Todd's biceps after 8 weeks? ____________________
   d. At this rate, how many weeks would it take to reach or exceed the total muscle increase predicted by the trainer? ____________________

Rodrigo puts his change into a bowl each evening. On Monday he puts 2 quarters in the bowl and decides to try and increase the amount each evening by at least 10 cents over the evening before. Choose the letter for the best answer.

3. Which series represents the minimum amount in the bowl Saturday morning?

   A $\sum_{k=1}^{5} 0.1(0.5)^{k-1}$

   B $\sum_{k=1}^{5} 0.5(0.1)^{k-1}$

   C $\sum_{k=1}^{5} 0.5 + 0.1(k-1)$

   D $\sum_{k=1}^{5} 0.1 + 0.5(k-1)$

4. What is the minimum amount in the bowl the following Monday morning?

   F \$3.50

   G \$5.60

   H \$6.80

   J \$7.60

Name ______________________ Class ______________ Date __________

12-3

Geometric Sequences and Series

Going Deeper

Essential question: *How can you write a rule for a geometric sequence and find the sum of a finite geometric series?*

Video Tutor

In a **geometric sequence**, the ratio of consecutive terms is constant. The constant ratio is called the **common ratio**, often written as r.

MCC9–12.F.BF.2

1 EXAMPLE Writing Rules for a Geometric Sequence

Makers of Japanese swords in the 1400s repeatedly folded and hammered the metal to form layers. The folding process increased the strength of the sword.

The table shows how the number of layers depends on the number of folds. Write a recursive rule and an explicit rule for the geometric sequence described by the table.

Number of Folds	***n***	1	2	3	4	5
Number of Layers	***f*(*n*)**	2	4	8	16	32

A Find the common ratio by calculating the ratios of consecutive terms.

$\frac{4}{2} =$ ____ $\frac{8}{4} =$ ____ $\frac{16}{8} =$ ____ $\frac{32}{16} =$ ____

The common ratio, r, is __________.

B Write a recursive rule for the sequence.

$f(1) =$ ____ and

The first term is __________.

$f(n) =$ ____ $\bullet$ ____ for $n \geq 2$

Every other term is the __________ of the previous term and the common ratio.

C Write an explicit rule for the sequence by writing each term as the product of the first term and a power of the common ratio.

n	***f*(*n*)**
1	$2(2)^0 = 2$
2	$2(2)^1 = 4$
3	$2(2)^{\square} = 8$
4	$2(2)^{\square} = 16$
5	$2(2)^{\square} = 32$

Generalize the results from the table: $f(n) =$ ____ $\bullet\ 2^{n-}$ 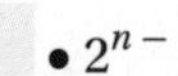

REFLECT

1a. Explain how you know that the sequence 4, 12, 36, 108, 324, ... is a geometric sequence.

1b. A geometric sequence has a common ratio of 5. If you know that the 6th term of the sequence is 30, how could you find the 7th term?

MCC9–12.F.BF.2

2 EXPLORE Writing General Rules for Geometric Sequences

Use the geometric sequence 6, 24, 96, 384, 1536, ... to help you write a recursive rule and an explicit rule for any geometric sequence. For the general rules, the values of *n* are consecutive integers starting with 1.

A Find the common ratio.

Numbers	**Algebra**
6, 24, 96, 384, 1536, ...	$f(1), f(2), f(3),$ ____ , ____ , ...
Common ratio = ____	Common ratio $= r$

B Write a recursive rule.

Numbers	**Algebra**
$f(1) =$ ____ and	Given $f(1)$,
$f(n) = f(n-1) \cdot$ ____ for $n \geq 2$	$f(n) = f(n-1) \cdot$ ____ for $n \geq 2$

C Write an explicit rule.

Numbers	**Algebra**
$f(n) =$ ____ $\cdot$ ____$^{n-1}$	$f(n) =$ ____ $\cdot$ ____$^{n-1}$

REFLECT

2a. The first term of a geometric sequence is 81 and the common ratio is $\frac{1}{3}$. Explain how you could find the 4th term of the sequence.

2b. What information do you need to know in order to find the 5th term of a geometric sequence by using its explicit rule?

2c. What is the recursive rule for the sequence $f(n) = 5(4)^{n-1}$?

Relating Geometric Sequences and Exponential Functions

The graph shows the heights to which a ball bounces after it is dropped. Write an explicit rule for the sequence of bounce heights.

A Represent the sequence in a table.

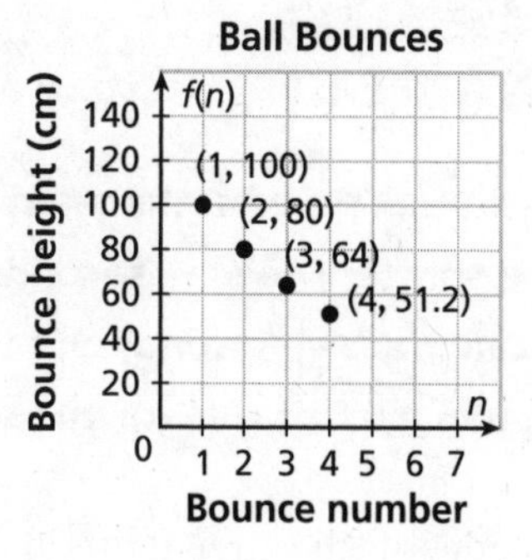

n	1	2	3	4
$f(n)$				

B Examine the sequence.

Is the sequence geometric? Explain.

____

What is the common ratio? ________

C Write an explicit rule for the sequence.

$f(n) = f(1) \cdot r^{n-1}$ Write the general rule.

$f(n) = \square \cdot \square^{n-1}$ Substitute ________ for $f(1)$ and ________ for r.

So, the sequence has the rule ____________________ where n is the bounce number and $f(n)$ is the ______________________________.

REFLECT

3a. A geometric sequence is equivalent to an exponential function with a restricted domain. On the graph above, draw an exponential curve that passes through the given points. Then write an exponential function of the form $f(n) = ab^n$ for the curve that you drew and give the function's domain.

____

3b. Show that the explicit rule for the sequence is equivalent to the exponential function. Justify the steps you take.

____

____

____

The explicit and recursive rules for a geometric sequence can also be written in subscript notation.

Explicit: $a_n = a_1 \cdot r^{n-1}$

Recursive: a_1 is given and $a_n = a_{n-1} \cdot r$ for $n \geq 2$

MCC9-12.F.LE.2

4 EXAMPLE Writing a Geometric Sequence Given Two Terms

The shutter speed settings on a camera form a geometric sequence where a_n is the shutter speed in seconds and n is the setting number. The fifth setting on the camera is $\frac{1}{60}$ second, and the seventh setting on the camera is $\frac{1}{15}$ second. Write an explicit rule for the sequence using subscript notation.

A Identify the given terms in the sequence.

$a_5 =$ ____ — The fifth setting is $\frac{1}{60}$ second, so the 5th term of the sequence is $\frac{1}{60}$.

$a_{\_} =$ ____ — The seventh setting is $\frac{1}{15}$ second, so the ________ term of the sequence is ________.

B Find the common ratio.

$a_7 = a_6 \cdot r$ — Write the recursive rule for a_7.

$a_6 =$ ____ $\cdot\ r$ — Write the recursive rule for a_6.

$a_7 =$ ____ $\cdot$ ____ $\cdot\ r$ — Substitute the expression for a_6 into the rule for a_7.

____ $=$ ____ $\cdot\ r^2$ — Substitute $\frac{1}{15}$ for a_7 and ________ for a_5.

____ $= r^2$ — Multiply both sides by 60.

____ $= r$ — Definition of positive square root

C Find the first term of the sequence.

$a_n = a_1 \cdot r^{n-1}$ — Write the explicit rule.

____ $= a_1 \cdot$ ____$^{_ - 1}$ — Substitute $\frac{1}{60}$ for a_n, ________ for r, and 5 for n.

$\frac{1}{60} = a_1 \cdot$ ____ — Simplify.

____ $= a_1$ — Divide both sides by 16.

D Write the explicit rule.

$a_n = a_1 \cdot r^{n-1}$ — Write the general rule.

$a_n =$ ____ $\cdot$ ____$^{n-1}$ — Substitute ________ for a_1 and ________ for r.

REFLECT

4a. When finding the common ratio, why can you ignore the negative square root of 4 when solving the equation $4 = r^2$?

4b. If you graphed the explicit rule for the sequence, what would the graph look like?

PREP FOR MCC9–12.A.SSE.4

5 EXPLORE Investigating a Geometric Series

A Start with a rectangular sheet of paper and assume the sheet has an area of 1 square unit. Cut the sheet in half and lay down one of the half-pieces. Then cut the remaining piece in half, and lay down one of the quarter-pieces. Continue the process: At each stage, cut the remaining piece in half, and lay down one of the halves. As you lay pieces down, arrange them to rebuild the original sheet of paper.

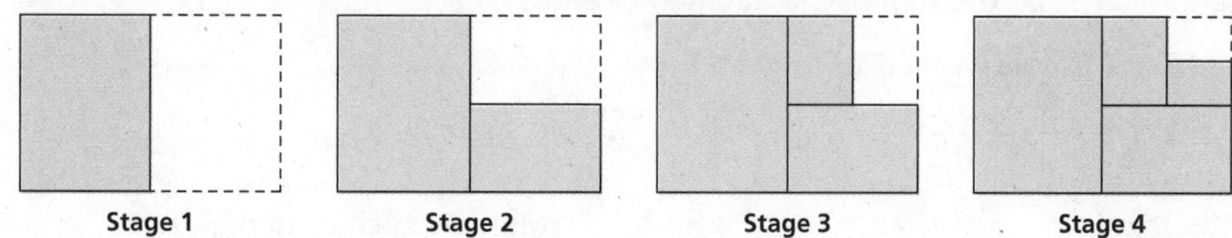

B Complete the table below by expressing the total area of the paper that has been laid down in two ways:

- as the sum of the areas of the pieces that have been laid down, and
- as the difference of 1 and the area of the remaining piece.

Stage	Sum of the areas of the pieces that have been laid down	Difference of 1 and the area of the remaining piece
1	$\frac{1}{2}$	$1 - \frac{1}{2} =$
2	$\frac{1}{2} + \quad = $	$1 - \quad =$
3	$\frac{1}{2} + \quad + \quad =$	$1 - \quad =$
4	$\frac{1}{2} + \quad + \quad + \quad =$	$1 - \quad =$

REFLECT

5a. Describe the sequence formed by the areas of the pieces that have been laid down.

5b. Make a generalization: What is the total area of the paper that has been laid down at the nth stage? Write the area as a sum and as a difference.

A **series** is the expression formed by adding the terms of a sequence. A **geometric series** is the expression formed by adding the terms of a geometric sequence. In the Explore, the areas $\frac{1}{2}, \frac{1}{4}, \frac{1}{8}$, and $\frac{1}{16}$ form a geometric sequence. The expression $\frac{1}{2} + \frac{1}{4} + \frac{1}{8} + \frac{1}{16}$ is a geometric series. You can derive a formula for the sum of a geometric series.

MCC9–12.A.SSE.4

6 EXPLORE Deriving a Formula for the Sum of a Geometric Series

Consider the geometric series $a_1 + a_1r + a_1r^2 + a_1r^3 + \cdots + a_1r^{n-1}$. The series has n terms. Let S_n be the sum of the geometric series.

A Find a simplified expression for $S_n - rS_n$.

$S_n = a_1 + a_1r + a_1r^2 + a_1r^3 + \cdots + a_1r^{n-1}$ Write S_n.

$rS_n = a_1r + a_1r^2 + a_1r^{\square} + a_1r^{\square} + \cdots + a_1r^{\square}$ Multiply each term of S_n by r.

Align like terms and subtract.

$$S_n = a_1 + a_1r + a_1r^2 + a_1r^3 + \cdots + a_1r^{n-1}$$

$$rS_n = a_1r + a_1r^2 + a_1r^3 + \cdots + a_1r^{n-1} + a_1r^n$$

$$S_n - rS_n = a_1 + \square + \square + \square + \cdots + \square - a_1r^n$$

So, $S_n - rS_n =$ ______________.

B Factor and divide by $1 - r$.

$S_n - rS_n = a_1 - a_1r^n$ Write the result from part A.

$S_n(1 - r) = a_1(\square - \square)$ Factor both sides.

$S_n = a_1\left(\frac{\square - \square}{1 - r}\right)$ Divide both sides by $1 - r$.

REFLECT

6a. In the first Explore, you found that $\frac{1}{2} + \left(\frac{1}{2}\right)^2 + \left(\frac{1}{2}\right)^3 + \cdots + \left(\frac{1}{2}\right)^n = 1 - \left(\frac{1}{2}\right)^n$.

Show that you get the same sum for the geometric series by using the formula you derived above.

6b. What restrictions are there on the values of r that can be used in the formula for the sum of a geometric series?

Sum of a Finite Geometric Series

The sum S_n of the geometric series $a_1 + a_1 r + a_1 r^2 + a_1 r^3 + \cdots + a_1 r^{n-1}$ is

$$S_n = a_1\left(\frac{1 - r^n}{1 - r}\right)$$

where r is the common ratio, $r \neq 1$, and n is the number of terms.

MCC9-12.A.SSE.4

7 EXAMPLE Finding the Distance Traveled by a Bouncing Ball

The following geometric sequence models n bounce heights of a ball, where the heights are measured in inches. (The initial height from which the ball is dropped before the first bounce is not part of this sequence.)

$$80, 80(0.8), 80(0.8)^2, \ldots, 80(0.8)^{n-1}$$

Based on the model, what is the total vertical distance that the ball travels in 10 bounces?

A Write a geometric series for the total vertical distance the ball travels.

On the first bounce, the ball travels 80 inches up and 80 inches down. On the second bounce, it travels 64 inches up and 64 inches down. On every bounce, the ball travels twice the bounce height. So, the following geometric sequence models the 10 distances traveled.

160, ______ (0.8), ______ (0.8)$^{\square}$, . . . , ______ (0.8)$^{\square}$

The following geometric series models the total distance traveled.

$S_n = 160 +$ ______ $(0.8) +$ ______ $(0.8)^{\square} + \cdots +$ ______ $(0.8)^{\square}$

B Use the formula for the sum of a finite geometric series.

In this case, $n =$ ________, $a_1 =$ ________, and $r =$ ________.

$S_n = a_1\left(\frac{1 - r^n}{1 - r}\right)$ Write the sum formula.

$= \square\left(\frac{1 - \square^{\square}}{1 - \square}\right)$ Substitute the values of n, a_1, and r.

$\approx \square$ Round to the nearest inch.

So, the ball travels approximately ________ inches in 10 bounces.

REFLECT

7a. Write and simplify an expression for the total distance the ball travels in n bounces. Check that your expression gives the correct result when $n = 10$.

____

An *annuity* is an account that is increased (or decreased) by equal deposits (or payments) that are made at regular intervals. The *future value* of an annuity is the total amount in the account at some time in the future.

MCC9-12.A.SSE.4

8 EXAMPLE Determining the Future Value of an Annuity

You deposit $1000 into a savings account at the end of each year for 10 years. The account earns 3% interest that is compounded annually. What is the future value of the annuity in 10 years?

A Develop a general formula for the future value of an annuity.

Suppose you deposit P dollars into the account at the end of each year for n years, and the account earns interest compounded annually at a rate i.

At the end of the first year, the total value of the annuity is P. At the end of the second year, interest is applied to the first deposit and there is a new deposit of P dollars, for a total value of $P(1 + i) + P$. Complete the table.

Year	Total Value of Annuity at End of Year
1	P
2	$P(1 + i) + P$
3	$P(1 + i)^{\square} + P(1 + i) + P$
⋮	⋮
n	$P(1 + i)^{\square} + P(1 + i)^{\square} + \cdots + P(1 + i)^2 + P(1 + i) + P$

Complete the equation for the total value A after n years.

$$A = P + P(1 + i) + P(1 + i)^2 + \cdots + P(1 + i)^{\square} + P(1 + i)^{\square}$$

This is a geometric series with $a_1 =$ ________ and $r =$ ________, so its sum is

$$A = a_1\left(\frac{1 - r^n}{1 - r}\right) = P\left(\frac{1 - (1 + i)^n}{1 - (1 + i)}\right) = P\left(\frac{(1 + i)^n - 1}{(1 + i) - 1}\right) = P\left(\frac{(1 + i)^n - 1}{\square}\right).$$

B Use the formula to find the future value of the annuity.

$A = P\left(\frac{(1 + i)^n - 1}{i}\right)$ Write the formula.

$= \square\left(\frac{\square^{\square} - 1}{\square}\right)$ Substitute 1000 for P, 0.03 for i, and 10 for n.

$\approx$ ________ Round to 2 decimal places.

So, the value of the annuity in 10 years is ________.

REFLECT

8a. Does your answer seem reasonable? How do you know?

8b. The total interest earned on an annuity is the future value minus the sum of the deposits. Write a formula for the total interest I of an annuity after n years with annual deposits of P dollars and interest compounded annually at rate i.

PRACTICE

Write a recursive rule and an explicit rule for each geometric sequence.

1. 9, 27, 81, 243, ...

---

2. 5, −5, 5, −5, ...

---

3. $12, 3, \frac{3}{4}, \frac{3}{16}, \ldots$

---

4. The table shows the beginning-of-month balances, rounded to the nearest cent, in Marla's savings account for the first few months after she made an initial deposit in the account.

Month	*n*	1	2	3	4
Account Balance ($)	***f*(*n*)**	2010.00	2020.05	2030.15	2040.30

a. Explain how you know that the sequence of account balances is geometric.

b. Write recursive and explicit rules for the sequence of account balances.

c. What amount did Marla deposit initially? Explain.

5. The graph shows the number of players in the first four rounds of the U.S. Open women's singles tennis tournament.

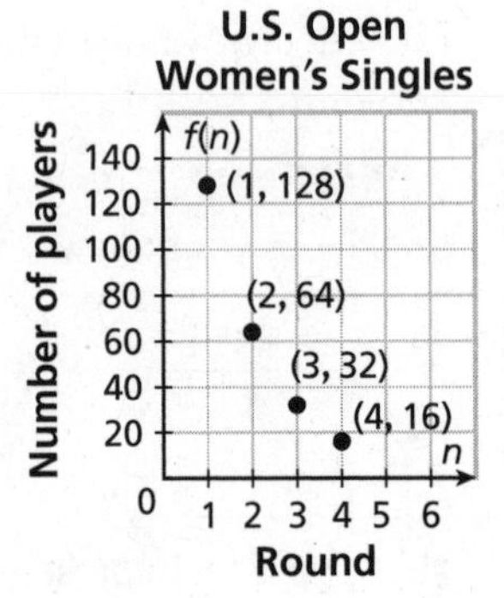

a. Write an explicit rule for the sequence of players in each round.

b. How many rounds are there in the tournament? (*Hint:* In the last round, only 2 players are left.)

6. The numbers of points that a player must accumulate to reach the next level of a video game form a geometric sequence, where a_n is the number of points needed to complete level *n*.

a. A player needs 1000 points to complete level 2 and 8,000,000 points to complete level 5. Write an explicit rule for the sequence using subscript notation.

b. How many points are needed for level 7? ____________

Write an explicit rule for each geometric sequence based on the given terms from the sequence. Assume that the common ratio *r* is positive.

7. $a_2 = 12$ and $a_4 = 192$

8. $a_5 = 0.32$ and $a_7 = 0.0128$

Each rule represents a geometric sequence. If the given rule is recursive, write it as an explicit rule. If the given rule is explicit, write it as a recursive rule. Assume that $f(1)$ is the first term of the sequence.

9. $f(n) = 6(3)^{n-1}$

____

10. $f(1) = 10; f(n) = f(n-1) \cdot 8$ for $n \geq 2$

____

11. An economist predicts that the cost of food will increase by 4% per year for the next several years.

a. Use the economist's prediction to write an explicit rule for a geometric sequence that gives the cost in dollars of a box of cereal in year n given that it costs \$3.20 in year 1.

____

b. What is the fourth term of the sequence, and what does it represent in this situation?

____

For each finite geometric series, n indicates the number of terms. Rewrite each series in the form $a_1 + a_1r + a_1r^2 + \cdots + a_1r^{n-1}$. Then find the sum.

12. $4 + 12 + 36 + \cdots + 8748; n = 8$

____

____

13. $10 + 5 + 2.5 + \cdots + 0.000003125; n = 6$

____

____

14. A ball is dropped from a height of 16 feet and allowed to bounce repeatedly. On the first bounce it rises to a height of 12 feet and then on each subsequent bounce it rises to 75% of its previous height.

a. Write a geometric sequence that models the first n bounce heights, in feet.

____

b. Write a geometric series to model the total vertical distance the ball travels as a result of n bounces. (Exclude the distance traveled before the first bounce.)

____

c. How far does the ball travel vertically as a result of the first 3 bounces? Show two ways to find the answer—by adding the first three terms of the series and by using a formula.

____

____

d. How far does the ball travel vertically as a result of the first 9 bounces?

____

15. Ali deposits $2000 into an account at the end of each year for 4 years. The account earns 5% interest compounded annually.

a. Complete the table to show the value of each deposit as well as the total value of the account at the end of the fourth year. For example, the value of the first deposit is $2000(1.05)^3 = \$2315.25$.

Value of first deposit	
Value of second deposit	
Value of third deposit	
Value of fourth deposit	
Total value of account	

b. Use the formula for the sum of a finite geometric series to find the total value of the account at the end of the fourth year.

16. Mr. Ortiz wants to save money for his grandson's future college costs. He plans to deposit $800 into an account at the end of each year. The account earns 6% interest compounded annually. What will be the value of the account in 18 years? Justify your answer.

17. Ms. Turner wants to accumulate $50,000 for her daughter's future college costs in 12 years. How much does she need to deposit into an account at the end of each year if the account earns 4% interest compounded annually? Explain.

18. In a single-elimination tournament, a competitor is eliminated after one loss. Suppose a single-elimination tennis tournament has 64 players. In the first round, 32 matches are played. In each subsequent round, the number of matches decreases by one half. How many matches are played in the tournament? Show how to find the answer two ways—by direct calculation and by a formula.

19. Nick works for a cleaning company. It takes him 2 hours 30 minutes to clean an office the first time. If he decreases his time by 5% on each subsequent visit, how much time will he spend cleaning the office during 10 visits? Justify your answer.

20. Midori earns $850 in her first month at a part time job. If she gets a 1% raise in each subsequent month, how much will she earn in a year? Justify your answer.

Name________________________ Class________________ Date____________

Additional Practice

Determine whether each sequence could be geometric or arithmetic. If possible, find the common ratio or difference.

1. 1.1, –3.3, 9.9, –29.7, 89.1, ...

____

2. –18, –7, 4, 15, 26, ...

____

3. 1, 2, 6, 24, 120, 720, ...

____

4. 3125, 2500, 2000, 1600, 1280, ...

____

Find the 10th term of each geometric sequence.

5. 1600, 800, 400, 200, ...

____

6. 0.0000001, 0.00001, 0.001, 0.1, ...

____

7. –64, 96, –144, 216, ...

____

8. 2, –6, 18, –54, ...

____

Find the 8th term of each geometric sequence with the given terms.

9. $a_3 = 12$ and $a_6 = 96$

____

10. $a_{15} = 100$ and $a_{17} = 25$

____

11. $a_{11} = -4$ and $a_{13} = -36$

____

12. $a_3 = -4$ and $a_5 = -36$

____

Find the geometric mean of each pair of numbers.

13. 2 and 8

____

14. 4 and 25

____

15. 2 and 3

____

Find the indicated sum for each geometric series.

16. S_7 for 14, 42, 126, 378, ...

____

17. $\sum_{k=1}^{8}(-4)^{k-1}$

____

Solve.

18. Deanna received an e-mail asking her to forward it to 10 other people. Assume that no one breaks the chain and that there are no duplicate recipients. How many e-mails will have been sent after 8 generations, including Deanna's?

____

Problem Solving

Crystal works at a tree nursery during the summer. She wonders why the lower branches of one particular type of tree drop off. The nurseryman explains that each layer of branches absorbs about 10% of the sunlight and lets the rest through to the next layer. If a layer receives less than 25% of the sunlight, those branches will drop off.

1. Crystal counts 7 distinct healthy layers on one tree. She wants to know how many more layers the tree will grow before starting to lose layers of branches.
   a. Write the rule for the *n*th term, a_n, of a geometric sequence. ________________
   b. If a_n represents the percent of sunlight reaching layer *n*, what is the value of a_1? How do you know?
   ____
   c. What is the value of *r*? What does it represent?
   ____
   d. Write the rule to find the percent of sunlight reaching layer 7. Solve for a_7. ________________
   e. About how many layers of branches will this tree have before a bottom layer drops off? ________________
2. The nurseryman points to a denser type of tree and states that only about 75% of sunlight gets through to each lower layer, but that a layer of this type of tree needs only about 15% of the original sunlight to survive.
   a. What percent of sunlight gets through to layer 7 of this tree? ________________
   b. How many layers of branches could this type of tree support? ________________

Jackson usually runs 8 laps around the football field and consistently completes the first lap in 3 minutes. During one practice session, his coach notes that it takes him 15% longer to complete each lap than the previous lap. Choose the letter for the best answer.

3. How long does it take Jackson to complete the eighth lap?
   A 5.25 min
   B 6.03 min
   C 6.93 min
   D 7.98 min

4. How long does it take Jackson to complete all 8 laps?
   F 9.18 min
   G 20.39 min
   H 41.18 min
   J 61.18 min

Name________________ Class____________ Date________

Performance Tasks

GPS COMMON CORE

MCC9-12.A.SSE.2
MCC9-12.A.APR.1
MCC9-12.F.BF.1a
MCC9-12.F.BF.2

★ **1.** Jeremy had a square piece of gift wrapping paper with a side length of x inches that he used to wrap a present. First he cut 6 inches off the right side of the paper and discarded the rectangular scrap. Next he cut 3 inches off the top of the paper and again discarded the rectangular scrap. What expression represents the total area in square inches of the scraps that he discarded? Justify your answer.

★ **2.** A customer at a self-storage facility was offered a choice between a storage unit shaped like a cube and another unit that is 2 feet longer, 5 feet wider, and 3 feet shorter than the first unit. The customer thinks that if the volume of the cube is x^3, the volume of the other unit would be $x^3 - 4x^2 - 11x + 30$. Is the customer correct? Factor the polynomial to check.

★ **3.** A Petri dish initially contains 1000 bacteria. The number of bacteria triples every 2 hours.

a. What type of sequence represents the number of bacteria in the population? Write the rule for the nth term of the sequence if n is the number of times the population has tripled.

b. What value of n represents 18 hours of growth? Explain how you know.

c. How many bacteria are in the culture after 18 hours?

continued

4. Alicia is building a block pyramid similar to the pyramid shown. The top level will always have two blocks. Alicia wants her pyramid to contain as many levels as possible.

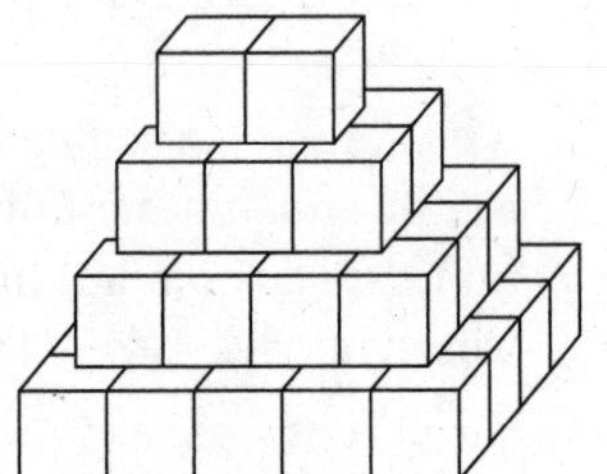

a. Make a table and a diagram. Number the levels starting from the top level.

b. The number of blocks in each level is $k(k+1)$ where k is the level number. Write a series to represent the total number of blocks in n rows.

c. How many levels can her pyramid have if Alicia has 200 blocks?

Name ______________________ Class ____________ Date ________

SELECTED RESPONSE

1. Which theorem states that if $f(x)$ is a polynomial of degree n, then $f(x)$ has at least one zero in the set of complex numbers?

A. Rational Zero Theorem

B. Factor Theorem

C. Remainder Theorem

D. Fundamental Theorem of Algebra

2. Which is a factored form of $x^4 - 16$?

F. $(x^2 - 2)(x^2 + 2)$

G. $(x^2 + 4)(x^2 - 2)(x^2 + 2)$

H. $(x^2 + 4)(x - 2)(x + 2)$

J. $(x^2 + 4)(x - 4)(x + 4)$

3. Christopher is drawing the graph of $f(x) = -x^5 + 2x^4 + x^3 + 3x^2 - 8x + 1$. How should he show the end behavior of the function?

A. $f(x) \to +\infty$ as $x \to +\infty$ and $f(x) \to -\infty$ as $x \to -\infty$

B. $f(x) \to -\infty$ as $x \to +\infty$ and $f(x) \to -\infty$ as $x \to -\infty$

C. $f(x) \to +\infty$ as $x \to +\infty$ and $f(x) \to +\infty$ as $x \to -\infty$

D. $f(x) \to -\infty$ as $x \to +\infty$ and $f(x) \to +\infty$ as $x \to -\infty$

4. Under which operation(s) is the set of polynomials closed?

F. addition only

G. addition and multiplication only

H. addition, subtraction, and multiplication only

J. addition, subtraction, multiplication, and division

5. Which expression is the expansion of $(x + 1)^4$?

A. $x^4 + 4x^3 + 6x^2 + 4x + 1$

B. $x^4 + 4x^3 + 6x^2 + 4x + 4$

C. $4x^4 + 4x^3 + 6x^2 + 4x + 1$

D. $4x^4 + 4x^3 + 6x^2 + 4x + 4$

6. If $x - a$ is a factor of a polynomial $p(x)$, which statement *must* be true?

F. $x + a$ is a factor of $p(x)$.

G. $p(a) = 1$

H. If $p(x)$ is divided by $x - a$, the remainder is 0.

J. If $p(x)$ is divided by $x - a$, the remainder is a.

7. Which factorization can you use to find the zeros of $f(x) = x^2 + 9$?

A. $(x + 3)(x - 3)$

B. $(x + 3i)(x - 3i)$

C. $(x + 3)(x + 3)$

D. $(x + 3i)(x + 3i)$

8. Which could be the rule for the function $f(x)$ whose graph is below?

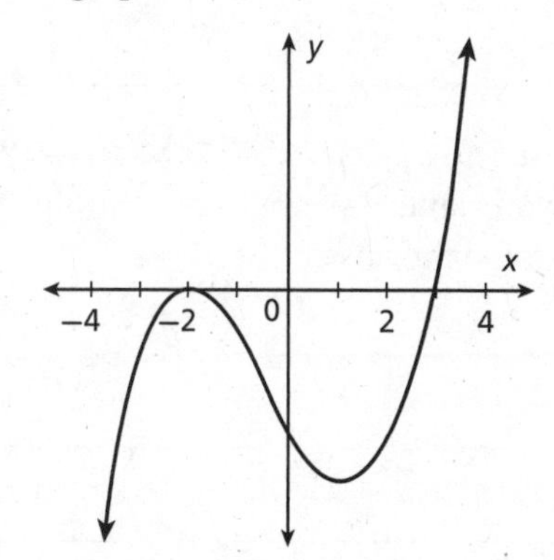

F. $f(x) = 2x^3 - 2x^2 - 16x + 24$

G. $f(x) = 2x^3 + 2x^2 - 16x - 24$

H. $f(x) = 2x^3 + 16x^2 + 42x + 36$

J. $f(x) = 2x^3 - 16x^2 + 42x - 36$

CONSTRUCTED RESPONSE

9. Morgan is considering two job offers. If she takes job A, she will earn \$3600 in her first month and then will get a 0.5% raise every month for 2 years. If she takes job B, she will earn \$3800 per month to start and will get a 1% raise at the end of every 3-month interval for 2 years. Which job will pay more during the first 2 years? Justify your answer.

10. Given the functions $p(x) = 3x^3 - 4x^2 + 7$ and $q(x) = 4x + 10 + 4x^2$, find $p(x) + q(x)$ and $p(x) - q(x)$.

11. Is -6 a zero of $f(x) = x^3 - 5x^2 - 8x + 12$? Show how you can use synthetic substitution to determine the answer.

For Items 12–15, use the figure and the information below.

You make a box by cutting out a square from each corner of a rectangular sheet of cardboard and folding up the flaps as shown below.

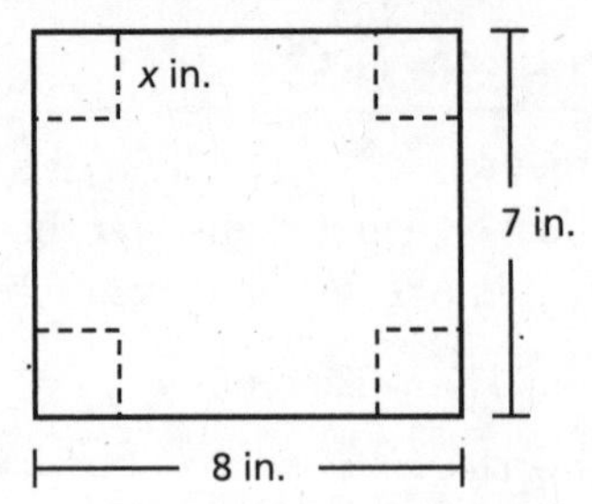

12. Write a function $V(x)$ to represent the volume of the box. Explain how you wrote $V(x)$.

13. What is the domain of $V(x)$? Justify your answer.

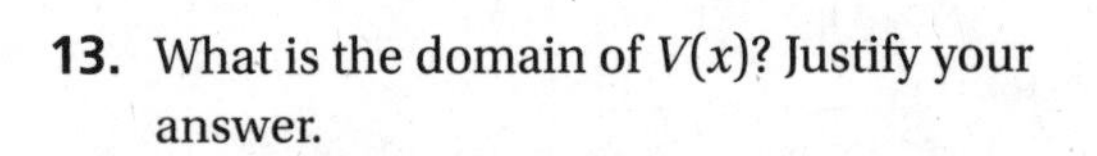

14. Write and solve an equation to find the two values of x that result in a box with a volume of 15 in.^{3} Use your calculator to help you solve the equation.

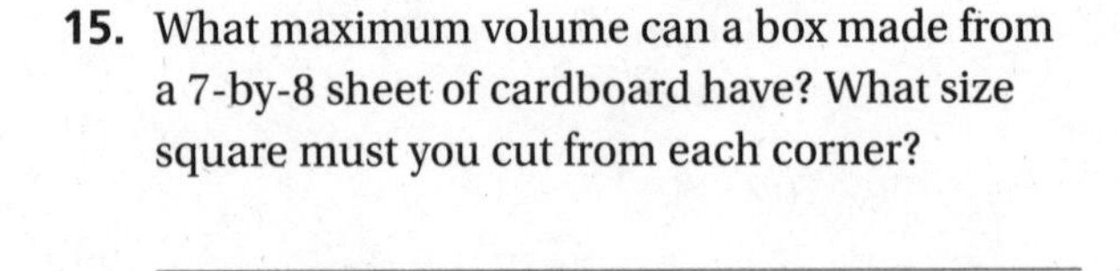

15. What maximum volume can a box made from a 7-by-8 sheet of cardboard have? What size square must you cut from each corner?

Rational and Radical Relationships

Module 13 Rational Functions

13-1	Variation Functions	MCC9-12.A.CED.2, MCC9-12.F.IF.4
13-2	Multiplying and Dividing Rational Expressions	MCC9-12.A.APR.6, MCC9-12.A.APR.7(+)
13-3	Adding and Subtracting Rational Expressions	MCC9-12.A.APR.6, MCC9-12.A.APR.7(+)
13-4	Rational Functions	MCC9-12.F.IF.4, MCC9-12.F.IF.7d(+)
13-5	Solving Rational Equations and Inequalities	MCC9-12.A.REI.2, MCC9-12.A.APR.6, MCC9-12.A.CED.1

Module 14 Radical Functions

14-1	Radical Functions	MCC9-12.F.IF.4, MCC9-12.F.IF.7b
14-2	Solving Radical Equations and Inequalities	MCC9-12.A.REI.2
	Performance Tasks	
	PARCC Assessment Readiness	

Unpacking the Standards

Understanding the standards and the vocabulary terms in the standards will help you know exactly what you are expected to learn in this unit.

MCC9-12.A.APR.7(+)

Understand that rational expressions form a system analogous to the rational numbers, closed under addition, subtraction, multiplication, and division by a nonzero rational expression; add, subtract, multiply, and divide rational expressions.

Key Vocabulary

rational expression *(expresión racional)* An algebraic expression whose numerator and denominator are polynomials and whose denominator is not 0.

closure *(cerradura)* A set of numbers is said to be closed, or have closure, under a given operation if the result of the operation on any two numbers in the set is also in the set.

What It Means For You

You can use the same operations and properties with rational expressions as with fractions. The results will be equivalent rational expressions.

EXAMPLE

Marcia plans to run for 40 minutes. She will run 20 minutes at a pace of x minutes per mile, and 20 minutes at a faster pace of $x - 1$ minutes per mile. The total distance she runs is the sum of the distances for each 20 minutes.

$$\frac{20}{x} + \frac{20}{x-1}$$

$$\frac{20}{x}\left(\frac{x-1}{x-1}\right) + \frac{20}{x-1}\left(\frac{x}{x}\right)$$

$$\frac{40x - 20}{x(x-1)}$$

If Marcia runs the first 20 minutes at 9 minutes per mile $(x = 9)$, she will run a total of about 4.7 miles.

UNIT 7

MCC9-12.N.RN.2

Rewrite expressions involving radicals and rational exponents using the properties of exponents.

Key Vocabulary

radical *(radical)* An indicated root of a quantity.

rational exponent *(exponente racional)* An exponent that can be expressed as $\frac{m}{n}$ such that if m and n are integers, then $b^{\frac{m}{n}} = \sqrt[n]{b^m} = \left(\sqrt[n]{b}\right)^m$.

What It Means For You

You can rewrite radical expressions using rational exponents. This lets you use the properties of exponents to simplify radical expressions.

EXAMPLE

$\sqrt[4]{10^3} \cdot \sqrt[4]{10^5} = 10^{\frac{3}{4}} \cdot 10^{\frac{5}{4}}$ $\sqrt[n]{a^m} = a^{\frac{m}{n}}$

$= 10^{\frac{3+5}{4}}$ *Product of powers*

$= 10^2$, or 100   *Simplify.*

GPS COMMON CORE **MCC9-12.F.IF.7**

Graph functions expressed symbolically and show key features of the graph…

Key Vocabulary

rational function *(función racional)* A function whose rule can be written as a rational expression.

zero of a function *(cero de una función)* For the function f, any number x such that $f(x) = 0$.

asymptote *(asíntota)* A line that a graph approaches as the value of a variable becomes extremely large or small.

square-root function *(función de raíz cuadrada)* A function of the form $f(x) = a\sqrt{x - h} + k$ where a, h, and k are constants and $a \neq 0$.

cube-root function *(función de raíz cúbica)* A function of the form $f(x) = a\sqrt[3]{x - h} + k$ where a, h, and k are constants and $a \neq 0$.

What It Means For You

There are many different ways to sketch the graph of a function besides making a table of values. Factoring can help you sketch the graph of a rational function. Using parent functions can help you sketch the graphs of square-root and cube-root functions.

EXAMPLE **Graphing a Rational Function**

Consider $f(x) = \dfrac{2x^2 - 2}{x^2 - 4} = \dfrac{2(x+1)(x-1)}{(x+2)(x-2)}$.

The factors in the numerator indicate the zeros.

The factors in the denominator indicate the vertical asymptotes.

The ratio of the leading coefficients of the numerator and denominator, 2, indicates a horizontal asymptote.

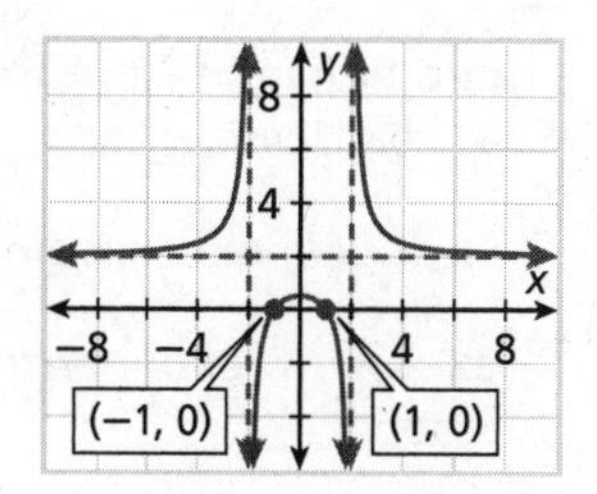

EXAMPLE **Graphing a Square Root Function**

The graph shows $f(x) = \sqrt{x}$ and $g(x) = 3\sqrt{x}$. Graph g is a vertical stretch of graph f by a factor of 3. Because the square root of a negative number is imaginary, the domain of each function is the nonnegative real numbers.

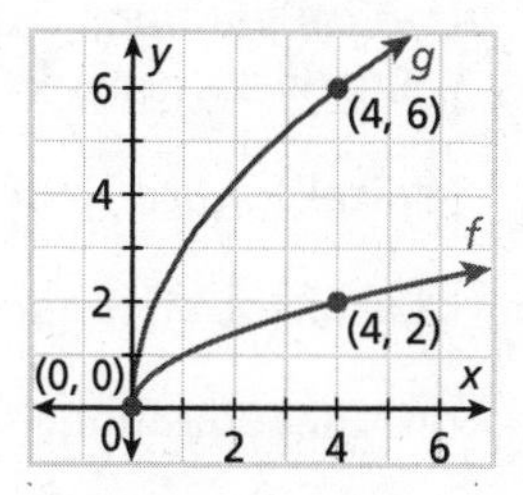

UNIT 7

MCC9-12.A.REI.2

Solve simple rational and radical equations… showing how extraneous solutions may arise.

Key Vocabulary

rational equation *(ecuación racional)* An equation that contains one or more rational expressions.

radical equation *(ecuación radical)* An equation that contains a variable within a radical.

extraneous solution *(solución extraña)* A solution of a derived equation that is not a solution of the original equation.

What It Means For You

When you solve rational or radical equations, you need to check your answers to be sure they are actually solutions.

EXAMPLE

$$\frac{2}{x-3} + \frac{1}{x} = \frac{x-1}{x-3} \qquad \textit{Given equation}$$

$$\left(\frac{2}{x-3} + \frac{1}{x}\right) \cdot x(x-3) = \left(\frac{x-1}{x-3}\right) \cdot x\,(x-3) \qquad \textit{Multiply by LCD.}$$

Simplifying gives $x^2 - 4x + 3 = 0$, which has solutions 3 and 1. However, 3 makes two of the original denominators 0, so it is an *extraneous solution*, and the only solution is 1.

Key Vocabulary

asymptote *(asíntota)* A line that a graph approaches as the value of a variable becomes extremely large or small.

branch of a hyperbola *(rama de una hipérbola)* One of the two symmetrical parts of the hyperbola.

closure *(cerradura)* A set of numbers is said to be closed, or have closure, under a given operation if the result of the operation on any two numbers in the set is also in the set.

cube-root function *(función de raíz cúbica)* A function of the form $f(x) = a\sqrt[3]{x-h} + k$ where a, h, and k are constants and $a \neq 0$.

end behavior *(comportamiento extremo)* The trends in the y-values of a function as the x-values approach positive and negative infinity.

excluded values *(valores excluidos)* Values of x for which a function or expression is not defined.

exponent *(exponente)* The number that indicates how many times the base in a power is used as a factor.

extraneous solution *(solución extraña)* A solution of a derived equation that is not a solution of the original equation.

UNIT 7

inverse variation *(variación inversa)* A relationship between two variables, x and y, that can be written in the form $y = \frac{k}{x}$, where k is a nonzero constant and $x \neq 0$.

radical *(radical)* An indicated root of a quantity.

radical equation *(ecuación radical)* An equation that contains a variable within a radical.

rational equation *(ecuación racional)* An equation that contains one or more rational expressions.

rational exponent *(exponente racional)* An exponent that can be expressed as $\frac{m}{n}$ such that if m and n are integers, then $b^{\frac{m}{n}} = \sqrt[n]{b^m} = \left(\sqrt[n]{b}\right)^m$.

rational expression *(expresión racional)* An algebraic expression whose numerator and denominator are polynomials and whose denominator is not 0.

rational function *(función racional)* A function whose rule can be written as a rational expression.

square-root function *(función de raíz cuadrada)* A function of the form $f(x) = a\sqrt{x-h} + k$ where a, h, and k are constants and $a \neq 0$.

zero of a function *(cero de una función)* For the function f, any number x such that $f(x) = 0$.

Name____________________ Class__________ Date__________

13-1

Variation Functions

Going Deeper

Essential question: *What is the effect of changing the value of a on the graph of $f(x) = \frac{a}{x}$?*

MCC9–12.F.IF.7d(+)

1 ENGAGE Understanding the Parent Function $f(x) = \frac{1}{x}$

The function $f(x) = \frac{1}{x}$ is the parent function of all functions of the form $g(x) = \frac{a}{x}$. The graph of $f(x) = \frac{1}{x}$ consists of two separate curves, one in Quadrant III and one in Quadrant I, called *branches*. As you can see from the tables and graph below, the ends of the branches approach the axes, which are called the graph's *asymptotes*.

$x < 0$	
x	$f(x)$
-5	$-\frac{1}{5}$
-2	$-\frac{1}{2}$
-1	-1
$-\frac{1}{2}$	-2
$-\frac{1}{5}$	-5

$x > 0$	
x	$f(x)$
$\frac{1}{5}$	5
$\frac{1}{2}$	2
1	1
2	$\frac{1}{2}$
5	$\frac{1}{5}$

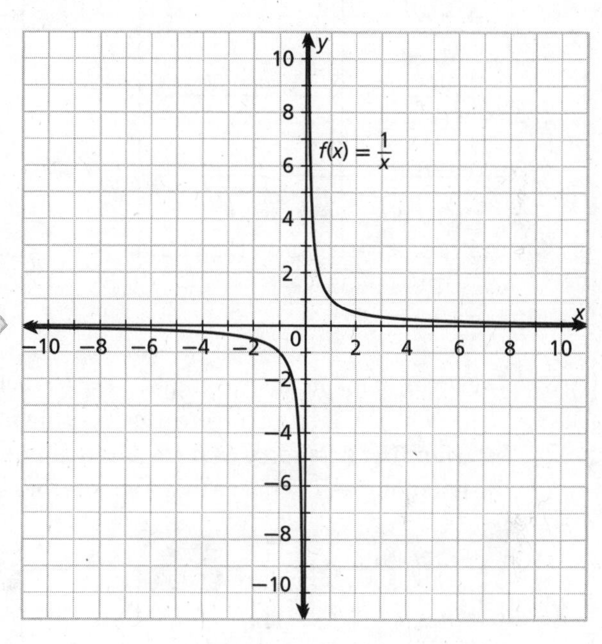

REFLECT

1a. What are the domain and range of the function?

____

1b. Is the function increasing or decreasing for $x < 0$? Is it increasing or decreasing for $x > 0$?

____

1c. If n is a nonzero number, both n and $\frac{1}{n}$ have the same sign. What does this fact tell you about the graph of the function $\frac{1}{x}$?

____

____

1d. If n is a nonzero number, then both $\left(n, \frac{1}{n}\right)$ and $\left(\frac{1}{n}, n\right)$ are points on the graph of the function. What does this fact tell you about the symmetry of the graph?

____

1e. The function's *end behavior* is determined by what happens to the value of $f(x)$ as the value of x increases or decreases without bound. The notation $x \to +\infty$, which is read "x approaches positive infinity," means that x is increasing without bound, while the notation $x \to -\infty$, which is read "x approaches negative infinity," means that x is decreasing without bound. Complete each table and then describe the function's end behavior.

x **increases without bound.**	
x	$f(x) = \frac{1}{x}$
100	
1000	
10,000	
100,000	

x **decreases without bound.**	
x	$f(x) = \frac{1}{x}$
−100	
−1000	
−10,000	
−100,000	

As $x \to +\infty$, $f(x) \to$ __________.

As $x \to -\infty$, $f(x) \to$ __________.

1f. The break in the function's graph at $x = 0$ is called an *infinite discontinuity*. To see why this is so, complete each table and then describe the function's behavior. The notation $x \to 0^+$ means that x approaches 0 from the right, while the notation $x \to 0^-$ means that x approaches 0 from the left.

x **approaches 0 from the right.**	
x	$f(x) = \frac{1}{x}$
0.01	
0.001	
0.0001	
0.00001	

x **approaches 0 from the left.**	
x	$f(x) = \frac{1}{x}$
−0.01	
−0.001	
−0.0001	
−0.00001	

As $x \to 0^+$, $f(x) \to$ __________.

As $x \to 0^-$, $f(x) \to$ __________.

MCC9–12.F.BF.3

2 EXAMPLE Graphing $g(x) = \frac{a}{x}$ when $a > 0$

Graph each function. (The parent function is shown in gray.)

A $g(x) = \frac{2}{x}$

$x < 0$	
x	$g(x) = \frac{2}{x}$
-4	
-2	
-1	
$-\frac{1}{2}$	

$x > 0$	
x	$g(x) = \frac{2}{x}$
$\frac{1}{2}$	
1	
2	
4	

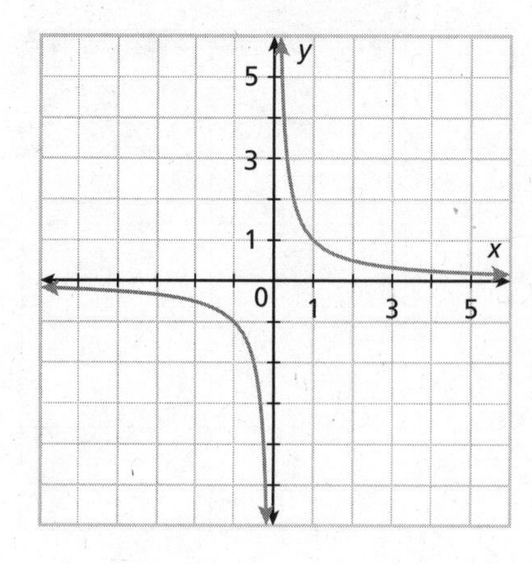

B $g(x) = \frac{0.4}{x}$

$x < 0$	
x	$g(x) = \frac{0.4}{x}$
-2	
-1	
-0.4	
-0.2	
-0.1	

$x > 0$	
x	$g(x) = \frac{0.4}{x}$
0.1	
0.2	
0.4	
1	
2	

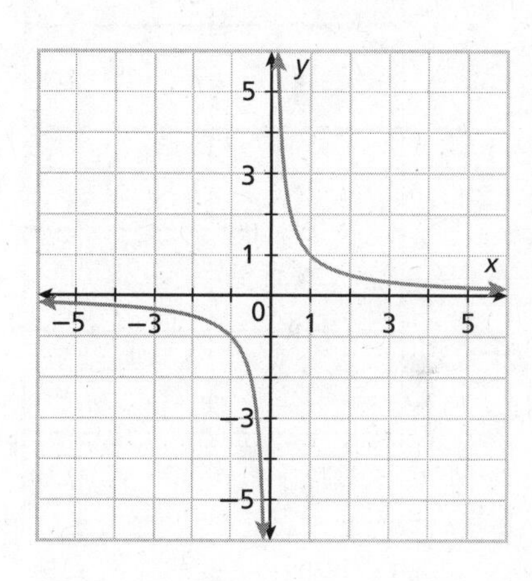

REFLECT

2a. You can obtain the graph of $g(x) = \frac{a}{x}$ from the graph of $f(x) = \frac{1}{x}$ by vertically stretching or shrinking it. Use this fact to complete the table.

Value of a in $g(x) = \frac{a}{x}$	Vertical stretch or shrink of the graph of f?
$a > 1$	
$0 < a < 1$	

MCC9–12.F.BF.3

3 EXAMPLE Graphing $g(x) = \frac{a}{x}$ when $a < 0$

Graph each function. (The parent function is shown in gray.)

A $g(x) = -\frac{2}{x}$

$x < 0$	
x	$g(x) = -\frac{2}{x}$
–4	
–2	
–1	
$-\frac{1}{2}$	

$x > 0$	
x	$g(x) = -\frac{2}{x}$
$\frac{1}{2}$	
1	
2	
4	

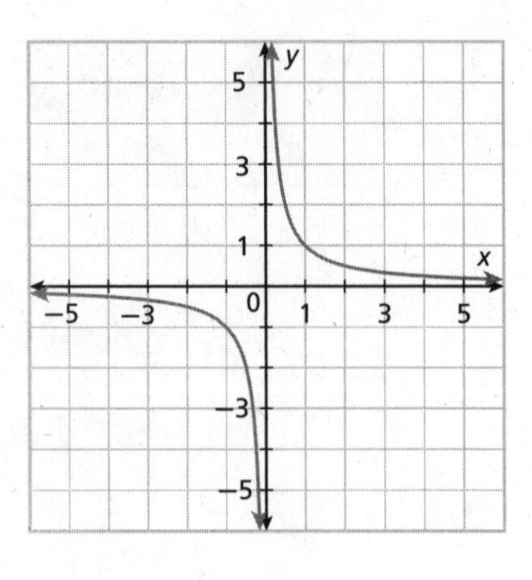

B $g(x) = -\frac{0.4}{x}$

$x < 0$	
x	$g(x) = -\frac{0.4}{x}$
–2	
–1	
–0.4	
–0.2	
–0.1	

$x > 0$	
x	$g(x) = -\frac{0.4}{x}$
0.1	
0.2	
0.4	
1	
2	

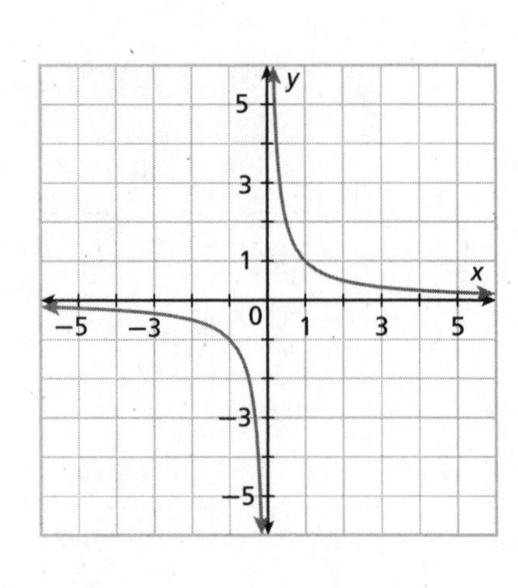

REFLECT

3a. Use the table below to summarize your comparisons of the graph of $g(x) = \frac{a}{x}$ with the graph of $f(x) = \frac{1}{x}$ for the given values of a.

Value of a in $g(x) = \frac{a}{x}$	Vertical stretch or shrink of the graph of f?	Also a reflection across the x-axis?
$a > 1$		
$0 < a < 1$		
$-1 < a < 0$		
$a < -1$		

Inverse Variation When the relationship between two real-world quantities x and y has the form $y = \frac{a}{x}$ for some nonzero constant a, the relationship is called *inverse variation* and y is said to *vary inversely* as x.

4 EXAMPLE Writing and Graphing an Equation for Inverse Variation

Mrs. Jacobs drives 30 miles to her job in the city. Her commuting time depends on her average speed, which varies from day to day as a result of weather and traffic conditions. Write and graph an equation that gives her commuting time as a function of her average speed.

A Use the formula $d = rt$ where d is distance, r is rate (average speed), and t is time to write t as a function of r given that $d = 30$.

$rt =$ ___ The product of rate and time gives distance.

$t = \frac{\quad}{r}$ Solve for t.

B Use the table to help you graph the function $t(r)$.

r	$t(r)$
10	
15	
30	
60	

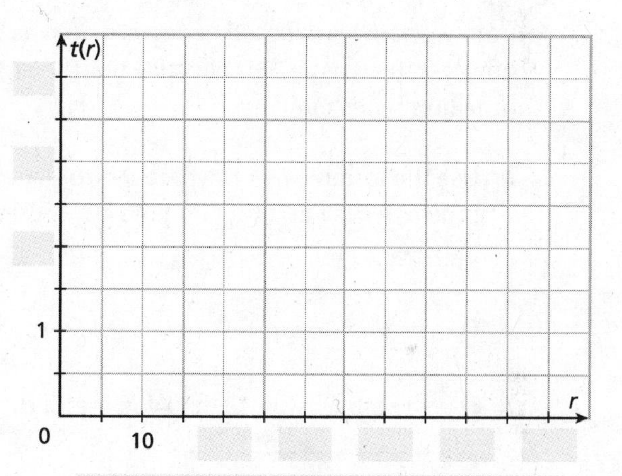

REFLECT

4a. Why does the graph consist only of the branch in Quadrant I?

____

4b. Do equal changes in average speed result in equal changes in commuting time? Give an example to support your answer.

____

____

PRACTICE

For each function, plot the points at which $x = \pm 1$, then draw the complete graph.

1. $f(x) = \frac{0.3}{x}$

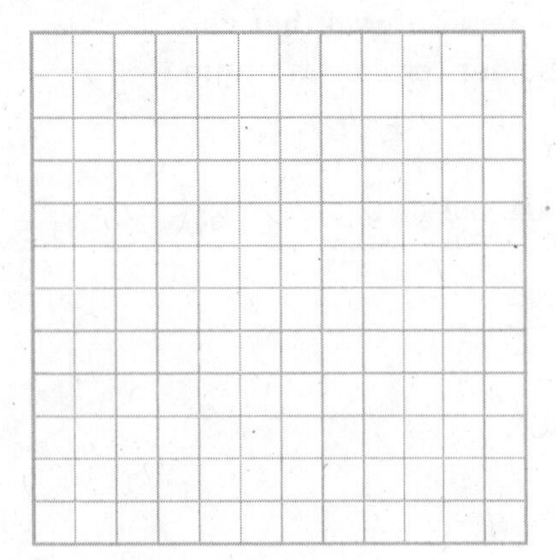

2. $f(x) = -\frac{4}{x}$

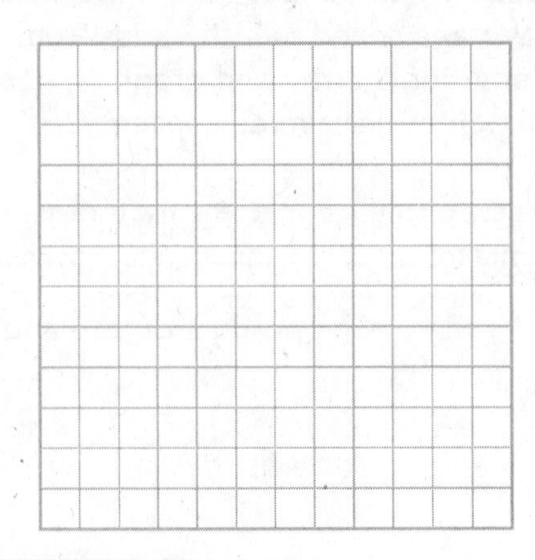

3. Shaun is paid $20 each week to mow a lawn. The time he spends mowing varies from week to week based on factors such as how much the grass has grown and how wet the grass is. His effective hourly pay rate is therefore a function of the time he spends mowing.

a. Use the formula $p = rt$ where p is total pay, r is hourly pay rate, and t is time to write r as a function of t given that $p = 20$. Describe the relationship between r and t.

____

b. Use the table below to help you graph the function $r(t)$.

t	$r(t)$
0.5	
1	
2	
2.5	

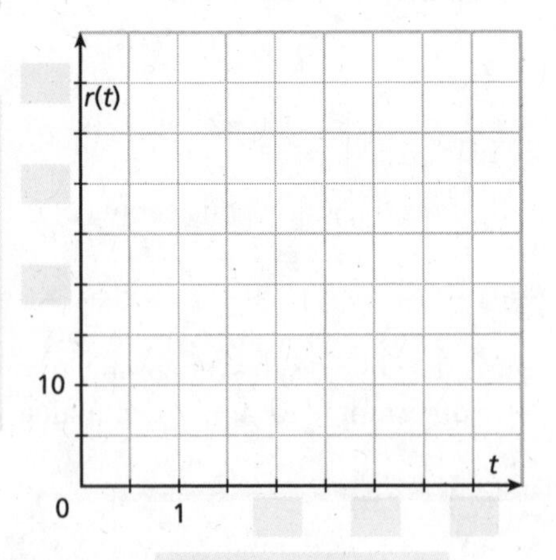

Name ______________________ Class ____________ Date ____________

13-1

Additional Practice

Graph each function.

1. $y = -\dfrac{5}{x}$

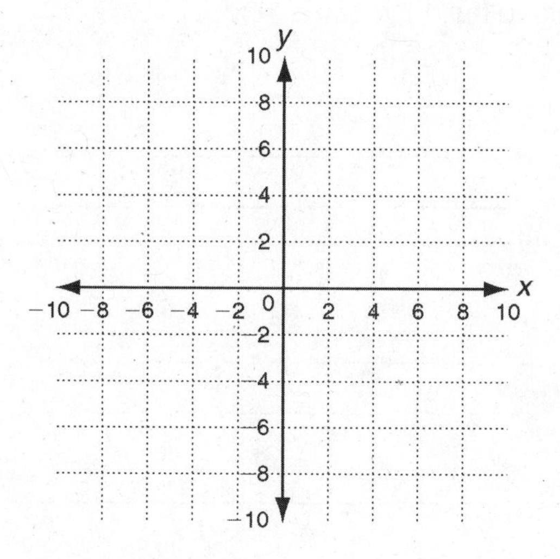

2. $y = \dfrac{15}{x}$

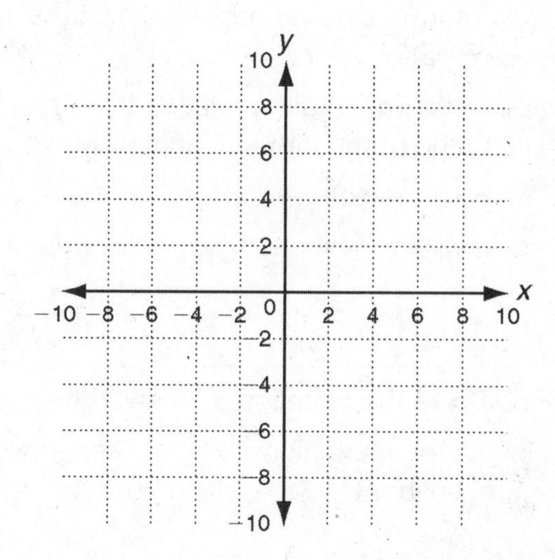

3. $y = \dfrac{2}{x}$

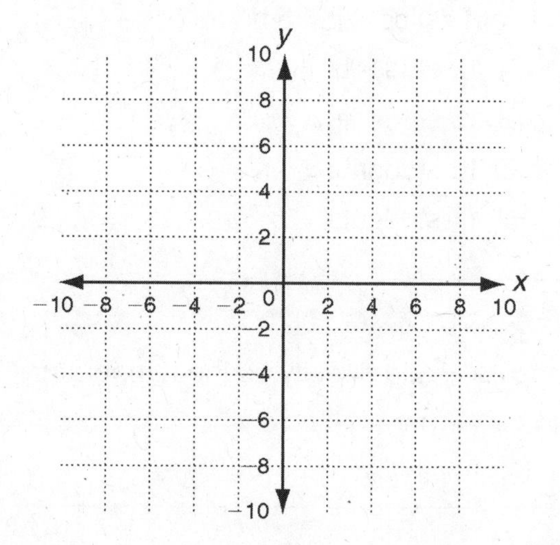

4. $y = \dfrac{4}{x}$

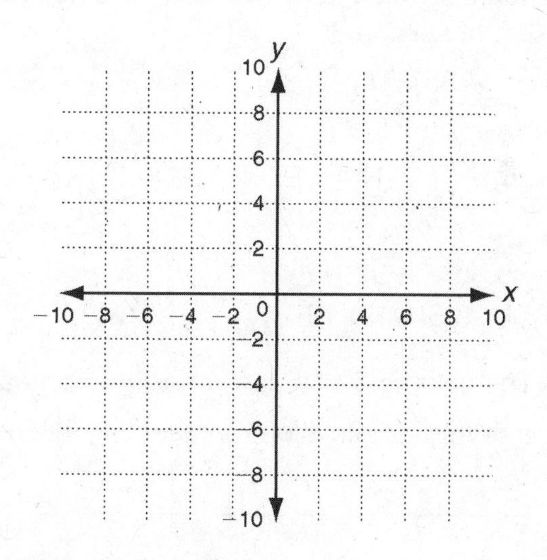

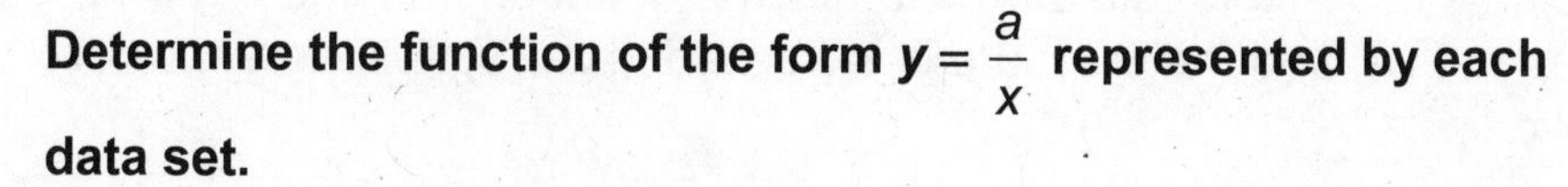

Determine the function of the form $y = \dfrac{a}{x}$ represented by each data set.

5.

x	2	3	4
y	8	12	16

____

6.

x	3	1	0.5
y	5	15	30

____

Problem Solving

Last semester five of Mr. Dewayne's students built a 7-foot sailboat in 195 working hours. The time, *t*, that it takes for a group of students to build a sailboat varies inversely as the number of students. Mr. Dewayne uses this data to plan activities for next semester.

1. How many working hours would it take 12 students to build the same kind of sailboat?
   a. Write an equation relating the time required to the number of students working. ________________
   b. Find the constant k. ________________
   c. Explain the meaning of k in terms of student hours.

   ____

   d. Solve the equation to answer the question. ________________
2. How many students would be needed to build a 7-foot sailboat in 75 working hours? ________________

Choose the letter for the best answer.

3. Which equation represents the number of hours it would take 15 students to build a 7-foot sailboat?

   A $\frac{195}{5} = \frac{t}{15}$

   B $\frac{t}{195} = \frac{15}{5}$

   C $(195)(5) = 15t$

   D $195t = (5)(15)$

4. How many students must Mr. Dewayne get to participate in order to build a 7-foot sailboat in 65 hours?

   A 14 students

   B 15 students

   C 16 students

   D 17 students

5. The volume V of a gas varies inversely as the pressure P and directly as the temperature T.
   a. Write an equation representing this relationship.

   ____

   b. A certain gas has a volume of 10 liters and a pressure of 1.5 atmospheres. If the gas is held at a constant temperature, and the pressure is increased to 3.5 atmospheres, what volume will the gas take up?

   ____

Name________________________ Class______________ Date__________

13-2

Multiplying and Dividing Rational Expressions

Going Deeper

Video Tutor

Essential question: *How do you find products and quotients of rational expressions?*

MCC9–12.A.APR.7(+)

1 EXAMPLE Multiplying Rational Expressions

Find the product: $\frac{5x}{x^2 + x - 2} \cdot \frac{3x - 3}{x^2 + 3x}$

$$\frac{5x}{x^2 + x - 2} \cdot \frac{3x - 3}{x^2 + 3x} = \frac{5x}{(x + 2)(\quad)} \cdot \frac{3(\quad)}{x(\quad)}$$

Factor each numerator and denominator, if possible.

$$= \frac{15x(\quad)}{x(x + 2)(\quad)(\quad)}$$

Multiply the numerators, and multiply the denominators.

$$= \frac{15}{(x + 2)(\quad)}$$

Simplify the product by dividing out any common factors in the numerator and the denominator.

REFLECT

1a. As a check on your work, show that $\frac{5x}{x^2 + x - 2} \cdot \frac{3x - 3}{x^2 + 3x}$ and the simplified expression for the product have the same value when $x = 2$.

____

1b. Suppose you decide to check your work by showing that the two expressions have the same value when $x = 0$. Describe what happens, and explain why it happens.

____

____

____

1c. The *excluded values* for a rational expression are any values of the variable for which the expression is undefined. Also, two expressions are *equivalent expressions* provided they have the same value for every value of the variable unless they are both undefined for that value of the variable. In order for the simplified expression for the product to be equivalent to $\frac{5x}{x^2 + x - 2} \cdot \frac{3x - 3}{x^2 + 3x}$, what excluded values must it have?

____

MCC9–12.A.APR.7(+)

2 EXAMPLE Dividing Rational Expressions

Find the quotient: $\frac{x-6}{x^2+2x-24} \div \frac{x^2-36}{x^2-4x}$

$$\frac{x-6}{x^2+2x-24} \div \frac{x^2-36}{x^2-4x} = \frac{x-6}{x^2+2x-24} \cdot \frac{x^2-4x}{\square}$$

Multiply by the reciprocal.

$$= \frac{x-6}{(x-4)(\square)} \cdot \frac{x(\square)}{(\square)(\square)}$$

Factor numerators and denominators.

$$= \frac{x(x-6)(\square)}{(x-4)(\square)(\square)(\square)}$$

Multiply the expressions.

$$= \frac{x}{(\square)^2}$$

Simplify.

REFLECT

2a. What are the excluded values for the simplified expression for the quotient?

____

2b. As a check on your work, show that $\frac{x-6}{x^2+2x-24} \div \frac{x^2-36}{x^2-4x}$ and the simplified expression for the quotient have the same value when $x = 1$.

____

MCC9–12.F.BF.1b

3 EXAMPLE Modeling with a Quotient of Rational Expressions

The expression $\frac{35E-125}{E(E-5)}$ represents the total gas consumed (in gallons) when Mr. Garcia drives 25 miles on a highway and 10 miles in a city to get to work. In the expression, *E* represents the fuel efficiency (in miles per gallon) of Mr. Garcia's car at highway speeds. Use the expression to find the average rate of gas consumed on the trip.

A Find the total distance that Mr. Garcia drives. ______________________________

B Use the verbal model to write an expression involving division for the average rate of gas consumed.

Average rate of gas consumed	=	Total gas consumed	÷	Total distance traveled

____

C Carry out the division to get a combined expression for the average rate of gas consumed.

REFLECT

3a. What unit of measurement applies to the expression for the average rate of gas consumed? Explain.

3b. Mr. Garcia's car has a highway fuel efficiency of E miles per gallon and a city fuel efficiency of $(E - 5)$ miles per gallon. If the distances driven on the highway and in the city are equal, then the average rate of gas consumed is given by $\left(\frac{1}{E} + \frac{1}{E-5}\right) \div 2 = \frac{E-5}{E(E-5)} + \frac{E}{E(E-5)}$. Carry out the operations in this expression to get a combined expression for the average rate of gas consumed. (Remember that to add two fractions with a common denominator, you keep the denominator and add the numerators.)

3c. Suppose Mr. Garcia drives 10 miles on a highway and 10 miles in a city to get to work. The combined expression for the total gas consumed is $\frac{10}{E} + \frac{10}{E-5}$, or $\frac{10(E-5)}{E(E-5)} + \frac{10E}{E(E-5)}$. Simplify the expression and then divide it by the total distance traveled to get a combined expression for the average rate of gas consumed. Compare this result with the one in the previous Reflect question.

3d. Show that $\left(\frac{d_1(E-5)}{E(E-5)} + \frac{d_2E}{E(E-5)}\right) \div (d_1 + d_2) = \frac{2E-5}{2E(E-5)}$ when $d_1 = d_2$ but not when $d_1 \neq d_2$.

PRACTICE

Find each product or quotient. State all excluded values.

1. $\frac{4x}{x-3} \cdot \frac{3x-9}{x^2}$

2. $\frac{3x+15}{x-2} \cdot \frac{7x-14}{x^2+5x}$

3. $\frac{x+1}{x^2+7x-8} \cdot \frac{x-1}{5x+5}$

4. $\frac{x^2+5x+6}{x^2-x+2} \cdot \frac{2x^2+8x+6}{x^2-3x-10}$

5. $\frac{5}{x^2-2x} \div \frac{3x}{x-2}$

6. $\frac{7x-21}{x^2+7x} \div \frac{x-3}{x^2-5x}$

7. $\frac{x^2+5x-6}{4x} \div \frac{x+6}{x^2-x}$

8. $\frac{x^2+5x+4}{x^2+4x} \div \frac{x^2-2x+1}{x^2-1}$

9. On his trip to work, Mr. Garcia drives at a speed of s miles per hour on the highway and $(s-30)$ miles per hour in the city. Recall that the distances he drives are 25 miles on the highway and 10 miles in the city.

a. Write an expression for the time that he spends driving on the highway and the time that he spends driving in the city.

b. His total time can be represented by the sum $\frac{25(s-30)}{s(s-30)} + \frac{10s}{s(s-30)}$ Rewrite this sum as a combined expression.

c. Find his average speed on the trip by dividing the total distance that he travels by the total time. Write the average speed as a quotient and then carry out the division.

Name ____________________ Class ____________ Date __________ 13-2

Additional Practice

Simplify. Identify any *x*-values for which the expression is undefined.

1. $\dfrac{x^2+3x+2}{x^2-3x-4}$

2. $\dfrac{4x^6}{2x^4}$

3. $\dfrac{x^2-x^3}{2x^2-5x+3}$

4. $\dfrac{x^3+x^2-20x}{x^2-16}$

5. $\dfrac{3x^2-9x-12}{6x^2+9x+3}$

6. $\dfrac{9-3x}{15-2x-x^2}$

Multiply. Assume all expressions are defined.

7. $\dfrac{4x+16}{2x+6} \bullet \dfrac{x^2+2x-3}{x+4}$

8. $\dfrac{x+3}{x-1} \bullet \dfrac{x^2-2x+1}{x^2+5x+6}$

Divide. Assume all expressions are defined.

9. $\dfrac{5x^6}{x^2y} \div \dfrac{10x^2}{y}$

10. $\dfrac{x^2-2x-8}{x^2-2x-15} \div \dfrac{2x^2-8x}{2x^2-10x}$

Solve. Check your solution.

11. $\dfrac{x^2+x-12}{x-3}=15$

12. $\dfrac{2x^2+8x-10}{2x^2+14x+20}=4$

Solve.

13. The distance, d, traveled by a car undergoing constant acceleration, a, for a time, t, is given by $d=v_0t+\dfrac{1}{2}at^2$, where v_0 is the initial velocity of the car. Two cars are side by side with the same initial velocity. One car accelerates, $a=A$, and the other car does not accelerate, $a=0$. Write an expression for the ratio of the distance traveled by the accelerating car to the distance traveled by the nonaccelerating car as a function of time.

Problem Solving

Anders designs a running field that consists of three concentric tracks as shown in the diagram.

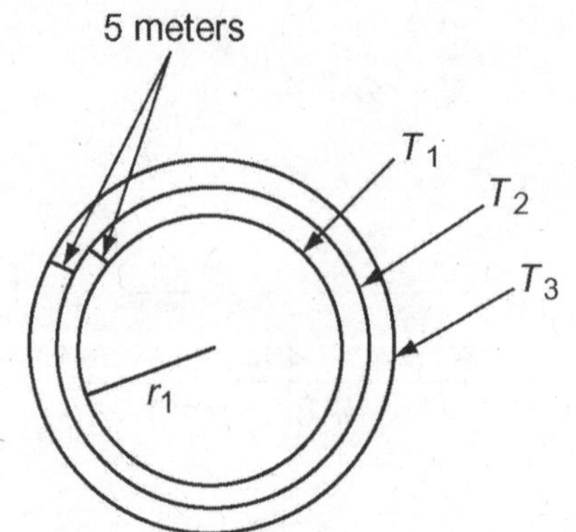

1. How do the lengths of each track compare?
   a. Write an equation for the length of the inner track, T_1, in terms of radius, r_1.

   ____

   b. Write an equation for the length of the middle track, T_2, in terms of radius r_1.

   ____

   c. Then write a rational expression for the ratio of the length of track T_2 to the length of track T_1 in terms of radius r_1. ______________________

2. Mari writes the expression $\frac{(r_1+10)(r_1-5)}{r_1^2-25}$ for the ratio of the length of the outer track, T_3, to that of the middle track, T_2. Anders thinks that is the wrong expression. Simplify Mari's expression to determine if she is correct. Explain.

   ____

   ____

3. Anders sets the radius of the inner track, T_1, at 70 meters.
   a. How many times longer is the middle track, T_2, than the inner track, T_1? ______________________
   b. How many times longer is the outer track, T_3, than the middle track, T_2? ______________________
   c. How many times longer is the outer track, T_3, than the inner track, T_1? ______________________

Choose the letter for the best answer.

4. How many times as large is the area enclosed by the outer track, T_3, than the area enclosed by the inner track, T_1?

   A $\left(\frac{10}{r_1}\right)$ B $\left(\frac{10}{r_1}\right)^2$

   C $\left(\frac{r_1+10}{r_1}\right)$ D $\left(\frac{r_1+10}{r_1}\right)^2$

5. What is the ratio of the area between the inner track and the outer track to the area enclosed by the inner track?

   A $20\left(\frac{r_1+5}{r_1^2}\right)$ B $\frac{(r_1+10)^2-1}{r_1^{\ 2}}$

   C $\pi\left(\frac{r_1+10}{r_1}\right)^2$ D $\pi\left(\frac{10}{r_1}\right)^2$

Name ________________________ Class ______________ Date __________

13-3

Adding and Subtracting Rational Expressions

Going Deeper

Video Tutor

Essential question: *How do you find sums and differences of rational expressions?*

PREP FOR MCC9-12.A.APR.7(+)

1 EXAMPLE Simplifying a Rational Expression

Simplify: $\frac{2x - 8}{x^2 - 6x + 8}$

Factor the numerator and the denominator. If there are any common factors, divide them out.

$\frac{2x - 8}{x^2 - 6x + 8} = \frac{2(\quad)}{(\quad)(x - 4)}$ Factor the numerator and the denominator.

$= \frac{2}{(\quad)}$ There is a common factor, so divide it out.

REFLECT

1a. The *excluded values* for a rational expression are any values of the variable for which the expression is undefined. What are the excluded values for $\frac{2x - 8}{x^2 - 6x + 8}$? What are the excluded values of the simplified form of this expression?

____

1b. The expression $\frac{2x - 8}{x^2 - 6x + 8}$ and its simplified form are called *equivalent expressions*. Equivalent expressions must have the same value for every value of the variable unless they are both undefined for that value of the variable. Is this true for $\frac{2x - 8}{x^2 - 6x + 8}$ and its simplified form when $x = 4$? If not, what can you do to make it true?

____

1c. Show that the expression $\frac{2x - 8}{x^2 - 6x + 8}$ and its simplified form have the same value when $x = 0$. How is this helpful? (Think about what you would know if the two expressions did *not* have the same value.)

____

1d. Error Analysis A student says that you can divide out 8 and x to simplify the expression $\frac{2x - 8}{x^2 - 6x + 8}$ as $\frac{2}{x - 6}$. Find the error in this reasoning.

____

____

MCC9–12.A.APR.7(+)

2 EXAMPLE Adding Rational Expressions

Find the sum: $\frac{x+2}{x^2+5x-6} + \frac{3}{x+6}$

$\frac{x+2}{x^2+5x-6} + \frac{3}{x+6} = \frac{x+2}{\square} + \frac{3}{x+6}$

Factor the first expression's denominator.

$= \frac{x+2}{\square} + \frac{3}{x+6} \cdot \frac{\square}{\square}$

Multiply the second expression by a form of 1 so that both expressions will have the same denominator.

$= \frac{x+2}{\square} + \frac{3(\square)}{(x+6)(\square)}$

Carry out the multiplication.

$= \frac{x+2+3(\square)}{\square}$

Now that both expressions have the same denominator, you can add the numerators.

$= \frac{\square}{\square}$

Simplify the numerator.

REFLECT

2a. As a check on your work, show that $\frac{x+2}{x^2+5x-6} + \frac{3}{x+6}$ and the expression for the sum have the same value when $x = 0$.

MCC9–12.A.APR.7(+)

3 EXAMPLE Subtracting Rational Expressions

Find the difference: $\frac{x-5}{x+2} - \frac{x+2}{x-5}$

$\frac{x-5}{x+2} - \frac{x+2}{x-5} = \frac{x-5}{x+2} \cdot \frac{\square}{\square} - \frac{x+2}{x-5} \cdot \frac{\square}{\square}$

Multiply each expression by a form of 1 so that both expressions will have the same denominator.

$= \frac{(\square)^2}{(x+2)(x-5)} - \frac{(\square)^2}{(x+2)(x-5)}$

Carry out the multiplications.

$= \frac{(\square)^2 - (\square)^2}{(x+2)(x-5)}$

Now that both expressions have the same denominator, you can subtract the numerators.

$= \frac{(\square) - (\square)}{(x+2)(x-5)}$

Square the binomials in the numerator.

$= \frac{\square}{(x+2)(x-5)}$

Simplify the numerator.

REFLECT

3a. As a check on your work, show that $\frac{x-5}{x+2} - \frac{x+2}{x-5}$ and the expression for the difference have the same value when $x = 0$.

3b. In the expression for the difference, is the numerator factorable? If so, can the expression be simplified? Explain.

MCC9–12.F.BF.1b

4 EXAMPLE Modeling with a Sum of Rational Expressions

The fuel efficiency of Mr. Garcia's car when driven at a typical highway speed is *E* miles per gallon. City driving reduces the fuel efficiency by 5 miles per gallon. Mr. Garcia drives 25 miles on a highway and 10 miles in a city to get to work. Write a rational expression that gives the total amount of gas consumed on Mr. Garcia's trip to work.

A Divide the distance traveled by the fuel efficiency to find an expression for the amount of gas consumed on each portion of the trip.

Gas consumed on highway = $\frac{\quad}{\quad}$ Gas consumed in city = $\frac{\quad}{\quad}$

B Use the verbal model to write an expression involving addition for the total gas consumed.

Total gas consumed	=	Gas consumed on highway	+	Gas consumed in city

C Carry out the addition to get a combined expression for the total gas consumed.

REFLECT

4a. Use unit analysis to show why dividing distance traveled by fuel efficiency gives the amount of gas consumed.

PRACTICE

Simplify each expression.

1. $\dfrac{2x-4}{3x-6}$

2. $\dfrac{4x+8}{8x+4}$

3. $\dfrac{2x-10}{x^2-3x-10}$

Find each sum or difference.

4. $\dfrac{x-5}{x+3}+\dfrac{x+4}{x-2}$

5. $\dfrac{3x}{2x+6}+\dfrac{x}{x^2+7x+12}$

6. $\dfrac{1}{x^2+2x+1}+\dfrac{1}{x^2-1}$

7. $\dfrac{7}{x^2-4x+4}-\dfrac{3x}{x-2}$

8. $\dfrac{x+2}{x-1}-\dfrac{x+8}{3x^2+3x-6}$

9. $\dfrac{x}{x^2-2x+1}-\dfrac{x}{x^2-1}$

10. Anita exercises by running and walking. When she runs, she burns c Calories per minute for a total of 500 Calories. When she walks, she burns $(c-8)$ Calories per minute for a total of 100 Calories.

a. Write an expression for the time that she spends running and another expression for the time that she spends walking.

b. Write two equivalent expressions for her total time.

11. a. In the second row of the table, write the result after performing the operation given in the first row of the table.

$\dfrac{x}{x+2}+\dfrac{1}{x^2-4}$	$\dfrac{x}{x+2}-\dfrac{1}{x^2-4}$	$\dfrac{x}{x+2}\cdot\dfrac{1}{x^2-4}$	$\dfrac{x}{x+2}\div\dfrac{1}{x^2-4}$

b. Do the results support or refute the claim that the set of all rational expressions is closed under all four basic operations? Explain.

c. Based on closure, what subset of real numbers is the set of rational expressions most like?

Name ________________ Class ________ Date ________

Additional Practice

Find the least common multiple for each pair.

1. $3x^2y^6$ and $5x^3y^2$

2. $x^2 + x - 2$ and $x^2 - x - 6$

Add or subtract. Identify any *x*-values for which the expression is undefined.

3. $\dfrac{2x-3}{x+4} + \dfrac{4x-5}{x+4}$

4. $\dfrac{x+12}{2x-5} - \dfrac{3x-2}{2x-5}$

5. $\dfrac{x+4}{x^2-x-12} + \dfrac{2x}{x-4}$

6. $\dfrac{3x^2-1}{x^2-3x-18} - \dfrac{x+2}{x-6}$

7. $\dfrac{x+2}{x^2-2x-15} + \dfrac{x}{x+3}$

8. $\dfrac{x+6}{x^2-7x-18} - \dfrac{2x}{x-9}$

Simplify. Assume all expressions are defined.

9. $\dfrac{\dfrac{x-1}{x+5}}{\dfrac{x+6}{x-3}}$

10. $\dfrac{\dfrac{12}{x+3}}{\dfrac{x^2+1}{x-2}}$

Solve.

11. A messenger is required to deliver 10 packages per day. Each day, the messenger works only for as long as it takes to deliver the daily quota of 10 packages. On average, the messenger is able to deliver 2 packages per hour on Saturday and 4 packages per hour on Sunday. What is the messenger's average delivery rate on the weekend?

Problem Solving

Vicki and Lorena motor downstream at about 6 knots (nautical miles per hour) in their boat. The return trip is against the current, and they can motor at only about 3 knots.

1. Vicki wants to find the average speed for the entire trip.
   a. Write an expression for the time it takes to travel downstream plus the time it takes for the return trip if the distance in each direction is *d*. ____________________
   b. What is the total distance they travel downstream and upstream in terms of *d*? ____________________
   c. Write an expression for their average speed using the expressions for the total time and the total distance. ____________________
   d. Vicki says that the average speed is 4 knots. Lorena says that the average speed is 4.5 knots. Explain who is correct and why.

   ____

2. If they delay the return trip until the current changes direction, they can motor back at 4 knots. What is the average speed for the entire trip under these conditions?

   ____

Zak runs at an average speed of 7.0 miles per hour during the first half of a race and an average speed of 5.5 miles per hour during the second half of the race. Choose the letter for the best answer.

3. Which expression gives Zak's average speed for the entire race?

   A $\frac{(7+5.5)}{2}$

   B $\frac{12.5(7+5.5)d}{2}$

   C $\frac{(38.5)d}{(7+5.5)}$

   D $\frac{2(38.5)d}{(7+5.5)d}$

4. If Zak runs the race in 1.25 hours, what is the length of the race in miles?

   A 3.85
   B 6.25
   C 7.7
   D 12.5

5. In a later race, Zak increased his average speed during the second half of the race to 6.0 miles per hour. What is his average speed for this race in miles per hour?

   A 6.42
   B 6.46
   C 6.52
   D 6.56

6. It took Zak 1.6 hours to run this later race. What is the length of this race in miles?

   A 5.17
   B 7.28
   C 9.55
   D 10.34

Name ______________________ Class ______________ Date ________

13-4

Rational Functions

Extension: Translating the Graph of $g(x) = \frac{a}{x}$

Essential question: *How does changing the values of the parameters affect the graph of more complicated rational functions?*

Video Tutor

You have seen that the graphs of functions of the form $g(x) = \frac{a}{x}$ are vertical stretches or shrinks, coupled with a reflection in the x-axis when $a < 0$, of the graph of the parent function $f(x) = \frac{1}{x}$. In this lesson, you will learn how the graphs of more complicated rational functions are related to the graph of the parent function.

MCC9–12.F.IF.7d(+)

1 EXAMPLE Graphing $s(x) = \frac{a}{x-h} + k$ when $a = 1$

Graph the function $s(x) = \frac{1}{x-3} + 2$.

A Determine the graph's horizontal asymptote. You know from examining the end behavior of the parent function that its graph has the x-axis as a horizontal asymptote. Now consider the end behavior of the given function.

x increases without bound.	
x	$s(x) = \frac{1}{x-3} + 2$
103	
1003	
10,003	
100,003	

x decreases without bound.	
x	$s(x) = \frac{1}{x-3} + 2$
−97	
−997	
−9997	
−99,997	

As $x \to +\infty$, $s(x) \to$ __________.

As $x \to -\infty$, $s(x) \to$ __________.

So, the graph's horizontal asymptote is the line __________.

B Determine the graph's vertical asymptote. You know that the parent function is undefined when $x = 0$. You also know from examining the behavior of the parent function near $x = 0$ that the graph has the y-axis as a vertical asymptote.

For what value of x is the given function undefined? __________

Complete the tables below to show that the graph's vertical asymptote is the line $x = 3$.

x approaches 3 from the right.	
x	$s(x) = \frac{1}{x-3} + 2$
3.01	
3.001	
3.0001	
3.00001	

x approaches 3 from the left.	
x	$s(x) = \frac{1}{x-3} + 2$
2.99	
2.999	
2.9999	
2.99999	

As $x \to 3^+$, $s(x) \to$ ________.

As $x \to 3^-$, $s(x) \to$ ________.

C Identify the coordinates of two reference points. You know that one branch of the graph of the parent function $f(x) = \frac{1}{x}$ includes the point (1, 1) while the other branch includes the point (−1, −1). These points are 1 unit to the right and 1 unit to the left of the vertical asymptote. What are the corresponding points on the graph of $s(x) = \frac{1}{x-3} + 2$?

____

D Draw the graph by first drawing the horizontal and vertical asymptotes as dashed lines and then plotting the reference points. Each branch of the graph should pass through one of the reference points and approach the asymptotes. (The graph of the parent function is shown in gray.)

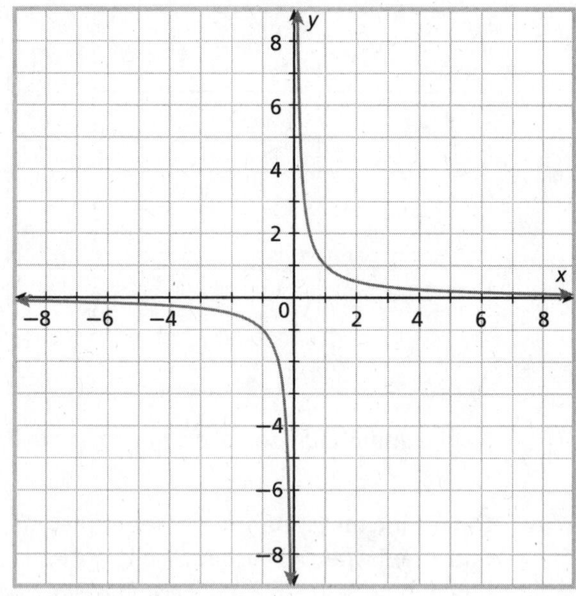

REFLECT

1a. Describe how to graph $s(x) = \frac{1}{x-3} + 2$ as a transformation of the graph of $f(x) = \frac{1}{x}$.

____

____

1b. What are the domain and range of the function $s(x) = \frac{1}{x-3} + 2$?

____

You have seen how to graph $s(x) = \frac{a}{x-h} + k$ when $a = 1$. The method is the same when $a \neq 1$, except that you translate the graph of $g(x) = \frac{a}{x}$ rather than the graph of $f(x) = \frac{1}{x}$.

MCC9–12.F.IF.7d(+)

2 EXAMPLE Graphing $s(x) = \frac{a}{x-h} + k$ when $a \neq 1$

Graph the function $s(x) = \frac{3}{x+2} + 1$.

A Identify the graph's horizontal asymptote. ______________

B Identify the graph's vertical asymptote. ______________

C Identify the coordinates of two reference points. You know that one branch of the graph of $g(x) = \frac{3}{x}$ includes the point (1, 3) while the other branch includes the point (−1, −3). These points are 1 unit to the right and 1 unit to the left of the vertical asymptote. What are the coordinates of the corresponding points on the graph of $s(x) = \frac{3}{x+2} + 1$?

____

D Draw the graph by first drawing the horizontal and vertical asymptotes as dashed lines and then plotting the reference points. Each branch of the graph should pass through one of the reference points and approach the asymptotes. (The graph of $g(x) = \frac{3}{x}$ is shown in gray.)

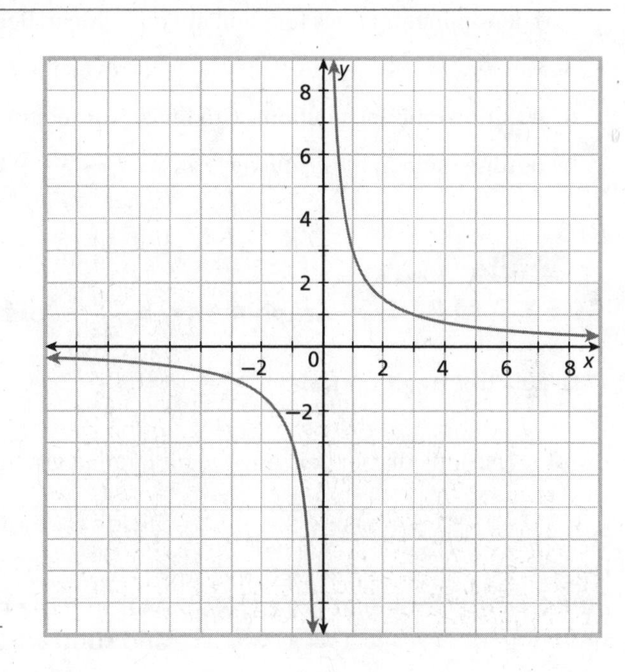

REFLECT

2a. Describe how to graph $s(x) = \frac{3}{x+2} + 1$ as a transformation of the graph of $f(x) = \frac{1}{x}$.

____

____

____

____

2b. Complete the table to summarize the characteristics of the graphs of the functions listed there.

	$f(x) = \frac{1}{x}$	$g(x) = \frac{a}{x}$	$s(x) = \frac{a}{x-h} + k$
Horizontal Asymptote	$y = 0$	$y = 0$	$y =$
Vertical Asymptote	$x = 0$	$x = 0$	$x =$
Reference Points	(1, 1), (−1, −1)	(1, a), (−1, −a)	(1 + ___, a + ___), (−1 + ___, −a + ___)

A **rational function** has the form $f(x) = \frac{p(x)}{q(x)}$ where $p(x)$ and $q(x)$ are polynomial functions and $q(x) \neq 0$. The functions that you have learned to graph are rational functions because they can be written as the ratio of two polynomials. For instance, you can write $f(x) = \frac{2}{x+1} + 3$ as $f(x) = \frac{2}{x+1} + 3 = \frac{2}{x+1} + \frac{3(x+1)}{x+1} = \frac{3x+5}{x+1}$. Notice that the numerator and denominator of this function are both linear. Because the process of writing $f(x) = \frac{a}{x-h} + k$ as $f(x) = \frac{bx+c}{dx+e}$ is reversible, you have a means of graphing rational functions with linear numerators and denominators by putting them in the *graphing form* $f(x) = \frac{a}{x-h} + k$.

MCC9–12.F.IF.7d(+)

3 EXAMPLE Graphing $f(x) = \frac{bx+c}{dx+e}$ when $d = 1$

Graph the function $f(x) = \frac{3x+2}{x-1}$.

A Use long division to write the function in graphing form.

$$x - 1\overline{)3x + 2} \quad \text{quotient } 3$$

Divide $3x$ by x and write down the quotient, 3.

$$\begin{array}{r} 3 \\ x-1\overline{)3x+2} \\ 3x-3 \\ \hline 5 \end{array}$$

Multiply the divisor, $x - 1$, by the quotient and subtract the result from the dividend, $3x + 2$, to get the remainder, 5.

So, the division of $3x + 2$ by $x - 1$ results in a quotient of 3 with a remainder of 5. Use the relationship below to rewrite the function's rule.

$$\frac{\text{dividend}}{\text{divisor}} = \text{quotient} + \frac{\text{remainder}}{\text{divisor}}$$

$$\frac{3x+2}{x-1} = \square + \frac{\square}{x-1}$$

Write the function in graphing form: ______________

B Use the graphing form to complete the information below about the graph. Then graph the function.

- Horizontal asymptote: ________
- Vertical asymptote: ________
- Reference point that is 1 unit to the right of the vertical asymptote: ________
- Reference point that is 1 unit to the left of the vertical asymptote: ________

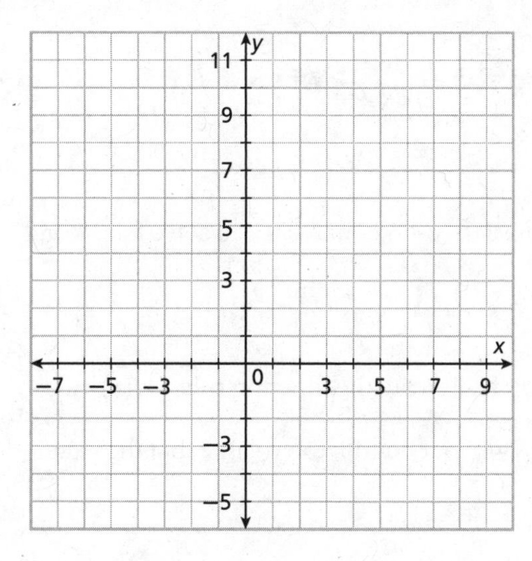

REFLECT

3a. Describe how you can find the vertical asymptote of the graph of $f(x) = \frac{3x + 2}{x - 1}$ without writing the function in graphing form first.

3b. If you divide the numerator and denominator of $f(x) = \frac{3x + 2}{x - 1}$ by x, you get $f(x) = \frac{3 + \frac{2}{x}}{1 - \frac{1}{x}}$. Use this form of the function to complete the table.

	The numerator approaches this value.	The denominator approaches this value.	The function approaches this value.
As *x* increases without bound			
As *x* decreases without bound			

3c. What does the table above tell you about the graph of the function?

The Reflect questions on the previous page suggest another way to find the asymptotes of the graph of $f(x) = \frac{bx + c}{dx + e}$:

- To find the vertical asymptote, set the denominator equal to 0 and solve for x. (You are finding the value of x for which the function is undefined. This value is sometimes called an *excluded value* because it cannot be included in the function's domain.)
- To find the horizontal asymptote, divide the numerator and the denominator of the function's rule by x, and then determine what value the function approaches as x increases or decreases without bound.

Graphing $f(x) = \frac{bx + c}{dx + e}$ when $d \neq 1$

Graph the function $f(x) = \frac{3x + 4}{4x - 5}$.

A Find the vertical asymptote. Set $4x - 5$ equal to 0 and solve for x to get

$x =$ ________.

B Find the horizontal asymptote. Rewrite the function rule as $f(x) = \frac{3 + \frac{4}{x}}{4 - \frac{5}{x}}$.

As x increases or decreases without bound, the y-value that the value of $f(x)$ approaches is $y =$ ________.

C Draw the graph after determining a reference point on each side of the vertical asymptote.

- A reference point to the right of the vertical asymptote: ________________
- A reference point to the left of the vertical asymptote: ________________

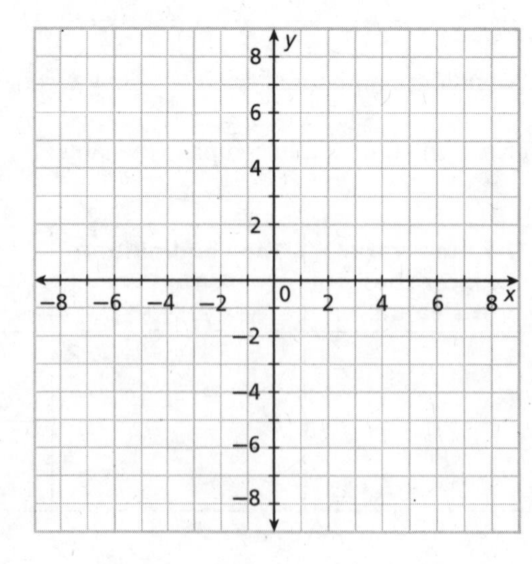

REFLECT

4a. State the domain and range of the function.

4b. Follow the steps below to write $f(x) = \frac{3x+4}{4x-5}$ in graphing form.

Step 1: Divide the numerator and denominator by the coefficient of x in the denominator.

$f(x) = \frac{\square x + 1}{x - \square}$

Step 2: Divide the numerator in Step 1 by the denominator in Step 1 using long division.

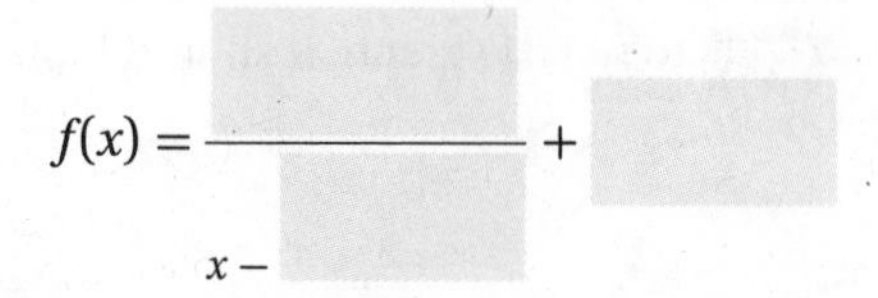

Step 3: Write the function in graphing form.

$f(x) = \frac{\square}{x - \square} + \square$

How does the graphing form help you check the graph that you drew?

MCC9–12.F.BF.1

5 EXAMPLE Modeling with Rational Functions

A chemist mixes 5 mL of an acid with 15 mL of water. The concentration of acid in the acid-and-water mix is $\frac{5}{5+15} = \frac{5}{20} = 25\%$. If the chemist adds more acid to the mix, then the concentration *C* becomes a function of the additional amount *a* of acid added to the mix. Write a rule for the function *C*(*a*) and then graph the function using a graphing calculator.

A Use the verbal model below to write the rule for $C(a)$.

$$\text{Concentration of acid in mix} = \frac{\text{Initial amount of acid} + \text{Additional acid}}{\text{Total amount of acid} + \text{Amount of water}}$$

B Determine a good viewing window by answering the following questions.

- What is a reasonable domain for the function? That is, what values can the variable a have in this situation?

- What concentration of acid does pure water have? What concentration of acid does pure acid have? So, what are the possible values of $C(a)$?

- On a graphing calculator, you will let x represent a and y represent $C(a)$. Specify a viewing window by stating the least and greatest x-values and the least and greatest y-values that you will use.

C Press WINDOW and set the viewing window. (Choose appropriate scales for the two axes.) Then press Y= and enter the rule for the function. Finally, press GRAPH to see the graph. It should look like the one shown.

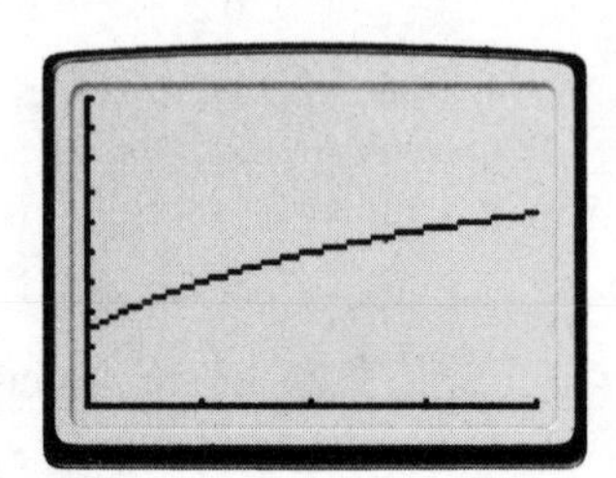

REFLECT

5a. Analyze the function's rule to determine the vertical asymptote of the function's graph. Why is the asymptote irrelevant in this situation?

5b. Analyze the function's rule to determine the horizontal asymptote of the function's graph. What is the relevance of the asymptote in this situation?

PRACTICE

Identify the asymptotes of the graph of each function.

1. $f(x) = \frac{5}{x-4}$

2. $f(x) = \frac{0.2}{x} - 1$

3. $f(x) = \frac{-4}{x+1} + 3$

4. $f(x) = \frac{11}{x-9} + 9$

Graph each function.

5. $f(x) = \frac{1}{x-2} + 4$

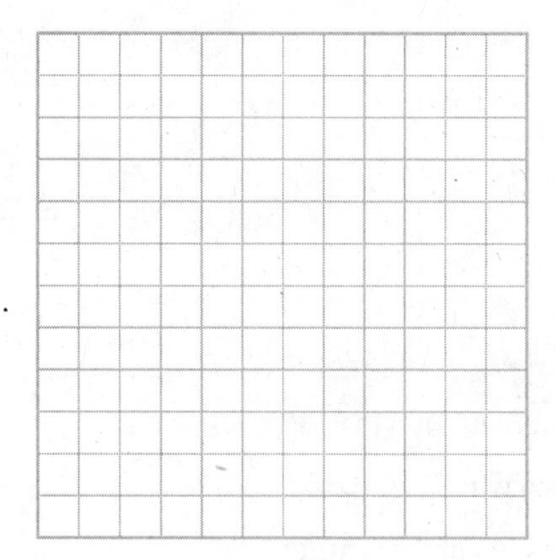

6. $f(x) = -\frac{1}{x+1} - 2$

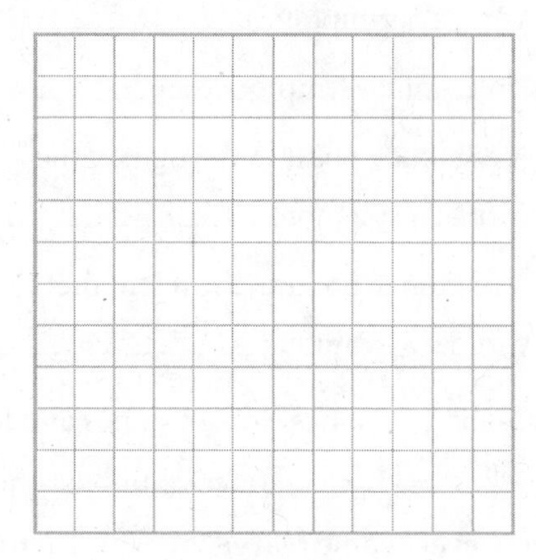

7. $f(x) = \frac{0.5}{x-1} - 3$

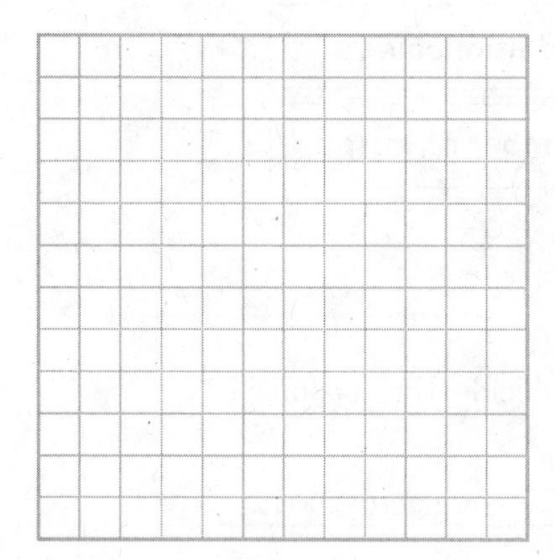

8. $f(x) = -\frac{2}{x+3} + 1$

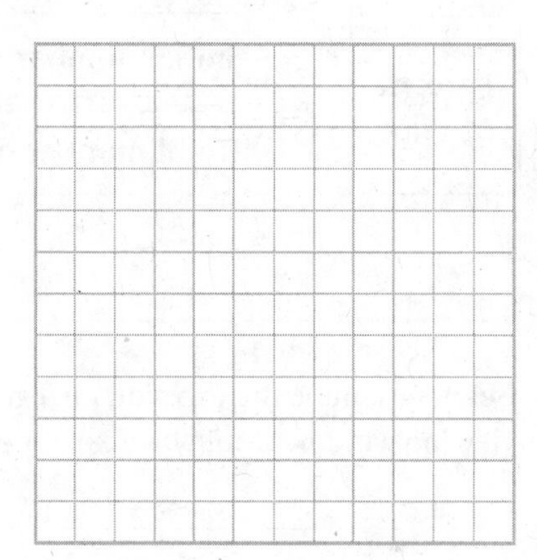

Write each function in graphing form and then graph the function.

9. $f(x) = \frac{3x-14}{x-5}$ ____________________

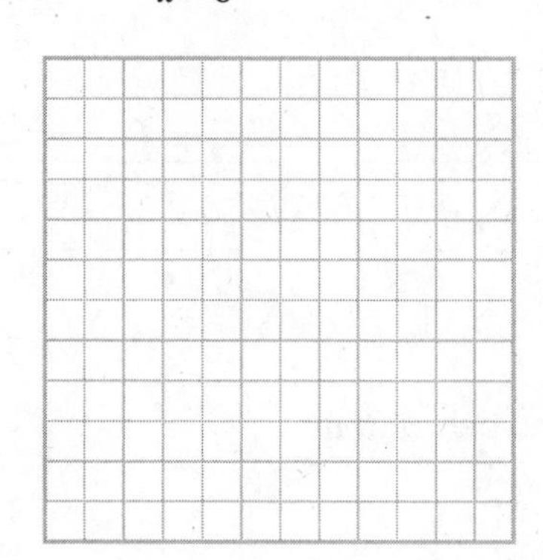

10. $f(x) = -\frac{4x+5}{x+2}$ ____________________

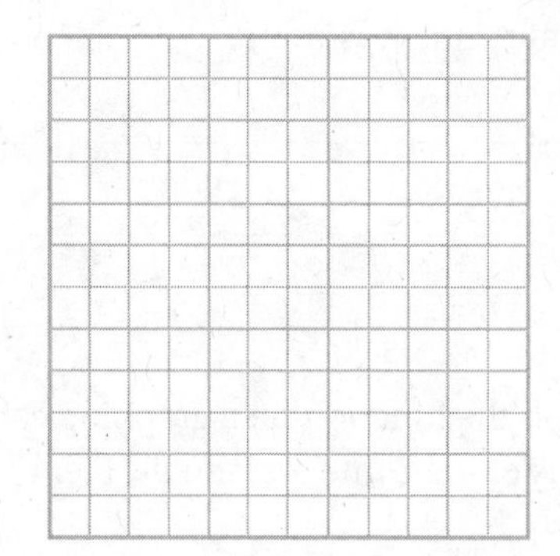

11. Graph $f(x) = \frac{2x + 1}{5x - 2}$ after finding the asymptotes and plotting a reference point on each side of the vertical asymptote.

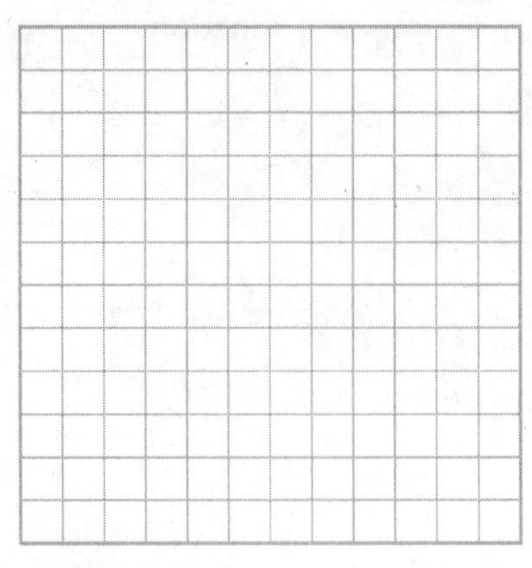

- Vertical asymptote: ___________
- Horizontal asymptote: ___________
- A reference point to the right of the vertical asymptote: ___________
- A reference point to the left of the vertical asymptote: ___________

12. A baseball team has won 18 games and lost 12. Its current percent of wins is $\frac{18}{18 + 12} = \frac{18}{30} = 0.6$, or 60%. Suppose the team experiences a winning streak where every game played is a win. Then its percent P of wins becomes a function of the number w of wins in the streak.

a. Use the verbal model below to write a rule for $P(w)$.

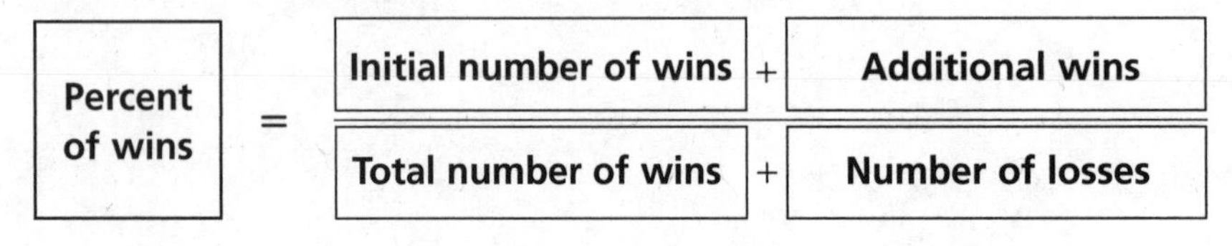

____

b. Before graphing the function on a graphing calculator, decide what a good viewing window would be. Explain your reasoning.

____

____

____

c. Again, before graphing the function on a graphing calculator, state what the graph's y-intercept is and whether the graph is increasing or decreasing. Explain your reasoning.

____

____

____

d. Graph the function on a graphing calculator. Describe the end behavior in terms of the context of the problem.

____

____

____

Name________________ Class__________ Date________

Additional Practice

Using the graph of $f(x)=\frac{1}{x}$ as a guide, describe the transformation and graph the function.

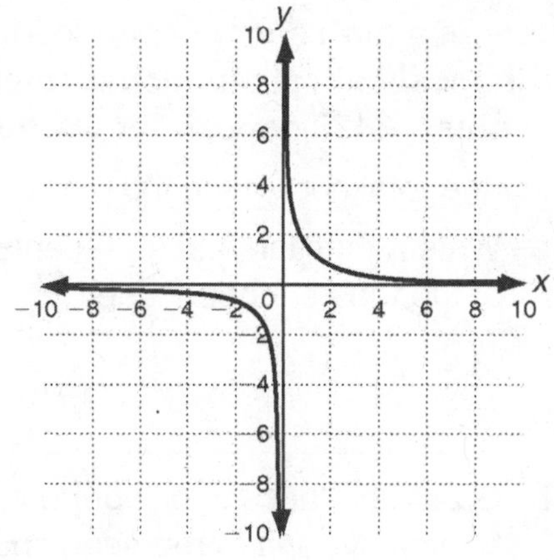

1. $g(x)=\dfrac{2}{x+4}$

____

Identify the asymptotes, domain, and range of each function.

2. $g(x)=\dfrac{1}{x-3}+5$ _______________________

____

3. $g(x)=\dfrac{1}{x+8}-1$ _______________________

____

Identify the zeros and asymptotes of the function. Then graph.

4. $f(x)=\dfrac{x^2+4x-5}{x+1}$

   a. Zeros:

   ____

   b. Vertical asymptote:

   ____

   c. Horizontal asymptote:

   ____

   d. Graph.

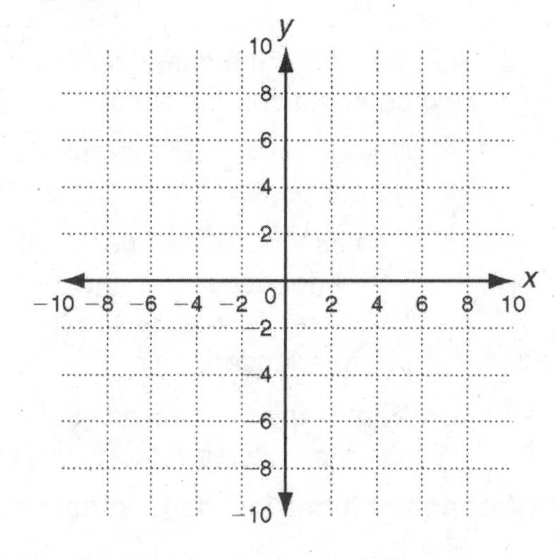

Solve.

5. The number, n, of daily visitors to a new store can be modeled by the function $n=\dfrac{250x+1000}{x}$, where x is the number of days the store has been open.

   a. What is the asymptote of this function and what does it represent? _______________________

   b. To the nearest integer, how many visitors can be expected on day 30? _______________________

Problem Solving

Members of a high school cheerleading squad plan a trip to support their robotics team at a regional competition. The trip will cost $70 per person plus a $420 deposit for the bus.

1. Find the total cost of the trip per cheerleader.

   a. Write a function that represents the total cost of the trip per cheerleader.

   ____

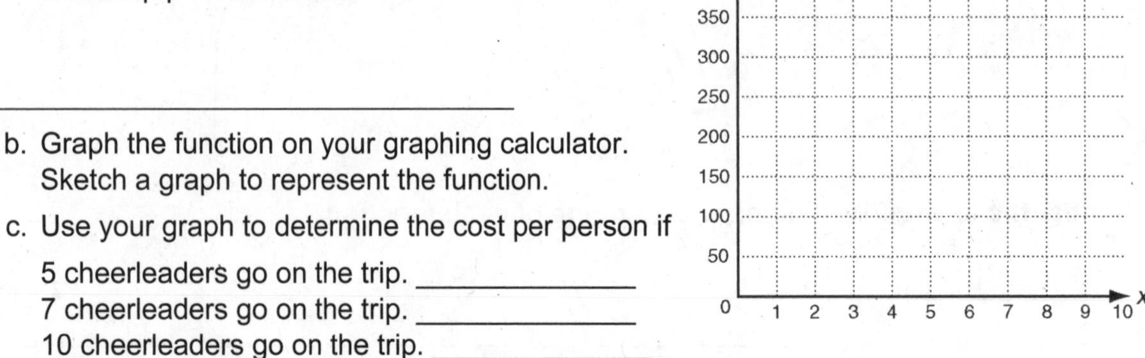

   b. Graph the function on your graphing calculator. Sketch a graph to represent the function.

   c. Use your graph to determine the cost per person if

   5 cheerleaders go on the trip. ____________
   7 cheerleaders go on the trip. ____________
   10 cheerleaders go on the trip. ____________

   d. What is the horizontal asymptote of the function? What does it mean in terms of the cost per person of the trip?

   ____

2. Stanton invites the cheerleaders to support the school's dive team at their next competition. The trip will cost $145 per person plus a $1000 deposit.

   a. Write a function to represent the cost of the trip per person. ________________

   b. What is the cost per person if

   5 cheerleaders go on the trip? ____________
   7 cheerleaders go on the trip? ____________
   10 cheerleaders go on the trip? ____________

   c. What is the increased cost for each of 10 cheerleaders to go with the dive team rather than to go with the robotics team? ____________

Choose the letter for the best answer.

3. The deposit for the bus on the robotics trip increases to $550. By how much does the cost per person increase if 10 cheerleaders go on the trip?

   A $13

   B $37

   C $83

   D $112

4. There are 15 cheerleaders signed up to go to the competition with the dive team. What is the cost per person to the nearest dollar?

   A $76

   B $103

   C $212

   D $304

Name________________ Class________________ Date________

13-5

Solving Rational Equations and Inequalities

Going Deeper

Video Tutor

Essential question: *What methods are there for solving rational equations?*

A rational equation consists of rational expressions and polynomials. You can solve a rational equation algebraically by finding the least common multiple (LCM) of the denominators of the rational expressions and multiplying each side of the equation by it. Doing so turns the equation into a polynomial equation.

MCC9–12.A.REI.2

1 EXAMPLE Solving a Rational Equation Algebraically

Solve $\frac{2}{x-1} = \frac{6}{x^2-x}$.

$\frac{2}{x-1} = \frac{6}{x^2-x}$ Write the equation.

$\frac{2}{x-1} = \frac{6}{x(\quad)}$ Factor each denominator.

$\frac{2}{x-1} \cdot x(\quad) = \frac{6}{x(\quad)} \cdot x(\quad)$ Multiply each side by the LCM.

$\frac{2x(\quad)}{x-1} = \frac{6x(\quad)}{x(\quad)}$ Carry out the multiplication.

$\quad = 6$ Simplify each side.

$x = \quad$ Solve for x.

REFLECT

1a. Evaluate each side of the equation when $x = 3$. What conclusion can you draw?

____

1b. What are the excluded values for each rational expression in the equation? Is the solution of the equation among the excluded values? Why is it important to know whether a solution is among the excluded values?

____

____

____

When solving rational equations algebraically, you must always check any apparent solutions to see if they are excluded values. If they are, then they are called **extraneous solutions** and must be rejected.

MCC9–12.A.REI.2

2 EXAMPLE Solving Rational Equations Having Extraneous Solutions

Solve $\frac{x}{x-2} + \frac{1}{x-4} = \frac{2}{x^2 - 6x + 8}$.

A Find the LCM of the denominators and multiply each side by it. Be sure to distribute the LCM to both rational expressions on the left side.

$$\frac{x}{x-2} + \frac{1}{x-4} = \frac{2}{x^2 - 6x + 8}$$

$$\frac{x}{x-2} + \frac{1}{x-4} = \frac{2}{(x-2)(\quad)}$$

$$\left[\frac{x}{x-2} + \frac{1}{x-4}\right](x-2)(\quad) = \frac{2}{(x-2)(\quad)} \cdot (x-2)(\quad)$$

$$\frac{x(x-2)(\quad)}{x-2} + \frac{(x-2)(\quad)}{x-4} = \frac{2(x-2)(\quad)}{(x-2)(\quad)}$$

$$x(\quad) + (x-2) = 2$$

$$\underline{\qquad\qquad} = 2$$

$$\underline{\qquad\qquad} = 0$$

B Solve the resulting quadratic equation by factoring.

$$(x+1)(\quad) = 0$$

$$x + 1 = 0 \quad \text{or} \quad \underline{\qquad} = 0$$

$$x = -1 \quad \text{or} \quad x = \underline{\quad}$$

C Classify each apparent solution as either an actual solution or an extraneous solution.

- -1 is an ______________ solution.
- __________ is an ______________ solution.

REFLECT

2a. Evaluate the left and right sides of the equation when $x = -1$.

____

MCC9–12.A.CED.1

3 EXAMPLE Modeling with Rational Equations

If you're in a canoe on a river and not paddling, you will travel in the same direction and at the same speed as the river's current. When you paddle *with* the current (downstream), the canoe's speed is the *sum* of your paddling speed and the current's speed. When you paddle *against* the current (upstream), the canoe's speed is the *difference* of your paddling speed and the current's speed.

Suppose you paddle a canoe at a steady speed of 4 miles per hour. You go 6 miles downstream and then 6 miles upstream to get back to where you started. The trip takes 4 hours. What is the speed of the current?

A Write expressions for the canoe's downstream and upstream speeds. Let s be the speed of the current.

Downstream speed = ______ Upstream speed = ______

B Divide the distance traveled in each direction by the canoe's speed in that direction to find the time for that part of the trip.

Downstream time = $\frac{\square}{\square}$ Upstream time = $\frac{\square}{\square}$

C Use the verbal model to write an equation that models the canoe trip.

Downstream time + **Upstream time** = **Total trip time**

____

D Solve the equation. Although can you solve the equation using algebra, you can also solve it using a graphing calculator. Treat the left side of the equation as a rational function $f(x)$. (You will need to substitute x for s when you enter the function on the graphing calculator.) Treat the right side of the equation as the constant function $g(x) = 4$.

- What viewing window should you use for graphing? Why?

____

____

____

- Enter the functions and graph them. At what point do the graphs intersect? Interpret the coordinates of this point in the context of the problem.

____

____

REFLECT

3a. The graph of $f(x)$ has a vertical asymptote at $x = 4$. Based on the context of the problem, why *should* there be a vertical asymptote at $x = 4$?

3b. Solve the equation in part C algebraically. How many solutions does the equation have? Do all the solutions make sense in the context of the problem? Why or why not?

PRACTICE

Solve each equation.

1. $\frac{3}{x+1} = \frac{1}{x^2 - 1}$

2. $\frac{2}{x} = x - 1$

3. $\frac{3}{2x} - \frac{5}{3x} = 2$

4. $\frac{x}{4} + 3 = \frac{x+4}{x-2}$

5. $\frac{x}{x-1} - \frac{3}{x} = \frac{1}{x^2 - x}$

6. $\frac{4}{x^2 - 4} - \frac{1}{x+2} = \frac{x-1}{x-2}$

7. Explain why the equation $\frac{x+1}{x-3} = \frac{4}{x-3}$ has no solution.

8. You paddle a canoe at a steady speed on a river where the current's speed is 1 kilometer per hour. You go 7.7 kilometers downstream and then 7.7 kilometers upstream to get back to where you started. The trip takes 3.6 hours.

a. Write a rational equation that models the problem. State what the variable in your equation represents.

b. Solve the equation and state the solution in terms of the context of the problem.

Additional Practice

Solve each equation.

1. $x - \frac{6}{x} = 5$

2. $\frac{15}{4} = \frac{6}{x} + 3$

3. $x = \frac{3}{x} + 2$

4. $\frac{4}{x^2 - 4} = \frac{1}{x - 2}$

Solve each inequality by using a graphing calculator and a table.

5. $\frac{6}{x+1} < -3$

6. $\frac{x}{x-2} \geq 0$

7. $\frac{2x}{x+5} \leq 0$

8. $\frac{-x}{x-3} \geq 0$

Solve each inequality algebraically.

9. $\frac{12}{x+4} \leq 4$

10. $\frac{7}{x+3} < -5$

11. $\frac{x}{x-2} > 9$

12. $\frac{2x}{x-5} \geq 3$

Solve.

13. The time required to deliver and install a computer at a customer's location is $t = 4 + \frac{d}{r}$, where t is time in hours, d is the distance, in miles, from the warehouse to the customer's location, and r is the average speed of the delivery truck. If it takes 6.2 hours for the employee to deliver and install a computer for a customer located 100 miles from the warehouse, what is the average speed of the delivery truck?

Problem Solving

Norton and Jessie have a lawn service business. Sometimes they work by themselves, and sometimes they work together. They want to know if it is worthwhile to work together on some jobs.

1. Norton can mow a large lawn in about 4.0 hours. When Norton and Jesse work together, they can mow the same lawn in about 2.5 hours. Jesse wants to know how long it would take her to mow the lawn if she worked by herself.

   a. Write an expression for Jessie's rate, using j for the number of hours she would take to mow the lawn by herself. ______________________

   b. Write an equation to show the amount of work completed when they work together. ______________________

   c. How long would it take Jessie to mow the lawn by herself? ______________________

2. Jessie can weed a garden in about 30 minutes. When Norton helps her, they can weed the same garden in about 20 minutes. Norton wants to know how long it would take him to weed the garden if he worked by himself.

   a. Write an expression for Norton's rate, using n for the number of hours he would take to weed the garden by himself. ______________________

   b. Write an equation to show the amount of work completed when they work together. ______________________

   c. How long would it take Norton to weed the garden by himself? ______________________

Choose the letter for the best answer.

3. Norton can edge a large lawn in about 3.0 hours. Jessie can edge a similar lawn in about 2.5 hours. Which equation could be used to find the time it would take them to edge that lawn if they worked together?

   A $\frac{1}{3} - \frac{1}{2.5} = \frac{1}{t}$

   B $\frac{1}{3} - \frac{1}{2.5} = t$

   C $\frac{1}{3} + \frac{1}{2.5} = \frac{1}{t}$

   D $\frac{1}{3} + \frac{1}{2.5} = t$

4. When Jessie helps Norton trim trees, they cut Norton's time to trim trees in half. What can be said about the time it would take Jessie to do the job alone?

   A Jessie would take the same amount of time as Norton.

   B Jessie would take half the time that Norton takes.

   C Jessie would take twice the time that Norton takes.

   D There is not enough information.

Name______________________ Class____________ Date__________

14-1

Radical Functions

Going Deeper

Essential question: *How can you graph transformations of the parent square root and cube root functions?*

Video Tutor

You can transform the parent square root and parent cube root functions by changing the values of *a*, *h*, and *k* in the general forms of the equations shown below.

$f(x) = a\sqrt{x-h} + k$ $\qquad$ $f(x) = a\sqrt[3]{x-h} + k$

MCC9-12.F.BF.3

1 EXAMPLE Changing the Value of *a*

Graph each radical function. Then describe the graph as a transformation of the graph of the parent function. (The graph of the parent function is shown.)

A $g(x) = 3\sqrt{x}$

x	g(x)
0	
1	
4	
9	
16	

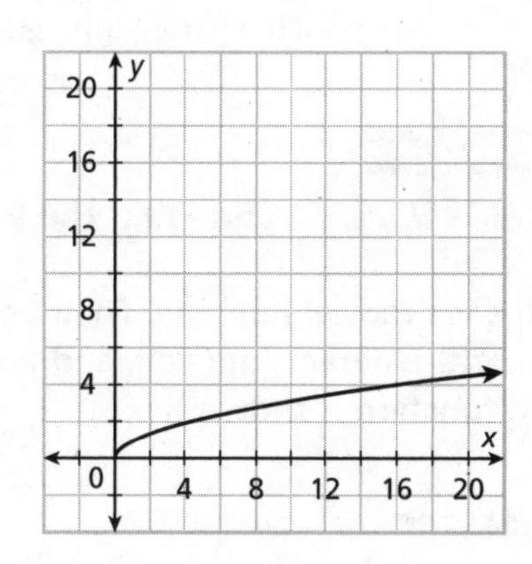

The graph of $g(x)$ is a vertical ______________ of the graph of the parent function by a factor of ________.

B $g(x) = 0.5\sqrt[3]{x}$

x	g(x)
−8	
−1	
0	
1	
8	

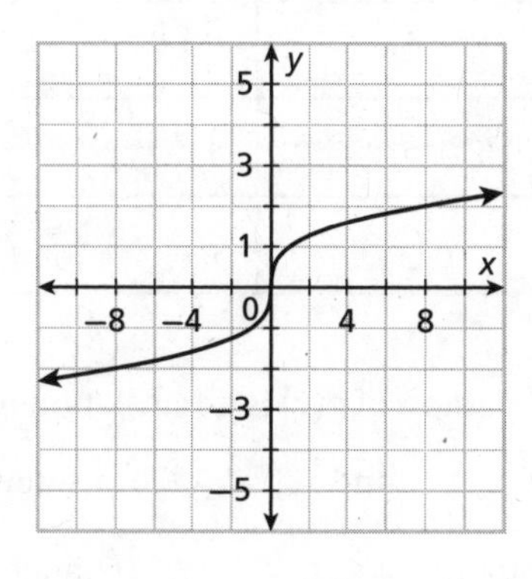

The graph of $g(x)$ is a vertical ______________ of the graph of the parent function by a factor of ________.

REFLECT

1a. In part A, why does it make sense to use x-values of 0, 1, 4, 9, and 16 when finding points on the graph of $g(x)$?

____

____

1b. Explain how you know in part B that the graph of $g(x)$ is a vertical shrink of the graph of the parent function.

____

____

1c. Generalize from your observations to complete the sentences below.

For $g(x) = a\sqrt{x}$ or $g(x) = a\sqrt[3]{x}$:

- when $|a| > 1$, the graph of $g(x)$ is a vertical ____________ of the graph of the parent function.
- when $0 < |a| < 1$, the graph of $g(x)$ is a vertical ____________ of the graph of the parent function.

MCC9–12.F.BF.3

2 EXAMPLE Changing the Values of *h* and *k*

Graph each radical function. Then describe the graph as a transformation of the graph of the parent function, and give its domain and range. (The graph of the parent function is shown.)

A $g(x) = \sqrt{x+4} - 3$

x	$g(x)$
−4	
−3	
0	
5	
12	

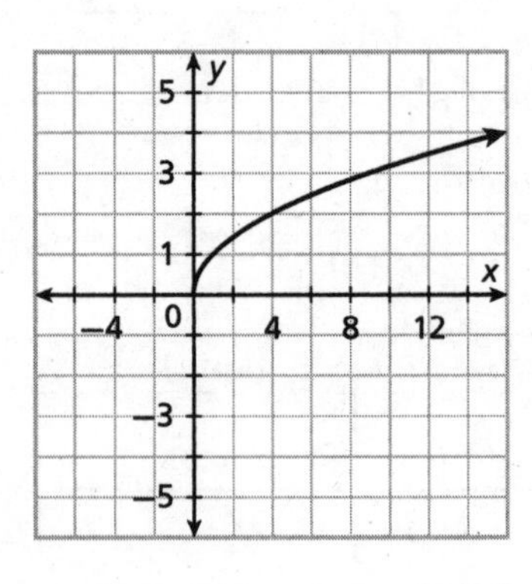

The graph of $g(x)$ is a translation of the graph of the parent function 4 units ____________ and ____________ units down.

Domain: $\{x \mid x \geq$ ______ $\}$ Range: $\{y \mid y \geq$ ______ $\}$

B $g(x) = \sqrt[3]{x-2} + 4$

x	$g(x)$
−6	
1	
2	
3	
10	

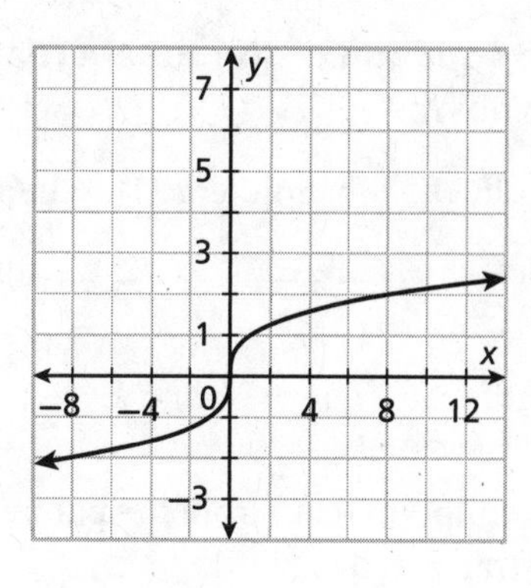

The graph of $g(x)$ is a translation of the graph of the parent function 2 units ________ and ________ units up.

Domain: ____________________ Range: ____________________

REFLECT

2a. How can you determine the domain of $g(x) = \sqrt{x+4} - 3$ by looking at its function rule?

____

____

____

2b. In part B, what are the values of h and k in $g(x) = \sqrt[3]{x-2} + 4$? What effect do h and k have on the function's graph?

____

____

____

2c. Generalize from your observations to complete the sentences below.
For $g(x) = \sqrt{x-h} + k$ and $g(x) = \sqrt[3]{x-h} + k$:

- the graph of $g(x)$ is a translation of the parent function $|h|$ units ____________ if $h < 0$ and h units ____________ if $h > 0$.
- the graph of $g(x)$ is a translation of the parent function $|k|$ units ____________ if $k < 0$ and k units ____________ if $k > 0$.

MCC9–12.F.BF.3

3 EXAMPLE Writing the Equation of a Radical Function

Write the equation of the square root or cube root function whose graph is shown.

A Identify the function type. The shape of the graph

indicates a ________________ function.

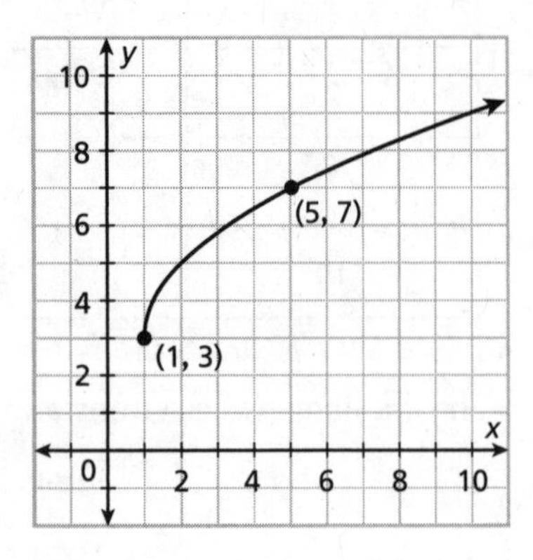

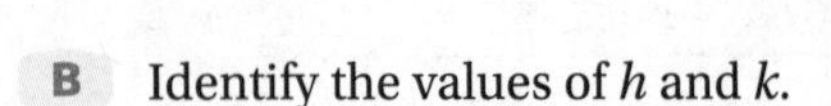

B Identify the values of h and k.

The endpoint (0, 0) from the parent square root function was translated to (1, 3).

$h =$ ______ $k =$ ______

The equation has the form $g(x) = a\sqrt{x - } + $.

C Use the point (5, 7) to identify a.

$g(x) = a\sqrt{x - 1} + 3$	Function form
______ $= a\sqrt{ - 1} + 3$	Substitute 7 for $g(x)$ and 5 for x.
$7 = a() + 3$	Simplify the radical.
______ $= a(2)$	Subtract 3 from both sides.
______ $= a$	Divide both sides by 2.

So, the equation of the function is $g(x) =$ ________________.

REFLECT

3a. Does the given graph represent a vertical stretch or a vertical shrink of the graph of the parent function? Does this agree with the value of a that you found? Explain.

____

3b. How can you identify the point to which (0, 0) from the graph of the parent function was translated in the graph of a square root function? in the graph of a cube root function?

____

____

____

PRACTICE

Graph each radical function. Then describe the graph as a transformation of the graph of the parent function, and give its domain and range. (The graph of the parent function is shown.)

1. $f(x) = 0.5\sqrt{x+2}$

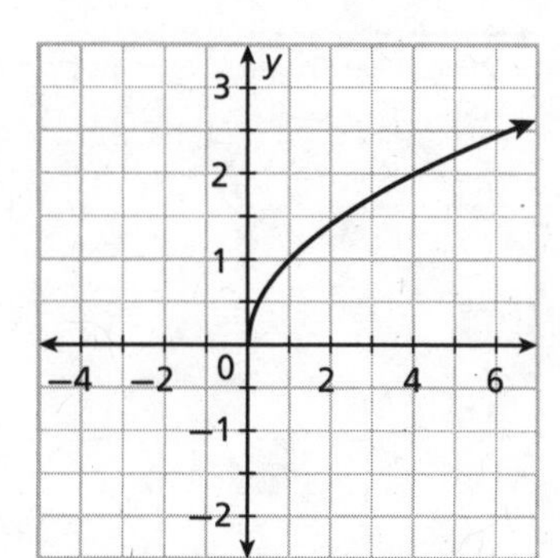

____

____

Domain: ______________________________

Range: ______________________________

2. $f(x) = 2\sqrt[3]{x} - 4$

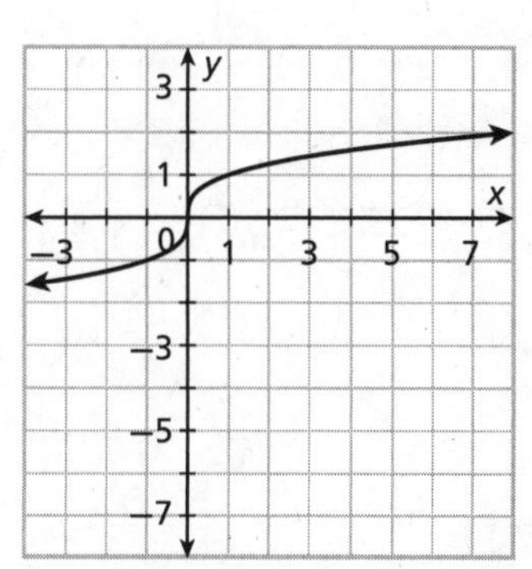

____

____

Domain: ______________________________

Range: ______________________________

3. $f(x) = -\sqrt{x} + 5$

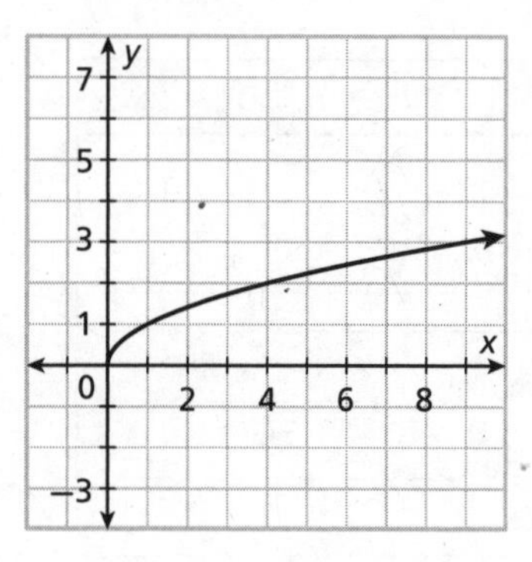

____

____

Domain: ______________________________

Range: ______________________________

4. $f(x) = -\sqrt[3]{x-1}$

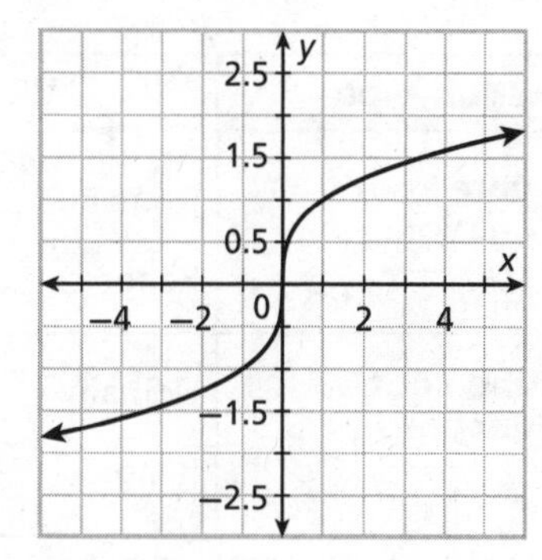

____

____

Domain: ______________________________

Range: ______________________________

Write the equation of the square root or cube root function whose graph is shown.

5. $f(x) =$ ______________________

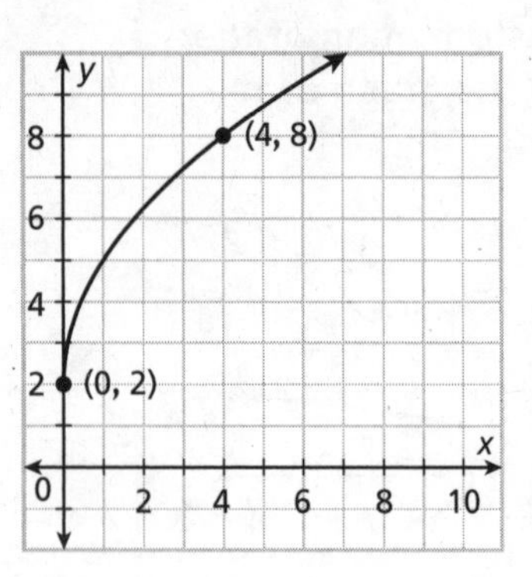

6. $f(x) =$ ______________________

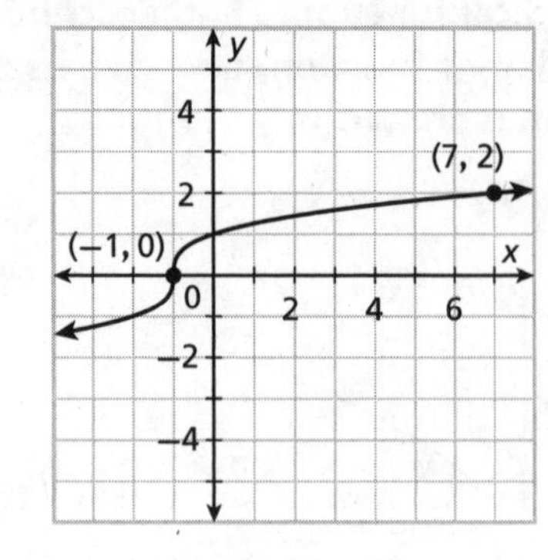

7. $f(x) =$ ______________________

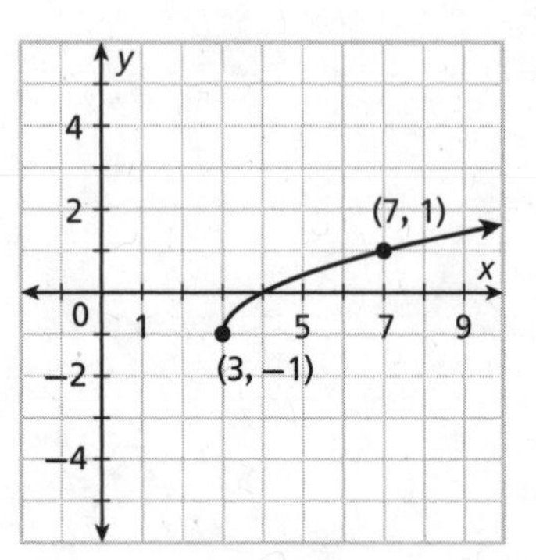

8. $f(x) =$ ______________________

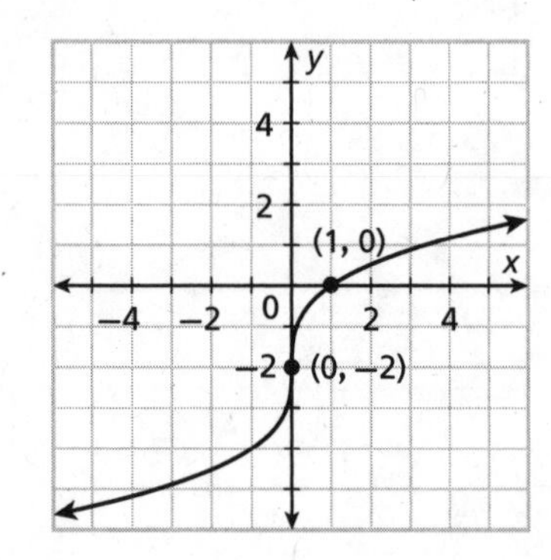

9. Complete the chart by writing the domains and ranges of each function type in terms of h and k.

Function Type	When $a > 0$	When $a < 0$
Square Root Functions $f(x) = a\sqrt{x - h} + k$	Domain: ______________ Range: ______________	Domain: ______________ Range: ______________
Cube Root Functions $f(x) = a\sqrt[3]{x - h} + k$	Domain: ______________ Range: ______________	Domain: ______________ Range: ______________

10. Which function has a greater minimum value, $f(x) = \sqrt{x - 4} - 1$ or the function whose graph is shown?

____

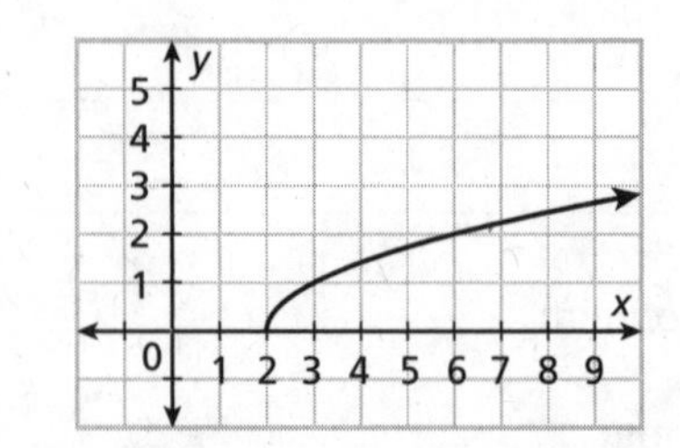

Name______________________ Class______________ Date____________ **14-1**

Additional Practice

Graph each function, and identify its domain and range.

1. $f(x) = \sqrt{x - 4}$

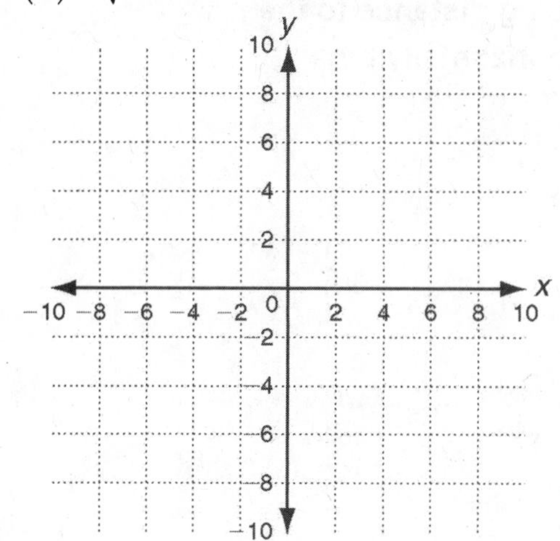

Domain: ______________________

Range: ______________________

2. $f(x) = \sqrt[3]{x} + 1$

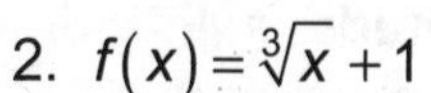

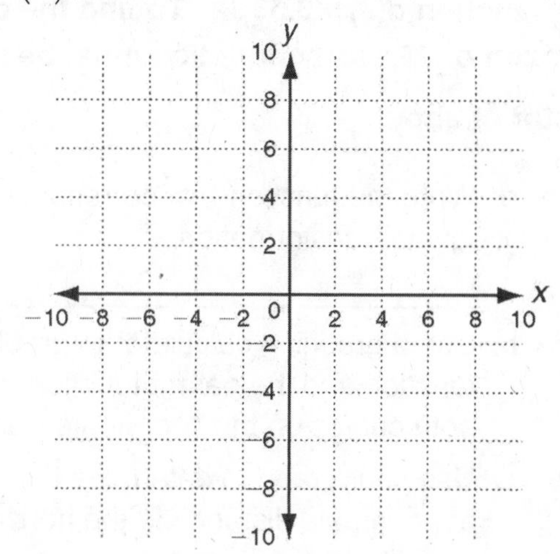

Domain: ______________________

Range: ______________________

Using the graph of $f(x) = \sqrt{x}$ as a guide, describe the transformation.

3. $g(x) = 4\sqrt{x + 8}$ ______________________________________

4. $g(x) = -\sqrt{3x} + 2$

____

Use the description to write the square root function g.

5. The parent function $f(x) = \sqrt{x}$ is reflected across the *y*-axis, vertically stretched by a factor of 7, and translated 3 units down. ______________________

6. The parent function $f(x) = \sqrt{x}$ is translated 2 units right, compressed horizontally by a factor of $\frac{1}{2}$, and reflected across the *x*-axis. ______________________

Solve.

7. For a gas with density, *n*, measured in atoms per cubic centimeter, the average distance, *d*, between atoms is given by $d = \left(\frac{3}{4\pi n}\right)^{\frac{1}{3}}$. The gas in a certain region of space has a density of just 10 atoms per cubic centimeter. Find the average distance between the atoms in that region of space.

____

Problem Solving

On Earth the distance, *d*, in kilometers, that one can see to the horizon is a function of altitude, *a*, in meters, and can be found using the function $d(a) = 3.56\sqrt{a}$. To find the corresponding distance to the horizon on Mars, the function must be stretched horizontally by a factor of about $\frac{9}{5}$.

1. a. Write the function that corresponds to the given transformation.

   ____

   b. Use a graphing calculator to graph the function and the parent function. Sketch both curves on the coordinate plane.

   c. Use your graph to determine the approximate distance to the horizon from an altitude of 100 meters:

   on Earth ____________________

   on Mars ____________________

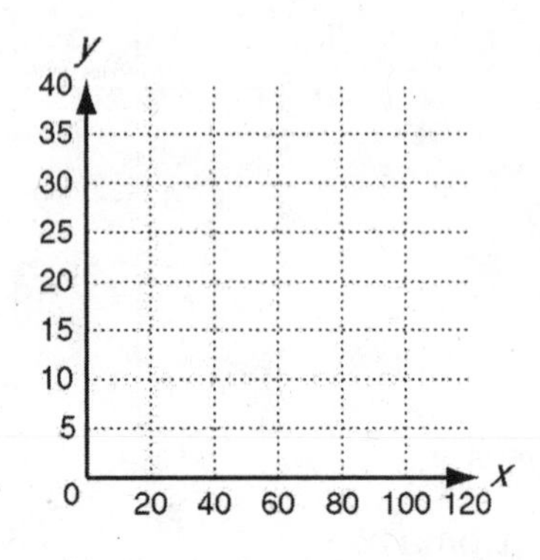

Choose the letter for the best answer.

2. Which equation represents the radius of a sphere as a function of the volume of the sphere?

   A $r = \sqrt[3]{\frac{3\pi}{4V}}$ C $r = \sqrt[3]{\frac{4V}{3\pi}}$

   B $r = \sqrt[3]{\frac{3V}{4\pi}}$ D $r = \sqrt[3]{\frac{4\pi}{3V}}$

4. Harry made a symmetrical design by graphing four functions, one in each quadrant. The graph of which function is in the third quadrant?

   A $f(x) = 4\sqrt{x}$ C $f(x) = -4\sqrt{x}$

   B $f(x) = 4\sqrt{-x}$ D $f(x) = -4\sqrt{-x}$

6. The hypotenuse of a right isosceles triangle can be written $H = \sqrt{2x^2}$, where *x* is the length of one of the legs. Which function models the hypotenuse when the legs are lengthened by a factor of 2?

   A $H = \sqrt{2x^2} + 2$ C $H = \sqrt{4x^2}$

   B $H = \sqrt{2x^2} + 4$ D $H = \sqrt{8x^2}$

3. Alice graphed a function that is found only in the first quadrant. Which function could she have used?

   A $f(x) = \sqrt{x+2}$ C $f(x) = \sqrt{x} + 2$

   B $f(x) = -\sqrt{x}$ D $f(x) = \sqrt{x-2}$

5. The side length of a cube can be represented by $s = \sqrt{\frac{T}{6}}$, where *T* is the surface area of the cube. What transformation is shown by $s = \sqrt{\frac{T}{3}}$?

   A Horizontal compression by a factor of 0.5

   B Horizontal stretch by a factor of 2

   C Vertical compression by a factor of 0.5

   D Vertical stretch by a factor of 2

Name ______________________ Class ______________ Date ______________

14-2

Solving Radical Equations and Inequalities

Going Deeper

Essential question: *How can you solve equations involving square roots and cube roots?*

Video Tutor

MCC9–12.A.REI.2

1 EXAMPLE Solving Simple Radical Equations

Solve each equation.

A $\sqrt{x+2} = 3$

$(\sqrt{x+2})^2 = 3^2$ — Square both sides of the equation.

$x + \square = \square$ — Simplify.

$x = \square$ — Solve for x.

Check your solution.

$\sqrt{x+2} = 3$ — Write the original equation.

$\sqrt{\square + 2} \stackrel{?}{=} 3$ — Substitute 7 for x.

$\square = 3$ — Simplify. The solution checks.

B $\sqrt[3]{12x} = 6$

$(\sqrt[3]{12x})^3 = 6^3$ — Cube both sides of the equation.

$\square = \square$ — Simplify.

$x = \square$ — Solve for x.

Check your solution.

$\sqrt[3]{12x} = 6$ — Write the original equation.

$\sqrt[3]{12(\square)} \stackrel{?}{=} 6$ — Substitute 18 for x.

$\square = 6$ — Simplify. The solution checks.

REFLECT

1a. Consider the function $f(x) = \sqrt{x+2}$. What are the domain and range of the function? Explain.

____

____

____

1b. Square both sides of the equation $\sqrt{x+2} = -3$ and solve for x as in part A. Is the value you get for x a solution of the equation? Explain.

____

1c. Consider the function $f(x) = \sqrt[3]{12x}$. What are the domain and range of the function?

____

1d. Cube both sides of the equation $\sqrt[3]{12x} = -6$ and solve for x as in Part B. Is the value you get for x a solution of the equation? Explain.

____

Because the ranges of square root functions are restricted, solving equations based on square root functions sometimes results in *extraneous solutions.* An **extraneous solution** is a solution of an intermediate equation that is not a solution of the original equation.

When solving square root equations, you must check all apparent solutions in the original equation to identify and rule out extraneous solutions.

Identifying Extraneous Solutions of Square Root Equations

Solve $\sqrt{x-3} + 5 = x$.

A Find the apparent solutions.

$\sqrt{x-3} + 5 = x$	Write the original equation.
$\sqrt{x-3} = x - \square$	Isolate the square root expression.
$(\sqrt{x-3})^2 = (x-5)^2$	Square both sides of the equation.
$x - 3 = x^2 - \square x + \square$	Simplify.
$0 = x^2 - \square x + \square$	Make one side of the quadratic equation equal 0.
$0 = (x - \square)(x - \square)$	Factor.
$x = \square$ or $x = \square$	Zero Product Property

B Check each apparent solution in the original equation to identify extraneous solutions.

Check $x = 7$.

$\sqrt{x - 3} + 5 = x$ — Write the original equation.

$\sqrt{ - 3} + 5 \stackrel{?}{=} $ — Substitute 7 for x.

$ + 5 = $ — Simplify. $x = 7$ is a solution.

Check $x = 4$.

$\sqrt{x - 3} + 5 = x$ — Write the original equation.

$\sqrt{ - 3} + 5 \stackrel{?}{=} $ — Substitute 4 for x.

$ + 5 \neq $ — Simplify. $x = 4$ is not a solution.

Because $x =$ ____ is extraneous, the only solution is $x =$ ____.

REFLECT

2a. Use a graphing calculator to graph the functions $f(x) = \sqrt{x - 3} + 5$ and $g(x) = x$ on the same screen. How could you use the graph to solve the equation $\sqrt{x - 3} + 5 = x$?

2b. What types of functions are $f(x)$ and $g(x)$?

2c. Does the graph show the extraneous solution of $\sqrt{x - 3} + 5 = x$? Explain.

2d. Use a graphing calculator to graph the functions $h(x) = -\sqrt{x - 3} + 5$ and $g(x) = x$ on the same screen. What do you notice about the point of intersection?

MCC9–12.A.REI.2

3 EXAMPLE Solving Cube Root Equations

Solve $2\sqrt[3]{x^2 - 8} + 3 = 2x - 1$.

$2\sqrt[3]{x^2 - 8} + 3 = 2x - 1$	Write the equation.
$2\sqrt[3]{x^2 - 8} = 2x - \square$	Isolate the cube root expression.
$\sqrt[3]{x^2 - 8} = x - \square$	Divide both sides by 2.
$\left(\sqrt[3]{x^2 - 8}\right)^3 = (x - 2)^3$	Cube both sides of the equation.
$x^2 - 8 = x^3 - \square x^2 + \square x - \square$	Expand $(x - 2)^3$.
$0 = x^3 - \square x^2 + \square x$	Make one side of the equation equal 0.
$0 = x(x - \square)(x - \square)$	Factor.
$x = \square$, $x = \square$, or $x = \square$	Zero Product Property

Check your solutions.

$2\sqrt[3]{x^2 - 8} + 3 = 2x - 1$	$2\sqrt[3]{x^2 - 8} + 3 = 2x - 1$	$2\sqrt[3]{x^2 - 8} + 3 = 2x - 1$
$2\sqrt[3]{0^2 - 8} + 3 \stackrel{?}{=} 2(\square) - 1$	$2\sqrt[3]{4^2 - 8} + 3 \stackrel{?}{=} 2(\square) - 1$	$2\sqrt[3]{3^2 - 8} + 3 \stackrel{?}{=} 2(\square) - 1$
$2(\square) + 3 \stackrel{?}{=} \square$	$2(\square) + 3 \stackrel{?}{=} \square$	$2(\square) + 3 \stackrel{?}{=} \square$
$\square = \square$	$\square = \square$	$\square = \square$

REFLECT

3a. Explain how you could use a graph to check your solutions.

____

____

____

____

3b. Cube root equations that have no restrictions on the variable do not yield extraneous solutions when solved. Why is it still important to check your solutions?

____

____

PRACTICE

Solve each equation.

1. $\sqrt{x+5} = 5$

2. $\sqrt[3]{4x} = -2$

3. $\sqrt{3x} = 9$

4. $\sqrt[3]{x+1} = 6$

5. $\sqrt{4x-7} = 5$

6. $\sqrt[3]{x-4} + 3 = -1$

7. $\sqrt{-3x-5} = x+3$

8. $\sqrt{12+2x} = x+2$

9. $\sqrt{-6x-14} = x+1$

10. $\sqrt{2x-7} = x-5$

11. $\sqrt{9x+90} = x+6$

12. $\sqrt[3]{1-x^2} = x+1$

13. $\sqrt[3]{9x^2+22x+8} = x+2$

14. $\sqrt[3]{x^2-x-1} = x-1$

Solve each equation by graphing.

15. $2\sqrt{x+1} = 3x+2$

16. $2\sqrt[3]{x+1} + 3 = -2x+1$

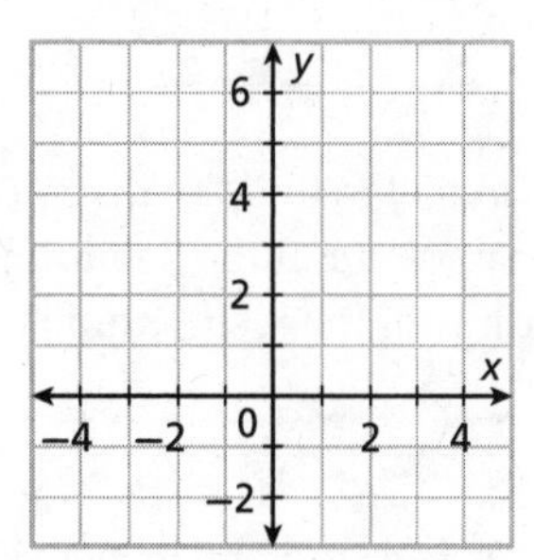

17. The function $s(l) = 1.34\sqrt{l}$ models the maximum speed s in knots for a sailboat with length l in feet at the waterline.

a. Use the model to find the length of a sailboat with a maximum speed of 12 knots. Round to the nearest foot.

b. Explain how you can check your solution using a graphing calculator. Then use the method you described to check your result.

18. The function $a(h) = 20\sqrt[3]{h - 8.3} + 40$ models the age a in years of a sassafras tree that is h meters high.

a. Use the model to find the height of the sassafras tree when it was 50 years old. Round to the nearest tenth of a meter.

b. Explain how you can check your solution using a graphing calculator. Then use the method you described to check your result.

19. When a car skids to a stop on a dry asphalt road, the equation $s = \sqrt{21d}$ models the relationship between the car's speed s in miles per hour at the beginning of the skid and the distance d in feet that the car skids.

a. Use the model to find the distance that a car will skid to a stop if it is traveling at 40 miles per hour at the beginning of the skid. Round to the nearest foot.

b. Use the model to find the distance that a car will skid to a stop if it is traveling at 20 miles per hour at the beginning of the skid. Round to the nearest foot. Compare this result with the result from part (a), where the speed was twice as great.

c. A car skids to a stop and leaves skid marks that are 65 feet long. The speed limit on the road is 35 miles per hour. Was the car speeding when it went into the skid? Explain.

Name______________________ Class______________ Date__________

Additional Practice

Solve each equation.

1. $\sqrt{x+6}=7$

2. $\sqrt{5x}=10$

3. $\sqrt{2x+5}=\sqrt{3x-1}$

4. $\sqrt{x+4}=3\sqrt{x}$

5. $\sqrt[3]{x-6}=\sqrt[3]{3x+24}$

6. $3\sqrt[3]{x}=\sqrt[3]{7x+5}$

7. $\sqrt{-14x+2}=x-3$

8. $(x+4)^{\frac{1}{2}}=6$

9. $4(x-3)^{\frac{1}{2}}=8$

10. $4(x-12)^{\frac{1}{3}}=-16$

Solve each inequality.

11. $\sqrt{3x+6}\leq 3$

12. $\sqrt{x-4}+3>9$

13. $\sqrt{x+7}\geq\sqrt{2x-1}$

14. $\sqrt{2x-7}>9$

Solve.

15. A biologist is studying two species of animals in a habitat. The population, p_1, of one of the species is growing according to $p_1=500t^{\frac{3}{2}}$ and the population, p_2, of the other species is growing according to $p_2=100t^2$ where time, t, is measured in years. After how many years will the populations of the two species be equal?

Problem Solving

The formula $s = \sqrt{30fd}$ can be used to estimate the speed, *s*, in miles per hour that a car is traveling when it goes into a skid, where *f* is the coefficient of friction and *d* is the length of the skid marks in feet.

1. How does the speed vary as the length of the skid marks? ____________________
2. Kody skids to a stop on a street with a speed limit of 35 mi/h. His skid marks measure 52 ft, and the coefficient of friction is 0.7. Kody says that he was driving only about 30 mi/h. Kody wants to prove that he was not speeding.
   a. Solve the equation for *d* in terms of *s*. ____________________
   b. How long would the skid marks be if he had been driving at a speed of 35 mi/h? ____________________
   c. Was Kody speeding or not? Explain how you know.

   ____

   d. Find his actual speed. ____________________
3. Ashley skids to a stop on a street with a speed limit of 15 mi/h to avoid a dog who runs into the street about 20 ft ahead of her. Ashley claims to have been going less than 15 mi/h. The coefficient of friction is 0.7.
   a. If Ashley were driving the speed limit, by what distance would she have missed the dog?

   ____

   b. If Ashley were driving less than 10 mi/h, by what distance would she have missed the dog?

   ____

Choose the letter for the best answer.

4. Barney was driving at 25 mi/h. A car pulls out 30 ft ahead of him. Which statement is true?
   A Barney hits the car.
   B Barney stops less than a foot from the car.
   C Barney misses the car by 3 ft.
   D Barney's skid marks measure 23 ft.

5. On a busy highway with a speed limit of 70 mi/h, a truck ahead of Verna jack-knifes across the road. Verna skids to a stop 10 ft short of the truck. Her skid marks measure 260 ft. Was Verna speeding?
   A Yes; her speed was 73.9 mi/h.
   B Yes; her speed was 75.3 mi/h.
   C No; her speed was 70 mi/h.
   D No; her speed was only 63 mi/h.

Name________________ Class____________ Date________

UNIT 7

Performance Tasks

GPS COMMON CORE

MCC9-12.A.APR.7(+)
MCC9-12.A.CED.1
MCC9-12.A.CED.2
MCC9-12.A.REI.2
MCC9-12.F.IF.7d(+)

★ **1.** A small company has a budget of $1500 to spend on office supplies for its workers. The function $E(x) = \frac{1500}{x}$ gives the amount that the company can spend on each employee. Is it possible for the amount of money per employee to be $0? Explain what feature of the graph of $E(x)$ tells you this.

★ **2.** Randall and Tiana ordered a pepperoni pizza and a cheese pizza of the same size. All the pieces of the pepperoni pizza were the same size, as were all the pieces of the cheese pizza, but the cheese pizza was cut into 4 more pieces than the pepperoni pizza. Tiana ate one piece of each pizza. Randall ate the rest of both pizzas. If the pepperoni pizza was cut into p pieces, what fraction of each pizza did Randall eat?

★★ **3.** In Major League baseball, the smallest allowable volume of a baseball is 92.06% of the largest allowable volume, and the range of allowable radii is 0.04 inches.

a. Suppose r is the largest allowable radius of a baseball in inches. Write expressions for the largest allowable volume of the baseball and the smallest allowable volume of the baseball, both in terms of r.

b. Write an equation that shows that the ratio of the smallest allowable volume to the largest allowable volume is 0.9206.

continued

c. Solve the equation in part **b** for r, and round r to the nearest hundredth of an inch. What are the smallest allowable radius and the largest allowable radius of a baseball?

4. Eva and Ty started jogging at the same time from opposite ends of a straight trail. Both jogged at a constant, but different, speed. When each of them reached the opposite end, he or she turned around and went back to where they started. The first time they met along the trail, they were 3 miles from Ty's end of the trail, and the second time they met, they had each turned around and were 2 miles from Eva's end of the trail.

a. Let the length of the trail be m miles. What was the total distance run by Ty and the total distance run by Eva the first time they met?

b. What was the total distance run by Ty and the total distance run by Eva the second time they met?

c. Set up an equation and solve for m to find the length of the trail. Why must the ratio of the total distances run the first time they met be equal to the ratio of the total distances run the second time they met?

Name ____________________ Class ______________ Date ________

SELECTED RESPONSE

1. What is the solution of the equation $\sqrt{x+27} = x - 3$?

A. $x = -9$ **C.** $x = 2$

B. $x = -2$ **D.** $x = 9$

2. Which best describes the graph of $g(x) = 4\sqrt[3]{x}$ as a transformation of the graph of $f(x) = \sqrt[3]{x}$?

F. vertical stretch by a factor of 4

G. vertical compression by a factor of $\frac{1}{4}$

H. translation 4 units up

J. translation 4 units to the right

3. A group of x friends splits the cost of a family-style dinner for \$50. In addition to the cost of the dinner, each person orders a \$5 dessert. Which function gives the amount $A(x)$ that each person pays?

A. $A(x) = \frac{x}{50} + 5$ **C.** $A(x) = \frac{50}{x} + 5$

B. $A(x) = \frac{x}{5} + 50$ **D.** $A(x) = \frac{5}{x} + 50$

4. What are the solutions of the equation $\frac{x}{x-1} + \frac{1}{x+2} = -\frac{3}{x^2+x-2}$?

F. $-1, -2$ **H.** -1

G. $-4, 1$ **J.** -4

5. Which function is the graphing form of $f(x) = \frac{4x+3}{x-1}$?

A. $f(x) = \frac{4}{x-1} + 7$

B. $f(x) = \frac{4}{x-1} - 1$

C. $f(x) = \frac{-1}{x-1} + 4$

D. $f(x) = \frac{7}{x-1} + 4$

6. The graph of which function is shown?

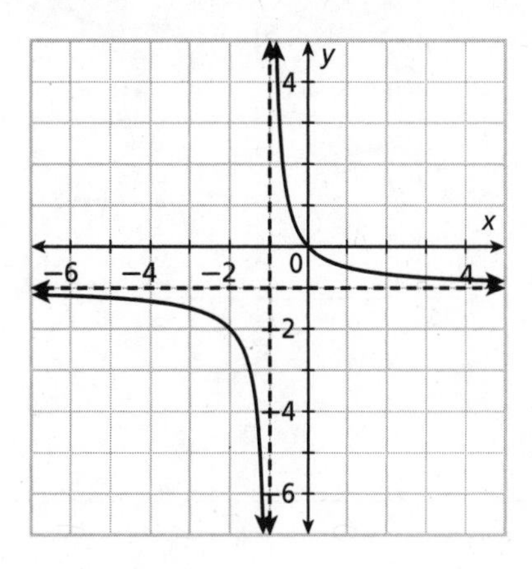

F. $f(x) = \frac{1}{x+1} + 1$

G. $f(x) = \frac{1}{x+1} - 1$

H. $f(x) = \frac{1}{x-1} + 1$

J. $f(x) = \frac{1}{x-1} - 1$

7. In which quadrants does the graph of $f(x) = \frac{3}{x}$ lie?

A. I and II **C.** II and IV

B. I and III **D.** III and IV

8. What is $\sqrt[5]{n^3}$ in rational exponent form?

F. $n^{\frac{5}{3}}$ **H.** n^{15}

G. $n^{\frac{3}{5}}$ **J.** n^8

9. Ronda began simplifying the expression $\sqrt{a} \cdot \sqrt[3]{a}$ by writing $a^{\frac{1}{2}} \cdot a^{\frac{1}{3}}$. What is the next step that she should take?

A. Write $a^{\frac{1}{2}} \cdot a^{\frac{1}{3}}$ as $a^{\frac{1}{2} \cdot \frac{1}{3}}$.

B. Write $a^{\frac{1}{2}} \cdot a^{\frac{1}{3}}$ as $\frac{1}{a^{\frac{1}{2} \cdot \frac{1}{3}}}$.

C. Write $a^{\frac{1}{2}} \cdot a^{\frac{1}{3}}$ as $a^{\frac{1}{2} + \frac{1}{3}}$.

D. Write $a^{\frac{1}{2}} \cdot a^{\frac{1}{3}}$ as $\frac{1}{a^{\frac{1}{2} + \frac{1}{3}}}$.

CONSTRUCTED RESPONSE

10. Graph $g(x) = \sqrt{x-1} + 2$ on the coordinate plane below. Then describe the graph of $g(x)$ as a transformation of the graph of the parent function $f(x) = \sqrt{x}$.

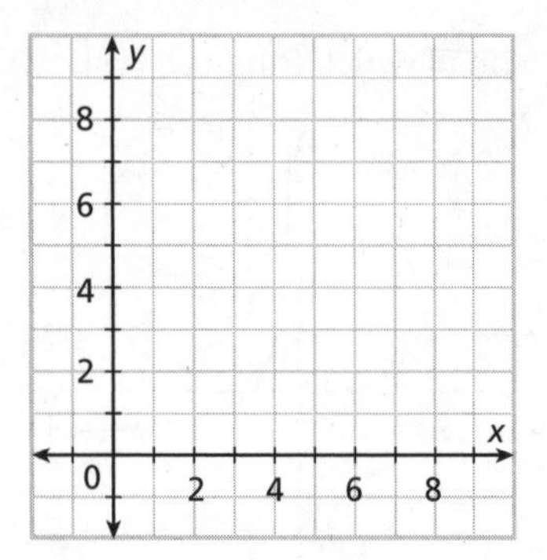

____

____

____

11. Kelsey is making bracelets to sell at a craft fair. She spends \$50 on a jewelry-making kit and \$.50 on beads for each bracelet. She plans to sell the bracelets for \$3 each.

a. Write and simplify a rule for the profit-per-bracelet function $P(b)$ if she sells b bracelets.

____

b. As the number of bracelets sold increases, what happens to the profit per bracelet?

____

____

12. Use the expressions $\frac{x}{x+1}$ and $\frac{1}{x^2+x}$ to complete the following.

a. Find the product of the expressions.

____

b. Find the quotient of the expressions (first expression divided by second expression).

____

____

c. Find the sum of the expressions.

____

d. Find the difference of the expressions (first expression minus second expression).

____

13. While canoeing on a river, your paddling speed is twice the river's current. You travel 3 miles downstream and then 3 miles upstream to get back to where you started.

a. Write a rule for $T(s)$, the function that gives your total trip time (in hours) as a function of the current's speed s (in miles per hour). The rule should involve a sum of two rational expressions. Carry out the addition to simplify the rule as much as possible.

____

b. Use the coordinate plane below to graph $T(s)$. Include axis labels and scales.

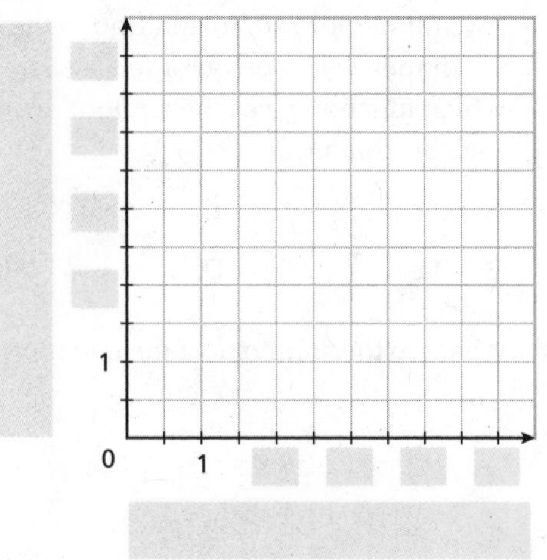

c. How is the graph of $T(s)$ related to the graph of the parent function $f(s) = \frac{1}{s}$?

____

d. Use the graph to estimate the current's speed when the total trip time is 2.5 hours.

____

e. Write and solve an equation to find the current's speed exactly when the total trip time is 2.5 hours.

____

UNIT 8

Exponential and Logarithms

	Module 15 Exponential and Logarithmic Functions	GPS COMMON CORE
15-1	Exponential Functions, Growth and Decay	MCC9-12.A.CED.2,MCC9-12.F.IF.7e
15-2	Inverses of Relations and Functions	MCC9-12.F.BF.4a
15-3	Logarithmic Functions	MCC9-12.F.BF.5, MCC9-12.F.IF.7e
	Module 16 Exponential and Logarithmic Equations	
16-1	Properties of Logarithms	MCC9-12.F.BF.5, MCC9-12.A.SSE.3, MCC9-12.F.IF.8b
16-2	Exponential and Logarithmic Equations and Inequalities	MCC9-12.F.LE.4, MCC9-12.A.SSE.3, MCC9-12.F.IF.8b
16-3	The Natural Base, *e*	MCC9-12.F.LE.4, MCC9-12.F.IF.7e
	Performance Tasks	
	PARCC Assessment Readiness	

UNIT 8

Unpacking the Standards

Understanding the standards and the vocabulary terms in the standards will help you know exactly what you are expected to learn in this unit.

MCC9-12.F.BF.5

Understand the inverse relationship between exponents and logarithms and use this relationship to solve problems involving logarithms and exponents.

Key Vocabulary

inverse function *(función inversa)*
The function that results from exchanging the input and output values of a one-to-one function. The inverse of $f(x)$ is denoted $f^{-1}(x)$.

logarithm *(logaritmo)*
The exponent that a specified base must be raised to in order to get a certain value.

What It Means For You

Logarithmic functions and exponential functions are inverse functions. The input of an exponential function is an exponent and the output is a power. The input of a logarithmic function is a power, and the output is an exponent.

EXAMPLE

When working with logarithms, remember that *a logarithm is an exponent*. In both equations below, b is the base, and the logarithm x is the exponent.

Exponential Equation **Logarithmic Equation**

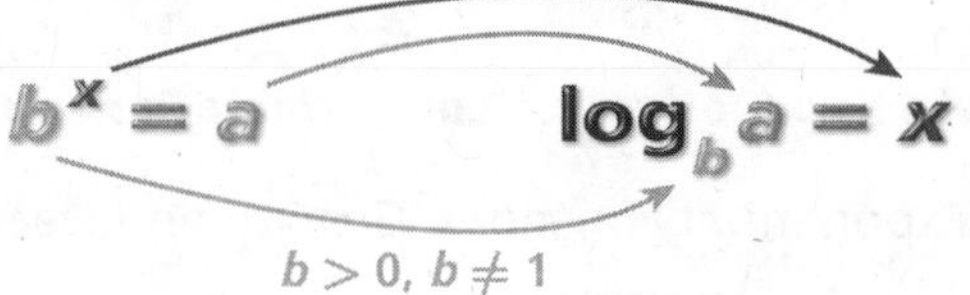

Read: b to the x equals a. Think: When I raise b to the xth power, I get a.	Read: log base b of a equals x. Think: x is the exponent on the base b that gives me a.

MCC9-12.F.IF.7e

Graph exponential and logarithmic functions, showing intercepts and end behavior, …

Key Vocabulary

exponential function *(función exponencial)* A function of the form $f(x) = ab^x$, where a and b are real numbers with $a \neq 0$, $b > 0$, and $b \neq 1$.

logarithmic function *(función logarítmica)* A function of the form $f(x) = \log_b x$, where $b \neq 1$ and $b > 0$, which is the inverse of the exponential function $f(x) = b^x$.

What It Means For You

Exponential functions represent growth or decay. Because exponential and logarithmic functions are inverse functions, the graph of an exponential function and its inverse logarithmic function are reflections in the line $y = x$.

EXAMPLE

For the function $f(x) = 3^x$, the input 2 gives the output 9. So, for the inverse function $f^{-1}(x) = \log_3 x$, the input 9 gives the output 2.
The y-intercept, 1, of $f(x) = 3^x$ is the x-intercept of $f^{-1}(x) = \log_3 x$.

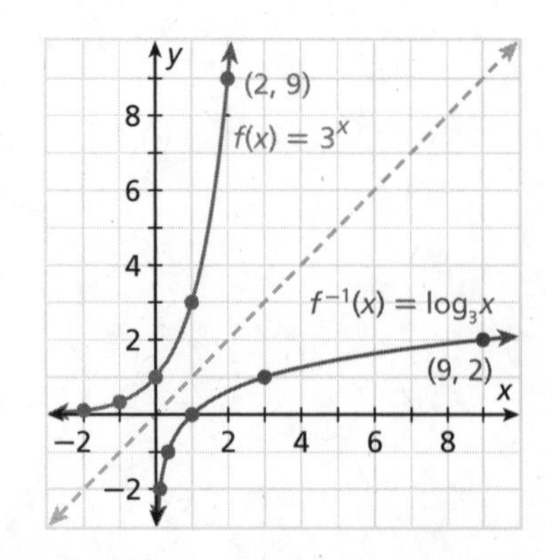

UNIT 8

MCC9-12.F.LE.4

For exponential models, express as a logarithm the solution to $ab^{ct} = d$ where a, c, and d are numbers and the base b is 2, 10, or e; evaluate the logarithm using technology.

Key Vocabulary

exponential equation
(ecuación exponencial) An equation that contains one or more exponential expressions.

What It Means For You

Because exponential and logarithmic functions are inverses, you can solve an exponential equation by taking the logarithm of both sides of the equation and using the properties of logarithms.

EXAMPLE

A veterinarian prescribes aspirin for a dog with arthritis. You can solve the exponential equation below to find out how many minutes it takes for the amount of aspirin in a 75 lb dog's system to drop from 325 mg to 50 mg.

$$50 = 325\left(\frac{1}{2}\right)^{\frac{t}{15}}$$

$$\frac{2}{13} = \left(\frac{1}{2}\right)^{\frac{t}{15}} \quad \text{Divide both sides by 325.}$$

$$\log\frac{2}{13} = \log\left(\frac{1}{2}\right)^{\frac{t}{15}} \quad \textit{Take the logarithm of both sides.}$$

Using the fact that $\log\left(\frac{1}{2}\right)^{\frac{t}{15}} = \frac{t}{15}\log\frac{1}{2}$, you can solve the equation above for t.

Using a calculator to evaluate the solution gives $t \approx 40.5$ minutes.

UNIT 8

Key Vocabulary

asymptote *(asíntota)* A line that a graph approaches as the value of a variable becomes extremely large or small.

base of an exponential function *(base de una función exponencial)* The value of b in a function of the form $f(x) = ab^x$, where a and b are real numbers with $a \neq 0$, $b > 0$, and $b \neq 1$.

common logarithm *(logaritmo común)* A logarithm whose base is 10, denoted $\log_{10}$ or just log.

end behavior *(comportamiento extremo)* The trends in the y-values of a function as the x-values approach positive and negative infinity.

exponential decay function *(decremento exponencial)* An exponential function of the form $f(x) = ab^x$ in which $0 < b < 1$. If r is the rate of decay, then the function can be written $y = a(1 - r)^t$, where a is the initial amount and t is the time.

exponential equation *(ecuación exponencial)* An equation that contains one or more exponential expressions.

exponential function *(función exponencial)* A function of the form $f(x) = ab^x$, where a and b are real numbers with $a \neq 0$, $b > 0$, and $b \neq 1$.

exponential growth function *(crecimiento exponencial)* An exponential function of the form $f(x) = ab^x$ in which $b > 1$. If r is the rate of growth, then the function can be written $y = a(1 + r)^t$, where a is the initial amount and t is the time.

inverse function *(función inversa)* The function that results from exchanging the input and output values of a one-to-one function. The inverse of $f(x)$ is denoted $f^{-1}(x)$.

logarithm *(logaritmo)* The exponent that a specified base must be raised to in order to get a certain value.

logarithmic function *(función logarítmica)* A function of the form $f(x) = \log_b x$, where $b \neq 1$ and $b > 0$, which is the inverse of the exponential function $f(x) = b^x$.

natural logarithm *(logaritmo natural)* A logarithm with base e, written as ln.

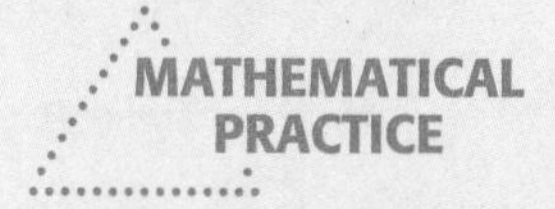

The Common Core Standards for Mathematical Practice describe varieties of expertise that mathematics educators at all levels should seek to develop in their students. Opportunities to develop these practices are integrated throughout this program.

1. **Make sense of problems and persevere in solving them.**
2. **Reason abstractly and quantitatively.**
3. **Construct viable arguments and critique the reasoning of others.**
4. **Model with mathematics.**
5. **Use appropriate tools strategically.**
6. **Attend to precision.**
7. **Look for and make use of structure.**
8. **Look for and express regularity in repeated reasoning.**

Name________________________ Class______________ Date__________

15-1

Exponential Functions, Growth and Decay

Going Deeper

Video Tutor

Essential question: *What are the characteristics of an exponential function?*

In an **exponential function**, the variable is an exponent. The parent function is $f(x) = b^x$, where b is any real number greater than 0, except 1.

MCC9–12.F.IF.7e

1 EXAMPLE Graphing $f(x) = b^x$ for $b > 1$

Graph $f(x) = 2^x$.

A Complete the table of values below.

B Plot the points on the graph and connect the points with a smooth curve.

x	$f(x) = 2^x$
−3	$2^{-3} = \frac{1}{2^3} = \frac{1}{8}$
−2	
−1	
0	
1	
2	
3	

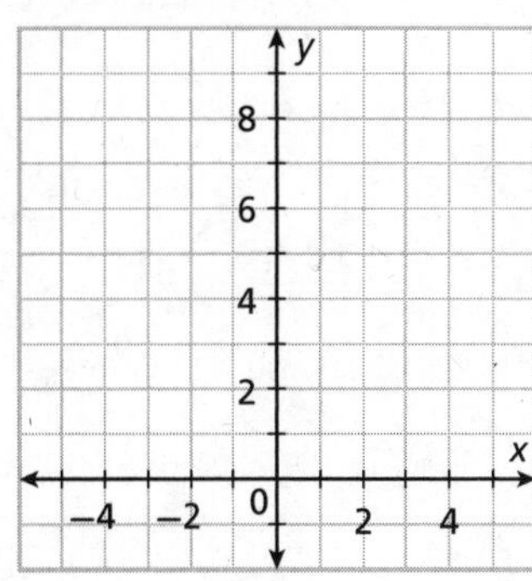

REFLECT

1a. What happens to $f(x)$ as x increases without bound? What happens to $f(x)$ as x decreases without bound?

____

____

1b. Does the graph intersect the x-axis? Explain how you know.

____

____

1c. What are the domain and range of $f(x)$?

____

MCC9–12.F.IF.7e

2 EXAMPLE Graphing $f(x) = b^x$ for $0 < b < 1$

Graph $f(x) = \left(\frac{1}{2}\right)^x$.

A Complete the table of values below.

B Plot the points on the graph and connect the points with a smooth curve.

x	$f(x) = \left(\frac{1}{2}\right)^x$
−3	$\left(\frac{1}{2}\right)^{-3} = (2)^3 = 8$
−2	
−1	
0	
1	
2	
3	

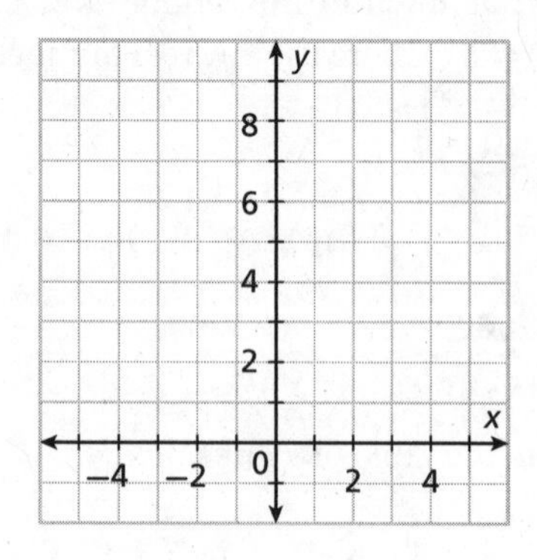

REFLECT

2a. What happens to $f(x)$ as x increases without bound? What happens to $f(x)$ as x decreases without bound?

2b. How do the domain and range of $f(x) = \left(\frac{1}{2}\right)^x$ compare to the domain and range of $f(x) = 2^x$?

2c. What do you notice about the y-intercepts of the graphs of $f(x) = \left(\frac{1}{2}\right)^x$ and $f(x) = 2^x$? Why does this make sense?

2d. What transformation can you use to obtain the graph of $f(x) = \left(\frac{1}{2}\right)^x$ from the graph of $f(x) = 2^x$?

---

3 ENGAGE Recognizing Types of Exponential Functions

A function of the form $f(x) = b^x$ is an **exponential growth function** if $b > 1$ and an **exponential decay function** if $0 < b < 1$.

Exponential Growth $f(x) = b^x$ for $b > 1$	Exponential Decay $f(x) = b^x$ for $0 < b < 1$
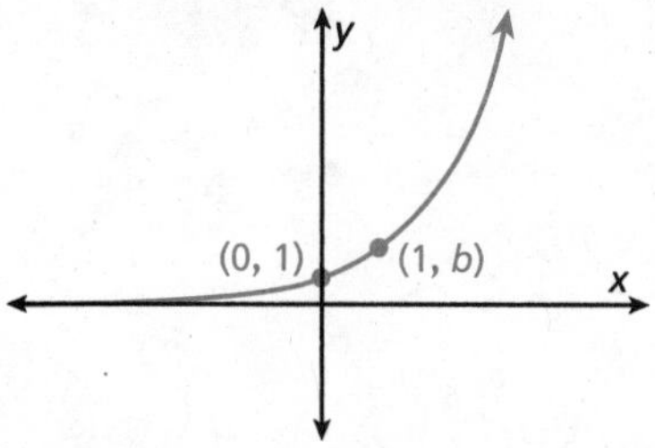 y; (0, 1); (1, b); x	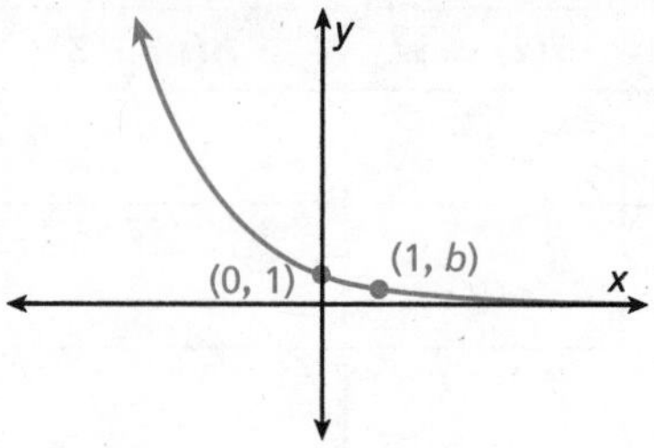 y; (0, 1); (1, b); x

REFLECT

3a. Describe the end behavior of an exponential growth function.

3b. Describe the end behavior of an exponential decay function.

3c. Explain why the point $(1, b)$ is always on the graph of $f(x) = b^x$.

3d. Explain why the point $(0, 1)$ is always on the graph of $f(x) = b^x$.

3e. Are $f(x) = 3^x$ and $g(x) = 5^x$ both exponential growth functions or both exponential decay functions? Although they have the same end behavior, how you do think their graphs differ? Explain your reasoning.

3f. Are $f(x) = \left(\frac{1}{3}\right)^x$ and $g(x) = \left(\frac{1}{5}\right)^x$ both exponential growth functions or both exponential decay functions? Although they have the same end behavior, how do you think their graphs differ? Explain your reasoning.

MCC9–12.F.LE.3

4 EXPLORE Comparing Linear, Cubic, and Exponential Functions

Compare each of the functions $f(x) = x + 3$ and $g(x) = x^3$ to the exponential function $h(x) = 3^x$ for $x \geq 0$.

A Complete the table of values for the three functions.

x	$f(x) = x + 3$	$g(x) = x^3$	$h(x) = 3^x$
0	3	0	1
1			
2			
3			
4			
5			

B The graph of $h(x) = 3^x$ is shown on the coordinate grid below. Graph $f(x) = x + 3$ on the same grid.

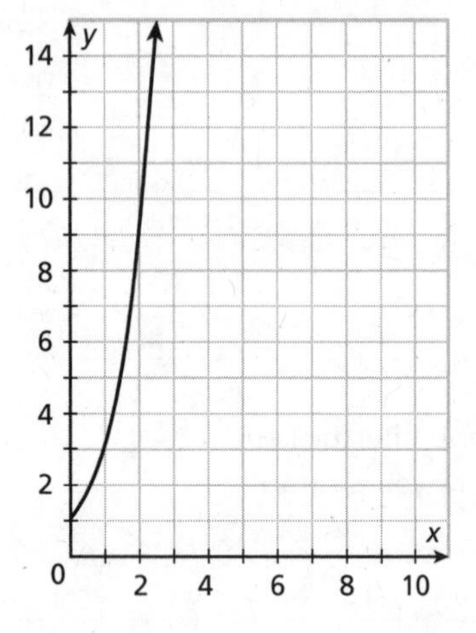

C The graph of $h(x) = 3^x$ is shown on the coordinate grid below. Graph $g(x) = x^3$ on the same grid.

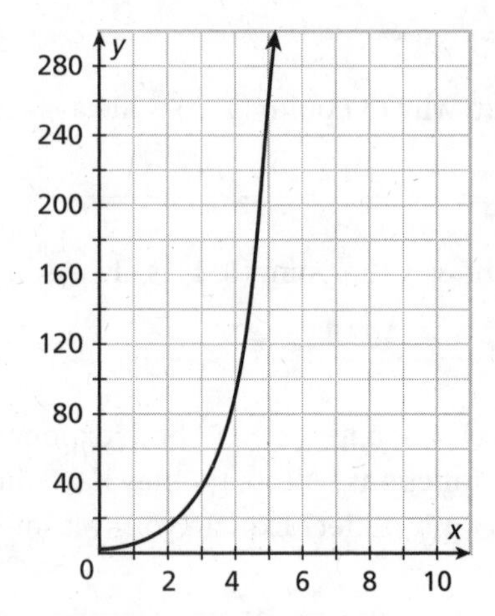

REFLECT

4a. How do the values of $h(x)$ compare to those of $f(x)$ and $g(x)$ as x increases without bound?

PRACTICE

Tell whether the function describes an exponential growth function or an exponential decay function. Explain how you know without graphing.

1. $f(x) = 0.9^x$

2. $g(x) = 4.5^x$

3. $h(x) = \left(\frac{5}{2}\right)^x$

4. $k(x) = \left(\frac{3}{4}\right)^x$

5. In an exponential function, $f(x) = b^x$, b is not allowed to be 1. Explain why this restriction exists.

6. Complete the table for $f(x) = 4^x$. Then sketch the graph of the function.

x	$f(x)$
−1	
0	
1	
2	
3	

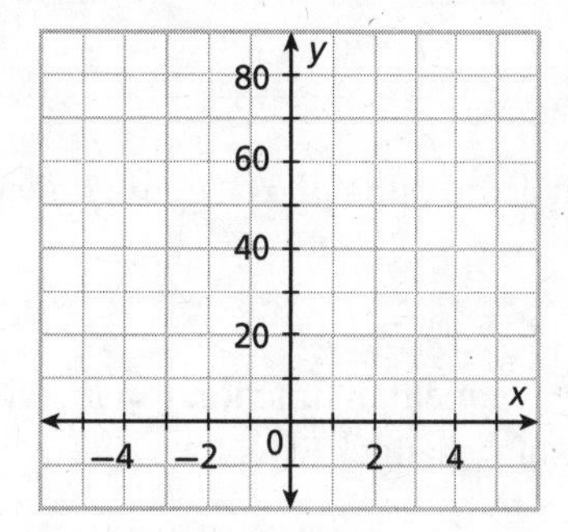

7. Complete the table for $f(x) = \left(\frac{1}{3}\right)^x$. Then sketch the graph of the function.

x	$f(x)$
−3	
−2	
−1	
0	
1	

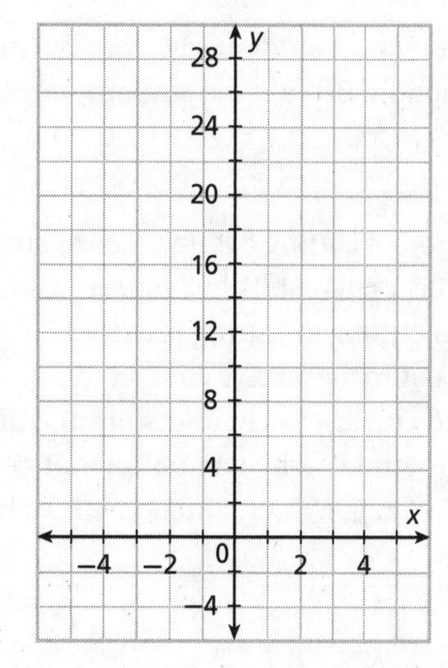

8. Compare the graph of $f(x) = 2^x$ to the graph of $g(x) = x^2$.

9. Enter the functions $f(x) = 10^x$ and $g(x) = \left(\frac{1}{10}\right)^x$ into your graphing calculator.

a. Look at a table of values for the two functions. For a given x-value, how do the corresponding function values compare?

b. Look at graphs of the two functions. How are the two graphs related to each other?

10. The graph of an exponential function $f(x) = b^x$ is shown.

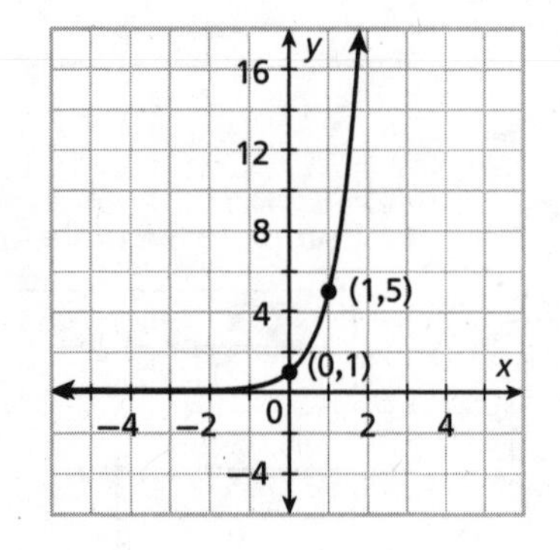

a. Which of the labeled points, (0, 1) or (1, 5), allows you to determine the value of b? Why doesn't the other point help?

b. What is the value of b? Explain how you know.

11. Given an exponential function $y = b^x$, when you double the value of x, how does the value of y change? Explain.

12. Given an exponential function $y = b^x$, when you add 2 to the value of x, how does the value of y change? Explain.

13. **Error Analysis** A student says that the function $f(x) = \left(\frac{1}{0.5}\right)^x$ is an exponential decay function. Explain the student's error.

14. One method of cutting a long piece of string into smaller pieces is to make individual cuts, so that 1 cut results in 2 pieces, 2 cuts result in 3 pieces, and so on. Another method of cutting the string is to fold it onto itself and cut the folded end, then fold the pieces onto themselves and cut their folded ends at the same time, and continue to fold and cut, so that 1 cut results in 2 pieces, 2 cuts result in 4 pieces, and so on. For each method, write a function that gives the number p of pieces in terms of the number c of cuts. Which function grows faster? Why?

Name_____________________ Class_____________ Date___________

Additional Practice

Tell whether the function shows growth or decay. Then graph.

1. $g(x) = -(2)^x$

____

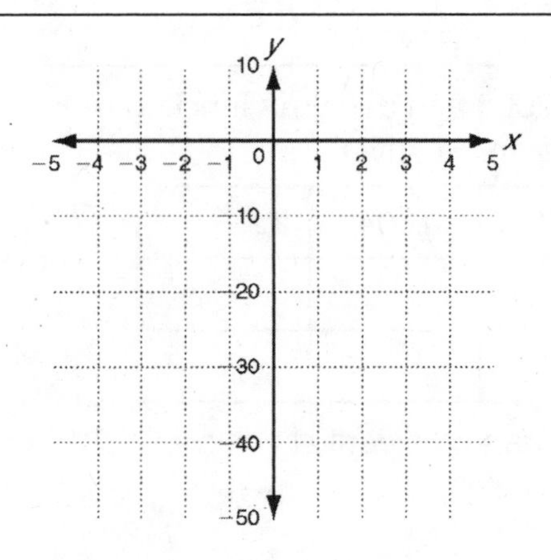

2. $h(x) = -0.5(0.2)^x$

____

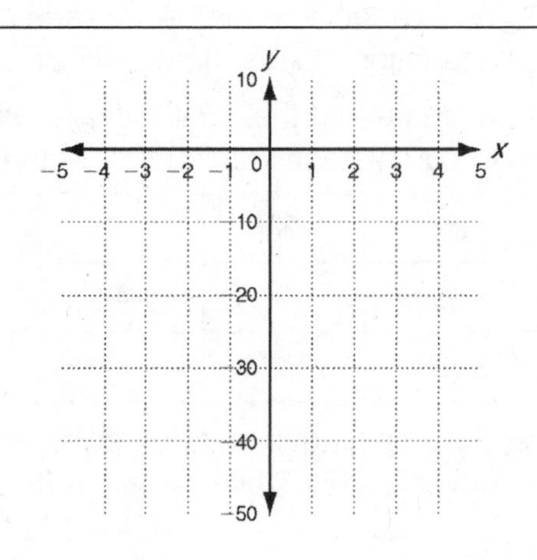

3. $j(x) = -2(0.5)^x$

____

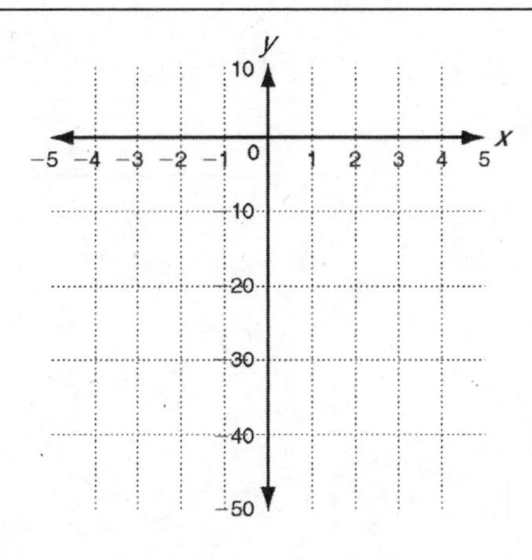

4. $p(x) = 4(1.4)^x$

____

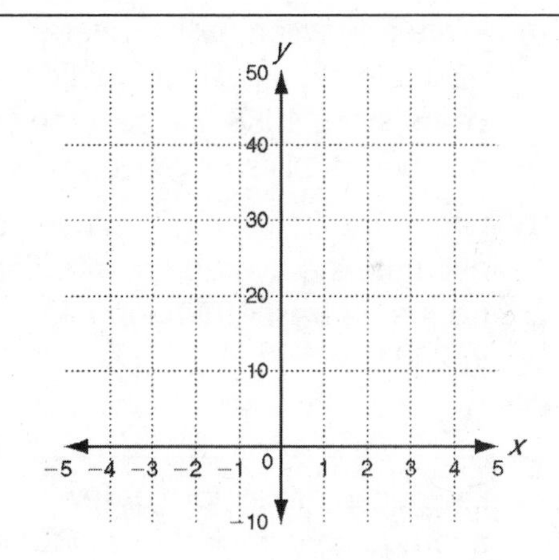

Solve.

5. A certain car's value depreciates about 15% each year. This is modeled by the function

   $V(t) = 20{,}000(0.85)^t$

   where $20,000 is the value of a brand-new model.

   a. Graph the function.

   b. Suppose the car was worth $20,000 in 2005. What is the first year that the value of this car will be worth less than half of that value?

   ____

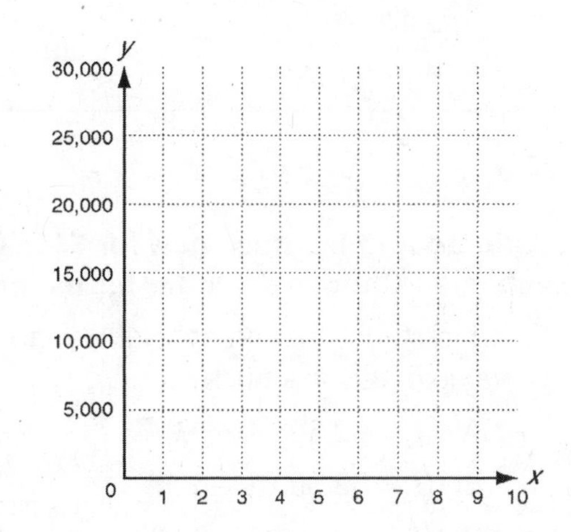

Problem Solving

Justin drove his pickup truck about 22,000 miles in 2004. He read that in 1988 the average residential vehicle traveled about 10,200 miles, which increased by about 2.9% per year through 2004.

1. Write a function for the average mileage, $m(t)$, as a function of t, the time in years since 1988. ________________

2. Assume that the 2.9% increase is valid through 2008 and use your function to complete the table to show the average annual miles driven.

Year	1988	1992	1996	2000	2004	2008
t	0	4				
m (t)	10,200					

3. Did Justin drive more or fewer miles than the average residential vehicle driver in 2004? by how much (to the nearest 100 miles)?

____

4. Later Justin read that the annual mileage for light trucks increased by 7.8% per year from 1988 to 2004.

   a. Write a function for the average miles driven for a light truck, $n(t)$, as a function of t, the time in years since 1988. He assumes that the average number of miles driven in 1988 was 10,200. ________________

   b. Graph the function. Then use your graph to estimate the average number of miles driven (to the nearest 1000) for a light truck in 2004.

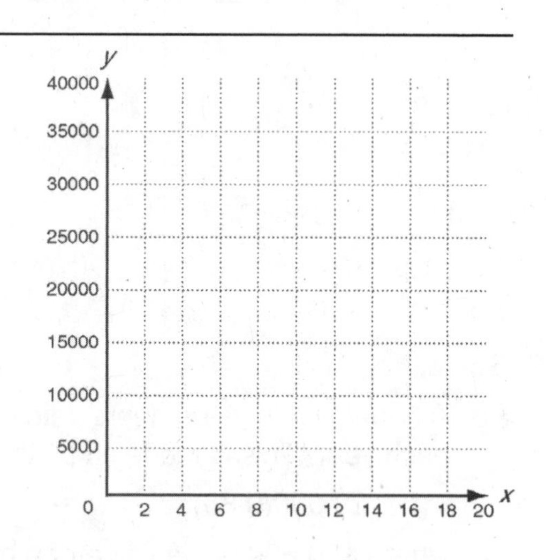

   ____

   c. Did Justin drive more or fewer miles than the average light truck driver in 2004? by how much?

   ____

Justin bought his truck new for $32,000. Its value decreases 9.0% each year. Choose the letter for the best answer.

5. Which function represents the yearly value of Justin's truck?

   A $f(t) = 32{,}000(1 + 0.9)^t$

   B $f(t) = 32{,}000(1 - 0.9)^t$

   C $f(t) = 32{,}000(1 + 0.09)^t$

   D $f(t) = 32{,}000(1 - 0.09)^t$

6. When will the value of Justin's truck fall below half of what he paid for it?

   F In 6 years

   G In 8 years

   H In 10 years

   J In 12 years

Name________________ Class________________ Date________________

15-2

Inverses of Relations and Functions

Going Deeper

Essential question: *How do you find the inverse of a function, and how is the original function related to its inverse?*

Video Tutor

PREP FOR MCC9-12.F.BF.4

1 ENGAGE Understanding the Inverse of a Function

The mapping diagram on the left shows a function. If you reverse the arrows in the mapping diagram as shown on the right, the original outputs become the inputs, and the original inputs become the outputs.

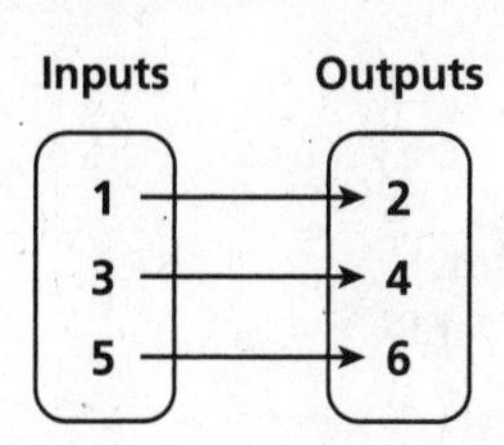

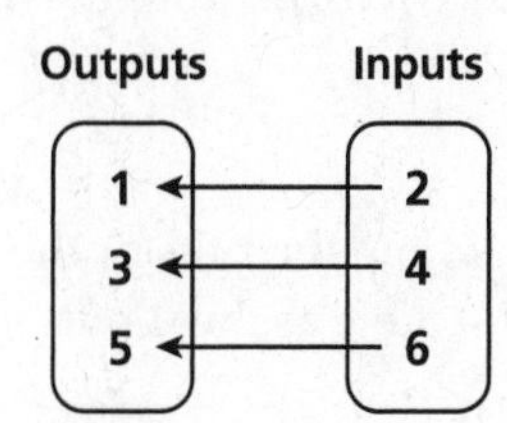

If you reverse the arrows in a mapping diagram of a function and the new mapping diagram also represents a function, this new function is said to be the *inverse* of the original function. Functions that undo each other are **inverse functions**.

The notation $f^{-1}(x)$ indicates the inverse of a function $f(x)$. The domain of $f^{-1}(x)$ is the range of $f(x)$, and the range of $f^{-1}(x)$ is the domain of $f(x)$.

REFLECT

1a. How do you know that each mapping diagram shows a function?

____

1b. The domain of a function $f(x)$ is the set {10, 20, 30}. What does this information tell you about $f^{-1}(x)$?

____

1c. If the graph of a function $f(x)$ includes the point (3, 0), what point must the graph of $f^{-1}(x)$ include? Explain.

____

MCC9-12.F.BF.4

2 EXPLORE Finding $f^{-1}(x)$ by Using Inverse Operations

Find the inverse function $f^{-1}(x)$ for the function $f(x) = 3x - 2$.

A Describe the sequence of operations performed on an input value x by the function $f(x)$.

- First, multiply by ________________.
- Second, ________________.

B Describe the inverse of each operation listed in step A, but in reverse order.

- First, add ______________.
- Second, ______________ by 3.

C Write a function rule for $f^{-1}(x)$ that matches the steps you described in step B.

$x +$ ☐ First, add 2 to the variable.

$\frac{x+2}{☐}$ Second, ______________ the sum by 3.

$f^{-1}(x) =$ ☐ Write the rule for the inverse function.

D Complete the tables to verify that you found the rule for the inverse function correctly. Use the outputs from the first table as the inputs for the second table.

Function $f(x) = 3x - 2$	
Input x	Output $f(x)$
0	
2	
4	
6	

Inverse Function	
Input x	Output $f^{-1}(x)$

REFLECT

2a. Explain how the tables show that you found the inverse of the function correctly.

____

____

2b. Why do you reverse the order of the steps when writing the inverse operations in part B?

____

____

____

2c. Could the rule for $f^{-1}(x)$ be written as $\frac{x}{3} + 2$? Explain why or why not.

____

____

MCC9–12.F.BF.4a

3 EXAMPLE Finding $f^{-1}(x)$ by Solving an Equation

Find the inverse function $f^{-1}(x)$ for the function $f(x) = 3x - 2$.

A Substitute y for $f(x)$, and then solve for x.

$\square = 3x - 2$ Replace $f(x)$ with y.

$y + \square = 3x$ Add 2 to both sides.

$\frac{y+2}{\square} = x$ Divide both sides by ______________.

B Write the rule for $f^{-1}(x)$.

$\frac{x+2}{3} = y$ Switch x and y in the equation from part A.

$\frac{x+2}{3} = f^{-1}(x)$ Replace y with $f^{-1}(x)$.

So, the inverse function is $f^{-1}(x) =$ ______________.

REFLECT

3a. How are the steps of solving the equation in part A similar to what you did when writing inverse operations in reverse order in the Explore?

____

3b. Why does it make sense to switch the variables when writing the inverse function?

____

____

MCC9–12.F.IF.7a

4 EXAMPLE Graphing a Function and Its Inverse

Graph the function $f(x) = 3x - 2$ and its inverse.

A Graph the function $f(x) = 3x - 2$.

The function is linear.

slope = $\square$; y-intercept = $\square$

B Graph the inverse function $f^{-1}(x)$.

From the previous Example, you know that $f^{-1}(x) = \frac{x+2}{3}$.

The function is linear.

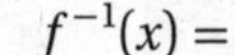 $\square\, x + \square$ Write in slope-intercept form.

slope = $\square$; y-intercept = $\square$

REFLECT

4a. Describe the relationship between coordinates of the points on the graph of a function and those on the graph of its inverse.

____

4b. Graph the line $y = x$ on the same coordinate plane as the graphs of $f(x)$ and $f^{-1}(x)$. Use the graph of $y = x$ to describe the graph of $f^{-1}(x)$ as a transformation of the graph of $f(x)$.

____

Real-World Functions The variables in functions that model real-world situations typically refer to the real-world quantities that they represent. For instance, the function that gives the amount a (in dollars) that you spend when you buy g gallons of gas for \$4 per gallon at a gas station is $a = 4g$. You can write $a(g) = 4g$ to emphasize the dependency of a on g.

You can find the inverse of a function that models a real-world situation by solving for the independent variable in terms of the dependent variable. You do not, however, switch the variables at the end of the process as you would switch x and y when finding the inverse of a purely mathematical function. The reason for not switching is that the variables have real-world meanings that cannot be interchanged.

In the case of the real-world function $a = 4g$, the inverse function is $g = \frac{a}{4}$, which gives the amount of gas (in gallons) that you can buy for a given amount of money (in dollars). To emphasize the dependency of g on a, you can write $g(a) = \frac{a}{4}$.

Finding the Inverse of a Real-World Function

Mr. Williams is driving on a highway at an average speed of 50 miles per hour. His destination is 100 miles away. The equation $d = 100 - 50t$ gives the distance d (in miles) that he has left to travel as a function of the time t (in hours) that he has been driving. Write and interpret the inverse of this function.

A Solve the equation for t.

$d = 100 - 50t$	Write the equation.
$d - \square = -50t$	Subtract 100 from both sides.
$\frac{d - \square}{\square} = t$	Divide both sides by -50.
$\square - \frac{d}{\square} = t$	Simplify the left side.

B Interpret the inverse function.

The inverse function gives the ____________________ that Mr. Williams has left to travel as a function of the ____________________ that he has driven.

REFLECT

5a. Use the inverse function to find the time that Mr. Williams has left to travel when he has driven 75 miles.

____

PRACTICE

Find the inverse function $f^{-1}(x)$ for each function $f(x)$.

1. $f(x) = x - 3$

$f^{-1}(x) =$ ______________________

2. $f(x) = \frac{x}{3}$

$f^{-1}(x) =$ ______________________

3. $f(x) = \frac{x+1}{6}$

$f^{-1}(x) =$ ______________________

4. $f(x) = -0.25x$

$f^{-1}(x) =$ ______________________

5. $f(x) = \frac{1}{2}x + 3$

$f^{-1}(x) =$ ______________________

6. $f(x) = 9 - 3x$

$f^{-1}(x) =$ ______________________

Graph each function and its inverse.

7. $f(x) = x + 2$

$f^{-1}(x) =$ ______________________

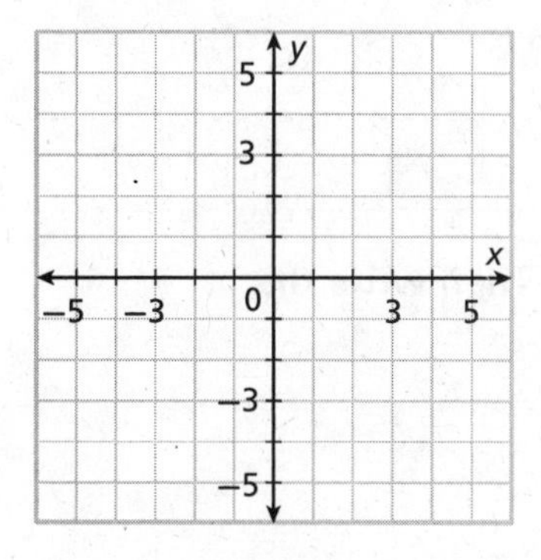

8. $f(x) = \frac{1}{4}x + \frac{1}{4}$

$f^{-1}(x) =$ ______________________

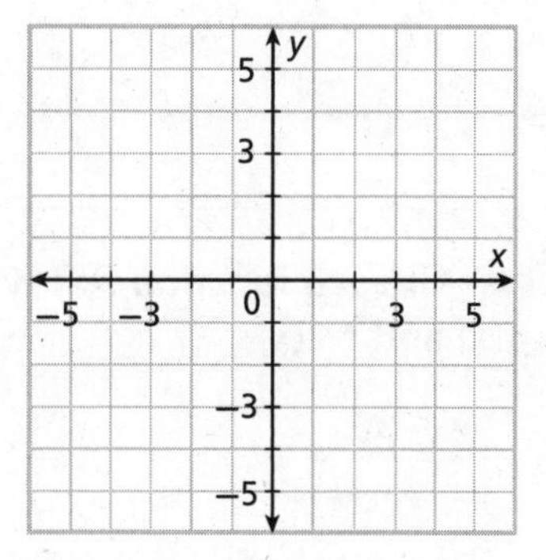

9. $f(x) = -\frac{1}{3}x - \frac{2}{3}$

$f^{-1}(x) =$ ______________________

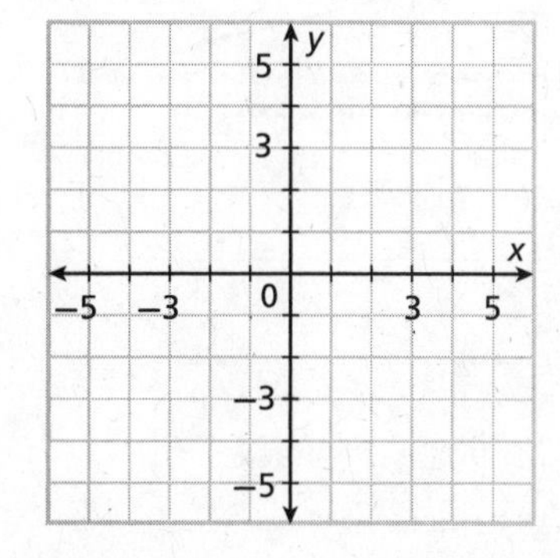

10. $f(x) = -5x$

$f^{-1}(x) =$ ______________________

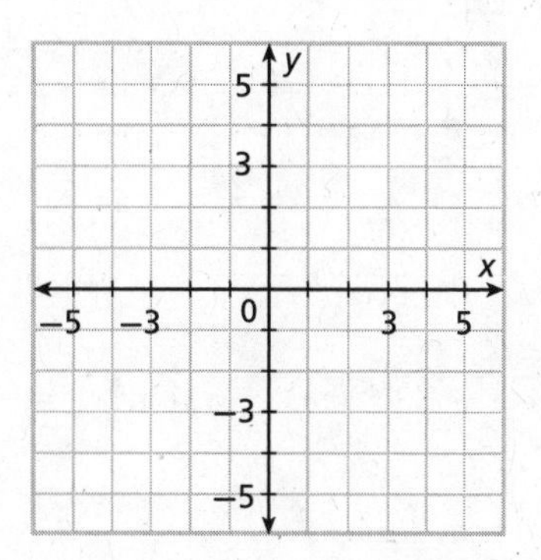

11. The function $A(h) = \frac{1}{2}(20)h$ gives the area A (in square inches) of a triangle with a base of 20 inches and height h (in inches). Write and interpret the inverse of this function.

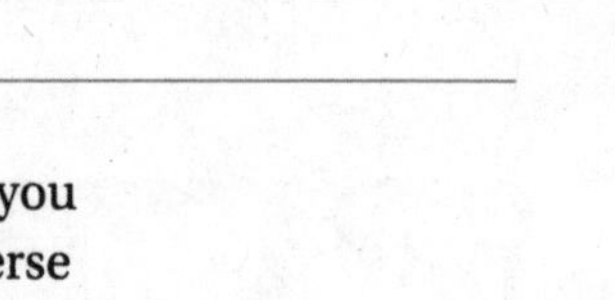

12. The function $a(t) = 8t + 10$ gives the amount a (in dollars) that you pay when you rent a kayak for \$10 and use it for time t (in hours). Write and interpret the inverse of this function.

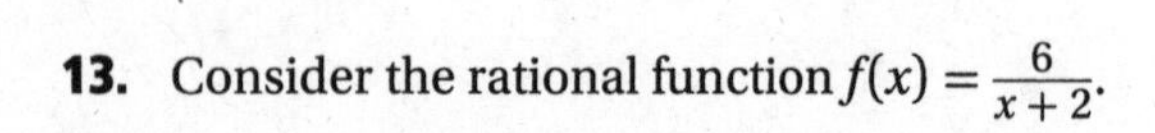

13. Consider the rational function $f(x) = \frac{6}{x+2}$.

a. What is the inverse of the function? ______

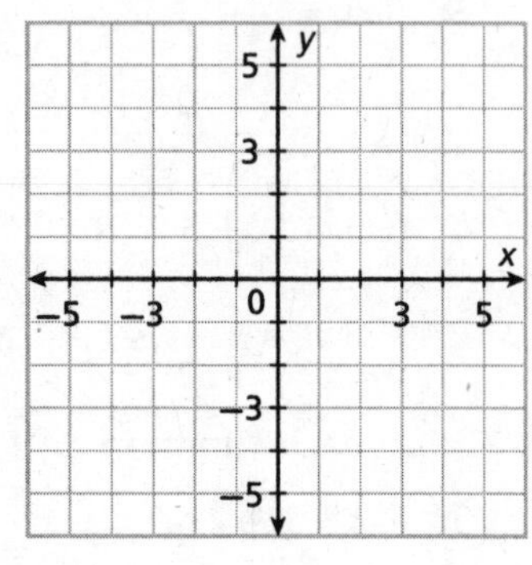

b. Graph the function and its inverse on the same coordinate plane. Then graph the line $y = x$. Describe the relationship between the graphs of $f(x)$ and $f^{-1}(x)$.

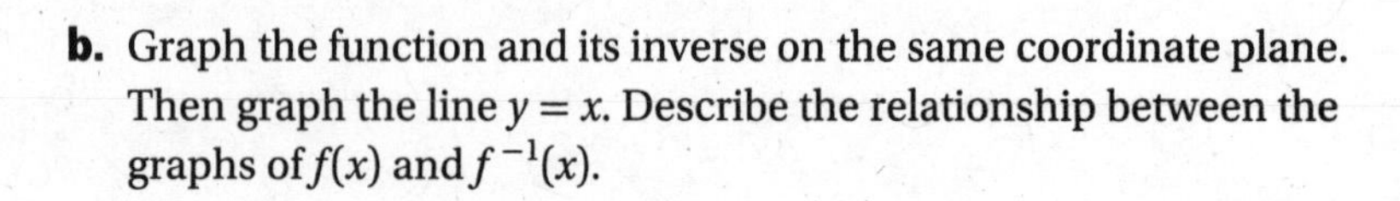

c. Give the domain and range of $f(x)$ and the domain and range of $f^{-1}(x)$. What is the relationship between the domains and ranges?

Graph the inverse of each function $f(x)$ whose graph is shown. Then write the rules for both $f(x)$ and $f^{-1}(x)$.

14.

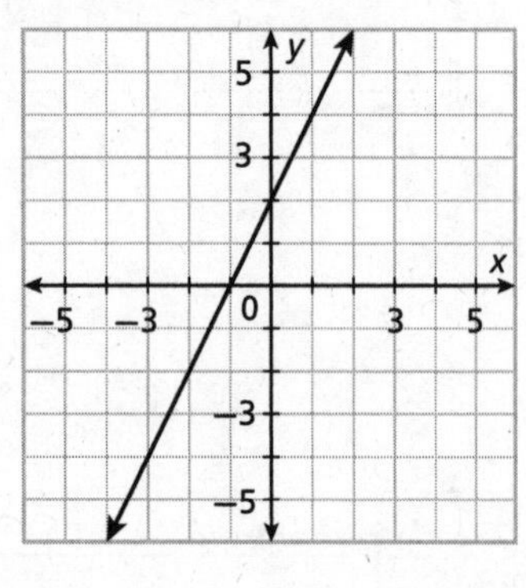

15.

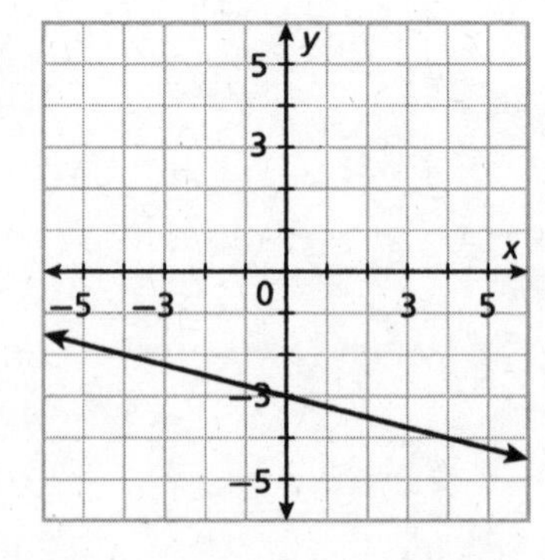

Name________________ Class________________ Date________________

15-2

Additional Practice

Use inverse operations to write the inverse of each function.

1. $f(x) = 15x - 10$ ________________
2. $f(x) = 10 - 4x$ ________________
3. $f(x) = 12 - 9x$ ________________
4. $f(x) = 5x + 2$ ________________
5. $f(x) = x + 6$ ________________
6. $f(x) = x + \frac{1}{2}$ ________________
7. $f(x) = -\frac{x}{12}$ ________________
8. $f(x) = \frac{x - 12}{4}$ ________________
9. $f(x) = \frac{3x + 1}{6}$ ________________

Graph each function. Then write and graph its inverse.

10. $f(x) = 2x - 4$

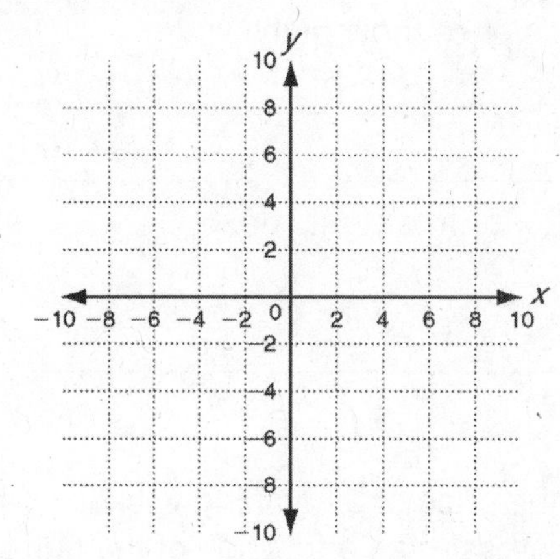

____

11. $f(x) = \frac{5}{2}x - 2$

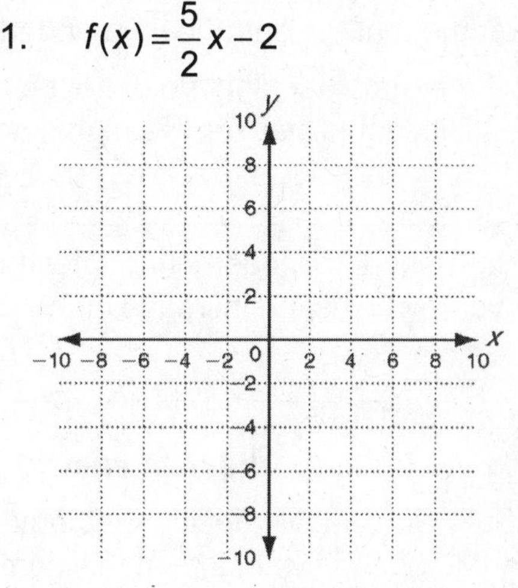

____

Solve.

12. Dan works at a hardware store. The employee discount is determined by the formula $d = 0.15\,(c - 10)$. Use the inverse of this function to find the cost of the item for which Dan received an $18.00 discount.

    a. Find the inverse function that models cost as a function of the discount. ________________

    b. Evaluate the inverse function for $d = 18$. ________________

    c. What was Dan's final cost for this item? ________________

Problem Solving

Sally and Janelle pay a total of $47.96 to camp for three nights at a state park. This includes a one-time park entrance fee of $5 and 9% sales tax. They paid $12 per night to stay for three nights last year, and the one-time park entrance fee was $5.

1. By how much per night has the price changed since last year?
   a. Write an equation for the total price, p, as a function of the price per night, n. ______________________
   b. Find the inverse function that models the price per night as a function of the total price. ______________________
   c. Evaluate the inverse function to find n, the price per night. ______________________
   d. By how much has the price per night changed since last year? ______________________
2. Sally is thinking about whether they want to stay at the park next year. Assume that the entrance fee and the sales tax rate will not change.
   a. If the price per night does not increase from this year's price, how much will it cost to stay for five nights next year?

   ____

   b. If the park management quotes them a price of $87.20 for five nights next year, what is the increase in the price per night?

   ____

Choose the letter for the best answer.

3. If Sally and Janelle decide that they want to spend five nights at this same park in the future and spend no more than $100, what is the maximum price per night that they can pay?
   A $16.00
   B $16.50
   C $17.00
   D $17.50
4. If the price of a camping vacation can be expressed as a function of the number of nights, what does the inverse function represent?
   F Number of nights as a function of the price per night
   G Number of nights as a function of the price of the vacation
   H Price of the vacation as a function of the price per night
   J Price of the vacation as a function of the number of nights

Name ____________________ Class ____________ Date ________

15-3

Video Tutor

Logarithmic Functions
Going Deeper

Essential question: *What are the characteristics of logarithmic functions?*

Recall that if $f(x)$ is a one-to-one function, then the graphs of $f(x)$ and its inverse, $f^{-1}(x)$, are reflections of each other about the line $y = x$. The domain of $f(x)$ is the range of $f^{-1}(x)$, and the range of $f(x)$ is the domain of $f^{-1}(x)$.

PREP FOR MCC9–12.F.IF.7e

1 EXPLORE Graphing the Inverse of an Exponential Function

The graph of $f(x) = 2^x$ is shown. Graph $f^{-1}(x)$ by following these steps.

A Complete the table by writing the image of each point on the graph of $f(x)$ after a reflection across the line $y = x$.

Point on the graph of $f(x)$	Point on the graph's image
(−2, 0.25) →	(0.25, −2)
(−1, 0.5) →	
(0, 1) →	
(1, 2) →	
(2, 4) →	

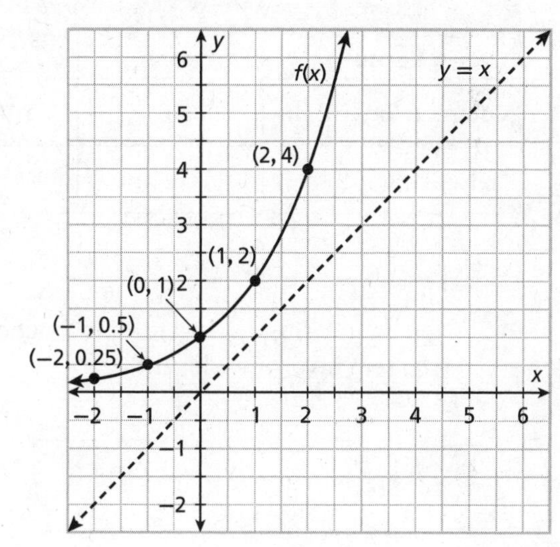

B Plot and label the image of each point on the coordinate plane.

C Use the images of the points to sketch the graph of $f^{-1}(x)$.

REFLECT

1a. What are the domain and range of $f^{-1}(x)$?

____

1b. Does the graph of $f^{-1}(x)$ have any asymptotes? Explain how you know.

____

____

1c. How do the values of $f^{-1}(x)$ change as x increases without bound?

____

MCC9–12.F.BF.5(+)

2 ENGAGE Defining Logarithmic Functions

A *logarithm* is the exponent to which a base must be raised in order to obtain a given value. For example, $2^3 = 8$, so the logarithm base 2 of 8 is 3, and you write $\log_2 8 = 3$.

Definition of Logarithm

For positive numbers y and b ($b \neq 1$), the **logarithm** of y with base b is written $\log_b y$ and is defined as follows:

$$\log_b y = x \text{ if and only if } b^x = y.$$

This definition means that every statement about exponents can be converted into an equivalent statement about logarithms, and vice versa. Note that you read $\log_b x$ as "the logarithm base b of x" or "log base b of x."

A **logarithmic function** with base b is the inverse of the exponential function with base b. For instance, the inverse of $f(x) = 2^x$ is $f^{-1}(x) = \log_2 x$, the graph of which you sketched in the Explore.

The table describes two special logarithms.

Special Logarithms		
Name	Base	Notation
Common logarithm	10	Write $\log x$ instead of $\log_{10} x$.
Natural logarithm	e	Write $\ln x$ instead of $\log_e x$.

The number e is the value that the expression $\left(1 + \frac{1}{x}\right)^x$ approaches as x increases without bound. e is an irrational number, approximately 2.72.

REFLECT

2a. Explain, in terms of a logarithmic function, how to write $7^2 = 49$ as an equivalent statement involving a logarithm.

2b. Explain, in terms of an exponential function, how to write $\log 1000 = 3$ as an equivalent statement involving an exponent.

2c. The input of $f(x) = 2^x$ is an exponent and the output is a power of 2. Describe the input and output of $f^{-1}(x) = \log_2 x$. Give a specific example.

2d. Find $\ln \frac{1}{e}$ by letting $\ln \frac{1}{e} = x$ and writing this statement in an equivalent form that involves an exponent. Explain your reasoning from that point on.

MCC9–12.F.BF.5(+)

3 EXAMPLE Evaluating Logarithmic Functions

Find each value of $f(x) = \log_2 x$.

A $f(16)$

Write the function's input as a power of 2. The function's output is the exponent.

$16 = 2^{\square}$, so $f(16) =$ ________.

B $f(64)$

$64 = 2^{\square}$, so $f(64) =$ ________.

C $f\left(\frac{1}{32}\right)$

$\frac{1}{32} = 2^{\square}$, so $f\left(\frac{1}{32}\right) =$ ________.

D $f\left(\frac{1}{8}\right)$

$\frac{1}{8} = 2^{\square}$, so $f\left(\frac{1}{8}\right) =$ ________.

E $f(1)$

$1 = 2^{\square}$, so $f(1) =$ ________.

REFLECT

3a. Is it possible to evaluate $f(0)$? Why or why not?

____

3b. For $f(x) = \log_2 x$, between which two integers does $f(40)$ lie? Explain.

____

____

3c. Estimate $g(95)$ for $g(x) = \log x$, without using a calculator. Explain.

____

____

3d. Without using a calculator, explain how you know that $\ln 20 > \log 20$.

____

____

MCC9–12.F.IF.7e

4 EXAMPLE Graphing a Logarithmic Function

Graph $f(x) = \log_{\frac{1}{2}} x$.

A What is the range of $f(x)$? (Think: what powers can you raise $\frac{1}{2}$ to?) ____________

What is the domain of $f(x)$? (Think: what values can be obtained by raising $\frac{1}{2}$ to a power?) ____________

B Complete the table of values.

x	$f(x)$
$\frac{1}{4}$	
$\frac{1}{2}$	
1	
2	
4	
8	

C Plot the points. Connect them with a smooth curve.

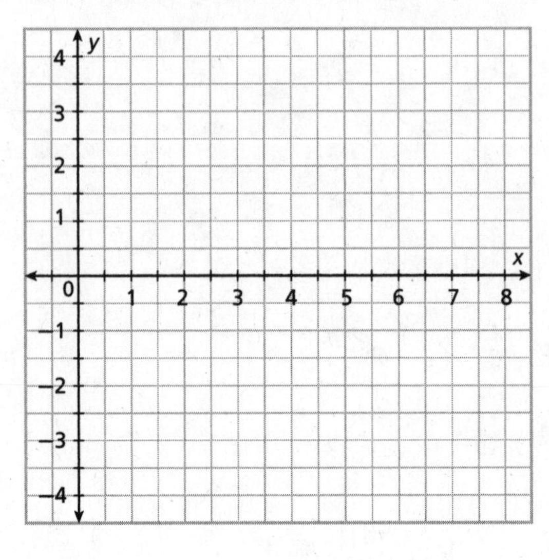

REFLECT

4a. How is the graph of $f(x) = \log_{\frac{1}{2}} x$ related to the graph of $f(x) = \log_2 x$ from the Explore? Why does this make sense?

____

____

____

____

4b. What point do the graphs of $f(x) = \log_{\frac{1}{2}} x$ and $f(x) = \log_2 x$ have in common? Why?

____

4c. Describe the end behavior of $f(x) = \log_{\frac{1}{2}} x$.

____

____

4d. How is the graph of $f(x) = \log_{\frac{1}{2}} x$ related to the graph of $f(x) = \left(\frac{1}{2}\right)^x$?

____

____

PRACTICE

1. The graph of $f(x) = 3^x$ is shown.

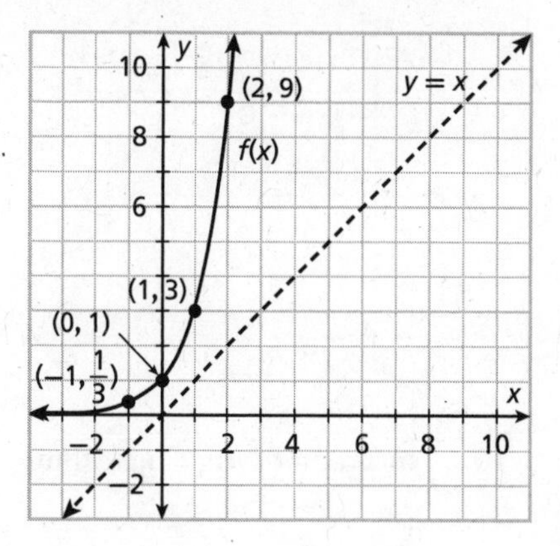

   a. Use the labeled points to help you draw the graph of $f^{-1}(x)$. Label the corresponding points on $f^{-1}(x)$.

   b. Write the inverse function, $f^{-1}(x)$, using logarithmic notation.

   ____

   c. State the domain and range of $f^{-1}(x)$.

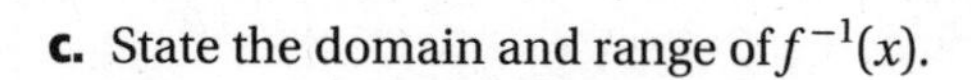

   ____

Find each value of $f(x) = \log_4 x$.

2. $f(16)$ ____________ 3. $f\left(\frac{1}{64}\right)$ ____________ 4. $f(4)$ ____________

Find each value of $f(x) = \log x$.

5. $f(10{,}000)$ ____________ 6. $f(0.1)$ ____________ 7. $f\left(\frac{1}{100}\right)$ ____________

Find each value of $f(x) = \log_{\frac{1}{4}} x$.

8. $f(16)$ ____________ 9. $f(1)$ ____________ 10. $f\left(\frac{1}{64}\right)$ ____________

Evaluate each expression.

11. $\log_8 64$ ____________ 12. $\log_2 1024$ ____________ 13. $\log 1{,}000{,}000$ ____________

14. For $f(x) = \log x$, between what two integers does $f(6)$ lie? Explain.

____

____

15. Explain how you can estimate the value of ln 10 without using a calculator.

____

____

16. What is the value of $\log_b b$ for $b > 0$ and $b \neq 1$? Explain.

____

Graph each logarithmic function.

17. $f(x) = \log_4 x$

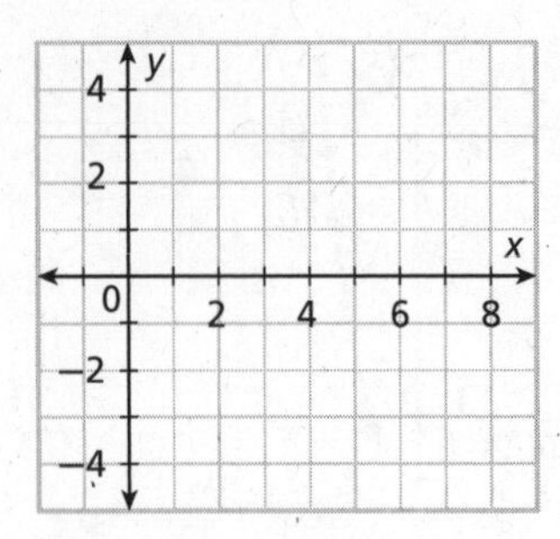

18. $f(x) = \log_{\frac{1}{3}} x$

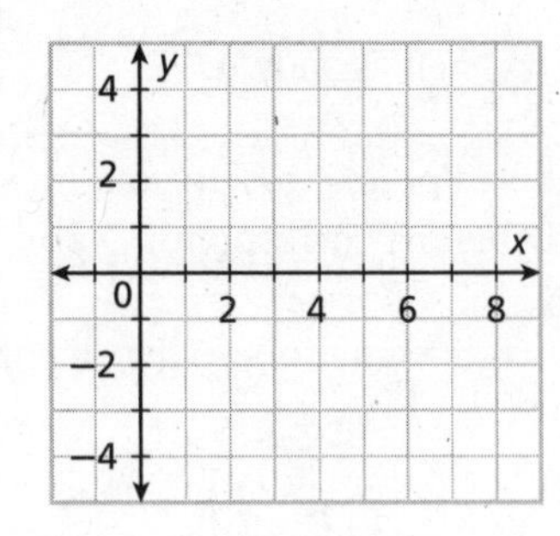

19. The graph of what logarithmic function is shown? Explain your reasoning.

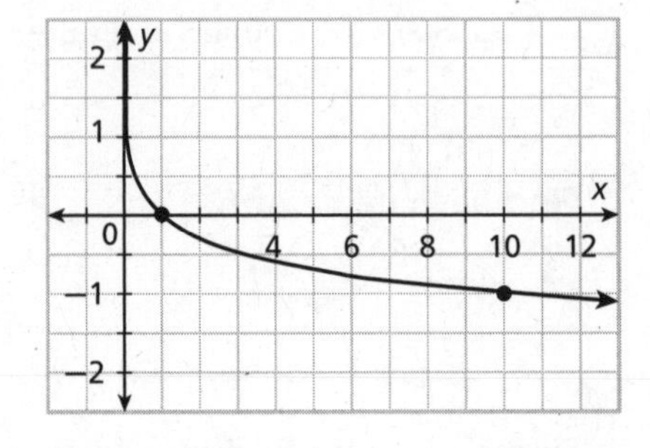

20. Name some values you would choose for x if you were plotting points to sketch the graph of $f(x) = \log x$ without using a calculator. Explain.

21. The graph of $f(x) = \log_b x$ passes through the points (1, 0) and (36, 2). What is the value of b? Explain.

22. When you fold a sheet of paper in half x times, the function $f(x) = 2^x$ gives the number of sections that are created by the folds.

a. Describe the input and output of the function $f^{-1}(x) = \log_2 x$ in the problem context.

b. Use $f^{-1}(x)$ to find the number of folds needed to create 64 sections.

c. Assume that a sheet of paper has an area of 1. Write an exponential function $g(x)$ that gives the area of a section of the paper after being folded in half x times.

d. Write the rule for $g^{-1}(x)$ and describe the function's input and output.

Name________________________ Class______________ Date__________

15-3

Additional Practice

Write each exponential equation in logarithmic form.

1. $3^7 = 2187$ ________
2. $12^2 = 144$ ________
3. $5^3 = 125$ ________

Write each logarithmic equation in exponential form.

4. $\log_{10} 100{,}000 = 5$ ________
5. $\log_4 1024 = 5$ ________
6. $\log_9 729 = 3$ ________

Evaluate by using mental math.

7. log 1,000,000 ________
8. log 10 ________
9. log 1 ________
10. $\log_4 16$ ________
11. $\log_8 1$ ________
12. $\log_5 625$ ________

Use the given *x*-values to graph each function. Then graph its inverse. Describe the domain and range of the inverse function.

13. $f(x) = 2^x$; $x = -2, -1, 0, 1, 2, 3, 4$

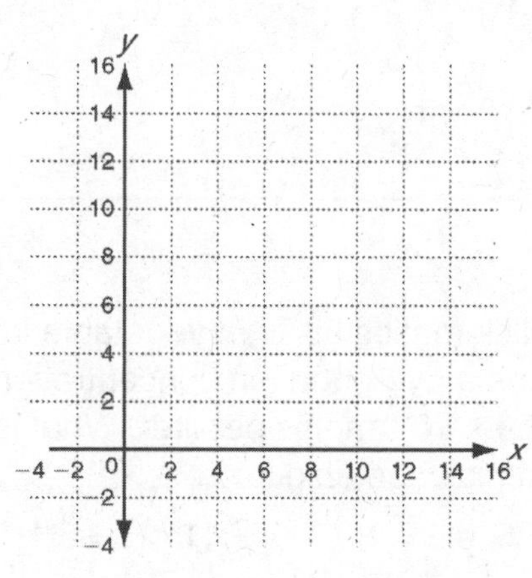

____

14. $f(x) = \left(\frac{1}{2}\right)^x$; $x = -3, -2, -1, 0, 1, 2, 3$

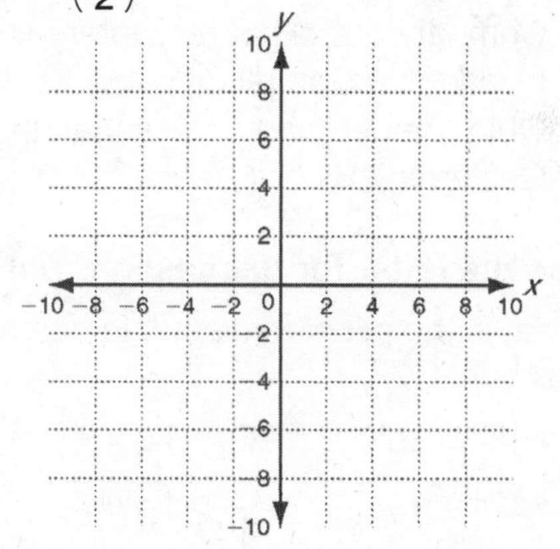

____

Solve.

15. The hydrogen ion concentration in moles per liter for a certain brand of tomato-vegetable juice is 0.000316.
    a. Write a logarithmic equation for the pH of the juice. ________
    b. What is the pH of the juice? ________

Problem Solving

The acidity of rainwater varies from location to location. Acidity is measured in pH and is given by the function $pH = -\log[H^+]$, where $[H^+]$ represents the hydrogen ion concentration in moles per liter. The table gives the $[H^+]$ of rainwater in different locations.

Hydrogen Ion Concentration of Rainwater	
Location	**$[H^+]$ (moles per liter)**
Central California	0.0000032
Eastern Texas	0.0000192
Eastern Ohio	0.0000629

1. Find the acidity of rainwater in eastern Ohio.
   a. Substitute the hydrogen ion concentration for rainwater in eastern Ohio in the function for pH.

   ____

   b. Evaluate the function. What is the acidity of rainwater in eastern Ohio to the nearest tenth of a unit?

   ____

2. Find how the acidity of rainwater in central California compares to the acidity of rainwater in eastern Ohio.
   a. Write a function for the acidity of rainwater in central California. ______________________
   b. Evaluate the function. What is the acidity of rainwater in central California to the nearest tenth of a unit? ______________________
   c. Compare the pH of rainwater in the two locations. Is the pH of rainwater in eastern Ohio greater than or less than that in central California? By how much? ______________________

Choose the letter for the best answer.

3. What is the pH of rainwater in eastern Texas?

   A pH = 3.7 C pH = 4.4
   B pH = 4.0 D pH = 4.7

4. Nick makes his own vegetable juice. It has a hydrogen ion concentration of 5.9×10^{-6} moles per liter. What is the pH of his vegetable juice?

   F pH = 4.9 H pH = 5.1
   G pH = 5.0 J pH = 5.2

5. What is the pH of a sample of irrigation water with a hydrogen ion concentration of 8.3×10^{-7} moles per liter?

   A pH = 6.1 C pH = 6.3
   B pH = 6.2 D pH = 6.4

6. What is the pH of a shampoo sample with a hydrogen ion concentration of 1.7×10^{-8} moles per liter?

   F pH = 7.4 H pH = 7.8
   G pH = 7.6 J pH = 8.0

Name________________________ Class______________ Date________

16-1

Properties of Logarithms

Going Deeper

Essential question: *How do you prove properties of logarithms?*

Video Tutor

MCC9–12.F.IF.2

1 EXPLORE Comparing Logarithmic Expressions

Use a calculator to evaluate each of the following expressions. When necessary, round your answers to three decimal places.

A $\log e$ ____________

B $\log 10e$ ____________

C $\log \frac{e}{10}$ ____________

D $\log e^{10}$ ____________

E $(\log e)(\ln 10)$ ____________

REFLECT

1a. How do $\log 10e$, $\log \frac{e}{10}$, and $\log e^{10}$ compare to $\log e$?

____

____

1b. How do you know that $\log e$ and $\ln 10$ are reciprocals? Given that the expressions are reciprocals, show another way to represent each expression.

____

____

MCC9–12.F.BF.5(+)

2 ENGAGE Properties of Logarithms

Recall that a logarithm is the exponent to which a base must be raised in order to obtain a given number. From this definition you can see that $\log_b b^m = m$. It follows that $\log_b b^0 = 0$, so $\log_b 1 = 0$. Also, $\log_b b^1 = 1$, so $\log_b b = 1$. These facts, and some additional properties of logarithms, are summarized below.

Properties of Logarithms For any positive numbers *a, m, n, b* ($b \neq 1$), and *c* ($c \neq 1$), the following properties hold.	
Definition-Based Properties	$\log_b b^m = m$ $\log_b 1 = 0$ $\log_b b = 1$
Product Property of Logarithms	$\log_b mn = \log_b m + \log_b n$
Quotient Property of Logarithms	$\log_b \frac{m}{n} = \log_b m - \log_b n$
Power Property of Logarithms	$\log_b m^n = n \log_b m$
Change of Base Property of Logarithms	$\log_c a = \frac{\log_b a}{\log_b c}$

REFLECT

2a. Use the definition of a logarithm to explain why $\log 10 = 1$ and $\ln e = 1$.

2b. Use the Product Property of Logarithms to explain why $\log 10e$ is 1 more than $\log e$.

2c. Use the Quotient Property of Logarithms to explain why $\log \frac{e}{10}$ is 1 less than $\log e$.

2d. Use the Power Property of Logarithms to explain why $\log e^{10}$ is 10 times $\log e$.

2e. Use the Change of Base Property to change the base of $\ln 10$ from e to 10. What does the result tell you about $\ln 10$?

2f. What is the relationship between $\log e$ and $\log \frac{1}{e}$? Explain your reasoning.

MCC9–12.F.BF.5(+)

3 EXAMPLE Proving the Product Property of Logarithms

Prove the Product Property of Logarithms.

A Given positive numbers m, n, and b ($b \neq 1$), show that $\log_b mn = \log_b m + \log_b n$.

To prove this property, convert statements about logarithms to statements about exponents. Then use properties of exponents.

Let $\log_b m = p$ and let $\log_b n = q$.

By the definition of a logarithm, $m = b^p$ and ____________.

B $\log_b mn = \log_b \left(\quad \right)$ — Substitution

$= \log_b b^{\square}$ — Product of Powers Property of Exponents

$= \square$ — Definition of a logarithm

$= \log_b m + \log_b n$ — Substitution

So, $\log_b mn = \log_b m + \log_b n$.

REFLECT

3a. Suppose $m = n$ in $\log_b mn$. What result do you get when you apply the Product Property of Logarithms? This result is a particular case of what other property of logarithms? Explain.

PRACTICE

1. Prove the Quotient Property of Logarithms. Justify each step of your proof.

2. Prove the Power Property of Logarithms. Justify each step of your proof.

3. When n is a positive integer, show how you can prove the Power Property of Logarithms using the Product Property of Logarithms. (*Hint:* When n is a positive integer, $m^n = m \cdot m \cdot m \cdot \dots \cdot m$ where m appears as a factor n times.)

Simplify each expression.

4. $\log_3 3^4$

5. $\log_7 7^5$

6. $\log_6 36^9$

7. $\log_{\frac{1}{10}} 10^3$

8. $\log_2 14 - \log_2 7$

9. $\log 25 + \log 4$

10. Your calculator has keys for evaluating only common logarithms and natural logarithms. Explain why you don't need a generic logarithm key where you must specify the base. Then describe how you can evaluate $\log_2 5$ using either one of your calculator's logarithm keys. Finally, find the value of $\log_2 5$ to 3 decimal places using each key to demonstrate that you get the same result.

11. On a graphing calculator, graph $y = \log \frac{10}{x}$ and $y = 1 - \log x$ in the same viewing window. What do you notice? Which property of logarithms explains what you see? Why?

12. On a graphing calculator, graph $y = \log 10^x$ and $y = x \log 10$ in the same viewing window.

a. What do you notice? Which property of logarithms explains what you see? Why?

b. What linear function are both functions equivalent to? Explain.

13. **Error Analysis** A student simplified $(\log_3 81)^2$ as shown at right. Explain and correct the student's error.

$(\log_3 81)^2$	
$= 2 \log_3 81$	Power Property of Logs
$= 2 \log_3 3^4$	Write 81 as a power of 3.
$= 2 \cdot 4$	Definition of logarithm
$= 8$	Multiply.

14. The formula $L = 10 \log \frac{I}{I_0}$ gives the sound level L (in decibels) for a sound with intensity I (in watts per square meter). I_0 is the threshold of human hearing, 10^{-12} watts/m^2.

a. Rewrite the formula by using the Quotient Property of Logarithms, substituting 10^{-12} for I_0 and simplifying.

b. Show how to use the formula from part (a) to find the intensity of a sound if its sound level L is 120 decibels.

Name________________ Class__________ Date________

Additional Practice

Express as a single logarithm. Simplify, if possible.

1. $\log_3 9 + \log_3 27$
2. $\log_2 8 + \log_2 16$
3. $\log_{10} 80 + \log_{10} 125$
4. $\log_6 8 + \log_6 27$
5. $\log_3 6 + \log_3 13.5$
6. $\log_4 32 + \log_4 128$

Express as a single logarithm. Simplify, if possible.

7. $\log_2 80 - \log_2 10$
8. $\log_{10} 4000 - \log_{10} 40$
9. $\log_4 384 - \log_4 6$
10. $\log_2 1920 - \log_2 30$
11. $\log_3 486 - \log_3 2$
12. $\log_6 180 - \log_6 5$

Simplify, if possible.

13. $\log_4 4^6$
14. $\log_5 5^{x-5}$
15. $7^{\log_7 30}$
16. $12^{\log_{12} 1}$
17. $\log_8 8^5$
18. $\log_3 9^4$

Evaluate. Round to the nearest hundredth.

19. $\log_{12} 1$
20. $\log_3 30$
21. $\log_5 10$

Solve.

22. The Richter magnitude of an earthquake, M, is related to the energy released in ergs, E, by the formula $M = \frac{2}{3}\log\left(\frac{E}{10^{11.8}}\right)$. Find the energy released by an earthquake of magnitude 4.2.

Problem Solving

Trina and Willow are researching information on earthquakes. One of the largest earthquakes in the United States, centered at San Francisco, occurred in 1906 and registered 7.8 on the Richter scale. The Richter magnitude of an earthquake, *M*, is related to the energy released in ergs, *E*, by the formula $M = \frac{2}{3}\log\left(\frac{E}{10^{11.8}}\right)$.

1. Find the amount of energy released by the earthquake in 1906.

   a. Substitute 7.8 for magnitude, *M*, in the equation. ________________

   b. Solve for the value of log *E*. ________________

   c. Willow says that *E* is equal to 10 to the power of the value of log *E*. Is she correct? What property or definition can be used to find the value of *E*? Explain.

   ____

   d. Trina says the energy of the 1906 earthquake was 3.16×10^{23} ergs. Willow says the energy was $10^{23.5}$ ergs. Who is correct? How do you know?

   ____

Choose the letter for the best answer.

2. An earthquake in 1811 in Missouri measured 8.1 on the Richter scale. About how many times as much energy was released by this earthquake as by the California earthquake of 1906?

   A 2.8

   B 3.0

   C 3.6

   D 5.7

3. Another large earthquake in California measured 7.9 on the Richter scale. Which statement is true?

   F 0.1 times as much energy was released by the larger earthquake.

   G The difference in energy released is 1.31×10^{23} ergs.

   H The energy released by the second earthquake was 3.26×10^{23} ergs.

   J The total energy released by the two earthquakes is equal to the energy released by an 8.0 earthquake.

4. Larry wrote the following: $\log 10^{0.0038} = 3.8 \times 10^{-3}$. Which property of logarithms did he use?

   A Product Property

   B Quotient Property

   C Inverse Property

   D Power Property

5. Vijay wants to change $\log_5 7$ to base 10. Which expression should he use?

   F $\frac{\log_{10} 7}{\log_{10} 5}$

   H $\frac{\log_{10} 7}{\log_5 5}$

   G $\frac{\log_{10} 5}{\log_{10} 7}$

   J $\frac{\log_7 5}{\log_{10} 7}$

Name____________________ Class__________ Date________

16-2

Exponential and Logarithmic Equations and Inequalities

Going Deeper

Video Tutor

Essential question: *What is the general process for solving exponential and logarithmic equations?*

An exponential equation is an equation in which the variable appears only as an exponent. The following property is useful for solving some types of exponential equations.

Property of Equality for Exponential Equations

For any positive number b other than 1, if $b^x = b^y$, then $x = y$.

MCC9–12.A.SSE.3c

1 EXAMPLE Solving Exponential Equations Algebraically

Solve each exponential equation.

A $2^{x-1} = 32$

$2^{x-1} = 2^{\square}$ Write 32 as a power of 2.

$x - 1 = \square$ Because the bases are equal, the exponents are equal.

$x = \square$ Solve for x.

B $9^{2x} = 27^{x+1}$

$(3^2)^{2x} = \left(\square\right)^{x+1}$ Write both bases as powers with a base of 3.

$3^{2 \cdot 2x} = 3^{\square}$ Power of a power property

$3^{4x} = 3^{\square}$ Simplify.

$4x = \square$ Because the bases are equal, the exponents are equal.

$x = \square$ Solve for x.

REFLECT

1a. Show how you can check that the solutions of the equations are correct.

____

____

1b. In the property of equality for exponential equations, explain why b cannot be equal to 1.

____

1c. How would you solve the equation in part A if 32 were replaced by 0.5?

____

MCC9–12.A.REI.11

2 EXAMPLE Solving an Exponential Equation with a Table

The equation $y = 4.1(1.33)^x$ models the population of the United States, in millions, from 1790 to 1890. In this equation, x is the number of decades since 1790, and y is the population in millions. In what year did the population reach 45 million?

A Write an equation and make a table of values to solve the equation.

When the population is 45 million, $y =$ _______.

To find the year when the population reached 45 million, solve the equation _______________.

Enter the expression $4.1(1.33)^x$ for Y_1 in your calculator's equation editor.

Set up a table by pressing 2nd WINDOW (TBLSET) and entering the values shown at right. Then press 2nd GRAPH (TABLE) to view the table.

TABLE SETUP
TblStart=0
ΔTbl=.1
Indpnt: Auto Ask
Depend: Auto Ask

X	Y_1
0	4.1
.1	4.2186
.2	4.3406
.3	4.4662
.4	4.5954
.5	4.7284
.6	4.8651

X=0

Scroll down until the value of Y_1 is approximately 45.

When Y_1 is approximately 45, $x =$ _______.

B Find the year when the population reached 45 million.

The population reached 45 million _______ decades after 1790.

This is _______ years after 1790.

So, the population reached 45 million in _______.

REFLECT

2a. The table includes the ordered pair (0.4, 4.5954). What does this ordered pair represent?

____

2b. Explain why it makes sense to use an increment of 0.1 for the table and not some other increment.

____

____

2c. Explain how you can check your solution.

____

____

2d. How could you solve the equation by using your calculator to graph $y = 4.1(1.33)^x$?

____

____

Solving an Exponential Equation by Graphing

Camilla invested $300 at 4% interest compounded continuously. Diego invested $275 at 6% interest compounded continuously. When will they have the same amount in their accounts? What will the amount be when this occurs?

A Write equations to represent the amount in each account. Use the fact that when an amount P is invested in an account that earns interest at a nominal rate r compounded n times per year, the amount in the account after t years is $A(t) = Pe^{rt}$.

Camilla: $A(t) = \square \cdot e^{\square \cdot t}$ — Substitute 300 for P and 0.04 for r.

Diego: $A(t) = \square \cdot e^{\square \cdot t}$ — Substitute 275 for P and 0.06 for r.

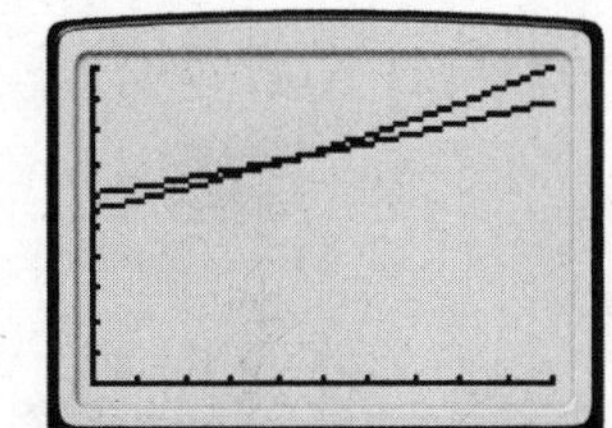

B Graph the equations.

Enter the equation for Camilla's account as Y_1 in your calculator's equation editor. Enter the equation for Diego's account as Y_2.

Graph both equations in the same viewing window. A good viewing in this situation is $0 \le x \le 10$ with a tick mark every 1 unit and $0 \le y \le 500$ with a tick mark every 50 units.

C Find the point of intersection of the graphs.

Press 2nd TRACE (CALC) and select **5:intersect** to find the point of intersection of the graphs.

The point of intersection is approximately ______________.

So, Camilla and Diego will have the same amount in their accounts after

approximately __________ years.

At this time, the amount in each account will be __________.

REFLECT

3a. Who has more money in his or her account after 3 years? How can you tell from the graphs?

____

____

3b. Suppose Camilla and Diego leave their money in their accounts for 10 years. At that time, who will have more money in his or her account? How much more?

____

3c. How can you observe the difference in the accounts after 10 years from the graphs of the equations?

____

You know that you can sometimes solve an exponential equation by writing both sides as powers with the same base. When that method is not possible, you can take a logarithm of both sides of the equation. This is justified by the following property.

Property of Equality for Logarithmic Equations

For any positive numbers x, y, and b ($b \neq 1$), $\log_b x = \log_b y$ if and only if $x = y$.

MCC9–12.F.BF.5(+)

4 EXAMPLE Taking the Common Logarithm of Both Sides

Solve $2^{x-3} = 85$. Give the exact solution and an approximate solution to three decimal places.

$2^{x-3} = 85$	Original equation
$\log 2^{x-3} = \log 85$	Take the common logarithm of both sides.
$\square \log 2 = \log 85$	Power Property of Logarithms
$\dfrac{\square \log 2}{\square} = \dfrac{\log 85}{\square}$	Divide both sides by log 2.
$\square = \dfrac{\log 85}{\log 2}$	Simplify.
$x = \dfrac{\log 85}{\log 2} + 3$	Solve for x to find the exact solution.
$x \approx \square$	Evaluate. Round to three decimal places.

REFLECT

4a. Why do you use the Power Property of Logarithms?

____

4b. How can you use estimation to check if your answer is reasonable?

____

____

____

You can also take the natural logarithm of both sides of an equation. It makes sense to take the natural logarithm, rather than the common logarithm, when the base is e.

MCC9–12.F.LE.4

5 EXAMPLE Taking the Natural Logarithm of Both Sides

Adam has $500 to invest for 4 years. He wants to double his money during this time. What interest rate does Adam need for this investment, assuming the interest is compounded continuously?

A Write an equation.

The formula for interest compounded continuously is $A = Pe^{rt}$ where A is the amount in the account, P is the principal, r is the annual rate of interest, and t is the time in years.

$P =$ __________ and A is the final amount after $t = 4$ years, so $A =$ __________.

The equation is ________________________.

B Solve the equation for r.

$\square = \square\, e^{4r}$	Write the equation.
$\square = e^{4r}$	Divide both sides by 500.
$\ln 2 = \ln e^{4r}$	Take the natural logarithm of both sides.
$\ln 2 = \square$	Power Property of Logarithms
$\ln 2 = \square$	Use the fact that ln e = 1.
$\frac{\ln 2}{4} = \frac{\square}{4}$ 	Divide both sides by 4.
$\square = r$	Solve for r to find the exact answer.
$\square \approx r$	Evaluate. Round to three decimal places.

So, Adam needs an interest rate of approximately __________%.

REFLECT

5a. What is the benefit of taking the natural logarithm of both sides of the equation, rather than the common logarithm?

____

5b. Describe two different ways to use your calculator to check your answer.

____

____

____

To solve a logarithmic equation in the form $\log_b x = a$, first rewrite the equation in exponential form ($b^a = x$) by using the definition of a logarithm. As you will see in the second part of the following example, you may first need to isolate the logarithmic expression on one side of the equation.

MCC9–12.F.BF.5(+)

6 EXAMPLE Solving a Logarithmic Equation Algebraically

Solve each logarithmic equation.

A $\log_3(x + 1) = 2$

$\square^2 = x + 1$ Definition of logarithm

$\square = x + 1$ Simplify.

$\square = x$ Solve for x.

B $7 + \log_3(5x - 4) = 10$

$\log_3(5x - 4) = \square$ Subtract 7 from both sides.

$\square^3 = 5x - 4$ Definition of logarithm

$\square = 5x - 4$ Simplify.

$\square = 5x$ Add 4 to both sides.

$\square = x$ Solve for x.

REFLECT

6a. How can you check your solution to part A by substitution?

____

____

6b. Your calculator has keys for evaluating only logarithms with a base of 10 or e. Use the Change of Base Property to rewrite the equation from part A so that the base of the logarithm is 10 or e. Then explain how to use graphing to check your solution.

____

____

6c. Explain how you could use graphing to check your solution to part B.

____

____

MCC9–12.A.REI.11

7 EXAMPLE Solving a Logarithmic Equation by Graphing

A telescope's limiting magnitude *m* is the brightness of the faintest star that can be seen using the telescope. The limiting magnitude depends on the diameter *d* (in millimeters) of the telescope's objective lens. The table gives two formulas relating *m* to *d*. One is a standard formula used in astronomy. The other is a proposed new formula based on data gathered from users of telescopes of various lens diameters.

Formulas for determining limiting magnitude from lens diameter	
Standard formula	$m = 2.7 + 5 \log d$
Proposed formula	$m = 4.5 + 4.4 \log d$

For what lens diameter do the two formulas give the same limiting magnitude?

A Use a graphing calculator. Enter $2.7 + 5 \log x$ as Y_1 and enter $4.5 + 4.4 \log x$ as Y_2.

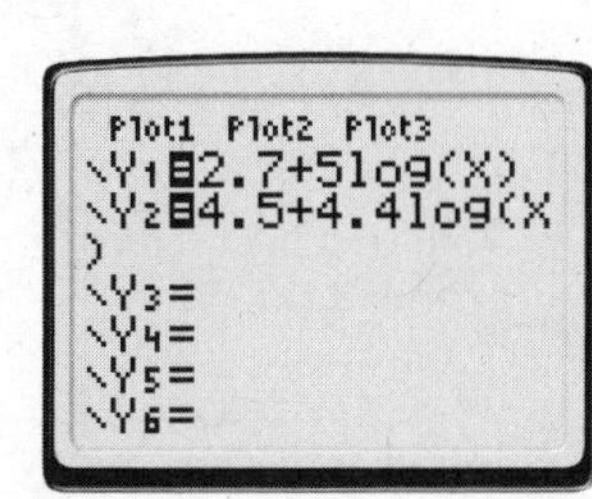

B Graph the two functions in the same viewing window. Use a window where $0 \le x \le 2000$ with a tick mark every 100 units and $0 \le y \le 20$ with a tick mark every 5 units.

C Press 2nd CALC TRACE and choose **5:intersect** to find the point of intersection of the graphs.

The coordinates of the point of intersection are ________________.

So, the two formulas give the same limiting magnitude for a lens diameter of ________________.

REFLECT

7a. What is the limiting magnitude that corresponds to this lens diameter? How do you know?

____

7b. What equation can you write in order to solve the problem algebraically?

____

7c. Show how to solve the equation algebraically. Justify each step. (*Hint:* First get all logarithmic expressions on one side of the equation and all non-logarithmic expressions on the other side of the equation.)

____

____

____

____

____

____

PRACTICE

Solve each exponential equation algebraically.

1. $16^{3x} = 64^{x+2}$

2. $\left(\frac{2}{5}\right)^{x+7} = \left(\frac{4}{25}\right)^{10}$

3. $27^x = \frac{1}{9}$

4. $6^{5x-1} = 36$

5. $0.01^{x+1} = 1000^{x-9}$

6. $625 = \left(\frac{1}{25}\right)^{x+3}$

7. $6^{x^2} = 36^8$

8. $0.75^{5x-2} = \left(\frac{27}{64}\right)^{x-6}$

9. $\left(\frac{1}{3}\right)^{x+2} = 81^{x-1}$

10. Show that you can solve $\frac{1}{4} = 16^{x+5}$ by writing both sides of the equation with a base of 2 or with a base of 4.

11. The equation $y = 87.3(1.07)^x$ models the population of a city, in thousands, from 1980 to 2010. In this equation, x is the number of years since 1980, and y is the population in thousands.

a. In what year did the population reach 150,000? __________

b. In what year did the population reach 250,000? __________

12. In the lower stratosphere (between 36,152 feet and 82,345 feet), the equation $p = 473.1e^{1.73 - 0.000048h}$ represents the atmospheric pressure p in pounds per square foot at altitude h feet.

a. At what altitude does the pressure equal 150 lb/ft^2? __________

b. At what altitude does the pressure equal 300 lb/ft^2? __________

13. Rima and Trevor both bought a car in 2010. Rima's car cost \$17,832 and Trevor's car cost \$22,575. Rima's car is depreciating at a rate of 11% per year and Trevor's car is depreciating at a rate of 13.5% per year.

a. Write each car's value as a function of time t (in years since 2010).

b. During what year will the cars have an equal value? At that time, what will the value of the cars be?

Solve. Give the exact solution and an approximate solution to three decimal places.

14. $6^x = 15$

15. $4^{2x} = 200$

16. $10^x = 35$

17. $10 + e^{\frac{x}{3}} = 4270$

18. $2^{9-x} + 3 = 62$

19. $e^{6x+1} = 530$

20. $3^{2x-1} = 14$

21. $210 + 4^x = 3 \cdot 4^x$

22. $11^{1-x} = 8$

23. What happens if you take the common logarithm of both sides of $5^x = -6$ in order to solve the equation? Why does this happen?

24. Kendra wants to double her investment of $4000. How long will this take if the annual interest rate is 4% compounded continuously? How long will this take if the annual interest rate is 8% compounded continuously? What effect does doubling the interest rate have on the time it takes the investment to double?

25. An account that earns interest at an annual rate of r earns more interest each year if the account is compounded, say n times per year (at a rate of r/n), than if it is compounded annually. The actual interest rate R earned is called the effective rate and r is called the nominal rate. For interest that is compounded continuously, R is given by $R = e^r - 1$. What is the nominal interest rate if R is 5.625%? Round to the nearest hundredth of a percent.

26. The equation $y = 4.1(1.33)^x$ models the population of the U.S., in millions, from 1790 to 1890. In this equation, x is the number of decades since 1790, and y is the population in millions. How many decades after 1790 did the population reach 28 million? Write an expression for the exact answer and give an approximate answer to the nearest tenth.

27. **Error Analysis** Identify and correct the error in the student work shown at right.

$$10^x = 20$$
$$\ln 10^x = \ln 20$$
$$x \ln 10 = \ln 20$$
$$x = \frac{\ln 20}{\ln 10} = \ln 2 \approx 0.693$$

____

____

Solve each logarithmic equation. Round to three decimal places if necessary.

28. $\log_7 (x - 5) = 2$ ______

29. $\log_4 (8x) = 3$ ______

30. $\log (7x - 1) = -1$ ______

31. $\ln(4x - 1) = 9$ ______

32. $11 + \log_4 (x + 1) = 15$ ______

33. $3 = \ln (3x + 3)$ ______

Solve by using the Product or Quotient Property of Logarithms so that one side is a single logarithm. Round to three decimal places if necessary.

34. $\log 20 + \log 10x = 5$ ______

35. $\ln x - \ln 6 = 3$ ______

36. $2.4 = \log 7 + \log 3x$ ______

For Exercises 37 and 38, use graphing to solve.

37. Charles collected data on the atmospheric pressure (ranging from 4 to 15 pounds per square inch) and the corresponding altitude above the surface of Earth (ranging from 1 to 30,000 feet). He used regression to write two functions that give the altitude above the surface of Earth given the atmospheric pressure.

$$f(x) = 66{,}990 - 24{,}747 \ln x$$

$$g(x) = -2870x + 40{,}393$$

a. At what atmospheric pressure(s) do the equations give the same altitude?

____

b. At what altitude(s) above Earth do these atmospheric pressures occur?

____

38. Elena and Paul determined slightly different equations to model the recommended height, in inches, of a tabletop for children x years old.

Elena: $y = 12.2 + 5.45 \ln x$

Paul: $y = 12.5 + 5.2 \ln x$

For what age do the models give the same tabletop height? What is that height?

____

Name________________ Class____________ Date__________

16-2

Additional Practice

Solve and check.

1. $5^{2x} = 20$ ______
2. $12^{2x-8} = 15$ ______
3. $2^{x+6} = 4$ ______
4. $16^{5x} = 64^{x+7}$ ______
5. $243^{0.2x} = 81^{x+5}$ ______
6. $25^{x} = 125^{x-2}$ ______
7. $\left(\frac{1}{2}\right)^{x} = 16^{2}$ ______
8. $\left(\frac{1}{32}\right)^{2x} = 64$ ______
9. $\left(\frac{1}{27}\right)^{x-6} = 27$ ______

Solve.

10. $\log_4 x^5 = 20$ ______
11. $\log_3 x^6 = 12$ ______
12. $\log_4 (x-6)^3 = 6$ ______
13. $\log x - \log 10 = 14$ ______
14. $\log x + \log 5 = 2$ ______
15. $\log (x+9) = \log (2x-7)$ ______
16. $\log (x+4) - \log 6 = 1$ ______
17. $\log x^2 + \log 25 = 2$ ______
18. $\log (x-1)^2 = \log (-5x-1)$ ______

Use a table and graph to solve.

19. $2^{x-5} < 64$ ______
20. $\log x^3 = 12$ ______
21. $2^x 3^x = 1296$ ______

Solve.

22. The population of a small farming community is declining at a rate of 7% per year. The decline can be expressed by the exponential equation $P = C(1 - 0.07)^t$, where P is the population after t years and C is the current population. If the population was 8,500 in 2004, when will the population be less than 6,000?

______

Problem Solving

Caffeine Content of Some Beverages	
Beverage	**Caffeine (mg per serving)**
Brewed coffee	103
Brewed tea	36
Iced tea	30
Cola	25

While John and Cody play their favorite video game, John drinks 4 cups of coffee and a cola, and Cody drinks 2 cups of brewed tea and a cup of iced tea. John recalls reading that up to 300 mg of caffeine is considered a moderate level of consumption per day. The rate at which caffeine is eliminated from the bloodstream is about 15% per hour.

1. John wants to know how long it will take for the caffeine in his bloodstream to drop to a moderate level.

   a. How much caffeine did John consume?

   ____

   b. Write an equation showing the amount of caffeine in the bloodstream as a function of time. ______________________

   c. How long, to the nearest tenth of an hour, will it take for the caffeine in John's system to reach a moderate level? ______________________

2. a. Cody thinks that it will take at least 8 hours for the level of caffeine in John's system to drop to the same level of caffeine that Cody consumed. Explain how he can use his graphing calculator to prove that.

   ____

   b. What equations did Cody enter into his calculator?

   ____

   c. Sketch the resulting graph.

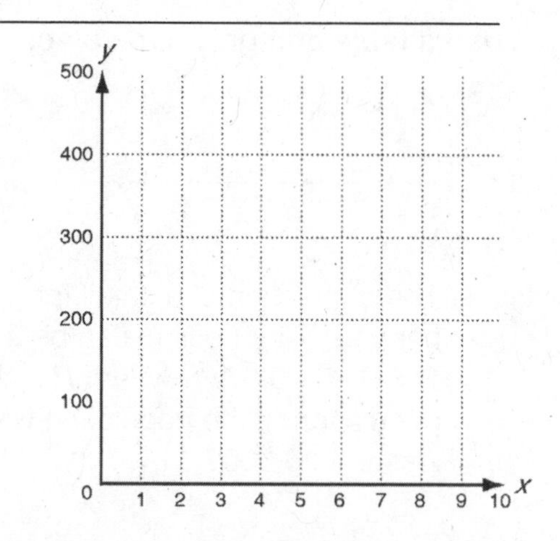

Choose the letter for the best answer.

3. About how long would it take for the level of caffeine in Cody's system to drop by a factor of 2?

   A 0.2 hour

   B 1.6 hours

   C 2.7 hours

   D 4.3 hours

4. If John drank 6 cups of coffee and a cola, about how long would it take for the level of caffeine in his system to drop to a moderate level?

   F 0.5 hour

   G 1.6 hours

   H 4.7 hours

   J 5.3 hours

Name________________________ Class__________ Date________

16-3

The Natural Base, e

Going Deeper

Essential question: *How does the graph of $f(x) = e^x$ compare to graphs of exponential functions with other bases?*

Video Tutor

MCC9–12.F.IF.2

1 EXPLORE Investigating $\left(1 + \frac{1}{x}\right)^x$

A Enter the expression $\left(1 + \frac{1}{x}\right)^x$ as Y_1 in your calculator's equation editor.

B Evaluate the function at the values of x shown in the table below. To do so, press VARS, select **Y-VARS**, and then select **1:Function**. In the function menu, select **1:Y_1**. Then use parentheses to evaluate the function at a value of x, as shown at right.

C Complete the table by writing all of the digits displayed on your calculator.

x	$\left(1 + \frac{1}{x}\right)^x$	x	$\left(1 + \frac{1}{x}\right)^x$
1	2	10,000	
10	2.59374246	100,000	
100		1,000,000	
1000		10,000,000	

D Find the value of e^1 on your calculator. To do so, press 2nd e^x LN and enter 1 as the exponent. Write all of the digits displayed on your calculator.

____

REFLECT

1a. What happens to the value of $1 + \frac{1}{x}$ as x increases without bound?

____

1b. What happens to the value of $\left(1 + \frac{1}{x}\right)^x$ as x increases without bound?

____

1c. What do you think is the connection between $\left(1 + \frac{1}{x}\right)^x$ and the number e?

____

MCC9–12.F.IF.7e

2 ENGAGE The Natural Base, e

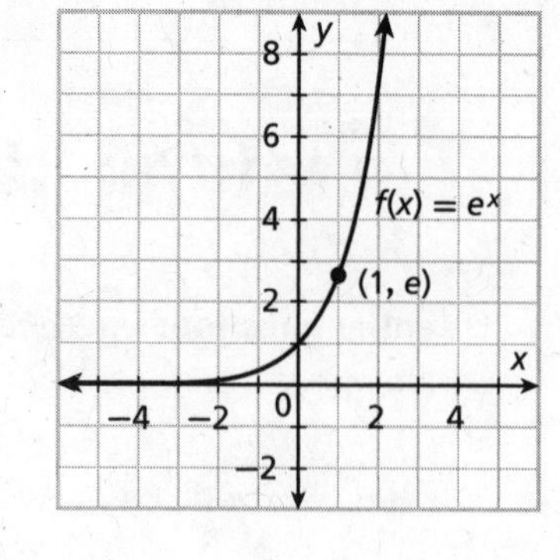

The number ***e*** is defined as the value that the expression $\left(1+\frac{1}{x}\right)^x$ approaches as x increases without bound. As you saw in the Explore, the decimal form of e is approximately 2.718281828. Despite the appearance of a pattern in the decimal digits, e is an irrational number whose actual decimal value neither repeats nor terminates. Like any other positive real number, e can be used as the base of an exponential function.

The graph of $f(x) = e^x$ is shown.

REFLECT

2a. Without graphing, explain how the graph of $f(x) = e^x$ compares to the graphs of $g(x) = 2^x$ and $h(x) = 3^x$.

____

____

MCC9–12.F.BF.3

3 EXAMPLE Graphing Transformations of $f(x) = e^x$

Graph each exponential function.

A $g(x) = e^{x+3}$

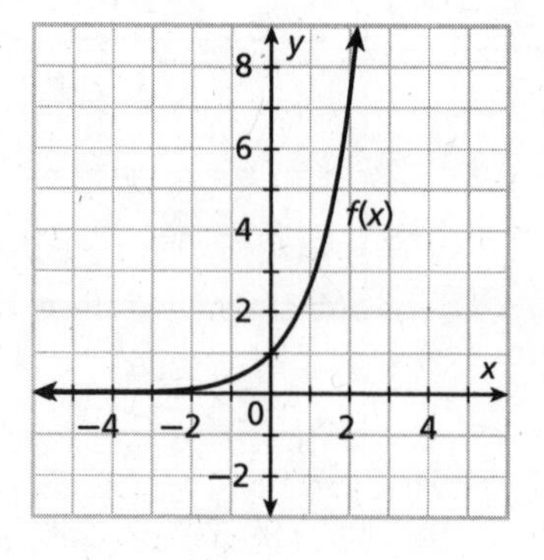

- First graph the parent function, $f(x) = e^x$. The graph of $f(x)$ is shown at right.
- The graph of $g(x)$ is a translation of the graph of $f(x)$ by how many units and in which direction?

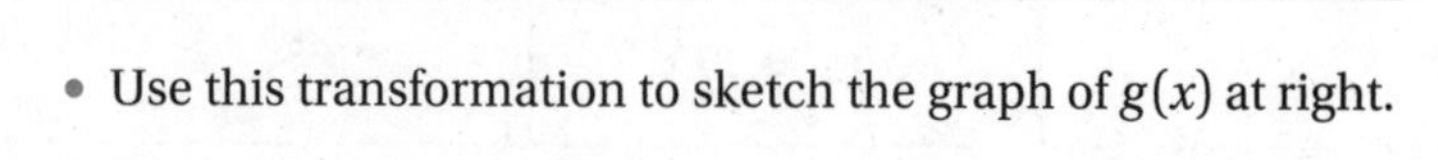

- Use this transformation to sketch the graph of $g(x)$ at right.

B $g(x) = \frac{1}{2}e^x + 1$

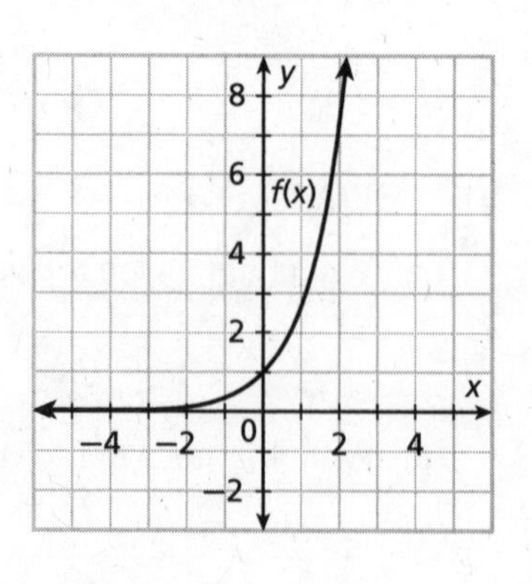

- First graph the parent function, $f(x) = e^x$. The graph of $f(x)$ is shown at right.
- The graph of $g(x)$ is a stretch or shrink of the graph of $f(x)$ in which direction and by what factor?

____

- The graph of $g(x)$ is also a translation of the graph of $f(x)$ by how many units and in which direction?

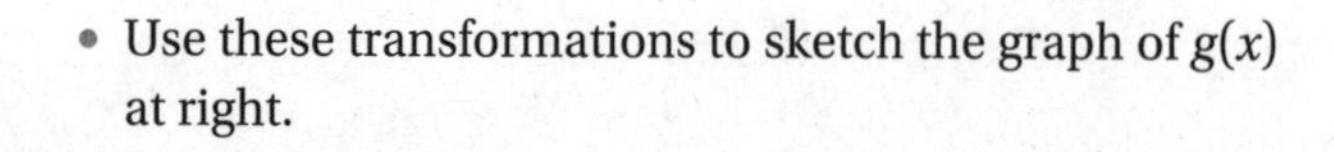

- Use these transformations to sketch the graph of $g(x)$ at right.

REFLECT

3a. Describe how the graph of $g(x)$ compares to the graph of $f(x) = e^x$.

____

The *effective rate of interest* on a deposit is the actual rate of interest earned, depending on the frequency of compounding. (*Nominal interest* does not take into account the frequency of compounding.) When an amount P is invested in an account earning interest at a nominal rate r compounded n times per year, the amount $A(t)$ in the account after t years is given by

$$A(t) = P\left(1 + \frac{r}{n}\right)^{nt}.$$

Consider what happens when the number n of compounding periods increases without bound; that is, when interest is compounded *continuously*.

$A(t) = P\left(1 + \frac{r}{n}\right)^{nt}$	Compound interest formula
$= P\left(1 + \frac{r}{mr}\right)^{mrt}$	Let $m = \frac{n}{r}$, so $n = mr$.
$= P\left(1 + \frac{1}{m}\right)^{mrt}$	Simplify.
$= P\left[\left(1 + \frac{1}{m}\right)^{m}\right]^{rt}$	Change the base of the exponential function.
$= Pe^{rt}$	As n increases without bound, so does m, and $\left(1 + \frac{1}{m}\right)^{m}$ approaches e.

So, when interest is compounded continuously, $A(t) = Pe^{rt}$ and the effective rate R is $e^r - 1$.

MCC9–12.F.IF.2

4 EXAMPLE Calculating Interest Compounded Continuously

Keiko invests \$2700 and earns 2.5% annual interest compounded continuously. What is the effective rate? How much will be in the account after 5 years?

A Find the effective rate.

$R = e^r - 1$	Use the formula for effective rate.
$= e^{\square} - 1$	Substitute 0.025 for r.
$\approx \square$	Evaluate. Round to 5 decimal places.

So, the effective rate is about 2.532%.

B Find the amount after 5 years.

$A(t) = Pe^{rt}$	Use the formula for interest compounded continuously.
$A(5) = \square \cdot e^{\square \cdot \square}$	Substitute 2700 for P, 0.025 for r, and 5 for t.
$\approx \square$	Evaluate. Round to the nearest hundredth.

So, the amount in Keiko's account after 5 years is ______________.

REFLECT

4a. Why does the variable n not appear in the formula $A(t) = Pe^{rt}$?

PRACTICE

Graph each exponential function.

1. $f(x) = e^{2x}$

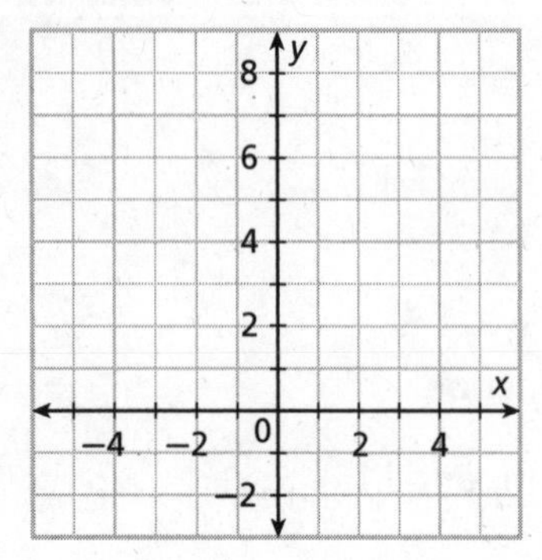

2. $f(x) = e^{-x} + 2$

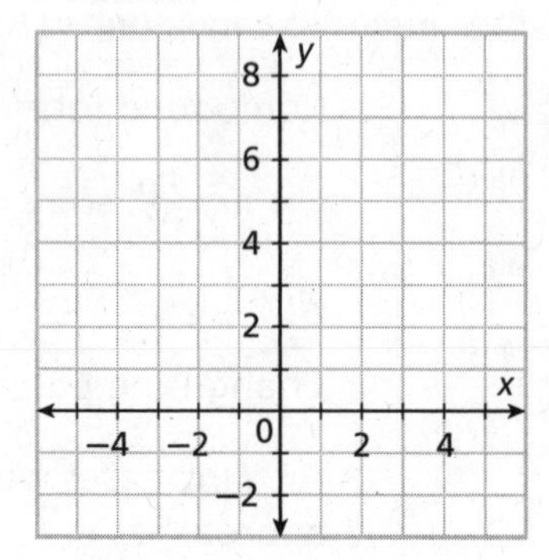

The graph of $f(x) = e^x$ is shown. Write the function rules for $g(x)$ and $h(x)$ based on the descriptions given. Then sketch the graphs of $g(x)$ and $h(x)$ on the same coordinate plane.

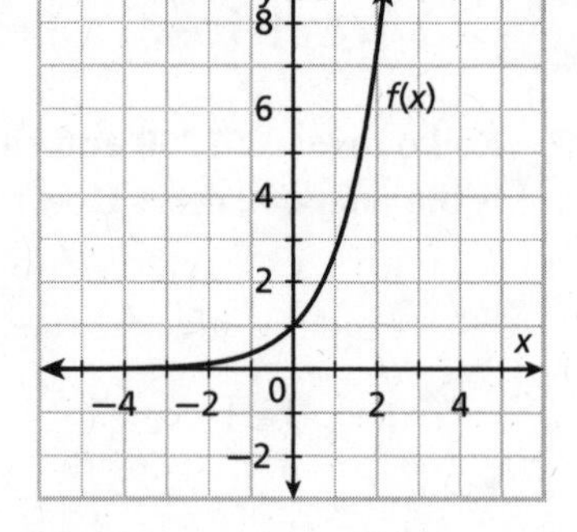

3. The graph of $g(x)$ is a horizontal shrink of the graph of $f(x)$ by a factor of $\frac{1}{3}$.

4. The graph of $h(x)$ is a horizontal translation of the graph of $f(x)$ to the right 3 units.

5. Carl invests \$3200 in an account that earns 3.1% annual interest compounded continuously. What is the effective rate? How much money will he have in his account after 7 years?

6. You plan to invest \$1000 in an account for one year. How much more money will you have at the end of the year if you choose an account that earns 6% annual interest compounded continuously versus an account that earns 6% annual interest compounded quarterly? Explain.

Name______________________ Class______________ Date__________

16-3

Additional Practice

Graph.

1. $f(x) = e^{2x}$

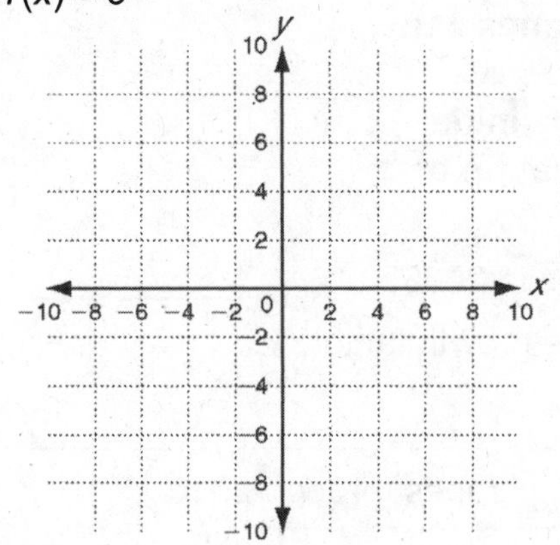

2. $f(x) = e^{0.5x}$

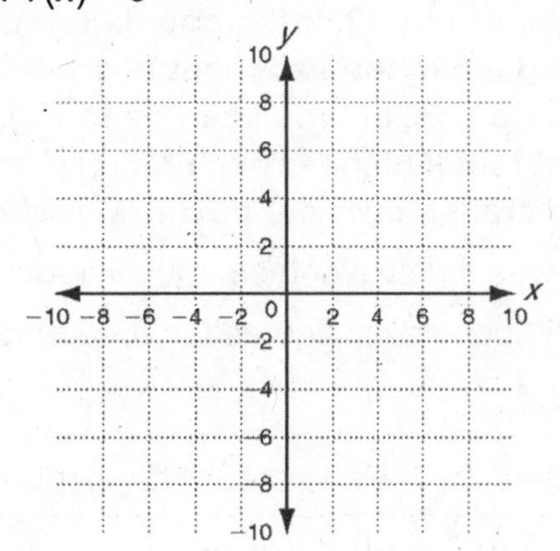

3. $f(x) = e^{1+x}$

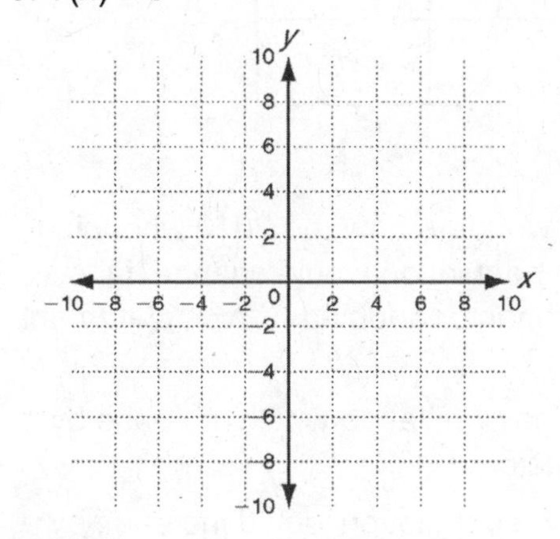

4. $f(x) = e^{2-x}$

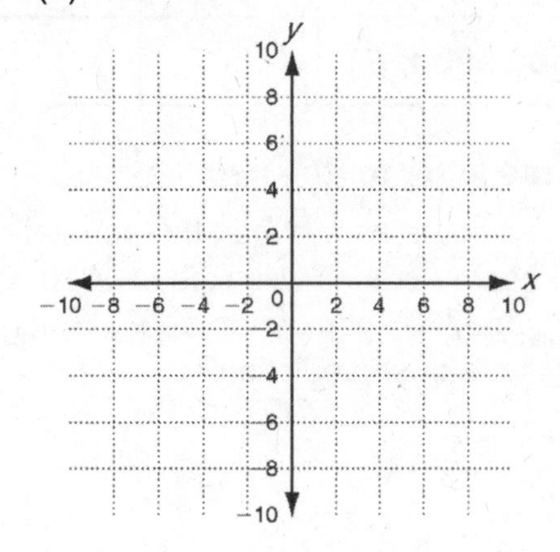

Simplify.

5. $\ln e^{x+2}$ ______________

6. $e^{\ln 2x}$ ______________

7. $e^{7 \ln x}$ ______________

8. $\ln e^{3x+1}$ ______________

9. $\ln e$ ______________

10. $\ln e^{2x+y}$ ______________

Solve.

11. Use the formula $A = Pe^{rt}$ to compute the total amount for an investment of $4500 at 5% interest compounded continuously for 6 years.

____

12. Use the natural decay function, $N(t) = N_0e^{-kt}$, to find the decay constant for a substance that has a half-life of 1000 years.

____

Problem Solving

Irene reads that the 2004 census of whooping cranes tallied 213 birds at one wildlife refuge in Texas. This number exceeded the 2003 record by 19. If the population of whooping cranes can be modeled using the exponential growth function $P_t = P_0 e^{kt}$, the population, P_t, at time t can be found, where P_0 is the initial population and k is the growth factor. Predict the population of whooping cranes over the next few years.

1. What was the size of the population of whooping cranes in 2003? ________________
2. Use the population figures for 2003 and 2004 to find the growth factor, k.

____

3. Complete the table to predict the population of whooping cranes through 2010.

Year	2006	2007	2008	2009	2010
t	3				
Population, P_t					

Choose the letter for the best answer.

4. Irene wants to know when the population of whooping cranes will exceed 1000. Using the 2003 population as P_0, which year is the best prediction?

A 2017

B 2019

C 2021

D 2023

5. Irene wonders how the 2010 whooping crane population would change if the growth factor doubled. Which statement is true?

F The population would increase by a factor of e^2.

G The population would increase by a factor of $e^{0.0934}$.

H The population would increase by a factor of $e^{(0.0934)(7)}$.

J The population would increase by a factor of $7e^2$.

6. How long will it take for an investment in an account paying 6% compounded continuously to double?

A 10.2 years

B 10.8 years

C 11.6 years

D 12.4 years

7. Darlene has a sample of a fossil that has 33% of its original carbon-14. Carbon-14 has a half-life of 5730 years. The decay constant for carbon-14 is 1.2×10^{-4}. Find the age of the fossil.

F About 7820 years

G About 8450 years

H About 8980 years

J About 9240 years

Name_______________ Class_______________ Date_______________

UNIT 8

Performance Tasks

GPS COMMON CORE

MCC9-12.A.CED.2
MCC9-12.F.IF.7e
MCC9-12.F.IF.8b
MCC9-12.F.BF.5
MCC9-12.F.LE.4

★ **1.** Ten years ago, a printing company charged $15 to produce 100 ten-page brochures. Every year, the cost increased by 2%. Write an exponential function to model the cost increases and use the function to find the cost of 100 ten-page brochures today.

★ **2.** A smoke detector contains a small amount of the radioactive element americium-241. How long will it take for one-third of the americium-241 to decay if its half-life is 432.2 years? Round your answer to the nearest whole year.

★★ **3.** Aaron invested $4000 in an account that paid an interest rate r compounded quarterly. After 10 years he has $5809.81. The compound interest formula is $A = P\left(1 + \frac{r}{n}\right)^{nt}$, where P is the principal (the initial investment), A is the total amount of money (principal plus interest), r is the annual interest rate, t is the time in years, and n is the number of compounding periods per year.

a. Divide both sides of the formula by P and then use logarithms to rewrite the formula without an exponent. Show your work.

b. Using your answer for part **a** as a starting point, solve the compound interest formula for the interest rate, r.

c. Use your equation from part **a** to determine the interest rate.

continued

4. The spread of a virus can be modeled by exponential growth, but its growth is limited by the number of individuals that can be infected. For such situations, the function $P(t) = \frac{Kpe^{rt}}{K + p(e^{rt} - 1)}$ can be used, where $P(t)$ is the infected population t days after the first infection, p is the initial infected population, K is the total population that can be infected, and r is the rate the virus spreads, written as a decimal.

a. A town of 10,000 people starts with 2 infected people and a virus growth rate of 20%. When will the growth of the infected population start to level off, and how many people will be infected at that point? Explain your reasoning, and include any graphs you draw, with or without technology.

b. When will the infected population equal the uninfected population?

Name ______________________ Class ______________ Date ________

SELECTED RESPONSE

1. If $f(x) = \log_3 x$, what is $f\left(\frac{1}{9}\right)$?

A. -2

B. $-\frac{1}{2}$

C. $\frac{1}{2}$

D. 2

2. Which is the solution of $10^{2x} = 319$?

F. $\log 17.86$

G. $2\log 319$

H. $\frac{\log 319}{2}$

J. $\frac{\log 319}{\log 20}$

3. Which equation has the same solution as $\log_4 (x + 7) = 5$?

A. $4^{x+7} = 5$

B. $4^5 = x + 7$

C. $5^{x+7} = 4$

D. $5^4 = x + 7$

4. Use inverse operations to write the inverse of $f(x) = x - \frac{4}{7}$.

F. $f^{-1}(x) = x + \frac{4}{7}$

G. $f^{-1}(x) = x + \frac{3}{7}$

H. $f^{-1}(x) = x - \frac{3}{7}$

J. $f^{-1}(x) = x - \frac{4}{7}$

5. Express $\log_3 81 - \log_3 3$ as a single logarithm. Simplify, if possible.

A. 3

B. $\log_3 3$

C. $\log_3 78$

D. 5

6. Latrell wants to double an investment of $3500 that earns interest at an annual rate of 6% compounded continuously. Which equation can he solve to find the doubling time t for this investment?

F. $7000 = 3500 \ln 0.06t$

G. $7000 = 3500e^{0.06t}$

H. $7000 = 3500(1.06)^t$

J. $7000 = 3500 \log_{0.06} t$

7. Alicia graphed an exponential function that has a y-intercept of 3. Which of the following functions could she have graphed?

A. $g(x) = 5^{x-3}$

B. $g(x) = 3(5)^x$

C. $g(x) = 5^x + 3$

D. $g(x) = 5^{3x}$

8. What is the inverse of $f(x) = 2x + 9$?

F. $f^{-1}(x) = \frac{x}{2} - 9$

G. $f^{-1}(x) = \frac{1}{2x + 9}$

H. $f^{-1}(x) = \frac{x - 9}{2}$

J. $f^{-1}(x) = \frac{2}{x - 9}$

9. An initial population of 900 frogs decreases at a rate of 14% per year. Which function gives the population after x years?

A. $f(x) = 900(1.14)^x$

B. $f(x) = 900(0.86)^x$

C. $f(x) = 900(0.14)^x$

D. $f(x) = 900 - 0.86^x$

10. The graph of $f(x)$ decreases as x decreases and increases as x increases. Which of these could be the function described?

F. $f(x) = 4.5(0.5)^x$

G. $g(x) = 4.5^{-2x}$

H. $h(x) = 4.5^{0.5x}$

J. $j(x) = 4.5^{-0.5x}$

11. Ron invests \$1200 at 4.5% compounded continuously and Dina invests \$1500 at 3% compounded continuously. When will they have the same amount in their accounts?

A. about 7 years **C.** about 14 years

B. about 8 years **D.** about 15 years

12. As x increases without bound, the graph of which function rises at the fastest rate?

F. $f(x) = 3^x$

G. $g(x) = 3x^2$

H. $h(x) = 5x + 30$

J. $j(x) = x^4 + 1$

CONSTRUCTED RESPONSE

13. The graph of $g(x)$ is a reflection in the x-axis and a vertical translation of the graph of $f(x) = \log_{\frac{1}{3}} x$. Write the equation of $g(x)$.

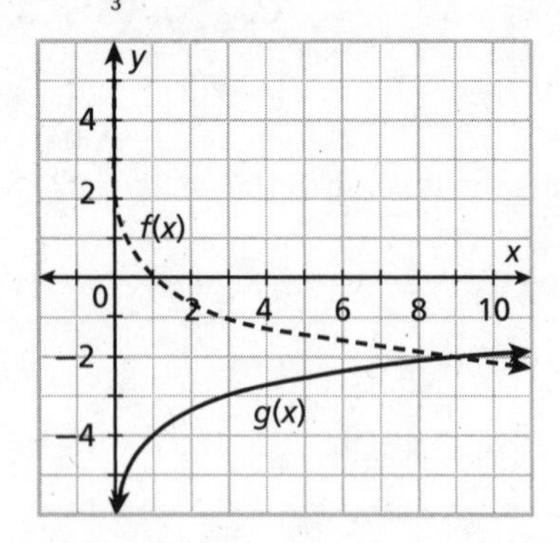

14. Explain how you can solve the exponential equation $5^{x+2} = 4^{3x}$ using your graphing calculator. Then give the approximate solution to two decimal places.

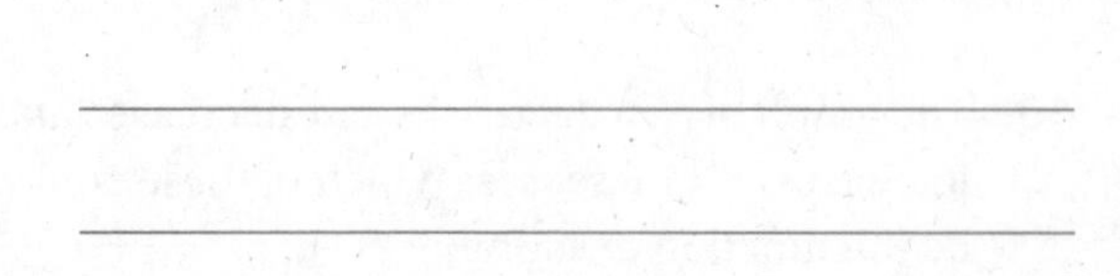

15. Consider the function $f(x) = \log_5 x$.

a. Complete the table.

x	$f(x)$
$\frac{1}{5}$	
1	
5	
25	

b. Sketch the graph of $f(x)$.

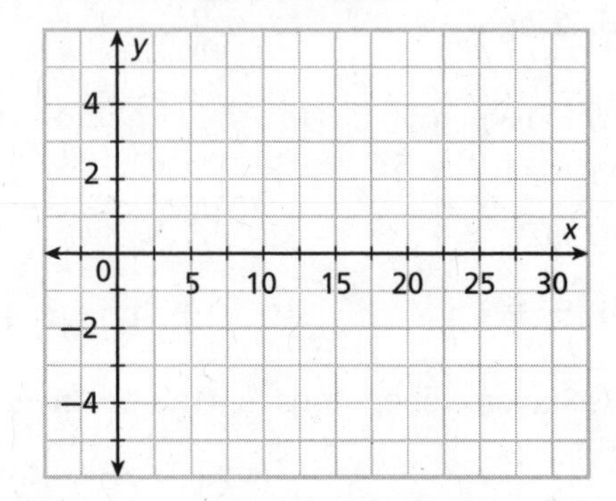

c. Give the equation of any asymptote for the graph of $f(x)$.

d. The function $g(x)$ is the inverse of $f(x)$. Write the equation for $g(x)$.

e. Name three points on the graph of $g(x)$ and tell how you can determine them by looking at the table or graph of $f(x)$.

f. The graph of $g(x)$ is the reflection of the graph of $f(x)$ across what line?

UNIT 9

Trigonometric Functions

UNIT 9

Unpacking the Standards

Understanding the standards and the vocabulary terms in the standards will help you know exactly what you are expected to learn in this unit.

MCC9-12.F.TF.2

Explain how the unit circle in the coordinate plane enables the extension of trigonometric functions to all real numbers, interpreted as radian measures of angles traversed counterclockwise around the unit circle.

Key Vocabulary

radian *(radian)* A unit of angle measure based on arc length. In a circle of radius r, if a central angle has a measure of 1 radian, then the length of the intercepted arc is r units.

trigonometric function *(función trigonométrica)* A function whose rule is given by a trigonometric ratio.

What It Means For You

You can measure angles in degrees or in radians. In a circle with radius r, an angle that forms an arc of length r measures 1 radian, or about 57°.

EXAMPLE

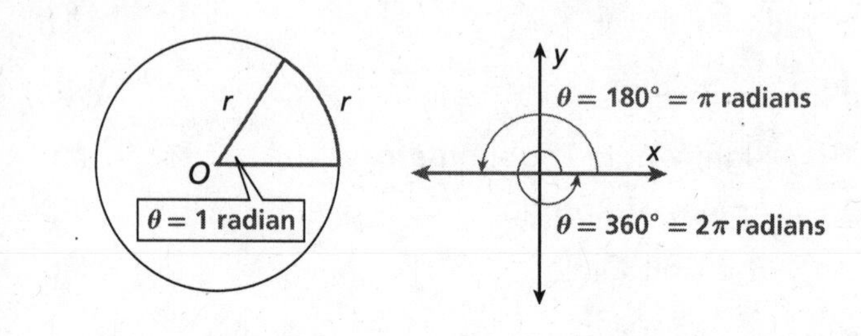

MCC9-12.F.IF.7e

Graph . . . trigonometric functions, showing period, midline, and amplitude.

Key Vocabulary

trigonometric function *(función trigonométrica)* A function whose rule is given by a trigonometric ratio.

periodic function *(función periódica)* A function that repeats exactly in regular intervals, called *periods.*

period of a periodic function *(periodo de una función periódica)* The length of a cycle measured in units of the independent variable (usually time in seconds). Also the reciprocal of the frequency.

amplitude *(amplitud)* The amplitude of a periodic function is half the difference of the maximum and minimum values (always positive).

What It Means For You

The graphs of trigonometric functions are curves that form repeating wave-like patterns.

EXAMPLE **Sine function $y = \sin x$**

$y = \sin x$
period $= 2\pi$
amplitude $= 1$

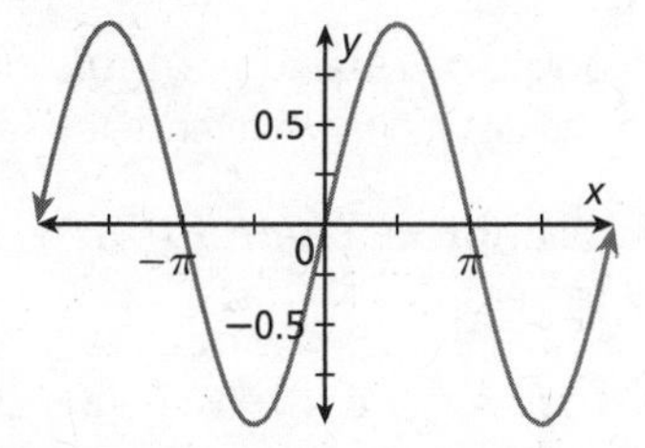

EXAMPLE **Cosine function $y = \cos x$**

$y = \cos x$
period $= 2\pi$
amplitude $= 1$

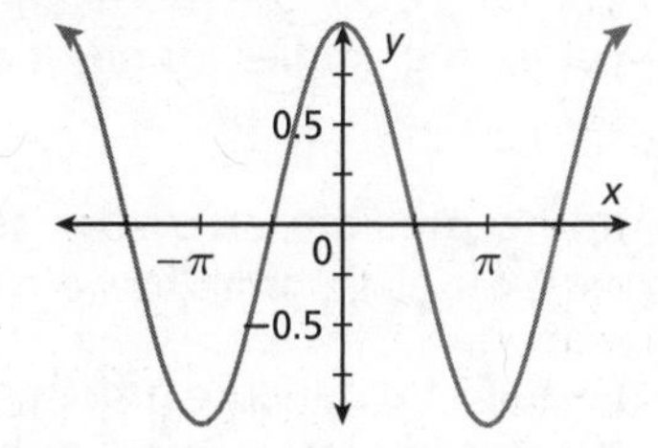

EXAMPLE **Tangent function $y = \tan x$**

$y = \tan x$
period $= \pi$
amplitude $=$ undefined

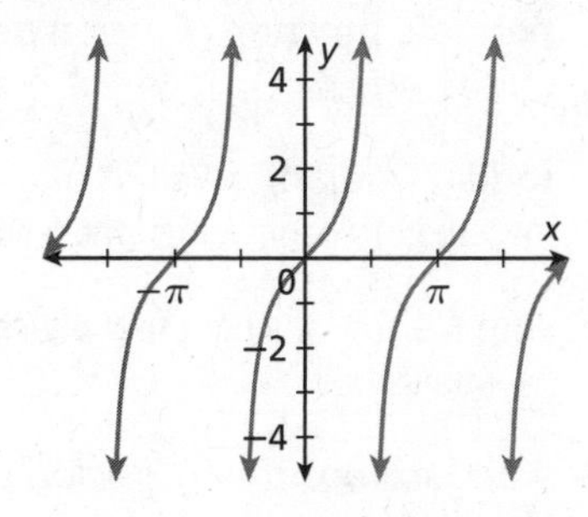

UNIT 9

Key Vocabulary

amplitude *(amplitud)* The amplitude of a periodic function is half the difference of the maximum and minimum values (always positive).

angle of rotation *(ángulo de rotación)* An angle formed by a rotating ray, called the terminal side, and a stationary reference ray, called the initial side.

asymptote *(asíntota)* A line that a graph approaches as the value of a variable becomes extremely large or small.

cosine *(coseno)* In a right triangle, the cosine of $\angle A$ is the ratio of the length of the side adjacent to $\angle A$ to the length of the hypotenuse.

coterminal angles *(ángulos coterminales)* Two angles in standard position with the same terminal side.

intercepted arc *(arco abarcado)* An arc that consists of endpoints that lie on the sides of an inscribed angle and all the points between the endpoints.

period of a periodic function *(periodo de una función periódica)* The length of a cycle measured in units of the independent variable (usually time in seconds). Also the reciprocal of the frequency.

periodic function *(función periódica)* A function that repeats exactly in regular intervals, called *periods*.

radian *(radian)* A unit of angle measure based on arc length. In a circle of radius r, if a central angle has a measure of 1 radian, then the length of the intercepted arc is r units.

sine *(seno)* In a right triangle, the ratio of the length of the side opposite $\angle A$ to the length of the hypotenuse.

standard position *(posición estándar)* An angle in standard position has its vertex at the origin and its initial side on the positive x-axis.

tangent of an angle *(tangente de un ángulo)* In a right triangle, the ratio of the length of the leg opposite $\angle A$ to the length of the leg adjacent to $\angle A$.

trigonometric function *(función trigonométrica)* A function whose rule is given by a trigonometric ratio.

unit circle *(círculo unitario)* A circle with a radius of 1, centered at the origin.

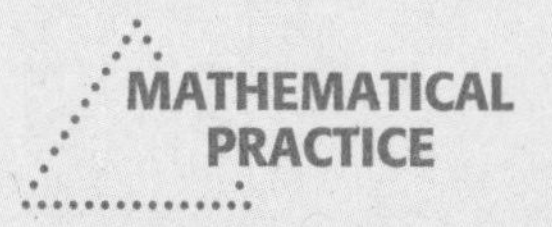

The Common Core Standards for Mathematical Practice describe varieties of expertise that mathematics educators at all levels should seek to develop in their students. Opportunities to develop these practices are integrated throughout this program.

1. **Make sense of problems and persevere in solving them.**
2. **Reason abstractly and quantitatively.**
3. **Construct viable arguments and critique the reasoning of others.**
4. **Model with mathematics.**
5. **Use appropriate tools strategically.**
6. **Attend to precision.**
7. **Look for and make use of structure.**
8. **Look for and express regularity in repeated reasoning.**

Name________________ Class____________ Date________

17-1

Right-Angle Trigonometry
Connection: Radian Measure

Essential question: *What is radian measure, and how are radians related to degrees?*

Video Tutor

MCC9–12.G.C.5

1 EXPLORE Finding the Ratio of Arc Length to Radius

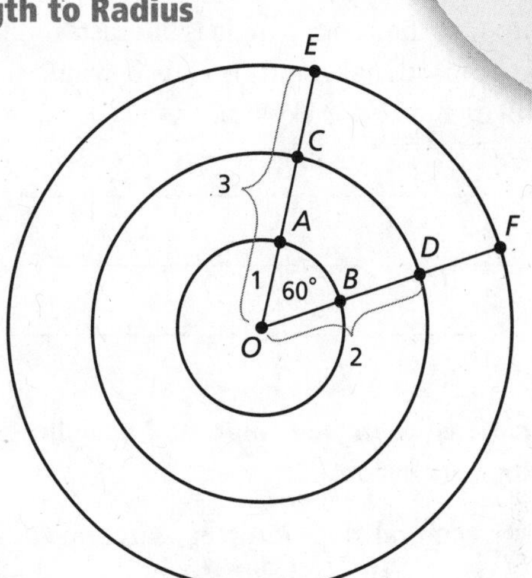

The diagram shows three circles centered at point O. The arcs between the sides of the 60° central angle are called **intercepted arcs**.

$\overparen{AB}$ is on the circle with radius 1 unit,

$\overparen{CD}$ is on the circle with radius 2 units, and

$\overparen{EF}$ is on the circle with radius 3 units.

Each intercepted arc has a different length, but because the arcs are intercepted by the same central angle, each length is the *same fraction* of the circumference of the circle containing the arc.

A Determine the fraction of each circle's circumference that the length of each arc represents.

- How many degrees are in a circle? __________
- What fraction of the total number of degrees in a circle is 60°? __________
- So, what fraction of the circumference of each circle is the length of each intercepted arc? __________

B Complete the table below. To find the length of the intercepted arc, use the fraction that you found in part A. Give all answers in terms of π.

Radius, r	Circumference, C ($C = 2\pi r$)	Length of Intercepted Arc, s	Ratio of Arc Length to Radius, $\frac{s}{r}$
1			
2			
3			

REFLECT

1a. What do you notice about the ratios in the fourth column of the table?

____

1b. When the ratio of the values of one variable y to the corresponding values of another variable x is a constant k, y is said to be *proportional* to x, and the constant k is called the *constant of proportionality*. Because $\frac{y}{x} = k$, you can solve for y to get $y = kx$. In the case of arcs intercepted by a 60° central angle, is arc length s proportional to radius r? If so, what is the constant of proportionality, and what equation gives s in terms of r?

1c. Suppose the central angle is 90° instead of 60°. Would arc length s still be proportional to radius r? If so, would the constant of proportionality still be the same? Explain.

Radian Measure In the Explore and its Reflect questions, you should have reached the following conclusions:

1. When a central angle intercepts arcs on circles that have a common center, the ratio of each arc length s to radius r is constant.

2. When the degree measure of the central angle changes, the constant also changes.

These facts allow you to create an alternative way of measuring angles. Instead of degree measure, you can use *radian measure*, defined as follows: If a central angle in a circle of radius r intercepts an arc of length s, then the angle's **radian measure** is $\theta = \frac{s}{r}$.

Relating Radians to Degrees

Let the degree measure of a central angle in a circle with radius r be $d°$, as shown. You can derive formulas that relate the *angle's* degree measure and its radian measure.

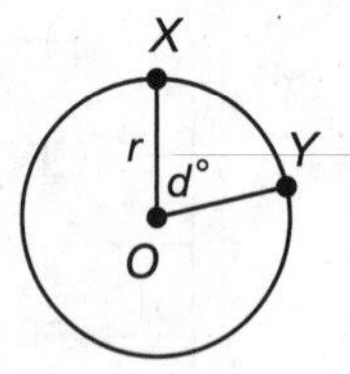

A Find the length s of the intercepted arc $\widehat{XY}$ using the verbal model below. Give the length in terms of π, and simplify.

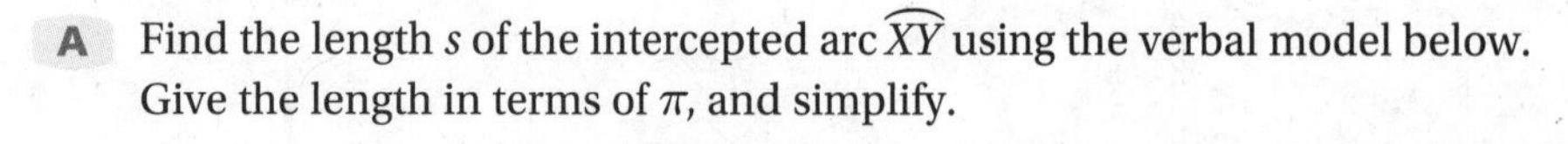

B Use the result from part A to write the angle's radian measure θ in terms of d to find a formula for converting degrees to radians.

$$\theta = \frac{s}{r} = \frac{\quad}{\quad} = \quad \cdot d^\circ$$

C Solve the equation from part B for d° to find a formula for converting radians to degrees.

$$d^\circ = \quad \cdot \theta$$

REFLECT

2a. What radian measure is equivalent to 360°? Why does this make sense?

____

____

Radian measures are usually written in terms of π, using fractions, such as $\frac{2\pi}{3}$, rather than mixed numbers.

MCC9-12.N.Q.1

3 EXAMPLE Converting Between Radians and Degrees

A Use the formula $\theta = \frac{\pi}{180^\circ} \cdot d^\circ$ to convert each degree measure to radian measure. Simplify the result.

Degree measure	Radian measure
15°	
45°	
90°	
120°	
135°	
165°	

B Use the formula $d^\circ = \frac{180^\circ}{\pi} \cdot \theta$ to convert each radian measure to degree measure. Simplify the result.

Radian measure	Degree measure
$\frac{\pi}{6}$	
$\frac{\pi}{3}$	
$\frac{5\pi}{12}$	
$\frac{7\pi}{12}$	
$\frac{5\pi}{6}$	
π	

REFLECT

3a. Which is greater, 1° or 1 radian? Explain.

____

3b. A radian is sometimes called a "dimensionless" quantity. Use unit analysis and the definition of radian to explain why this description makes sense.

____

____

PRACTICE

1. Convert each degree measure to radian measure. Simplify the result.

Degree measure	18°	24°	72°	84°	108°	126°	132°
Radian measure							

2. Convert each radian measure to degree measure. Simplify the result.

Radian measure	$\frac{\pi}{15}$	$\frac{\pi}{5}$	$\frac{4\pi}{15}$	$\frac{3\pi}{10}$	$\frac{8\pi}{15}$	$\frac{13\pi}{15}$	$\frac{9\pi}{10}$
Degree measure							

3. When a central angle of a circle intercepts an arc whose length equals the radius of the circle, what is the angle's radian measure? Explain.

____

4. A *unit circle* has a radius of 1. What is the relationship between the radian measure of a central angle in a unit circle and the length of the arc that it intercepts? Explain.

____

5. A pizza is cut into 8 equal slices.

a. What is the radian measure of the angle in each slice? __________

b. If the length along the outer edge of the crust of one slice is about 7 inches, what is the *diameter* of the pizza to the nearest inch? (Use the formula $\theta = \frac{s}{r}$, but note that it gives you the radius of the pizza.) __________

Name________________________ Class______________ Date__________

Additional Practice

Convert each measure from degrees to radians or from radians to degrees.

1. $\frac{5\pi}{12}$ 2. 215° 3. $-\frac{29\pi}{18}$

________ ________ ________

4. –180° 5. $\frac{5\pi}{3}$ 6. $-\frac{7\pi}{6}$

________ ________ ________

7. 400° 8. $\frac{3\pi}{10}$ 9. 35°

________ ________ ________

Use the unit circle to find the exact value of each trigonometric function.

10. $\cos\frac{2\pi}{3}$ 11. $\tan\frac{5\pi}{4}$ 12. $\tan\frac{5\pi}{6}$

________ ________ ________

13. sin 315° 14. cos 225° 15. tan 60°

________ ________ ________

Use a reference angle to find the exact value of the sine, cosine, and tangent of each angle.

16. 150° 17. –225° 18. –300°

________ ________ ________

19. $\frac{11\pi}{6}$ 20. $-\frac{2\pi}{3}$ 21. $\frac{5\pi}{4}$

________ ________ ________

Solve.

22. San Antonio, Texas, is located about 30° north of the equator. If Earth's radius is about 3959 miles, approximately how many miles is San Antonio from the equator?

____

Problem Solving

Gabe is spending two weeks on an archaeological dig. He finds a fragment of a circular plate that his leader thinks may be valuable. The arc length of the fragment is about $\frac{1}{6}$ the circumference of the original complete plate and measures 1.65 inches.

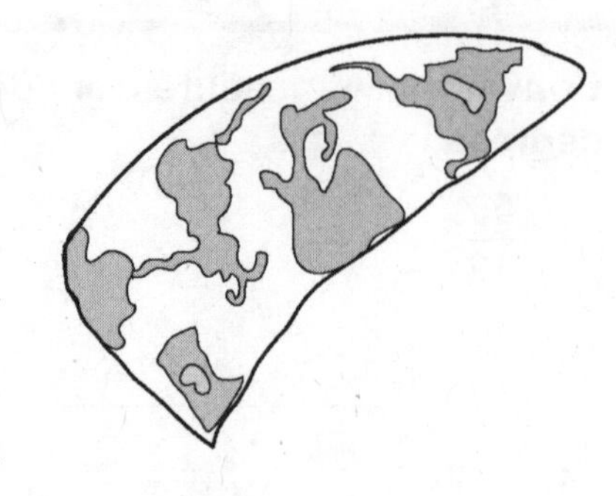

1. A similar plate found earlier has a diameter of 3.14 inches. Could Gabe's fragment match this plate?
   a. Write an expression for the radius, r, of the earlier plate. ________
   b. What is the measure, in radians, of a central angle, θ, that intercepts an arc that is $\frac{1}{6}$ the length of the circumference of a circle? ________
   c. Write an expression for the arc length, S, intercepted by this central angle. ________
   d. How long would the arc length of a fragment be if it were $\frac{1}{6}$ the circumference of the plate? ________
   e. Could Gabe's plate be a matching plate? Explain.

   ____

   ____

2. Toby finds another fragment of arc length 2.48 inches. What fraction of the outer edge of Gabe's plate would it be if this fragment were part of Gabe's plate? ________

The diameter of a merry-go-round at the playground is 12 feet. Elijah stands on the edge and his sister pushes him around. Choose the letter for the best answer.

3. How far does Elijah travel if he moves through an angle of $\frac{5\pi}{4}$ radians?

   A 12.0 ft   C 23.6 ft

   B 15.1 ft   D 47.1 ft

4. Through what angle does Elijah move if he travels a distance of 80 feet around the circumference?

   F $\frac{40}{3}\pi$ radians   H $\frac{40}{3}$ radians

   G $\frac{80}{3}$ radians   J $\frac{20}{3}$ radians

Virgil sets his boat on a 1000-yard course keeping a constant distance from a rocky outcrop. Choose the letter for the best answer.

5. If Virgil keeps a distance of 200 yards, through what angle does he travel?

   A 5π radians   C 10 radians

   B 5 radians   D 10π radians

6. If Virgil keeps a distance of 500 yards, what fraction of the circumference of a circle does he cover?

   F $\frac{1}{\pi}$ H $\frac{3}{4\pi}$

   G $\frac{\pi}{3}$ J $\frac{3\pi}{4}$

Name ______________________ Class ______________ Date ______________

17-2

Angles of Rotation

Extension: The Unit Circle

Essential question: *What is an angle of rotation, and how is it measured?*

MCC9–12.F.TF.1

1 ENGAGE Understanding Angles of Rotation

In trigonometry, an **angle of rotation** is an angle formed by the starting and ending positions of a ray that rotates about its endpoint. The angle is in **standard position** in a coordinate plane when the starting position of the ray, or **initial side** of the angle, is on the positive x-axis and has its endpoint at the origin. To show the amount and direction of rotation, a curved arrow is drawn to the ending position of the ray, or **terminal side** of the angle.

In geometry, you were accustomed to working with angles having measures between 0° and 180°. In trigonometry, angles can have measures greater than 180° and even less than 0°. To see why, think in terms of *revolutions*, or complete circular motions. Let θ be an angle of rotation in standard position.

- If the rotation for θ is less than 1 revolution in a counterclockwise direction, then the measure of θ is between 0° and 360°.
- If the rotation for θ is more than 1 revolution but less than 2 revolutions in a counterclockwise direction, then the measure of θ is between 360° and 720°, as shown at the left below.
- If the rotation for θ is less than 1 revolution in a clockwise direction, then the measure of θ is between 0° and −360°, as shown at the right below.

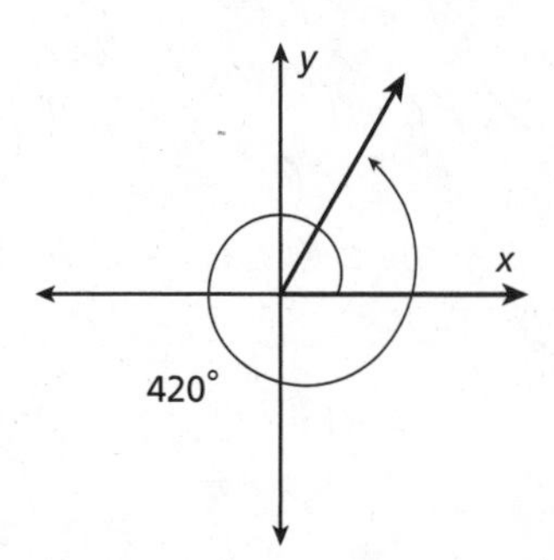

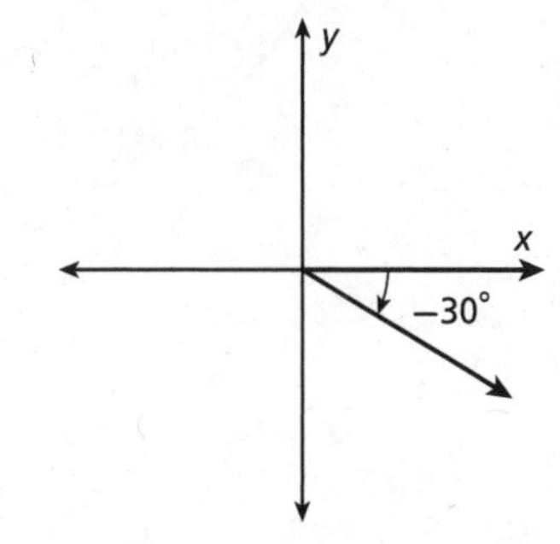

In general, when a rotation is counterclockwise, the measure of θ is positive, and when a rotation is clockwise, the measure of θ is negative.

In the illustrations above, the measures of angles of rotation are given in degrees, but if a circle is introduced into the coordinate plane, you can think in terms of arc lengths and use radian measure instead.

The **unit circle** is a circle that has a radius of 1 unit and is centered at the origin. Think of θ, an angle of rotation in standard position, as traversing an arc on the unit circle. Recall that radian measure was defined in Lesson 8-1 as $\theta = \frac{s}{r}$ where s is the arc length and r is the radius of the circle. Since $r = 1$ in this case, the radian measure of θ is simply the arc length: $\theta = s$. (Note: Throughout this unit, the symbol θ will be used to represent both an angle of rotation and its measure. For instance, "angle θ" refers to an angle, while "$\theta = \pi$" refers to an angle's measure.)

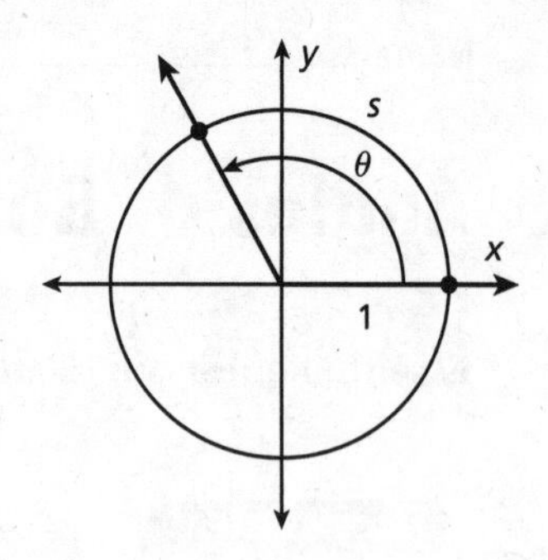

REFLECT

1a. The unit circle below shows the measures of angles of rotation that are commonly used in trigonometry. Radian measures appear outside the circle, and equivalent degree measures appear inside the circle. Provide the missing measures.

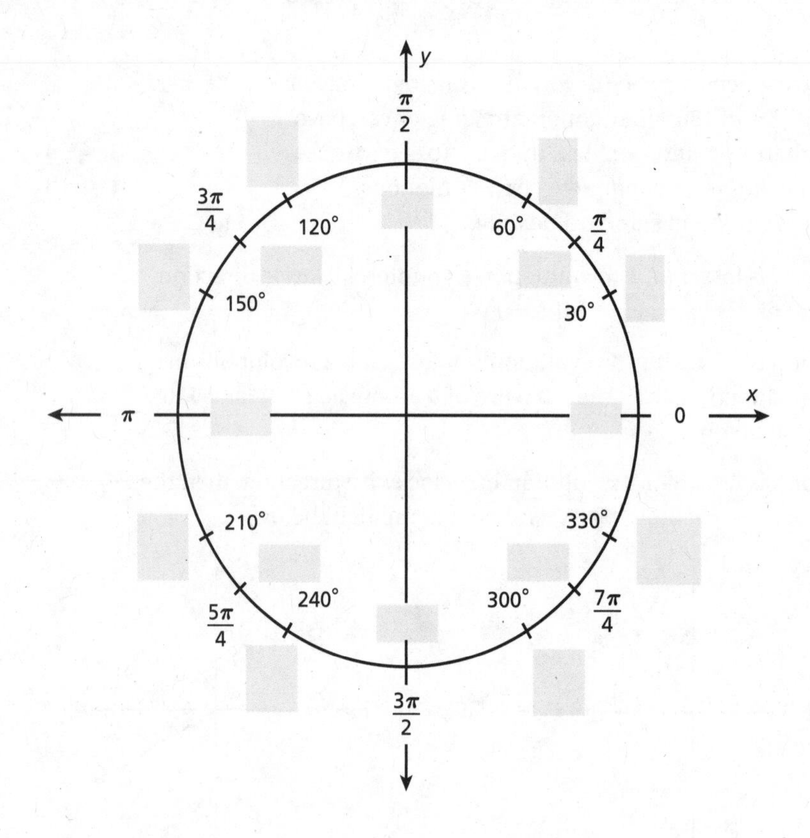

1b. Explain how you can use the diagram above to draw an angle of rotation with a measure of 570°.

MCC9–12.F.TF.1

2 EXAMPLE Drawing Angles of Rotation

Draw each angle of rotation with the given measure.

A **450°**

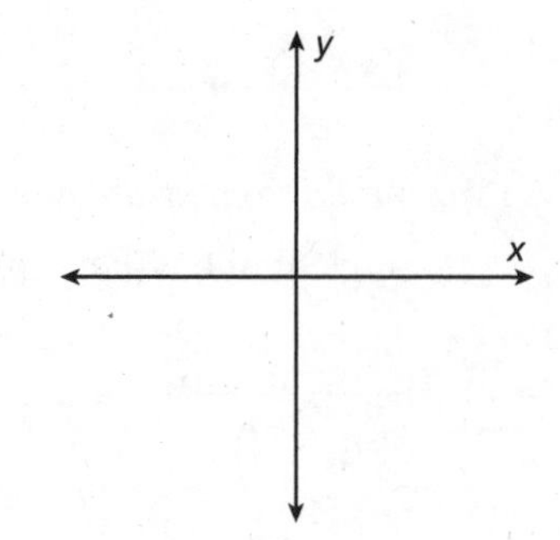

Recognize that 450° represents 1 revolution counterclockwise (360°) plus 90° more. Draw the angle's initial side on the positive x-axis. Then draw a spiraling arrow from the initial side in a counterclockwise direction. The spiral should complete a full circle and then go a quarter of a circle farther. Draw the angle's terminal side where the arrow ends.

B $-\frac{5\pi}{4}$

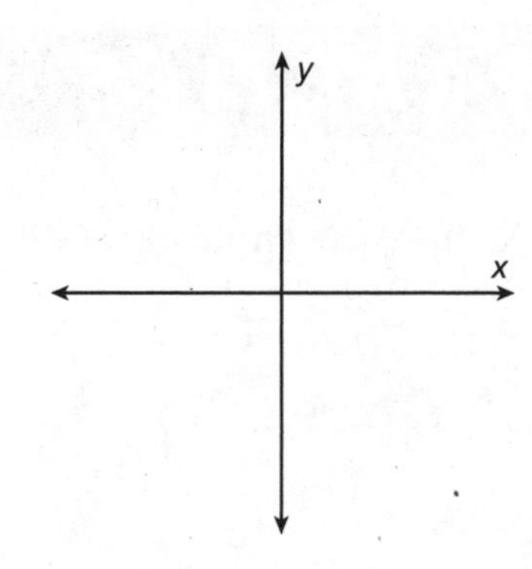

Recognize that $-\frac{5\pi}{4}$ represents $\frac{1}{2}$ revolution clockwise $(-\pi)$ plus $-\frac{\pi}{4}$ more. Draw the angle's initial side on the positive x-axis. Then draw a spiraling arrow from the initial side in a clockwise direction. The spiral should complete a half circle and then go an eighth of a circle farther. Draw the angle's terminal side where the arrow ends.

REFLECT

2a. Is the measure of an angle of rotation in standard position completely determined by the position of its terminal side? Explain.

____

____

Angles of rotation in standard position that have the same terminal side are called **coterminal**.

MCC9–12.F.TF.1

3 EXAMPLE Finding Coterminal Angles

Find the measure of a positive angle and a negative angle that are coterminal with each given angle.

A **−30°**

For a positive coterminal angle, add 360°: $-30° + 360° =$ __________

For a negative coterminal angle, subtract 360°: $-30° - 360° =$ __________

B $\frac{4\pi}{3}$

For a positive coterminal angle, add 2π: $\frac{4\pi}{3} + 2\pi =$ __________

For a negative coterminal angle, subtract 2π: $\frac{4\pi}{3} - 2\pi =$ __________

REFLECT

3a. Describe a general method for finding the measure of *any* angle that is coterminal with a given angle.

____

3b. Find the measure between 720° and 1080° of an angle that is coterminal with an angle that has a measure of −30°. Explain your method.

____

PRACTICE

Draw the angle of rotation with each given measure.

1. −180°

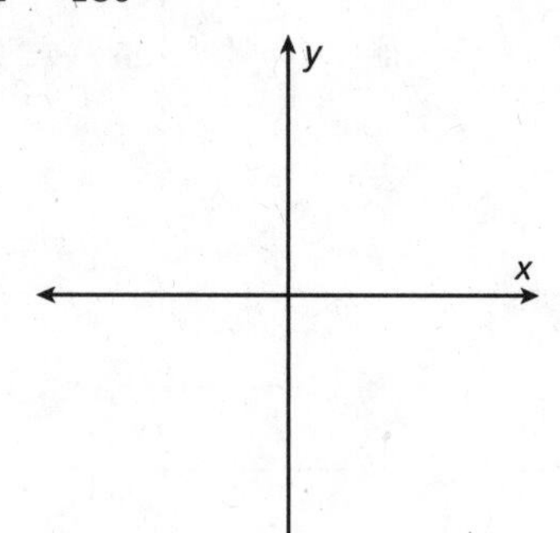

2. 405°

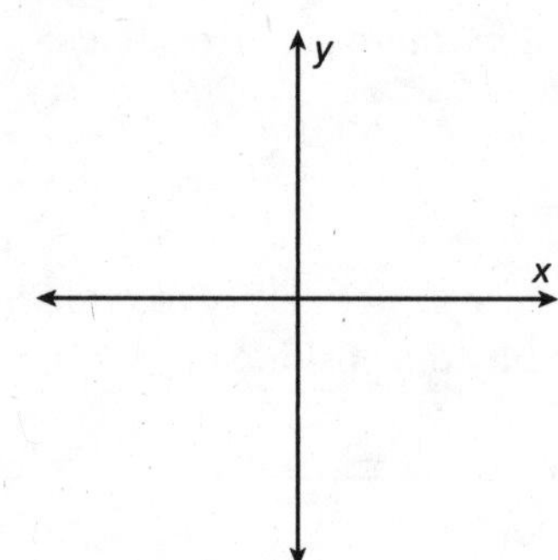

3. $-\frac{2\pi}{3}$

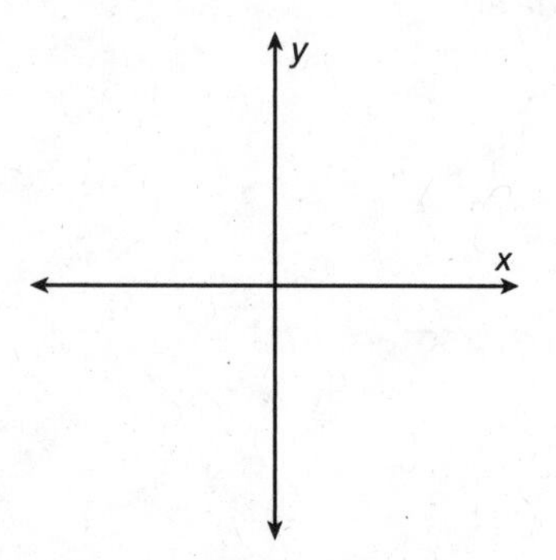

4. $\frac{15\pi}{4}$

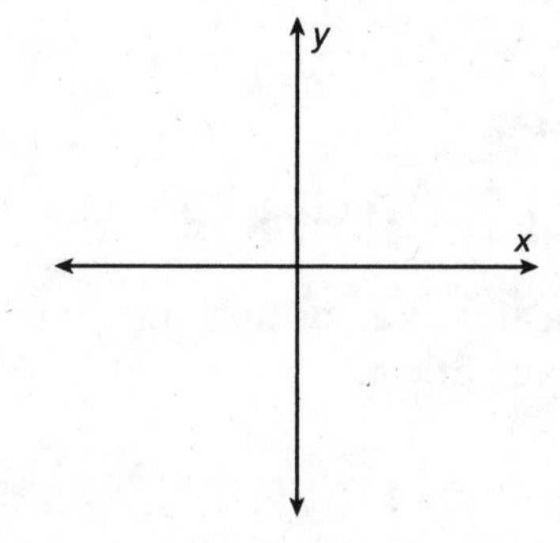

Find the measure of a positive angle and a negative angle that are coterminal with each given angle.

5. −10° ____________________

6. 500° ____________________

7. $-\frac{7\pi}{6}$ ____________________

8. $\frac{11\pi}{4}$ ____________________

Name________________________ Class________________ Date____________

17-2

Additional Practice

Draw an angle with the given measure in standard position.

1. $-420°$

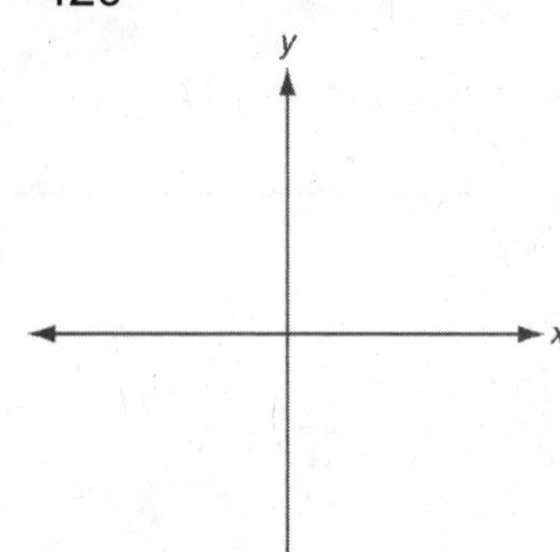

2. $405°$

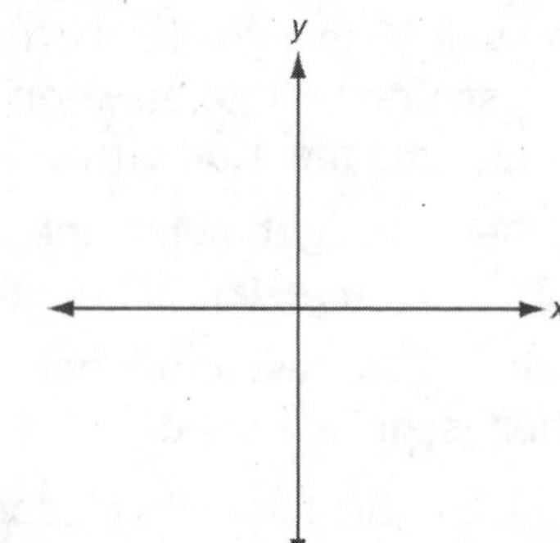

3. $-450°$

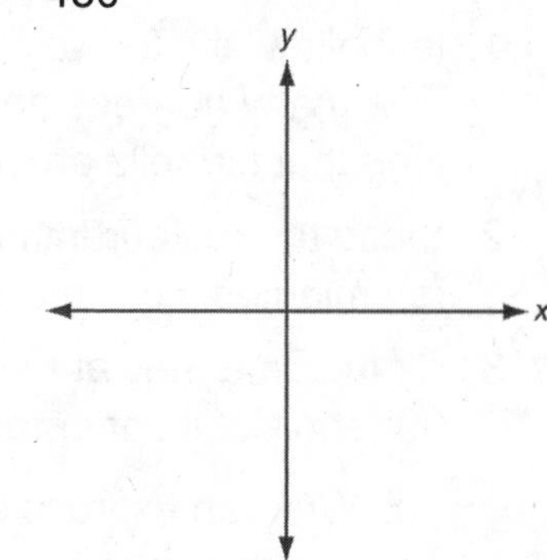

Find the measures of a positive angle and a negative angle that are coterminal with each given angle.

4. $\theta = 425°$ ____________
5. $\theta = -316°$ ____________
6. $\theta = -800°$ ____________
7. $\theta = 281°$ ____________
8. $\theta = -4°$ ____________
9. $\theta = 743°$ ____________

Find the measure of the reference angle for each given angle.

10. $\theta = 211°$ ____________
11. $\theta = -755°$ ____________
12. $\theta = -555°$ ____________
13. $\theta = 119°$ ____________
14. $\theta = -160°$ ____________
15. $\theta = 235°$ ____________

***P* is a point on the terminal side of *θ* in standard position. Find the exact value of the six trigonometric functions for *θ*.**

16. $P(-5, 5)$ ____________
17. $P(2, 9)$ ____________
18. $P(-7, -5)$ ____________

Solve.

19. A circus performer trots her pony into the ring. The pony circles the ring 22 times as the performer flips and turns on the pony's back. At the end of the act, the pony exits on the side of the ring opposite its point of entry. Through how many degrees does the pony trot during the entire act? ____________

Problem Solving

Isabelle and Karl agreed to meet at the rotating restaurant at the top of a tower in the town center. The restaurant makes one full rotation each hour.

1. Isabelle waits for Karl, who arrives 30 minutes later. Through how many degrees does the restaurant rotate between the time that Isabelle arrives and the time that Karl arrives? ____________

2. Since the restaurant is busy, they don't get menus for another ten minutes. How much farther has the restaurant rotated? ____________

3. By the time they are served dinner, the restaurant has rotated to an angle 30° short of its orientation when Isabelle arrived.

   a. Write an expression for the length of time that Isabelle has been there. ____________

   b. How long has she been there? ____________

   c. How long has Karl been there? ____________

   d. How far has the restaurant rotated since Karl arrived? ____________

4. When their bill comes, it includes a note that the restaurant has rotated 840° since Isabelle arrived.

   a. How long has it been since they were served dinner? ____________

   b. How many rotations has the restaurant made since Isabelle arrived? ____________

   c. How far is the restaurant from its orientation when Karl arrived? ____________

5. On their way out, they stop and look at a map. A museum is located at a point northeast of the tower with coordinates (3, 2).

   a. Write the trigonometric function for the angle that the line from the tower to the museum makes with a line due north from the tower. ____________

   b. Isabelle says that the museum is exactly 4 kilometers from the tower. How much farther north is the museum than the tower? ____________

An advertisement on a kiosk near the bus stop rotates through 765° while Aaron waits for his bus. Choose the letter for the best answer.

6. What is the difference in the orientation of the advertisement between when Aaron arrived at the bus stop and when the bus came?

   A 45°

   B 90°

   C 315°

   D 405°

7. If the advertisement rotates at a rate of one rotation every 10 minutes, how long does Aaron wait for his bus?

   F Less than 2 min

   G Between 2 min and 10 min

   H Between 10 min and 20 min

   J More than 20 min

Name______________________ Class______________ Date__________

17-3

The Unit Circle

Connection: The Sine, Cosine, and Tangent Functions

Essential question: *How can the sine, cosine, and tangent functions be defined using the unit circle?*

Video Tutor

MCC9–12.F.TF.2

1 EXPLORE Extending the Definitions of Sine, Cosine, and Tangent

In geometry, you learned that sine, cosine, and tangent are ratios of the lengths of the sides of a right triangle. In particular, if θ is an acute angle in a right triangle, then:

$$\sin \theta = \frac{\text{opposite}}{\text{hypotenuse}}$$

$$\cos \theta = \frac{\text{adjacent}}{\text{hypotenuse}}$$

$$\tan \theta = \frac{\text{opposite}}{\text{adjacent}}$$

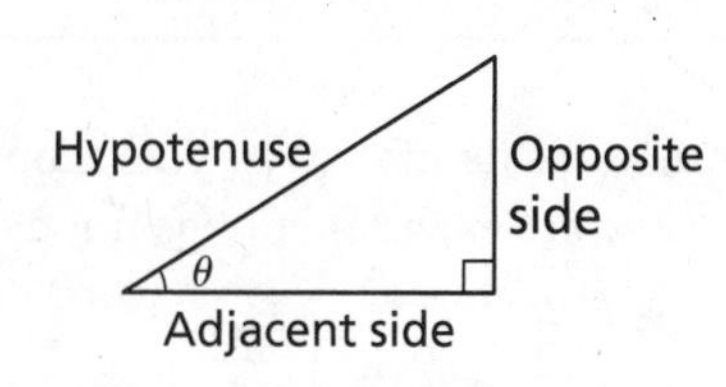

You can extend these definitions using angles of rotation and the unit circle. The diagram below shows the terminal side of an angle θ intersecting the unit circle at a point (x, y). A perpendicular is drawn from this point to the x-axis in order to form a right triangle.

A Use the coordinates of the intersection point to label the length of each side of the triangle in the diagram. (Remember that the circle has a radius of 1.)

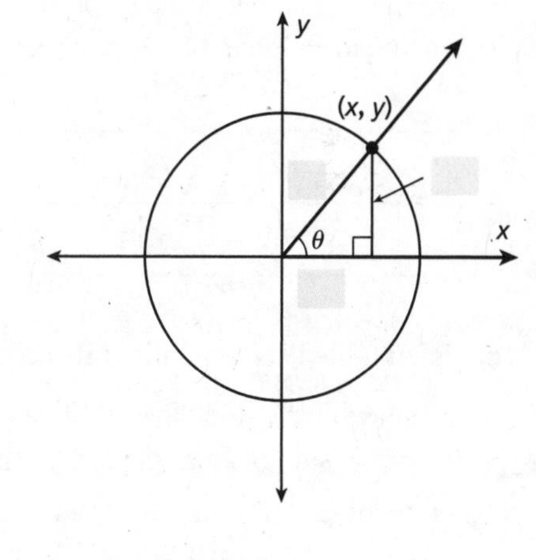

B Use the lengths from part A to find the values of $\sin \theta$, $\cos \theta$, and $\tan \theta$.

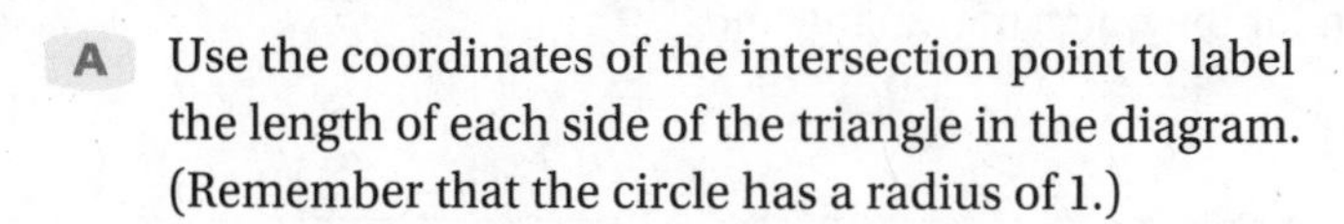

$\sin \theta = \frac{\text{opposite}}{\text{hypotenuse}} =$ __________

$\cos \theta = \frac{\text{adjacent}}{\text{hypotenuse}} =$ __________

$\tan \theta = \frac{\text{opposite}}{\text{adjacent}} =$ __________

REFLECT

1a. Explain why sine, cosine, and tangent, as defined above, are functions.

____

____

____

1b. Although you can think of x and y as lengths when the terminal side of θ lies in Quadrant I, you know that the values of x and/or y are negative in other quadrants. Dropping the idea of lengths and simply accepting that $\sin\theta = y$, $\cos\theta = x$, and $\tan\theta = \frac{y}{x}$ no matter where the terminal side of θ lies, complete the table by stating the sign of each function's values in each quadrant.

	Sign of Function's Values in Quadrant			
Trigonometric function	**I**	**II**	**III**	**IV**
$\sin\theta$				
$\cos\theta$				
$\tan\theta$				

1c. Are the sine, cosine, and tangent functions defined at all points on the unit circle? If not, identify the points where each function is not defined, and state any restrictions on the value of θ.

1d. What are the maximum and minimum x- and y-coordinates of points on the unit circle? What does this mean for the range of the sine and cosine functions?

1e. Each table lists several points on the unit circle near $(0, 1)$. If each point is on the terminal side of an angle θ, find the value of $\tan\theta$. Then describe what happens to $\tan\theta$ the closer θ gets to 90°.

Point on terminal side of θ	Value of $\tan\theta$
$\left(\frac{3}{5}, \frac{4}{5}\right)$	
$\left(\frac{5}{13}, \frac{12}{13}\right)$	
$\left(\frac{7}{25}, \frac{24}{25}\right)$	

Point on terminal side of θ	Value of $\tan\theta$
$\left(-\frac{3}{5}, \frac{4}{5}\right)$	
$\left(-\frac{5}{13}, \frac{12}{13}\right)$	
$\left(-\frac{7}{25}, \frac{24}{25}\right)$	

Domain and Range The table below describes the domain and range of each trigonometric function.

Function	Domain	Range
Sine ($\sin\theta = y$)	θ can be any angle of rotation.	$-1 \le \sin\theta \le 1$
Cosine ($\cos\theta = x$)	θ can be any angle of rotation.	$-1 \le \cos\theta \le 1$
Tangent $\left(\tan\theta = \frac{y}{x}\right)$	θ cannot be an odd multiple of 90° or $\frac{\pi}{2}$.	All real numbers

MCC9–12.F.TF.3(+)

2 EXPLORE Identifying Reference Angles

Let θ' be an angle with a measure between 0 and $\frac{\pi}{2}$, and let (x, y) be the coordinates of the point of intersection of the terminal side of θ' and the unit circle. You can find three other angles related to θ' through reflections in the axes.

A Draw the reflection of the terminal side of θ' in the y-axis. Consider this to be the terminal side of an angle θ with a measure between 0 and 2π. Label the coordinates of the point of intersection of the terminal side of θ and the unit circle.

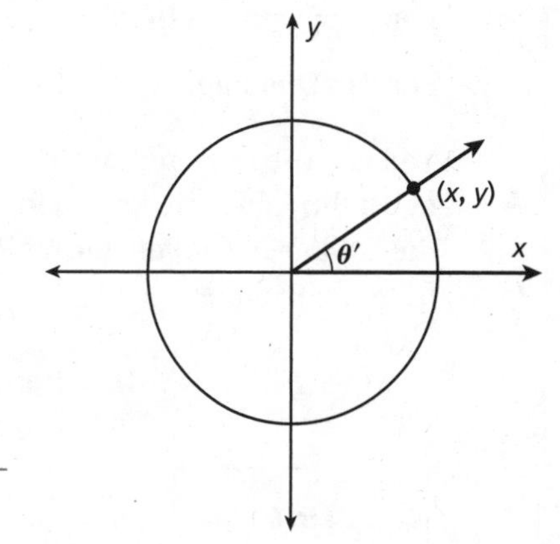

- In what quadrant is the terminal side of θ? ____________
- Due to the reflection, the positive angle that the terminal side of θ makes with the *negative* x-axis is θ'. What is the sum of the measures of θ and θ'? __________

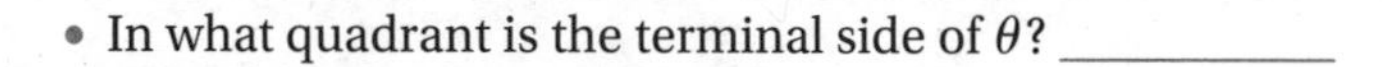

- Write θ' in terms of θ. ____________

B Draw the reflection of the terminal side of θ' in the x-axis. Consider this to be the terminal side of an angle θ with a measure between 0 and 2π. Label the coordinates of the point of intersection of the terminal side of θ and the unit circle.

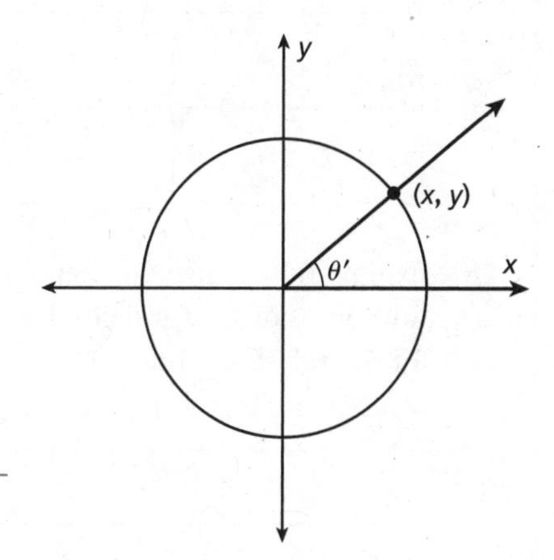

- In what quadrant is the terminal side of θ? __________
- Due to the reflection, the positive angle that the terminal side of θ makes with the *positive* x-axis is θ'. What is the sum of the measures of θ and θ'? __________

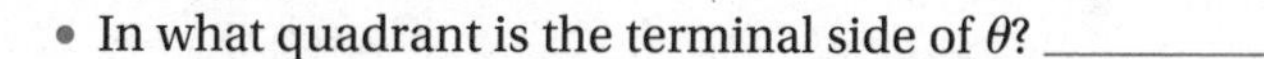

- Write θ' in terms of θ. ______________

C Draw the reflection of the terminal side of θ' in *both* axes. (First reflect in one axis, then reflect the image in the other axis.) Consider this to be the terminal side of an angle θ with a measure between 0 and 2π. Label the coordinates of the point of intersection of the terminal side of θ and the unit circle.

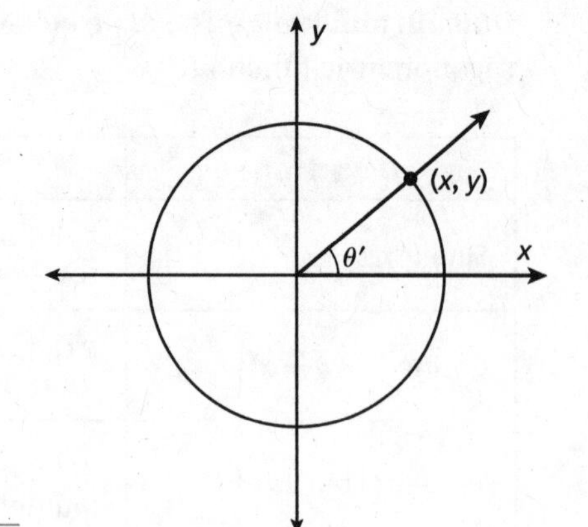

- In what quadrant is the terminal side of θ? __________
- Due to the reflection, the positive angle that the terminal side of θ makes with the *negative* x-axis is θ'. By how much do the measures of θ and θ' differ? ______
- Write θ' in terms of θ. ______________

REFLECT

2a. The **reference angle** θ' for an angle θ with a measure between 0 and 2π is the acute angle formed by the terminal side of θ and the x-axis.

For θ in Quadrant I, $\theta' = \theta$.

For θ in Quadrant II, $\theta' = \pi - \theta$.

For θ in Quadrant III, $\theta' = \theta - \pi$.

For θ in Quadrant IV, $\theta' = 2\pi - \theta$.

You can use reference angles to find the values of sine, cosine, and tangent of θ if the values are known for θ'. Suppose that $\sin\theta' = y$ and $\cos\theta' = x$ as in the Explore. Complete the table using the coordinates of the intersection points from the Explore.

	Quadrant I $0 < \theta < \frac{\pi}{2}$	Quadrant II $\frac{\pi}{2} < \theta < \pi$	Quadrant III $\pi < \theta < \frac{3\pi}{2}$	Quadrant IV $\frac{3\pi}{2} < \theta < 2\pi$
$\sin\theta$				
$\cos\theta$				
$\tan\theta$				

2b. Explain how to use the diagram at right to determine the values of $\sin\theta$ and $\cos\theta$ when the values are known for the reference angle θ'.

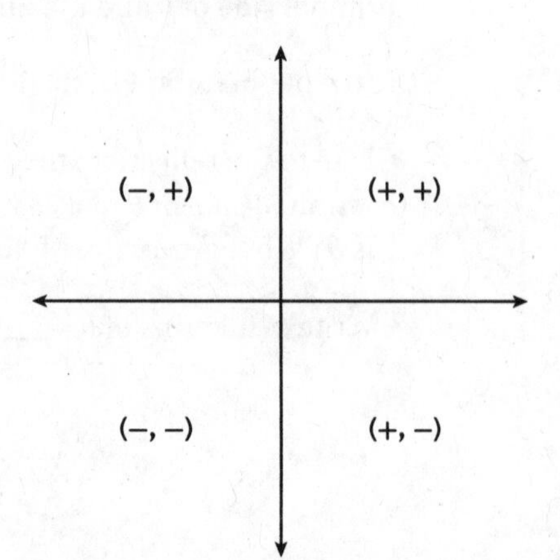

____

____

____

____

____

____

Special Angles In geometry, you studied two special right triangles: 30°-60°-90° and 45°-45°-90° triangles. You can use these triangles to find exact values for the trigonometric functions of angles with measure 30°, 45°, and 60° $\left(\text{or, in radians, } \frac{\pi}{6}, \frac{\pi}{4}, \text{ and } \frac{\pi}{3}\right)$ or of any angle having one of these angles as a reference angle.

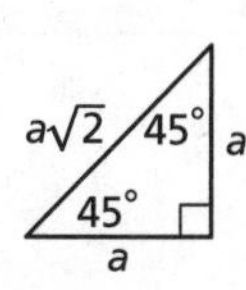

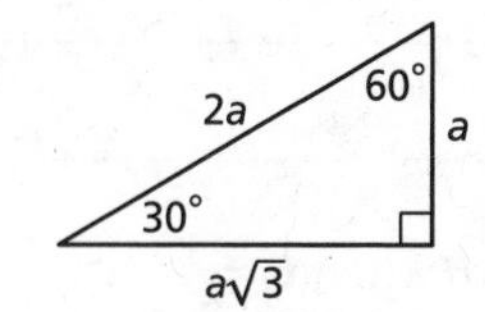

MCC9–12.F.TF.3(+)

3 EXAMPLE Finding Sine, Cosine, and Tangent of Special Angles

Find $\sin\theta$, $\cos\theta$, and $\tan\theta$ when $\theta = \frac{\pi}{3}, \frac{2\pi}{3}, \frac{4\pi}{3}$, and $\frac{5\pi}{3}$.

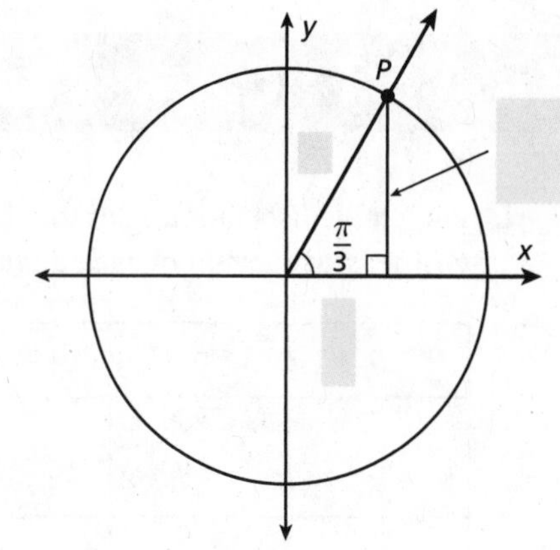

A The diagram shows an angle of $\frac{\pi}{3}$ and the unit circle. Use the side-length relationships in a 30°-60°-90° triangle to label the side lengths of the triangle formed by dropping a perpendicular from the point P where the angle's terminal side intersects the unit circle.

What are the coordinates of P? _______________

B Find each function value.

$\sin\frac{\pi}{3} =$ ________

$\cos\frac{\pi}{3} =$ ________

$\tan\frac{\pi}{3} =$ ________

C Recognize that $\frac{\pi}{3}$ is the reference angle for $\frac{2\pi}{3}, \frac{4\pi}{3}$, and $\frac{5\pi}{3}$. Complete the table, remembering that the quadrant in which the terminal side of an angle lies determines the signs of the trigonometric functions of the angle.

θ	Quadrant	$\sin\theta$	$\cos\theta$	$\tan\theta$
$\frac{2\pi}{3}$				
$\frac{4\pi}{3}$				
$\frac{5\pi}{3}$				

REFLECT

3a. Explain why $\frac{\pi}{3}$ is the reference angle for $\frac{2\pi}{3}$, $\frac{4\pi}{3}$, and $\frac{5\pi}{3}$.

3b. Explain how to find $\sin\theta$, $\cos\theta$, and $\tan\theta$ when $\theta = \frac{16\pi}{3}$.

PRACTICE

1. Each table lists four angles that have the same reference angle. Find the sine, cosine, and tangent of each angle.

θ	$\sin\theta$	$\cos\theta$	$\tan\theta$
$\frac{\pi}{6}$			
$\frac{5\pi}{6}$			
$\frac{7\pi}{6}$			
$\frac{11\pi}{6}$			

θ	$\sin\theta$	$\cos\theta$	$\tan\theta$
$\frac{\pi}{4}$			
$\frac{3\pi}{4}$			
$\frac{5\pi}{4}$			
$\frac{7\pi}{4}$			

2. If the terminal side of an angle falls on one of the axes, the angle is called a *quadrantal angle*. The table below lists the four quadrantal angles from 0 to 2π (not including 2π). Complete the table by giving the coordinates of the point where each angle's terminal side intersects the unit circle, and then find the values of sine, cosine, and tangent.

θ	Intersection point	$\sin\theta$	$\cos\theta$	$\tan\theta$
0				
$\frac{\pi}{2}$				
π				
$\frac{3\pi}{2}$				

Additional Practice

Find the value of the sine, cosine, and tangent functions for θ.

1. 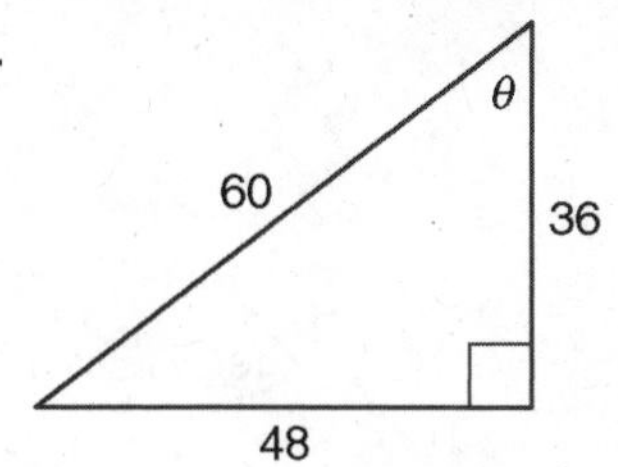

2. 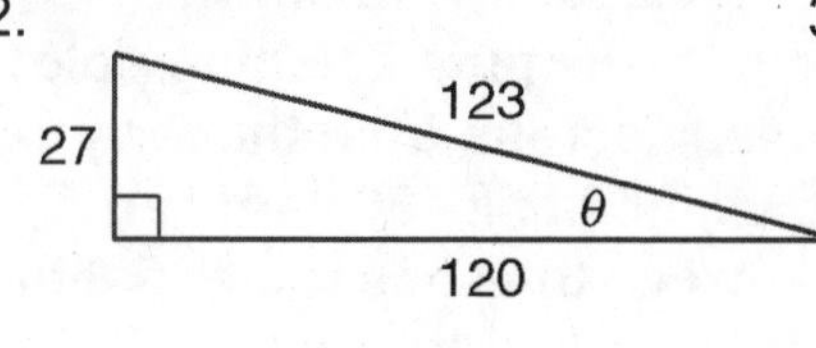

3. 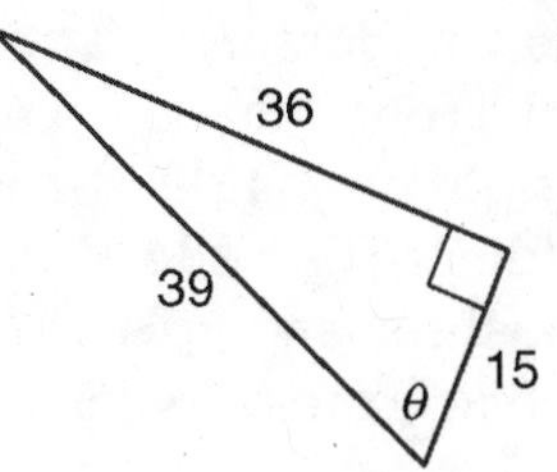

________________ ________________ ________________

Use a trigonometric function to find the value of x.

4. 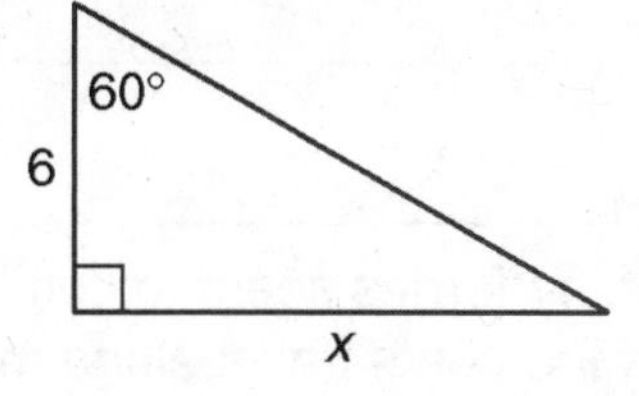

5. 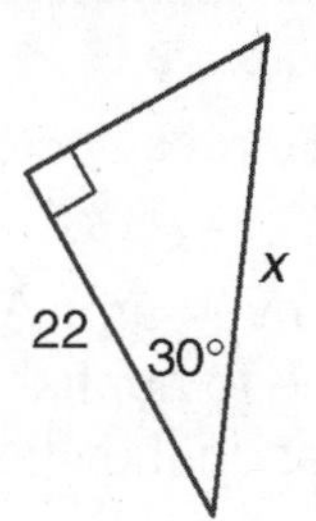

6. 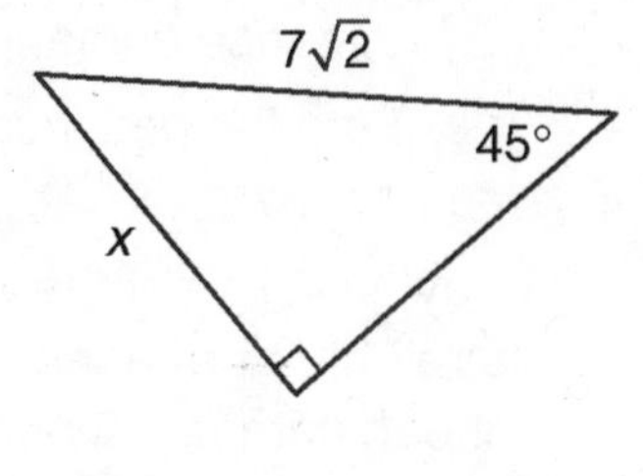

________________ ________________ ________________

Find the values of the six trigonometric functions for θ.

7. 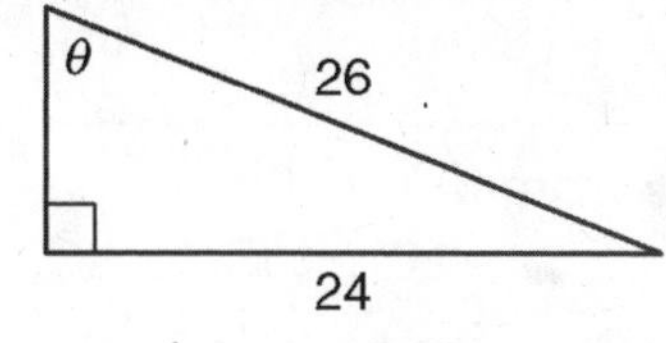

8. 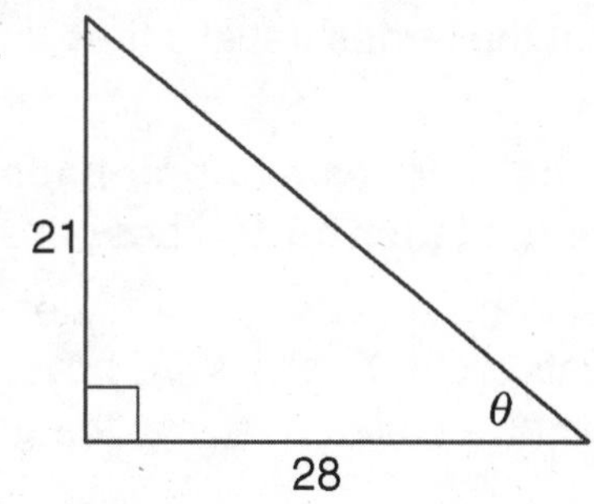

9. 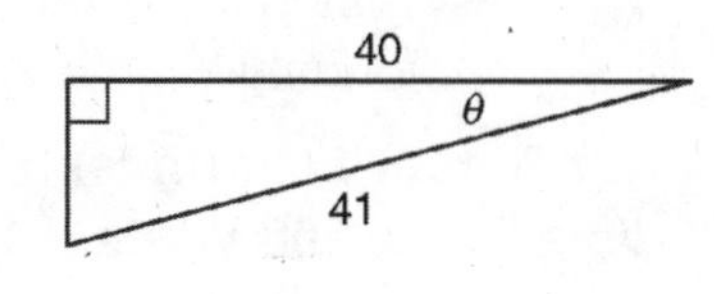

________________ ________________

________________ ________________ ________________

Solve.

10. A water slide is 26 feet high. The angle between the slide and the water is 33.5°. What is the length of the slide? ________________

11. A surveyor stands 150 feet from the base of a viaduct and measures the angle of elevation to be 46.2°. His eye level is 6 feet above the ground. What is the height of the viaduct to the nearest foot? ________________

12. The pilot of a helicopter measures the angle of depression to a landing spot to be 18.8°. If the pilot's altitude is 1640 meters, what is the horizontal distance to the landing spot to the nearest meter? ________________

Problem Solving

Kayla is fishing near the ferry landing near her home. She wonders how far the ferries actually travel when they cross the river. To find out, she puts a fishing pole upright on the riverbank directly across from the ferry landing. Then she walks down the bank 180 yards and measures an angle of 75° between the lines to her fishing pole and the ferry landing on the opposite bank.

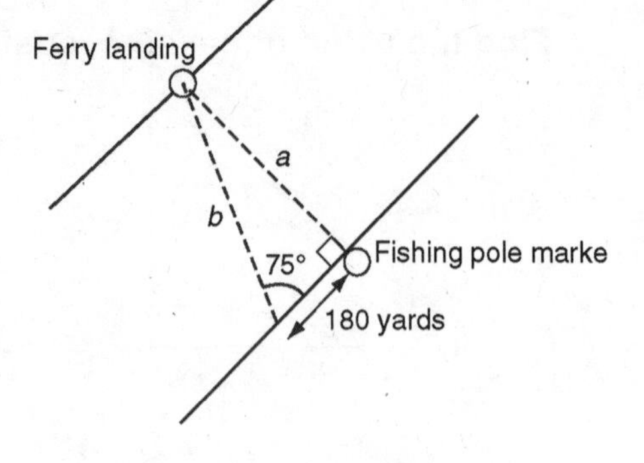

1. Find the distance directly across the river.
   a. On the diagram, name the side of the triangle that represents the distance Kayla wants to determine. ________________
   b. Write a trigonometric function that relates the known distance and angle to the required distance. ________________
   c. Find the distance to the nearest yard directly across the river. ________________
2. Kayla walks another 200 yards down the riverbank. At this point the ferries seem to come straight at her at an angle of 60° to the line to her fishing pole. If the boats travel along this line to compensate for the current, how far do they travel?
   a. How far is she from her fishing pole now? ________________
   b. Write the trigonometric function that relates this distance and angle to the required distance, *c*. ________________
   c. What is the distance that the ferries travel if they travel along this line? ________________

At a hot-air balloon festival, Luis watches a hot-air balloon rise from a distance of 200 yards. Choose the letter for the best answer.

3. From Luis's position, the balloon seems to hover at an angle of elevation of 50°. Which trigonometric function gives the height of the balloon, *h*?

   A 200 sin 50°

   B 200 tan 50°

   C $\frac{200}{\cos 50°}$

   D $\frac{200}{\cot 50°}$

4. After a short while, the balloon seems to hover at an angle of 75°. How high is it off the ground now?

   F 193 yd

   G 207 yd

   H 746 yd

   J 773 yd

Olivia has a pool slide that makes an angle of 25° with the water. The top of the slide stands 4.5 feet above the surface of the water. Choose the letter for the best answer.

5. How far out into the pool will the slide reach?

   A 2.1 ft

   B 5.0 ft

   C 7.6 ft

   D 9.7 ft

6. The slide makes a straight line into the water. How long is the slide?

   F 5.0 ft

   G 7.6 ft

   H 9.7 ft

   J 10.6 ft

Name_______________________ Class_______________ Date_________

18-1

Graphs of Sine and Cosine

Going Deeper

Essential question: *What are the key features of the graphs of the sine, cosine, and tangent functions?*

Graphing $f(\theta) = \sin\theta$

Graph $f(\theta) = \sin\theta$ for $0 \le \theta \le 2\pi$.

A Complete the axis labels on the coordinate plane below. The θ-axis shows angle measures in radians. The $f(\theta)$-axis shows the function values.

B Complete the table of values.

θ	0	$\frac{\pi}{6}$	$\frac{\pi}{2}$	$\frac{5\pi}{6}$	π	$\frac{7\pi}{6}$	$\frac{3\pi}{2}$	$\frac{11\pi}{6}$	2π
$f(\theta) = \sin\theta$									

C Plot the points from the table and draw a smooth curve through them.

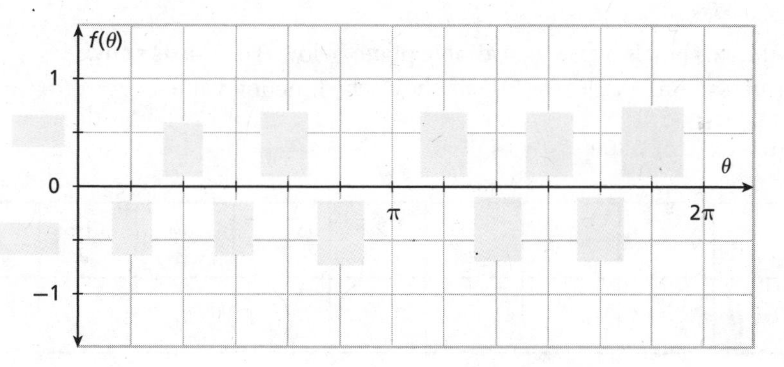

REFLECT

1a. Give a decimal approximation of $\sin\frac{\pi}{3}$. Check to see if the curve that you drew passes through the point $\left(\frac{\pi}{3}, \sin\frac{\pi}{3}\right)$. What other points can you check based on the labeling of the θ-axis?

____

____

1b. On the interval $0 \leq \theta \leq 2\pi$, where does the sine function have positive values? Where does it have negative values?

1c. List the θ-intercepts of the graph of $f(\theta) = \sin\theta$ on the interval $0 \leq \theta \leq 2\pi$. What do you think the next positive θ-intercept will be? Explain.

1d. What are the minimum and maximum values of $f(\theta) = \sin\theta$ on the interval $0 \leq \theta \leq 2\pi$? Where do the extreme values occur in relation to the θ-intercepts?

1e. Describe a rotation that will map the curve onto itself over the interval $0 \leq \theta \leq 2\pi$.

Graphing $f(\theta) = \cos\theta$

Graph $f(\theta) = \cos\theta$ for $0 \leq \theta \leq 2\pi$.

A Complete the axis labels on the coordinate plane below. The θ-axis shows angle measures in radians. The $f(\theta)$-axis shows the function values.

B Complete the table of values.

θ	0	$\frac{\pi}{3}$	$\frac{\pi}{2}$	$\frac{2\pi}{3}$	π	$\frac{4\pi}{3}$	$\frac{3\pi}{2}$	$\frac{5\pi}{3}$	2π
$f(\theta) = \cos\theta$									

C Plot the points from the table and draw a smooth curve through them.

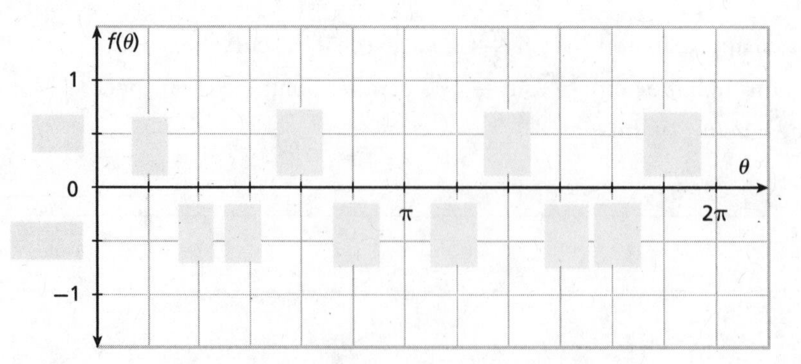

REFLECT

2a. On the interval $0 \leq \theta \leq 2\pi$, where does the cosine function have positive values? Where does it have negative values?

2b. List the θ-intercepts of the graph of $f(\theta) = \cos\theta$ on the interval $0 \leq \theta \leq 2\pi$. What do you think the next positive θ-intercept will be? Explain.

2c. What are the minimum and maximum values of $f(\theta) = \cos\theta$ on the interval $0 \leq \theta \leq 2\pi$? Where do the extreme values occur in relation to the θ-intercepts?

MCC9–12.F.IF.7e

3 ENGAGE Understanding the Properties of the Graphs

In the preceding Explores, you graphed the sine and cosine functions over the interval $0 \leq \theta \leq 2\pi$, which represents all angles of rotation within the first counterclockwise revolution that starts at 0. What you drew are not the complete graphs, however. They are simply one *cycle* of the graphs.

As you will see in the next Explore, the graphs of sine and cosine consist of repeated cycles that form a wave-like shape. When a function repeats its values over regular intervals on the horizontal axis as the sine and cosine functions do, the function is called **periodic**, and the length of the interval is called the function's **period**.

The wave-like shape of the sine and cosine functions has a "crest" (where the function's maximum value occurs) and a "trough" (where the function's minimum value occurs). Halfway between the "crest" and the "trough" is the graph's **midline**. The distance that the "crest" rises above the midline or the distance that the "trough" falls below the midline is called the graph's **amplitude**.

REFLECT

3a. Complete the table.

Function	Properties of Function's Graph		
	Period	Midline	Amplitude
$f(\theta) = \sin\theta$			
$f(\theta) = \cos\theta$			

MCC9–12.F.TF.4(+)

4 EXPLORE Extending the Graphs of Sine and Cosine

Use the cycle shown for the first counterclockwise revolution (starting at 0 and ending at 2π) to extend the graphs of the sine and cosine functions to the right (second counterclockwise revolution) and to the left (first clockwise revolution).

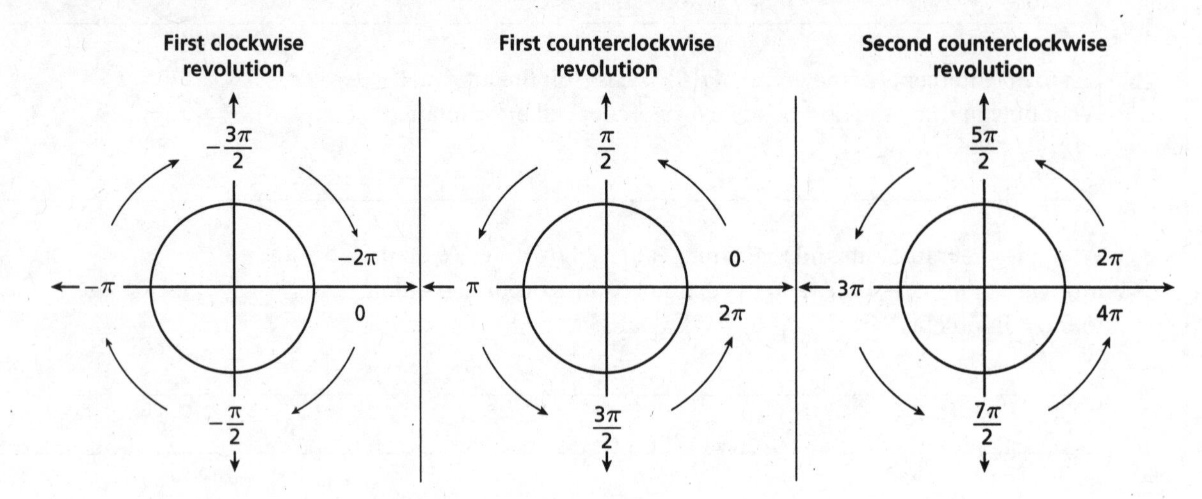

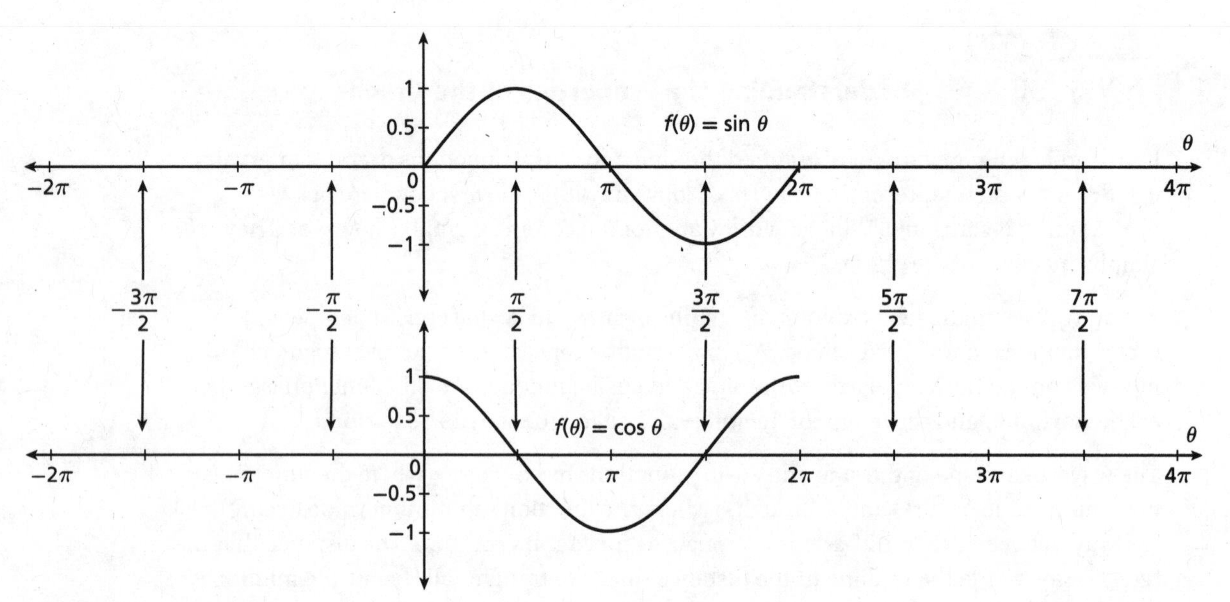

REFLECT

4a. The graphs show that sine and cosine are periodic functions. Explain why this is so by referring to angles of rotation and the unit circle.

____

____

4b. The graphs show that $\sin(-\theta) = -\sin\theta$ and $\cos(-\theta) = \cos\theta$. Explain why this is so by referring to angles of rotation and the unit circle.

____

____

MCC9–12.F.IF.7e

5 EXPLORE Graphing $f(\theta) = \tan \theta$

Graph $f(\theta) = \tan \theta$ for $0 \le \theta \le 2\pi$.

A Complete the axis labels on the coordinate plane in part D. The θ-axis shows angle measures in radians. The $f(\theta)$-axis shows the function values.

B Complete the table of values. The dashes that appear as function values for $\theta = \frac{\pi}{2}$ and $\theta = \frac{3\pi}{2}$ indicate that $f(\theta)$ is undefined.

θ	0	$\frac{\pi}{4}$	$\frac{\pi}{2}$	$\frac{3\pi}{4}$	π	$\frac{5\pi}{4}$	$\frac{3\pi}{2}$	$\frac{7\pi}{4}$	2π
$f(\theta) = \tan \theta$			—				—		

C Examine the behavior of the function near $\theta = \frac{\pi}{2}$ and $\theta = \frac{3\pi}{2}$. For each table below, use a calculator set in radian mode to find the approximate values of $\sin \theta$ and $\cos \theta$, then use the fact that $\tan \theta = \frac{\sin \theta}{\cos \theta}$ to find the value of $\tan \theta$. Note that $\frac{\pi}{2} \approx 1.5708$ and $\frac{3\pi}{2} \approx 4.7124$. After examining the values of $\tan \theta$, complete the summary statement below the table.

θ	$\sin \theta$	$\cos \theta$	$\tan \theta$
1.50			
1.55			
1.57			

As $\theta \to \frac{\pi}{2}^-$, $\tan \theta \to$ ________.

θ	$\sin \theta$	$\cos \theta$	$\tan \theta$
1.65			
1.60			
1.58			

As $\theta \to \frac{\pi}{2}^+$, $\tan \theta \to$ ________.

θ	$\sin \theta$	$\cos \theta$	$\tan \theta$
4.50			
4.70			
4.71			

As $\theta \to \frac{3\pi}{2}^-$, $\tan \theta \to$ ________.

θ	$\sin \theta$	$\cos \theta$	$\tan \theta$
5.00			
4.75			
4.72			

As $\theta \to \frac{3\pi}{2}^+$, $\tan \theta \to$ ________.

D Draw the vertical asymptotes found in part C as dashed lines. Then plot the points from part B and draw smooth curves that pass through the plotted points and approach the asymptotes.

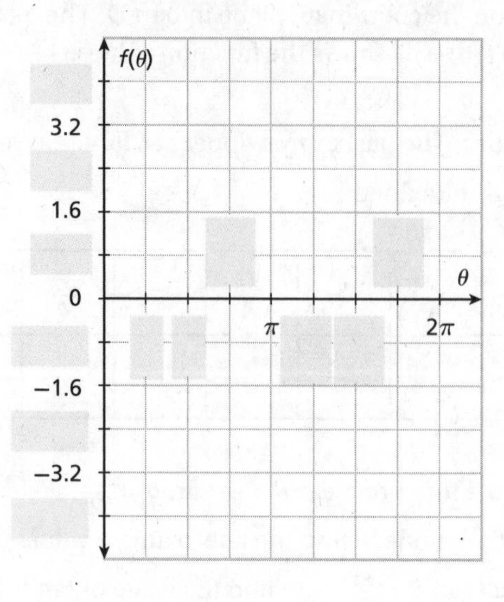

REFLECT

5a. What is the relationship between $\frac{\pi}{4}$ and 0.8? Why is 0.8 a good interval to use for the vertical axis?

5b. On the interval $0 \le \theta \le 2\pi$, where does the tangent function have positive values? Where does it have negative values?

5c. List the θ-intercepts of the graph of $f(\theta) = \tan \theta$ on the interval $0 \le \theta \le 2\pi$. What do you think the next positive θ-intercept will be? Explain.

5d. How many times does the tangent function run through all of its values on the interval $0 \le \theta \le 2\pi$? What, then, is the function's period?

5e. Does the tangent function have minimum or maximum values? Explain.

5f. The points where $\tan \theta = \pm 1$ serve as handy reference points when graphing the tangent function. What line lies halfway between them? (Note that this line is called the graph's *midline* even though the tangent function does not have minimum or maximum values.)

MCC9–12.F.TF.4(+)

6 EXPLORE Extending the Graph of Tangent

Use the cycle shown for the first counterclockwise revolution (starting at 0 and ending at 2π) to extend the graph of the tangent function to the right (second counterclockwise revolution) and to the left (first clockwise revolution).

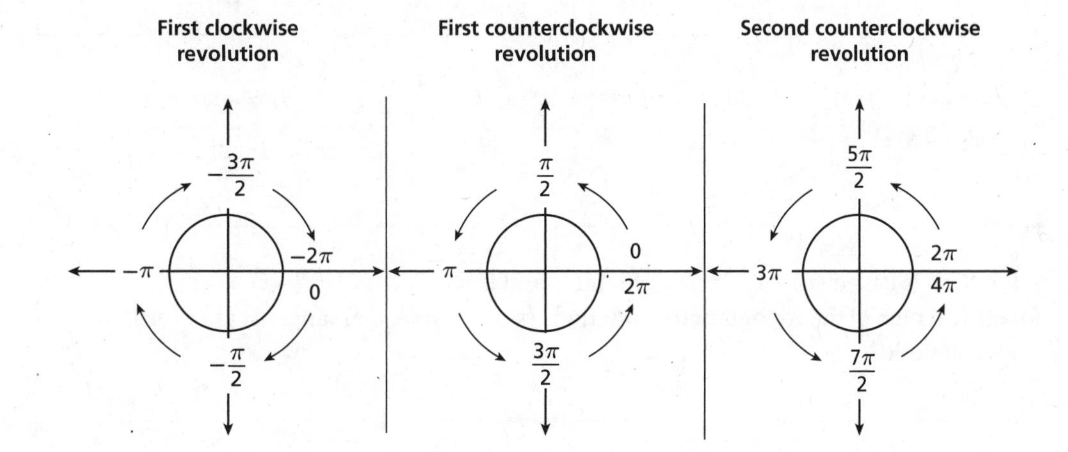

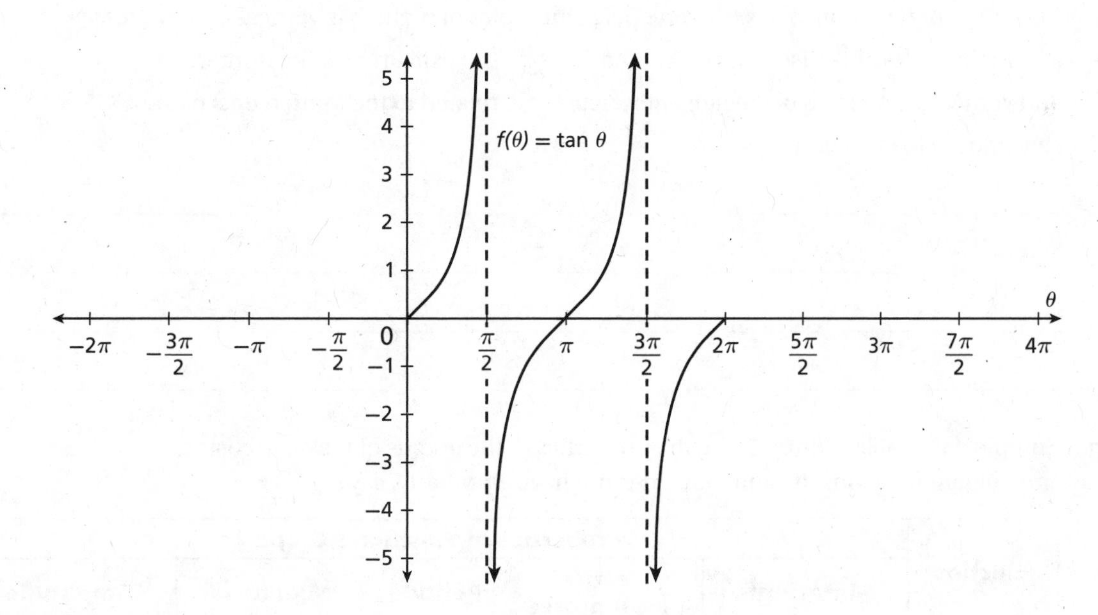

REFLECT

6a. The graph shows that tangent is a periodic function. Explain why this is so by referring to angles of rotation and the unit circle.

6b. Error Analysis A student says that there are 8 cycles of the tangent function on the interval $-8\pi \le \theta \le 8\pi$, because $\frac{16\pi}{2\pi} = 8$. Explain the error in the student's reasoning.

6c. The graph shows that $\tan(-\theta) = -\tan\theta$. Explain why this is so by referring to angles of rotation and the unit circle.

6d. Show that $\tan(-\theta) = -\tan\theta$ using these facts: $\tan\theta = \frac{\sin\theta}{\cos\theta}$, $\sin(-\theta) = -\sin\theta$, and $\cos(-\theta) = \cos\theta$.

6e. A function is called *even* if $f(-x) = x$ for all x, and it is called *odd* if $f(-x) = -f(x)$ for all x. Which of the trigonometric functions (sine, cosine, and tangent) are even? Which are odd?

6f. The graph of $f(\theta) = \tan\theta$ has θ-intercepts at multiples of π and has vertical asymptotes at odd multiples of $\frac{\pi}{2}$. Use the fact that $\tan\theta = \frac{\sin\theta}{\cos\theta}$ to explain how the θ-intercepts and vertical asymptotes of the tangent function are related to the θ-intercepts of the sine and cosine functions.

6g. Complete the table to summarize the properties of the graphs of the sine, cosine, and tangent functions. If a function does not have a property, say so.

Function	Properties of Function's Graph				
	θ-intercepts	Vertical asymptotes	Period	Midline	Amplitude
$f(\theta) = \sin\theta$					
$f(\theta) = \cos\theta$					
$f(\theta) = \tan\theta$					

Name________________________ Class________________ Date____________

18-1

Additional Practice

Identify whether each function is periodic. If the function is periodic, give the period.

1.
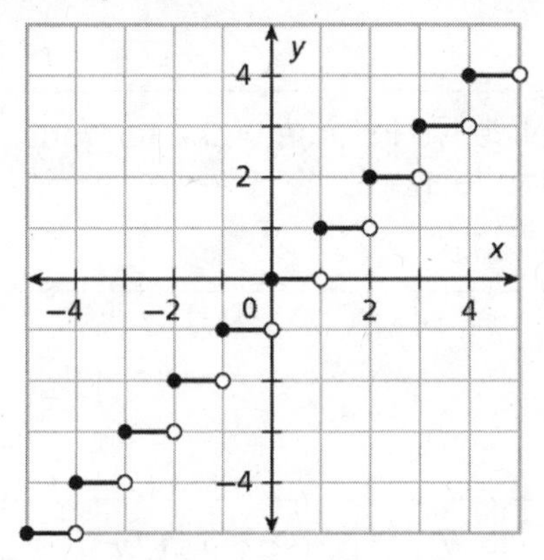

____

2.
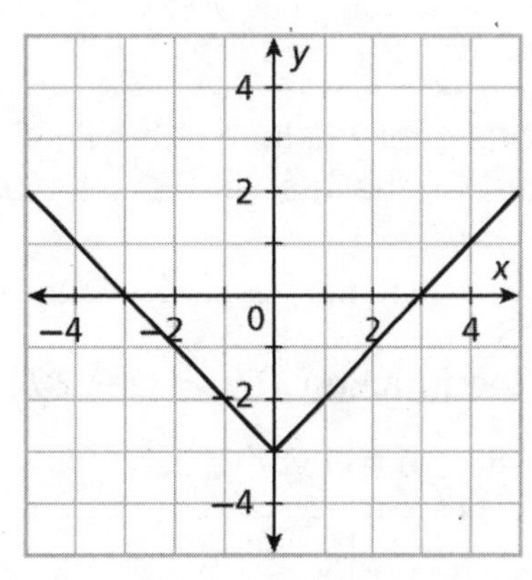

____

3.
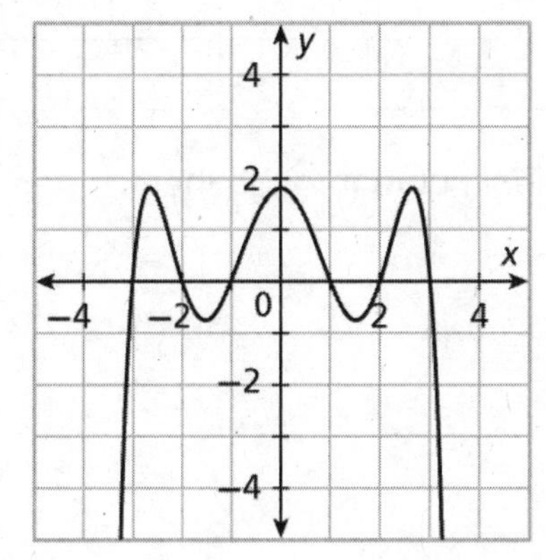

____

4.
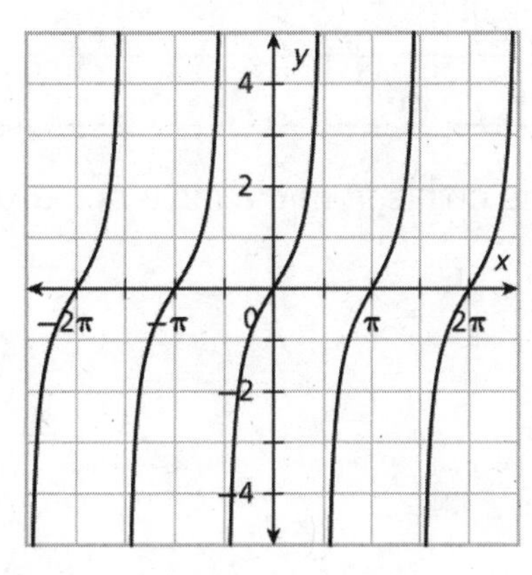

____

5.
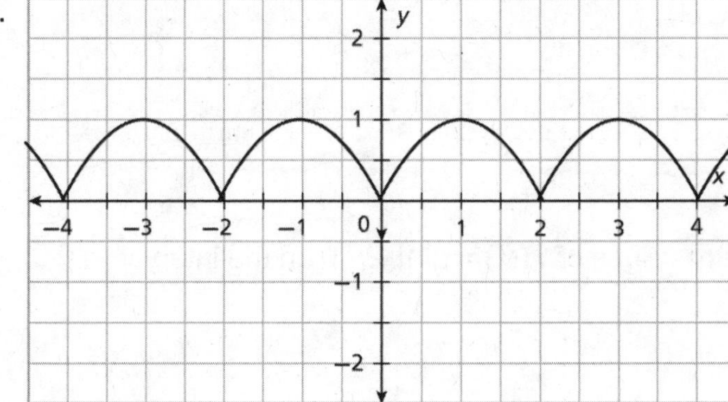

____

Problem Solving

1. Use the periodicity of the sine and cosine graphs to write an expression showing the general form of the values for which $\cos(x) = \sin(x)$.

____

2. The *cotangent* function, abbreviated cot(*x*), is the multiplicative inverse of the tangent function. On the interval $0 \le x \le 2\pi$, where is cot(*x*) not defined?

____

Consider the function $f(\theta) = \sin(2\theta)$.

3. Complete the table of values.

θ	0	$\frac{\pi}{6}$	$\frac{\pi}{2}$	$\frac{5\pi}{6}$	π	$\frac{7\pi}{6}$	$\frac{3\pi}{2}$	$\frac{11\pi}{6}$	2π
2θ									
$f(\theta) = \sin 2\theta$									

4. Plot the points from the table and draw a smooth sinusoidal curve through them.

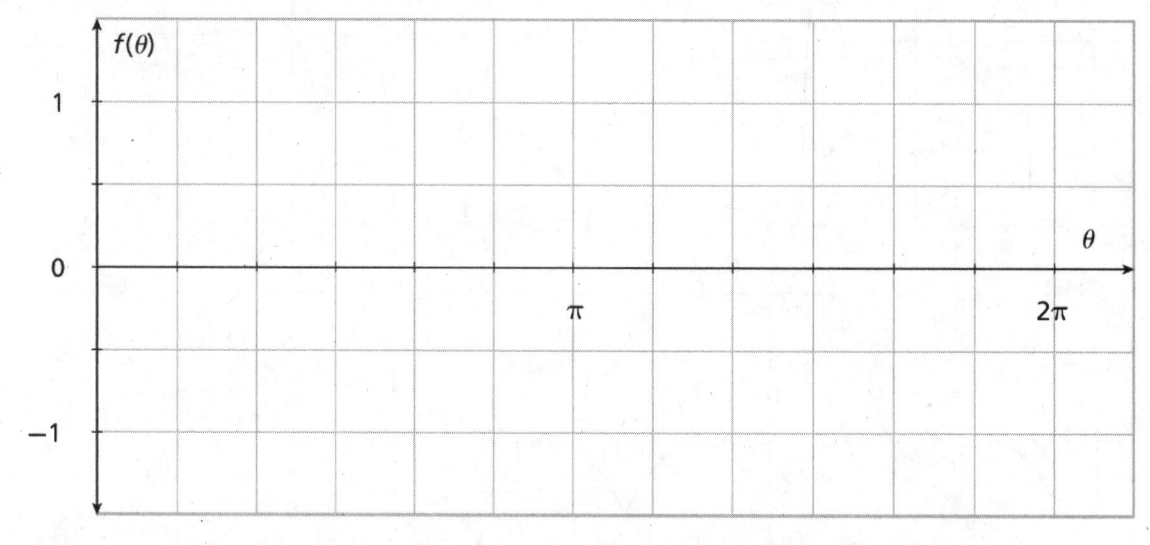

5. What do the maximum and minimum values of $f(\theta) = \sin(2\theta)$ on the interval $0 \le \theta \le 2\pi$ appear to be?

____

6. What is the period of $f(\theta) = \sin(2\theta)$? ______________________

Name________________________ Class______________ Date________

18-2

Graphs of Other Trigonometric Functions

Extension: Transformations of Trigonometric Graphs

Essential question: *How do the constants a, b, h, and k in the functions* $g(\theta) = a \sin b(\theta - h) + k$, $g(\theta) = a \cos b(\theta - h) + k$, *and* $g(\theta) = a \tan b(\theta - h) + k$ *affect their graphs?*

Video Tutor

MCC9–12.F.IF.7e

1 ENGAGE — Recognizing Key Points and Asymptotes on Parent Graphs

In this lesson you will graph functions of the form $g(\theta) = a \sin b\theta$, $g(\theta) = a \cos b\theta$, and $g(\theta) = a \tan b\theta$. You have already seen the graphs of the *parent* functions (when $a = 1$ and $b = 1$). One cycle of the graph of each parent function is shown below along with five key points or asymptotes from that cycle.

Graph of $f(\theta) = \sin \theta$ on the interval $0 \le \theta \le 2\pi$

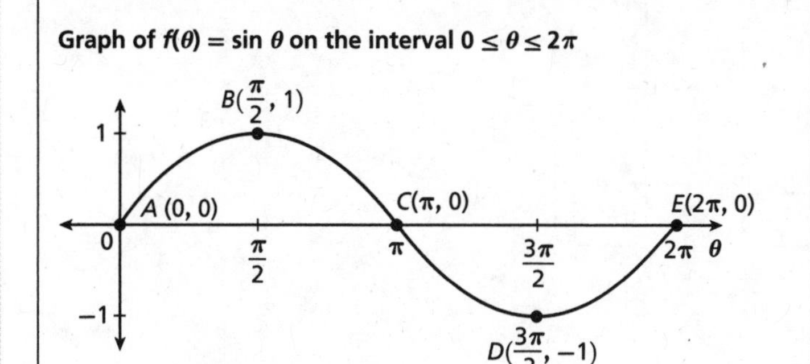

Graph of $f(\theta) = \cos \theta$ on the interval $0 \le \theta \le 2\pi$

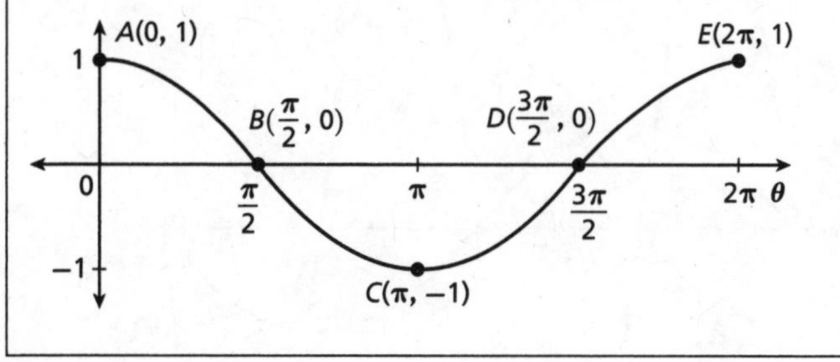

Graph of $f(\theta) = \tan \theta$ on the interval $-\frac{\pi}{2} < \theta < \frac{\pi}{2}$

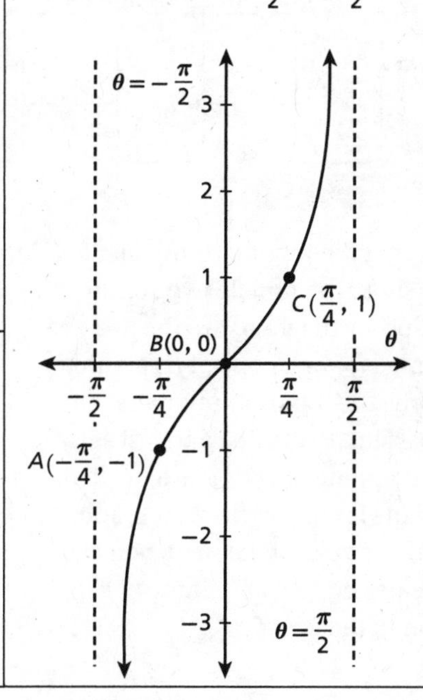

REFLECT

1a. Describe the key points for the sine and cosine curves.

____

____

1b. Points A and C on the tangent curve are called *halfway* points. Why?

____

____

2 ENGAGE Understanding Transformations of Trigonometric Graphs

If $f(\theta)$ is one of the three parent trigonometric functions, then the constants a and b in $g(\theta) = af(b\theta)$ alter the graph of $f(\theta)$ in particular ways. Notice that the constant a appears *outside* the function and therefore acts on f's output values, while the constant b appears *inside* the function and therefore acts on f's input values. For instance, consider the function $g(\theta) = 3 \sin 2\theta$ whose parent function is $f(\theta) = \sin \theta$. The mapping diagram below shows what happens when $0, \frac{\pi}{4}, \frac{\pi}{2}, \frac{3\pi}{4}$, and π are used as inputs for g.

Input for g	$\times 2$ →	Input for f	f →	Output for f	$\times 3$ →	Output for g
0	→	0	→	0	→	0
$\frac{\pi}{4}$	→	$\frac{\pi}{2}$	→	1	→	3
$\frac{\pi}{2}$	→	π	→	0	→	0
$\frac{3\pi}{4}$	→	$\frac{3\pi}{2}$	→	-1	→	-3
π	→	2π	→	0	→	0

Notice that the input-output pairs for $f(\theta) = \sin \theta$ (the middle two sets in the mapping diagram) are the five key points for one cycle of f's graph. Similarly, the input-output pairs for $g(\theta) = 3 \sin 2\theta$ (the first and last sets in the mapping diagram) are the five key points for one cycle of g's graph. From the graphs at the right, you can see the period and amplitude of g in relation to those of f.

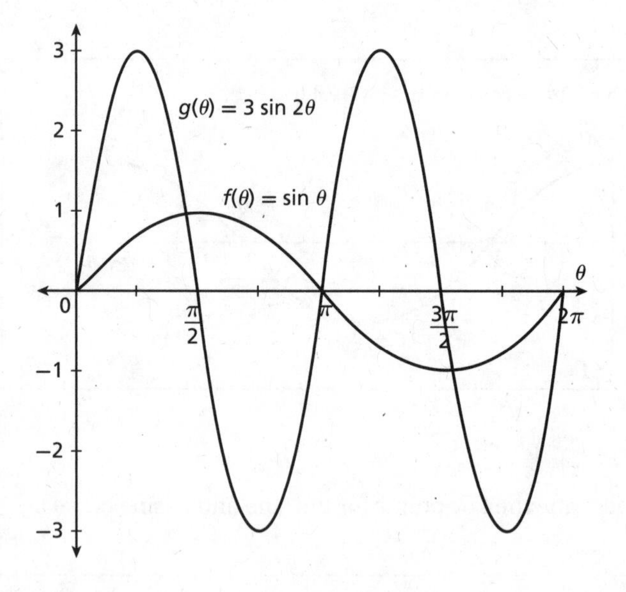

Function	Period	Amplitude
$f(\theta) = \sin \theta$	2π	1
$g(\theta) = 3 \sin 2\theta$	π	3

REFLECT

2a. Describe how you can obtain the period and amplitude for $g(\theta) = 3 \sin 2\theta$ using the constants 3 and 2 from the function's rule.

____

____

2b. In terms of transformations, the change in the period is the result of horizontally shrinking the graph of f by a factor of $\frac{1}{2}$ (since $\pi = \frac{1}{2}(2\pi)$). How would you characterize the change in the amplitude in terms of transformations?

____

Graphing $g(\theta) = a \cos b\theta$

Graph one cycle of $g(\theta) = -3 \cos \frac{\theta}{2}$.

A Determine the function's period. One cycle of the graph of the parent function, $f(\theta) = \cos \theta$, begins at 0 and ends at 2π. One cycle of the graph of g also begins at 0 but ends when $\frac{\theta}{2} = 2\pi$, or $\theta = 4\pi$.

So, the function's period is __________.

B Use the period to determine the five key input values for g. Those five values divide the interval $0 \le \theta \le 4\pi$ into four equal parts. So, the first input value is 0, and the second is $\frac{4\pi}{4} = \pi$. These values are entered in the first column of the table at the right. Complete the rest of the first column.

C Determine the output values for the key input values. Remember that g multiplies each output value from the parent function by -3. For instance, when $\theta = 0$, the parent function's output value is 1, but the output value for g is $-3 \cdot 1 = -3$. Complete the second column of the table.

Key input-output pairs	
θ	$g(\theta)$
0	
π	

D Plot the key points on the coordinate plane shown. Then use them to draw one cycle of the graph of $g(\theta) = -3 \cos \frac{\theta}{2}$. One cycle of the graph of the parent function is shown in gray for comparison.

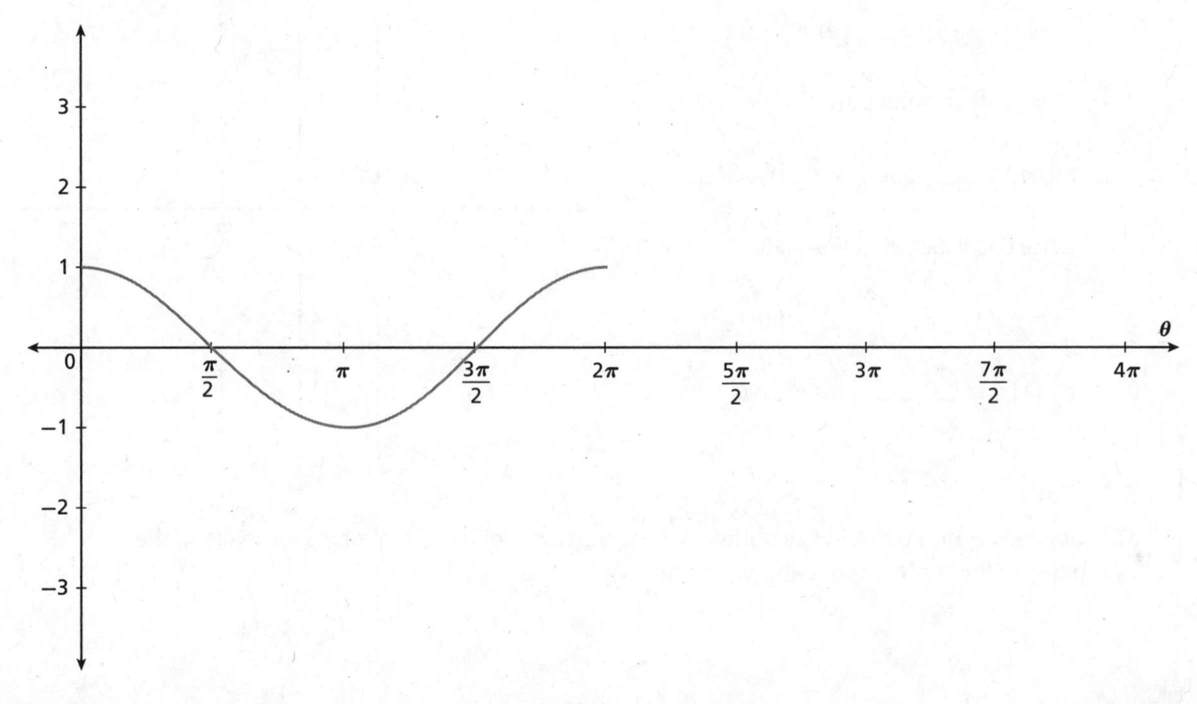

REFLECT

3a. Describe how the graph of f is transformed to obtain the graph of g.

____

____

3b. Error Analysis A student said that the amplitude of the graph of g is -3. Describe and correct the student's error.

____

____

MCC9-12.F.IF.7e

4 EXAMPLE Graphing $g(\theta) = a \tan b\theta$

Graph one cycle of $g(\theta) = \frac{1}{2} \tan \frac{\theta}{3}$.

A Determine the graph's asymptotes. The graph of the parent function, $f(\theta) = \tan \theta$, has asymptotes at $\theta = -\frac{\pi}{2}$ and $\theta = \frac{\pi}{2}$. The graph of g has asymptotes at $\frac{\theta}{3} = -\frac{\pi}{2}$, or $\theta =$ __________, and $\frac{\theta}{3} = \frac{\pi}{2}$, or $\theta =$ __________.

B Determine the graph's three key points.

- One point is where the graph crosses its midline (the θ-axis). For the parent function, this occurs when $\theta = 0$. For g, this occurs when $\frac{\theta}{3} = 0$, or $\theta =$ __________. So, the graph of g crosses its midline at the point __________.
- The other two points are the *halfway* points. For the parent function, these points are $\left(-\frac{\pi}{4}, -1\right)$ and $\left(\frac{\pi}{4}, 1\right)$.

  For g, the θ-values are $\frac{\theta}{3} = -\frac{\pi}{4}$, or $\theta =$ ________, and $\frac{\theta}{3} = \frac{\pi}{4}$, or $\theta =$ ________.

  The corresponding $g(\theta)$-values are $\frac{1}{2}(-1) =$ __________ and $\frac{1}{2}(1) =$ __________, respectively.

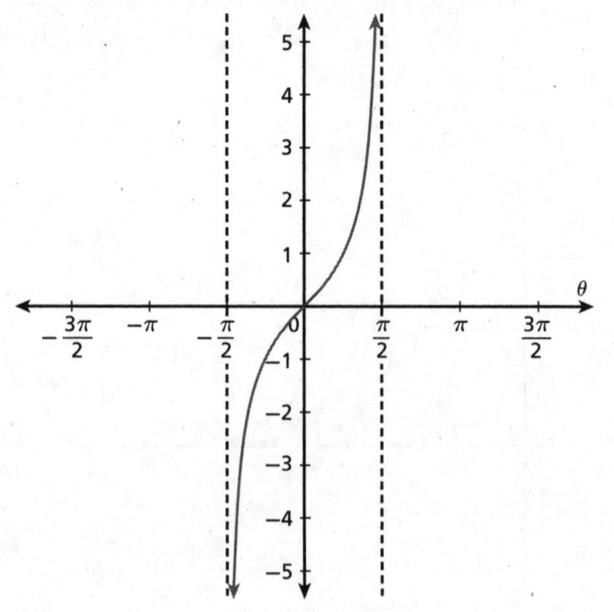

C Use the asymptotes and key points to draw one cycle of the graph of g. One cycle of the parent function's graph is shown in gray.

REFLECT

4a. Describe how the graph of f is transformed to obtain the graph of g.

____

MCC9–12.F.BF.3

5 ENGAGE Understanding Transformations of Trigonometric Graphs

You have learned how the constants a and b in the functions $f(\theta) = a \sin b\theta$, $f(\theta) = a \cos b\theta$, and $f(\theta) = a \tan b\theta$ affect the period and amplitude of their graphs. Now you will examine how the constants h and k in $g(\theta) = f(\theta - h) + k$ alter the graph of $f(\theta)$.

Notice that the constant h appears *inside* the function and therefore acts on f's input values, while the constant k appears *outside* the function and therefore acts on f's output values. For instance, consider the function $g(\theta) = 3 \sin 2\left(\theta - \frac{\pi}{2}\right) + 1$, the result of introducing the constants $h = \frac{\pi}{2}$ and $k = 1$ in the function $f(\theta) = 3 \sin 2\theta$. The mapping diagram below shows what happens when $\frac{\pi}{2}, \frac{3\pi}{4}, \pi, \frac{5\pi}{4}$, and $\frac{3\pi}{2}$ are used as inputs for g.

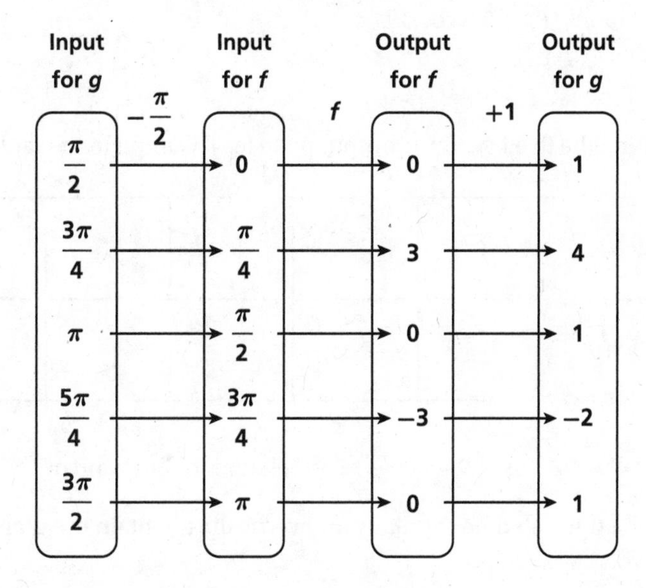

Notice that the input-output pairs for $f(\theta) = 3 \sin 2\theta$ (the middle two sets in the mapping diagram) are the five key points for one cycle of f's graph. Similarly, the input-output pairs for $g(\theta) = 3 \sin 2\left(\theta - \frac{\pi}{2}\right) + 1$ (the first and last sets in the mapping diagram) are the five key points for one cycle of g's graph. From the graphs at the right, you can see that g's graph is a translation of f's graph.

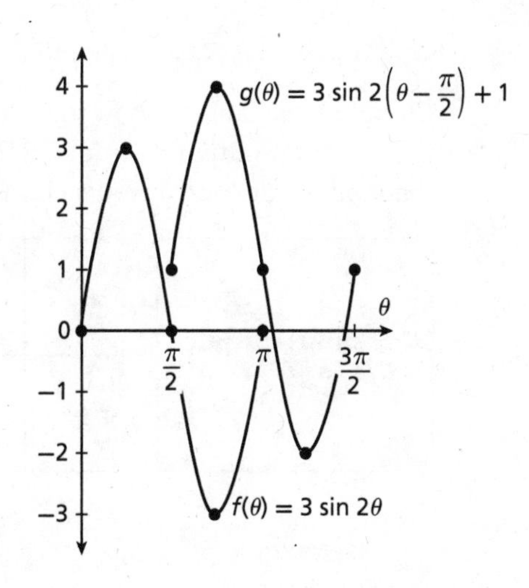

REFLECT

5a. In terms of the constants $h = \frac{\pi}{2}$ and $k = 1$, describe how the graph of f is translated to obtain the graph of g.

5b. The constants h and k in $g(\theta) = f(\theta - h) + k$ change where a cycle begins and ends as well as what the maximum and minimum values are, but do the constants change the period and amplitude? Explain.

MCC9–12.F.IF.7e

6 EXAMPLE Graphing $g(\theta) = a \cos b(\theta - h) + k$

Graph one cycle of $g(\theta) = 0.5 \cos 3\left(\theta - \frac{\pi}{3}\right) - 1.5$.

A Think about the related function $f(\theta) = 0.5 \cos 3\theta$.

- What is the period of f? ___________
- Use the period to determine the five key input-output pairs for f. Complete the table.

Key input-output pairs for f	θ	0				
	$f(\theta)$					

B Think about the graph of $g(\theta) = 0.5 \cos 3\left(\theta - \frac{\pi}{3}\right) - 1.5$ in relation to the graph of f.

- How must the graph of f be translated horizontally and vertically to obtain the graph of g? (Note that $k < 0$ in this case.)

- Complete the table to show the effect of the horizontal and vertical translations on the key input-output pairs for f. Remember that a horizontal translation affects only the input values and a vertical translation affects only the output values.

Key input-output pairs for g	θ					
	$g(\theta)$					

C Plot the key points for the graph of g and use them to draw one cycle of the graph. One cycle of the graph of f is shown in gray for comparison.

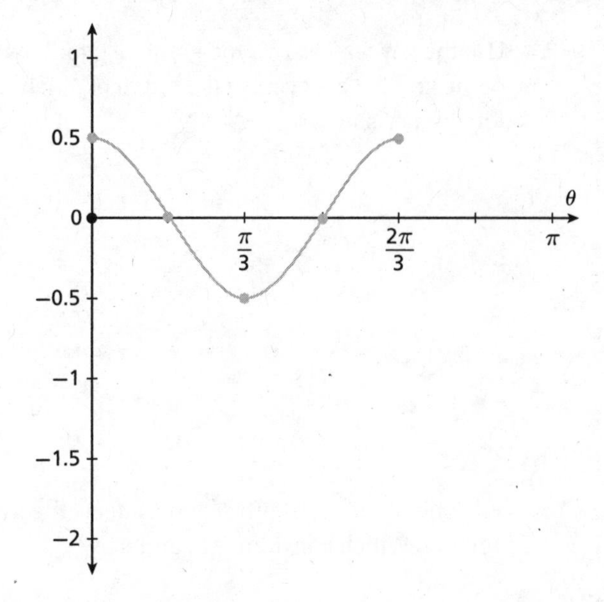

REFLECT

6a. If $g(\theta) = 0.5 \cos 3\left(\theta + \frac{\pi}{3}\right) - 1.5$ instead of $g(\theta) = 0.5 \cos 3\left(\theta - \frac{\pi}{3}\right) - 1.5$, what changes about how the graph of f is translated to obtain the graph of g?

____

MCC9–12.F.IF.7e

7 EXAMPLE Graphing $g(\theta) = a \tan b(\theta - h) + k$

Graph one cycle of $g(\theta) = 2 \tan \frac{1}{2}(\theta + \pi) + 3$.

A Think about the related function $f(\theta) = 2 \tan \frac{\theta}{2}$.

- What is the period of f? __________
- Use the period to determine the key features of the graph of f. Complete the table.

Key features of the graph of *f*	Equations of asymptotes	Coordinates of midline crossing	Coordinates of halfway points

B Think about the graph of $g(\theta) = 2 \tan \frac{1}{2}(\theta + \pi) + 3$ in relation to the graph of f.

- How must the graph of f be translated horizontally and vertically to obtain the graph of g? (Note that $h < 0$ in this case.)

____

- Complete the table to show the effect of the horizontal and vertical translations on the key features of the graph of f.

Key features of the graph of *f*	Equations of asymptotes	Coordinates of midline crossing	Coordinates of halfway points

C Use the key features for the graph of g to draw one cycle of the graph. One cycle of the graph of f is shown in gray for comparison.

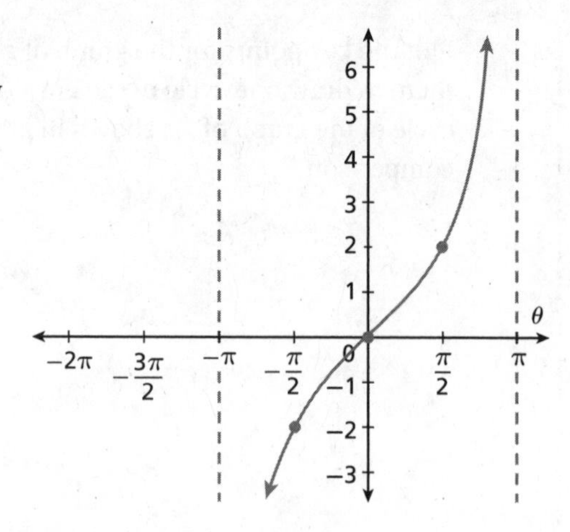

REFLECT

7a. Only one of the constants h and k affects the asymptotes for the graph of a tangent function. Which constant is it, and why?

7b. Only one of the constants h and k affects the midline for the graph of a trigonometric function. Which constant is it, and why?

MCC9–12.F.IF.7e

8 EXAMPLE Modeling the Motion of a Paddle Wheel

A side view of a riverboat's paddle wheel is shown. The paddle wheel has a diameter of 16 feet and rotates at a rate of 1 revolution every 4 seconds. Its lowest point is 2 feet below the water line.

The function $h(t) = 8 \sin \frac{\pi}{2}(t - 1) + 6$ models the motion of the paddle labeled P. The function gives the "height" (which is negative when the paddle is below the water line) at time t (in seconds). Graph the function on the interval $0 \leq t \leq 6$.

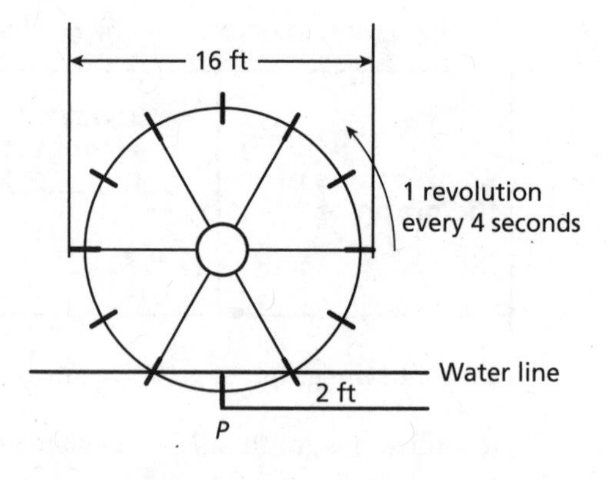

A Complete the table for the related function $f(t) = 8 \sin \frac{\pi}{2}t$.

Key input-output pairs for f						
	t	0				
	$f(t)$					

B Identify the translations to obtain the graph of h from the graph of f, then complete the table for h.

Amount and direction of horizontal translation: ______________________

Amount and direction of vertical translation: ______________________

Key input-output pairs for *h*	***t***					
	h(t)					

C Plot the key points for the graph of h and use them to draw one cycle of the graph. One cycle of the graph of f is shown in gray for comparison.

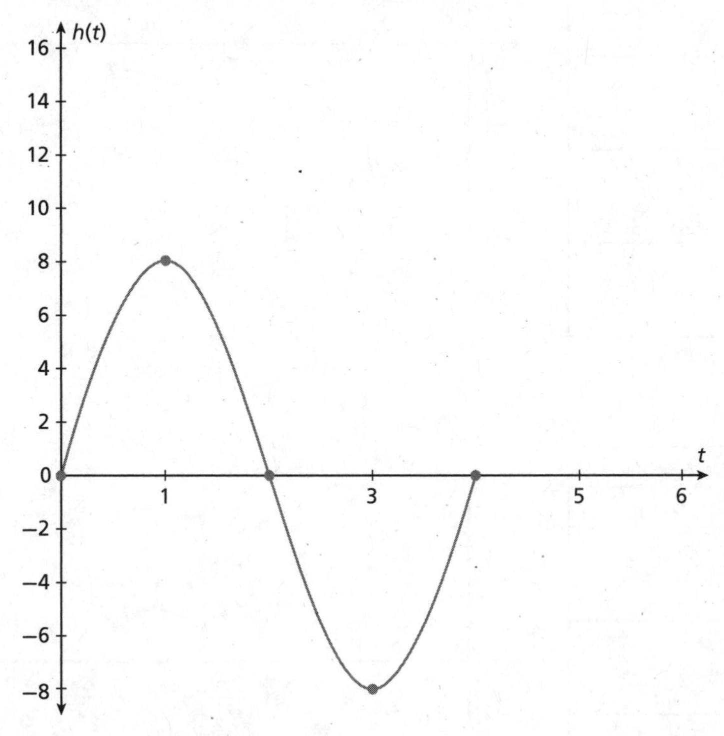

D Extend the graph one quarter of a cycle to the left and to the right in order to show the graph over the interval $0 \le t \le 6$.

REFLECT

8a. What is the significance of the graph's t-intercepts in the context of the situation?

____

8b. What is the significance of the maximum and minimum values of h in the context of the situation?

____

____

____

PRACTICE

For Exercises 1–3, complete each table with the key points or asymptotes for one cycle of the graph of each function, then graph the cycle. (One cycle of the graph of the parent function is shown in gray.)

1. $g(\theta) = -2 \sin 4\theta$

Key input-output pairs	
θ	$g(\theta)$

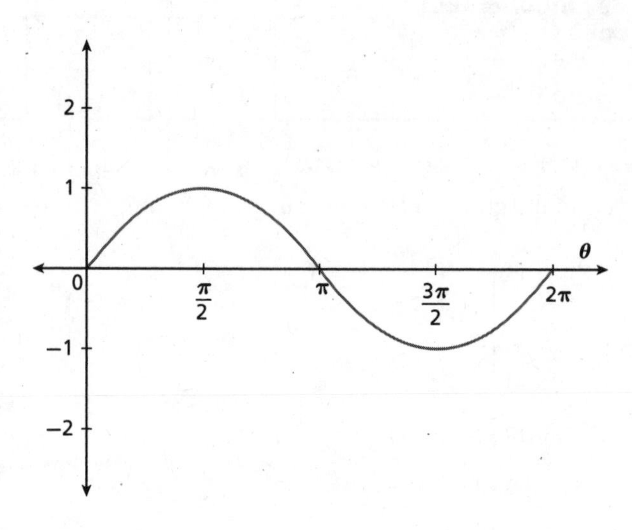

2. $g(\theta) = 0.75 \cos \frac{2\theta}{3}$

Key input-output pairs	
θ	$g(\theta)$

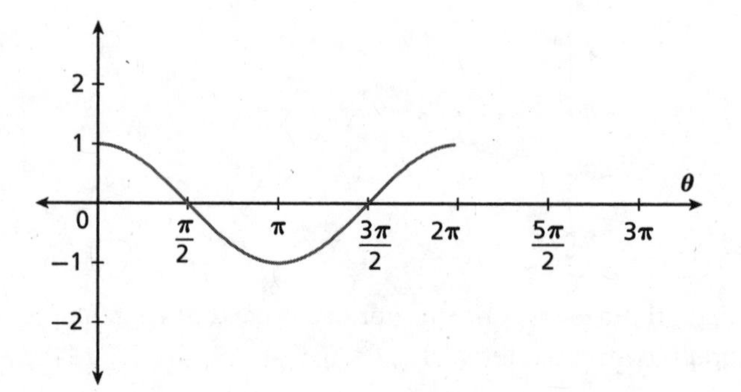

3. $g(\theta) = -\tan 2\theta$

Key features of graph	
Equation of left asymptote	
Equation of right asymptote	
Coordinates of midline crossing	
Coordinates of left halfway point	
Coordinates of right halfway point	

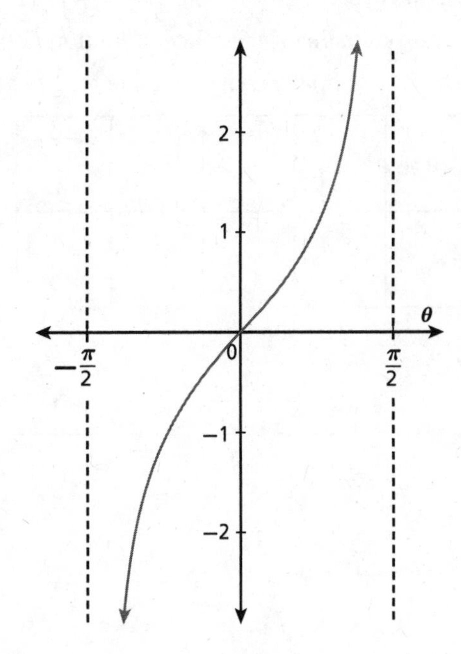

4. One cycle of the graph of a sine function is shown along with the five key points for the cycle. Use the points to determine a rule for the function.

$g(\theta) =$ ____

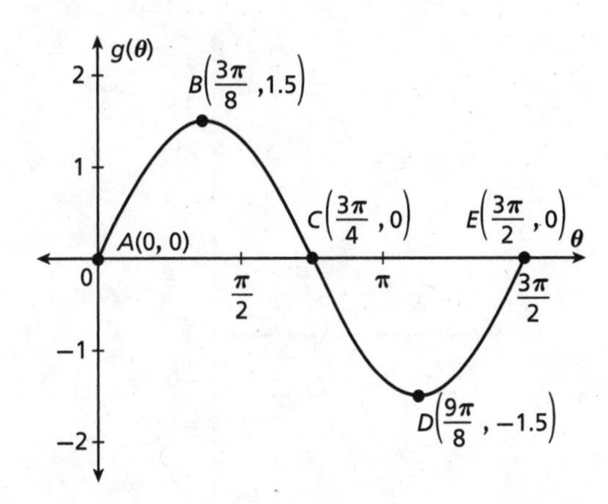

5. What are the period and amplitude of the graph of $g(\theta) = a \sin b\theta$ where $a \neq 0$ and $b > 0$? (Give your answers in terms of a and b.)

____

6. What is the period of the graph of $g(\theta) = a \tan b\theta$ where $a \neq 0$ and $b > 0$? What are the coordinates of the halfway points on one cycle of the graph? (Give your answers in terms of a and b.)

____

7. Graph one cycle of $g(\theta) = 2 \sin \frac{2}{3}\left(\theta - \frac{\pi}{4}\right) - 1$ by first completing the table of key input-output pairs for the related function $f(\theta) = 2 \sin \frac{2}{3}\theta$, then completing the table for g, and finally using the table for g to graph the cycle.

θ	0				
$f(\theta)$					

θ					
$g(\theta)$					

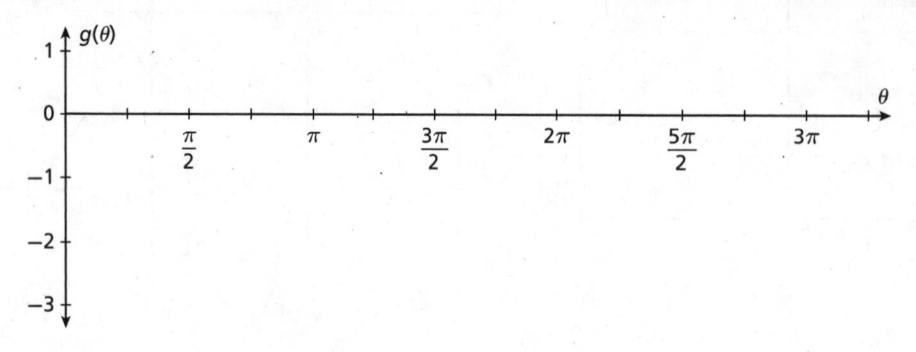

8. Graph one cycle of $g(\theta) = \frac{1}{2} \tan 2\left(\theta + \frac{\pi}{2}\right) + \frac{1}{2}$ by first completing the table of key features for the graph of the related function $f(\theta) = \frac{1}{2} \tan 2\theta$, then completing the table for g, and finally using the table for g to graph the cycle.

	Graph of *f*	Graph of *g*
Asymptotes		
Midline crossing		
Halfway points		

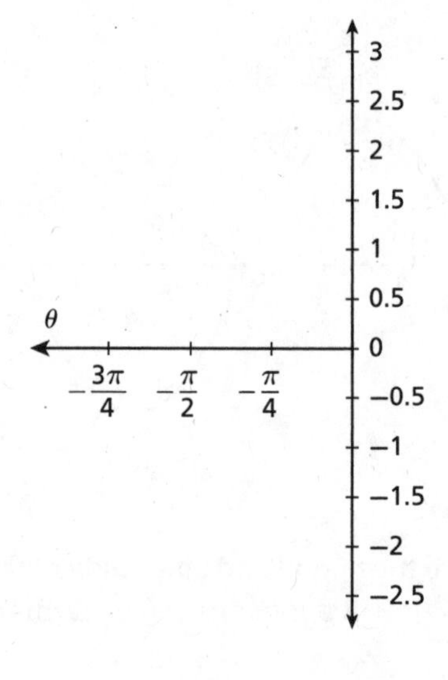

9. Suppose a working scale model of a riverboat has a paddle wheel that is 8 inches in diameter, rotates at a rate of 1 revolution every 2 seconds, and dips 0.5 inch below the water line. The function $h(t) = 4 \sin \pi(t - 0.5) + 3.5$ gives the "height" (in inches) of one paddle at time t (in seconds). Graph the function on the interval $0 \le t \le 4$.

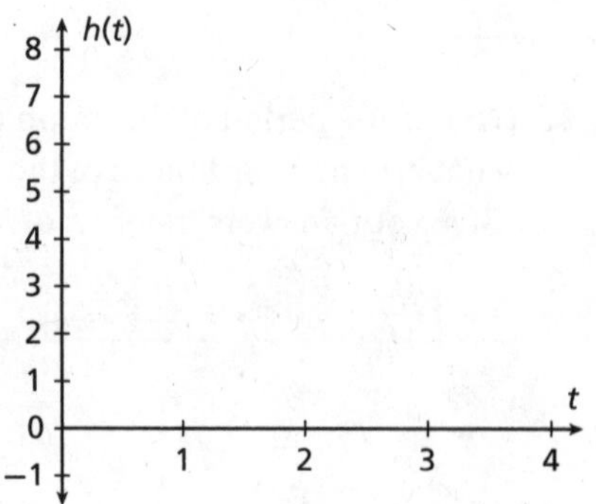

Name______________________ Class______________ Date____________

18-2

Additional Practice

Using $f(x) = \sin x$ or $g(x) = \cos x$ as a guide, graph each function. Identify the amplitude and period.

1. $b(x) = -5\sin\pi x$

2. $k(x) = 3\cos 2\pi x$

________________________ ________________________

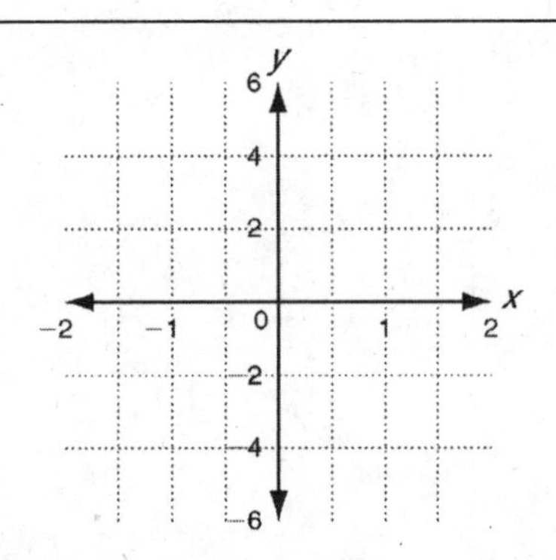

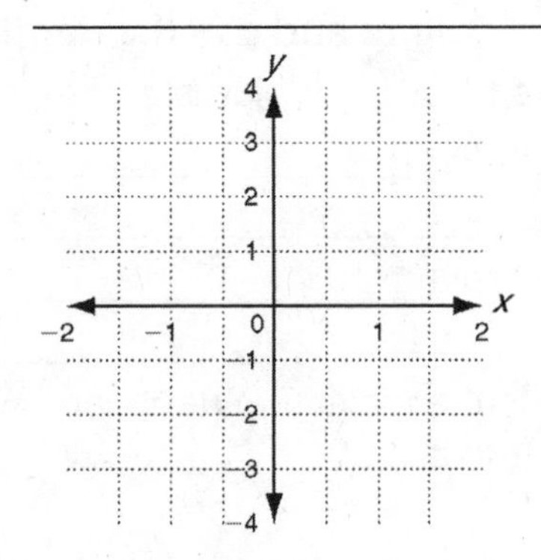

Using $f(x) = \sin x$ or $g(x) = \cos x$ as a guide, graph each function. Identify the x-intercepts and phase shift.

3. $h(x) = \sin\left(x + \dfrac{\pi}{4}\right)$

4. $h(x) = \cos\left(x - \dfrac{\pi}{4}\right)$

________________________ ________________________

________________________ ________________________

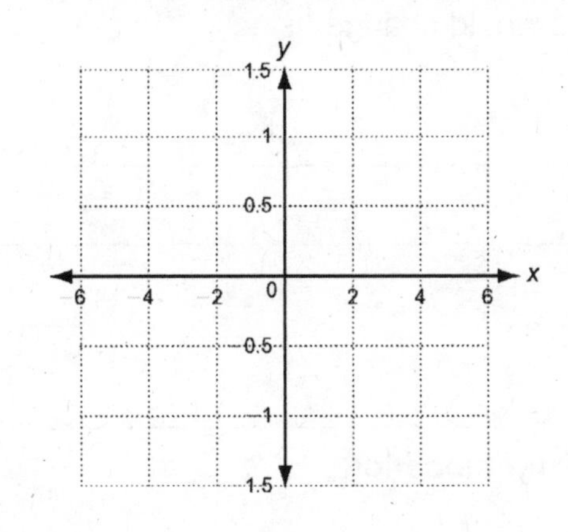

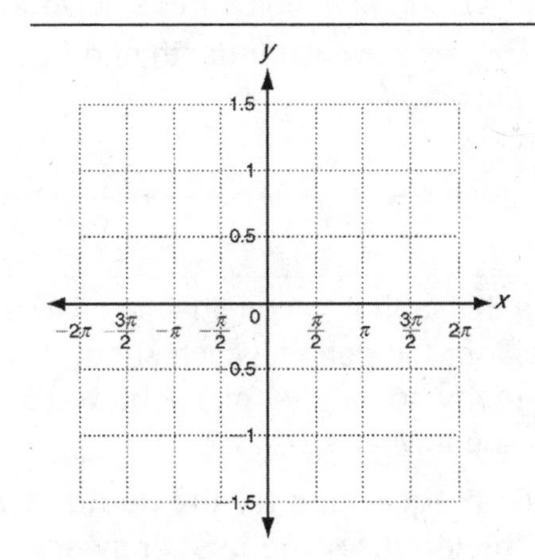

Solve.

5. a. Use a sine function to graph a sound wave with a period of 0.002 second and an amplitude of 2 centimeters.

   b. Find the frequency in hertz for this sound wave.

________________________ s

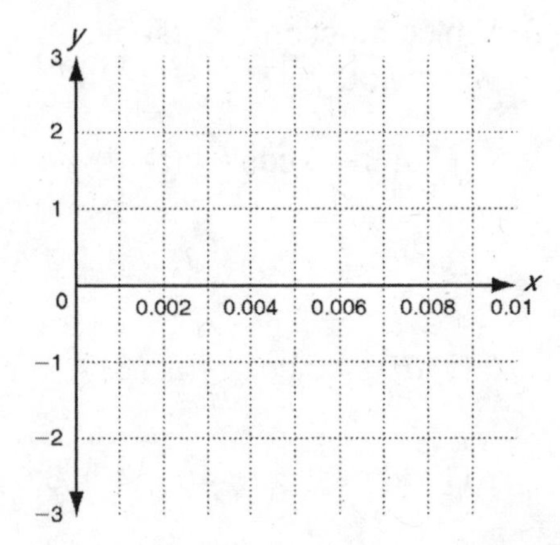

Problem Solving

As a result of the tide, the depth of the water in the bay varies with time. According to the harbormaster, the depth can be modeled by the function $d(t) = 2.5\cos\left(\frac{\pi}{6}\right)(t-2)+4$, where t is the number of hours since midnight, and d is the depth in meters.

1. Identify the following features of the graph of the function.
   a. Amplitude ______________
   b. Period ______________
   c. Phase shift ______________
   d. Vertical shift ______________
   e. What is the maximum depth and when does that occur?

      ____

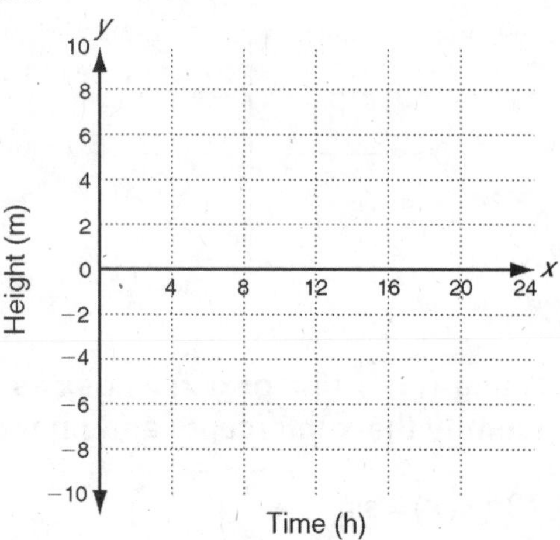

   f. What is the minimum depth and when does that occur?

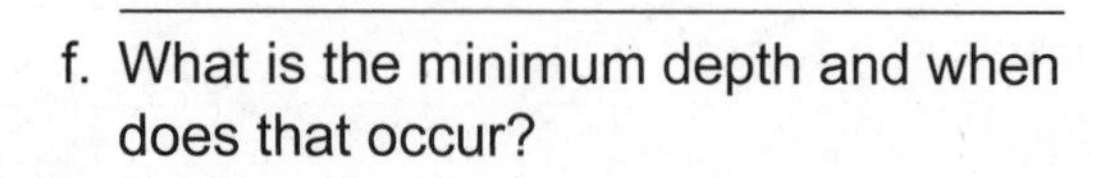

      ____

2. Graph the function for 24 hours.
3. How many high tides occur in 24 hours? ______________
4. Jim thinks that the amplitude and the vertical shift should be reversed.
   a. Write the equation for this new function. ______________
   b. Explain how water depth and frequency of tides would change using Jim's function.

   ____

   ____

5. Petra thinks that the original function is correct, except for the period, which should be 24. If so, how many hours after midnight would the first high and low tides occur? ______________

Jim looks at equations for the depth of water in different locations. Choose the letter for the best answer.

6. Which function represents a location that will dry out?

   A $d(t) = 5\cos\frac{\pi}{12}(t-1)+4$

   B $d(t) = 4\cos\frac{\pi}{8}(t-2)+4.5$

   C $d(t) = 3\cos\frac{\pi}{6}(t-3)+5$

   D $d(t) = 2\cos\frac{\pi}{4}(t-4)+5.5$

7. How deep is the water at 1:00 A.M. in a location where the water depth t hours after midnight is modeled by $d(t) = 1.25\cos\frac{\pi}{12}(t-1)+6$?

   F 4.75 m

   G 5.75 m

   H 7.25 m

   J 8.25 m

Name________________ Class__________ Date________

18-3

Fundamental Trigonometric Identities

Going Deeper

Video Tutor

Essential question: *How can you use a given value of one of the trigonometric functions to calculate the values of the other functions?*

You may have noticed that because $\sin \theta = y$, $\cos \theta = x$, and $\tan \theta = \frac{y}{x}$ you can write the identity $\tan \theta = \frac{\sin \theta}{\cos \theta}$. In the following Explore, you will derive another identity based on the Pythagorean Theorem, which is why the identity is known as a *Pythagorean* identity.

MCC9–12.F.TF.8

1 EXPLORE Deriving a Pythagorean Identity

The terminal side of an angle θ intersects the unit circle at the point (a, b), as shown.

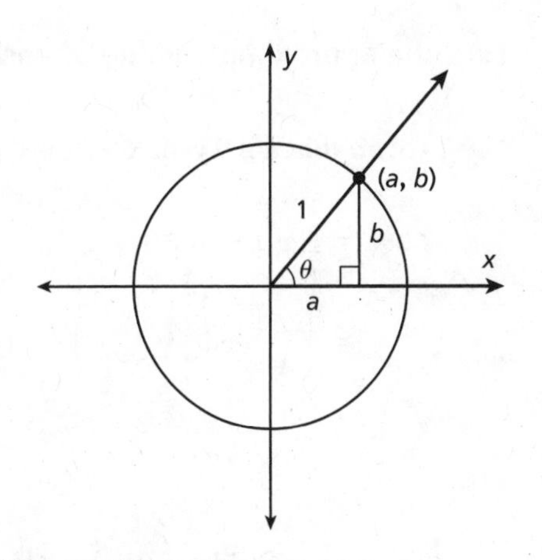

A Write a and b in terms of trigonometric functions involving θ.

$a =$ ____________

$b =$ ____________

B Apply the Pythagorean Theorem to the right triangle in the diagram. When a trigonometric function is squared, it is common practice to write the exponent immediately after the name of the function. For instance, write $(\sin \theta)^2$ as $\sin^2 \theta$.

$a^2 + b^2 = c^2$ — Write the Pythagorean Theorem.

$(\quad)^2 + (\quad)^2 = \quad^2$ — Substitute for a, b, and c.

$\quad + \quad = \quad$ — Square each expression.

REFLECT

1a. The identity is typically written with the sine function first. Write the identity this way, and explain why it is equivalent to the one in Step B.

____

1b. Confirm the Pythagorean identity for $\theta = \frac{\pi}{3}$.

____

1c. Confirm the Pythagorean identity for $\theta = \frac{3\pi}{4}$.

____

Rewriting the Identity You can rewrite the identity $\sin^2\theta + \cos^2\theta = 1$ to express one trigonometric function in terms of the other. As shown below, each alternate version of the identity involves positive and negative square roots. You determine which sign to use based on knowing the quadrant in which the terminal side of θ lies.

Solve for $\sin\theta$:

$$\sin^2\theta + \cos^2\theta = 1$$
$$\sin^2\theta = 1 - \cos^2\theta$$
$$\sin\theta = \pm\sqrt{1 - \cos^2\theta}$$

Solve for $\cos\theta$:

$$\sin^2\theta + \cos^2\theta = 1$$
$$\cos^2\theta = 1 - \sin^2\theta$$
$$\cos\theta = \pm\sqrt{1 - \sin^2\theta}$$

MCC9–12.F.TF.8

2 EXAMPLE Using the Pythagorean Identity

Find the approximate value of each trigonometric function.

A **Given that $\sin\theta = 0.766$ where $0 < \theta < \frac{\pi}{2}$, find $\cos\theta$.**

$\cos\theta = \pm\sqrt{1 - \sin^2\theta}$ Use the identity solved for $\cos\theta$.

$= \pm\sqrt{1 - (\quad)^2}$ Substitute for $\sin\theta$.

$\approx \pm$ ______ Evaluate using a calculator. Round to the nearest thousandth.

The terminal side of θ lies in Quadrant ______, where $\cos\theta$ ______ 0.

So, $\cos\theta \approx$ ______.

B **Given that $\cos\theta = -0.906$ where $\pi < \theta < \frac{3\pi}{2}$, find $\sin\theta$.**

$\sin\theta = \pm\sqrt{1 - \cos^2\theta}$ Use the identity solved for $\sin\theta$.

$= \pm\sqrt{1 - (\quad)^2}$ Substitute for $\cos\theta$.

$\approx \pm$ ______ Evaluate using a calculator. Round to the nearest thousandth.

The terminal side of θ lies in Quadrant ______, where $\sin\theta$ ______ 0.

So, $\sin\theta \approx$ ______.

REFLECT

2a. In part A, suppose $\frac{\pi}{2} < \theta < \pi$ instead of $0 < \theta < \frac{\pi}{2}$. How does this affect the value of $\cos\theta$?

______

______

2b. In part B, suppose $\frac{3\pi}{2} < \theta < 2\pi$ rather than $\pi < \theta < \frac{3\pi}{2}$. How does this affect the value of $\sin\theta$?

____

____

2c. In part A, explain how to find the approximate value of $\tan\theta$. Then find it.

____

Other Identities If you multiply both sides of the identity $\tan\theta = \frac{\sin\theta}{\cos\theta}$ by $\cos\theta$, you get the identity $\sin\theta = \tan\theta\cos\theta$. And if you divide both sides of $\sin\theta = \tan\theta\cos\theta$ by $\tan\theta$, you get the identity $\cos\theta = \frac{\sin\theta}{\tan\theta}$.

MCC9-12.F.TF.8

3 EXAMPLE Using an Identity That Involves Tangent

Given that $\tan\theta \approx -2.327$ where $\frac{\pi}{2} < \theta < \pi$, find the approximate values of $\sin\theta$ and $\cos\theta$.

A Write $\sin\theta$ in terms of $\cos\theta$.

$\sin\theta = \tan\theta\cos\theta$ — Use the identity $\sin\theta = \tan\theta\cos\theta$.

$\approx$ ______ $\cos\theta$ — Substitute the value of $\tan\theta$.

B Use the Pythagorean identity to find $\cos\theta$. Then find $\sin\theta$.

$\sin^2\theta + \cos^2\theta = 1$ — Use the Pythagorean identity.

$(\text{\_\_\_\_\_\_}\cos\theta)^2 + \cos^2\theta \approx 1$ — Substitute for $\sin\theta$.

______ $\cos^2\theta + \cos^2\theta \approx 1$ — Square.

______ $\cos^2\theta \approx 1$ — Combine like terms.

$\cos^2\theta \approx$ ______ — Solve for $\cos^2\theta$.

$\cos\theta \approx \pm$ ______ — Solve for $\cos\theta$.

The terminal side of θ lies in Quadrant ________, where $\cos\theta$ ________ 0.

So, $\cos\theta \approx$ ________________, and $\sin\theta \approx -2.327\cos\theta \approx$ ________________.

REFLECT

3a. When you multiplied the given value of $\tan\theta$ with the calculated value of $\cos\theta$ in order to find the value of $\sin\theta$, was the product positive or negative? Explain why this is the result you'd expect.

3b. If $\tan\theta = 1$ where $0 < \theta < \frac{\pi}{2}$, show that you can solve for $\sin\theta$ and $\cos\theta$ exactly using the Pythagorean identity. Why is this so?

PRACTICE

Find sin θ and tan θ for each given value of cos θ.

1. $\cos\theta = 0.596,\ 0 < \theta < \frac{\pi}{2}$

$\sin\theta \approx$ ________, $\tan\theta \approx$ ________

2. $\cos\theta = 0.985,\ \frac{3\pi}{2} < \theta < 2\pi$

$\sin\theta \approx$ ________, $\tan\theta \approx$ ________

3. $\cos\theta = -0.342,\ \frac{\pi}{2} < \theta < \pi$

$\sin\theta \approx$ ________, $\tan\theta \approx$ ________

4. $\cos\theta = -0.819,\ \pi < \theta < \frac{3\pi}{2}$

$\sin\theta \approx$ ________, $\tan\theta \approx$ ________

Find cos θ and tan θ for each given value of sin θ.

5. $\sin\theta = 0.186,\ 0 < \theta < \frac{\pi}{2}$

$\cos\theta \approx$ ________, $\tan\theta \approx$ ________

6. $\sin\theta = 0.756,\ \frac{\pi}{2} < \theta < \pi$

$\cos\theta \approx$ ________, $\tan\theta \approx$ ________

7. $\sin\theta = -0.644,\ \frac{3\pi}{2} < \theta < 2\pi$

$\cos\theta \approx$ ________, $\tan\theta \approx$ ________

8. $\sin\theta = -0.328,\ \pi < \theta < \frac{3\pi}{2}$

$\cos\theta \approx$ ________, $\tan\theta \approx$ ________

Find sin θ and cos θ for each given value of tan θ.

9. $\tan\theta = 0.301,\ 0 < \theta < \frac{\pi}{2}$

$\sin\theta \approx$ ________, $\cos\theta \approx$ ________

10. $\tan\theta = 2.416,\ \pi < \theta < \frac{3\pi}{2}$

$\sin\theta \approx$ ________, $\cos\theta \approx$ ________

11. $\tan\theta = -0.739,\ \frac{\pi}{2} < \theta < \pi$

$\sin\theta \approx$ ________, $\cos\theta \approx$ ________

12. $\tan\theta = -3.305,\ \frac{3\pi}{2} < \theta < 2\pi$

$\sin\theta \approx$ ________, $\cos\theta \approx$ ________

Name________________ Class__________ Date__________

Additional Practice

Prove each trigonometric identity.

1. $\cos^4\theta - \sin^4\theta + \sin^2\theta = \cos^2\theta$

2. $\left(\dfrac{\cos^2\theta}{\sin^2\theta}\right)\cos^2\theta = \left(\dfrac{\cos^2\theta}{\sin^2\theta}\right) - \cos^2\theta$

3. $\tan^2\theta - \tan^2\theta\sin^2\theta = \sin^2\theta$

4. $\dfrac{1+\dfrac{\cos\theta}{\sin\theta}}{\dfrac{\cos\theta}{\sin\theta}(\sin\theta + \cos\theta)} = \dfrac{1}{\cos\theta}$

Find $\sin\theta$ and $\cos\theta$ for each given value of $\tan\theta$.

5. $\tan\theta \approx -2.185,\ \dfrac{3\pi}{4} < \theta < 2\pi$

6. $\tan\theta \approx -0.143,\ \dfrac{\pi}{2} < \theta < \pi$

Solve.

7. Use the equation $mg\sin\theta = \mu mg\cos\theta$ to determine the angle at which a waxed wood block on an inclined plane of wet snow begins to slide. Assume $\mu = 0.17$.

Problem Solving

The advertisement for a new shoe promises runners less slip. The coefficient of friction (μ) between concrete and a new material used in the sole of this shoe is 1.5. The force of friction that causes slip is equal to $mg \sin \theta$, where m is a runner's mass and g is the acceleration due to gravity. The force that prevents slip is $\mu mg \cos\theta$.

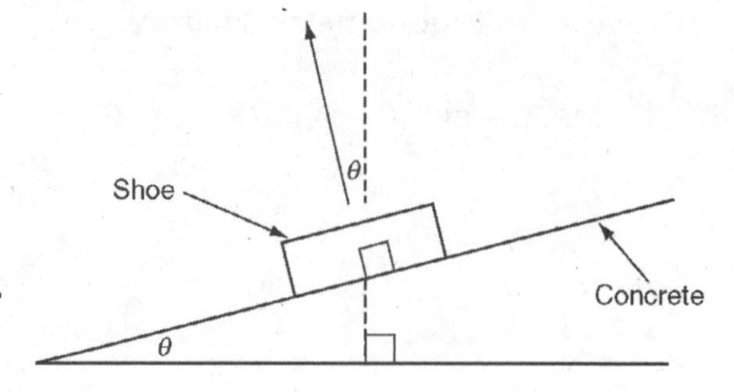

1. Mukisa wants to know what this new shoe will do for his performance.
   a. At the instant of slip, the force that causes slip is equal to the force that prevents it. Write an equation to show this relationship. ______________________
   b. Rewrite the equation with trigonometric expressions on one side of the equation, and substitute the coefficient of friction for the new material. ______________________
   c. Use a trigonometric identity to rewrite the equation using only the tangent function. ______________________
   d. Solve for θ, the angle at which the new shoe will start to slip. ______________________
2. Mukisa wonders how his old shoes compare to these new shoes. The label on the box of his old shoes states that the coefficient of friction is 1.3.
   a. Write an equation to find the angle at which a shoe with a coefficient of friction of 1.3 will slip. ______________________
   b. At what angle will this shoe start to slip? ______________________
   c. Suggest how the new shoes might improve Mukisa's performance.

____

An advertisement states, "Use this wax and your skis will slide better than silk on silk!" The coefficient of friction for silk on silk is 0.25. The coefficient of friction for waxed wood on wet snow is 0.14. The equation $mg \sin\theta = \mu mg \cos\theta$ can be used to find the angle at which a material begins to slide. Choose the letter for the best answer.

3. Which expression gives the angle at which silk begins to slide on silk?
   A $\cos^{-1}(0.25)$
   B $\sin\left(\dfrac{1}{0.25}\right)$
   C $\tan\left(\dfrac{1}{0.25}\right)$
   D $\tan^{-1}(0.25)$

4. At what angle would a waxed wooden ski begin to slide on wet snow?
   F 2°
   G 8°
   H 12°
   J 14°

Performance Tasks

GPS COMMON CORE

MCC9-12.F.IF.7e
MCC9-12.F.TF.1
MCC9-12.G.SRT.8

1. When a road has a 6% grade, it rises a vertical distance of 6 ft over a horizontal distance of 100 ft. One of the steepest roads in the U.S. is in San Francisco. Filbert Street between Hyde and Leavenworth has a grade of 31.5%. What is the angle that corresponds to this grade? Round to the nearest tenth of a degree.

2. The center of a circular wall clock is 8 feet, or 96 inches, from a classroom floor, and the minute hand is 6 inches long. Ross wants to model the distance of the tip of the minute hand from the floor as a function of the number of minutes past 12:00 PM by using the cosine function. Write the model function, where $D(t)$ is the distance from the floor in inches and t is the number of minutes past 12:00 PM.

3. A DVD's rotational speed varies from 1530 revolutions per minute (rpm) when the inner edge is being read to 630 rpm when the outer edge is being read.

a. What is the total rotation of the DVD in radians after 10 seconds if the computer is reading data on the outer edge? Write your answer in terms of π and show your work.

b. In 10 seconds, what linear distance is covered by the part of the DVD that passes under the reader head from part **a**, which is about 6 cm from the center of the DVD? Round to the nearest centimeter and show your work.

c. If the computer is reading data on the inner edge (about 2.5 cm from the center of the DVD), what linear distance is covered by the part of the DVD that passes under the reader head in 10 seconds? Round to the nearest centimeter and show your work.

continued

4. Belinda recorded the dew point in her hometown in degrees Fahrenheit each day for a year (not a leap year) and entered the data into her graphing calculator, with x representing the number of days since January 1 and $x = 0$ as January 1. She then performed a sinusoidal regression as shown.

```
SinReg
 y=a*sin(bx+c)+d
 a=25.00086565
 b=.0172134442
 c=-1.583657028
 d=39.99903543
```

a. What is the model function? What is the function's period and amplitude? (Answers can be rounded to two decimal places, but don't round when calculating.)

b. Use the model function to find the approximate dew point on February 20. Also, determine on what day(s) the model says the dew point was 55°F by using your graphing calculator.

c. What is the phase shift of the model function?

Name ______________________ Class ______________ Date ________

SELECTED RESPONSE

1. An angle θ whose vertex is at the center of a unit circle intercepts an arc whose length is $\frac{2}{3}$ of the circle's circumference. What is the radian measure of θ if $0 < \theta < 2\pi$?

   A. $\frac{2}{3}$ **C.** $\frac{4\pi}{3}$

   B. $\frac{2\pi}{3}$ **D.** $-\frac{4\pi}{3}$

2. For which value of θ does $\tan \theta = 1$?

   F. $\frac{\pi}{6}$ **H.** $\frac{\pi}{3}$

   G. $\frac{\pi}{4}$ **J.** $\frac{\pi}{2}$

3. An angle θ whose vertex is at the center of a circle of radius 4 units intercepts an arc whose length is 6π units. What is the radian measure of θ if $0 < \theta < 2\pi$?

   A. $\frac{3}{4}$ **C.** $\frac{3\pi}{2}$

   B. $\frac{2}{3\pi}$ **D.** $-\frac{\pi}{2}$

4. If $0 < \theta < \frac{\pi}{2}$, which of the following is equal to $\sin \theta$?

   F. $\sin\left(\frac{\pi}{2} + \theta\right)$

   G. $\sin(\pi - \theta)$

   H. $\sin(\pi + \theta)$

   J. $\sin(2\pi - \theta)$

5. If $\cos \theta = 0.342$ where $\frac{3\pi}{2} < \theta < 2\pi$, what is the approximate value of $\sin \theta$?

   A. 0.940

   B. 0.883

   C. −0.883

   D. −0.940

6. If $f(\theta) = \sin \theta$, what is $f\left(\frac{5\pi}{3}\right)$?

   F. $-\frac{\sqrt{3}}{2}$

   G. $-\frac{1}{2}$

   H. $\frac{1}{2}$

   J. $\frac{\sqrt{3}}{2}$

Use the following information for Items 7–10.

In the window of a jewelry store, rings are displayed on a rotating turntable. The function

$$d(t) = 3 \sin \pi t + 4$$

models a particular ring's distance (in inches) from the window at time t (in minutes).

7. How fast (in revolutions per minute, or rpm) is the turntable rotating?

   A. 1 rpm **C.** 3 rpm

   B. 2 rpm **D.** 4 rpm

8. What is the ring's maximum distance from the window?

   F. 1 inch **H.** 5 inches

   G. 3 inches **J.** 7 inches

9. An employee at the jewelry store made a change to the display so that the distance function is now $d(t) = 3 \sin \pi t + 3.5$. Which of the following describes the change?

   A. The employee moved the ring closer to the center of the turntable.

   B. The employee moved the ring farther from the center of the turntable.

   C. The employee moved the turntable closer to the window.

   D. The employee moved the turntable farther from the window.

CONSTRUCTED RESPONSE

10. a. Using the original distance function $d(t) = 3 \sin \pi t + 4$ as described on the preceding page, graph the function on the interval $0 \le t \le 6$. Include labels and scales for the axes.

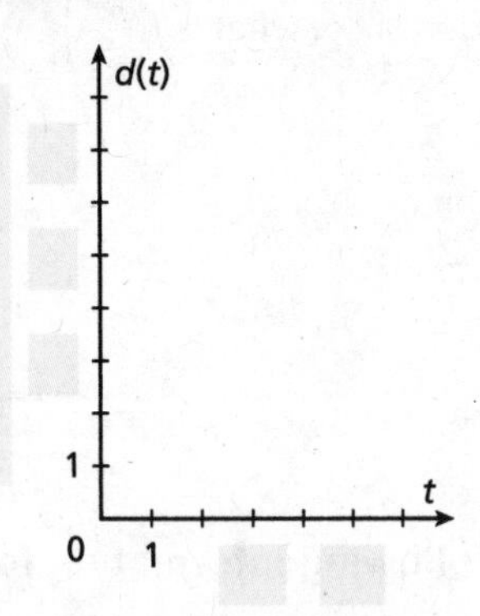

b. Identify the graph's period, amplitude, and midline.

______

______

11. If $\theta = 10$ radians, explain how you know that $\cos \theta < 0$ without using a calculator to find $\cos \theta$.

______

______

______

______

______

______

12. A reflector is attached to a spoke on a bicycle wheel. When the wheel rotates, the reflector is 4 inches above the ground at its lowest point and 22 inches above the ground at its highest point.

a. Write a rule for the function $h(t)$ that gives the height h (in inches) of the reflector at time t (in seconds) when the wheel rotates at a rate of 2 revolutions per second. Assume the following:

- The x-axis is at ground level.
- The y-axis passes through the center of the wheel.
- The reflector starts at the point (9, 13).

Note that the wheel rotates *clockwise*, so angles of rotation must be negative.

______

b. Graph $h(t)$ on the interval $0 \le t \le 2$. Include labels and scales for the axes.

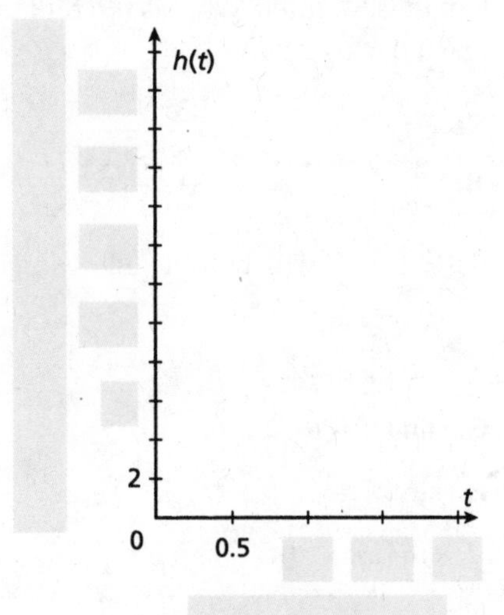

c. Suppose the wheel's rotational speed is increased to 3 revolutions per second. How must you alter the height function's rule? What effect does this change have on the function's graph?

______

______

______

Mathematical Modeling

GPS COMMON CORE

Unpacking the Standards

Understanding the standards and the vocabulary terms in the standards will help you know exactly what you are expected to learn in this unit.

GPS COMMON CORE **MCC9-12.F.IF.7b**

Graph … piecewise-defined functions, including step functions and absolute value functions.

Key Vocabulary

piecewise function *(función a trozos)* A function that is a combination of one or more functions.

step function *(función escalón)* A piecewise function that is constant over each interval in its domain.

absolute-value function *(función de valor absoluto)* A function whose rule contains absolute-value expressions.

What It Means For You

You can use piecewise-defined functions to model applications that are described by different functions over different parts of their domain.

EXAMPLE

The function for topsoil prices is a step function consisting of three constant functions:

$y = 10$, for $0 \le x < 5$

$y = 7$, for $5 \le x < 25$

$y = 5$, for $x \ge 25$

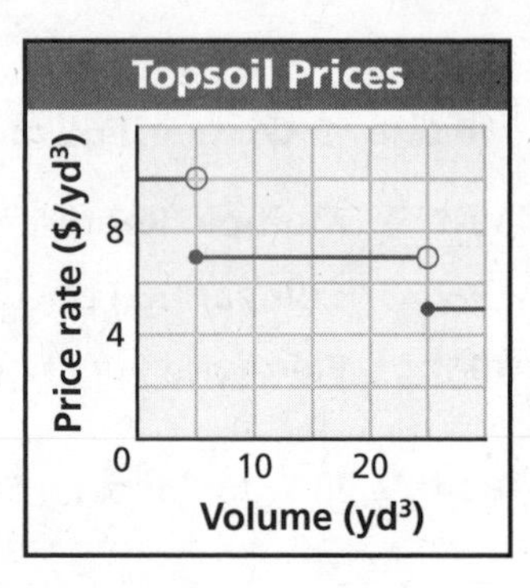

UNIT 10

GPS COMMON CORE **MCC9-12.F.BF.3**

Identify the effect on the graph of replacing $f(x)$ by $f(x) + k$, $kf(x)$, $f(kx)$, and $f(x + k)$ for specific values of k (both positive and negative); find the value of k given the graphs. …

Key Vocabulary

transformation *(transformación)* A change in the position, size, or shape of a figure or graph.

What It Means For You

The effects of adding or multiplying by constants in the equations of functions are predictable: they cause transformations of the parent graph such as translating it, stretching it, or reflecting it.

EXAMPLE

The graph shows the parent absolute-value function $f(x) = |x|$ and the results of several transformations.

$f(x) = |x|$

A: $f(x) = -|x|$

B: $f(x) = |x + 2|$

C: $f(x) = 2|x - 3| + 1$

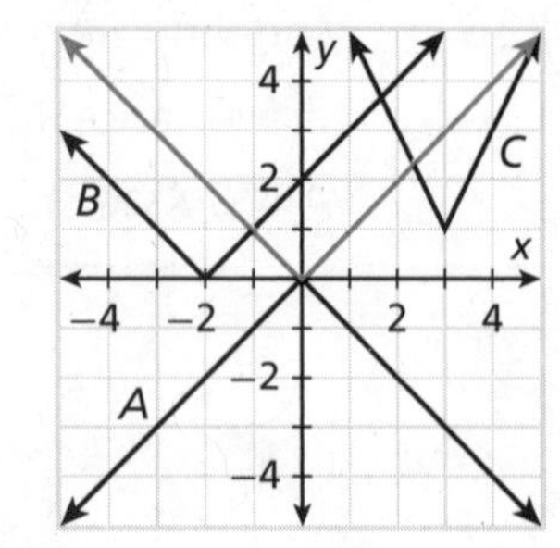

MCC9-12.F.BF.4b(+)

Verify by composition that one function is the inverse of another.

Key Vocabulary

composition of functions *(composición de funciones)* The composition of functions f and g, written as $(f \circ g)(x)$ and defined as $f(g(x))$ uses the output of $g(x)$ as the input for $f(x)$.

inverse function *(función inversa)* The function that results from exchanging the input and output values of a one-to-one function. The inverse of $f(x)$ is denoted $f^{-1}(x)$.

What It Means For You

Functions that are inverses "undo" each other. A function takes an input value x and assigns an output value. The inverse function takes this output value as an input and returns it to its original value, x.

EXAMPLE

Let $f(x) = 0.5x - 1$ and $g(x) = 2x + 2$.

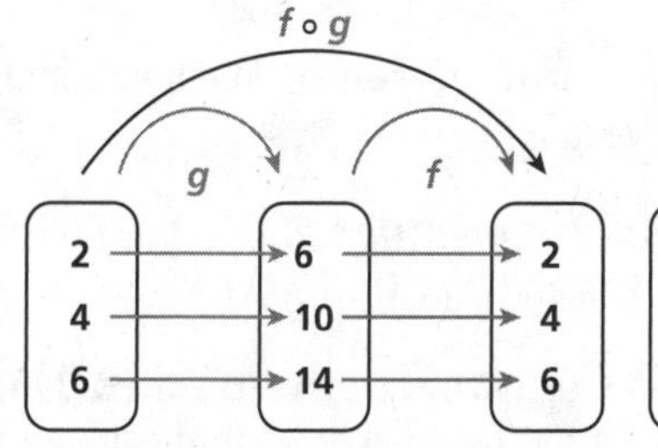

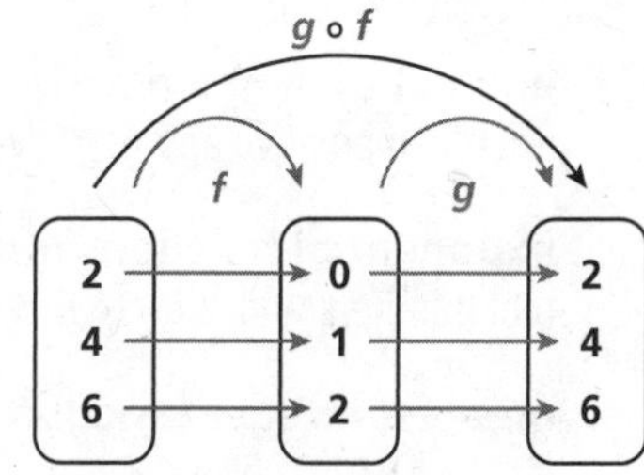

Because $f(g(x)) = x$ and $g(f(x)) = x$, $f(x)$ and $g(x)$ are inverses.

MCC9-12.F.LE.1

Distinguish between situations that can be modeled with linear functions and with exponential functions.

Key Vocabulary

linear function *(función lineal)* A function that can be written in the form $f(x) = mx + b$, where x is the independent variable and m and b are real numbers. Its graph is a line.

exponential function *(función exponencial)* A function of the form $f(x) = ab^x$, where a and b are real numbers with $a \neq 0$, $b > 0$, and $b \neq 1$.

What It Means For You

Linear and exponential functions both model growth (or decay), but while a linear function models a *constant amount* of growth for equal intervals, an exponential function models a *constant factor* of growth for equal intervals.

EXAMPLE **Linear growth**

Mass (kg)	4	5	6	7	8	9	10
Length (cm)	30.6	32	33.4	34.8	36.2	37.6	39

+1.4 +1.4 +1.4 +1.4 +1.4 +1.4

For each additional kilogram, the length increases by an amount of 1.4 centimeters.

EXAMPLE **Exponential growth**

Time (yr)	5	6	7	8	9	10
Buffalo	124	150	185	213	261	322

×1.2 ×1.2 ×1.2 ×1.2 ×1.2

For each additional year, the number of buffalo increases by a factor (to the nearest tenth) of 1.2.

UNIT 10

Key Vocabulary

absolute-value function *(función de valor absoluto)* A function whose rule contains absolute-value expressions.

composition of functions *(composición de funciones)* The composition of functions f and g, written as $(f \circ g)(x)$ and defined as $f(g(x))$, uses the output of $g(x)$ as the input for $f(x)$.

cube-root function *(función de raíz cúbica)* A function of the form $f(x) = a\sqrt[3]{x - h} + k$ where a, h, and k are constants and $a \neq 0$.

end behavior *(comportamiento extremo)* The trends in the y-values of a function as the x-values approach positive and negative infinity.

exponential function *(función exponencial)* A function of the form $f(x) = ab^x$, where a and b are real numbers with $a \neq 0$, $b > 0$, and $b \neq 1$.

greatest integer function *(función de entero mayor)* A function denoted by $f(x) = [x]$ or $f(x) = \lfloor x \rfloor$ in which the number x is rounded down to the greatest integer that is less than or equal to x.

inverse function *(función inversa)* The function that results from exchanging the input and output values of a one-to-one function. The inverse of $f(x)$ is denoted $f^{-1}(x)$.

linear function *(función lineal)* A function that can be written in the form $f(x) = mx + b$, where x is the independent variable and m and b are real numbers. Its graph is a line.

logarithmic function *(función logarítmica)* A function of the form $f(x) = \log_b x$, where $b \neq 1$ and $b > 0$, which is the inverse of the exponential function $f(x) = b^x$.

one-to-one function *(función uno a uno)* A function in which each y-value corresponds to only one x-value. The inverse of a one-to-one function is also a function.

parabola *(parábola)* The shape of the graph of a quadratic function. Also, the set of points equidistant from a point F, called the focus, and a line d, called the *directrix*.

piecewise function *(función a trozos)* A function that is a combination of one or more functions.

polynomial function *(función polynomial)* A function whose rule is a polynomial.

quadratic function *(función cuadrática)* A function that can be written in the form $f(x) = ax^2 + bx + c$, where a, b, and c are real numbers and $a \neq 0$, or in the form $f(x) = a(x - h)^2 + k$, where a, h, and k are real numbers and $a \neq 0$.

residual *(residuo)* The signed vertical distance between a data point and a line of fit.

square root function *(función de raiz cuadrada)* A function of the form $f(x) = a\sqrt{x - h} + k$ where a, h, and k are constants and $a \neq 0$.

step function *(función escalón)* A piecewise function that is constant over each interval in its domain.

transformation *(transformación)* A change in the position, size, or shape of a figure or graph.

vertex form of a quadratic function *(forma en vértice de una función cuadrática)* A quadratic equation written in the form $f(x) = a(x - h)^2 + k$, where a, h, and k are constants and (h, k) is the vertex.

Name________________________ Class________________ Date__________

19-1

Video Tutor

Multiple Representations of Functions

Focus on Modeling

Essential question: *How can you use an exponential function to model population growth and find an annual growth rate?*

The United States government performs a census every 10 years. The census data from 1790 to 1890 are given in the table below. How can you use the data to predict the population in 1845 and 1990?

1 Model the population from 1790 to 1890.

A Complete the table. Round the population (in millions) to the nearest tenth.

Census Year	Decades Since First Census	Population	Population (in millions)
1790	0	3,929,214	3.9
1800		5,308,483	
1810		7,239,881	
1820		9,638,453	
1830		12,866,020	
1840		17,069,453	
1850		23,191,876	
1860		31,443,321	
1870		39,818,449	
1880		50,189,209	
1890		62,979,766	

B Use your graphing calculator to determine the exponential regression equation for the data as follows.

- Let the *x*-values be the number of decades since 1790. Enter these values in list L_1.
- Let the *y*-values be the population in millions. Enter these values in list L_2.
- Find the exponential regression equation by pressing STAT, selecting the **CALC** menu, and then selecting **0:ExpReg**.

Write the exponential regression equation below, rounding the values of *a* and *b* to two decimal places.

REFLECT

1a. Write the regression equation in the form of an exponential growth function, $y = a(1 + r)^t$. What does r represent?

2 Determine how well the model fits the data.

A Plot the 11 data points (*decades since first census, population in millions*) on the coordinate plane below.

B Graph the exponential regression equation on the same coordinate plane.

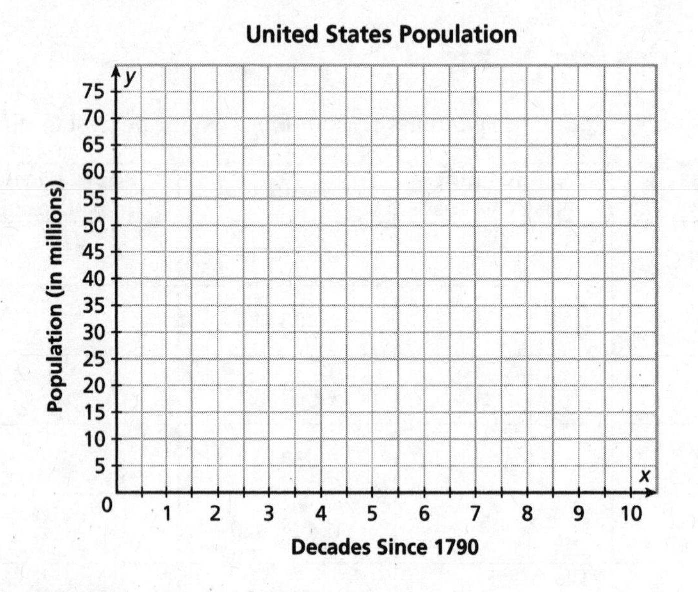

C Press 2nd STAT (LIST) and select **7:RESID** to access a list of residuals. List the residuals in order. Round each residual to two decimal places.

REFLECT

2a. Do you think an exponential model is a good fit for the data? Explain.

2b. Press 2nd Y= (STAT PLOT) to create a scatterplot of the residuals. (Use L_1 as Xlist and RESID as Ylist.) What does the residual plot suggest for x-values greater than 8?

3 Write the exponential model in other forms.

A What property of exponents tells you that $y = 4.09\left(1.33^{\frac{1}{10}}\right)^{10x}$ is an equivalent form of the exponential model?

B Rewrite $y = 4.09\left(1.33^{\frac{1}{10}}\right)^{10x}$ by evaluating the base. Round the base to two decimal places.

C Based on the rewritten model, what was the annual growth rate of the U.S. population for the period 1790–1890?

REFLECT

3a. What does x represent in the rewritten model?

3b. Suppose a student used the equation $y = 4.09(1.03)^x$ as an exponential model for the population. What would these x-values represent?

4 Use the model to make predictions.

A Use the exponential model you wrote in step 1B to predict the population in 1845. State what value you used for x.

B Use the exponential model you wrote in step 1B to predict the population in 1990. State what value you used for x.

REFLECT

4a. How confident are you of the predicted population for 1845? Explain.

4b. Knowing that a residual is the difference between an actual value and a predicted value, would you say that your prediction of the population in 1845 might be a little too high or a little too low? Explain.

4c. The census for 1990 showed that the U.S. population was 248,718,302. Compare this to your prediction. What does this tell you about the growth rate of the population for the period 1890–1990 relative to the growth rate for the period 1790–1890?

4d. Explain the difference between the predicted population and the actual population for 1990.

EXTEND

1. Use the data in the population table (still stored in your calculator as L_1 and L_2) to determine the quadratic regression equation. Round the values of *a*, *b*, and *c* to three decimal places.

2. List the residuals for the quadratic regression in order. Round each residual to the nearest hundredth.

3. Is the quadratic regression equation a better fit for the data than the exponential model? Explain.

4. Use the quadratic model to predict the population in 1990. Compare this prediction to the one you obtained from the exponential model.

5. On your calculator, graph the data and both regression equations in the same window. Discuss how the graphs compare. (*Hint:* To make the graphs, perform the regressions again with the arguments shown at right. This stores the regression equations as Y_1 and Y_2.)

Additional Practice

Use a graphing calculator to determine the exponential regression equation for the data. Round the values of *a* and *b* to two decimal places.

1.

x	0	5	10	15	20
$f(x)$	4.2	5.7	7.3	9	11

____

2.

x	−1	0	1	2	3
$f(x)$	8.2	7.8	7.4	7.1	6.8

____

Write the equation in the form of an exponential growth function, $y = a(1 + r)^t$, or an exponential decay function, $y = a(1 \tilde{\ } r)^t$.

3. $y = 1.2(0.85)^t$ ________________________

4. $y = 3.85(1.07)^t$ ________________________

The population of the city of Lincoln over the period from 1970 to 2010 can be modeled by the equation $y = 3.35(1.18)^x$ where x is the number of decades since 1970.

5. Write an equivalent model that represents the *annual* change in population (to two decimal places) over that same period. ________________________

6. Compare the growth rate per decade with the growth rate per year.

____

A scatterplot of a data set and the graph of an exponential model for the data are shown.

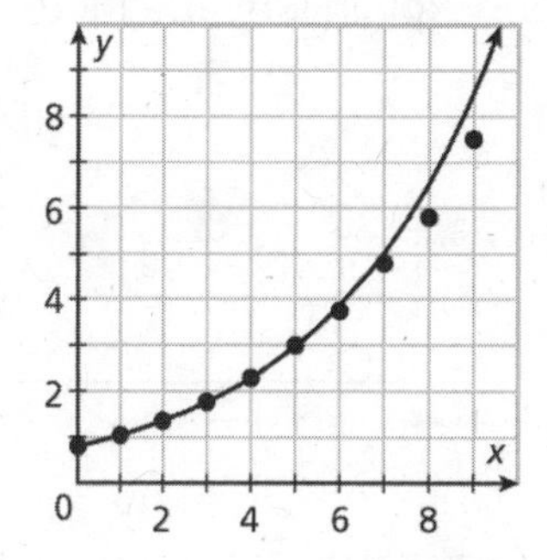

7. Tell whether the model does or does not appear to be a good fit for the data. Explain your reasoning.

____

____

8. Can you use your model to predict the value of y for $x = 15$? Explain why you would or would not want to do so.

____

____

Problem Solving

The table shows the population (in millions) of the state of Georgia according to census results for 1920–2010.

Decades since 1920	Population (in millions)	Decades since 1920	Population (in millions)
0	2.90	5	4.59
1	2.91	6	5.46
2	3.12	7	6.48
3	3.44	8	8.19
4	3.94	9	9.69

1. Use a graphing calculator to find the exponential regression equation for the data. Round the values of *a* and *b* to two decimal places. ________________
2. Rewrite your equation from Exercise 1 so that it demonstrates the growth rate per decade. ________________
3. What is the growth rate per *year* (to two decimal places)? ________________

The coordinate grid shows a scatterplot of the data.

4. Use the grid to graph your equation from Exercise 1.
5. Explain why the model is or is not a good fit for the data.

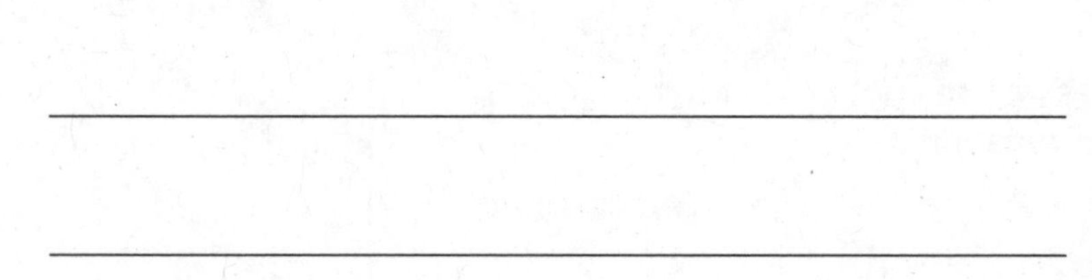

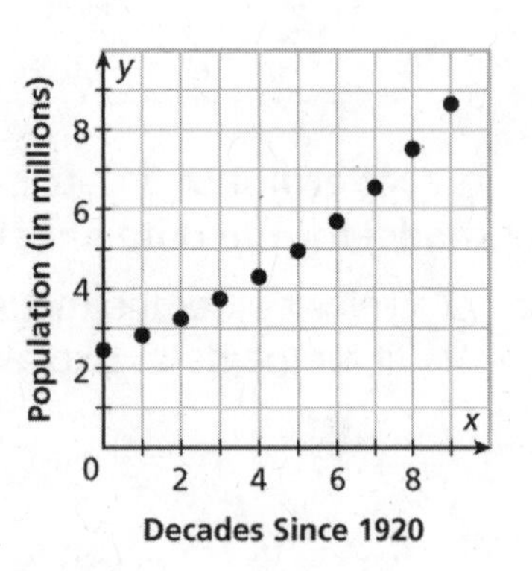

Use the table above and your answers to Exercises 1–5. Choose the letter for the best answer.

6. Use your graph to predict the population of Georgia in 1995.
   A 7 million
   B 9 million
   C 70 million
   D 90 million

7. Use the table and your equation to approximate the residual for 1960.
   F 0.36
   G 0.23
   H −0.23
   J −0.36

Name________________________ Class______________ Date__________

19-2

Comparing Functions

Going Deeper

Essential question: *How can you compare two different functions each presented in a different way?*

MCC9-12.F.IF.9

Video Tutor

1 EXAMPLE Identifying and Comparing Functions

Classify each of the functions *f* and *h* shown below. Then compare any maxima and minima, and the intervals where the graphs are increasing or decreasing.

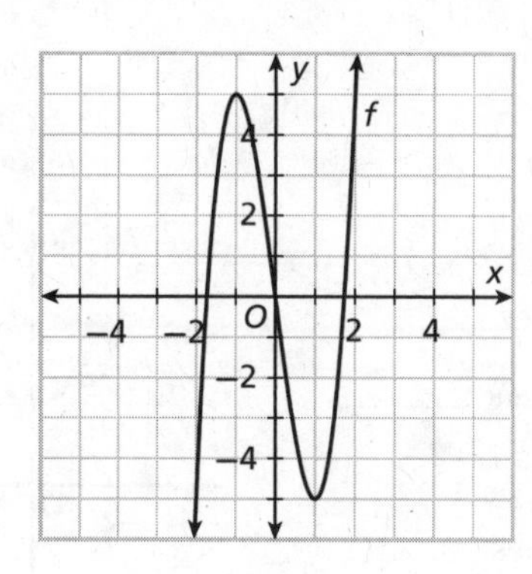

x	$h(x)$
−5	4
−2	2
1	0
4	−2

A Graph h on the same set of axes as f. Connect the points with a smooth line or curve.

The graph shows that f is a ______________, ______________ function and that h is a ______________ function.

B f has a local maximum at ______________ and a local minimum at ______________. The function increases for x-values from negative infinity to ______, ______________ for x-values from -1 to ______, then ______________ for x-values from ______ to ______________.

h has ______ minima or maxima. The function ______________ for x-values from ______________ to ______________.

REFLECT

1a. Could you have used tables to compare f and h? Is there an advantage to using graphs instead?

____

1b. What type of function is $g(x) = (x - 1)^2$? Compare any maxima and minima of g to those for the function f in Explore 1.

____

____

MCC9–12.F.LE.3

2 EXPLORE Identifying Functions and Comparing End Behavior

A Classify functions f and g.

x	−1	0	1	2	3	4
$f(x)$	0.5	1	2	4	8	16

$g(x) = x^2 + 2$

The table for f shows that changes in x are constant, and the ratios of the values of $f(x)$ are constant, so f is ________________.

g is ________________ because the function rule is written in the form

________________.

B Graph both functions and investigate their end behavior.

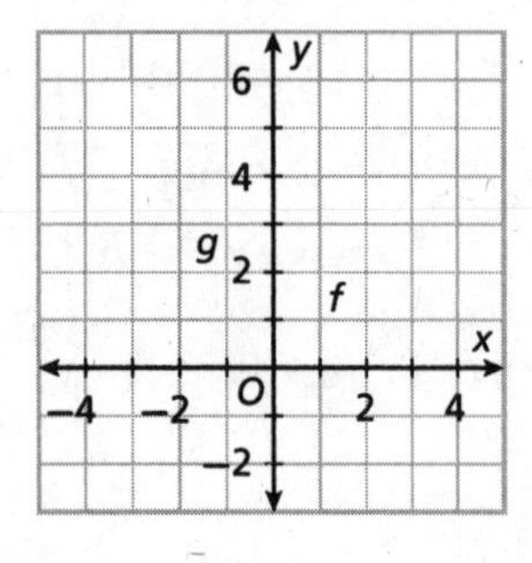

End behavior of f:

As x approaches positive infinity ($x \to +\infty$), $f(x)$ approaches ________.

As x approaches negative infinity ($x \to -\infty$), $f(x)$ approaches ________.

End behavior of g:

As x approaches positive infinity ($x \to +\infty$), $g(x)$ approaches ________.

As x approaches negative infinity ($x \to -\infty$), $g(x)$ approaches ________.

REFLECT

2a. In Explore 2, is $f(x)$ always less than $g(x)$? Explain.

PRACTICE

1. Classify each of the functions shown below. Then compare the end behavior of the functions.

$j(x) = \frac{1}{x} + 3$

The function k has constant first differences of −2 and a y-intercept at (0, 3).

Name________________ Class________ Date________

Additional Practice

Compare the end behavior for each pair of functions.

1. $f(x) = x^4 - x^2 + 4x$ and $g(x) = -5x + 2$

____

2. $f(x) = x^3$ and $g(x) = -x^2$

____

3. $f(x) = -x^4 - 3x^3$ and $g(x) = \sqrt{x}$

____

4. $f(x) = \frac{1}{x}$ and $g(x) = x\ln 2$

____

Determine which function matches the graphical representation shown.

5.

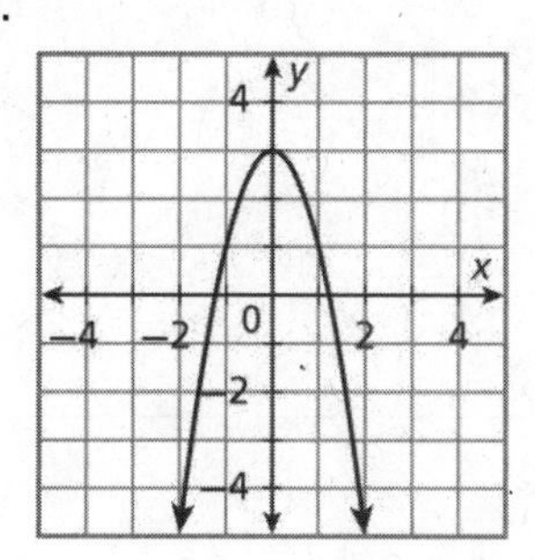

____

6.

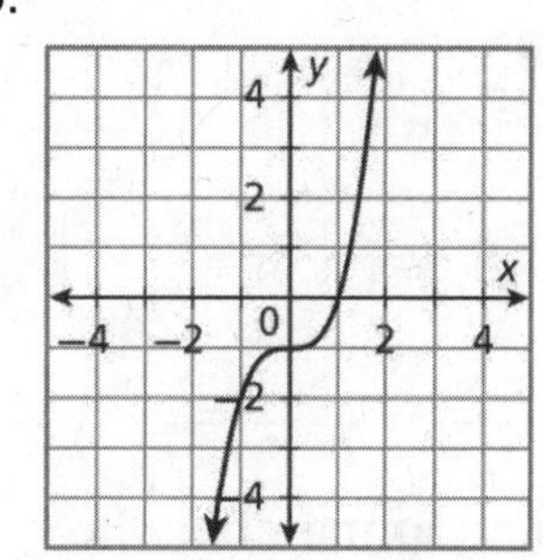

____

7. Find the average rate of change for the data in the following chart, over the given range.

x	2	4	6	8	10	12	14
y	1.5	6	10.5	15	19.5	24	28.5

____

Problem Solving

Sketch the graph of the function.

1. The quadratic function passes through points (–2, 0) and (2, 0). Find the point that represents the vertex.

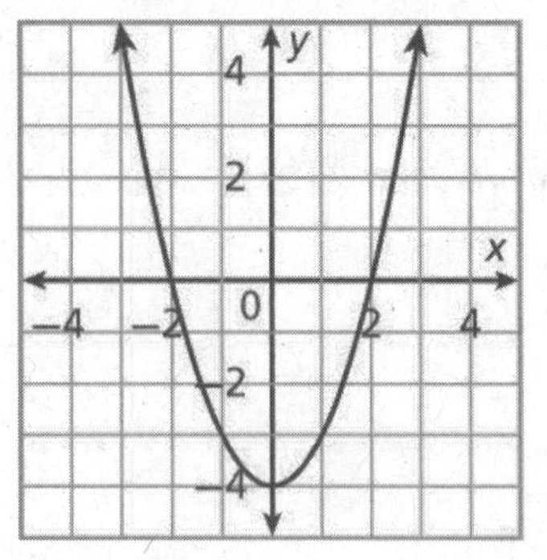

Solution:
Step 1: Plot the zeros.
Step 2: Find the vertex.
$(x + 2)(x - 2) = x^2 - 4$
vertex: (0, -4)
Step3: Sketch the graph.

2. The cubic function passes through points (–2, 16), (–1, 2), (1, –2), and (2, –16). Find the point that represents the zero.

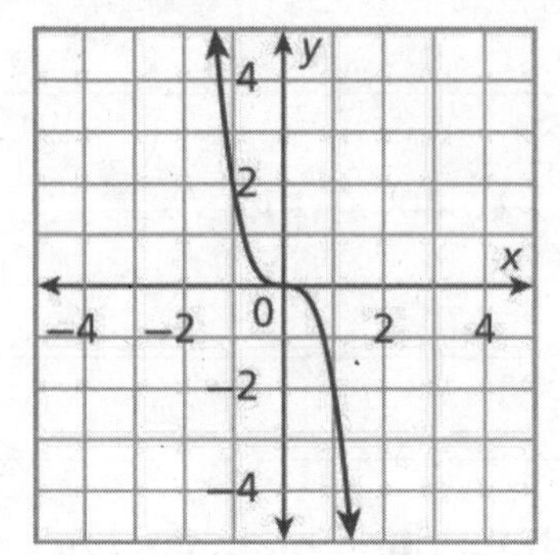

Determine which function matches the graph shown.

3.

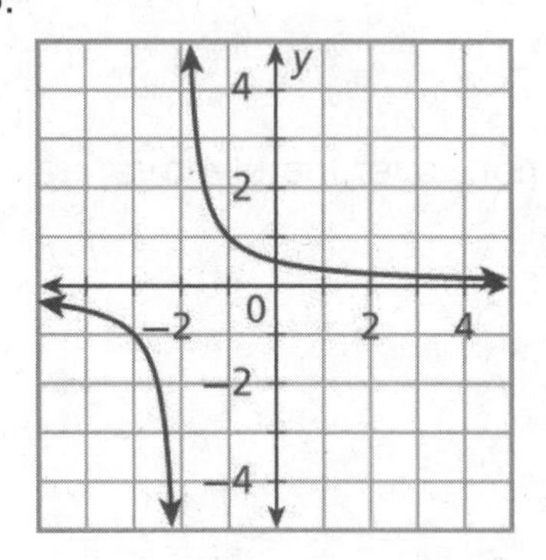

A $y = \ln x$

B $y = \log x$

C $y = \dfrac{1}{x+2}$

4.

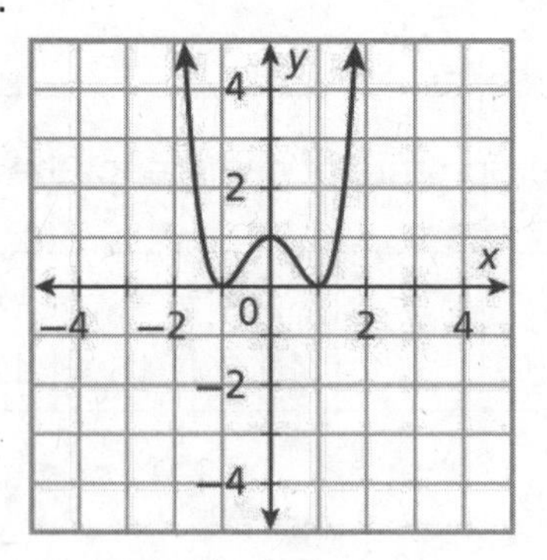

F $y = x^2 + 1$

G $y = x^2 - 2x + 1$

H $y = x^4 - 2x^2 + 1$

Name________________________ Class______________ Date__________

19-3

Piecewise Functions

Going Deeper

Video Tutor

Essential question: *How are piecewise functions and step functions different from other functions?*

A **piecewise function** is a function whose definition changes over different parts of its domain. The **greatest integer function** is a piecewise function whose rule is denoted by $[\![x]\!]$, which represents the greatest integer less than or equal to x. To evaluate a piecewise function for a given value of x, substitute the value of x into the rule for the part of the domain that includes x.

MCC9-12.F.IF.2

1 EXAMPLE Evaluating Piecewise Functions

A **Find $f(-3), f(-0.2), f(0)$, and $f(2)$ for $f(x) = \begin{cases} -x & \text{if } x < 0 \\ x+1 & \text{if } x \geq 0 \end{cases}$.**

$-3 < 0$, so use the rule $f(x) = -x$: $f(-3) = -(-3) =$ ________

$-0.2 < 0$, so use the rule ____________: $f(-0.2) = -(-0.2) =$ ________

$0 \geq 0$, so use the rule $f(x) = x + 1$: $f(0) = 0 + 1 =$ ________

$2 \geq 0$, so use the rule ____________: $f(2) =$ ________ $=$ ________

B **Find $f(-3), f(-2.9), f(0.7)$, and $f(1.06)$ for $f(x) = [\![x]\!]$.**

The greatest integer function $f(x) = [\![x]\!]$ can also be written as shown below. Complete the rules for the function before evaluating it.

$$f(x) = \begin{cases} \vdots & \\ -3 & \text{if } -3 \leq x < -2 \\ \square & \text{if } -2 \leq x < -1 \\ -1 & \text{if } \square \leq x < \square \\ \square & \text{if } 0 \leq x < 1 \\ 1 & \text{if } \square \leq x < \square \\ 2 & \text{if } \square \leq x < \square \\ \vdots & \end{cases}$$

For any number x that is less than -2 and greater than or equal to -3, the greatest of the integers less than or equal to x is -3.

-3 is in the interval $-3 \leq x < -2$, so $f(-3) = -3$.

-2.9 is in the interval $-3 \leq x < -2$, so $f(-2.9) =$ ____________.

0.7 is in the interval ____________, so $f(0.7) =$ ____________.

1.06 is in the interval ____________, so $f(1.06) =$ ____________.

REFLECT

1a. Why should the parts of the domain of a piecewise function $f(x)$ have no common x-values?

1b. For positive numbers, how is applying the greatest integer function different from the method of rounding to the nearest whole number?

MCC9–12.F.IF.7b

2 EXAMPLE Graphing Piecewise Functions

Graph each function.

A $f(x) = \begin{cases} -x & \text{if } x < 0 \\ x + 1 & \text{if } x \geq 0 \end{cases}$

Complete the table. Use the values to help you complete the graph. Extend the pattern to cover the entire domain on the grid.

x	−3	−2	−1	−0.9	−0.1
f(x)	3	2		0.9	

x	0	0.1	0.9	1	2
f(x)	1	1.1			3

The transition from one rule, $-x$, to the other, $x + 1$, occurs at $x = 0$. Show an open dot at (0, 0) because the point is not part of the graph. Show a closed dot at (0, 1) because the point is part of the graph.

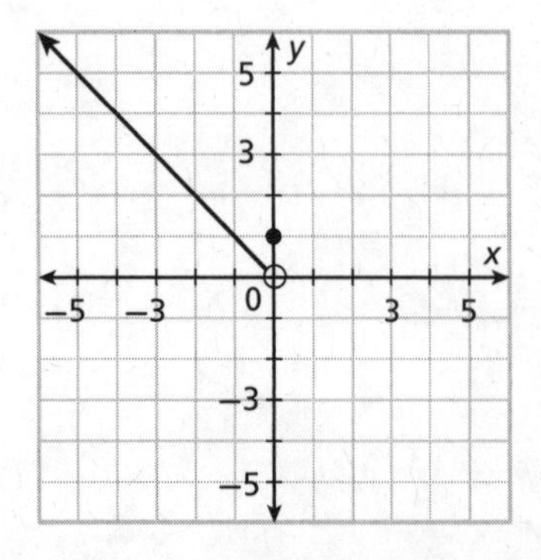

B $f(x) = [\![x]\!]$

Complete the table. Use the values to help you complete the graph. Extend the pattern to cover the entire domain on the grid.

x	−4	−3.9	−3.1	−3	−2.9
f(x)	−4	−4		−3	

x	−2.1	−2	−1.5	−1	0
f(x)		−2			0

x	1	1.5	2	3	4
f(x)					4

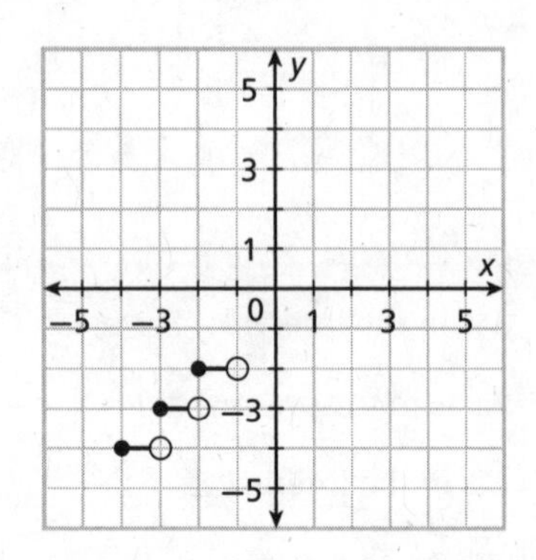

REFLECT

2a. Why does the first graph use rays and not lines?

2b. The greatest integer function is an example of a **step function**, a piecewise function that is constant for each rule. Use the graph of the greatest integer function to explain why such a function is called a step function.

2c. Does the greatest integer function have a maximum or minimum value? Explain.

MCC9–12.F.BF.1

3 EXAMPLE Writing and Graphing a Piecewise Function

On his way to class from his dorm room, a college student walks at a speed of 0.05 mile per minute for 3 minutes, stops to talk to a friend for 1 minute, and then to avoid being late for class, runs at a speed of 0.10 mile per minute for 2 minutes. Write a piecewise function for the student's distance from his dorm room during this time. Then graph the function.

A Express the student's distance traveled d (in miles) as a function of time t (in minutes). Write an equation for the function $d(t)$.

$$d(t) = \begin{cases} \_\_\_\_ t & \text{if } 0 \le t \le 3 \\ 0.15 & \text{if } 3 < t \le \_\_\_\_ \\ 0.15 + 0.10(t - 4) & \text{if } 4 < t \le \_\_\_\_ \end{cases}$$

← He travels at 0.05 mile per minute for 3 minutes.

← Distance traveled is constant for 1 minute.

← Add the distance traveled at 0.10 mile per minute to the distance already traveled.

B Complete the table.

t	0	1	2	3
d(t)				

t	4	5	6
d(t)			

C Complete the graph.

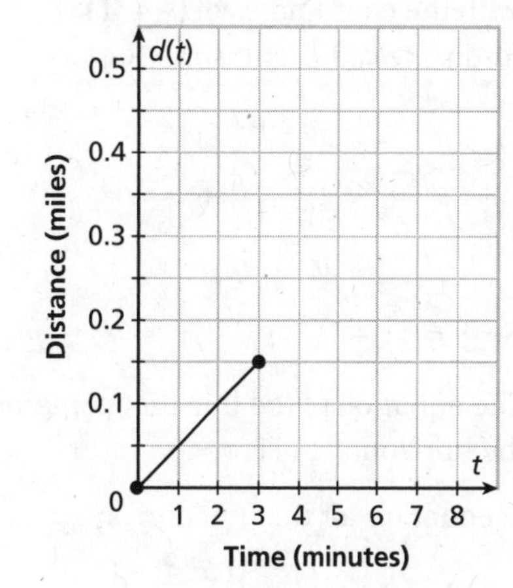

REFLECT

3a. Why is the second rule for the function $d(t) = 0.15$ instead of $d(t) = 0$?

____

3b. Why is the third rule for the function $d(t) = 0.15 + 0.10(t - 4)$?

____

____

MCC9–12.F.IF.5

4 EXAMPLE Writing a Function When Given a Graph

Write the equation for each function whose graph is shown.

A

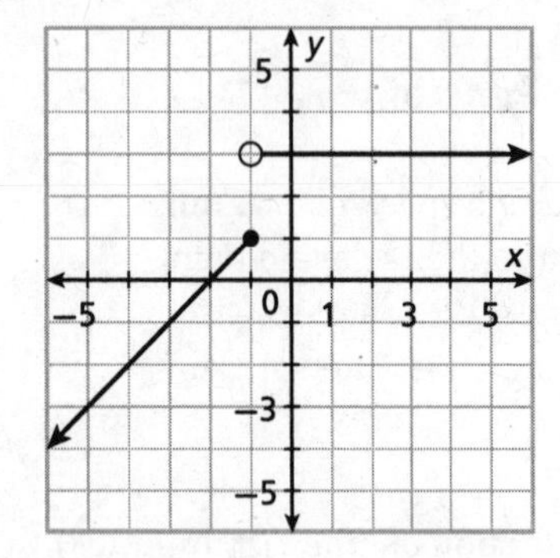

Find the equation for each ray:

- Find the slope m of the line that contains the ray on the left. Use $(-4, -2)$ and $(-1, 1)$.

$$m = \frac{1 - (\quad)}{-1 - (\quad)} = \frac{3}{3} = 1$$

Substitute this value of m along with the coordinates of $(-1, 1)$ into $y = mx + b$ and solve for b.

$$y = mx + b$$

$$\quad = 1(\quad) + b$$

$$\quad = b$$

So, $y = 1x + \quad$.

- The equation of the line that contains the horizontal ray is $y = \quad$.

The equation for the function is:

$$f(x) = \begin{cases} \quad & \text{if } x \le -1 \\ \quad & \text{if } x > -1 \end{cases}$$

B

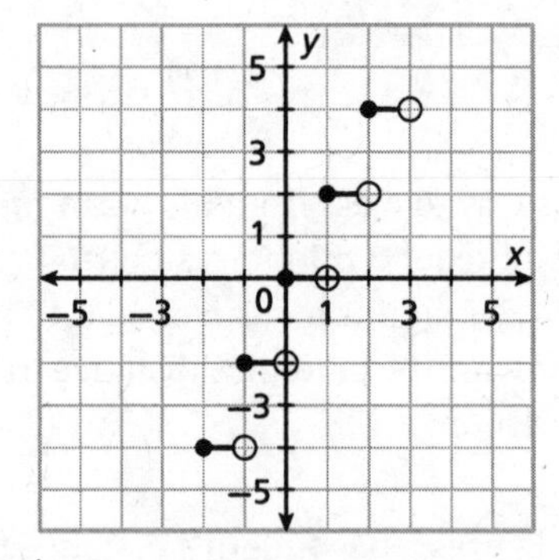

Write a rule for each horizontal line segment.

$$f(x) = \begin{cases} -4 & \text{if } -2 \le x < -1 \\ \quad & \text{if } -1 \le x < 0 \\ 0 & \text{if } 0 \le x < 1 \\ \quad & \text{if } 1 \le x < 2 \\ \quad & \text{if } 2 \le x < 3 \end{cases}$$

Although the graph shows the function's domain to be $-2 \le x < 3$, assume that the domain consists of all real numbers and that the graph continues its stair-step pattern for $x < -2$ and $x \ge 3$.

Notice that each function value is ________ times the corresponding value of the greatest integer function.

The equation for the function is:

$$f(x) = \quad [\![x]\!]$$

REFLECT

4a. When writing a piecewise function from a graph, how do you determine the domain of each rule?

4b. How can you use y-intercepts to check that your answer in part A is reasonable?

PRACTICE

Graph each function.

1. $f(x) = \begin{cases} -x + 1 & \text{if } x < 0 \\ x & \text{if } x \geq 0 \end{cases}$

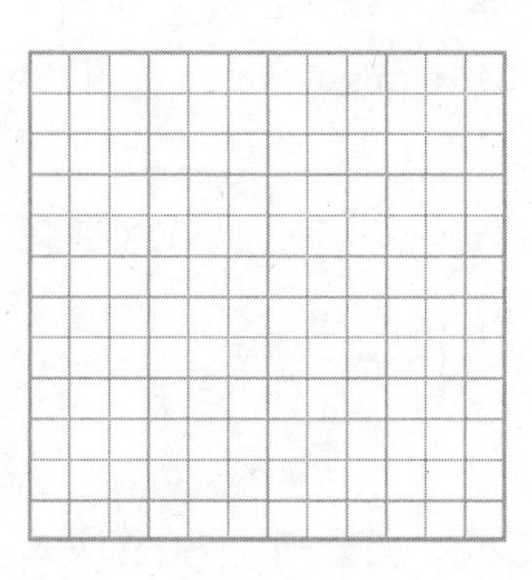

2. $f(x) = \begin{cases} -1 & \text{if } x < 1 \\ 2x - 2 & \text{if } x \geq 1 \end{cases}$

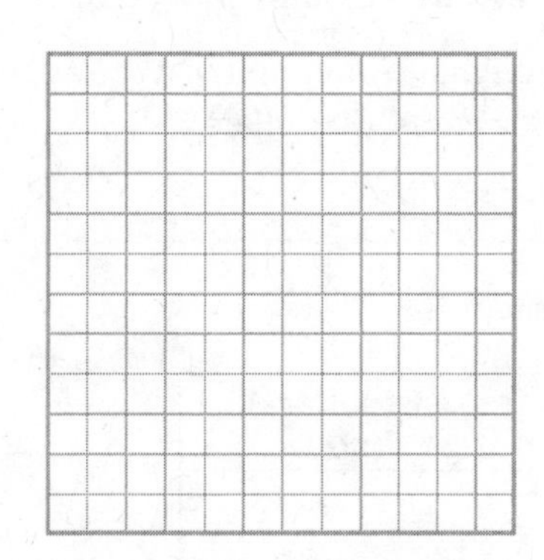

3. $f(x) = [\![x]\!] + 1$

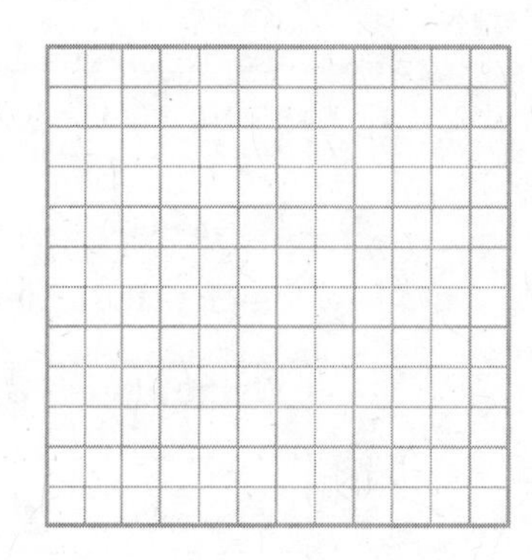

Write the equation for each function whose graph is shown.

4.

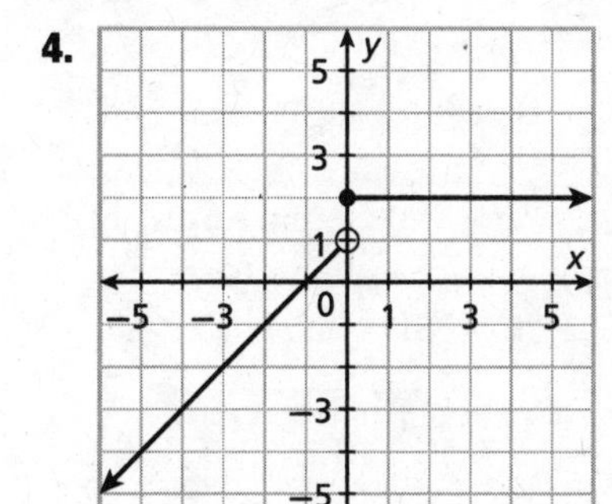

5.

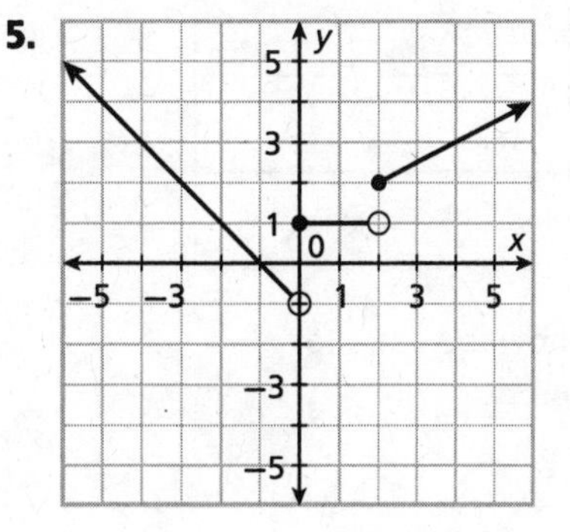

6.

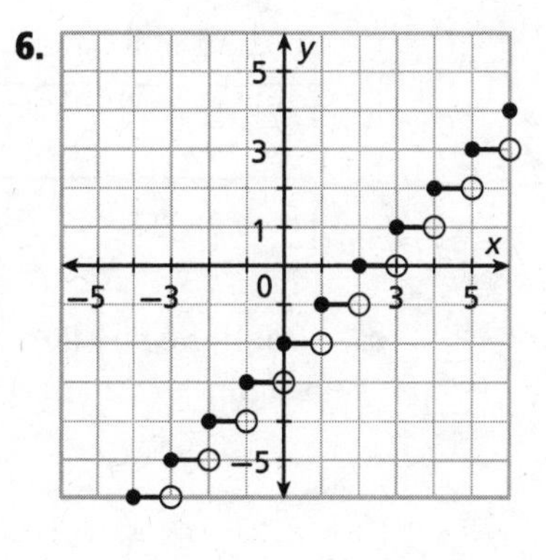

---

7. A garage charges the following rates for parking (with an 8 hour limit):

$4 per hour for the first 2 hours

$2 per hour for the next 4 hours

No additional charge for the next 2 hours

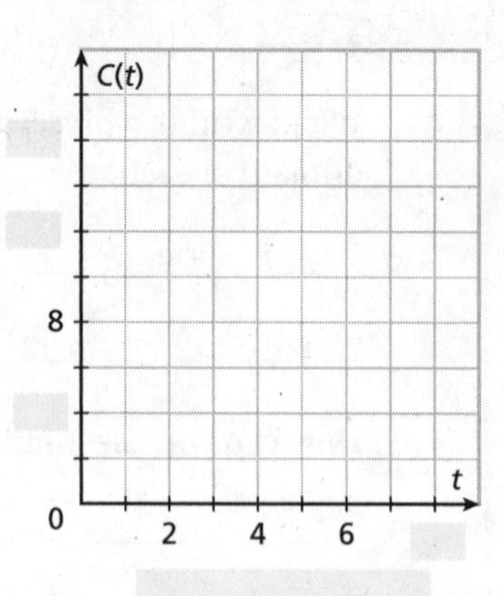

a. Write a piecewise function that gives the parking cost C (in dollars) in terms of the time t (in hours) that a car is parked in the garage.

____

b. Graph the function. Include labels to show what the axes represent and to show the scales on the axes.

8. The cost to send a package between two cities is $8.00 for any weight less than 1 pound. The cost increases by $4.00 when the weight reaches 1 pound and again each time the weight reaches a whole number of pounds after that.

a. For a package having weight w (in pounds), write a function in terms of $[\![w]\!]$ to represent the shipping cost C (in dollars).

____

b. Complete the table.

Weight (pounds) w	Cost (dollars) $C(w)$
0.5	
1	
1.5	
2	
2.5	

c. Graph the function. Show the costs for all weights less than 5 pounds.

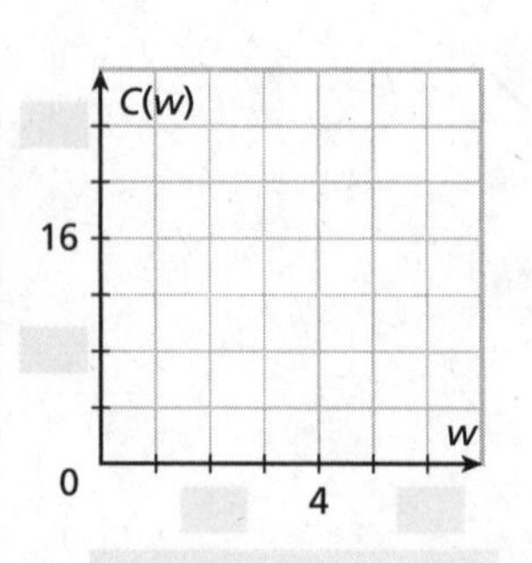

Name______________________ Class______________ Date__________

19-3

Additional Practice

Evaluate each piecewise function for $x = -8$ and $x = 5$.

1. $f(x)=\begin{cases} 2x & \text{if } x<0 \\ 0 & \text{if } x\ge 0 \end{cases}$

____

2. $g(x)=\begin{cases} 2-x & \text{if } x\le 5 \\ -x^2 & \text{if } 5<x<8 \\ 6 & \text{if } 8\le x \end{cases}$

____

3. $h(x)=\begin{cases} 2x+4 & \text{if } x\le -8 \\ -1 & \text{if } -8<x<5 \\ x^2 & \text{if } 5\le x \end{cases}$

____

4. $k(x)=\begin{cases} 15 & \text{if } x\le -5 \\ x & \text{if } -5<x<1 \\ 7-\dfrac{x}{2} & \text{if } 1<x \end{cases}$

____

Graph each function.

5. $f(x)=\begin{cases} 6 & \text{if } x<-2 \\ 3x & \text{if } -2\le x \end{cases}$

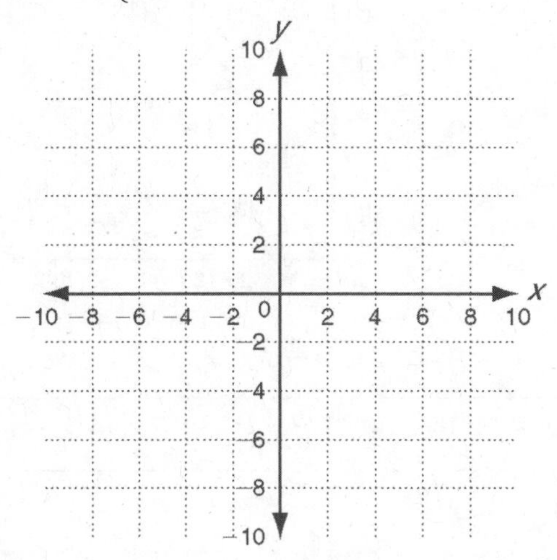

6. $g(x)=\begin{cases} 12-x & \text{if } x\le 5 \\ x+2 & \text{if } 5<x \end{cases}$

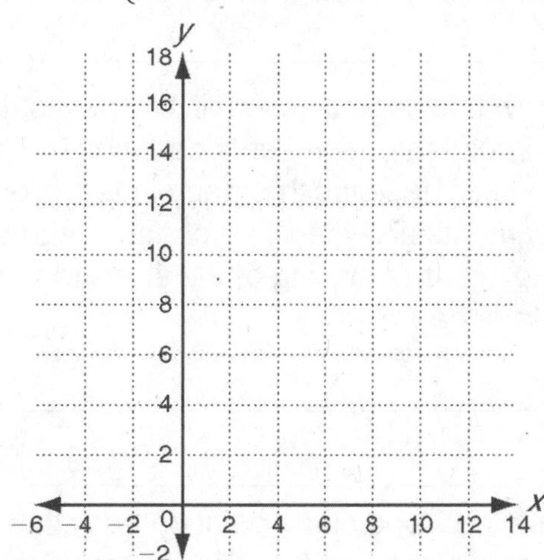

Solve.

7. An airport parking garage costs \$20 per day for the first week. After that, the cost decreases to \$17 per day.

   a. Write a piecewise function for the cost of parking a car for x days. _______________________

   b. What is the cost to park for 10 days? _______________________

   c. Ms. Anderson went on two trips. On the first, she parked at the garage for 5 days; on the second, she parked at the garage for 8 days. What was the difference in the cost of parking between the two trips? _______________________

Problem Solving

Roscoe earns $9.50 per hour at the woodcrafts store for up to 40 hours per week. For each hour over 40 hours he earns $13.00 per hour. Company policy limits his hours to no more than 60 per week. Roscoe wants to know how much he can earn in a week.

1. Complete the table to show his earnings for 30, 40, 50, and 60 hours per week.

Hours per Week (t)	Roscoe's Earnings, $E(t)$				
	Hours ≤ 40 ($9.50 per h)		Hours > 40 ($13.00 per h)		Total Earnings
30	30	$285	0	$0	$285
40					
50					
60					

2. Graph earnings as a function of hours worked, using the data from the table. Roscoe thinks the points lie in a straight line. Is he correct?

____

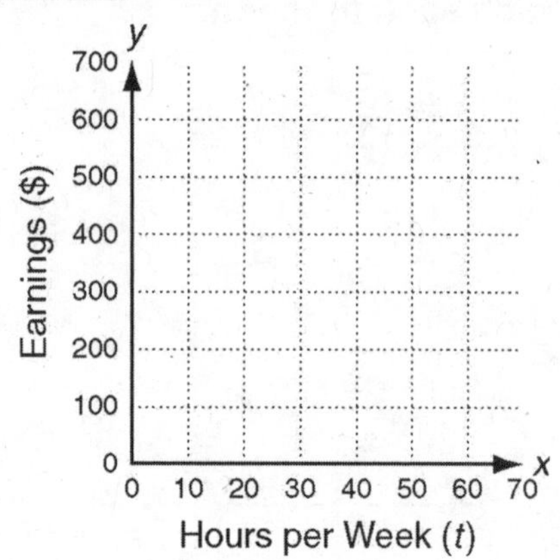

3. Draw line segments to join the points, including the point that represents earnings for 0 hours worked. Describe the graph in terms of line segments and the slope of each segment. Explain the meaning of the slope in terms of rate of pay.

____

____

4. Use the slope and a point on each line segment to write a piecewise function for earnings $E(t)$ as a function of hours worked (t). ______________________________

Choose the letter for the best answer.

5. How much will Roscoe earn if he works 56.5 hours in one week?

A $594.50

B $610.00

C $625.50

D $734.50

6. Roscoe earned $471 last week. How many hours did he work?

F 45

G 47

H 49

J 51

Name________________________ Class______________ Date__________

20-1

Transforming Polynomial Functions

Going Deeper

Essential question: *What are the effects of the constants a, h, and k on the graph of $f(x) = a(x - h)^n + k$?*

Video Tutor

In this lesson, you will explore transformations of the graph of $f(x) = x^n$. First, you will focus on translations.

MCC9–12.F.BF.3

1 EXAMPLE Graphing $f(x) = x^n + k$

Graph each function.

A $g(x) = x^4 - 1$

Complete the table of values and use it to help you graph the function. The graph of the parent function $f(x) = x^4$ is shown.

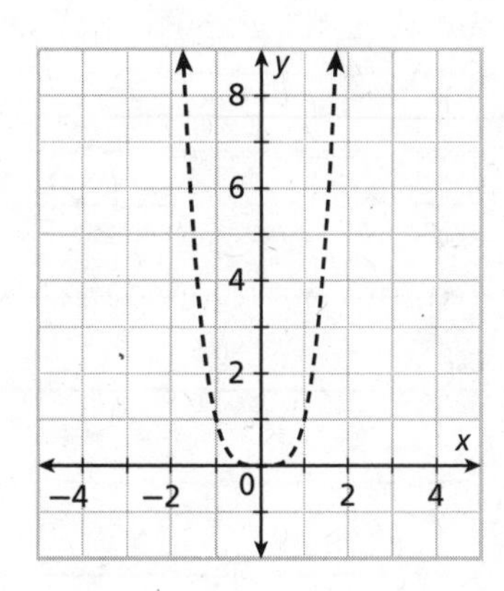

x	$g(x)$
−2	
−1	
0	
1	
2	

B $h(x) = x^3 + 2$

Complete the table of values and use it to help you graph the function. The graph of the parent function $f(x) = x^3$ is shown.

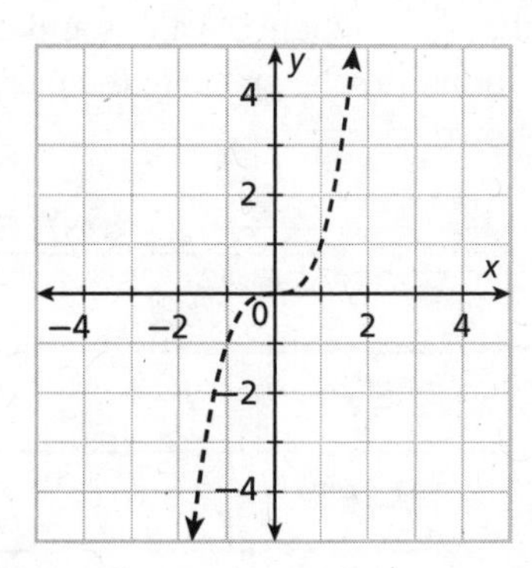

x	$h(x)$
−2	
−1	
0	
1	
2	

REFLECT

1a. How is the graph of $g(x)$ related to the graph of its parent function?

1b. How is the graph of $h(x)$ related to the graph of its parent function?

1c. In general, how do you think the graph of $j(x) = x^n + k$ is related to the graph of its parent function?

MCC9–12.F.BF.3

2 EXAMPLE Graphing $f(x) = (x - h)^n$

Graph each function.

A $g(x) = (x - 3)^4$

Complete the table of values and use it to help you graph the function. The graph of the parent function $f(x) = x^4$ is shown.

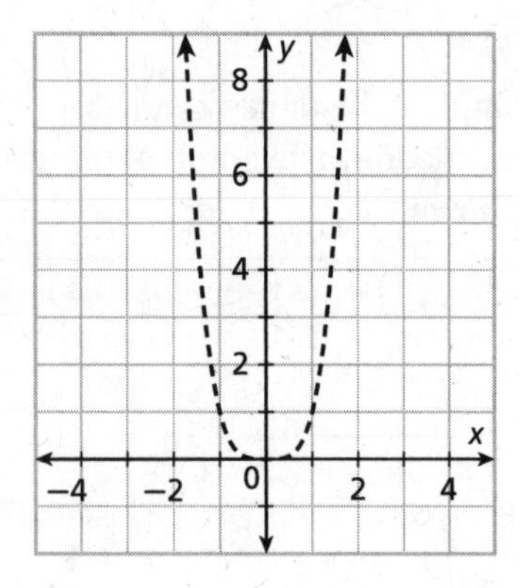

x	$g(x)$
1	
2	
3	
4	
5	

B $h(x) = (x + 1)^3$

Complete the table of values and use it to help you graph the function. The graph of the parent function $f(x) = x^3$ is shown.

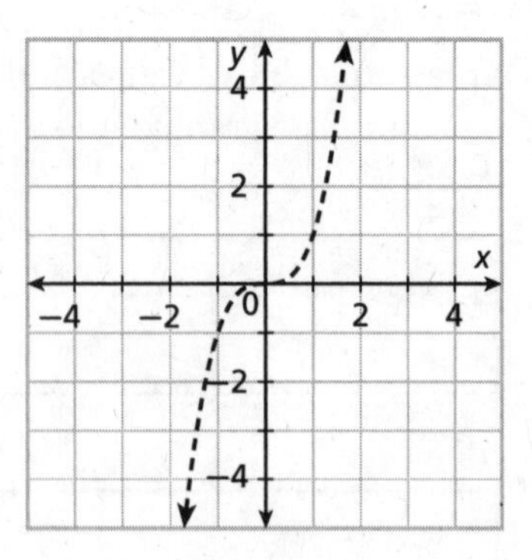

x	$h(x)$
–3	
–2	
–1	
0	
1	

REFLECT

2a. How is the graph of $g(x)$ related to the graph of its parent function?

2b. How is the graph of $h(x)$ related to the graph of its parent function?

2c. In general, how do you think the graph of $j(x) = (x - h)^n$ is related to the graph of its parent function?

MCC9–12.F.BF.3

3 EXAMPLE Graphing $f(x) = (x - h)^n + k$

Graph $g(x) = (x - 2)^3 + 1$.

A The graph of the parent function, $f(x) = x^3$, is shown. Determine how the graph of $g(x)$ is related to the graph of $f(x)$.

Since $g(x) = (x - 2)^3 + 1$, $h =$ ________ and $k =$ ________.

Complete the table to describe how the graph of the parent function must be translated to obtain the graph of $g(x)$.

Type of Translation	Number of Units	Direction
Horizontal		
Vertical		

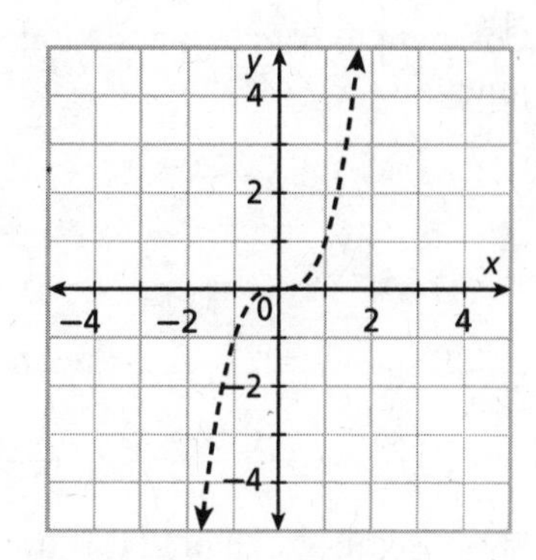

B Use the translations you identified to help you draw the graph of $g(x)$.

REFLECT

3a. Compare the domain and range of $g(x) = (x - 2)^3 + 1$ to the domain and range of the parent function $f(x) = x^3$.

3b. How is the graph of $h(x) = (x + 17)^8 - 6$ related to the graph of $f(x) = x^8$?

MCC9–12.F.BF.3

4 EXAMPLE Writing the Equation of a Function

The graph of $g(x)$ is the graph of $f(x) = x^4$ after a horizontal and vertical translation. Write the equation of $g(x)$.

A Complete the table to describe how the graph of the parent function must be translated to obtain the graph of $g(x)$. (*Hint:* Consider how the "turning point" (0, 0) on the graph of $f(x)$ must be translated to obtain the turning point on the graph of $g(x)$.)

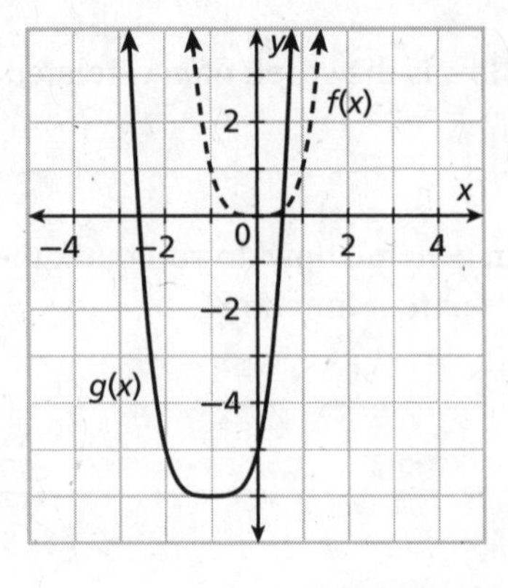

Type of Translation	Number of Units	Direction
Horizontal		
Vertical		

B Determine the values of h and k in the equation $g(x) = (x - h)^4 + k$.

Based on the translations, $h =$ __________ and $k =$ __________.

So, $g(x) =$ ____________________.

REFLECT

4a. Compare the domain and range of $g(x)$ to the domain and range of the parent function $f(x) = x^4$.

4b. Suppose the graph of $g(x)$ is translated 3 units right and 2 units up to give the graph of $h(x)$. Explain how you can write the equation of $h(x)$.

4c. In general, do translations change the end behavior of a function of the form $f(x) = x^n$? Give a specific example.

As you have learned, the values of h and k in the function $f(x) = a(x - h)^n + k$ correspond to a horizontal and vertical translation of the graph of the parent function. Now you will investigate the effects of the constant a.

Graphing $f(x) = ax^n$

Graph each pair of functions.

A $g(x) = \frac{1}{4}x^4$ and $h(x) = -\frac{1}{4}x^4$

Complete the table of values and use it to help you graph the functions. The graph of the parent function $f(x) = x^4$ is shown.

x	*g(x)*	*h(x)*
−2		
−1		
0		
1		
2		

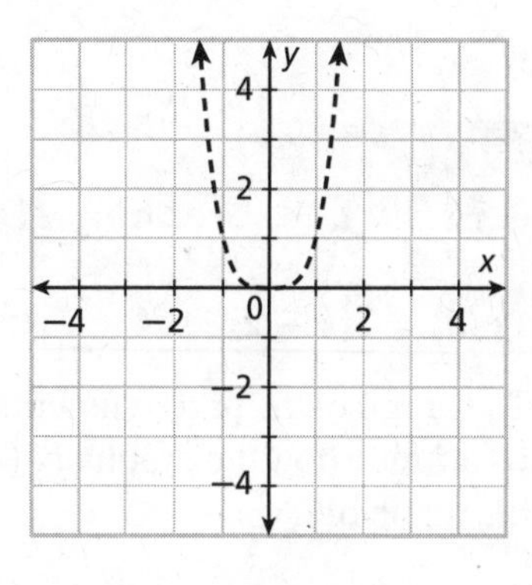

B $g(x) = 2x^3$ and $h(x) = -2x^3$

Complete the table of values and use it to help you graph the functions. The graph of the parent function $f(x) = x^3$ is shown.

x	*g(x)*	*h(x)*
−2		
−1		
0		
1		
2		

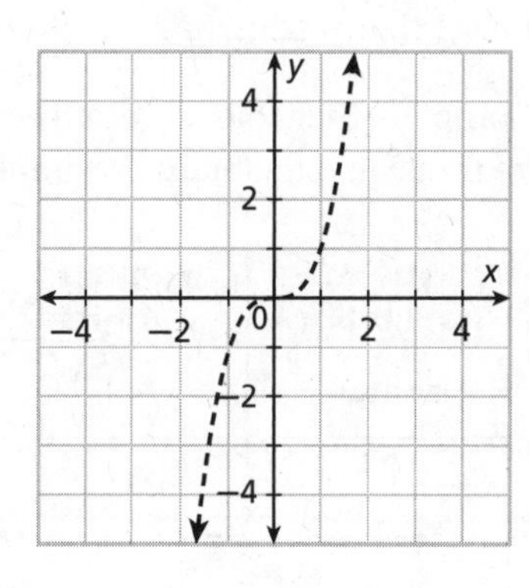

REFLECT

5a. How is the graph of $f(x) = ax^n$ related to the graph of the parent function $f(x) = x^n$ when $a > 1$? when $0 < a < 1$?

5b. How is the graph of $f(x) = ax^n$ related to the graph of the parent function $f(x) = x^n$ when $a < -1$? when $-1 < a < 0$?

5c. How is the end behavior of the graph of $f(x) = ax^n$ related to the end behavior of the graph of the parent function $f(x) = x^n$?

Graphing $f(x) = a(x - h)^n + k$

Graph $g(x) = 3(x - 2)^4 - 4$.

A The graph of the parent function $f(x) = x^4$ is shown. Determine how the graph of $g(x)$ is related to the graph of $f(x)$.

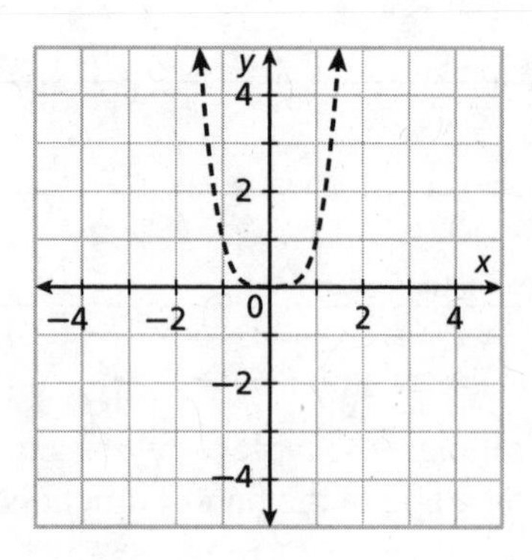

First perform any vertical stretches, shrinks, and reflections.

For $g(x)$, $a =$ __________. The graph of $f(x)$ is stretched vertically and there is no reflection.

B For $g(x)$, $h =$ __________ and $k =$ __________.

Complete the table to describe how the graph of the parent function must be translated to obtain the graph of $g(x)$.

Type of Translation	Number of Units	Direction
Horizontal		
Vertical		

C Use the transformations you identified to help you draw the graph of $g(x)$.

REFLECT

6a. Describe how you think the graph of $g(x) = -0.5(x + 1)^5 - 1$ is related to the graph of the parent function $f(x) = x^5$. Check your prediction by graphing the functions on your calculator.

7 EXAMPLE Writing the Equation of a Function

The graph of $g(x)$ is the graph of $f(x) = x^3$ after a series of transformations. Write the equation of $g(x)$.

A Complete the table to describe how the graph of the parent function must be translated to obtain the graph of $g(x)$. (*Hint:* Consider how the "symmetry point" (0, 0) on the graph of $f(x)$ must be translated to obtain the symmetry point on the graph of $g(x)$.)

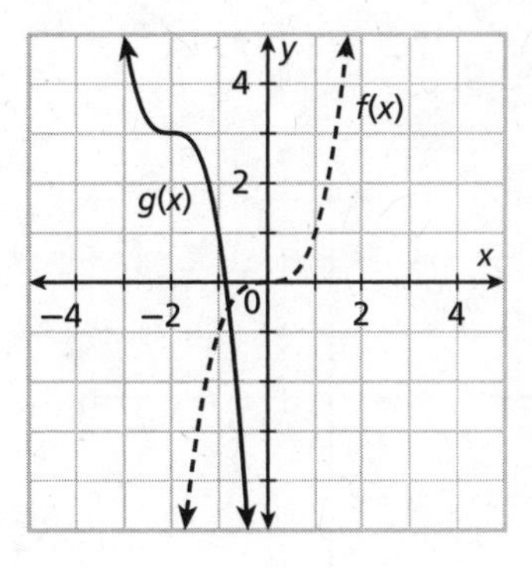

Type of Translation	Number of Units	Direction
Horizontal		
Vertical		

So, $h =$ __________ and $k =$ __________.

B Determine the value of a in the equation $g(x) = a(x - h)^3 + k$.

The image of the point (0, 0) is __________.

The image of the point (1, 1) is __________.

The vertical distance between (0, 0) and (1, 1) is 1 unit.

The vertical distance between the images of (0, 0) and (1, 1) is __________ units.

This means that $|a| =$ __________.

The graph of the parent function is reflected across the x-axis, so a __________ 0.

So, the value of a is __________.

C Use the values of h, k, and a to write the equation: $g(x) =$ ______________________________.

REFLECT

7a. The graph of $g(x)$ contains (−3, 5). Check that your equation from part C is correct by showing that (−3, 5) satisfies the equation.

____

____

7b. Suppose the graph of $g(x)$ is translated 4 units right and 5 units down to give the graph of $h(x)$. What is the equation of $h(x)$?

____

7c. The transformation of $f(x)$ into $g(x)$ above involved all of translation, reflection, and stretching. Would it change the final equation to perform these transformations in a different order? Why or why not?

____

PRACTICE

Graph each function.

1. $f(x) = x^3 - 2$

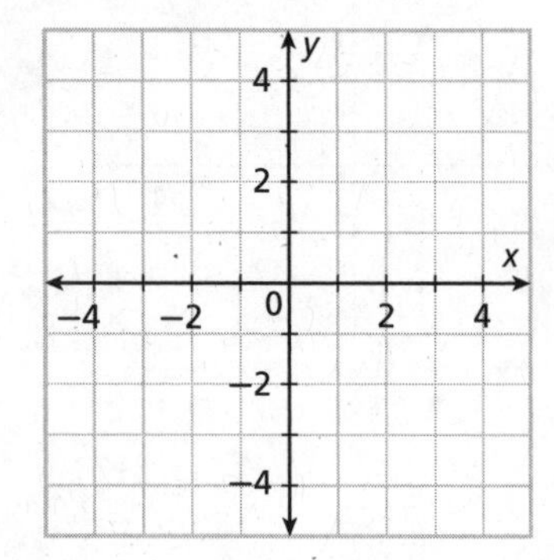

2. $f(x) = x^6 + 1$

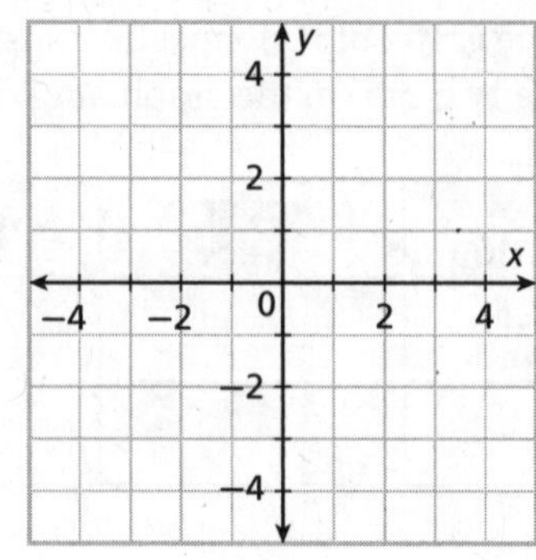

3. $f(x) = (x + 2)^4$

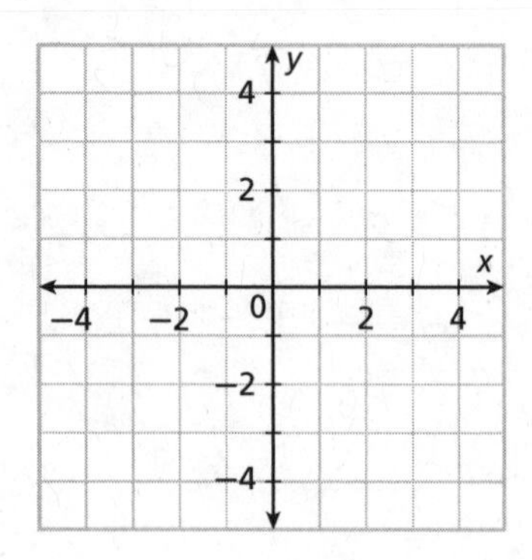

4. $f(x) = (x - 3)^5$

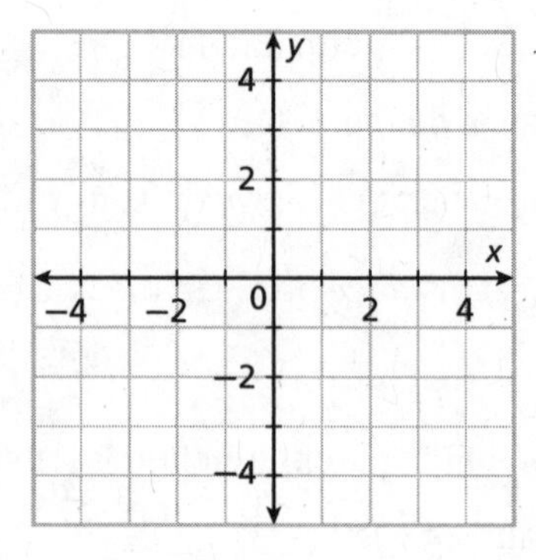

5. $f(x) = (x - 1)^4 + 2$

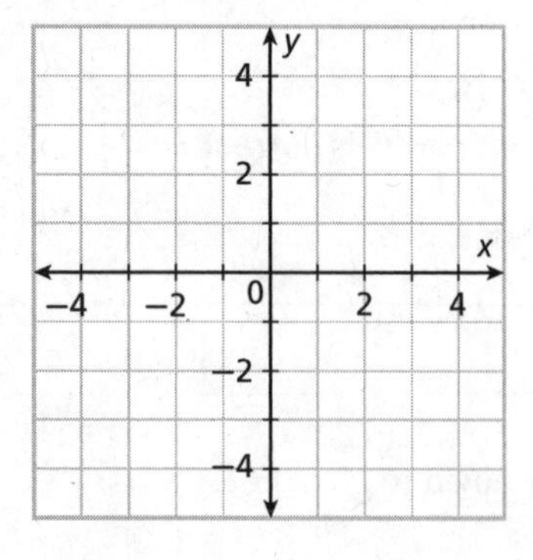

6. $f(x) = (x + 2)^3 - 2$

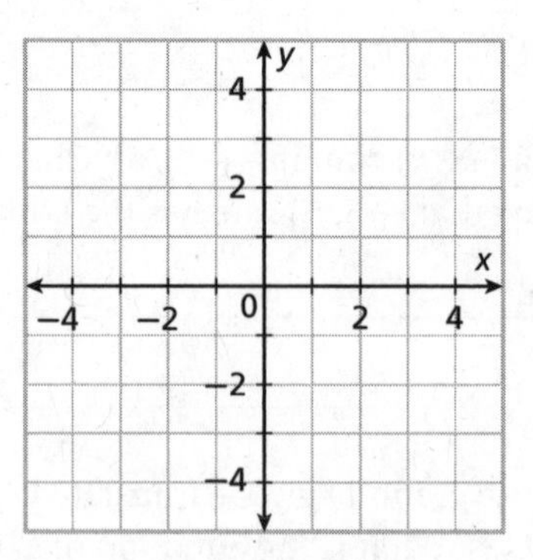

7. Without graphing, explain how the graph of $g(x) = (x - 5)^7 - 1.3$ is related to the graph of $f(x) = x^7$.

Graph each function.

8. $f(x) = 2x^4$

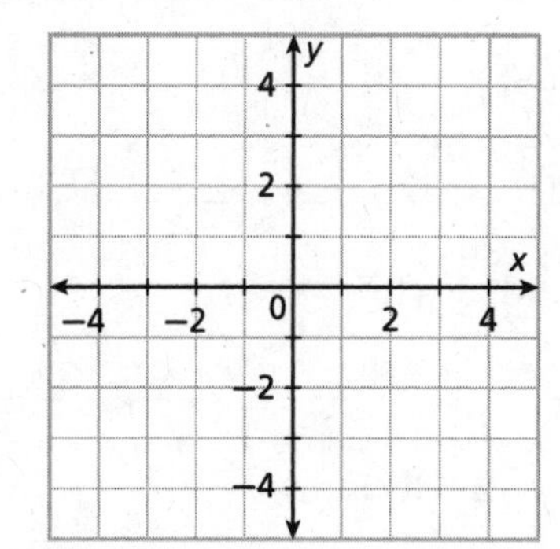

9. $f(x) = -\frac{1}{2}x^3$

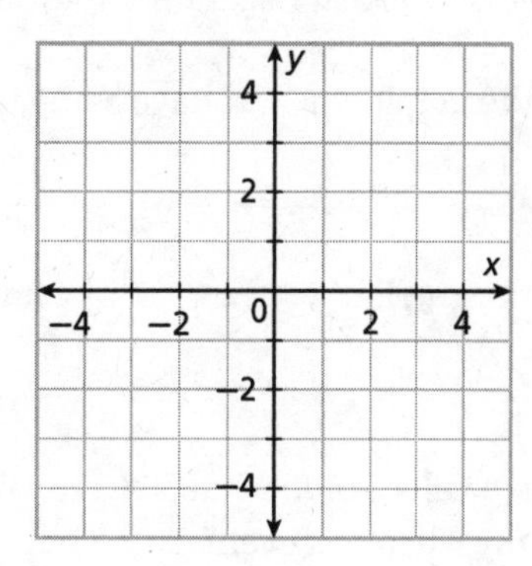

10. $f(x) = -(x - 3)^4 + 1$

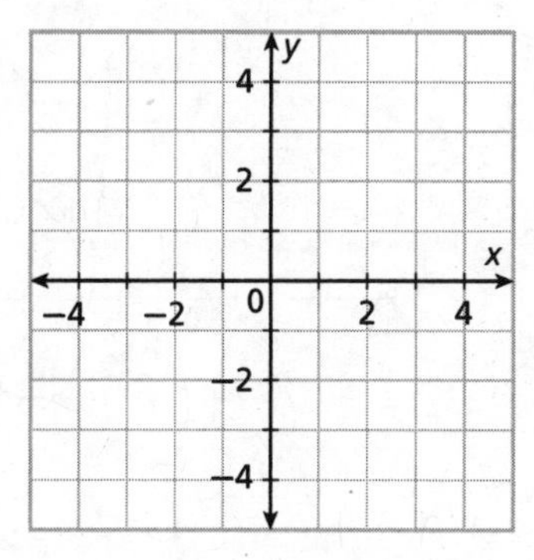

11. $f(x) = 2(x + 1)^3 - 2$

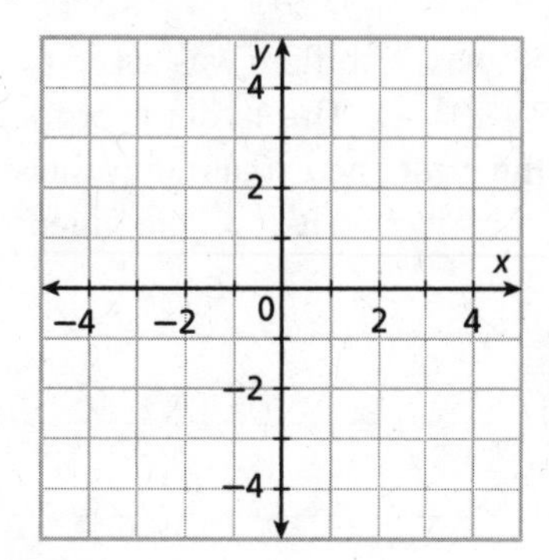

The graph of $g(x)$ is the graph of $f(x) = x^3$ after a horizontal and vertical translation. Write the equation of $g(x)$.

12.

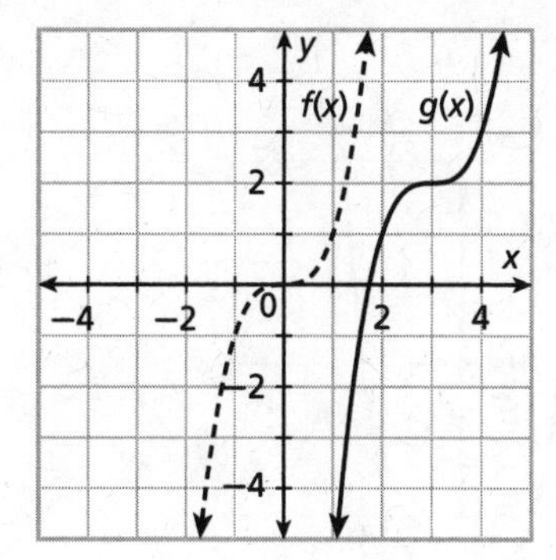

____

13.

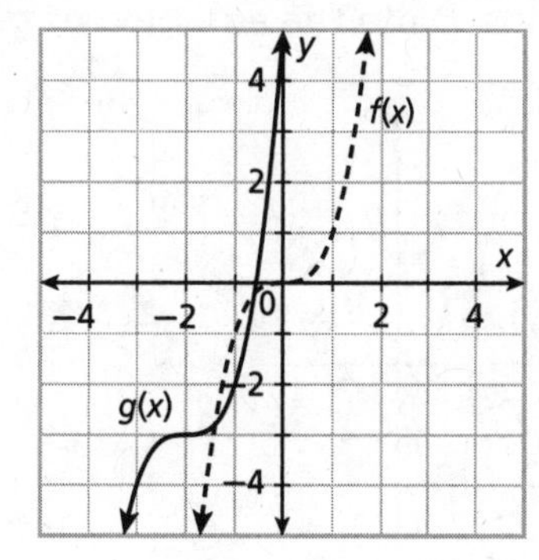

____

14. Suppose you translate the graph of $y = (x - 2)^5 - 7$ left 4 units and up 3 units. What is the equation of the resulting graph?

____

15. A turning point on the graph of a function is a point where the graph changes from increasing to decreasing, or from decreasing to increasing. A turning point corresponds to a local maximum or local minimum.

a. Does the graph of $y = x^4$ have a turning point? If so, what is it?

b. Does the graph of $y = (x + 5)^4 + 4$ have a turning point? If so, what is it?

c. For even values of n, what is the turning point of $y = (x - h)^n + k$? Why is this true only when n is even?

16. **Error Analysis** A student was asked to graph the function $g(x) = (x + 3)^4 - 2$. The student's work is shown at right. Identify the error and explain how the student should have graphed the function. Graph the function correctly.

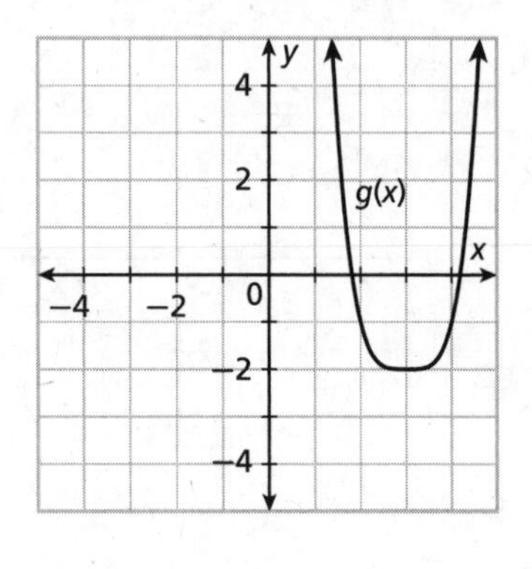

The graph of $g(x)$ is the graph of $f(x) = x^4$ after a series of transformations. Write the equation of $g(x)$.

17.

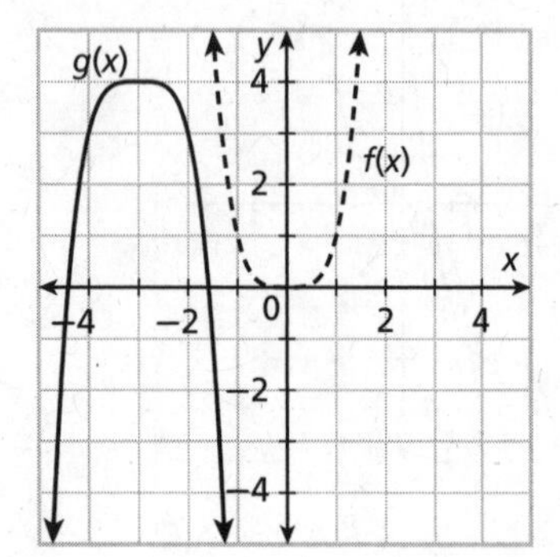

18.

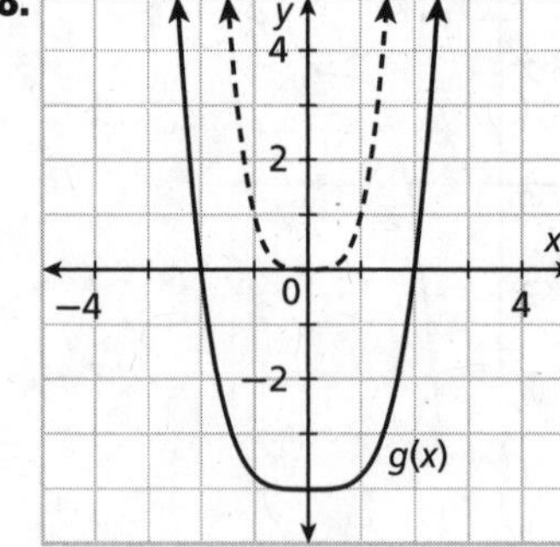

19. $S(x) = \frac{4}{3}\pi\left(\frac{x}{2}\right)^3$ gives the volume of a sphere with diameter x, and $C(x) = x^3$ gives the volume of a cube with edge length x. Explain why the volume of a sphere with diameter x is less than the volume of a cube with edge length x.

Name ________________ Class ________ Date ________

20-1

Additional Practice

For $f(x) = x^3 + 1$, write the rule for each function and sketch its graph.

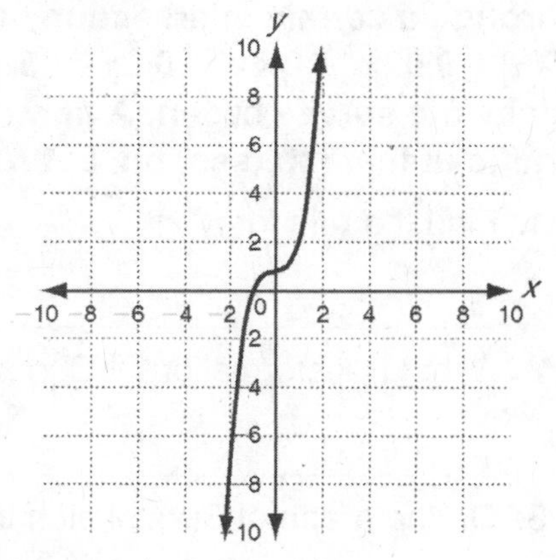

1. $g(x) = f(x + 4)$

____

2. $g(x) = 3f(x)$

____

3. $g(x) = f\left(\frac{1}{2}x\right)$

____

Let $f(x) = -x^3 + 4x^2 - 5x + 12$. Write a function $g(x)$ that performs each transformation.

4. Reflect $f(x)$ across the y-axis

____

5. Reflect $f(x)$ across the x-axis

____

Let $f(x) = x^3 + 2x^2 - 3x - 6$. Describe $g(x)$ as a transformation of $f(x)$ and graph.

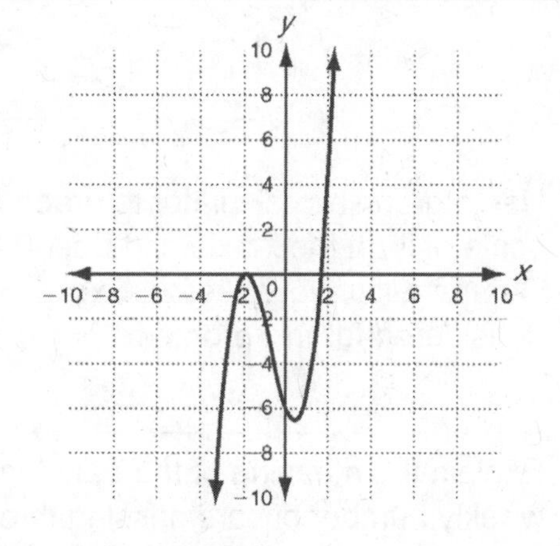

6. $g(x) = \frac{1}{4}f(x)$

____

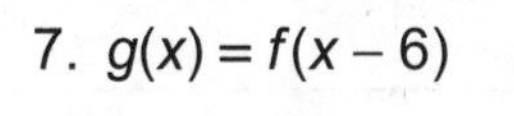

7. $g(x) = f(x - 6)$

____

Write a function that transforms $f(x) = x^3 + 4x^2 - x + 5$ in each of the following ways. Support your solution by using a graphing calculator.

8. Move 6 units up and reflect across the y-axis. ______________________

9. Compress vertically by a factor of 0.25 and move 3 units right. ______________________

Solve.

10. The number of participants, N, in a new Internet political forum during each month of the first year can be modeled by $N(t) = 4t^2 - t + 2000$, where t is the number of months since January. In the second year, the number of forum participants doubled compared to the same month in the previous year. Write a function that describes the number of forum participants in the second year.

____

Problem Solving

A traffic engineer determines that the number of cars passing through a certain intersection each week can be modeled by $C(x) = 0.02x^3 + 0.4x^2 + 0.2x + 35$, where x is the number of weeks since the survey began. A new road has just opened that affects the traffic at that intersection. Let $N(x) = C(x) + 200$.

1. Find the rule for $N(x)$.

____

2. What transformation of $C(x)$ is represented by $N(x)$?

____

3. On the graph of $C(x)$, sketch the graph for $N(x)$.

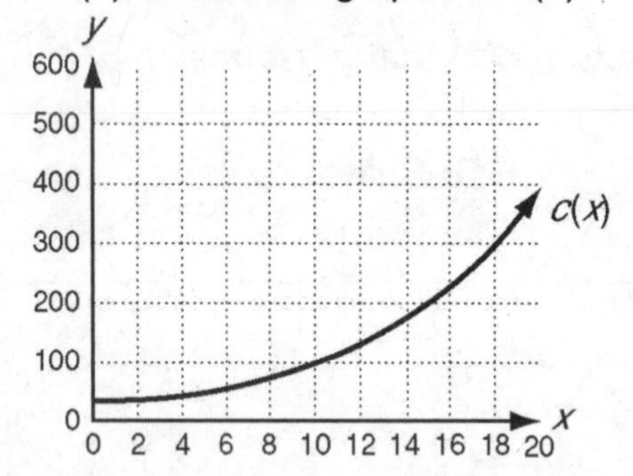

4. Use a graphing calculator to graph $N(x)$. Use a window from 0 to 20 with a scale of 1 on the x-axis and from 0 to 500 with a scale of 1 on the y-axis. Compare it to your sketch. Explain why only the values in Quadrant 1 are considered for this problem.

____

5. Explain the meaning of the transformation of $C(x)$ into $N(x)$ in terms of the weekly number of cars passing through the intersection.

____

6. Emergency roadwork temporarily closes off most of the traffic to this intersection. Write a function $R(x)$ that could model the effect on $C(x)$ Explain how the graph of $C(x)$ might be transformed into $R(x)$.

____

7. Describe the transformation $2C(x)$ by writing the new rule and explaining the change in the context of the problem.

____

Name______________________ Class______________ Date__________

20-2

Transforming Exponential and Logarithmic Functions

Going Deeper

Video Tutor

Essential question: *How does changing the values of a, h, and k affect the graph of* $f(x) = a\log_b(x - h) + k$?

A general logarithmic function has the form $f(x) = a\log_b(x - h) + k$ where $b > 0$ ($b \neq 1$) and a, h, and k are real numbers. The effect of changing the parameters a, h, and k in a logarithmic function is similar to the effect of changing these parameters in other types of functions.

MCC9–12.F.BF.3

1 EXAMPLE Changing the Values of *h* and *k*

The graph of $f(x) = \log_2 x$ is shown. Graph $g(x) = \log_2(x - 3)$ and $h(x) = \log_2(x - 3) + 2$.

A Complete the table of values.

x	g(x)	h(x)
3.5		
4		
5		
7		
11		

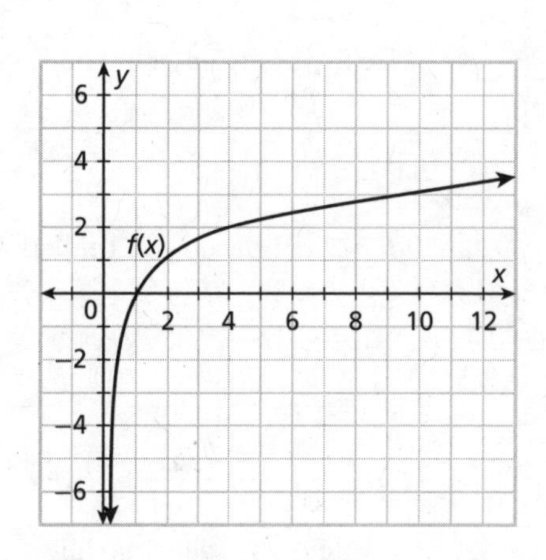

B Plots the points from your table.

C Use the points to help you sketch and label the graphs of $g(x)$ and $h(x)$.

REFLECT

1a. How does the graph of $g(x)$ compare to the graph of $f(x)$?

____

1b. How does the graph of $h(x)$ compare to the graph of $f(x)$?

____

1c. In general, how do you think the graph of $j(x) = \log_b(x - h) + k$ is related to the graph of the parent function, $f(x) = \log_b(x)$?

____

____

____

MCC9–12.F.BF.3

2 EXAMPLE Changing the Value of *a*

The graph of $f(x) = \log_{\frac{1}{2}} x$ is shown. Graph $g(x) = 2\log_{\frac{1}{2}} x$ and $h(x) = -\frac{1}{2}\log_{\frac{1}{2}} x$.

A Complete the table of values.

x	$g(x)$	$h(x)$
1		
2		
4		
8		

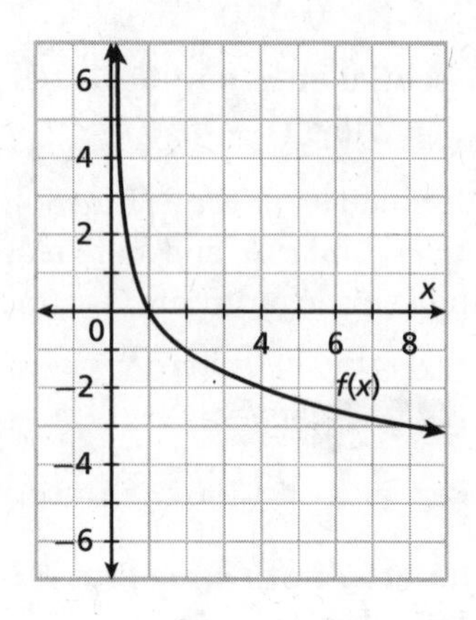

B Plots the points from your table.

C Use the points to help you sketch and label the graphs of $g(x)$ and $h(x)$.

REFLECT

2a. For $a > 0$, how do you think the value of a affects the graph of $j(x) = a\log_b x$?

2b. How does the value of a affect the graph of $j(x) = a\log_b x$ when $a < 0$?

2c. The graph of $j(x) = a\log_b x$ always has what point in common with the graph of $f(x) = \log_b x$? Explain why.

2d. Without graphing, explain how the graph of $j(x) = 0.25\log_{\frac{1}{2}}(x + 6)$ would compare to the graph of $f(x)$. Discuss asymptotes, end behavior, and intercepts.

MCC9–12.F.BF.3

3 EXAMPLE Writing an Equation from a Graph

The graph of $g(x)$ is the graph of $f(x) = \log_{\frac{1}{4}} x$ after a horizontal translation, a reflection in the x-axis, and a vertical translation. Write the equation of $g(x)$.

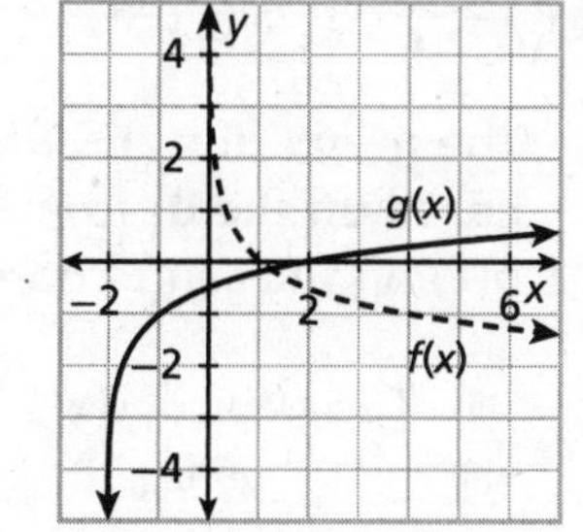

A Let $g(x) = a \log_{\frac{1}{4}} (x - h) + k$. Find the value of h.

The vertical asymptote of $g(x)$ is the line __________.

The vertical asymptote of the parent function $f(x)$ is $x = 0$. This means

$f(x)$ is translated __________ units to the left and so $h =$ __________.

B Find the value of a.

Since the graph of the parent function $f(x)$ is reflected across the

x-axis, the sign of a is __________. Since it was given that the transformation did not

involve a stretch, $a =$ __________.

C Find the value of k.

Consider the point $(4, -1)$ on the graph of $f(x)$ and the sequence of transformations that maps it to the corresponding point on the graph of $g(x)$.

The horizontal translation maps $(4, -1)$ to $(2, -1)$. Then the reflection across the x-axis maps $(2, -1)$ to $(2, 1)$. Finally, the vertical translation maps $(2, 1)$ to $(2, 0)$.

The final transformation is a translation of __________ unit(s) down, so $k =$ __________.

D Write the equation.

Using the values of the parameters from above, $g(x) =$ ______________.

REFLECT

3a. How can you use the x-intercept of the graph of $g(x)$ to check that you wrote a correct equation?

____

____

3b. Given the graph of a function $f(x) = ab^{x-h} + k$, which parameter (a, h, or k) is determined by the location of the graph's asymptote? Given the graph of a function $g(x) = a \log_b (x - h) + k$, which parameter ($a$, h, or k) is determined by the location of the graph's asymptote? Explain each of your answers.

____

____

____

____

PRACTICE

The graph of $f(x) = \log_3 x$ is shown. Write the function rules for $g(x)$ and $h(x)$ based on the descriptions given. Then sketch and label the graphs of $g(x)$ and $h(x)$ on the same coordinate plane.

1. The graph of $g(x)$ is the translation of the graph of $f(x)$ to the right 4 units and up 3 units.

   ____

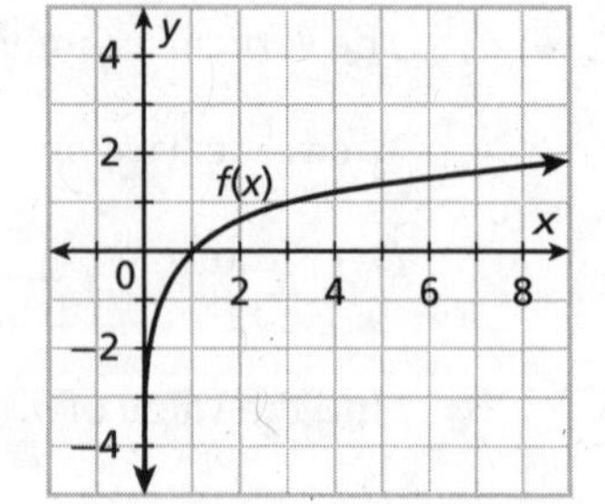

2. The graph of $h(x)$ is the reflection of the graph of $f(x)$ over the x-axis followed by a translation down 2 units

   ____

The graph of $f(x) = \log_{\frac{1}{3}} x$ is shown. Write the function rules for $g(x)$ and $h(x)$

based on the descriptions given. Then sketch and label the graphs of $g(x)$ and $h(x)$ on the same coordinate plane.

3. The graph of $g(x)$ is a vertical shrink of the graph of $f(x)$ by a factor of $\frac{1}{3}$ and a reflection across the x-axis.

   ____

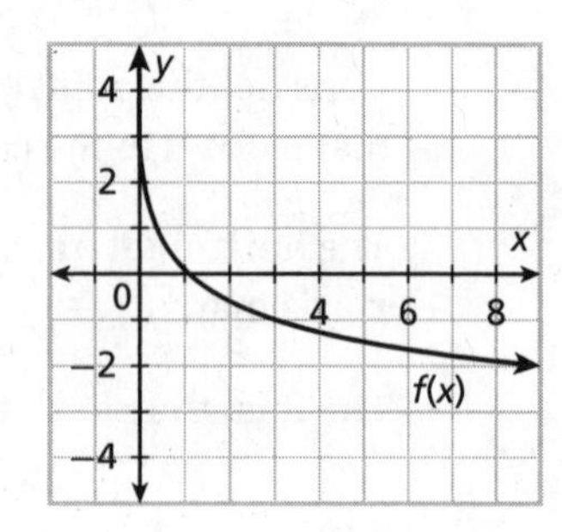

4. The graph of $h(x)$ is a vertical stretch of the graph of $f(x)$ by a factor of 2 and a translation 3 units up.

   ____

Use the graphs of $f(x)$, $g(x)$, and $h(x)$ for Exercises 5 and 6.

5. The graph of $g(x)$ is the graph of $f(x) = \log_2 x$ after a vertical shrink and a horizontal translation. Write the equation of $g(x)$.

   ____

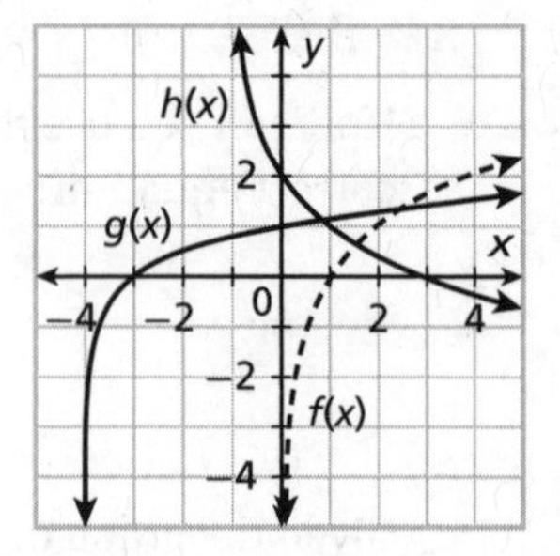

6. The graph of $h(x)$ is the graph of $f(x) = \log_2 x$ after a horizontal translation, a reflection in the x-axis, and a vertical translation. Write the equation of $h(x)$.

   ____

7. The table below lists some characteristics of the graph of the function $f(x) = \log_b x$. Complete the table by listing the corresponding characteristics of the graph of $g(x) = a \log_b (x - h) + k$.

Function	Asymptote	Reference point 1	Reference point 2
$f(x) = \log_b x$	$x = 0$	(1, 0)	(b, 1)
$g(x) = a \log_b (x - h) + k$			

8. In this exercise, you will make a conjecture about horizontal stretches and shrinks of the graphs of logarithmic functions.

a. Let $f(x) = \log_2 8x$ and $g(x) = \log_2 x + 3$. Complete the table. Then graph $f(x)$ and $g(x)$ on the coordinate plane at right.

x	f(x)	g(x)
1		
2		
4		
8		

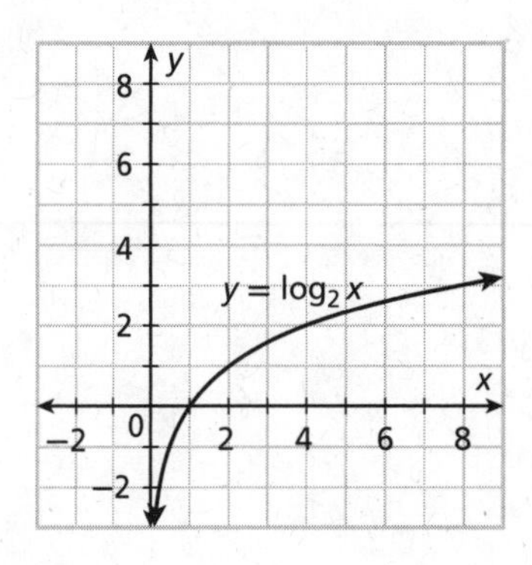

b. Describe the graphs of $f(x)$ and $g(x)$ as transformations of the parent base 2 logarithmic function.

____

____

c. Let $h(x) = \log_2 \frac{1}{2}x$ and $j(x) = \log_2 x - 1$. Complete the table. Then graph $h(x)$ and $j(x)$ on the coordinate plane at right.

x	h(x)	j(x)
1		
2		
4		
8		

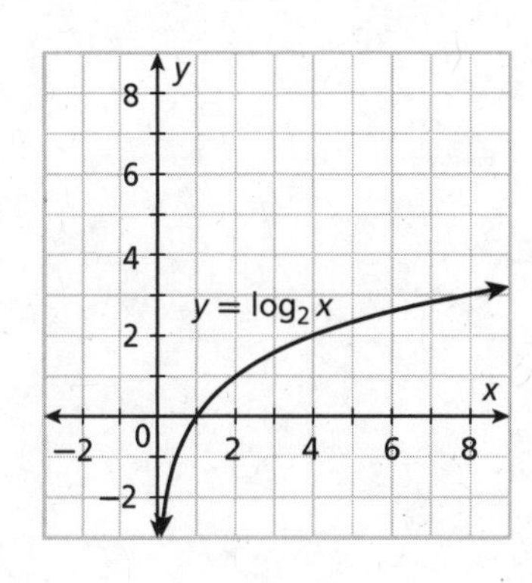

Continued

d. Describe the graphs of $h(x)$ and $j(x)$ as transformations of the parent base 2 logarithmic function.

e. The rules for the functions $f(x)$ and $h(x)$ have the form $\log_2 cx$ while the rules for the functions $g(x)$ and $j(x)$ have the form $\log_2 x + k$. Write the values of k in $g(x)$ and $j(x)$ as logarithms with base 2.

f. Summarize the relationship between a horizontal stretch or horizontal shrink of the graph of a logarithmic function and a translation of the graph.

Name________________________ Class______________ Date______________

20-2

Additional Practice

Graph each function. Find the asymptote. Tell how the graph is transformed from the graph of its parent function.

1. $f(x) = 5(2^x)$

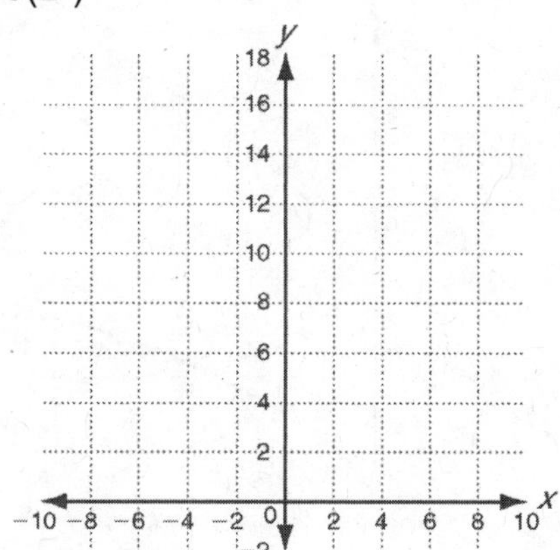

2. $f(x) = 5^{\frac{x}{4}}$

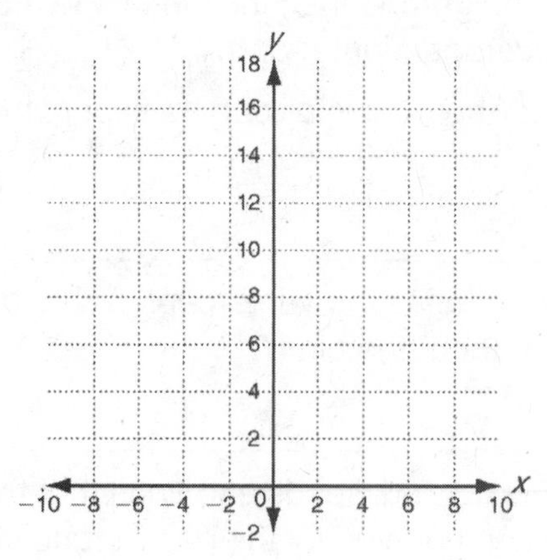

3. $f(x) = \log(x + 5)$

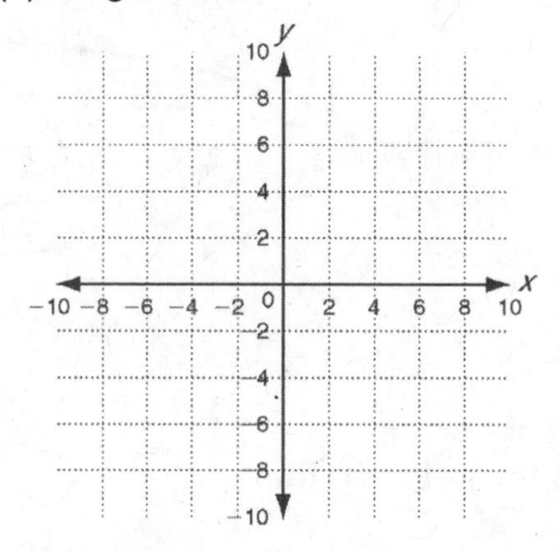

4. $f(x) = 3 + \ln x$

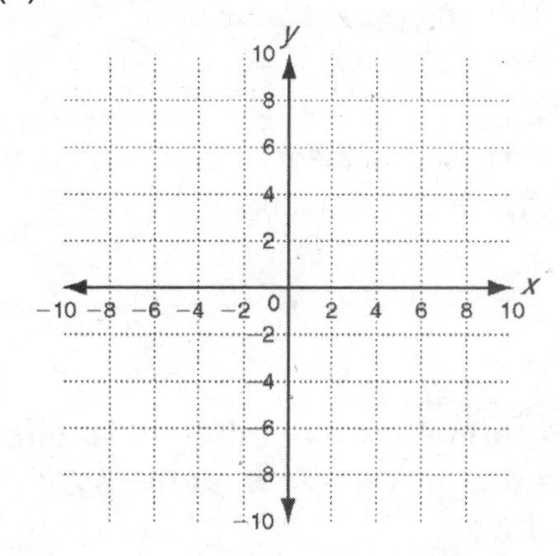

Write each transformed function.

5. The function $f(x) = \log(x + 1)$ is reflected across the y-axis and translated down 4 units. ______________

6. The function $f(x) = -8^{x-3}$ is reflected across the x-axis, compressed horizontally by a factor of 0.2, and stretched vertically by a factor of 2. ______________

Solve.

7. The function $A(t) = Pe^{rt}$ can be used to calculate the growth of an investment in which the interest is compounded continuously at an annual rate, r, over t years. What annual rate would double an investment in 8 years?

____

Problem Solving

Alex is studying a new species of hybrid plant. The average height of the plant can be modeled by the function $h(t) = 2 \ln (t + 1.25)$, where h is the height in feet and t is the number of weeks after planting.

1. Alex graphs the function to see the rate an average plant grows.

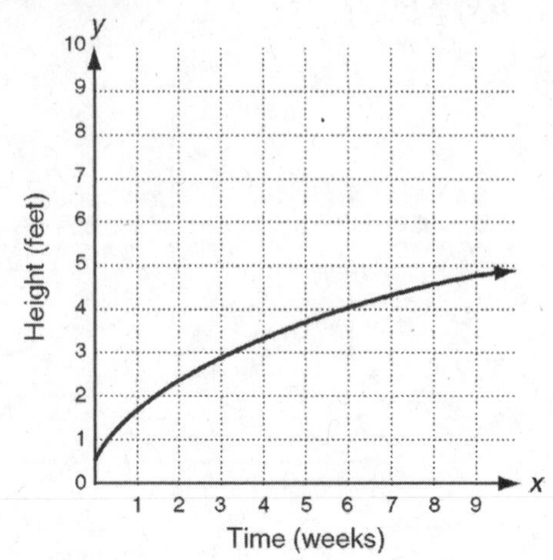

   a. About how tall can he expect the plant to be after 3 weeks?

   ____

   b. What is the y-intercept? What does it tell Alex about the plant?

   ____

2. Alex plants seeds and finds that the height is now modeled by the parent function.

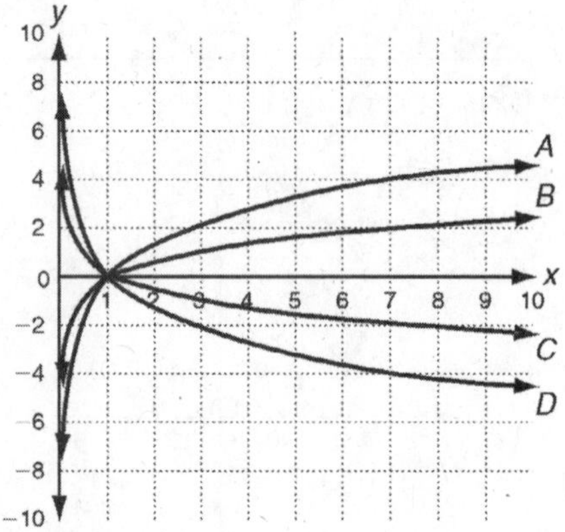

   a. Give the parent function $g(t)$. ______________

   b. Describe how the function $h(t)$ is transformed from the parent function.

   ____

   c. Choose the letter of the graph that represents the parent function.

   ____

Alex experiments with different fertilizers and finds that he can change the growth curve of the hybrid plant. Choose the letter for the best answer.

3. Alex finds that the height of the plants can now be modeled by the function $f(t) = 1.5 \ln (t + 1) + 0.4$. Which statement describes the transformation from the parent function?

   A Translation 0.4 unit up and 1 unit left; vertical stretch by 1.5

   B Translation 1 unit up and 0.4 unit right; vertical stretch by 1.5

   C Translation 0.4 unit down and 1 unit left; horizontal stretch by 1.5

   D Translation 1 unit down and 0.4 unit right; horizontal stretch by 1.5

4. Alex looks at the graph of the growth of his plants after trying a different fertilizer. The graph is transformed from the parent function by a vertical compression by a factor of 0.5 and a translation 1 unit right. Which function describes this transformation?

   F $k(t) = 2 \ln (t + 1)$

   G $k(t) = 2 \ln (t - 1)$

   H $k(t) = 0.5 \ln (t - 1)$

   J $k(t) = 0.5 \ln (t + 1)$

Name________________________ Class________________ Date____________

20-3

Transforming Functions
Extension: Transformations of Exponential Functions

Video Tutor

Essential question: *How do transformations of exponential functions compare with transformations of other function types?*

The following table summarizes how the values of the parameters a, h, and k affect the graph of an exponential growth function $f(x) = ab^{x-h} + k$.

Parameter	Effect
h	If $h > 0$, the graph of the parent function is translated $\lvert h \rvert$ units to the right. If $h < 0$, the graph of the parent function is translated $\lvert h \rvert$ units to the left.
k	If $k > 0$, the graph of the parent function is translated $\lvert k \rvert$ units up. If $k < 0$, the graph of the parent function is translated $\lvert k \rvert$ units down.
a	If $a > 1$, the graph of the parent function is stretched vertically by a factor of a. If $0 < a < 1$, the graph of the parent function is shrunk vertically by a factor of a.

Using the properties of exponents, you can rewrite the expression $ab^{x-h} + k$ as follows:

$$ab^{x-h} + k = ab^x \cdot b^{-h} + k = (ab^{-h})b^x + k$$

where ab^{-h} is a constant because a, b, and h are constants. This means that the parameter h in the function $f(x) = ab^{x-h} + k$ can be eliminated by combining it with the parameter a. Therefore, when you are asked to find the equation of an exponential growth function, you can assume that it has the form $f(x) = ab^x + k$.

MCC9–12.F.BF.3

1 EXAMPLE Writing an Exponential Growth Equation from a Graph

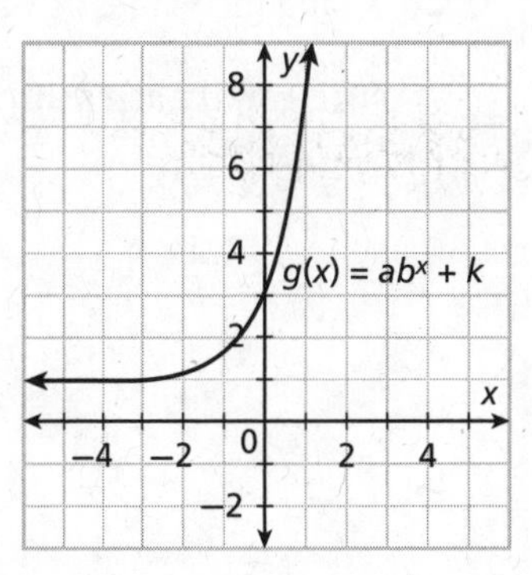

A Find the value of k. $y = 1$ is a horizontal asymptote of the graph of g, so the parent function is transformed vertically. $k =$ ________.

B If g is transformed so the x-axis is the asymptote of the graph, the y-intercept of the graph is 2. The y-intercept of the parent exponential growth function $f(x) = b^x$ is 1, so f is stretched vertically by a factor of 2, and $a =$ ________.

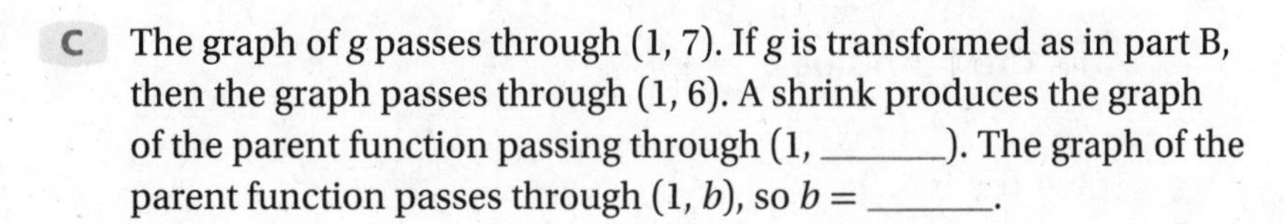

C The graph of g passes through (1, 7). If g is transformed as in part B, then the graph passes through (1, 6). A shrink produces the graph of the parent function passing through (1, ________). The graph of the parent function passes through (1, b), so $b =$ ________.

D The equation of g is $g(x) =$ ________________.

REFLECT

1a. How did you use the fact that the graph of g passes through (1, 7) to find a point through which the parent function passes?

____

____

1b. What is the parent function of g? How is the graph of g related to the graph of its parent function?

____

____

You can find the parent function of an exponential decay function in the same way as you did for an exponential growth function in Example 1, by assuming the equation has the form $f(x) = ab^x + k$.

MCC9–12.F.BF.3

2 EXAMPLE Writing an Exponential Decay Equation from a Graph

A Find the value of k. $y = -1$ is a horizontal asymptote of the graph of g, so the parent function is transformed vertically. $k =$ ______.

B The equation of g has the form $y = ab^x - 1$ and the graph passes through (0, 1).

$y = ab^x - 1$	Write the equation of g.
$\square = ab^{\square} - 1$	Substitute 0 for x and 1 for y.
$\square = \square - 1$	Simplify.
$a = \square$	Solve for a.

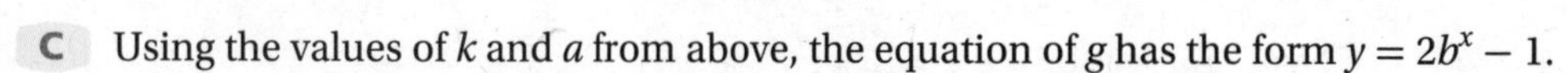

C Using the values of k and a from above, the equation of g has the form $y = 2b^x - 1$.

The graph passes through (−1, 5).

$y = 2b^x - 1$	Write the equation of g.
$\square = 2b^{\square} - 1$	Substitute −1 for x and 5 for y.
$\square = \square - 1$	Simplify.
$\square = \square$	Add 1 to both sides.
$b = \square$	Solve for b.

D The equation of g is $g(x) =$ ______________.

REFLECT

2a. What is the parent function of g?

2b. How is the graph of g related to the graph of its parent function?

Consider two linear functions $f(x) = x$ and $g(x) = 3x$. By simply multiplying by 3, you can transform f into g. Can an exponential function be transformed into another through a combination of a vertical translation and stretching or shrinking?

MCC9–12.F.BF.3

3 EXAMPLE The Uniqueness of Parent Functions

A Let $f(x) = 3^x$ and $g(x) = ab^x + k$. Transform f by stretching/shrinking it vertically by a factor of a and translating vertically by k units. What is the equation of transformed f?

B Compare the equations of transformed f and g. If f and g are equal, what must be true about b?

REFLECT

3a. What conclusion can you draw concerning the possibility of transforming $f(x) = 3^x$ into a different exponential function $g(x) = ab^x + k$, with $b \neq 3$? Explain.

3b. Through translation and stretching or shrinking, can you transform $f(x) = 3^x$ into $g(x) = 6^x$? Explain.

3c. Do you agree or disagree with the following statement? "The functions $y = 2^x$, $y = 3^x$, $y = 4^x$, and so on, are each parent functions of an exponential family and not simply transformations of one another." Explain your reasoning.

PRACTICE

1. **Error Analysis** A student is told that the graph shown at right is a vertical translation of $f(x) = 1.5^x$ and determines that the equation of the function must be $f(x) = 1.5^x - 3$ because the y-intercept is -3. Explain and correct the error in the student's reasoning.

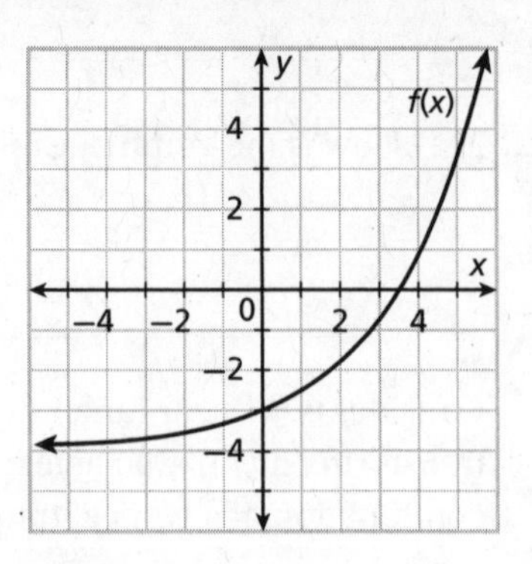

____

____

____

Write an equation of the exponential function $g(x)$ whose graph is shown.

2.

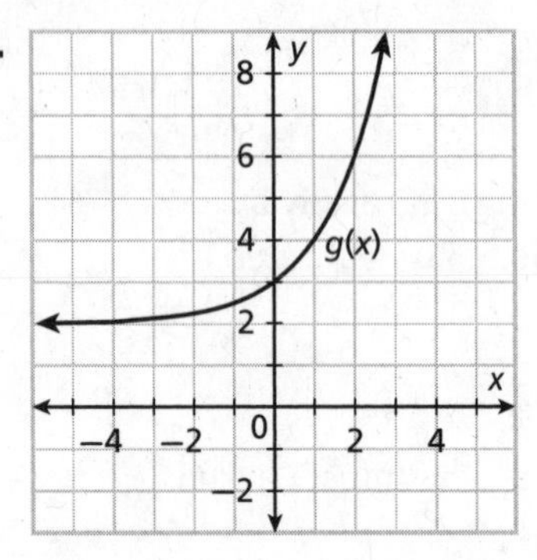

____

3.

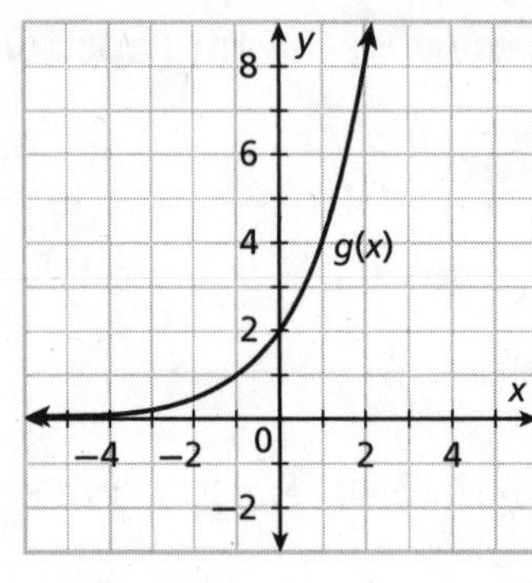

____

4.

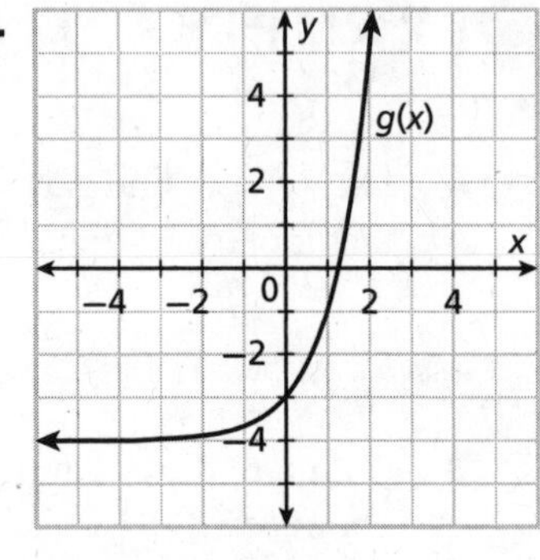

____

5.

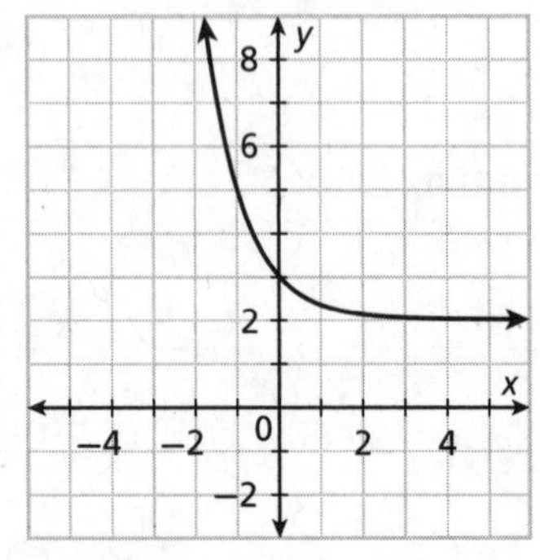

____

6.

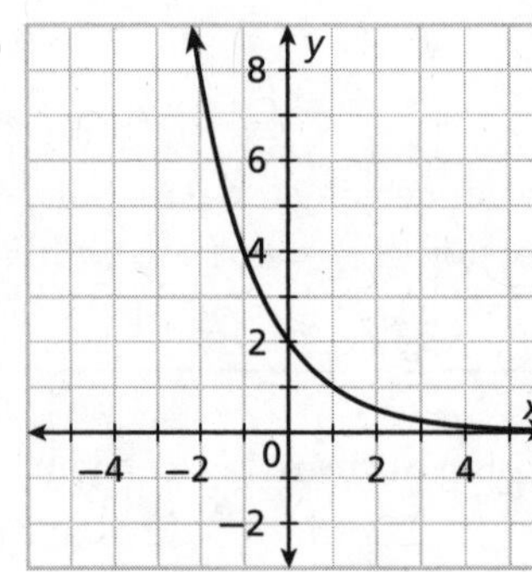

____

7.

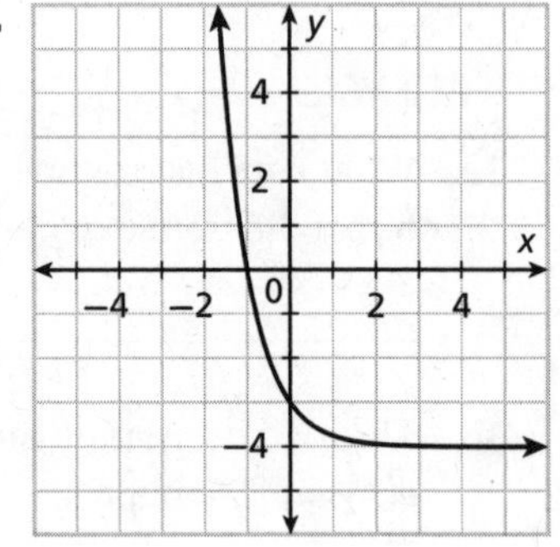

____

Consider the functions $f(x) = 2(5^x)$ and $g(x) = 2\left(\frac{1}{5}\right)^x$.

8. Can you describe a vertical translation, vertical shrink, vertical compression, or some combination of those transformations of f that will produce g? Explain.

____

____

9. Can you describe a different type of transformation of f that will produce g? Explain.

____

____

Additional Practice

Write an equation of the exponential function $h(x)$ whose graph is shown.

1. ________________________

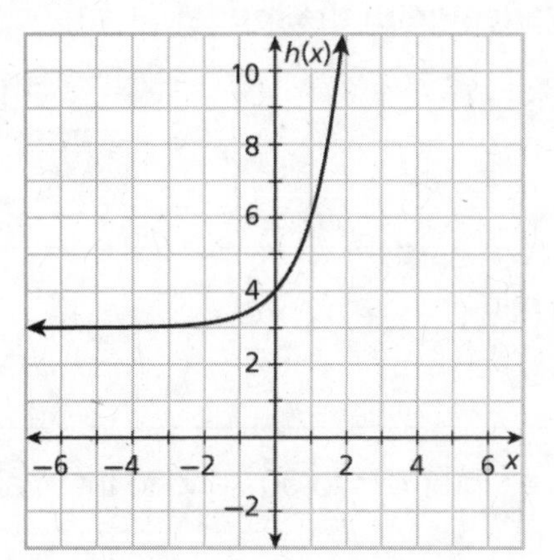

2. ________________________

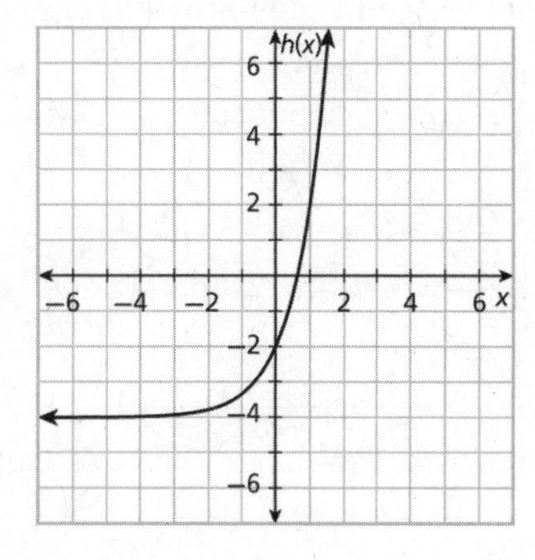

3. ________________________

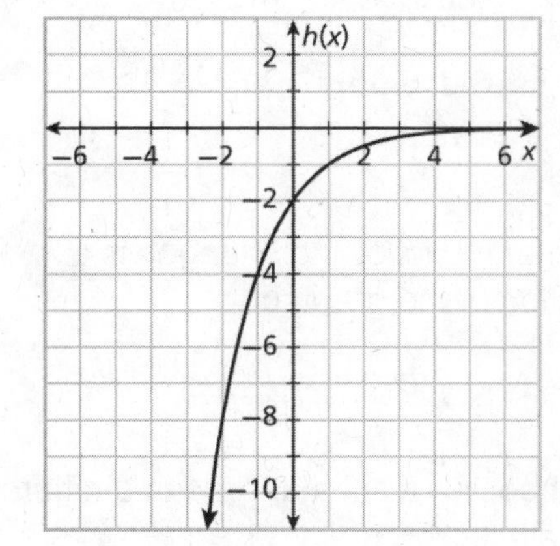

4. ________________________

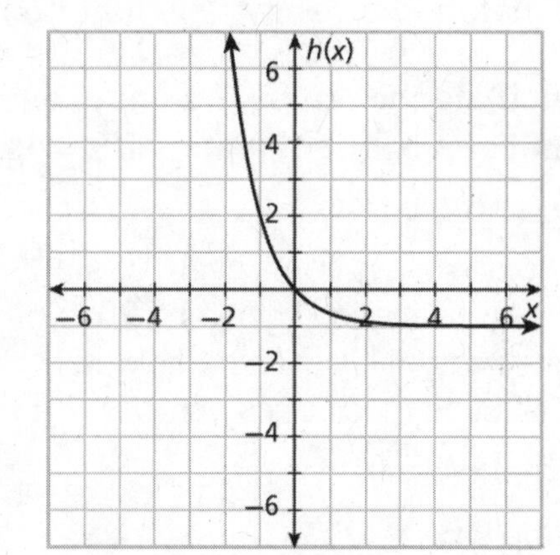

5. ________________________

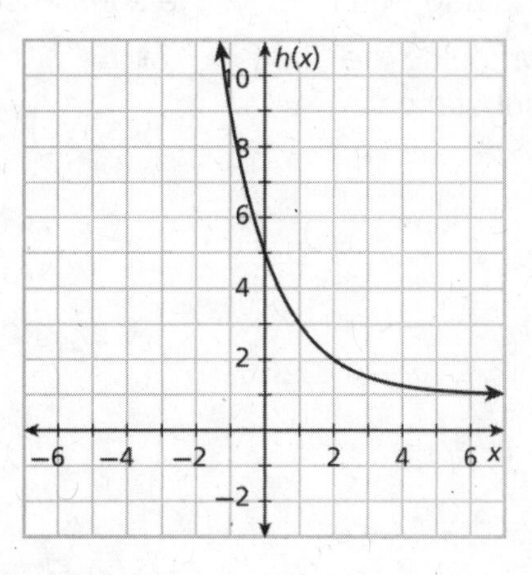

6. ________________________

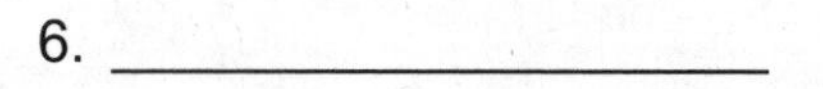

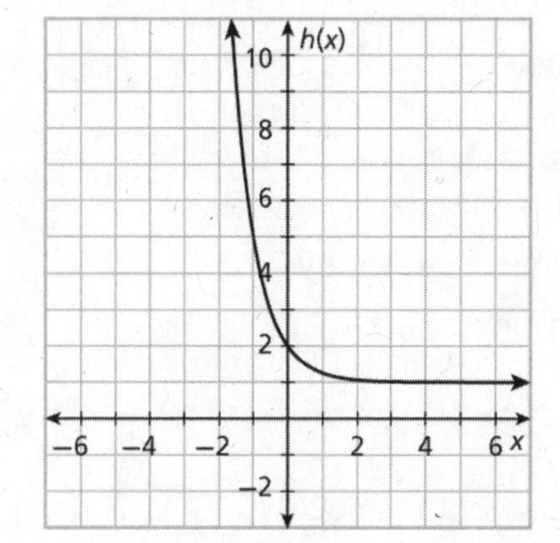

Problem Solving

A dose of a synthetic compound breaks down in the bloodstream over time. The amount of the compound in the blood with an initial dose of A_0 mg, under some conditions, is given by $A = A_0(0.97^t)$, where t is the time in minutes. The standard dose is 20 mg. Describe how each of the following changes would be reflected in the model.

1. The initial dose is changed from 20 mg to 10 mg.

____

2. The breakdown of the compound does not begin for 10 minutes.

____

3. The breakdown time period is decreased from one-minute intervals to 30-second intervals.

____

The half-life of a radioactive material is the time it takes for half of the amount of material to decay. The function $N(t) = N_0\left(\frac{1}{2}\right)^{t/t_{1/2}}$ can be used to calculate the remaining undecayed amount of material, where N_0 is the initial amount of material, $t_{1/2}$ is the half-life of the substance, and t is time.

4. Suppose sample A contains 10 lb of material and sample B contains 20 lb of the same material. Which sample will have half of its mass decay first?

   A sample A

   B sample B

   C They will both reach half of their respective initial mass simultaneously.

   D not enough information

5. Suppose the half-life of a substance were twice as long. What kind of transformation would the graph of the function undergo?

   F vertical stretch by 2

   G vertical shift by 2

   H horizontal compression by $\frac{1}{2}$

   J none of the above

6. Which of the following changes is a reflection of the graph of $N(t) = N_0\left(\frac{1}{2}\right)^{t/t_{1/2}}$?

   A choosing a substance with a different half-life

   B graphing the amount of decayed material in the sample

   C starting with more of the substance

   D graphing the "third-life" of the substance

Name______________________ Class______________ Date__________

21-1

Operations with Functions

Going Deeper

Essential question: *When you perform operations with functions, how does the graph of the resulting function compare with the original graphs?*

The sum of two functions, $f + g$, can be found graphically using the graphs of f and g.

MCC9–12.F.BF.1b

1 EXAMPLE Adding Functions Graphically and Algebraically

Given $f(x) = 4$ and $g(x) = \frac{2}{5}x - 2$, sketch the graph of $f + g$ using the graphs of f and g. Then find $f + g$ algebraically and use your answer to check your graph.

A Graph f and g.

Draw vertical arrows from x-axis to the graph of g.

"Add" these arrows to the graph of f by placing the tail end of each arrow on the graph of f at the corresponding x-value. The first one has been done for you.

Draw a line to connect the heads of the arrows. The resulting line is the graph of $f + g$.

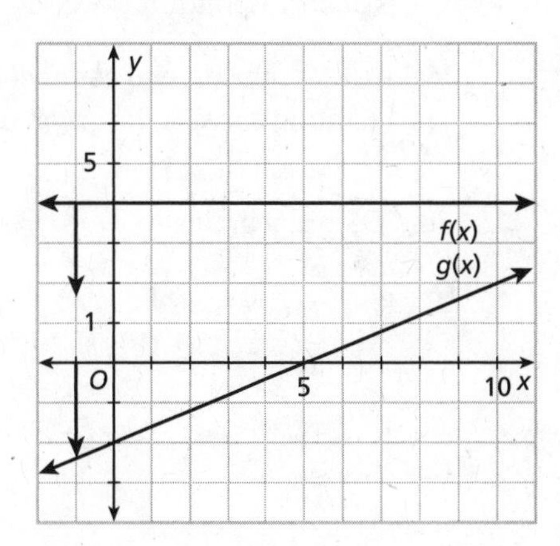

B Find $(f + g)(x)$ algebraically.

$(f + g)(x) = f(x) + g(x)$

$= \_\_\_ + \frac{2}{5}\_\_\_ - \_\_\_$ Substitute function rules.

$= \frac{2}{5}\_\_\_ + \_\_\_$ Combine like terms.

Graph $(f + g)(x)$ on the graph above to check your sketch in part A.

REFLECT

1a. Compare the graphs of $g(x)$ and $(f + g)(x)$ in Example 1.

____

1b. Suppose $f(x)$ is a constant function and $g(x)$ is a linear function. What will the graph of $(f + g)(x)$ look like? Explain.

____

____

____

The difference of two functions, $f - g$, can be found graphically using the graphs of f and g. When the graph of f lies above the graph of g, the difference $f - g$ is positive. When the graph of f lies below the graph of g, the difference $f - g$ is negative.

MCC9–12.F.BF.1b

2 EXAMPLE Subtracting Functions Graphically and Algebraically

Given $f(x) = \frac{1}{2}x^2 - 4x + 11$ and $g(x) = -\frac{1}{4}x^2 + 2x + 2$, sketch the graph of $f - g$ using the graphs of f and g. Then find $f - g$ algebraically and use your answer to check your graph.

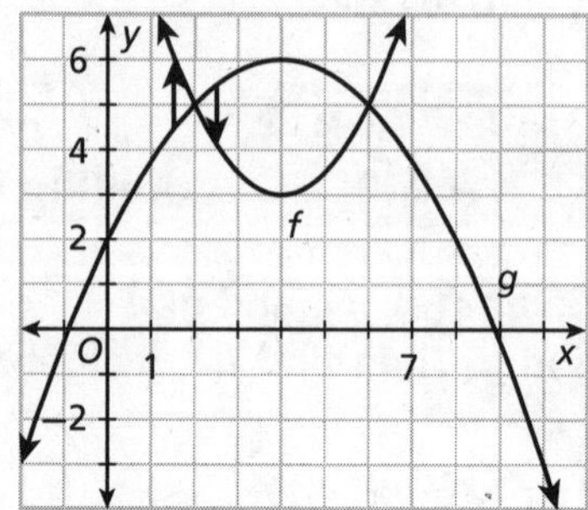

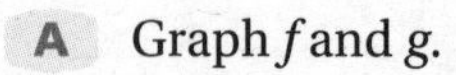

A Graph f and g.

Draw vertical arrows from the graph of g to the graph of f. Two have been done for you.

Redraw the arrows with the tail end of each arrow on the x-axis at corresponding x-values.

Make a smooth curve to connect the arrowheads. The resulting curve is the graph of $f - g$.

B Find $f - g$ algebraically.

$(f - g)(x) = f(x) - g(x)$

$= \frac{1}{2}\_\_\_\_ - \_\_\_\_ + \_\_\_\_ - \left(-\frac{1}{4}\_\_\_\_ + \_\_\_\_ + \_\_\_\_\right)$ Substitute function rules.

$= \frac{1}{2}\_\_\_\_ - \_\_\_\_ + \_\_\_\_ + \frac{1}{4}\_\_\_\_ - \_\_\_\_ - \_\_\_\_$ Distributive Property

$= \frac{3}{4}\_\_\_\_ - \_\_\_\_ + \_\_\_\_$ Combine like terms.

Graph $f - g$ on the graph above to check your sketch in part A.

REFLECT

2a. Compare the graphs of f and $f - g$ in Example 2.

____

____

2b. Suppose f and g are quadratic functions, and the coefficients of the x^2-terms are not equal. What will the graph of $f - g$ look like? Explain.

____

____

____

MCC9–12.F.BF.1b

3 EXAMPLE Multiplying and Dividing Functions

Given $f(x) = x^2 - 6x + 5$ and $g(x) = x - 1$, find the given function. Then compare the graph of the resulting function to the graphs of the original functions.

A fg

$(fg)(x) = f(x) \cdot g(x)$

$= \_\_\_\_\_\_ \cdot \_\_\_\_\_\_$

$= \_\_\_\_\_\_$

$= \_\_\_\_\_\_$

Graph f, g, and fg on the same set of axes.

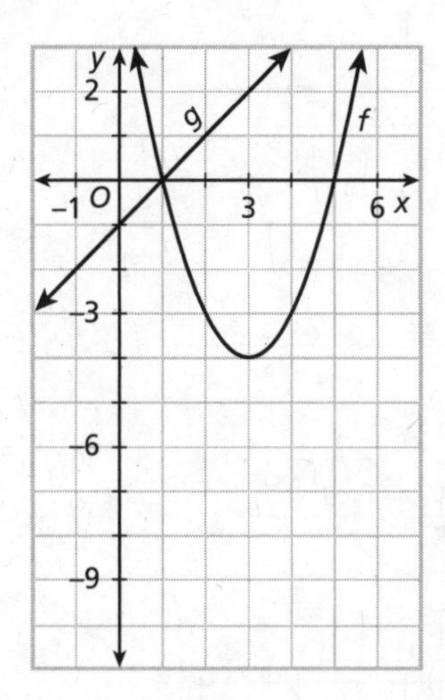

The graph of fg shows a cubic function.

The graph of f is a parabola, and the graph of g is a line.

B $\frac{f}{g}$

$\left(\frac{f}{g}\right)(x) = \_\_\_\_\_\_$

$= \_\_\_\_\_\_$

$= \_\_\_\_\_\_$

$= x - 5$, where $x \neq 1$

Graph f, g, and $\frac{f}{g}$ on the same set of axes.

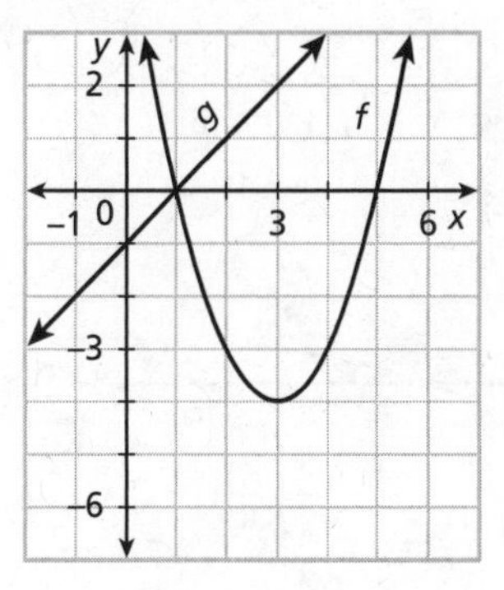

The graph of $\frac{f}{g}$ is the graph of g translated down 4 units, where $x \neq 1$.

REFLECT

3a. Explain why the graph of the product of the quadratic function and the linear function shows a cubic function in part A of Example 3.

____

____

____

____

3b. Is the graph of the quotient of a quadratic function and a linear function always a line? Explain.

____

____

____

PRACTICE

Sketch the graph of the sum or difference of the functions using the graphs of $f(x)$ and $g(x)$. Then find the sum or difference of the functions algebraically and use your answer to check your sketch.

1. $f(x) = \frac{1}{4}x + 3$, $g(x) = -\frac{1}{4}x + 2$

$(f + g)(x) =$ ___________

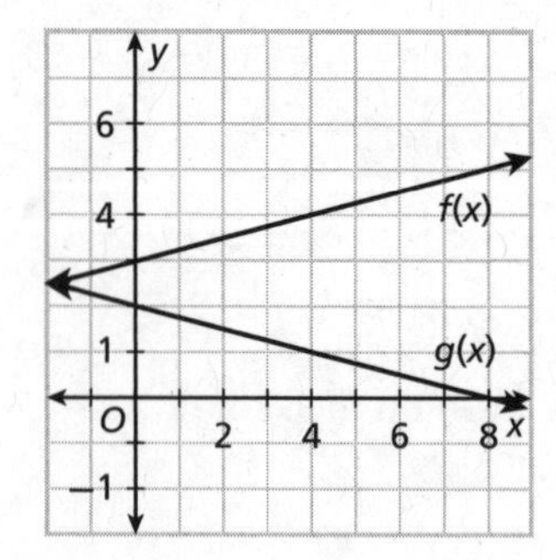

2. $f(x) = 2^x$, $g(x) = 3$

$(f + g)(x) =$ ___________

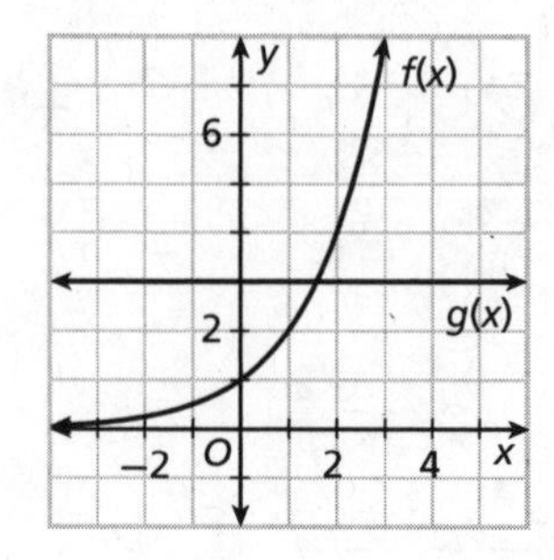

3. $f(x) = \log_3 x + 5$, $g(x) = 6$

$(f - g)(x) =$ ___________

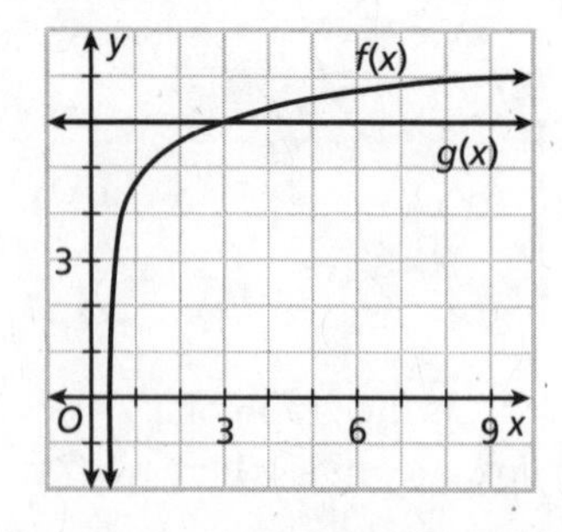

4. $f(x) = x + 4$, $g(x) = x^2 - 2x + 4$

$(f - g)(x) =$ ___________

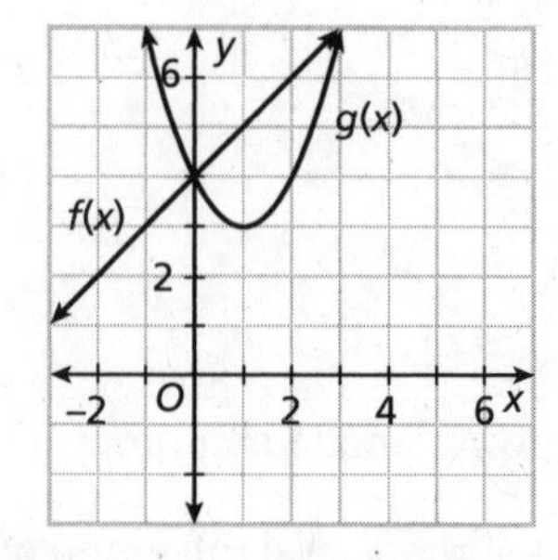

Find each function using $f(x)$ and $g(x)$. Then compare the graph of the resulting function to the graphs of the original functions.

5. Find $(fg)(x)$ when $f(x) = \frac{1}{3}x + 2$ and $g(x) = 3$.

____

____

6. Find $\left(\frac{f}{g}\right)(x)$ when $f(x) = x^3 - 4x^2 + x + 6$ and $g(x) = x - 2$.

____

____

7. In Exercises 2, 3, and 5, one of the given functions is a constant function. How does adding or subtracting a constant to a function appear to affect the graph of the function? How does multiplying a function by a constant appear to affect the graph of a function?

____

____

Name ________________ Class ________ Date ________

Additional Practice

Use the following functions for Exercises 1–16.

$f(x) = \frac{1}{2x}$ $g(x) = x^2$ $h(x) = x - 8$ $k(x) = \sqrt{x}$

Find each function.

1. $(gk)(x)$ ________
2. $(g + h)(x)$ ________
3. $(g - h)(x)$ ________
4. $(fg)(x)$ ________
5. $(gh)(x)$ ________
6. $\left(\frac{f}{g}\right)(x)$ ________
7. $\left(\frac{g}{k}\right)(x)$ ________
8. $(fk)(x)$ ________
9. $(h - g)(x)$ ________

Find each value.

10. $(gk)(9)$ ________
11. $\left(\frac{g}{h}\right)(-2)$ ________
12. $(gh)(-4)$ ________
13. $\left(\frac{f}{f}\right)(732)$ ________
14. $\left(\frac{g}{f}\right)(3)$ ________
15. $(fg)(136)$ ________
16. Find $\left(\frac{f}{g}\right)(2)$ when $f(x) = x^3 - 5x^2 + 7x - 2$ and $g(x) = x - 2$.

Problem Solving

In an airport, Roberta is walking on a moving walkway, in the direction the walkway is moving. Her speed relative to the walkway is given by the function $G(x) = 2x^2 - 4x + 2$. The walkway's speed relative to the ground is given by the function $H(x) = 1.5x^2 - 3x - 1$.

1. Write an expression showing Roberta's total speed, relative to the ground.

____

2. Shortly after stepping on the walkway, Roberta realizes she forgot to buy a postcard in the gift shop behind her. She turns around and walks backwards, against the flow of the walkway. Write an expression showing Roberta's total speed, relative to the ground, after she has turned around.

____

3. Write a pair of functions (of x) j and k such that the following equation is true:

$$\left(\frac{j}{k}\right)(2) = 5$$

$j(x) =$ ____________________ $k(x) =$ ____________________

4. An industrial engineer models a company's sales, in units sold, with the function $S(t) = 18t - 1950$ and the company's factory's output, in units produced, by $P(t) = 17t + 1800$. Write a function representing the inventory of the company's warehouse, which holds the units the company produces but has not yet sold.

$I(t) =$ ____

Name________________________ Class________________ Date____________

21-2

Functions and Their Inverses

Going Deeper

Essential question: *What are the inverses of quadratic and cubic functions and how do you find them?*

Video Tutor

PREP FOR MCC9–12.F.BF.4d(+)

1 ENGAGE Understanding One-to-One Functions

A function is **one-to-one** if each output of the function is paired with exactly one input. Only one-to-one functions have inverses that are also functions.

Recall that the graph of $f^{-1}(x)$ is the reflection of the graph of $f(x)$ across the line $y = x$.

Linear functions with nonzero slopes are always one-to-one, so their inverses are always functions.

Quadratic functions with unrestricted domains are not one-to-one. The reflection of the parabola labeled $g(x)$ across the line $y = x$ is not a function.

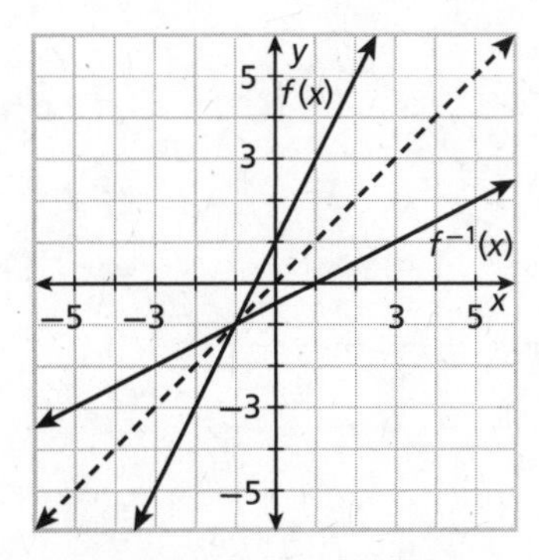

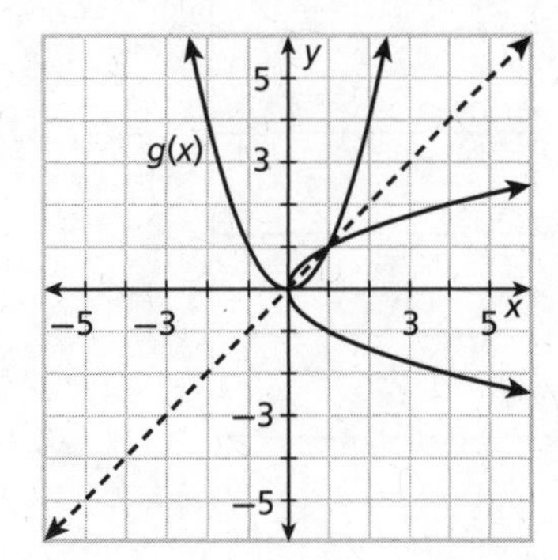

REFLECT

1a. Why is a linear function with a nonzero slope a one-to-one function? Why is a linear function not one-to one if the slope is 0?

____

____

____

1b. Why is the quadratic function $g(x)$ not one-to-one?

____

____

1c. Explain why the reflection of the graph of $g(x)$ across the line $y = x$ is not a function.

____

____

1d. Consider the quadratic function $g(x) = x^2$. How could you restrict its domain so that the resulting function is one-to-one? Explain. Graph the function for the restricted domain.

____

____

____

MCC9–12.F.BF.4d(+)

2 EXAMPLE Graphing the Inverse of $f(x) = ax^2$ with $x \geq 0$

Graph the function $f(x) = 0.5x^2$ for the domain $x \geq 0$. Then graph its inverse, $f^{-1}(x)$, and write a rule for the inverse function.

A Complete a table of values to graph $f(x)$ for nonnegative values of x.

x	$f(x)$
0	
1	
2	
3	
4	

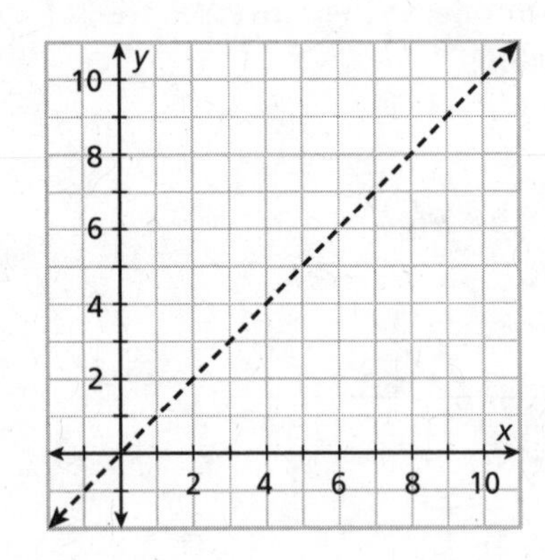

B Complete the table below by finding the image of each point on the graph of $f(x)$ after a reflection across the line $y = x$. To reflect a point across $y = x$, switch the x- and y-coordinates of the point.

Points on the graph of $f(x)$	(0,)	(1,)	(2,)	(3,)	(4,)
Points on the graph of $f^{-1}(x)$	(0,)	(0.5,)	( )	( )	( )

C Use the table from part B to graph $f^{-1}(x)$.

D Write a rule for $f^{-1}(x)$.

____ $= 0.5x^2$	Replace $f(x)$ with y.
____ $y = x^2$	Multiply both sides by 2.
$\sqrt{}$ $= x$	Use the definition of positive square root.
$\sqrt{2}$ $=$ ____	Switch x and y to write the inverse.
$\sqrt{2x} =$ ____	Replace y with $f^{-1}(x)$.

REFLECT

2a. When solving the equation $2y = x^2$ for x in part D, you use the definition of a positive square root. Why can you ignore negative square roots?

2b. How else could you restrict the domain of $f(x)$ in order to get an inverse that is a function? What is the inverse function given that restriction?

MCC9–12.F.BF.4

3 ENGAGE Understanding Square Root Functions

A quadratic function of the form $f(x) = ax^2$ for $x \geq 0$ is a one-to-one function, so its inverse is also a function. In general, the inverse of $f(x) = ax^2$ for $x \geq 0$ is the *square root function* $g(x) = \sqrt{\frac{x}{a}}$.

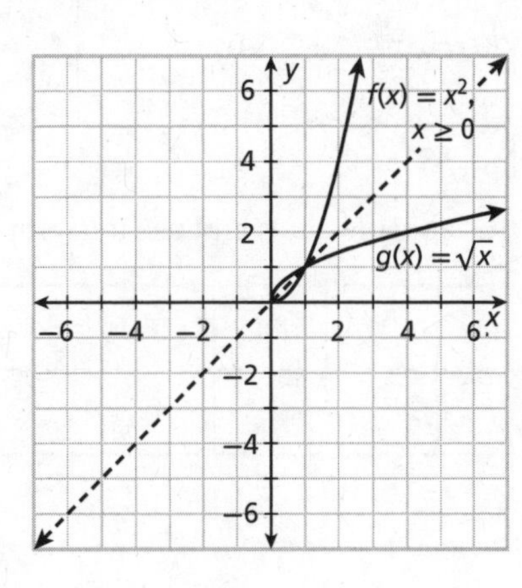

A **square root function** is a function whose rule involves $\sqrt{x}$. The parent square root function is $g(x) = \sqrt{x}$. The graph shows that $g(x) = \sqrt{x}$ is the inverse of $f(x) = x^2$ for $x \geq 0$.

A square root function is defined only for values of x that make the expression under the radical sign nonnegative.

REFLECT

3a. What are the domain and range of the parent square root function $g(x) = \sqrt{x}$? Explain.

3b. When $a > 1$, the graph of $f(x) = ax^2$ for $x \geq 0$ is a vertical stretch by a factor of a of the graph of the parent quadratic function for $x \geq 0$. When $a > 1$, is the graph of $g(x) = \sqrt{\frac{x}{a}}$ a horizontal stretch or a horizontal shrink by a factor of a of the graph of the parent square root function? Explain.

MCC9–12.A.CED.2

4 EXAMPLE Modeling the Inverse of a Quadratic Function

The function $d(t) = 16t^2$ gives the distance d in feet that a dropped object falls in t seconds. Write and graph the inverse function $t(d)$ to find the time t in seconds it takes for an object to fall a distance of d feet. Then estimate how long it will take a penny dropped into a well to fall 48 feet.

A Write the inverse function.

The original function is a _______________ function with a domain restricted to $t \geq$ _________.

The function fits the pattern $f(x) = ax^2$ for $x \geq 0$, so its inverse will have the form $g(x) = \sqrt{\frac{x}{a}}$.

Original Function	Inverse Function
$d(t) = 16t^2$ for $t \geq 0$	$t(d) = \sqrt{\frac{\square}{\square}}$ for $d \geq 0$

B Complete the table of values and use it to graph the function $t(d)$.

d	0	4	16	36	64	100
t						

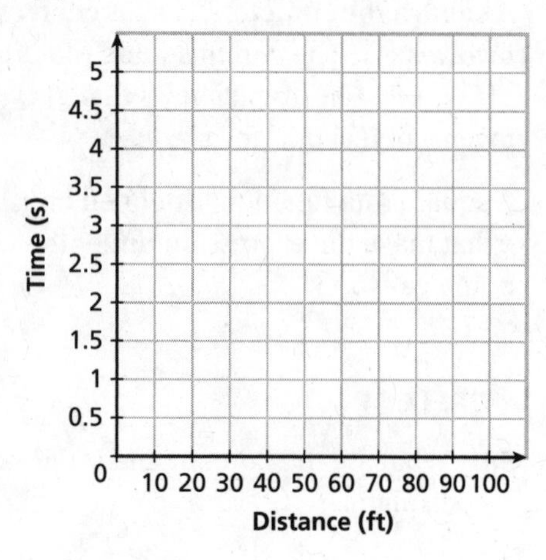

C Use the function $t(d)$ to estimate how long it will take a penny to fall 48 feet.

$t(d) = \sqrt{\frac{d}{16}}$ Write the function.

$t(48) = \sqrt{\frac{\square}{16}}$ Substitute 48 for d.

$t(48) = \sqrt{\square}$ Simplify.

$t(48) \approx \square$ Use a calculator to estimate.

So, it will take about _____________ seconds for a penny to fall 48 feet.

REFLECT

4a. Explain why the domain is restricted to $t \geq 0$ for the original function $d(t) = 16t^2$.

4b. Describe another way that you could estimate the time it would take a penny to fall 48 feet.

MCC9–12.F.BF.4a

5 ENGAGE Understanding the Cube Root Function

A table of values for the parent cubic function, $f(x) = x^3$, is shown below, along with its graph.

x	$f(x)$
−2	−8
−1	−1
0	0
1	1
2	8

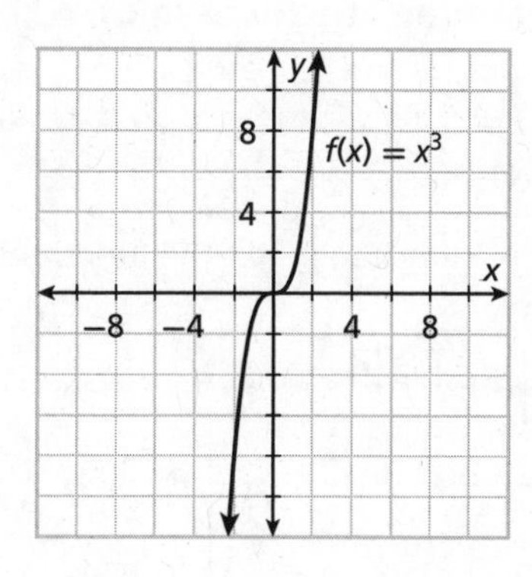

Because $f(x) = x^3$ is a one-to-one function, its inverse is also a function. The inverse of $f(x) = x^3$ is the *cube root function* $g(x) = \sqrt[3]{x}$.

A **cube root function** is a function whose rule involves $\sqrt[3]{x}$. The parent cube root function is $g(x) = \sqrt[3]{x}$.

A table of values for $g(x) = \sqrt[3]{x}$ is shown below, along with its graph.

x	$g(x)$
−8	−2
−1	−1
0	0
1	1
8	2

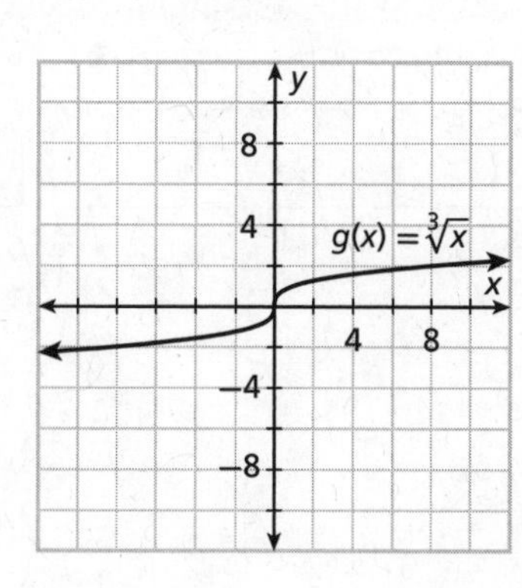

REFLECT

5a. Explain how the values in the tables for $f(x) = x^3$ and $g(x) = \sqrt[3]{x}$ show that the graphs of these functions are reflections of each other across the line $y = x$.

5b. Is $g(x) = \sqrt[3]{x}$ also a one-to-one function? Explain.

5c. What are the domain and range of $f(x) = x^3$?

5d. What are the domain and range of $g(x) = \sqrt[3]{x}$?

MCC9–12.F.BF.4

6 EXAMPLE Graphing the Inverse of $f(x) = ax^3$

Graph the function $f(x) = 0.5x^3$. Then graph its inverse, $f^{-1}(x)$, and write a rule for the inverse function.

A Complete the table of values to graph the function $f(x) = 0.5x^3$.

x	$f(x)$
−2	
−1	
0	
1	
2	

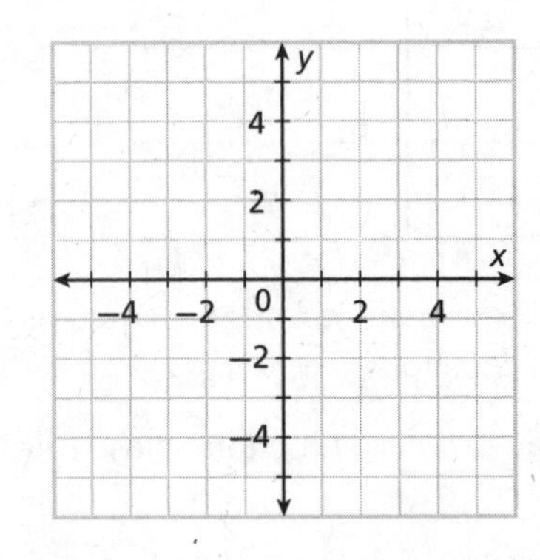

B Complete the table below by finding the image of each point on the graph of $f(x)$ after a reflection across the line $y = x$.

Points on the graph of $f(x)$	(−2,)	(−1,)	(0,)	(1,)	(2,)
Points on the graph of $f^{-1}(x)$	(−4,)	(−0.5,)			

C Use the table from part B to graph $f^{-1}(x)$.

D Write a rule for $f^{-1}(x)$.

$\square = 0.5x^3$	Replace $f(x)$ with y.
$\square\, y = x^3$	Solve for x. Multiply both sides by 2.
$\sqrt[3]{\square} = x$	Use the definition of cube root.
$\sqrt[3]{2\square} = \square$	Switch x and y to write the inverse.
$\sqrt[3]{2x} = \square$	Replace y with $f^{-1}(x)$.

REFLECT

6a. What is the inverse of the function $f(x) = ax^3$?

____

6b. When $0 < a < 1$, the graph of $f(x) = ax^3$ is a vertical shrink by a factor of a of the graph of the parent cubic function. When $0 < a < 1$, is the graph of $f^{-1}(x) = \sqrt[3]{\frac{x}{a}}$ a horizontal stretch or a horizontal shrink by a factor of a of the graph of the parent cube root function? Explain.

____

____

____

____

____

6c. Complete the chart below by describing the graph of each function as a transformation of the graph of its parent function.

Value of a	$f(x) = ax^3$	$g(x) = \sqrt[3]{\frac{x}{a}}$
$a > 1$		
$0 < a < 1$		

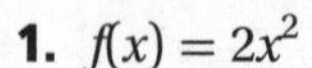

Graph the function *f(x)* for the domain $x \geq 0$. Then graph its inverse, $f^{-1}(x)$, and write a rule for the inverse function.

1. $f(x) = 2x^2$

$f^{-1}(x) =$ ______

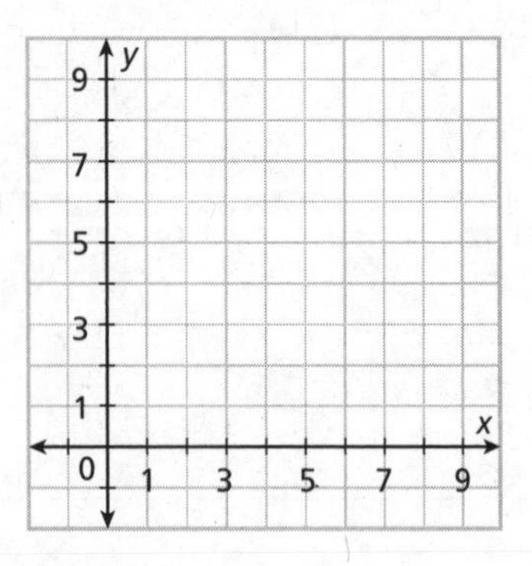

2. $f(x) = -x^2$

$f^{-1}(x) =$ ______

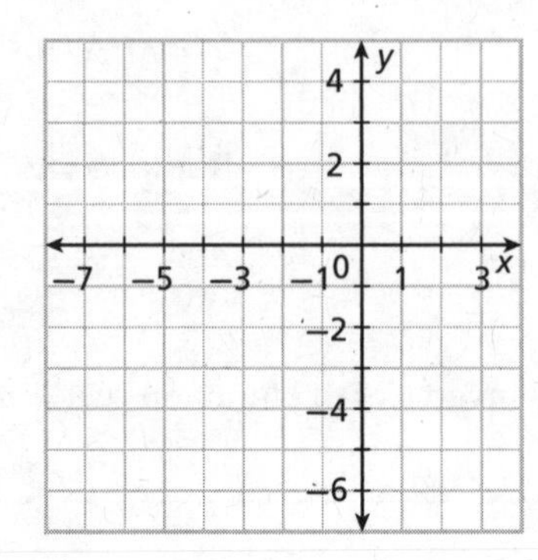

3. $f(x) = \frac{1}{3}x^2$

$f^{-1}(x) =$ ______

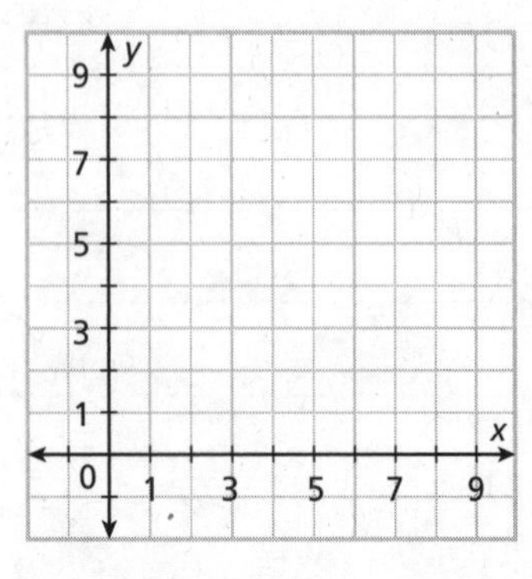

4. $f(x) = -\frac{1}{2}x^2$

$f^{-1}(x) =$ ______

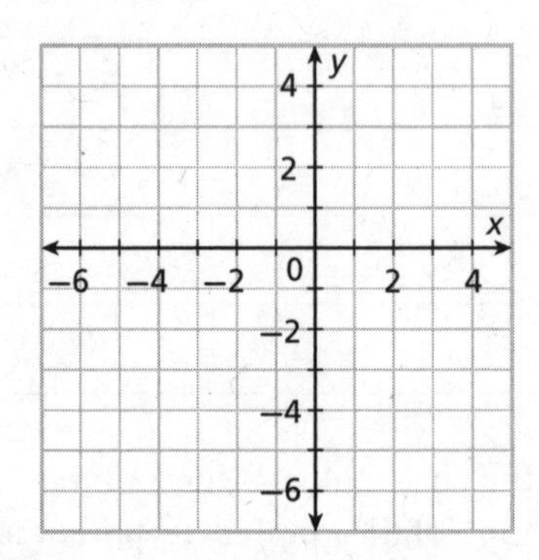

5. A company manufactures square tabletops that are covered by 16 square tiles. If s is the side length of each tile in inches, then the area A of a tabletop in square feet is given by $A(s) = \frac{1}{9}s^2$.

a. Write and graph the inverse function $s(A)$ to find the side length of the tiles in inches for a tabletop with an area of A square feet.

______

b. What is the side length of the tiles that make up a tabletop with an area of 4 square feet?

______

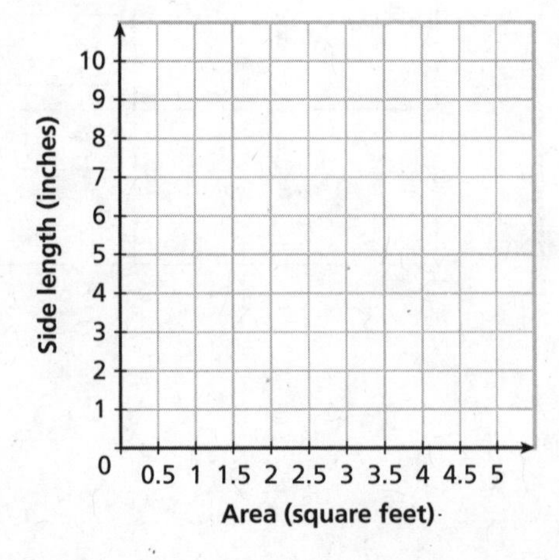

6. The function $A(r) = \pi r^2$ gives the area A in square meters of a circle with a radius of r meters.

a. Write and graph the inverse function $r(A)$ to find the radius in meters of a circle with an area of A square meters.

____

b. Estimate the radius of a circular swimming pool that has a surface area of 120 square meters.

____

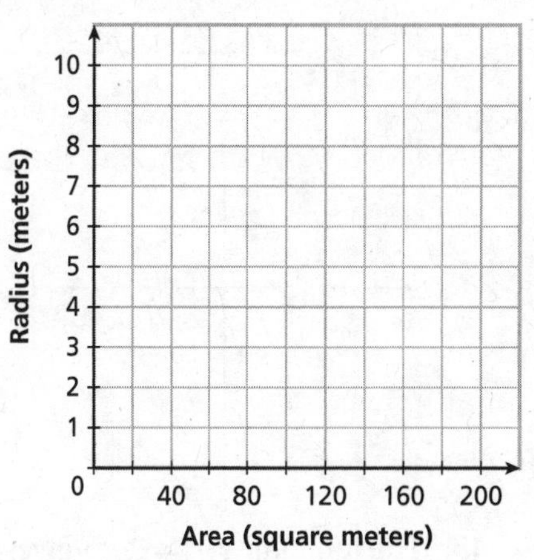

Graph each square root function $g(x)$. (The graph of the parent function is shown.) Then describe $g(x)$ as a transformation of the parent square root function.

7. $g(x) = \sqrt{\frac{x}{3}}$

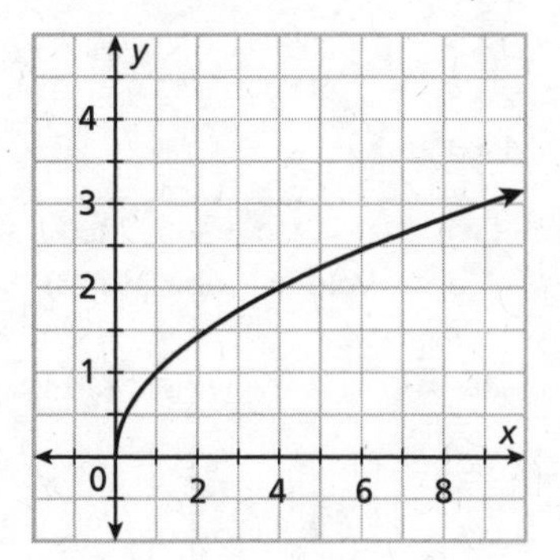

____

____

8. $g(x) = \sqrt{4x}$

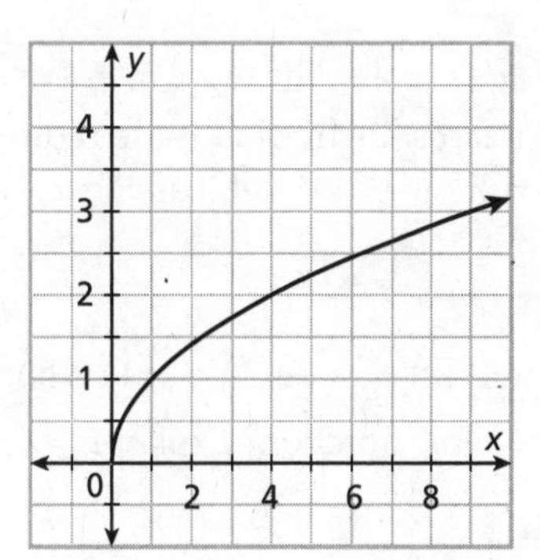

____

____

Graph the function $f(x)$. Then graph its inverse, $f^{-1}(x)$, and write a rule for the inverse function.

9. $f(x) = 2x^3$

$f^{-1}(x) =$

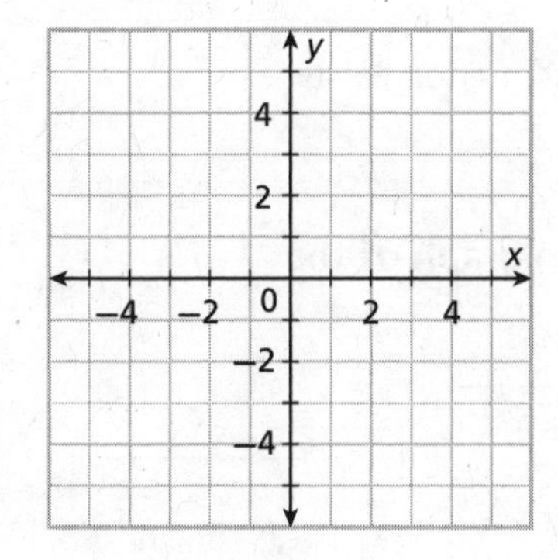

10. $f(x) = -x^3$

$f^{-1}(x) =$

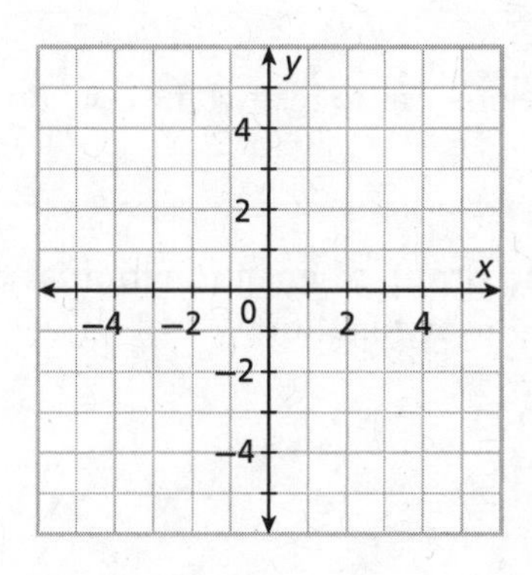

11. $f(x) = \frac{1}{4}x^3$

$f^{-1}(x) =$ ______________________

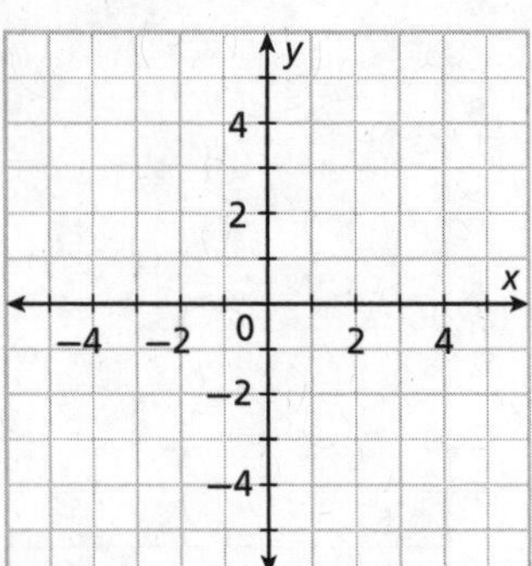

12. $f(x) = -\frac{1}{3}x^3$

$f^{-1}(x) =$ ______________________

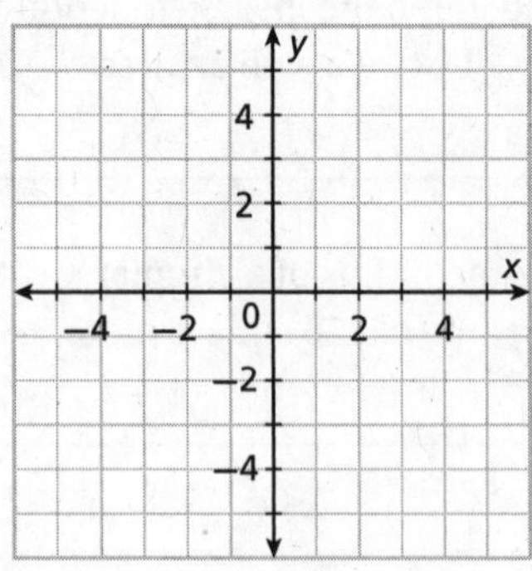

13. The function $V(r) = \frac{4}{3}\pi r^3$ gives the volume V in cubic inches of a sphere with a radius of r inches.

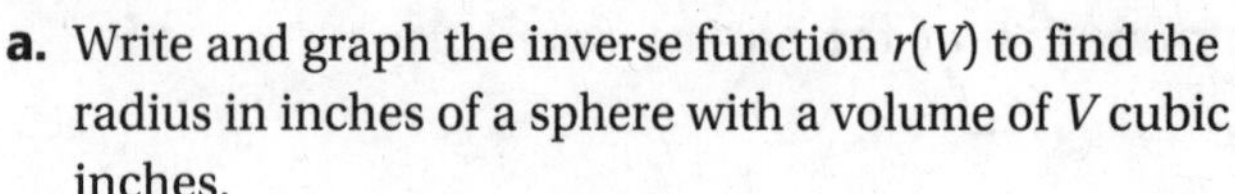

a. Write and graph the inverse function $r(V)$ to find the radius in inches of a sphere with a volume of V cubic inches.

____

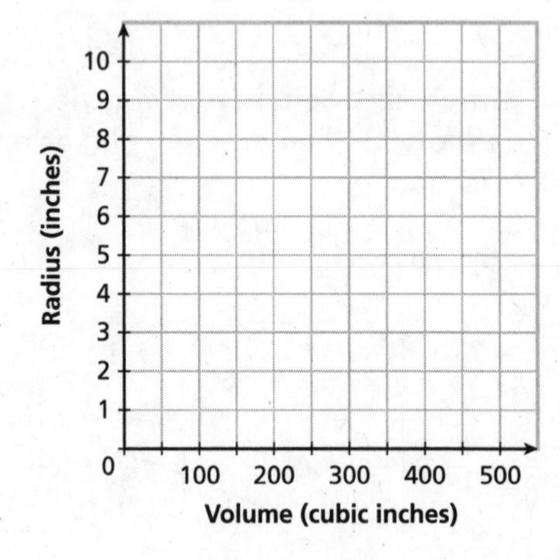

b. To the nearest inch, what is the radius of a basketball with a volume of 455 cubic inches?

____

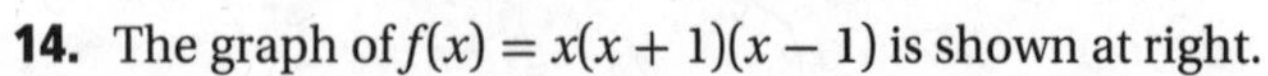

14. The graph of $f(x) = x(x + 1)(x - 1)$ is shown at right.

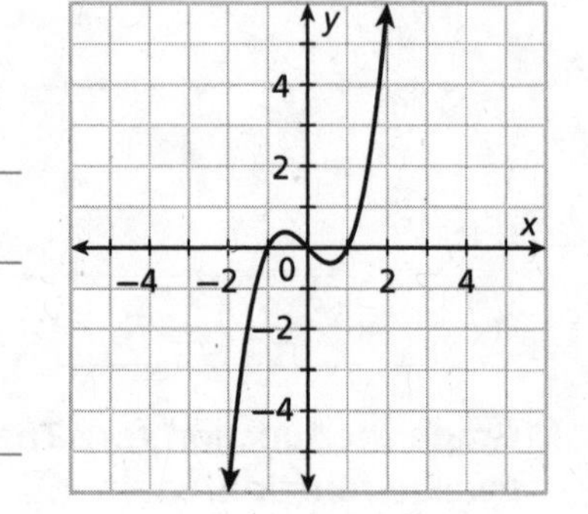

a. Is $f(x)$ a cubic function? Explain.

____

____

b. Is $f(x)$ a one-to-one function? Explain.

____

____

c. Does an inverse function for $f(x)$ exist? Explain.

____

d. Give one way to restrict the domain of $f(x)$ so that an inverse function exists.

____

Describe the graph of each function as a transformation of the graph of the parent cube root function.

15. $g(x) = 4\sqrt[3]{x}$

____

____

16. $g(x) = \sqrt[3]{8x}$

____

____

Additional Practice

Find the inverse of each function. Determine whether the inverse is a function and state its domain and range.

1. $k(x) = 10x + 5$

2. $d(x) = 6 - 2x$

3. $f(x) = (x - 5)^2$

4. $g(x) = \dfrac{4 - x}{2}$

5. $h(x) = \sqrt{x^2 - 9}$

6. $b(x) = 2\log x$

7. $m(x) = e^{x - 5}$

8. $w(x) = \left(\dfrac{x - 3}{2}\right)^6$

Solve.

9. So far, Rhonda has saved $3000 for her college expenses. She plans to save $30 each month. Her college fund can be represented by the function $f(x) = 30x + 3000$.

   a. Find the inverse of $f(x)$.

   b. What does the inverse represent?

   c. When will the fund reach $3990?

   d. How long will it take her to reach her goal of $4800?

Problem Solving

A juice drink manufacturer is designing an advertisement for a national sports event on its cans. The lateral surface area of the cans is given by the function $L(h) = 2.5\pi h$, where h is the height of the can. The total surface area of the can is given by the function $T(h) = 2.5\pi(h + 1.25)$.

1. The graphic designer needs to know how the height of the can varies as a function of the lateral surface area.

   a. Find the inverse, $h(L)$, of the function $L(h)$.

   ____

   b. Explain the meaning of the inverse function.

   ____

   c. If the lateral surface area of one can is 35.34 in^2, what is the height of this can? ______________

Choose the letter for the best answer.

2. The manufacturer produces cans in different sizes. The height of one can is 5.5 in. The designer is planning to use only half the lateral surface area of this can. What is this area?

   A 8.8 in^2

   B 11.0 in^2

   C 21.6 in^2

   D 43.2 in^2

4. The total surface area of one size of can is 45.16 in^2. What is the height of this can?

   A 3.5 in.

   B 4.5 in.

   C 5.5 in.

   D 6.5 in.

3. The designer is studying the possibility of using the total surface area of each can. Which function gives height, $h(T)$, as a function of total surface area, T?

   F $h(T) = \dfrac{T}{2.5\pi} - 1.25$

   G $h(T) = \dfrac{T}{2.5\pi} + 1.25$

   H $h(T) = (2.5\pi)(T - 1.25)$

   J $h(T) = (2.5\pi)(T + 1.25)$

5. The designer updates an old advertisement that covers the lateral surface area, L, of a can to create a new advertisement that covers the total surface area, T, of the can. Which function gives this area?

   F $T = (2.5\pi)(L + 1.25)$

   G $T = (2.5\pi)(L - 1.25)$

   H $T = L - 2.5\pi(1.25)$

   J $T = L + 2.5\pi(1.25)$

Name ______________________ Class ______________ Date ________

22-1

Curve Fitting with Polynomial Models

Focus on Modeling

Video Tutor

Essential question: *How can you use polynomial functions to model and solve real-world problems?*

You are making an open rectangular box for an art project. To make the box, you cut out a square from each corner of a rectangular piece of cardboard and fold up the flaps to create an open box as shown below.

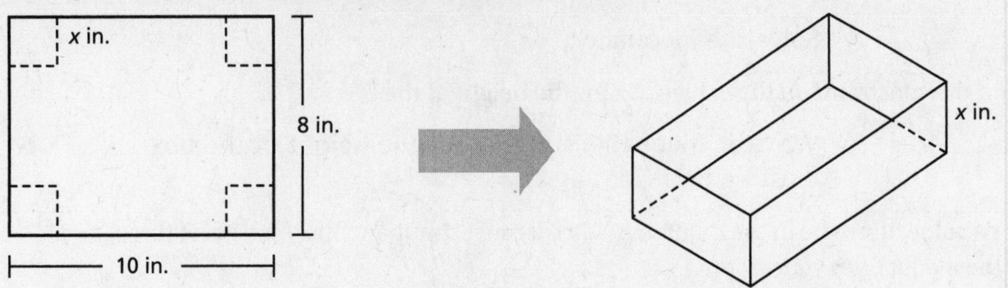

The original rectangular piece of cardboard is 10 inches long and 8 inches wide. If x is the side length in inches of each square that is cut from the corners, what value or values of x will result in a box with a volume of 48 in.^{3}? Is this the greatest possible volume? Explain.

1 Write a volume function.

A Use the figure to help you write expressions for the length, width, and height of the box.

Length of box: $10 - 2x$

Width of box: ______________________

Height of box: ______________________

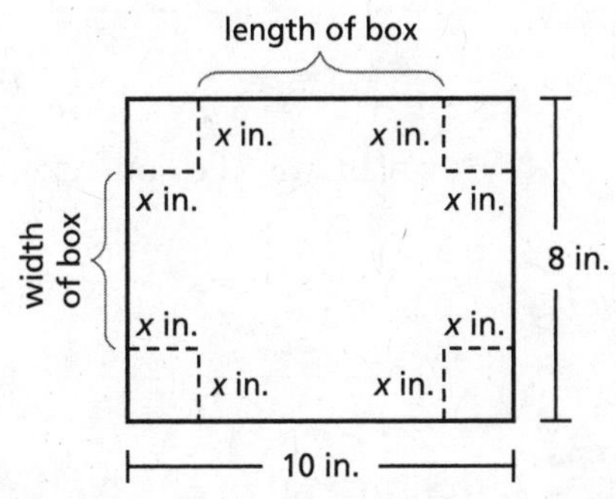

B The volume of the box is the product of the length, width, and height. Use the expressions you wrote above to write a function $V(x)$ that models the volume of the box.

____

REFLECT

1a. What units are associated with the expressions for the length, width, and height? What are the units for the volume of the box?

____

1b. How can you use your function $V(x)$ to find the volume of the box when squares with sides of length 3 inches are cut from the corners of the cardboard? What are the dimensions of the box in this case?

____

2 Determine the domain of the volume function.

A To find the domain of the volume function, use the fact that each dimension of the box must be positive.

Find the constraint on the values of x for the length of the box.

$10 - 2x > 0$ Write an inequality stating that the length of the box must be positive.

__________ Solve the inequality.

Find the constraint on the values of x for the width of the box.

__________ > 0 Write an inequality stating that the width of the box must be positive.

__________ Solve the inequality.

Find the constraint on the values of x for the height of the box.

__________ Write an inequality stating that the height of the box must be positive.

B For a value of x to be in the domain of $V(x)$, it must simultaneously satisfy all three of the inequalities you wrote.

So, the domain of $V(x)$ is all x such that __________ $< x <$ __________.

REFLECT

2a. What would happen to the volume if x took on either of the endpoint values in the domain inequality? Explain why this makes sense in the context of the problem.

____

____

2b. Explain why the domain of $V(x)$ is not $0 < x < 5$.

____

____

3 Write and solve an equation.

A Multiply the factors in $V(x)$ to write $V(x)$ as a polynomial in standard form.

$V(x) =$ ____

B To find the value of x that results in a box with a volume of 48 in.^{3}, set the polynomial $V(x)$ equal to 48. Write the resulting equation.

____

C Write your equation in the form $p(x) = 0$. To make calculations easier, divide both sides of your equation by the greatest common factor of the coefficients of $p(x)$.

____

D Solve the equation. First determine the possible rational zeros of $p(x)$.

______

Use synthetic substitution to find a zero of $p(x)$. Then factor $p(x)$ completely to find the remaining zeros.

The zeros of $p(x)$ are ______.

E Interpret the results. Which of the zeros are in the domain of $V(x)$?

______

For each of these zeros, what are the corresponding dimensions of the box?

______

______

REFLECT

3a. Check that the values of x that you found above result in a box with a volume of 48 in.^{3}

______

______

3b. Given that it's possible to create a box with a volume of 48 in.^{3}, do you think it's possible to create a box with a volume of 24 in.^{3}? Explain.

______

______

4 Graph the volume function and determine the local maximum.

A Use a graphing calculator to graph the volume function $V(x)$.

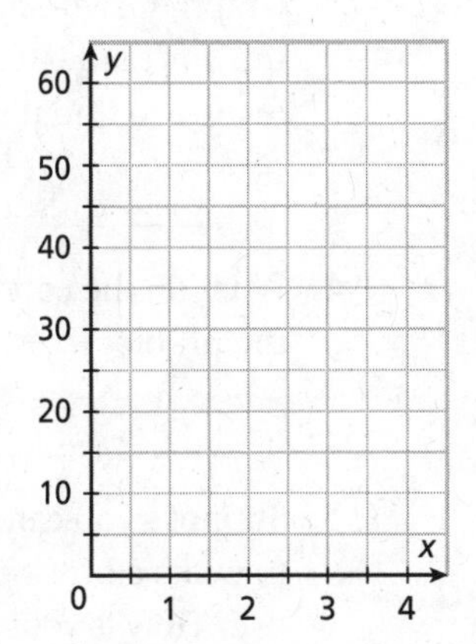

Step 1: Enter $V(x)$ in the equation editor.

Step 2: Use the domain of $V(x)$ and the fact that the volume can be at least 48 in.^{3} to help you choose an appropriate viewing window.

Step 3: Graph the function. Sketch the graph on the coordinate plane at right.

B Find the maximum value of the function within the domain.

Step 1: Press 2nd TRACE (CALC), then select **4:maximum.**

Step 2: Use the arrow keys to move along the graph to select a left bound, a right bound, and a guess. Press ENTER after each of these.

At what point does the maximum value occur? Round the coordinates to the nearest tenth.

______

REFLECT

4a. Interpret the result. What do the coordinates of the point where the maximum value occurs represent in the context of the problem?

4b. How does your graph of $V(x)$ support the domain you found earlier?

4c. You know that $V(x)$ has a maximum value on the domain $0 < x < 4$, but does $V(x)$ have a maximum value when the domain is not restricted (that is, when x can be any real number)? Explain.

EXTEND

1. Suppose you have a second piece of cardboard that is 16 inches long and 6 inches wide. What is the volume function for this box when squares of side length x are cut from the corners of the cardboard?

2. What is the domain of this volume function?

3. Graph this volume function in the same viewing window as the volume function for the box made from the 10-by-8 piece of cardboard. Then use the calculator's Intersect feature to find the coordinates of the point or points where the graphs intersect.

4. What do the coordinates of the points of intersection represent in the context of the problem?

5. Suppose you can make a box from only one of the pieces of cardboard and you want to make a box with the greatest possible volume. Which piece of cardboard should you use? How is your answer supported by the graphs of the volume functions?

Name ______________________ Class ______________ Date __________

Additional Practice

The diagrams show patterns for making two boxes. For each box, a square of side length *x* centimeters is cut from each corner of a rectangular piece of cardboard. The flaps are folded up to form the box. Use the diagrams for Exercises 1–4.

Box A

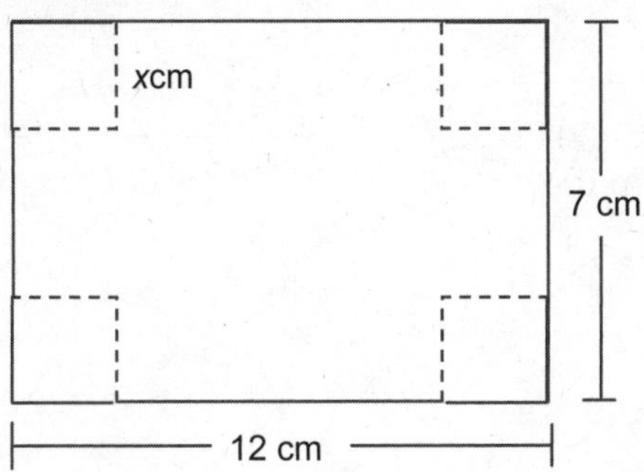

Box B

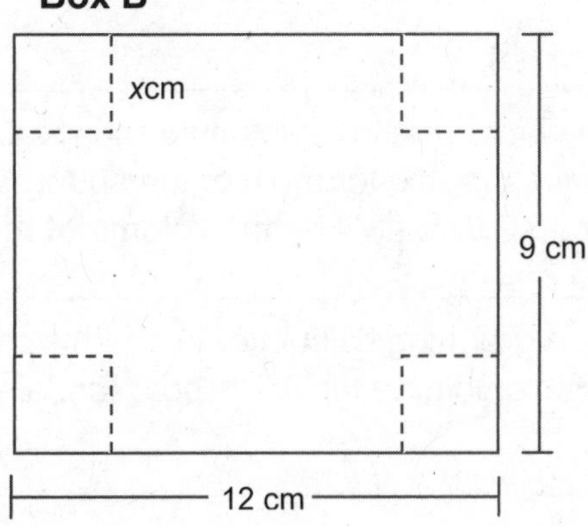

1. Write a function $V(x)$ that models the volume of each box. Find the domain of each function.

   Box A ______________________________

   Box B ______________________________

2. Find the volume of each box if a square of side length 1 centimeter is cut from each corner.

   Box A ______________ **Box B** ______________

3. For each function, multiply the factors in $V(x)$ to write it as a polynomial in standard form.

   Box A ______________________________

   Box B ______________________________

4. Graph each function on a graphing calculator. Which box could have a volume of 80 cubic centimeters? How do you know? Then find the value of *x* that produces a volume of 80 cubic centimeters.

   ____

   ____

   ____

   ____

Problem Solving

Sue cuts identical squares out of the corners of the cardboard square shown, then folds up the flaps to make a box. Use this information for Exercises 1–3.

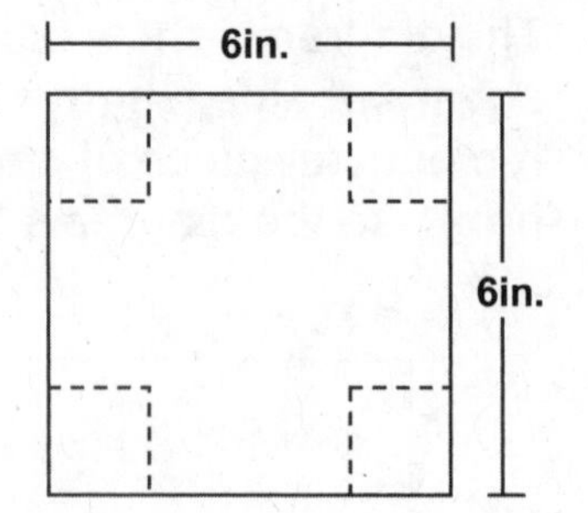

1. Describe the possible side lengths Sue can use for the squares she cuts from the corners of the box.

____

2. Sue wants the box to be cube-shaped. What side length should she use for each of the squares she cuts from the corners? What will be the volume of the box?

____

3. Use a graphing calculator to find the maximum possible volume for Sue's box. Explain your procedure.

____

____

Choose the best answer.

A rectangular prism has sides of length x, $0.5x$, and $x - 1$ inches. Its volume is 9 cubic inches. Use this information for Exercises 4–6.

4. Which equation models the situation?

   A $0.5x^3 - 0.5x = 9$

   B $0.5x^3 - 0.5x^2 = 9$

   C $0.5x^2 - 0.5x^2 = 9$

   D $(0.5x)(x - 1) = 9$

5. What are the possible rational solutions of the equation in Exercise 1?

   F $\pm\frac{1}{1}, \pm\frac{1}{2}, \pm\frac{1}{3}, \pm\frac{1}{6}, \pm\frac{1}{9}, \pm\frac{1}{18}$

   G $\pm\frac{1}{1}, \pm\frac{2}{1}, \pm\frac{3}{1}, \pm\frac{6}{1}, \pm\frac{9}{1}, \pm\frac{18}{1}$

   H $\pm\frac{1}{1}, \pm\frac{3}{1}, \pm\frac{9}{1}$

   J $\pm\frac{1}{1}, \pm\frac{1}{3}, \pm\frac{1}{9}$

6. What is the length of the shortest side of the prism?

   A 1 in. C 2 in.

   B 1.5 in. D 3 in.

7. The volume of a rectangular prism is 225 cubic centimeters. The base of the prism is a square, and the height of the prism is 4 centimeters greater than a side length of the base. What is the height of the prism?

   A 4 cm C 9 cm

   B 5 cm D 25 cm

8. A pyramid-shaped sculpture has a volume of 18 cubic inches. The length of a side of the square base of the pyramid is 3 inches less than the height of the pyramid. What equation could model this situation?

   A $x^3 - 3x^2 = 18$

   B $x^3 - 3x^2 = 54$

   C $x^3 - 6x^2 + 9x = 18$

   D $x^3 - 6x^2 + 9x = 54$

Name________________ Class__________ Date__________

22-2

Curve Fitting with Exponential and Logarithmic Models

Focus on Modeling

Essential question: *How can you model the time it takes a radioactive substance to decay as a function of the percent of the substance remaining?*

Video Tutor

Radioactive substances decay to other substances over time. The half-life of a radioactive substance is the time it takes for one-half of the substance to decay. How can you determine the length of time it takes a given radioactive substance to decay to a specified percent?

1 Model radioactive decay with an exponential function.

A The isotope bismuth-210 has a half-life of 5 days. Complete the table showing the decay of a sample of bismuth-210.

Number of Half-Lives	Number of Days (t)	Percent of Isotope Remaining (p)
0	0	100
1	5	50
2	10	
3		
4		

B Write the decay rate r as a fraction. ______________

C Write an expression for the number of half-lives in t days. ______________

D Write an exponential decay function that models this situation. The function $p(t)$ should give the percent of the isotope remaining after t days.

____

REFLECT

1a. Show how to check that your model is correct by letting $t = 10$ and comparing the resulting value of $p(t)$ to the value in the table.

____

____

1b. Find $p(t)$ when $t = 0$, 1, and 8. Explain what these values represent.

1c. Every 5 days, the amount of bismuth-210 decreases by 50%. By what percent does the amount of bismuth-210 decrease *each day*? Explain.

1d. Describe the end behavior of $p(t)$ as t increases without bound.

2 Convert the exponential decay function to a logarithmic function.

A The function $p(t) = 100\left(\frac{1}{2}\right)^{\frac{t}{5}}$ gives the percent of bismuth-210 that remains after t days. Describe the domain and range of this function.

B Write the inverse of the decay function by solving for t. Use p in place of $p(t)$.

$p = 100\left(\frac{1}{2}\right)^{\frac{t}{5}}$	Given
$\square = \left(\frac{1}{2}\right)^{\frac{t}{5}}$	Divide both sides by 100.
$\log_{\square}\left(\square\right) = \frac{t}{5}$	Definition of logarithm
$5\log_{\square}\left(\square\right) = t$	Multiply both sides by 5.

REFLECT

2a. Describe the domain and range of the logarithmic function.

2b. Verify that the logarithmic model is correct by substituting 50 for p. What is the resulting value of t? Explain why this result makes sense.

3 Convert to a common logarithm.

A Rewrite your logarithmic function with a common logarithm. Where appropriate, round to two decimal places.

$t = 5 \log_{\frac{1}{2}}\left(\frac{p}{100}\right)$ — Given

$= 5 \cdot \frac{\log \square}{\log \square}$ — Change of Base Property

$= \frac{5}{\log \square} \cdot \log \square$ — Write the denominator as part of the first factor.

$= \square \log \square$ — Evaluate the first factor. Round to two decimal places.

B Write the function without a fraction.

$t = -16.61\left(\log \square - \log \square\right)$ — Quotient Property of Logarithms

$= -16.61\left(\log \square - \square\right)$ — Evaluate log 100.

$= -16.61 \log \square + \square$ — Distributive Property

$= \square - 16.61 \log \square$ — Commutative Property of Addition

REFLECT

3a. What is the benefit of rewriting the function so that it involves a common logarithm?

3b. The final form of the logarithmic function includes rounded numbers. Check the accuracy of the function by substituting 50 for *p* and evaluating the expression with your calculator. Do you get the expected result? Explain.

3c. Explain how you can find out how long it takes until 5% of the bismuth-210 remains. Round to the nearest tenth of a day.

3d. To emphasize that *t* is a function of *p*, write the equation of the logarithmic function using function notation.

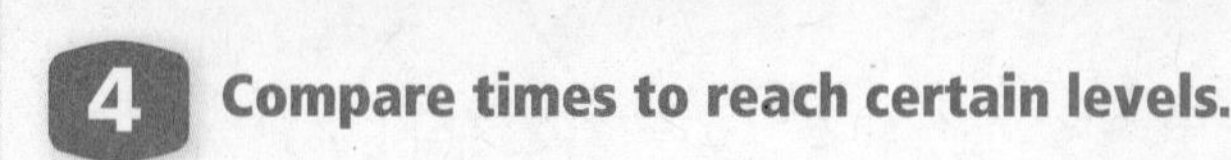

4 Compare times to reach certain levels.

You can use your calculator, as follows, to compare the amounts of time it takes the percent of bismuth-210 to drop from 100% to 75%, from 75% to 50%, and from 50% to 25%.

A Enter the logarithmic function from step 3 into the equation editor of your graphing calculator.

B Press 2nd WINDOW (TBLSET). Then set the TblStart value at 100 and the ΔTbl value to -25.

C Look at the table of values. How many days does it take for the percent to drop from 100% to 75%? from 75% to 50%? from 50% to 25%?

REFLECT

4a. Why is there an ERROR message in the table in the row corresponding to the value $x = 0$?

4b. Make a conjecture about how the amount of time it takes for bismuth-210 to drop from 70% to 60% compares to the amount of time it takes to drop from 20% to 10%. Then check your conjecture using a graphing calculator.

EXTEND

1. As a sample of bismuth-210 decays, the sample is transformed into a mixture of bismuth-210 and other isotopes in its decay chain. The time needed for the amount of the other isotopes to reach a certain percent of the sample can be obtained from the logarithmic model for bismuth-210 by replacing p in the function's rule. Write a function that gives the time t needed for the amount of the other isotopes to reach p percent of the sample. (*Hint:* Consider how the percent of bismuth-210 and the percent of the other isotopes are related.)

2. Use the function you wrote in Exercise 1 to determine the time needed for the other isotopes to reach 75% of the sample amount. Explain why your result makes sense.

Name ____________ Class ____________ Date ____________

Additional Practice

Determine whether f is an exponential function of x. If so, find the constant ratio.

1.

x	–1	0	1	2	3
$f(x)$	9	3	1	0.3	0.9

____

2.

x	–1	0	1	2	3
$f(x)$	0.01	0.03	0.15	0.87	5.19

____

3.

x	–1	0	1	2	3
$f(x)$	$\frac{5}{6}$	$\frac{5}{2}$	7.5	22.5	67.5

____

4.

x	–1	0	1	2	3
$f(x)$	1	0.5	0.33	0.25	0.2

____

Use exponential regression to find a function that models the data.

5.

x	1	2	3	4	5
$f(x)$	14	7.1	3.4	1.8	0.8

____

6.

x	2	12	22	32	42
$f(x)$	5	20	80	320	1280

____

Solve.

7. a. Bernice is selling seashells she has found at the beach. The price of each shell depends on its length. Find an exponential model for the data.

Length of Shell (cm)	5	8	12	20	25
Price ($)	2	3.5	5	18	40

____

b. What is the length of a shell selling for $9.00? ______________________

c. If Bernice found a 40 cm Conch shell. How much could she sell it for? ______________________

8. a. Use logarithmic regression to find a function that models this data.

Time (min)	1	2	3	4	5
Speed (m/s)	1.5	6.2	10.6	12.9	14.8

____

b. When will the speed exceed 20 m/s? ______________________

c. What will the speed be after 1 hour? ______________________

22-2 ...em Solving

1. ... ll group of farmers joined together to grow and sell wheat in 1985. The table shows how their production of wheat increased over 20 years.

Wheat Produced by Growers Co-op						
Years After 1985	3	6	10	13	16	20
Wheat (tons)	70	105	150	210	340	580

a. Find an exponential model for the data. ____________

b. Use the model to predict when their wheat production will exceed 2000 tons. ____________

2. The table shows the U.S. production of tobacco from 1997 to 2002.

Tobacco Production						
Years After 1996	1	2	3	4	5	6
Tobacco (× 100,000 pounds)	1787	1480	1293	1053	992	890

a. Find a logarithmic model for the data. ____________

b. Use the model to predict when tobacco production could fall below 50,000,000 pounds. ____________

Robert recently discovered a forgotten student loan bill. The amount due after 10 years is now $10,819.33. He found some old statements and determined that after 7 years the bill was $8831.80 and after 5 years he owed $7714.03. Choose the letter for the best answer.

3. Which function models the data?

A $S(x) = 5000(1.07)^x$

B $S(x) = 1.07(5000)^x$

C $S(x) = 5500(1.07)^x$

D $S(x) = 1.07(5500)^x$

4. How much did Robert borrow initially?

F $5750

G $5500

H $5250

J $5000

5. Robert is planning to pay the loan in full next year. How much will he owe then?

A $12,092.14

B $11,925.07

C $11,869.33

D $11,576.69

6. What is the interest rate on Robert's student loan?

F 7%

G 6%

H 5%

J 4%

Name _______________ Class _______________ Date _______________

Modeling Real-World Data

Focus on Modeling

Essential question: *How can you model age as a function of body mass index given a data set?*

Video Tutor

Body mass index (BMI) is a measure used to determine healthy body mass based on a person's height. BMI is calculated by dividing a person's mass in kilograms by the square of his or her height in meters. The median BMI measures for a group of boys ages 2 to 10 years are given in the chart below.

Age of Boys	2	3	4	5	6	7	8	9	10
Median BMI	16.6	16.0	15.6	15.4	15.4	15.5	15.8	16.2	16.6

How can you use the data to develop a model for predicting the age of a boy with a given BMI?

1 Write a model of boys' median BMI as a function of age.

A Create a scatter plot for the data in the table, treating age as the independent variable x and median BMI as the dependent variable y.

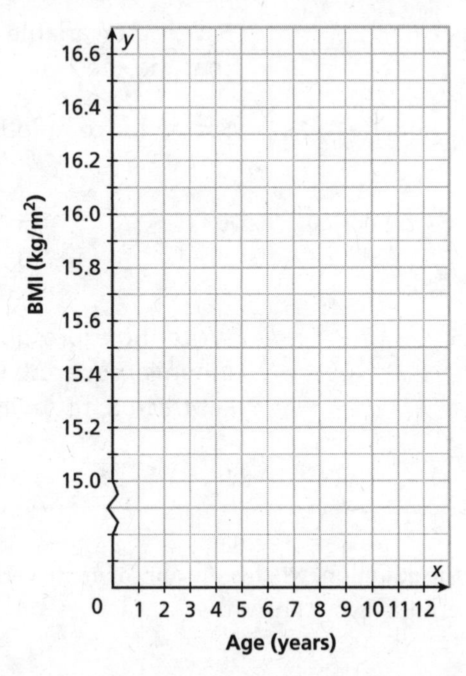

B Use a graphing calculator to find a quadratic regression model of the data.

- Enter the data into two lists. First, enter the ages in L_1 and the median BMI measures in L_2.
- Use the quadratic regression feature. Press STAT, select **CALC**, and then select **5:QuadReg**. Enter the independent variable, L_1, followed by a comma, and then the dependent variable, L_2. Press ENTER.

he values for a, b, and c correspond to the values in the standard form of a quadratic function, $f(x) = ax^2 + bx + c$. Record each value to three significant digits to complete the quadratic model below.

$f(x) =$ ______ $x^2 -$ ______ $x +$ ______

REFLECT

1a. Explain why it is appropriate to use a quadratic model for this data set, rather than another type of model, such as linear or cubic.

____

1b. Use a calculator to make a scatter plot of the data and then graph $f(x)$ on the same screen. Is the model a good fit for the data? Explain.

____

____

2 Write the quadratic model in vertex form.

Complete the square to write the function in vertex form, $f(x) = a(x - h)^2 + k$.

$f(x) = 0.0763x^2 - 0.897x + 18.0$ — Write the equation in standard form.

$f(x) =$ ______ $(x^2 - 11.76x) + 18.0$ — Factor the variable terms so that the coefficient of x^2 is 1.

$f(x) = 0.0763\left(x^2 - 11.76x + \square\right) + 18.0 - \square$ — Set up for completing the square.

$f(x) = 0.0763\left(x^2 - 11.76x + \text{______}\right) + 18.0 - 0.0763 \cdot$ ______ — Complete the square: $\left(\frac{11.76}{2}\right)^2 =$ ______

$f(x) = 0.0763\left(x - \text{______}\right)^2 + 15.4$ — Write the expression in parentheses as a binomial squared. Simplify the product being subtracted, rounding to 3 significant digits.

REFLECT

2a. Based on the vertex form of the equation, what is the approximate vertex of the graph of $f(x)$? Explain how you determined your answer.

____

____

2b. Do the coordinates you found for the vertex agree with the information in the scatter plot? Explain.

2c. Interpret the meaning of the vertex in the context of the problem.

2d. Give the domain of $f(x)$ based on the data set.

3 Graph and write the inverse of the quadratic model.

A Because $f(x)$ is quadratic, it is not one-to-one and its inverse is not a function. Restrict the domain of $f(x)$ to values of x for which $f(x)$ is increasing so that its inverse will be a function. What is the restricted domain of $f(x)$?

B Enter the coordinates of the vertex in the first row of the table below. Complete the table of values and use it to graph $f(x)$ with the restricted domain. Round the values of $f(x)$ to the nearest tenth.

x	f(x)
5.88	
7	
8	
9	
10	

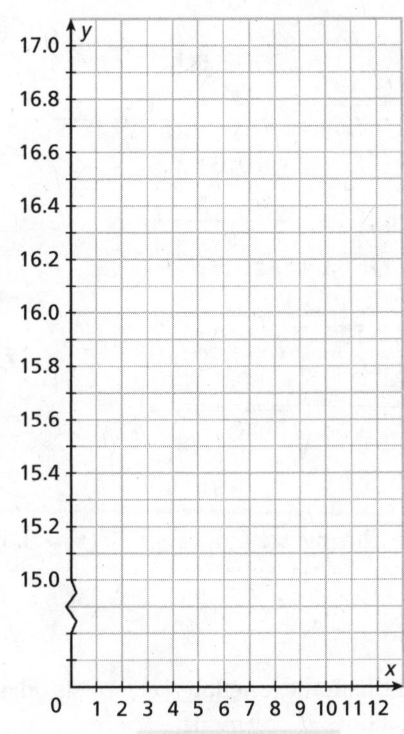

C Find the images of each of the points in the table in part B after reflection over the line $y = x$. Record the coordinates of the points below.

t the points from part C and draw a smooth curve through them to graph the
verse function, $f^{-1}(x)$.

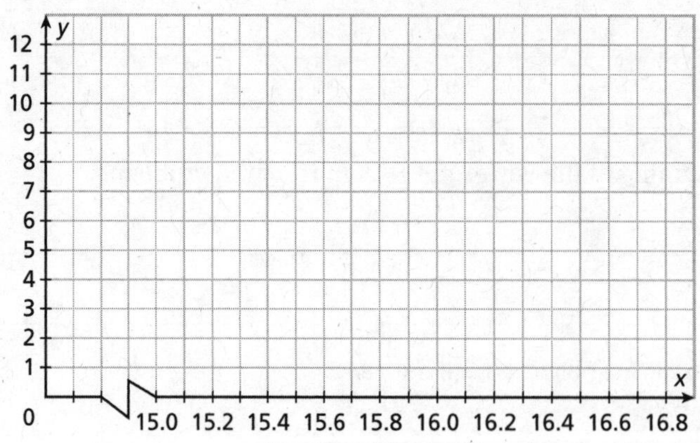

E Write a rule for $f^{-1}(x)$.

$f(x) = 0.0763\left(x - \square\right)^2 + \square$	Write equation of $f(x)$.
$y = 0.0763\left(x - \square\right)^2 + \square$	Replace $f(x)$ with y.
$y - \square = 0.0763\left(x - \square\right)^2$	Subtract 15.4 from both sides.
$\frac{1}{0.0763}\left(y - \square\right) = \left(x - \square\right)^2$	Divide both sides by 0.0763.
$\sqrt{\frac{1}{0.0763}}\sqrt{y - \square} = x - \square$	Use the definition of positive square root.
$\sqrt{\frac{1}{0.0763}}\sqrt{y - \square} + \square = x$	Add 5.88 to both sides.
$\sqrt{\frac{1}{0.0763}}\sqrt{x - \square} + \square = y$	Switch x and y to write inverse.
$3.62\sqrt{x - \square} + \square \approx f^{-1}(x)$	Simplify and replace y with $f^{-1}(x)$.

So, the inverse function is $f^{-1}(x) \approx 3.62\sqrt{x - \square} + \square$.

REFLECT

3a. The quadratic function $f(x)$ models boys' median BMI as a function of age. What does $f^{-1}(x)$ model?

3b. Why does it make sense to make the least x-value in the domain of $f(x)$ be 5.88 when finding the inverse function?

3c. What are the domain and range of $f(x)$? of $f^{-1}(x)$?

3d. Use a graphing calculator to graph $f(x)$, $f^{-1}(x)$, and the line $y = x$ in the same window. How can you use these graphs to check that you found the inverse function correctly?

EXTEND

Use the inverse function $f^{-1}(x)$ to make predictions for Exercises 1 and 2. (In Exercise 2, allow the domain to include x-values greater than 10.)

1. A boy over the age of 6 has a BMI of 15.9. How old do you expect him to be, to the nearest tenth of a year?

2. A boy over the age of 6 has a BMI of 20.4. How old do you expect him to be, to the nearest tenth of a year?

3. Which of your predictions, the one in Exercise 1 or the one in Exercise 2, do you think is more reliable? Explain your reasoning.

4. Over what interval, if any, does the inverse function $f^{-1}(x)$ increase? Over what interval, if any, does it decrease? Does this make sense given what you know about $f(x)$?

odel you found for $f^{-1}(x)$ applies to boys aged 5.88 years or older. der how you could change your model so that it applies to boys 5.88 years or younger.

low else could you restrict the domain of $f(x) = 0.0763(x - 5.88)^2 + 15.4$ o find an inverse that is a function?

____

b. Complete the table of values and use it to graph $f(x)$ with the restricted domain. Round the values of $f(x)$ to the nearest hundredth.

x	f(x)
2	
3	
4	
5.88	15.4

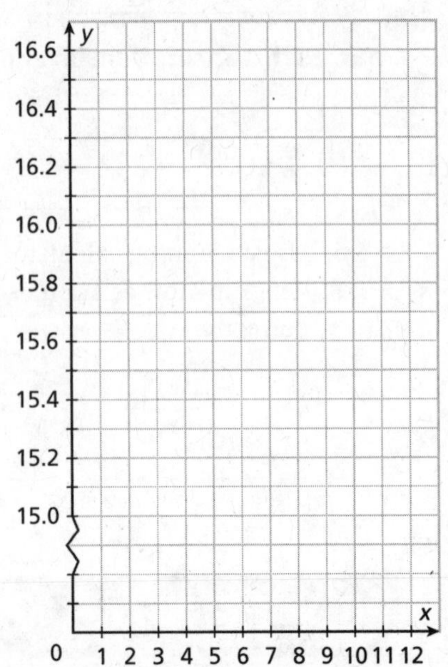

c. What is the range of $f(x)$ with the restricted domain?

____

d. Graph the inverse of $f(x)$ with the restricted domain. Give the domain and range of the inverse.

Domain:

____

Range:

____

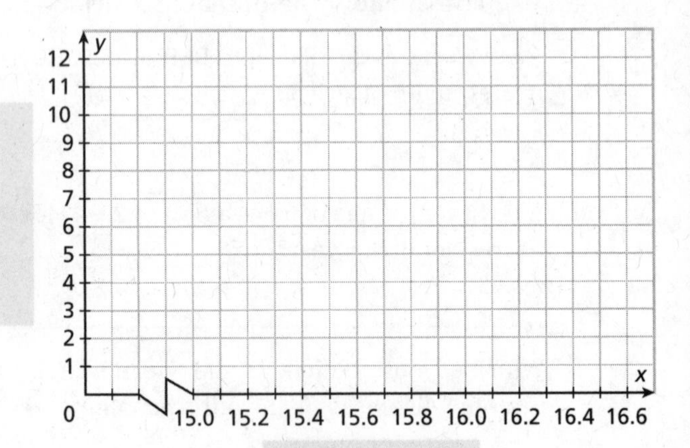

e. The equation of $f^{-1}(x)$ when the domain of $f(x)$ is restricted to $\{x \mid 5.88 \le x \le 10\}$ is $f^{-1}(x) = 3.62\sqrt{x - 15.4} + 5.88$. What is the equation of $f^{-1}(x)$ when the domain of $f(x)$ is restricted to $\{x \mid 2 \le x \le 5.88\}$? Explain.

____

____

____

Name________________________ Class____________ Date__________

Additional Practice

Use constant differences or ratios to determine which parent function would best model the given data set.

1.

x	12	16	20	24	28
y	0.8	3.6	16.2	72.9	328.05

____

2.

x	13	19	25	31	37	43
y	−1	17	35	53	71	89

____

3.

x	2	7	12	17	22
y	−100	−55	40	185	380

____

4.

x	0.10	0.37	0.82	1.45	2.26
y	0.3	0.6	0.9	1.2	1.5

____

Write a function that models the data set.

5.

x	2.2	2.6	3.0	3.4	3.8
y	0.68	4.52	9.0	14.12	19.88

____

6.

x	−5	0	5	10	15	20
y	8	6	4	2	0	−2

____

7.

x	0.3	0.7	1.1	1.5	1.9
y	2.5	3	3.6	4.32	5.184

____

8.

x	0.06	0.375	0.96	1.815	2.94
y	0.2	0.5	0.8	1.1	1.4

____

9.

x	−6	1	8	15	22
y	15	1	30.12	102.36	217.72

____

10.

x	0.32	2.07	4.8	8.51	13.2
y	0.9	1.6	2.3	3.0	3.7

____

Solve.

11. The table shows the population growth of a small town.

Years after 1974	1	6	11	16	21	26	31
Population	662	740	825	908	1003	1095	1200

a. Write a function that models the data. ________________________

b. Use your model to predict the population in 2020. ________________________

22-3

m Solving

nows the population of Lincoln Valley over the last 7 years. ǐe town council is developing long-range plans and is considering how the population might grow in the future if the current trend continues.

Lincoln Valley Population 2000–2006							
Year	1	2	3	4	5	6	7
Population	1049	1137	1229	1326	1434	1542	1662

1. What is the independent variable? What is the dependent variable? Assign x or y to each variable.

____

2. Make a scatter plot of the data. Do the data form a linear pattern? For this to be true, explain what must be true about finite differences.

____

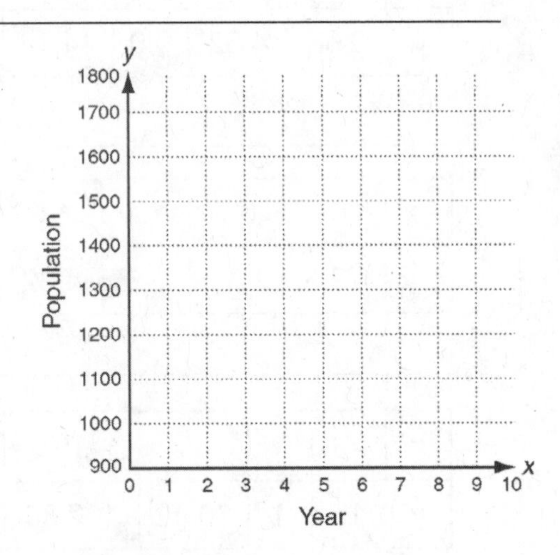

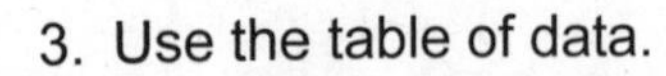

3. Use the table of data.

   a. Find the first differences.

   ____

   b. Find the second differences.

   ____

   c. Find the third differences.

   ____

   d. Find the ratios between y-values.

   ____

4. What kind of function will best describe the data? Justify your conclusion.

____

Choose the letter for the best answer.

5. Which function best models the given data?

   A $y = 101.9x + 932.1$

   B $y = 3.1x^2 + 77.0x + 969.6$

   C $y = 996.6x^{0.233}$

   D $y = 974.9(1.08)^x$

6. Predict the population of Lincoln Valley in 2012.

   F 2270

   G 2450

   H 2650

   J 2860

Name_______________ Class_______________ Date__________

UNIT 10

Performance Tasks

GPS COMMON CORE

MCC9-12.F.BF.3
MCC9-12.F.IF.7b

★ **1.** Insurance policy A states, "If your monthly income decreases by d dollars, we will pay d dollars per month." Insurance policy B states, "If your monthly income decreases by p percent, we will pay p percent of your resulting monthly income per month." For both policies, write a function $f(x)$ for your income after the decrease and a function $g(x)$ for your income after the insurance policy. Use composites of these functions to explain which policy pays out more.

★ **2.** A doctor has found that the amount of aspirin in milligrams in the body of one of his patients can be modeled by the function $a(t) = 325e^{-0.2166t}$, where t is the number of hours since the patient took the aspirin. What transformations must be applied to the function $f(t) = e^t$ in order to produce this function?

3. A veterinarian is attempting to determine a function that converts a dog's age from dog years into human years, and she knows that a newborn puppy has a human age the same as that of a newborn baby. She also knows that a dog that is 1 year old in dog years has a human age of 15 years, while a dog that is 2 years old has a human age of 24 years. In addition, she knows that for every year a dog ages after age 2, its human age increases by 4 years.

a. Write three points, with the x-coordinates being a dog's age in dog years at 0, 1, and 2 years, and the y-coordinates being the dog's age in human years. Find a quadratic function that models this data.

b. Write 2 more points, with the x-coordinates being the dog's age in dog years at 3 and 4 years, and the y-coordinates being the dog's age in human years. Write a linear function that fits these two points.

continued

a piecewise function that converts a dog's age in dog years into human years. Does it r which part of the function you use to convert 2 dog years into human years? Why or not?

4. A single person's federal income tax bracket is determined by his or her taxable income as shown in the table.

2011 Federal Income Tax Brackets	
Tax Rate	**Taxable Income**
10%	\$0 to \$8,500
15%	\$8,500 to \$34,500
25%	\$34,500 to \$83,600
28%	\$83,600 to \$174,400
33%	\$174,400 to \$379,150
35%	\$379,150 and above

a. A person with \$50,000 in taxable income pays 10% on the income up to \$8,500, 15% on the income between \$8,500 and \$34,500, and 25% on the income between \$34,500 and \$50,000. How much would the person pay in income tax?

b. Write a piecewise function $T(n)$ that can be used to calculate the amount of federal income tax owed based on taxable income. Then use the function to verify the amount of income tax you calculated in part **a**, showing your work.

c. What percentage of their entire income would a person with \$50,000 in taxable income actually pay in income tax?

Name ________________ Class ____________ Date ________

SELECTED RESPONSE

1. Given $f(x) = -5x - 2$ and $g(x) = 2x - 7$, find $h(x) = f(x) - g(x)$.

   A. $h(x) = -3x - 9$

   B. $h(x) = -7x - 9$

   C. $h(x) = -7x + 5$

   D. $h(x) = -7x - 5$

2. You graph the function $f(x) = 300(1.015)^x$, which gives the total amount in your account after x years of interest that is compounded annually. The function $g(x)$ gives the amount in your account if you make the same initial investment, but at a rate of interest of 2.3% compounded annually. How would the graph of $g(x)$ compare to the graph of $f(x)$?

   F. It would have the same y-intercept, but rise more quickly over time.

   G. It would have the same y-intercept, but rise less quickly over time.

   H. It would have a greater y-intercept and rise more quickly over time.

   J. It would have a greater y-intercept and rise less quickly over time.

3. The function $d(t) = 4.9t^2$ models the distance in meters an object falls after t seconds where $t \geq 0$. Which function $t(d)$ best models the time in seconds that it will take an object to fall d meters?

   A. $t(d) = 0.20\sqrt{d}$

   B. $t(d) = 0.45\sqrt{d}$

   C. $t(d) = 2.2\sqrt{d}$

   D. $t(d) = 4.9\sqrt{d}$

4. Which function is graphed below?

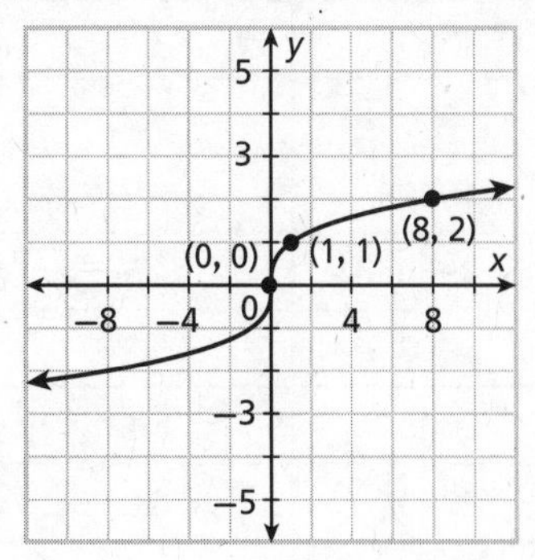

   F. $f(x) = \sqrt{x}$ **H.** $f(x) = x^3$

   G. $f(x) = \sqrt[3]{x}$ **J.** $f(x) = \frac{1}{x^3}$

5. The graph below is a horizontal and vertical translation of the graph of $f(x) = \left(\frac{3}{4}\right)^x$.

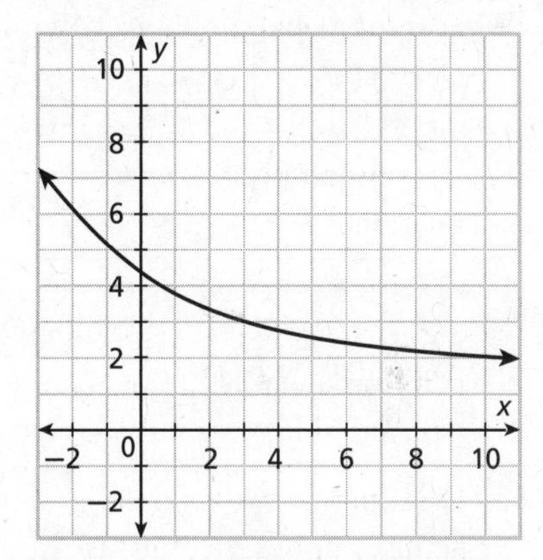

   What is the equation of the graph?

   A. $y = \left(\frac{3}{4}\right)^{x-2} + 3$ **C.** $y = \left(\frac{3}{4}\right)^{x+3} + 2$

   B. $y = \left(\frac{3}{4}\right)^{x-3} + 2$ **D.** $y = \left(\frac{3}{4}\right)^{x+2} + 3$

6. The graph of $g(x)$ is the graph of $f(x) = \log x$ translated 6 units to the right and shrunk vertically by a factor of $\frac{1}{4}$. Which is the equation of $g(x)$?

   F. $g(x) = \frac{1}{4}\log(x - 6)$

   G. $g(x) = \frac{1}{4}\log(x + 6)$

   H. $g(x) = 4\log(x - 6)$

   J. $g(x) = 4\log(x + 6)$

RESPONSE

ws the total world population
2010 according to data from the
Bureau.

Year	Population (in billions)
1950	2.6
1960	3.0
1970	3.7
1980	4.5
1990	5.3
2000	6.1
2010	6.9

a. Find the exponential regression equation, using the number of decades since 1950 as x-values. Round the values of a and b to two decimal places.

____

b. What is the population's growth rate? Tell how you know.

____

____

c. Show how to transform the equation to find the annual growth rate.

____

____

____

d. Do you think the exponential model is a good fit for the data? Use residuals to explain.

____

____

____

____

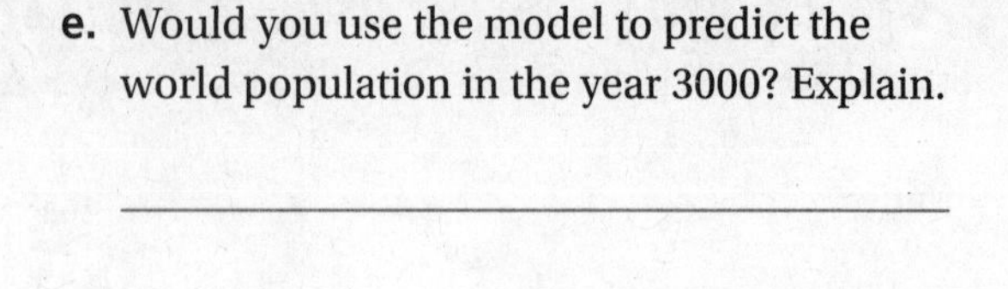

e. Would you use the model to predict the world population in the year 3000? Explain.

____

____

____

____

8. A taxicab driver charges \$6.00 for any distance less than 1 mile. For distances of 1 mile or more, he charges \$6.00 plus \$3.00 for each complete mile.

a. Write the equation for the function $C(d)$, which gives the cost C (in dollars) of riding in the taxicab for a distance d (in miles).

____

b. Graph the function to show the costs for all distances less than 5 miles. Include labels and scales on your graph.

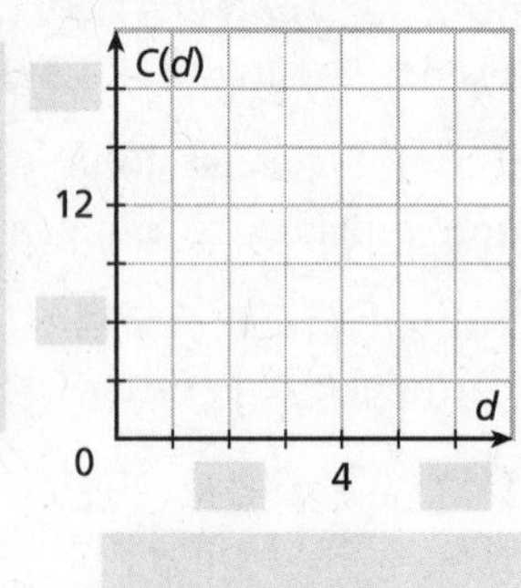

9. Find the inverse function of $f(x) = x^2 + 3$ by using algebra. Include any necessary restrictions on the domain of $f(x)$.

____

____

____

____

____

____